"Barra's enthusiasm for his subject is contagious, his eye for the human foible compassionate and his eye for the off fact is irrepressible."—Michael Skube, *Atlanta Journal-Constitution*

"Barra is no garden variety deconstructionist. . . . [He] lines up the mythmaking process in his crosshairs."—*Chicago Tribune*

"A fascinating glimpse into a rowdy, turbulent period."—*Cincinnati Enquirer*

"Wyatt Earp's hell-for-leather charge into the rugged territory between history and legend has never been better charted."—*San Diego Union-Tribune*

"[Barra] offers fascinating and provocative insights into how various individuals manipulated and twisted aspects of Earp's life for their own purpose."—Jay Freeman, *Booklist*

"Barra is an author who revels in history's stubborn complexities."—*Kansas City Star*

"Barra has done his homework and in the process accomplished something of a paradox-with-a-half-twist: hero-making in pursuit of truth."—John Anderson, *Newsday*

"The grand narrative of the frontier is one of America's great stories. And [this book] is a passionate but cold-eyed look at a big chunk of that story, and why it became the clouded mix of truth and exaggeration that still provides the nation with inspiration today."—*Associated Press*

"Barra's book meticulously re-examines the recoverable facts and many myths. . . . [His] digressive approach proves an effective tool in his successful effort to debunk Wyatt's debunkers."—Gregg Rickman, *San Francisco Chronicle*

"Finally, a chronicle of the most famous lawman in American history that is as fascinating as the man himself."—Steve Straessle, *Arkansas Democrat-Gazette*

"Allen Barra, one of the country's best sportswriters, tells this epic American story with great affection and skill, in one of the most engaging books about the American West since Thomas Berger's *Little Big Man*."—*American Way*

"Barra does an admirable job of discounting the stories and outright lies told by Earp's contemporaries by using firsthand accounts and newspaper stories of the time."—*Publishers Weekly*

Inventing Wyatt Earp

His Life and Many Legends

Allen Barra

With a new introduction by the author

University of Nebraska Press
Lincoln and London

To mom, who never lost faith

Library of Congress Cataloging-in-Publication Data
Barra, Allen.
Inventing Wyatt Earp: his life and many legends / Allen Barra;
with a new introduction by the author.
p. cm.
Originally published: New York: Caroll & Graf, c1998.
Includes bibliographical references and index.
ISBN 978-0-8032-2058-4 (pbk.: alk. paper)
1. Earp, Wyatt, 1848–1929. 2. Southwest, New—History—1848–.
3. Frontier and pioneer life—Southwest, New. 4. Peace officers—
Southwest, New—Biography. 5. United States marshals—Southwest,
New—Biography. I. Title.
F786.E18B37 2008
978'.02092—dc22
[B]   2008038484

Introduction to the
Bison Books Edition

In the ten years since *Inventing Wyatt Earp* was first published, a great deal has occurred in the odd little world known as Earpiana.

First, Glenn G. Boyer's 1976 book *I Married Wyatt Earp* (*IMWE*) has been exposed—I used the word "fraud" in writing about it for the *New York Times* and "hoax" in *American Heritage* magazine, so I may as well repeat them here. The so-called Clum Manuscript, which Boyer claimed to have spliced into the Cason Manuscript (the as-yet-unpublished memoirs of Josephine Sarah Marcus Earp), does not exist. The University of Arizona Press, after a deplorable period of evasion and foot-dragging, finally withdrew the book from its catalogue. The major credit for this victory must go to Tony Ortega, currently the editor in chief of the *Village Voice* in New York. As a reporter for the *Phoenix New-Times* in 1999, he obtained access to the University of Arizona's files and revealed, step-by-step, how Boyer snookered the press's editors. (Those wishing to read Ortega's story can find it at http://www.phoenixnewtimes .com/1999-03-04/news/i-varied-wyatt-earp/full.)

Paula Mitchell Marks, when faced with the evidence of Boyer's deceit, rewrote passages of her 1989 study of the O.K. Corral gunfight *And Die in the West* to reflect the new revelations. I've chosen not to do something similar with *Inventing Wyatt Earp* for several reasons. First, thanks to researchers such as Jeff Morey, Jack Burroughs, and Gary Roberts, there was already much skepticism about the authenticity of *IMWE* when I began researching my book in 1993; that skepticism is expressed in numerous passages of *In-*

venting Wyatt Earp. Second, not all of Boyer's book is written from whole cloth, and in several instances his novelistic revisions suggest the actual thoughts of Josephine from her memoirs. As of this writing there are, sadly, no plans to publish the Cason Manuscript, but a remarkable Arizona researcher, Carol Mitchell (whose grandfather Jim Mitchell was a friend of Wyatt), is currently working on a definitive biography of one of the frontier's most extraordinary women.

A much more serious case of fraud in Earp research has only slowly come to light. One of the first things I noticed when I began studying the available Earp material was that there seemed to be little evidence to support just about anything in Frank Waters's hugely influential 1960 work *The Earp Brothers of Tombstone* (*EBOT*). Waters presented the book as the memoirs of Virgil Earp's widow, Allie, but after interviewing Waters by phone and examining his papers, I could find almost nothing in his interviews with Allie to justify *EBOT*'s contention that Wyatt was a crooked card shark and a murderer or that he carried on a flagrant affair with Josephine—Sadie, as she would later be known and possibly as she was known in Tombstone. In fact, I could find nothing from any source—not newspapers, journals, letters, memoirs, recollections from interviews, or even rumors—to indicate such a liaison at that time. While it's fairly obvious that the couple did know each other in Tombstone, it is highly unlikely they could have been carrying on any kind of relationship there without somebody noticing. There is nothing in the surviving recollections of Allie Earp to suggest such an affair; for that matter, it isn't clear from comments made by Allie in Waters's original manuscript, titled "Tombstone Travesty," that she took any notice of Josephine while the Earps were in Tombstone. It looks very much as if Waters, together with the late Arizona researcher and alleged document thief John Gilchriese, simply invented a great many stories about Wyatt and put them in Allie's voice for *EBOT*. The interested reader is obliged to seek out the most detailed study of Waters's chicanery in *Travesty: Frank Waters' Earp Agenda Exposed* (2005), a fine piece of historical detective work by S. J. Reidhead.

Waters's fraud with *The Earp Brothers of Tombstone* is a great deal more serious from a historical perspective than Boyer's with *I Married Wyatt Earp*. For one thing, Waters was a Pulitzer Prize winner and a historian of some repute. His book influenced virtually every work about Earp and Tombstone from 1960 to the mid-1990s, from literary (Paula Mitchell Marks's *And Die in The West* and David Thomson's 1990 novel *Silver Light*) to film. However, after grave doubts about Waters's veracity began to come to light, it's an encouraging sign that most recent books on Earp (particularly Casey Tefertiller's *Wyatt Earp: The Life Behind the Legend* [1997], Bruce Olds's superb Doc Holliday novel *Bucking the Tiger* [2001], Steven Lubet's definitive study of the O.K. Corral gunfight and its legal aftermath *Murder in Tombstone* [2004], and Gary Roberts's biography *Doc Holliday: The Life and Legend* [2006]) have discarded Boyer's and Waters's depiction of Earp altogether.

Not all fiction writers have followed suit. Skepticism regarding Waters did not reach Thomas Berger in time to influence his 1999 novel *The Return of Little Big Man*. Larry McMurtry, alas, refuses to let history get in the way of a rollicking good story; in his 1996 *Telegraph Days* he still has Wyatt as the hard-drinking, lecherous bully of *The Earp Brothers of Tombstone*. Nor did recent Earp research have an impact on David Milch's view of Wyatt in the final season of the cult-favorite HBO series *Deadwood*. Milch has Morgan Earp gunning down a Pinkerton detective in cold blood in the streets of the mining camp and Wyatt lying about his exploits with the stage line that ran in and out of the town. (I don't know why, since his employment there was a matter of record.)

One of the most gratifying developments since the publication of *Inventing Wyatt Earp* is the number of people from all walks of life who have contacted me with odd and interesting bits of information. This is as good a place as any to mention them. Sportscaster Bob Costas directed me to a Billy Crystal movie, *Forget Paris*, in which Crystal's character, abed in a hospital, complains of a fellow patient's cough: "I pay for a private room, they put me next to Doc Holliday." A reader in England sent me a newspaper clipping regarding the death of one Rod Earp of Gloucestershire, who claimed to be the great-grandson of Wyatt and who, according to his stepson Stephen, "Never went to see the films that came out about Wyatt Earp and didn't have any books about him, but he could fire two guns at the same time, hitting both targets accurately." I always wondered how target shooting was received by the good folks of Gloucestershire, until I saw the English comedy *Hot*

Fuzz; apparently such gunplay is the norm in sleepy English villages. Dennis O'Brien, a retired police officer from Long Island, contributed a newspaper item about a Texas postal worker who was convicted by a federal jury of e-mailing threats such as "Judgment Day will come. It will be a shootout at the O.K. Corral."

My late cousin Bart Anello of Elkins Park, Pennsylvania, dug up a second Earp-related cartoon by Gary Larsen, this one with the Earps and some cowboys playing "Dodge ball" in the streets of Dodge City. Well, you'd have to see it. Bart also tracked down a gold pocket watch given to Bat Masterson by a colleague in the newspaper business. The owner, a distant relative of Bat's, was trying to sell it to collectors without his mother's knowledge. I'll always wonder where the watch wound up.

Jeff Morey found a blood-chilling version of "O.K. Corral" by Walter Brennan in which the only actor to portray Old Man Clanton tells the story of the gunfight from the perspective of . . . Johnny Behan! Terry Gross of NPR's *Fresh Air* clued me in to the availability on CD of the Ken Darby Singers rendition of the theme from the Wyatt Earp TV series. Bruce Olds, author of *Bucking the Tiger*, informed me that in a very bad 1987 movie, *Assassination*, Charles Bronson's Secret Service agent tells first lady Jill Ireland that he "grew up in Tombstone, Arizona. My father went there to write a book about Wyatt Earp and stayed on."

In 2002 my family and I had the pleasure of meeting Bob and Melba Matson, who have done yeoman work in preserving the Wyatt Earp Birthplace Museum in Monmouth, Illinois. Since then, we have been back twice to the fine little town of Monmouth for its annual celebrations.

In 2004 journalist and TV producer Bill Kurtis invited me and my family to Arizona for the shooting of one of his *Investigating History* segments, "Wyatt Earp at the O.K. Corral." The show was shot partly at what remains of the set of the movie *Tombstone* at Mescal, Arizona. If you've ever wondered what it's like to spend time on a movie set of a western town, I can only tell you that in my experience it is: cold. Mescal is on an elevated plain, and when the wind and sleet come in from the north, there is no shelter, particularly not behind the thin, noninsulated walls of a movie set. If I hadn't been rescued by Tombstone historian Sherry Monahan and her husband, Larry, I might not have survived to write this. I'm fairly certain the reenactor playing Billy Clanton froze to death on the ground of the lot in back of the O.K. Corral. Other scenes for the show were filmed at Old Tucson Studios. In one scene prior to the gunfight, you can see my wife, Jonelle, and my daughter, Maggie, then age twelve, crossing the street in full period costume.

In 2005 I had a very pleasant conversation with Wyatt Earp of Ocean County, Democratic Party county chairman and secretary commissioner of the election board of Ocean. Mr. Earp informed me that, according to family history, Wyatt visited relatives in New Jersey in the early part of the twentieth century and, along with his friend Bat Masterson, who took the train down from New York, visited the beach resort of Long Branch. The detail gives some credibility to the story, as the Long Branch Saloon in Dodge City was named for the New Jersey town by coowner and Wyatt's friend Will Harris, whose family enjoyed outings at the resort. If Mr. Earp's family history is correct, this would be the only known sighting of the original Wyatt east of Illinois. If Wyatt were to travel via a time machine to visit his descendants in Ocean County today, he might be dismayed to find that they are staunch Democrats.

Max Allen Collins's novel *Black Hats* was published in 2007 by William Morrow. The story concerns the elderly Wyatt's fictitious journey to New York in the 1920s to team up with Bat Masterson and help rescue the son of Doc Holliday and Kate Elder from Al Capone and his gang. (Collins's graphic novel *Road to Perdition*, written under the pseudonym of Patrick Culhane, was turned into a popular film with Tom Hanks.) "The notion for this novel," Collins writes in the afterword, "grew out of the publication of two fine biographies, *Wyatt Earp: The Life Behind the Legend* by Casey Tefertiller, and *Inventing Wyatt Earp: His Life and Many Legends* by Allen Barra." In a subsequent phone conversation, Mr. Collins informed me he has hopes for a TV film based on *Black Hats*; Kurt Russell, with a little makeup and gray-tinted hair, would make a fine elderly Wyatt.

In 2007 ten-year-old Nicholas Ward of Brooklyn, son of author Nathan Ward and grandson of historian Geoffrey Ward, couldn't wait to tell me after seeing *Shanghai Noon* that Owen Wilson's train-robbing character, Roy O'Bannon, finally reveals to Jackie Chan's Shanghai Kid that his "real name is Wyatt Earp." "That's a terrible cowboy name," says Chan.

Jeff Morey has completed an extraordinary docudrama for the
BBC, *The Wild West Gunfight at the O.K. Corral*, which is the best
retelling of the events up to and after the O.K. Corral gunfight that
I've ever seen. The program has aired in Britain, and here's hoping
they find a distributor for American television.

I'd also like to thank four people to whom I shamefully did not
give enough credit for the first edition of *Inventing Wyatt Earp*.
Richard Snow, editor of *American Heritage* magazine for many
years, was instrumental in helping me sort through boxes of photo-
copies of the Stuart Lake papers at the Huntington Library, without which my book could not have been written. Howell Raines,
then the editorial-page editor of the *New York Times*, and the late
film critic Pauline Kael both recommended me for the Huntington,
and Ms. Virginia J. Renner was very helpful in assisting me with
paperwork.

Kent Carroll of Carroll and Graf has left that publishing house,
which is now part of Perseus Books. Before he left, Kent happily informed me that sales of *Inventing Wyatt Earp* were on the verge of
passing up those of all previous Earp books except, of course, Stuart
Lake's *Frontier Marshal*. (I believe John M. Myers's *Last Chance:
Tombstone's Early Years* [1950] was the previous second-best seller.)
Lake has a head start of nearly seventy years on me, so I doubt I'll
catch up, but second place isn't bad.

I'd like to thank the good folks at Old Town Helena, Alabama,
and Wild West City in Netcong, New Jersey (which is about an
hour's ride from where I write this). Their regular reenactments of
the O.K. Corral gunfight have helped keep the event prominent
in the public's mind. Both of their versions make up in vitality for
what they lack in historical accuracy.

And, finally, thanks to *True West* editor Bob Boze Bell for having
lent me his distinctive artwork, used in every edition of *Inventing Wyatt Earp*, including this one; and Tom Swanson and Alicia
Christensen of the University of Nebraska Press (as well as Gary
Dunham, now of SUNY Press) for their care and patience in making
this edition possible and keeping Wyatt Earp alive well into the
twenty-first century. With a little luck, we'll beat Stuart Lake yet.

Contents

Introduction to the Bison Books Edition   v

Preface   1

Introduction   4

1. Wyatt: The Odyssey   19

2. "Bloody Kansas"—Wyatt Earp in Wichita   36

3. On to Dodge City   54

4. Tombstone: The Iliad   91

5. "Three Men Hurled into Eternity"—
   The Streetfight in Tombstone   139

6. Wyatt Earp on Trial   178

7. Wyatt Earp Unleashed: The Vendetta Ride   231

8. Putting Clothes on a Ghost:
   The Life and Legend of Doc Holliday   286

9. The Lion in Autumn   306

10. Hollywood Gunfighter   329

11. Print the Legend   375

12. Wyatt Redux   396

Bibliography   406

Index   413

An anecdotal and legendary history can be truer than the truth itself.
—ERNEST RENAN, *nineteenth-century French historian*

This is the West, Sir. When the legend becomes fact, print the legend.
—From JAMES WARNER BELLAHS's *screenplay for*
The Man Who Shot Liberty Valance

Preface

H. F. Sills was a thirty-six-year-old Canadian-born train engineer from Las Vegas, Nevada, who saw the wide open silver mining camp of Tombstone, Arizona, for the first time on October 25, 1881. Laid off from the Atchison, Topeka, and Santa Fe Railroad, he was making use of the company's Tombstone hospital facilities to recover from a slight injury. Like all newcomers to Tombstone—the town "had a man for breakfast" was a popular line—Sills had heard blood-curdling tales of street violence and while walking the town's bustling but peaceful streets on the afternoon of October 26, he must have wondered if he'd get to see some action.

According to testimony Sills would later give at the O.K. Corral hearing, some time around two o'clock he "saw four or five men standing in front of the O.K. Corral, talking of some trouble they had with Virgil Earp, and they made threats at the time, that on meeting him they would kill him on sight. Some of the party spoke up at the time and said that they would kill the whole party of the Earps when they met them." Two of the men making the threats were wearing guns "in plain sight." Sills couldn't say if the others were armed.

The engineer didn't know the men. He would later learn that they were Issac "Ike" Clanton and his younger brother Billy, and their friends, the McLaury brothers, Frank and Tom. The fifth man was probably William "Billy the Kid" Claiborne, who had nicknamed himself in honor of the young outlaw who had recently been slain a

1

few days' ride from Tombstone in Fort Sumner, New Mexico. Sills paid no attention to their dress—the high boots, gaudy shirts with colored bandannas, and flat-brimmed hats; such going-to-town outfits were common to small ranchers in the Southwest when taking a break in the big city. He probably did not know that the men were referred to, or referred to themselves as "Cowboys," and if he did know, he must have thought the term a bit strange.

Sills also didn't know who the Earps were, a point that was to assume great importance at the subsequent hearing, where most of the other witnesses were wildly partisan. He asked passersby if they could point out Virgil Earp; Virgil was identified as the tall, severe-looking man with the drooping mustache standing in front of Hafford's saloon on the corner of Allen and Fourth Streets. With him were two other men who bore a striking resemblance to Virgil Earp; Sills would later learn that they were his younger brothers, Wyatt and Morgan. All were dressed in impeccable white shirts and long coats—it was chilly on the afternoon of October 26 and patches of snow were on the ground—with black flattop sombreros of the kind worn by Mexican ranch owners. Standing with them was a fourth man Sills also did not know. He was about as tall as the Earps, but thinner, and gave the appearance of a gentleman. Sills had never heard of Doc Holliday, either.

When Sills was told that Virgil was the town marshal, he must have been a little shaken: Was it possible that five men, ranchers or herders, would so brazenly discuss the killing of policemen within earshot of townspeople? Sills called Virgil Earp to one side and told him what he had heard.

If Virgil Earp was gruff to Sills, it was because he had serious business on his mind. For some time now townspeople had been giving Virgil reports on the Cowboys' threats, but he wasn't sure how seriously they should be taken. Sills seemed calm and objective; his warning helped to make up Virgil's mind.

Thirty minutes later the Earps and Holliday started from the corner at Hafford's and turned right up Fourth Street. From there, they walked about three hundred feet to Fremont Street, turned left, and walked another three hundred or so feet to Fly's Photography Studio in back of the O.K. Corral, where they would find the Cowboys and immortality. Sills remembered that the marshal stopped at a building to pick up a shotgun, then gave it to Holliday, who concealed it under his long overcoat. Virgil Earp accepted Doc's cane in return.

Trailing the Earp party by about two hundred feet, Sills watched them "go up and speak to the other party. I wasn't close enough to hear their conversation, but saw them pull out their revolvers immediately." Virgil, Sills said, threw up his hands and spoke, but he couldn't hear what the marshal said.

H. F. Sills was the most important witness to testify in the hearing. The first men to fire their guns, he claimed, were Billy Clanton and Wyatt Earp. Only two other witnesses would support that claim: Virgil and Wyatt Earp.

About half a minute after the first two shots were fired, every participant in the fight was dead or wounded, except for Wyatt Earp.

History does not record what became of H. F. Sills after he gave his testimony.

Introduction

Two years ago this summer, I took a walking tour from my home in South Orange, New Jersey, looking for traces of Wyatt Earp's legend. My first stop, the town post office, pictured Wyatt on the wall in its "Heroes of the West" series. The portrait on the stamp is an odd one, showing him not in his familiar black frock coat and flat-brimmed sombrero but wearing a white, soft-brimmed model of the kind Henry Fonda wore in *My Darling Clementine* (which is probably what the artist was trying to copy). Around his neck is an old-fashioned yellow bandanna. The effect is to make Wyatt Earp look like a cowboy, but, as Arizona historian Bob Boze Bell phrased it, "Wyatt was many things in his life, but never a cowboy."

I pick up my mail; there's a newsletter from the National Writer's Union promising a "Shootout at the E-Rights Corral." At the corner newsstand the *Wall Street Journal* has an editorial cartoon with President Clinton walking into an "O.K. Corral" showdown with Congress (presumably, in this scenario Newt Gingrich is Ike Clanton). The local paper, the *Newark Star-Ledger*, has a story on alleged police abuse with a quote from a sociologist about the danger of what crime writer Joseph Wambaugh called "the Wyatt Earp syndrome," that is, the tough cop attitude. We can only hope that it was a coincidence that a *People* magazine story on Mark Fuhrman pictured him sitting in front of a poster from the movie *Tombstone*. At Computer City, I find a CD-Rom game, "Wyatt Earp's West," which includes a Wyatt Earp quiz. (Sample question: "How many Earp

4

brothers were there?" Their answer: "Three." There were five—actually, six, if you include a half brother, Newton.)

Later that day I pick up my daughter, Maggie, at Western Day at her grade school. The sign above the gym entrance says, of course, "O.K. Corral." In the gym, there's a pile of books left for the kids' amusement. I find a copy of *Fievel Goes West* from the Stephen Speilberg film about the Jewish mouse who goes to the frontier in search of the legendary "Law Dog" Wylie Burp. (Burp's voice in the film is supplied by James Stewart, who in fact played Earp in John Ford's 1964 film, *Cheyenne Autumn*.) In the movie, Fievel's sister, Tanya, wants to leave New York for the West to become a stage performer: Did Speilberg know that Wyatt's wife of forty-seven years, Josephine Marcus, was Jewish, an actress, and born in New York?

In South Orange, New Jersey, a place Wyatt Earp probably never got within a thousand miles of, I found references to him everywhere—except in the library. My local library had nothing at all on Earp except a couple of essays contained in coffee table anthologies on the Old West, a battered copy of the hugely popular *Wyatt Earp, Frontier Marshal*, Stuart Lake's highly fictionalized 1931 biography, the book that began Earp's legend, and Frank Waters's *The Earp Brothers of Tombstone*. Both books contain much fiction, and as a result so did most of the subsequent newspaper and magazine articles on Earp to be found in the library.

Every American knows the name of Wyatt Earp; he may well be one of the two or three dozen most famous Americans. As a cultural icon, he is ubiquitous. Don Imus, the most popular radio personality in the country, named his son Wyatt. When Muhammad Ali refused induction into the U.S. Army, he told reporters, "All a man has got to show for his time here on earth is what kind of name he had. Jesus. Columbus. Daniel Boone. Now, Wyatt Earp . . . who would have told him when he was fighting crooks and standing up for his principles that there'd be a television show about him? That kids on the street would say, 'I'm Wyatt Earp. Reach.'"

America's most popular western movie icons, John Wayne and Clint Eastwood, borrowed heavily from Earp's legend in creating their screen personas. (In *Coogan's Bluff*, when Eastwood's Arizona cop arrives in New York City, Lee J. Cobb's police captain cautions him, "This isn't the O.K. Corral," and contemptuously refers to him

as "Wyatt.") Earp's image so dominates the western that it's practically impossible to mention a western made since the mid-1930s that
can't be connected in some way either with Earp's real life story or
with another Earp movie. Jeff Morey, an Earp historian in California, swears he can connect any movie ever made in Hollywood with
Wyatt Earp in less than six moves. (Six Degrees of Wyatt Earp?)
Morey may be able to do just that. Earp's image is so pervasive it
transcends westerns. *Easy Rider,* written by Terry Southern and
Dennis Hopper (who grew up in Dodge City hearing stories about
Wyatt), the bikers played by Peter Fonda and Hopper are named for
the two great parallel legends of the American West, Wyatt Earp
and Billy the Kid. When director Brian DePalma and screenwriter
David Mamet revived *The Untouchables,* they didn't go to Eliot
Ness's story but to Wyatt Earp's. Their film version has almost nothing to do with Ness's struggle against Al Capone, but is instead a
compendium of plot situations from various Earp films. (As popular
culture critic Robert Warshow noted, the classic Hollywood gangster
films were really urban westerns.) Earp is practically a symbol of our
national resolve. A couple of years ago when a Marine colonel in
charge of a peace keeping force landed in Somalia, he boldly announced, "This may be Dodge City, but we're Wyatt Earp."

Earp's fame isn't limited to the English-speaking world. Cruising
the Internet I found a news item about a U.N. official from Pakistan
who accused the United States of displaying "a Wyatt Earp attitude"
in foreign affairs.

The Gunfight at The O.K. Corral, or the street fight in Tombstone, as it should properly be called, is so much a part of America
folklore that scarcely a public confrontation of any kind can occur
without someone evoking it. When Pat Buchanan kicked off his bid
for the presidency in Arizona in the 1996 Republican primary he
posed for pictures, replete with gunbelt, in front of the O.K. Corral.
(Had Buchanan been standing there on October 26, 1881, he would
have missed the fight—it took place a block away at a lot in back of
the corral.) Which vote was Buchanan courting, I wonder, the old
Clanton-Cowboy-Democratic coalition or the decendents of the Republican Earps? The words *Democrat* and *Republican* mean something a great deal different now from what they did in 1881. (If
Virgil or Wyatt had found this NRA supporter posing for pictures wearing a Colt .45 in public, they'd have clubbed him—or

"buffaloed" him in the parlance of the time—hauled him off to jail, and fined him $25 for carrying firearms within the city limits.)

Almost everyone knows the name of Wyatt Earp, but scarcely anyone knows anything about him. Many think they do because they've read the Sunday supplement article or seen any of the dozen or so movies that told the "real" story. On the day I write this, television offers two competing visions: Burt Lancaster as a plaster saint Wyatt Earp in *Gunfight at the O.K. Corral,* made in 1957 at the peak of the Eisenhower years, or *Doc,* a 1970 fable with a Vietnam War subtext, from a script by Pete Hamill and featuring Harris Yulin's Wyatt Earp as a sneering, homosexual bully.

So confused are most journalists about the basic facts of Earp's life that when *Tombstone* with Kurt Russell and Val Kilmer, became a success in the winter of 1994, many critics attacked it for being "revisionist," which was ludicrous since *Tombstone* was the first film to present at least a broad outline of the facts of Earp's life.

On the whole, academics have fared no better than journalists when it comes to Wyatt Earp. John Mack Faragher, a historian of the American frontier in the department of history at Yale University and author of a superb biography of Daniel Boone, wrote about Earp in the 1995 book *Past Imperfect—History According to the Movies.* "The real Earp," says Faragher,

> was a frontier demimonde—sometime lawman but full-time gambler, confidence man, associate of prostitutes and pimps. . . . he kept company with the saloon crowd and quickly developed a reputation as a bad case . . . Southeastern Arizona at the time was torn by conflict between the Republican business community and the mostly Democratic ranchers of the arid countryside. The "Cowboys," as the Republican *Tombstone Epitaph* labeled the ranchers, were led by Newman "Old Man" Clanton and his hot-headed sons and were backed by such violent gunmen as "Curly" Bill Brocius and Johnny Ringo. The trouble in Tombstone was just one episode in a series of local wars that pitted men with traditional rural values and Southern sympathies against mostly Yankee capitalist modernizers. As the hired guns of the businessmen in town, the Earps became the enemies of the Clantons.

Not all of what Faragher says is wrong, but even the parts that are half right need to be put in perspective, including the idea that there was a frontier "demimonde" for Wyatt Earp to inhabit. The entire frontier was a demimonde, one where social lines merged and mingled constantly, where a popular madam could be shot by accident in the bed belonging to the mayor of Dodge City and his wife while they were out of town, as Dora Hand was in 1878; where the Rev. Endicott Peabody, friend to Wyatt Earp and, later, tutor to Franklin D. Roosevelt, could build his church just a few blocks from Tombstone's red light district; where Wyatt Earp and Bat Masterson could spend their Saturday nights in Dodge City saloons and their Sunday mornings as church deacons without being considered hypocrites.

Wyatt Earp didn't "associate" with prostitutes and pimps; he lived with them. It was his business to do so. A local tradition in Kansas says that Wyatt's second wife, Mattie, was a former prostitute; on the frontier it wasn't uncommon to meet one future's spouse during a business transaction. The charge that Earp was a confidence man is based not on Wyatt's years on the frontier but on an incident that happened in Los Angeles in 1911 when he was sixty-three. (The actual charge was "misdemeanor of conspiracy to violate gambling laws.")

Wyatt certainly was a gambler, a fact he never denied. Nearly every peace officer on the frontier gambled, as did a great many males of every occupation and persuasion. Gambling was a perfectly respectable profession in the West of the 1870s and '80s, and the bad press Wyatt got for his gambling came not in the Old West but many years later when America reformed and Earp didn't. Josephine Marcus liked to tell a story that she picked up from Tombstonians about the Reverend Peabody going to the Oriental Saloon in search of funds to build the first Protestant church in southeast Arizona. Wyatt had been winning at cards, and he placed a stack of bills in front of Peabody. "Here's my contribution," he said. Then, to the rest of the players, "Now each of you has to give the same." St. Paul's stands to this day, around the corner and less than a block from the lot where the O.K. Corral gunfight took place. Everyone knows of Wyatt Earp's participation in the shootout, but it's doubtful that one in a thousand tourists who pass by St. Paul's knows of Wyatt Earp's contribution to Episcopalianism.

As for "keeping company with the saloon crowd," Wyatt Earp

would certainly have pleaded guilty. Saloons in the Old West were music, dance, and social gathering halls, even for nondrinkers like Wyatt. Earp put the matter succinctly to Stuart Lake when the latter asked why he had spent so much time in saloons: "We had no YMCAs."

Regarding the more serious charge that the Earps were merely the "hired guns" of Republican capitalists, Faragher neglects to mention that some of the "traditional rural values" those Democratic Cowboys adhered to included cattle rustling, stagecoach robbery, and, occasionally, murder. Had Faragher been living in Tombstone in the 1880s it's not inconceivable that he would have been as pro-Earp as other educated Republican Easterners of that period.

Richard Slotkin, in his popular 1992 sociohistorical work *Gunfighter Nation—The Myth of the Frontier in Twentieth-Century America* writes about the gunfight at the O.K. Corral that "The national fame of that incident was itself an artifact of Hollywood culture. Neither Earp nor the gunfight had enjoyed any great notoriety outside Arizona until 1920, when the aged Wyatt appeared on a movie lot in Pasadena hoping to cash in on the enthusiasm for 'authentic' Western figures." Mr. Slotkin is dead wrong, but he's on to something. Identified as "The Gunfight at the O.K. Corral," the Tombstone streetfight's national fame was an "artifact" of Hollywood culture; the fight itself didn't happen at the corral and it wasn't generally called the "Gunfight at the O.K. Corral" until the movie of that name was released in 1958. But by 1958 Wyatt Earp had already been world famous for decades. The actual gunfight, no matter what it was called, had been written about in *The New York Times, Harper's Weekly, Scribner's, Police Gazette,* and many other publications long before Hollywood got hold of it. Hollywood just put a catchy tag on an incident that had been part of Western folklore for half a century before its first depiction on screen. (As Bob Boze Bell has remarked, "The Gunfight in the Lot in Back of the O.K. Corral Next to Fly's Photography Studio" would never make it on to a movie marquee.) And if Wyatt's visit to a movie set in 1920, where his friend William S. Hart was filming *Wild Bill Hickok,* helped make Earp nationally famous, it was one heck of a delayed reaction. The first Wyatt Earp movie, *Law and Order* with Walter Huston, would not be made till 1932, by which time Wyatt had been dead for three years.

Faragher and Slotkin, like too many modern historians who write

about the Old West—Paula Mitchell Marks, author of the highly
successful 1989 book, *And Die in the West, The Story of the Gunfight
at the O.K. Corral* could be included here—have taken Wyatt Earp's
debunkers at their word: Having proven that the Wyatt Earp of the
early films and of the 1950s television series was a false idol, they
assumed there was nothing more to say about the man. In spite of
the debunkers, almost as if to spite them, Wyatt Earp goes right on
being famous. At a time when once invincible folk figures such as
Davy Crockett, Wild Bill Hickok, and Buffalo Bill have faded, Wyatt Earp seems more contemporary than ever.

Why, despite the enormous interest in Wyatt Earp and his legend, is most of the print material available on him dubious or just
plain bogus? The answer is largely due to the hoards of partisan
Earpianists who bought up or stole many of the letters and documents and falsified many more. Even careful scholars who have
tested the validity of each source have found that a great many gaps
exist in the record, and letters and key documents (such as the original transcript from the O.K. Corral hearing) no longer exist or were,
for years, in the hands of private collectors. Quite probably many
more key documents are still in their hands.

Another reason for the lack of reliable material on Earp is Stuart
Nathaniel Lake. In 1931 Houghton Mifflin published Lake's *Wyatt
Earp, Frontier Marshal,* supposedly Wyatt's autobiography, to almost
unanimous acclaim and enormous sales. It would not be an exaggeration to call Frontier Marshal one of the great mythmaking American
books of the twentieth century; despite numerous debunkings, Lake's
Wyatt Earp remains, in the minds and hearts of millions, as solid a
symbol of America's frontier as Walt Disney's Davy Crockett.

Though Lake met with Wyatt only a few times, most of *Frontier
Marshal* was written in the first person. Lake insisted on the veracity
of his text, and we now know that he received several letters from
Earp as well as hundreds more from Wyatt's friends and acquaintances. He also made liberal use of the Flood manuscript, an earlier,
failed attempt at an autobiography that Earp prepared with a family
friend named John Flood. From this rich source material, Lake wrote
a terrific novel, putting most of the story in Wyatt's voice.

Lake's narrative is far from worthless, but the myths he created
around Earp became so popular and have been retold in so many
different forms that even now, nearly seventy years later, it is as

necessary to refer to his text in discussing Earp as it would be to refer to Polybius in a life of Hannibal, or to the Scottish bard Blind Harry in a life of William Wallace. Regarding Wyatt's years in railroad and buffalo camps and his first years as a Kansas police officer, Lake is almost all we have to go by, that and some tantalizing scraps of letters and newspaper clippings. Not until he reached Wichita in 1874 did Earp begin to leave a definable paper trail, and after that the voluminous material that collected around him—one researcher intimates that "Earp papers" could fill five volumes—was already beginning to be colored by the mythmaking process that was building around him. The real problem with *Frontier Marshal* is not that Lake exaggerated or distorted Earp's life; Wyatt's later critics and debunkers are guiltier of that. The problem is that by oversimplifying the man and the controversies in which he was involved, Lake obscured for two generations the fact that the real Wyatt Earp was more interesting and his life more exciting than anyone except Wyatt's most intimate friends knew.

Stuart Lake was not, as many now believe, the man who "created" Wyatt Earp or made him famous. For most of his lifetime Earp was something of a celebrity, though his fame was largely confined to the West. Bat Masterson, Wyatt's lifelong friend and colleague on the Dodge City police force, helped revive Earp's fame with a celebrated 1907 article for the Hearst magazine *Human Life*. After World War I, numerous magazine and book writers turned their attention to Tombstone and its glory years; when they went back to Arizona for firsthand accounts, Wyatt's friends—the Republican avatars of Eastern concerns mentioned by our modern academies—had long since left. Tombstone had practically become a ghost town, and the only ones left to tell the story were old timers who knew or sympathized with the Cowboy rustlers who Earp fought against. The Earps were resented by many of these folks practically upon their arrival in Tombstone—they were Yankees and Union supporters, they were townspeople, they were adept at making a buck, and, perhaps most important of all, they wore federal badges.

This last point cannot be too fully emphasized: Wyatt Earp was a federal officer for brief periods from late 1879 to 1881 under his brother Virgil, who was a U.S. deputy marshal for southeastern Arizona Territory and who had the power to appoint deputies. After Virgil was shot and crippled, Wyatt asked for and received the deputy marshal's appointment. Yet, his image has come to dominate that of all other U.S. marshals of the time. When Tommy Lee Jones's federal marshal arrives on the scene in *The Fugitive*, the local sheriff caustically announces, "Okay, fellows, Wyatt Earp is here." When Michael Keaton's FBI agent in *Out of Sight* knocks on Jennifer Lopez's door, her father, Dennis Farina, calls out, "Honey, Wyatt Earp is here." It's important to note that the strong identification with federal law is not one Earp made for himself, but one that his enemies chose to emphasize. During the Vendetta Ride in 1882 when Wyatt was avenging his brothers, Democratic newspapers in Arizona Territory wrote repeatedly of the "federal abuse of power" exercised by Earp.

The western far right's paranoia regarding the federal government is no new thing, and we can see it in its nascent form in the frontier cattle and mining town clashes of the 1870s and '80s. It was out of these clashes that the legends of both Wyatt Earp Superman (which most Americans still hold) and Wyatt Earp Bogeyman (still prevalent in much of Arizona and the southwest) were born. Both legends have numerous partisans to this day, as anyone who has browsed through a bookstore in Tombstone, Arizona, can testify.

Earp was the central figure in two best-selling books years before Stuart Lake. William "Billy" Breakenridge, sometimes deputy sheriff to John Behan, Wyatt's chief rival in Tombstone and a pretty fair myth-spinner in his own right, wrote a self-serving book on Tombstone called *Helldorado*. Published in 1928 by the highly respected Boston house, Houghton Mifflin, *Helldorado* placed Wyatt Earp— not his brother Virgil, who was the Tombstone town marshal and U.S. deputy sheriff—in the center of the southeastern Arizona conflict and in a largely negative light. Since many Eastern readers were still not clear as to who Wyatt Earp was, *Helldorado* had the odd effect of adding to a legend that Breakenridge was trying to diminish.

Tombstone—An Iliad of the Southwest, by the then well-known Chicago journalist Walter Noble Burns, was the first nationally popular book to feature Wyatt Earp. In 1926 Burns, a crime reporter in Al Capone's Chicago, had published *The Saga of Billy the Kid*, resuscitating the Kid's name and starting a boom for true (well, quasi-true) stories of the Old West. The Saga of Billy The Kid went on to become the most successful nonfiction western book of all time—as of this writing it is still in print, though Burns's name is long forgotten. Not long after the publication of *Billy the Kid,* Burns went to Arizona to seek traces of the Southwest's other great legend, Wyatt Earp. The trail eventually led him to California, where he found Earp unwilling to speak except on the subject of Doc Holliday. Burns (who also interviewed Billy Breakenridge) found enough gold in the conversation to make *Tombstone* a best-seller, but Wyatt, who believed Burns was working on a biography of Doc, was horrified to see himself propped up as "The Lion of Tombstone." Why couldn't these writers leave an old man in peace?

Tombstone officially signaled the start of a national interest in Wyatt's adventures, but by the time Burns died in 1932, Wyatt Earp, the American frontier version of a tragic hero, had been eclipsed by the more simplistic Earp created by Stuart Lake. Lake's Earp was the lawman hero Americans were looking for in the 1930s. Weary of the excesses of the Prohibition era and the gangsters it spawned, many Americans felt that something had gone awry with American society. A spate of books on the western frontier indicated a renewed interest in what were regarded as traditional American values, and the handiest symbol of those values was Wyatt Earp. Lake was fully willing to buff up *Frontier Marshal* for Hollywood just as he had buffed up Wyatt's life for *Frontier Marshal.* With each new telling Wyatt became more righteous and less complex until, in the late 1950s, a man who had once stolen a horse and who left Arizona under the shadow of a warrant for murder now had his name on comic book covers and lunchboxes.

The Wyatt Earp of Stuart Lake's *Frontier Marshal* was constructed on the legendary edifice of the West's first great Northern gunfighter, Wild Bill Hickok. Lake, in effect, made Wyatt the inheritor of Hickok's Yankee, cattle town supercop image (an image, ironically, that fit Wyatt better than Hickok, who was a bad policeman). In addition, Lake's Earp was part Bat Masterson (who supplied Lake with much color and background information), part Bill Tilghman, Charlie Bassett, and Neal Brown (Wyatt's colleagues on the Dodge City police force), and part Virgil Earp (Wyatt's older brother who was much closer to the model of a conventional frontier lawman than Wyatt), with a bit of Doc Holliday thrown in. (It was Doc, not Wyatt, who had a reputation as a gunfighter in his own lifetime.)

But by far the biggest part of *Wyatt Earp, Frontier Marshal* came from Wyatt's own life. That Stuart Lake's account of Wyatt Earp's life contains much fiction cannot be denied, but it's also true that Lake wrote what he did because the people he spoke to and corresponded with, people who had seen Earp in action on the frontier, all saw Wyatt as larger than life. There was something about Wyatt that made him a lightning rod for myth. Hollywood didn't create the Wyatt Earp legend; it perpetuated and reinvented it. If the real Wyatt Earp was never quite the hero of the early movies and TV shows inspired by Stuart Lake, there was nonetheless something about him that, when weighed against men of his own time and place, caused people to see him as extraordinary.

In his eighty-one years Wyatt Earp proved to be a remarkably complex man, composed of many seemingly contradictory parts. He was a farmer, pioneer, teamster, stage coach driver, shotgun guard, buffalo hunter, boxing promoter and referee, church deacon, lumber hauler, saloon keeper, gambler, faro dealer, prospector, detective, bounty hunter, body guard, Wells Fargo agent, horse breeder, movie advisor, and, always, adventurer. He was also a lawman; he was never a county sheriff or town marshal of Wichita, Dodge City, Tombstone, or any other place, but he was a first-rate peace officer idolized by his colleagues and feared by his enemies. Wyatt Earp was a lawman for perhaps five or six years of his life, and yet became the most famous law enforcer in American history. He was never a gunfighter or a killer, but, on the contrary, respected for his uncanny ability to keep peace while avoiding violent confrontations. Yet his name will always be associated with a thirty-second gunfight that made him a symbol of a "gunfighter nation." He had, perhaps, a bit of the con artist in him, but he was no fraud.

That a study of Wyatt Earp's life is needed may be doubted; he wasn't a pivotal figure in the settling of the West or even in the cow towns or mining camps he lived and worked in. But surely history is more than a study of social and economic factors. And if history isn't more than the study of such things, legend certainly is. Was King Arthur important? Was a deer poacher named Robin Hood? As *Tombstone* screenwriter Kevin Jarre has suggested, Wyatt Earp's life might be the last chance we have to see the folk process by which fact is turned into legend and legend to myth. And Wyatt Earp's importance as a symbol of the Old West cannot be exaggerated.

*   *   *

This book isn't a biography, at least not in the usual sense. I hope anyone wishing to know the facts of Wyatt Earp's life will come away satisfied that they have a definite sense of the man and the environment that produced him. My real subject, though, is the Wyatt Earp *legend*: How it came into being and evolved over the decades and why is has been constantly been resurrected and reinvented. Though most of the printed material available on Earp is either bogus or tainted with questionable source material, there are a few good source books for those seeking more basic information on certain aspects of Earp's life. Alford Turner's *The Earps Talk* (Creative Publishing, 1992), for instance, reprints several newspaper interviews with Wyatt and Virgil as well as the complete texts of their testimony before the O.K. Corral inquest. The lost documents are included, along with other testimony, in *The O.K. Corral Inquest*, edited by Turner (Creative Publishing, 1992).

The Earp Papers—In a Brother's Image by Don Chaput (Affiliated Writers of America, Inc.) is a superb collection of newspaper articles, legal documents, and other papers that cover the entire span of the Earp brothers' lives. Casey Tefertiller's assiduously researched *Wyatt Earp—The Life Beyond the Legend* (John Wiley and Sons, 1997) contains much more information than this volume on Wyatt's post-Arizona life, particularly the forty-seven years Wyatt and Josephine were together. Tefertiller, a Bay Area journalist, talked to surviving family and friends and has put together the most complete picture to date of the strange, lifelong match between two adventurers of vastly different backgrounds.

As my focus is the development of the Earp legend, I've tended to skim through the decades after Tombstone except for incidents that are pertinent to my story, but for those interested there are numerous short books and pamphlets that cover aspects of Wyatt's life such as *The Earps' Last Frontier—Wyatt and Virgil Earp in the Nevada Mining Camps, 1902–1905* by Jeffrey M. Kintop and Guy Lewis Rocha, from Great Basin Press. And, of course, Stuart Lake's *Wyatt Earp, Frontier Marshal* is readily available in a 1994 Pocket Book edition, and has all manner of wonderful (but, alas) unverifiable tales of Wyatt's boyhood and teenage years.

Beyond that, the study of Earp's life and legend become a maze that constantly weaves from folklore to history and then back again. I couldn't have made the journey without several people who steered me through these previously uncharted waters. I start with Kevin Jarre, a great writer, whose original script for the movie *Tombstone* is the great unpublished Wyatt Earp novel. Jarre brought me to Bob Boze Bell, author, artist, folklorist, and radio show host, whose *Illustrated Life and Times of Wyatt Earp* and *Doc Holliday* companion volume first brought Tombstone to life for me. Bell also contributed many of the photos in this volume and contributed to the cover design.

Bob Palmquist, a Tucson lawyer, was absolutely indispensable in leading me through the ramifications of Arizona territorial law in the 1870s and '80s, particularly as to how it related to the aftermath of the O.K. Corral gunfight. Bob also contributed valuable research on Earp in Kansas and in popular literature.

Bob McCubbin, an El Paso archivist, gave freely from a library on the Old West so huge he still hasn't missed the books I stole from him. Ruth and Aaron Cohen of Guidon Books and Tom Swinford of T. P. Swinford Bookseller in Scottsdale, Arizona, the two best western bookstores in the country, worked overtime to find me important materials all of the in print and most of the out-of-print books I mention in this volume can be purchased through their stores. Jacob Reiss of the Highland Booksmith in Birmingham, Alabama; Peter Ryby of the Montclair Book Center in Montclair, New Jersey; and Ray Boas of Ray Boas, Bookseller in New Preston, Connecticut—the three best all-around book stores in the country—went out of their way to find me out-of-print volumes. Make that the four best bookstores: The folks at paper Treasures in New Market, Virginia, were constantly coming up with all kinds of wonderful things, including the October 28, 1881, edition of *The New York Times* with the account of the O.K. Corral gunfight.

Carl Chafin, a California researcher, provided me with Josephine Marcus's original, unadulterated memoirs, and previously untranscribed sections of journals by the Tombstone diarist George Parsons. Jack Burrows, the author of *John Ringo, The Gunfighter Who Never Was,* was a constant supporter who generously shared his time and materials and clearheaded view of what happened in southeast Arizona from 1879 to 1882. Thanks as well to Peter Blodgett of Huntington Library, where Stuart Lake's papers are kept; to Megan Hahn of the New York Historical Society and to Paul Johnson, a New York Earp researcher who guided me to the McLaury family letters there; to Jim Dunham and Paul Northrup for riding me through the country where so much of this happened; to Casey Tefertiller, for giving of time and materials while he worked to get his own book out; to Stuart Lake's daughter, Carolyn, for information on her father and his work; and to the late Richard Erwin and the late Frank Waters, who, though his conclusion on Earp turned out to be different from mine, graciously allowed me to interview him.

I'd also like to thank the folks at the Bancroft Library, the Kansas State Historical Society, the Arizona Historical Society, the University of Arizona Special Collections, the Iowa State Historical Society, the Arizona State Historical Collection, and all the newspapers around the country that granted me "friend of" status in researching and sending me information, with a special nod to the *Chicago Tribune*.

Special thanks is owed to Ike Clanton, whose drunken antics the night before and the day of the gunfight in Tombstone made this book possible.

Finally, some special thanks: to Jonelle Bonta, who took time from her own busy career (and whose own book has probably been delayed by a year because of me) for typing and proofreading every page of this book; to Kent Carroll of Carroll & Graf, the only editor I approached who didn't say "but the Costner movie failed at the box office," and who is a real editor in the old fashioned sense of the word and left his imprint on every chapter of his book; and, finally, to Jeff Morey, researcher supreme, who, more than anyone else, is responsible for keeping the image of the real Wyatt Earp alive. There has not been a decent book on Wyatt Earp or the O.K. Corral written in the last ten years that doesn't owe him an enormous debt. Thanks especially for introducing me, while we were in Arizona, to the dangers of "Uncle Ned" history, as in "My Uncle Ned knew the man who knew the *real* story of Wyatt Earp."

And, before I get on with the story, I'd like to thank my late father, Alfred Barra, who bequested me his copies of Burns's *Tombstone* and Lake's *Frontier Marshal,* complete with all the related clippings he had saved over the years sticking out of them. Dad, though I never would have admitted this to you ten years ago, you were right all along: The Earps were the good guys, the Clantons and the Cowboys were the bad guys.

I don't know where else to fit this in, but thanks to my daughter, Margaret Elizabeth, who, one day when she was four, cuddled close to me while we were watching a scary part of Snow White where the heroine goes into the forest alone. "Daddy," she whispered, "she's scared. She needs Wyatt Earp to help her."

1

Wyatt: The Odyssey

I f the story of Wyatt Earp is the story of the West, as Bat Master-son claimed, then the white two-story structure where Wyatt was born on March 19, 1848, is a disappointment. Tourists visiting the Wyatt Earp Birthplace Museum in Monmouth, Illinois, expect something more western. "People tell us, 'We thought it would be more like a ranch or a log cabin'," a staff member explains. "One guy from England even expected mud walls. He felt the house didn't 'symbolize' Wyatt Earp." But then, Wyatt never spent much time in houses.

According to an early biographer, John Flood, many years after leaving home Wyatt became nostalgic for the house and returned to Illinois: "The dear old Monmouth was not the Monmouth as he had remembered it; everything had changed. The great, high fences that he had to climb up to look over when he was a boy seemed dwarfed and shrunken now . . . the woods and fields were not the great, unexplored horizons that they used to be. The rivers and streams seemed narrow and diminutive, and the rolling hills had lost their enchantment." Wyatt's nostalgia for Illinois is unrecorded elsewhere, but the state did leave its stamp on him and his two older brothers. The most celebrated peace officers of the cattle town era—Wild Bill Hickok, the Earp brothers, the Masterson brothers—lived in Illinois as young men and grew up in the same pro-Union, Republican, progressive, antislavery atmosphere that spawned Abraham Lincoln. (Several other prominent lawmen were raised in neighboring states;

the great Bill Tilghman, whom Wyatt and Bat Masterson would know in Dodge City, grew up in equally pro-Union Iowa.) The Earps had southern roots, and their father, Nicholas Porter Earp, remained a southerner at heart all his life, but three of Wyatt's brothers, including his half brother, Newton, would fight for the Union, and Wyatt would try to.

Nick Earp, a wheat, corn, and tobacco farmer, storekeeper, constable, cooper, justice of the peace, wagon master, judge, and bootlegger, to name just a few of his occupations, was born in North Carolina in 1813, the son of Walter and Martha Earp. Nicholas had eight brothers and sisters, and most of the Earps currently living in the United States can trace their ancestry back to this family or to a branch in Virginia and the Carolinas.[1]

The principal scholars of the Earp family tree, Mrs. Esther L. Irvine (whose research is in the Colton Public Library in Colton, California) and Effie Earp Cramer (whose materials are at the Wyatt Earp Birthplace Museum in Monmouth, Illinois), traced the American Earps from Anglo-Saxon/Celtic roots. Thomas Earp, born in Ireland and come to the new world from England in the early 1700s, is generally accepted as the first immigrant. In 1789 Josiah Earp became the first "Fighting Earp," enlisting in the Colonial Army in Maryland. Soon after the war Phillip became the first Earp with "itchy feet," moving through at least three other states before settling in Kentucky, which is where Wyatt's grandfather, Walter Earp, raised most of his children.[2] In 1836 Walter's son Nicholas married a Kentucky girl, Abigail Storm, the daughter of a neighboring farmer. Within two years, Nicholas lost a daughter, Mariah Ann, and then Abigail herself to an unspecified illness.

Left with a two-year-old son, Newton Jasper, to care for, Nicholas quickly sought and found a new wife. On July 30, 1840, he married Virginia Ann Cooksey, who would become the mother of the five full Earp brothers—James, Virgil, Wyatt, Morgan, and Warren— and three daughters—Martha and Virginia Ann, who died as children, and Adelia.

The strange odyssey of Nicholas's life would cover nearly 8,000 miles by wagon and railroad over four decades. Soon after James (1841) and Virgil (1843) were born, he moved his family from Kentucky to Wyatt's birthplace in Monmouth, Illinois, a community of perhaps one thousand people. His brother, Lorenzo Dow Earp, had

visited the growing town and written glowingly about it. Other family members went, too; Walter Earp was to be buried there after
earning the honorary title of "judge" for being a notary public and
performing wedding ceremonies. Life was good in Monmouth for all
the Earps, especially Nicholas, who worked a small farm, kept a
saloon, and also served as justice of the peace. In the Birthplace
Museum there is record of his having been elected captain of a "big
hunt"—presumably for bear—in the forests that surrounded the
town. In his spare time, he discussed and argued politics.

The Earps had scarcely settled in Monmouth when the news of
the impending war with Mexico was the talk of the town square.
Nicholas Earp led the cheers for Manifest Destiny, enlisting in a
company of volunteer Monmouth dragoons captained by a man
named Wyatt Berry Stapp. Captain Stapp thought well of Nicholas
Earp and made him a third sergeant; Nicholas, after being shipped
home in December 1847 (because of a leg injury from a mule kick),
named his next child for his old company commander.

A little more than a year after his return Nick was on the move
again, this time leaving behind his father and brothers for Pella in
Marion County, Iowa, where the U.S. government had granted
Nicholas Earp 160 acres. For the next six years Nick farmed, repaired
harnesses, and followed in his father's footsteps as a notary public
and justice of the peace. He also acquired several additional pieces of
land. And then, in 1856, for no apparent reason, he pulled up stakes
yet again and moved to Illinois. In less than two years, he moved his
family back to Pella. Between moves, Nick and Ginnie Ann had
three more children, Morgan (born in 1851), Warren (1855), and
Virginia Ann (1858). James and Virgil had now lived in seven
homes.

For the first and only time in his life, Nick Earp tried to become a
full-time farmer. (But he would also be listed in the census as a
cooper. Nick always seemed to be in preparation for whatever direction the economy might swing.) The urge didn't last long. None of
the Earp men ever stuck with farming; Wyatt hated it the most. For
him, the only redeeming feature of brutal, late-nineteenth-century
farmwork was the time he got to spend around horses; learning to
ride also meant the freedom to learn shooting and hunting. For a
while, life was idyllic. Then, both of Wyatt's younger sisters died,
most likely from one of the unnamed fevers that periodically swept

through the region, and Nick reacted by moving again, buying a place back in Monmouth for the healthy sum of $2,000. Two years later, probably to evade several steep fines for bootlegging—a craft he presumably picked up in Kentucky—Nick moved his brood back again to Pella. The fines remain unpaid.

During the family's second stay in Pella, the Civil War broke out. James and Virgil, and their half-brother Newton, enlisted in the Union army. Curiously, all three traveled to another district to sign up, even though Nick, a deputy provost marshal for his congressional district, could have sworn them in. The explanation was probably their political differences; the boys regarded themselves as Lincoln men, and Nick, though he disliked slavery, was vehemently opposed to the abolition of slavery. He hadn't enlisted in the war to take the Southwest from Mexico to give the federal government the power to take away a citizen's property (or punish him for making his own whiskey).

Domineering as he was and would remain, Nick Earp stuck to his principle of encouraging his boys to think for themselves. Years later Wyatt would quote his father as saying: " 'Religion is a matter which every man must settle for himself. Your mother and I tried to make you children understand your responsibilities, to yourselves and to others; beyond that we did not expect to accomplish much.' " This stood for politics as well. There is no indication of animosity on Nick's part that some of his sons chose to fight for the Union.

All three young Earps achieved creditable war records—James was severely wounded and sent home in 1863, while Newton, in a second tour of duty, reached the rank of sergeant—marred only by Virgil's court-martial, probably for fighting, a minor offense that cost him half a month's pay and didn't interfere with an honorable discharge. Nick, back in Pella, recruited and drilled local companies.

Wyatt, thirteen in 1861, stayed home, hoeing his father's corn, hating the task but producing, in the opinion of one neighbor, an excellent crop. One day he heard a bugle ring—possibly from a regiment his father was training—and determined that he, too, must be a part of it all. He ran away to the recruiting office at Ottumwa, a river port where Union soldiers were transported east—how he got to the town, a good half-day journey by wagon, isn't clear—and to his chagrin, he found his father waiting there. Wyatt was promptly hauled back to the farm for punishment. About to be switched,

Wyatt took quick advantage when his father pushed a protesting Ginnie Ann aside. He rushed his father, shouting, "You can't hit my mother!" Nicholas, who had no intention of hitting anyone but Wyatt, was taken aback by his son's pluck and audacity and, stopping a moment to think things over, decided against the switching. This was the first of many stories that would collect around Wyatt's legend where he diverted trouble through a combination of fast thinking and fast action.

By the spring of 1864 the Earps once more were packed and ready to travel, this time to California, with a wagon train of less than a dozen families, and Nick leading the trek. Wyatt, at sixteen, would never have so settled a life again as the one he had left in Iowa. He had nothing but adventure on his mind, and soon he would get it. In Omaha, Wyatt was unsettled by the first gunfight he had ever witnessed (whether or not a man was killed is unclear). Many years later he told Stuart Lake of some hair-raising Indian clashes, in one of which our young hero fended off an Indian attack by stampeding several hundred horses and oxen into their ranks. What a small wagon train was doing with several hundred draught animals was not explained. The sudden appearance of so many horses and oxen must have startled the whites as much as the Indians.

Somewhere in this fracas Wyatt took potshots at braves not much older than himself. So, in the space of a few weeks, sixteen-year-old Wyatt had been introduced to frontier violence. He had seen a man shot, and now he had taken a shot at a man himself. He also learned when not to shoot. One Earp historian relates a story Wyatt told to his nephew, Bill Miller, about a Paiute who had been hanging around the Earp campfire. Nicholas lost his temper and kicked him in the seat of his pants:

> "I was expecting trouble," Wyatt said, "and got my gun as soon as we saw this Indian, who'd been hanging around begging and probably trying to steal and generally making a nuisance of himself. He wasn't the only one. I stood out of the way behind a wagon. He pulled a knife and Pa pulled a six-shooter and I would have shot him if he hadn't put his knife away and left. I had him covered and come close to shooting, except that Pa got in the way. If

he'd have got Pa, I aimed to cut him down. I had a six-shooter in my belt and could have stood the ten others off. There wasn't a one of them with any sand if you stood up to them, but they all had mean tempers and they were all thieves."

This is an uncharitable view of Plains Indians, but most pioneers never saw them under other circumstances. Only a few years after the Earps' encounter, Mark Twain was to describe the first Indians he saw as "prideless beggars . . . hungry, always hungry, and yet never refusing anything that a hog would eat, though often eating what a hog would decline." The white man's romanticizing of the Plains Indians would not begin for several decades.

While on a stopover in Utah, young Wyatt supposedly met his first frontier legend, the most respected scout and mountain man of his day, Jim Bridger. Unfortunately, Lake's is the only account that places Bridger among the Earp party in that period, which probably means that Wyatt learned about hunting and fishing either from some other veteran mountain man or from his own father, who taught him to shoot game and handle draught animals. Nick Earp was a stern wagon master, which was needed on this trip since, like many pioneer parties, this one engaged in petty feuds and squabbles and constantly threatened to bog down or split up (and given the elder Earp's temper, it's likely he instigated more than a few incidents). Whatever Nicholas Earp's flaws as a community leader, he got the wagon train through without a single loss.

By the end of the year, the Earps were in San Bernardino. "Around a table loaded with the fruits and sweetmeats of a southern clime," Flood wrote, "a family of five children and a father and a mother"—four children, actually, since James left the party before it arrived in California—"were seated at a feast of glorious thanksgiving in the little village of San Bernardino on Christmas Day of Eighteen Hundred and Sixty-Four. There were evidences of their recently having come through an ordeal. The men didn't show the effects, their skins were weathered and bronzed, but upon the countenances of the mother and her daughter there were still the signs of fatigue." One can only imagine what their reaction would have been if they had been told that before the next decade was out they'd be making the trip again.

*   *   *

"It had been anticipated," wrote Stuart Lake in one of *Frontier Marshal*'s seminal mythmaking passages, "that Wyatt would continue the study of law in California, but the taste of life he had enjoyed during the covered wagon journey made him loathe to return to books . . . by spring he had set his own mind definitely against any vocation that might hold him from adventuring." Lake got the last part right; the stuff about studying law was fiction. In San Bernardino Wyatt plowed his father's farm, a task he enjoyed no more in lush California than he had in arid Iowa, and waited for an opportunity to bolt. Finally, he and Nick had a falling out, more than likely resorting to their fists, and Wyatt was on his own.

Work wasn't hard to find. By the end of the Civil War San Bernardino was a boomtown of more than two thousand, much larger than a pueblo down the road named Los Angeles. Prospectors, hunters, cattlemen, lumberjacks, soldiers, and freighters filled the streets; a husky teenager might have his pick from a variety of jobs. Wyatt liked the freighters best: They worked with horses and mules and they traveled. His first job offer came when a driver for the San Bernardino–Los Angeles line broke his leg: "Who'll take your place?" the owner asked the driver. "Get Nicholas Earp's boy Wyatt," the driver advised. "You've got bad horses and bad men to handle on that run and young Wyatt can do both." Wyatt had been a master of horses and wagons since the age of fourteen, but it's not likely that anyone with valuable freight to ship would entrust it to a seventeen year old, no matter what his reputation, especially on a route that covered sixty hard miles through mountain passes and desert. Although no records prove Wyatt ever drove a stage in California, Virgil, who was five years older, did drive for a Gen. Phineas Banning, one of southern California's early stage line operators. Virgil probably let Wyatt go along on some runs, which allowed Wyatt to later pad his resume with "Stage Driver."

Carrying heavy freight was no easier work than farming, but at least you moved while you worked. Wyatt hauled freight, first in heavy wagons from San Bernardino to Salt Lake City, and then with Virgil over the same route for San Francisco–based freighter Charles Chrisman. He also signed on to grade the Union Pacific railroad line, which took him all the way to Julesburg, Colorado. By 1869, at age twenty-one, Wyatt had already traveled several thousand miles.

He would have a long way to go before he would match his peripatetic father. Nick had now moved five times and lived in four states from Kentucky to California. In 1868, he took Ginnie Ann and the three children remaining at home—Morgan, Warren, and Adelia—and moved back to the Midwest. This time, they could take the train, or at least take it from Wyoming (where Wyatt and Virgil accompanied them to) all the way to Illinois. The strapping, six-foot-tall Earp brothers then found work as freighters and hunters of game for crews in the railroad camps. In their spare time they learned to gamble and fight and watch their backs. They also developed a lifelong interest in boxing.

"Railway construction camps in the Wyoming of 1868," wrote Lake,

> were populated by rough and boisterous fellows, but Wyatt Earp did not remember them as spontaneously wild or genuinely bad in comparison with cow camps and mining towns. They were strung across the state, at approximately twenty-mile intervals, with about two hundred men in each camp. Laborers, for the greater part, were veterans of the Civil War—from both armies—earning one to two dollars a day and board. They were a hard-driven, hard-working crowd inured to the hardest living, and they found their recreation in hard drinking and hard fighting. They carried guns at their work as protection against Indian attacks, but in settling differences among themselves usually laid weapons aside and fought with fists. Possibly war had provided a sufficiency of gunplay; at any rate, Wyatt could remember but one instance in which he saw railroad workers choose pistols to settle a quarrel.

Boxing in the railroad camps was governed by London Prize Ring rules, though *governed* may not be an accurate term, as there was little in London Prize Ring that wasn't allowed. Butting, eye gouging, hair pulling, ear biting, rabbit punching, and tripping were all common, though spitting was frowned upon. A Dodge City Times account of a bare knuckles bout staged while Wyatt was assistant marshal, though somewhat exaggerated, gives an idea of what went on at a match:

On last Tuesday morning the champion prizefight of
Dodge City was indulged in by Messrs. Nelson Whitman
and the noted Red Hanley, familiarly known as 'the Red
Bird from the South. . . .' During the forty-second
round Red Hanley implored Norton [the referee] to take
Nelson off for a little while till he could have time to put
his right eye back where it belonged, set his jawbone, and
have the ragged edge trimmed off his ears where they had
been chewed the worst. This was against the rules of the
ring so Norton declined, encouraging him to bear it as
well as he could and squeal when he got enough. About
the sixty-fourth round Red squealed unmistakably and
Whitman was declared the winner. The only injury sustained by the loser in this fight were two ears chewed off,
one eye busted and the other disabled, right cheek bone
caved in, bridge of the nose broken, seven teeth knocked
out, one jawbone mashed, one side of the tongue bit off,
and several other unimportant fractures and bruises. Red
retires from the ring in disgust.

The real job of referees like Wyatt wasn't so much to see that such
fights were clean—what would constitute dirty?—as to simply keep
the fighters fighting instead of wrestling and butting.

At one match held near Cheyenne, Wyoming, on July 4, 1869,
Mike Donovan, a seasoned pro, beat a young boxer named John
Shanssey so badly that the latter retired from the ring. Donovan went
on to become a well-known heavyweight; Shanssey was later to become mayor of Yuma, Arizona. Wyatt, acting as a bookie for the
camp laborers, met both men before the bout. The meeting was to
prove momentous for Wyatt. Years later, when Earp was in Fort
Griffin, Texas, possibly in search of "Dirty" Dave Rudabaugh, Shanssey introduced him to a notorious dentist-turned-gambler named
John "Doc" Holliday.

There is no account of Wyatt stepping into the ring himself, but
he must have learned something of the fistic arts in the camps.
Thirty-five years later Bat Masterson would recall in his magazine
profile of Wyatt that he:

never at any time in his career, resorted to the pistol ex-
cepting in such cases where such a course was absolutely
necessary. Wyatt could scrap with his fists, and had often
taken all the fight out of bad men, as they were called,
with no other weapons than those provided by Nature.
There were few men in the West who could whip Earp in
a rough-and-tumble fight thirty years ago, and I suspect
that he could give a tough youngster a hard tussle eight
now, even if he is sixty-one years of age.

Given Wyatt's love for the rough-and-tumble life of the camps, it
seems inexplicable that he would suddenly chuck it all away for a
normal life in a settled town. From the Plains, Wyatt went to join
Nicholas and Ginnie Ann in Lamar, Missouri. It was to be his first
try at settling down until his old age. Wyatt never talked about
Lamar to John Flood or Stuart Lake or anyone. In fact, it wasn't
until a couple of decades after *Frontier Marshal* was published that
researchers even found out that the Earps had lived in Missouri.
No one knows why Nick chose Lamar, though the 240 acres of
property he had acquired not far from his brother's farm could well
have been reason enough. That the family never spoke of Lamar is
unsurprising—nothing of any consequence happened there. Except
to Wyatt, and he had good reason to forget.

It was the fall of 1869 in sleepy, settled Lamar that the most
famous lawman of the American West actually got his first law appointment. The official title wasn't the familiar "marshal" or "sheriff"
of frontier towns, but the more staid "constable." On September
24 of that same year Wyatt's half-brother, Newton, announced his
candidacy when the position came up for election. This would later
be cited as an example of Wyatt's opportunism, but in fact it was
Newton who ran against Wyatt, who already had the job. There is
no indication that either brother harbored ill feelings over the election; Newton would later name his son after Wyatt.

Actually, Wyatt and Newton may have run against each other
simply to keep the job in the family. Nick had already served a stint
as town constable—that was in addition to running a small farm,
operating a small grocery store and restaurant, and serving as a justice of the peace. With Nick as a justice and Wyatt as a policeman,
the Earps had the law business—such as the law business was in

Lamar, Missouri, in 1870—in their pocket. The voters were happy enough with the arrangement. "This is a good appointment," wrote someone in the *Southwest Missourian* when Wyatt first got the job, "and when our city dads get the machine in grinding order lawbreakers had better watch out." Possibly in anticipation of Wyatt's future reputation, lawbreakers such as Missouri's Jesse James and Cole Younger heeded the warning. No major crimes were committed in Lamar during the period—a good thing, since Barton County, where Lamar is located, didn't have a jail in 1870.

Twenty-nine Missouri voters gave Wyatt Earp the only elective position he ever held, although, technically, he never held it because he never assumed office. In fact Wyatt may have won the election only because of a sympathy vote. Sometime in late 1869, he met a girl named Urilla Sutherland, the daughter of a Lamar hotel keeper named James Sutherland. More about who Urilla (or Rilla or Willa) Sutherland was and how Wyatt met her is not known. Local tradition says she was younger than Wyatt when they married, and Wyatt had just turned twenty-two. Her parents must have approved of the match; Nicholas, too, since he performed the ceremony. The couple purchased a lot on the outskirts of Lamar for $50. A little more than nine months later Wyatt would put it up for sale.

Urilla Sutherland died, possibly of typhus but almost certainly while in childbirth. Shortly after the Earp brothers (Virgil and Wyatt and perhaps Newton, since James and Morgan were away and Warren too young) got into a brawl with Urilla's brothers, who apparently blamed Wyatt for their sister's death. *Why* they blamed Wyatt isn't clear. The logical reason would seem to be that they thought Urilla was too young to have married and believed her to have been seduced by the older Wyatt.[3]

The following year brought a minor court action involving $20 that Wyatt either stole or borrowed and failed to pay back (the court records aren't clear). The case was eventually dismissed, but Wyatt wasn't there to know about it. He was engaged—or appears to have been engaged—in perhaps the most serious clash with the law he would ever have.

The known facts are that three men named Wyatt S. Earp, Edward Kennedy, and John Shown were charged, according to the document in the U.S. Federal Records, with stealing two horses each from one William Keys. Who Kennedy and Shown were is not known.[4] John Shown's wife gave a statement that adds both color and confusion to the incident:

> I know Wyatt S. Earp and Ed Kennedy. They got my husband drunk near Ft. Gibson, I.T. [Indian Territory] about the 28th of March 1871. They went and got Mr. Jim Keys' horses [apparently William Keys' brother], and put my husband on one and he led the other, and told him to ride 50 miles towards Kansas and then they would hitch the horses to a wagon, and he could ride. I went with these two men and met my husband 50 miles North of Ft. Gibson, and rode with these two men [Earp and Kennedy] in a hack. On meeting my husband they took the two horses out of the hack and put in the two he had. Earp drove on toward Kansas for three full nights. (We laid over days). About three o'clock of the third night James M. Keys overtook us. My husband John Shown said he could have the horses—the other left. Earp and Kennedy told Keys that my husband stole the horses. They also said that if Shown (my husband) turned state's evidence then they would kill him.

Earp and Shown made the $500 bail, which they subsequently skipped. Kennedy was acquitted on June 8, 1871, which means there had been a trial. The names of Wyatt Earp and John Shown were never again mentioned in connection with the case. What's the explanation? The most likely one is that Earp, Shown, and Kennedy were rank amateurs as horse thieves. Shown appears as the less guilty partner and he skipped; Kennedy appears as more guilty than Shown, but he was tried and acquitted. Kennedy's acquittal suggests that the statement by Shown's wife was self-serving nonsense; it's possible that she was even involved in whatever crime was attempted.[5] There is no other apparent explanation for why she went along on the ride.

If this was Wyatt Earp, our Wyatt Earp, then the horse theft episode left him at a crossroads.[6] He was twenty-three with no family of his own and no profession. One career possibility was outlawing—he certainly had the skill with guns and horses to make a first-rate holdup man. Instead, he took up a profession where an enterprising young man could make a good deal of money the honest way if he applied himself and didn't mind days of scorching heat and choking dust, swarms of insects, occasional nights spent in rain and mud, the threat of Indians and stampedes, the unceasing roar of heavy rifles in his ears, and the all-pervading smell of gunsmoke, offal, and rotting carcasses.

For a couple of years after the death of his wife, Wyatt Earp was a loner; he would retain some of the qualities of a loner the rest of his life. There are no records or even hints of romantic involvements with women and not many of friendships with men. The one person who later recalled Wyatt at this age was Bat Masterson, who remembered him as "about twenty-six years old"—actually he was twenty-four—"and weighing in the neighborhood of 160 pounds, all of it muscle. He stood six feet in height, with light blue eyes, and a complexion bordering on the blond." Bat met Wyatt on the Plains where, like hundreds of other young men with no other hopes of employment, they killed buffalo.

"I'll admit," Wyatt later said, "that in 1871 no buffalo hunter of my acquaintance—myself, least of all—planned his work as a crusade for civilization; but in a sense it was that. I went into the business to make money while enjoying life that appealed to me."[7]

Wyatt's fellow hunters were disgusted by his practice of assisting his hired man in butchering the animals. Hunters—those who could afford their own guns and ammunition and could hire someone to do the skinning—were supposed to be above such filthy work. Earp seemed to give butchering no second thought. By joining in the cutting, Wyatt, who had no capital, was able to kill and skin the twenty to twenty-five buffalo per day needed to make a profit and to keep expenses down by working with only one other man and one wagon. As for the danger of Indians or buffalo stampedes, Stuart Lake wrote: "The Indian hazard offered no great deterrent to a man of Wyatt's temperament than the possibility that he might be caught by the hoofs or horns of a stampeding buffalo herd. Face to face with either danger, he would do what he might."

If we are to trust Lake, Wyatt also gave no thought to the proper weapon with which to hunt buffalo. The twelve-plus pound, .50 caliber Sharps rifle was, because of its power and range, the almost unanimous choice among buffalo hunters, "but notable among its drawbacks were the cost of ammunition and the fact that the rifle's accuracy was seriously affected by rapid fire." (The gun had to be watered down constantly to keep from overheating.) Wyatt, according to Lake, chose instead, "a breech-loading gun, with apparatus for reloading shells, and this, with a supply of powder, lead, and caps, was to constitute his hunting arsenal." Lake went on: "At any range under one hundred yards, he could score as accurately with his shotgun as any rifleman." Someone, probably Wyatt or Bat Masterson, was pulling Lake's leg. One hundred feet, not one hundred yards, would have been closer to the effective range of any shotgun available in the early 1870s, and even at one hundred feet the pellets from such a weapon would not have been able to do much more than annoy a buffalo.[8] Wyatt must have shot buffalo, like most other hunters, with a Sharps, and he made a good enough living at it to go out on several hunts.[9]

Earp made no extravagant claims for himself as a buffalo hunter but took notice of the prowess of his associates: "The known record kill from a single stand was held by Tom Nixon, a famous shot who made headquarters at Dodge. He downed one hundred and twenty animals without moving his rest-sticks, but he ruined his Sharps rifle." And: "The best authenticated total for a season's kill was set by Billy Tilghman. He took thirty-three hundred hides between September 1 of one year and April 1 of the next; no buffalo hunter I know ever topped that score."

Old West scholars will recognize "Billy" Tilghman as the future Bill Tilghman, regarded by many as the most efficient peace officer of the Plains states. Most of the great Kansas peace officers met on the buffalo-strewn plains—Masterson, Tilghman, Charlie Bassett, and Neal Brown were just four of the buffalo hunters who would one day comprise the most famous peacekeeping force of the cattle town era in Dodge City. There were also some future desperadoes in the buffalo camps, including Dutch Henry and Hendry Brown—Stuart Lake would later splice their names to Dutch Henry Brown, the villain played by Stephen McNally in the 1950 James Stewart movie *Winchester '73* Among such men, Wyatt made an impression. Billy Dixon, who knew Wyatt in the camps, recalled to Bat Masterson that

Wyatt was a shy young man with few intimates. With casual acquaintances he seldom spoke unless spoken to.

When he did say anything, it was to the point, without fear or favor, which wasn't relished by some; but that never bothered Wyatt. To those who knew him well he was a genial companion. He had the most even disposition I ever saw; I never knew him to lose his temper. He was more intelligent, better educated, and far better mannered than the majority of his associates, which probably did not help them to understand him. His reserve limited his friendships, but more than one stranger, down on his luck, has had firsthand evidence of Wyatt's generosity. I think his outstanding quality was the nicety with which he gauged the time and effort for every move. That, plus his absolute confidence in himself, gave him the edge over the run of men.

Bill Tilghman recalled something else: "In all the years during which I was intimately associated with Wyatt, as a buffalo hunter and a peace officer, I never knew him to take a drink of liquor."

By 1872, it seems, the popular image of Wyatt Earp that remains today was already becoming fixed in people's minds. To those he regarded as friends, he awarded a fierce, familylike loyalty; strangers saw the calm confidence of a man not to be trifled with, a man Bat Masterson would later call "absolutely destitute of physical fear." Wyatt Earp was acquiring, in the parlance of his place and time, a reputation.

At the beginning of 1873, Wyatt still had no clear idea of what profession he was going to follow, but he had a clear-headed vision of where the money was going. He could see the buffalo giving way to Texas cattle; six years later he would foresee the decline of the cattle towns and the rise of the mining camps. But for now, all roads were leading to Abilene, Caldwell, Ellsworth, Wichita, and a huge buffalo camp making the transition to cow town, Dodge City. Wyatt was twenty-five years old. He sold his buffalo gun and set out for Kansas.

Notes

1. I encountered the Virginia branch of the clan in the town of New Market, Virginia, where I had just purchased a copy of the

October 28, 1881, "New York Times" with an account of the O.K. Corral gunfight. As I was leaving town I saw a shingle at an art gallery that read Judith Earp Delaughter. Ms. Delaughter shared phone numbers of other Earps and anecdotes that are used in this book.

2. In a newly printed pamphlet, *Wyatt Earp: Facts, Volume 1*, Glenn G. Boyer contends that Walter was one-quarter Cherokee, the son of Phillip Earp and Sally Vaughan, who was the daughter of William Vaughan and a full-blooded Cherokee woman, Fair-O-Bee Looney. Boyer's new series of pamphlets on Earp genealogy are available from Historical Research Associates, Rodeo, New Mexico.

3. That they "had" to marry because Wyatt got Urilla pregnant, as some have speculated, isn't likely: The evidence indicates she died almost nine months from the time of their marriage. For good measure, there's also an intriguing but unsubstantiated tale that the fight wasn't about Urilla but about a still the Sutherlands operated that was in competition with Nick's and that Wyatt, as constable, destroyed.

4. One version of this story has Wyatt being arrested and ignominiously hauled in chains to a stockade. The source of the story appears to be a rabid anti-Earp biographer from the 1950s, Ed Bartholomew, and as such is highly suspect.

5. It may be that Wyatt Earp was a fugitive from justice, as Earp debunker Ed Bartholomew would later claim. But despite much national publicity during the next several decades, no one ever attempted to serve a federal warrant on him.

6. Glenn Boyer, in the December 1993 issue of *True West*, suggests the possibility that it might have been another "Wyatt S. Earp, of whom there are more than a few in the public records of the time." If so, this would explain why no one has ever heard mention of men named Kennedy and Shown in any accounts of Wyatt Earp's life. This is certainly possible, given the odd number of people named Earp who lived in the area, but no one has yet discovered another Wyatt S. Earp.

7. John Gilchriese, an Earp researcher from Arizona, has claimed in interviews that Wyatt was an "unsuccessful buffalo hunter." But he has never revealed on what evidence he based this conclusion.

8. Actually, that wasn't the strangest claim made for Wyatt The Buffalo Hunter. In his popular book, *Cowboy Capital of the World—*

The Saga of Dodge City, Samuel Carter made the bizarre assertion that Wyatt shot buffalo from horseback like Buffalo Bill Cody, of whom Wyatt was supposed to have been a "disciple." Mr. Carter died several years ago, and no one has been able to discover his source for this claim.

9. Lee Silva, a California-based researcher, disputes the point about shotguns and buffalo hunting, writing that Lake was correct in saying that Wyatt "loaded into the shotgun shell and fired through the smooth-bore barrel of a breechloading cartridge shotgun, the same as round lead balls were shot through the smooth bore muzzle-loading muskets of the Civil War period and before." I remain skeptical. My information on buffalo hunting came from an interview with David A. Dary, author of the 1974 volume *The Buffalo Book* (The Swallow Press, Inc.). According to Dary's letter to me, "The single slug shotgun was costly, inaccurate, and inefficient, at least the guns that were used in the late 1860s and early 1870s. You can find little evidence of anyone using such a method to hunt buffalo. When metallurgy became more sophisticated, using a single slug in a shotgun became a fairly common method of hunting, not just out West, but in the Northeast as well. But not in the late 1860s and early 1870s."

2

"Bloody Kansas"—Wyatt Earp in Wichita

From the mid-1850s till the interruption of the Civil War, and then again from the late '60s to the mid '70s, Kansas was the focus of far more national attention than its relatively sparse population merited. More than neighboring Missouri, Kansas was the battleground for the pre–Civil War violence that swept the border— "Bleeding Kansas," a New York editorialist called the state that had been ravaged by John Brown, Quantrill's Raiders, and scores of other notorious and desperate men. At the same time, the southwestern corner of the state was serving as a base from which much of the rest of the West would eventually be settled.

After the Civil War, with astonishing swiftness, the enormous buffalo herds, most of which migrated through Kansas, were decimated. The killing of the buffalo was an industry in Kansas, from supplying the hunters to skinning to the shipping of hides. Kansans who made their fortune in buffalo, such as future Dodge City mayor Bob Wright, soon found to their delight that the elimination of wild beasts paved the way for a more profitable industry based on domesticated animals. By the early 1870s, Kansas was the cattle-shipping center of the world, and the center of the cattle-shipping center was Wichita. Wyatt Earp, with his uncanny instinct for where the money would be, was there by 1874, right on time to catch the tide.

Wichita originated in 1864 as a trading post set up near a village of peaceful Wichita Indians. It remained one till the Atchison, Topeka, and Santa Fe Railroad built a branch line there in 1872.

Within a year, herds that would once have been driven to Abilene stopped at Wichita. From January to December 1874, nearly one-quarter of a million steers were shipped from Wichita to points north and east. A visiting easterner estimated the population of Wichita at that time to be about twelve hundred, though he may have included the hundreds of transients who passed in and out of every week on the way to points south and west. (Two such transients, headed for New Mexico, were a young woman with the surname of Antrim, thought to be from New York, and her teenaged son, William, who would be known before the decade was out as Billy the Kid. One native of Wichita recollected that they lived in an apartment just north of the courthouse, where Wyatt Earp worked.)

Wichita vied with Abilene before it and Dodge City after it for the unofficial title of the wickedest city on the plain; signs were placed on cattle routes that promised dust-choked rovers that "Everything goes in Wichita." Texas cowhands often complained about the rough treatment they received at the hands of Kansas peace officers, but none of them ever complained that the signs offered false advertising. A St. Louis paper described the town as "a brevet hell after sundown" with brass bands, piano music, and whip cracking in public streets contributing to the general merriment.

All night drinking and gambling were so common that in the middle of a trial, when a snake crawled into the court room, the judge reassured everyone, "Don't worry, it's real." Wichita also gave the thrill-starved drovers something they couldn't get back home: lewd stage shows with professional (in the sense that they were paid) actresses. There were even reports of races between naked saloon girls. Prostitution, surprisingly, was a small industry; the city marshal's report for late 1872 lists just four brothels and fourteen prostitutes at the height of the livestock shipping season. Of course, these were licensed prostitutes, and the likelihood of fierce competition from unlicensed practitioners cannot be discounted.

On October 29, 1874, at the peak of Wichita's cattle season, Wyatt Earp got his first known newspaper write-up:

> The Higgenbottom outfit, who attempted to jump the country at an expense of twenty or thirty thousand dollars to Wichita, it appears among other games stuck M. R. Moser for a new wagon, who instead of putting himself in

communication by telegraph with the outside world just
got two officers, John Behrens and Wiatt Earp, to light
out upon the trail. These boys fear nothing and fear nobody. They made about seventy-five miles from sun to
sun, across trackless prairies, striking the property and the
thieves near the Indian line. To make a long and exciting
story short, they just leveled a shotgun and a six shooter
upon the scallywags as they lay concealed in some brush,
and told them to "dough over," which they did.

While not the stuff from which pulp westerns were made, the report
has all the ingredients of many classic Earp stories to follow: a hard,
relentless ride in pursuit of a criminal, a complete lack of fear in
performance of a job, and an ending in which the quarry is brought
back alive. From a historical standpoint, there's only one thing odd
about it: City records indicate that Earp was appointed a policeman
on April 21, 1875, about six months after the capture of the Higgenbottom gang.

Why is Earp listed as an officer? He may have been working for a
private detective agency or been employed as a kind of auxiliary cop,
a "special officer" paid from bag money put up by wealthy private
citizens—most likely store owners and saloon keepers—with a stake
in keeping the peace. If nothing else, the item confirms the suspicions of historians who contend that cow town newspapers told only
a part of the story of frontier law enforcement.

For instance, Dave Leahy, a newspaperman and friend of Earp's
in Wichita, later wrote in a letter to Stuart Lake that "Bill Smith, the
marshal, was desperately in need of a man who had nerve enough to
wear a star—for it was a dangerous occupation in those days. He saw
Earp, a stranger, in the street one day and, sizing him up as a man
who might be fit, he asked him if he would care to take the position.
Wyatt agreed and Bill told Mayor Hope that he would put him to
work."[1]

In *Frontier Marshal* Stuart Lake awarded Wyatt the job on the
basis of a far more dramatic encounter: the arrest, in Ellsworth, Kansas, of the great Texas gunfighter Ben Thompson. The Ben Thompson story is the most colossal whopper in all of *Frontier Marshal*; the
tale was repeated on the TV series and in so many subsequent magazine articles and children's books that it became a cornerstone of the

Wyatt Earp legend—and did much to damage Wyatt Earp's reputation when it was later disproved.

Today Ben Thompson's name is remembered only by a handful of western buffs, but in his day Thompson was far better known than Wyatt Earp. English born and Texas bred, Thompson was sort of the Lou Gehrig or Jimmy Foxx of gunfighters in his day, with Wild Bill Hickok generally accorded the status of Babe Ruth. They were champions of their respective regions, Thompson having fought in the Confederate army, Hickok in the Union. The two legends never faced each other. Since Stuart Lake was erecting Wyatt's legend over Wild Bill Hickok's, Lake gave him the confrontation with Ben Thompson that Hickok never had.

"I met Wild Bill Hickok in Kansas City in 1871," Wyatt is quoted as saying. "Jack Gallagher, the celebrated scout, was there; and I remember Jack Martin, Billy Dixon, Jim Hanrahan, Tom O'Keefe, Cheyenne Jack, Billy Ogg, Bernardo Carlisle, Old Man Keeler, Kirk Jordan, and Andy Johnson. The names may not mean much to another century, but in my younger days each was a noted man. Much that they accomplished has been ignored by the records of their time, but every one made history." Probably not coincidentally, they also made the pages of Frank Wilstach's highly colored 1926 biography, *Wild Bill Hickok*, which served, in part, as a model for Lake's *Frontier Marshal*. Wyatt might have met all of those local legends on the buffalo hunting and gambling circuit in 1871, but it's doubtful that Wild Bill was among them. Hickok's best biographer, Joseph Rosa, has established that in April 1871, when Lake has Wyatt riding into Kansas City, Wild Bill was sworn in as town marshal of Abilene. "Hickok," says Lake's Wyatt, "was regarded as the deadliest pistol shot alive, as well as a man of great courage. The truth of certain stories about Bill's achievements may have been open to debate, but he had earned the respect paid to him." This sounds less like Wyatt Earp than Stuart Lake, as if someone was anticipating future controversy for his version of Wyatt Earp.

To appreciate the status later accorded Wyatt Earp, it's necessary to understand the awe in which Hickok was held by his contemporaries. By the time of his death in 1876, the dime novelists—Ned Buntline, J. W. Buel, Prentice Ingraham—had long since established Bill as the archetypal gunfighter, "The Prince of Pistoleers." And before the dime novelists, who cashed in on the legend, there were the Eastern journalists, who created it. The man who took Hickok's local legend East, and then all over the world, was Col. George Ward Nichols.[2]

Nichols was one of America's first celebrity journalists. In 1866 he journeyed to Kansas to profile Wild Bill Hickok for *Harper's New Monthly* magazine. The profile gave America its first vivid look at a new kind of frontiersman who would come to dominate the world's image of the American West, the pistoleer, shootist, or gunfighter. Nichols turned Hickok, while he was still alive, into the country's biggest frontier hero since Davy Crockett and made him the first legendary peace officer of the American West.

The real Wild Bill was a successful Civil War scout, Indian fighter, and buffalo hunter, but on his record as a policeman, Hickok, according to historian Leon Metz, "would have had a hard time getting a job as a dog catcher." No matter. The profile was not of Hickok but of a kind of hero that America was ready to believe in. "I never," Wild Bill allegedly told the journalist Henry M. Stanley (he of Dr. Livingston fame), "killed one man without good cause." With one or two notable exceptions, particularly that of Phil Coe, he might have been right.

More than any other shooting in the Old West before the O.K. Corral, Hickok's killing of Phil Coe revealed the tensions and antagonisms that remained just below the surface of the cow towns and mining camps. In 1871, Hickok was hired by the city fathers of the booming cow town of Abilene to keep the unruly drovers, most of them Texans, in check. One night, Hickok heard Coe discharge a pistol in the street in defiance of city ordinance and rushed out of a saloon to investigate. Accounts of what happened next vary. According to a Texas paper, Coe was "murdered at Abilene, Kansas, by a notorious character known as 'Wild Bill.'" An anti-Hickok witness, a Texan, said that Hickok drew two pistols and killed Coe on the spot—a split second after accidentally killing his own friend, Mike Williams, a special deputy employed by a nearby theater. (Hence the popular story that Hickok killed "his own deputy.") Other witnesses, all Kansans, said that Coe had a pistol in his hand when Hickok confronted him. More than likely, words ensued. In the Phil Coe sequence from Walter Hill's 1995 film, *Wild Bill*, Jeff Bridges booms, "I'm a Union man. I fought your kind in the war," which sounds about right. Coe then raised his pistol—or Hickok thought he was about to.

The reaction to the Coe shooting is like a minipreview of the post–O.K. Corral controversy ten years later, with partisan witnesses telling wildly divergent stories. The Kansans, most of them Republicans, regarded all cowhands as "Texans"—no matter where they were from—and all Texans as potential threats. (Coe wasn't a cowhand, but most of his friends were.) Hickok was probably guilty of some degree of manslaughter, at least by modern standards, but the prevailing opinion at the time was that peace officers needed to be given considerable discretion in dealing with town violence.

The Texans, of course, saw it another way. Most of the drovers were simply rowdy, good-natured Southern boys releasing a little tension after grueling trail drives. But even bullets fired in celebration could kill; one native of Caldwell recalled watching a Texan send a bullet through a bedroom window and quoted a Greek aphorism, "The boys throw stones in jest, but the frogs die in earnest."

Many Kansans didn't see the jest in the Texans' rough humor; the memory of "Bleeding Kansas" was still fresh. Irregulars from both sides of the conflict made much of Kansas and Missouri a living hell during the war years and spawned such postwar Confederate idols as Jesse and Frank James and Cole Younger, all of whom were still very much active in the 1870s. That most of the Texans now riding into Kansas had never been there before or were too young to have served in the Confederate Army was of no account. In 1868 Kansas passed a law forbidding "vagrants, drunks, or former Confederate soldiers" from carrying "pistols, bowie knives, or other deadly weapons" into the state under penalty of a stiff fine and up to three months in jail. The law fails to specify how peace officers decided who, in a crowd of herders, were the "former Confederates." Apparently anyone who sounded Southern was considered a former Confederate.

Of course, in practice such laws were difficult to enforce—most cattlemen were not about to surrender their God-given right to firearms without a debate. In spring of 1870 Abilene passed its own ordinance against the carrying of firearms by anyone within the city limits; it was scorned and disregarded by the swarms of Texas drovers, who riddled the ordinance posters with bullets and tore down the town jail. No townspeople were killed, but hundreds were certainly terrified. To understand the importance of policemen such as Earp, Masterson, and Tilghman is to understand that the real problem wasn't townsfolk cowering in fear so much as the possibility of townsfolk arming themselves to fight the Civil War again. The threat of vigilante action was anathema to the Kansas cattle town businessmen, to whom the drovers were economic life's blood. The business faction wanted the cattlemen held in check, not driven away, and as historian Robert Dykstra noted, towns like Ellsworth learned, after experiments with vigilante justice, "that the intricacies of repressing violence could not be entrusted to unfit personnel and an emotionally aroused populace." "Unfit personnel" meant not just vigilantes but, ultimately, men like Hickok, whose confrontational tactics were bad for business. Earp's method, perfected by the time he reached Dodge City, was to isolate the leader in the group of troublemakers, close on him, clamp down on his gun hand, and lay the barrel of his own gun across the transgressor's crown. By the standards of frontier justice in the 1870s this was humane; one might ask if it is any less so today. Indeed, the chief reason Wyatt Earp gained such a reputation as a hard cop in Kansas is that everyone he clashed with lived to tell about it.[3]

"The most important lesson I learned from those proficient gunfighters," Lake's Wyatt says in *Frontier Marshal*, "was that the winner of a gunplay usually was the man who took his time. The second was that, if I hoped to live long on the frontier, I would shun flashy trickshooting—grandstand play—as I would poison."

This sounds very much like something Wyatt would say, and the way he would have said it. It also sounds very much like Bat Masterson, who did say it and who was probably Lake's source. In the most quoted and anthologized passage from all of *Frontier Marshal*, Lake puts in Wyatt's mouth the distilled wisdom of three decades of frontier lawmen: "When I say that I learned to take my time in a gunfight, I do not wish to be misunderstood, for the time to be taken was only that split fraction of a second that means the difference between deadly accuracy with a six-gun and a miss. . . . Mentally deliberate, but muscularly faster than thought, is what I mean." Bat Masterson added to this the element of nerve, which he distinguished from courage. Courage helped you confront your trouble; nerve helped you stay cool in the confrontation. Wyatt Earp, said Bat, was possessed of both characteristics.

According to Wyatt, the inspiration for all his gunfighting wisdom was Wild Bill himself:

That summer in Kansas City he performed a feat of pistol-shooting which often has been cited as one of the most remarkable on record. . . .

Diagonally across Market Street, possibly one hundred yards away, was a saloon, and on the side-wall toward the police station a sign that carried a capital letter O. The sign ran off at an angle from Hickok's line of sight, yet, before anyone guessed what his target was, Wild Bill had fired five shots from the gun in his right hand, shifted weapons, and fired five more shots. Then he told Tom to send someone over to look at the O. All ten of Bill's slugs were found inside the ring of that letter.

That was shooting. . . . It may surprise some to know that a man of Hickok's skill could make a six-gun effective up to four hundred yards.

In the 1950s, anthologies edited by Bernard DeVoto and other historians quoted this passage as straight from the mouth of Wyatt Earp. In fact, Earp never said it. The story was concocted by Stuart Lake at his myth-mongering best. Wyatt may have met Hickok—he never mentioned it to anyone if he did—but he never saw Hickok or anyone else fire ten shots into the O on a side of a wall at a range of 100 yards; the idea of Hickok emptying both Colts into a wall next to a police station is in itself ludicrous.

As the years went on, the story of Wild Bill's shooting into the O evolved from a story Wyatt told to something Wyatt did. Typical is a passage from *The Picture Story of Wyatt Earp, The Most Colorful Marshal of the Old West* children's book. It's the Texas gunfighter, Ben Thompson, who shoots the cork through the bottle. Young Wyatt, "slow-tempered and fast-drawing," decides to show Thompson some real shooting:

His right hand dropped to his holster and came up with a gun. Five shots ripped out so fast they sounded like one. Then Wyatt pulled the gun on his left hip. Five more shots followed just as swift.

"Now, Pete," said Wyatt as he holstered his guns, "suppose you step over to Ord's store and look at the two O's in his sign."

In a few minutes Pete was back. "Boss," he reported to the square-set man, "there's five shot holes in one O and five shot holes in the other."

The square-set man walked up to Wyatt and stuck out his hand.

"My name's Ben Thompson."

"Mine's Wyatt Earp."

Earp did meet Ben Thompson somewhere, but no one knows the place and time.

The legend has Wyatt, a complete unknown, riding into the thriving cattle station of Ellsworth in 1873 just after Thompson's brother Billy killed the county sheriff, a man named Whitney, in what was probably an accident stemming from Thompson's resisting arrest. The young, unarmed Wyatt, appalled that no arrests were made, sarcastically remarks to the mayor, "Nice police force you have got." The mayor challenges Wyatt to take the job; Wyatt borrows two gun belts and Colts—"New guns and holsters," he says, "might have slowed me down"—and walks down the main street to confront Thompson.

"What do you want, Wyatt?" says Thompson, the use of the first name implying that Thompson knows Earp from somewhere. "I want you, Ben," Wyatt replies. "I'd rather talk than fight," Thompson says. "I'll get you either way," says Wyatt, without halting his stride.

Thompson shrugs; he'll take his chances in court, apparently in the knowledge that wealthy Texans will get preferential treatment in Kansas courts. The judge fines him just $25 for his part in the shooting for "disturbing the peace." Wyatt, the spiritual father of Dirty Harry, tosses his badge away in disgust and walks off. "Ellsworth," he says, "figures sheriffs at $25 a head. I don't figure the town's my size." The one part of the story that rings true is Lake's assertion that the judge "knocked the charge down from accessory to murder after considering 'the economic importance of the Texas men to the community.'"

Does the most famous Earp story from his Kansas years have a basis in fact? Thompson was arrested in Ellsworth after his brother killed Sheriff Whitney, but it was by a local deputy named Ed Hogue who, ironically, would later be arrested by Earp for a misdemeanor in Dodge. When Wyatt got into a scrape with some Texans in Wichita the next year he told them, according to the Flood manuscript, to "Go back uptown and ask Ben Thompson. He was in Abilene, he will tell you." Nothing more is known about the incident, but if Wyatt was using Ben Thompson as a character witness Thompson must have had some respect for him.

And the respect may well have stemmed from a near confrontation in Ellsworth. William Box Hancock, a cowhand of the period, left a manuscript with the Oklahoma Historical Society in which he claimed that Earp did arrest Thompson. When Josephine "Sadie" Marcus, Wyatt's third wife, prepared her memoirs, she included a passage in which Wyatt is quoted as saying, "I just kept looking him (Thompson) in the eye as I walked toward him. And when he started talking to me, I knew I had him . . . and that's all there was to it."

Whatever happened between Wyatt and Ben Thompson, it created no lingering animosity.

According to I Married Wyatt Earp, sometime in the late 1880s, well after the troubles in Tombstone, Sadie and Wyatt were having dinner in Austin, Texas, when Thompson—short, heavyset, and by this time bald—came to their table. "Well I'll be jiggered if it isn't Wyatt Earp!" Thompson said. Wyatt told Sadie that "Ben and I know each other from the Kansas days." Her impression was that the notorious Thompson, now the Austin City marshal, didn't look like he'd harm a fly, regardless of what they said about him. "They probably made most of it up anyhow," she wrote, "just as they have about Wyatt."

Abel Head "Shanghai" Pearce was the most colorful cattle king in the history of movies and television. In real life, he was more so. Like Thompson, Pearce was not a Texan by birth—he was from Rhode Island, of all places. The six-foot, five-inch-tall cow dealer got into the beef business as a butcher in the Confederate army and got his nickname after the war; he loved to strut into a new town in high boots with huge rowels, and someone thought he looked "like a Shanghai rooster."

Millions of American schoolboys who came of age in the 1950s know that Wyatt Earp—a.k.a. Hugh O'Brian, Burt Lancaster, and Joel McCrea—arrested the famous Shanghai and backed down a score of his men in the process. Every Earp researcher who came along after that knows that Wyatt Earp or Stuart Lake was a bald-faced liar and made that story up, since not one newspaper story of the era supports it. But though Lake may have exaggerated, the evidence indicates that something happened involving either Pearce or another cattle baron like him, and that it made an impression on the people who saw it.

Lake didn't make up the Shanghai Pearce arrest story. If it was made up, it was made up by Wyatt or his first biographer, John Flood. Flood's account begins with Sam Botts—a real Wichita officer whom Flood identifies as Potts—arresting the drunken, boisterous and hugely influential cattleman. Pearce—identified as "Cad" Pearce, probably because of Wyatt's seventy-six year old memory—knows that the Wichita city fathers don't want to alienate a man who brings a fortune to the town's economy with each herd, so he gets huffy with the portly, unimpressive Potts and resists arrest (or, as Flood phrases it, "He was for the law which . . . looked upon him patronizingly when he was in his cups and chose to be ugly").

At this point, Wyatt Earp steps in. Though Wyatt is identified in both Flood's and Lake's accounts as a Wichita policeman, he wasn't working for the force yet. Why did he interfere? Probably, as he was on the "special" payroll, a rented cop who assisted regular police when the cattle herds hit town. "Give me that gun," Wyatt says to Pearce, "or I'll break your arm." Pearce's friends show up. Faced with the muzzles of several guns, Wyatt flees down the alley and into a side door where he grabs a shotgun he has stashed. When Pearce and his victorious mob come around the corner, they find Wyatt waiting, along with Potts, Marshal Smith, and James Earp—the only instance, by the way, when Wyatt's oldest brother is said to have picked up a gun in his brother's defense.

Pearce surrenders; Wyatt becomes famous; and Wichita gratefully offers him a job as chief deputy. The accounts of this story are similar in Flood and Lake, with the difference that Lake decides the cattleman must indeed have been Shanghai Pearce. It certainly could have been; the logical place for Pearce at the height of the cattle season was Wichita. Wyatt thought he had arrested "Cad" Pearce, and if it wasn't Shanghai Pearce he arrested, then it was at least some Texas cattle baron. Historians hostile to Earp have pointed out the lack of newspaper substantiation for Wyatt's cattle town deeds, but in fact surviving newspapers scarcely contain any stories about clashes between *any* Kansas police and Texans in this period. (Virtually the only exceptions involved killings, which had to be mentioned.) Kansas papers of the period invariably wrote of Earp in glowing terms, using phrases like "doing a splendid job" or "adding new laurels" to his record, but seldom mention specifics and never when dealing with Texas cowhands. This is absurd, since keeping the Texans in line was precisely the reason Earp was hired. A number of Old West researchers now believe that Kansas papers simply regarded *all* news about clashes between Kansas police officers and Texans to be bad for business and pressured the local papers (with whom they advertised) into practicing self-censorship.

A strong back-up to this theory—and an equally strong back-up for the story of the Shanghai Pearce arrest—comes from the veteran Wichita newspaperman, Dave Leahy, a friend of Earp's in Wichita, who recalls Wyatt having been in "two big fights" when "the Texans wanted to capture the town. The story of those two fights would almost fill a book." If they are so noteworthy, one wants to ask, then why didn't Leahy, a journalist, write about them at the time they occurred? The only logical answer is that he wasn't allowed to, just as Dodge City reporters wouldn't write of similar clashes in later years.

If anything, Leahy's letter seems more action-packed than the Pearce stories in Flood or Lake. In fact, though Lake is often and, rightfully, accused of coloring Wyatt's adventures, some of his accounts of Earp's most famous confrontations, when looked at carefully, appear almost subdued. For instance, the arrest of Shanghai Pearce, presented by Lake in *Frontier Marshal*, comes off as an entirely plausible event. No extravagant claims are made; no one is gunned down. Wyatt doesn't outdraw twenty Texans or even one; Wyatt even admits that he retreated in order to get a better tactical position. The point to Lake's story doesn't seem to be to show off Wyatt's courage so much as his cleverness in the strategic placing of his shotgun—an important detail, since we know he and Bat Masterson used the same tactic to great advantage in Dodge. (We will see it again four years later in the famous Clay Allison confrontation.)

Another point to Earp's story is that he was able to bring off the arrest without shooting anyone; surely no peace officer of the Old West bragged so much about how many men he *didn't* kill. "Wyatt had hopes," Lake wrote, "of getting into action on his own before any posse of citizens could reach Pearce and the Cowboys. Not only was there a chance that he could save some needless killing; in his first big play as a Wichita police officer, the Texas men now had him studded." In other words, Wyatt wasn't going to let any Texans get away with treeing him, especially in a situation where he might make a good impression on his bosses. Both these motives fit the Wyatt Earp we will come to know.

Another piece of evidence that some important arrest had been made is that a short time after the period Lake was writing about Wyatt was offered a deputy's badge. Not the chief deputy's badge that Lake claimed for him, but a deputy's badge. According to the Wichita papers, he made solid if unspectacular use of it.

In May 1875, the *Wichita Beacon* has Wyatt arresting a horse thief he might have killed, firing, in the paper's words, "one shot across his poop deck to bring him to." (Perhaps he was lenient in memory of his own horse theft three years earlier.) Another item talks of an arrest made by Wyatt and town marshal Mike Meagher of a wagon thief and two of his accomplices.

There are three other Wichita newspaper items that mention Earp. On January 12, 1876, the *Beacon* reported

> Last Sunday night (January 9), while policeman Earp was sitting with two or three others in the back room of the Custom House Saloon, his revolver slipped from his holster, and falling to the floor, the hammer was resting on the cap, is supposed to have struck the chair, causing a discharge of one of the barrels. The ball passed through his coat, struck the north wall then glanced off and passed out through the ceiling. It was a narrow escape and the occurrence got up a lively stampede from the room. One of the demoralized was under the impression that someone had fired through the window from the outside.

In *Frontier Marshal* Earp goes on at length about how "professionals" always kept a single action revolver with the hammer resting on an empty chamber; we may assume that this is the incident that taught him the wisdom of such precautions.[4]

A December 15, 1875, item is more illuminating:

On last Wednesday (December 8), policeman Earp found a stranger lying near the bridge in a drunken stupor. He took him to the "cooler" and on searching him found in the neighborhood of $500 on his person. He was taken next morning, before his honor, the police judge, paid his fine for his fun like a little man and went on his way rejoicing. He may congratulate himself that his lines, while he was drunk, were cast in such a pleasant place as Wichita as there are but few other places where that $500 bank roll would have been heard from. The integrity of our police force has never been seriously questioned.

Wyatt would to be accused of complicity in more than one bunco operation in his eighty-one years, but even his enemies have never been able to pin a dishonest incident to him while he served on a police force.[5]

Wyatt's tour of duty began and ended with fights. On his first day in Wichita he got into a fistfight with one Doc Black, a hotel owner who was bullying a young boy. Wyatt cleaned Doc's clock and was arrested for his trouble by Marshal Bill Smith. Rather than throw him in jail, Smith and the mayor concluded that anyone who could handle Black might make a pretty good peace officer. (Dave Leahy remembered Doc Black as someone who kept trespassers off his property with a pitchfork. Leahy also recalled that "Doc Black was not the town bully. . . . Mrs. Black was the bully of Doc's family.")

Almost a year from the time Earp was appointed, he was involved in another scuffle, this time with Bill Smith. The popular version of The Beacon's reporting of the incident is the one that appears in Frank Waters's Earp-debunking *The Earp Brothers of Tombstone*: "On last Sunday night a difficulty occurred between Policeman Erp (sic) and Wm. Smith, candidate for city marshal. Erp was arrested for violation of the peace and order of the city and was fined on Monday afternoon by his honor Judge Atwood, $30 and cost, and was relieved from the police force." Waters was right as far as he quoted. What Waters (and a score of historians who followed him) *didn't* quote at the end of the item put a different spin on the story:

The remarks that Smith was said to have made in regard to the marshal sending for Erp's brothers to put them on the police force furnished no just grounds for an attack, and upon ordinary occasions we doubt if Erp would have given them a second thought. The good order of the city was properly vindicated in the fining and dismissal of Erp. It is but justice to Earp to say he has made an excellent officer, and hitherto his conduct has been *unexceptionable*. (Italics mine)

Smith, who was running for the marshal's post, must have accused Mike Megher, who had the job, of agreeing to hire Wyatt's brothers (meaning Virgil and Morgan, since James was happily tending bar with no intention of getting out into the law enforcement business). This is almost certainly what Wyatt did have in mind, though why it became a political issue remains a mystery. Ironically, the accusations didn't hurt Megher, who was reelected.

Though it was embarrassing at the time, Earp's dismissal did nothing to hurt his standing with the leading citizens in Wichita. Seven years later in a testimony sent to Tombstone during the O.K. Corral inquest, Charles Hatton, a city attorney during Earp's tour of duty, added a personal note: "I take great pleasure in saying that Wyatt S. Earp was one of the most efficient officers that Wichita ever had and I can safely testify that Mr. Earp is in every sense reliable and a trustworthy gentleman." Jimmy Cairns, who also signed the document and served with Wyatt on the Wichita police (and would later become Bat Masterson's brother-in-law), was quoted through Dave Leahy as saying that "Wyatt Earp was the most dependable pal" he had during his career as a police officer and that "he was a clean fellow through and through." Leahy added that Wyatt Earp "was the bravest man himself whom I have ever known intimately," with the possible exception of the famed Pinkerton agent Charlie Siringo. If Wyatt didn't leave Wichita with all his dignity, he at least left with a reputation.

He wasn't the only Earp in Wichita that year with a reputation. In *Why the West Was Wild*, a comprehensive search of newspaper files and records of the cattle town era, Nyle H. Miller and Joseph W. Snell report that

Bessy Earp, wife of James, Wyatt's brother, was fined Wichita police court in May 1874, for being a prostitute.

So was Sally Earp, who apparently shared the same dwelling, but for whom no other identification has been found. Bessy and Sally were each fined $8 and $2 in court costs. Sally's name appears regularly in the city's prostitute file list through February 1875 and Bessy's through March 1875.

Miller and Snell were fine researchers, but in this case their conclusions aren't supported by the slim evidence. The name in the court records is spelled "Betsy," not Bessy, as Miller and Snell wrote, and no one has ever been able to figure out who Sally Earp was or if she was any relation to James or Wyatt. (Some have speculated that it was Celia, Wyatt's second wife, otherwise known as Mattie, but this is quite a stretch. No one knows where Wyatt met Mattie, and there is no evidence she was with him in Wichita.) Betsy could well have been James Earp's Bessie, and it's far from the realm of possibility that their relationship was, at least in part, professional.[6] But James was the loner among the brothers, and if he was pimping in Wichita he was more than likely running a one-man show.

Except for a brief sojourn into Texas, Wyatt would not see his older brother again for four years. In need of work, he headed for the frontier boomtown most in need of his unique talents.

Notes

1. Leahy's memory may be faulty on this: most accounts from Wichita in late '74 and for the first half of '75 have Mike Megher, not Bill Smith, as town marshal. Smith was the man Earp would later be accused of slugging, an incident that would lead to his dismissal.

2. A study of George Ward Nichols's life and career might yield some interesting facts about American journalism in the second half of the nineteenth century, particularly as it pertained to the building of frontier legends. We know little about Nichols, except that he died in Cincinnati in 1885 and at the time of his death was president of the Cincinnati College of Music. But he was a journalist of note in the 1860s, surely one of the best-paid journalists in America. Among my father's books I found a volume entitled *The Story of the Great March—From the Diary of a Staff Officer.* The inscription on the title page reads "By Brevet Major George Ward Nichols, Aide-de-Camp to General Sherman." Nichols accompanied Sherman on his famous march through Georgia to the sea; his

brevet, however it was earned, must have come before this appointment, as it's difficult for an aide-de-camp to win medals for bravery. My father's copy was published in 1866, by which time it was
already in its twenty-fourth printing. There's no hint of the original
publication date; it may have come out during the war, with much
of it appearing first in magazine form. Nichols must have already
been something of a celebrity himself when he met Hickok in
Springfield in 1865.

3. In Thomas Berger's great western novel *Little Big Man*, the
hero, Jack Crabb, encounters the young Wyatt Earp in a buffalo
hunting camp in Kansas. "He didn't look special to me," observes
Jack, "but he had some of the assurance of Custer and Hickok, if
not the long hair." Jack and Wyatt get into a brawl—Crabb belches
and Earp thinks Jack has called his name—and Jack goes for his
gun. Wyatt clubs him across the head with his gun barrel:

> This was the technique called "buffaloing," and it was
> Wyatt Earp's favorite when he became a marshal later
> on. In all his violent life, he only killed two or three
> men, but he buffaloed several thousand, I guess he was
> the meanest man I ever run across. In a similar circum-
> stance, Wild Bill would have killed his opponent. Not
> Earp, he was too mean. To draw on you meant he
> considered you a worthy antagonist; but he didn't; he
> thought most other people was too inferior to kill, so
> he would just crack their skulls. I don't know how it
> worked, but when he looked at you as if you was gar-
> bage, you might not have agreed with him, but you
> had sufficient doubt to stay your gun hand a minute,
> and by then he had cold-cocked you.

James Dunham, an advisor to movie and TV westerns and a western gun showman, points out that the passage is accurate except for
one point. Earp probably didn't start "buffaloing" until 1873, which
is when the Colt Peacemaker was issued. The only sidearm that
could have served for the purpose was the famous army model with
a 7 1/2 inch barrel. If Earp had clubbed someone with the standard
1857 cap and ball Colt, he'd have misaligned his own gun.

4. A letter from Earp to Lake asked the author to leave the
embarrassing incident out of his book.

5. This is as good a place as any to deal with an oft-quoted letter
in Frank Waters's *The Earp Brothers of Tombstone* that alleges that
Wyatt was a card cheat. The letter, from Floyd Benjamin Streeter,
claims that

Wyatt Earp drifted into Hays occasionally in the early days. The father of our Hays newspaperman was a pioneer businessman here and played cards a good deal, so was acquainted with members of the gambling fraternity. He says he never knew Wild Bill Hickok to cheat at cards, but said that he and his friends had little use for Earp because he was up to some dishonest tricks every time he played.

I am inclined to write this off as "Uncle Ned history," common to Southwestern folklore, as in "My Uncle Ned knew a man who knew the truth. . . ." In the first place, no one knows where the Streeter letter is, or for that matter where Waters's papers and original manuscript are. In view of how many anti-Earp incidents Waters seems to have fabricated—as we'll see later—and considering that no other articles or books on Earp contain an accusation of cheating, it's probably best to dismiss the story. Card players who cheated, by the way, didn't last long on the frontier. Rigged faro games, however, were another matter. Most faro games were rigged simply to keep the house from losing more money than it had at hand.

6. It's unlikely that "Bessy" or "Sally" Earp, whoever they were, were fined for being prostitutes. What's likely is that they were fined for being *unlicensed* prostitutes. Since this item is the source for all later stories about the Earp brothers' activities as pimps, it demands some examination. The Earps, like a great many Old West peace officers studied in a modern light, appear to be pimping until one understands how the law and prostitution really worked on the frontier. A good example of how the system worked is found in Don Chaput's fine biography, *Virgil Earp—Western Peace Officer*:

> A misunderstanding developed between Marshal Earp and Emma Parker, a madame who operated a house of ill fame. She had been licensed as a "Class Two" establishment, which operated in cycles of thirteen day licensing periods. On September 27, she refused to pay the fee, stating she intended to contest the case. Virgil filed a report on the matter. This is not mentioned here because it is a significant event. Rather, it adds to the picture of what constituted a month's work for a city marshal; collecting taxes, getting meals for prisoners, cleaning the hand cuffs, licensing whores, arresting drunks, and fining "fast riders."

3

On to Dodge City

At the heart of Wyatt Earp's legend is the fact that his name is indelibly linked to the Old West's most famous mining camp, Tombstone, and its most famous cattle town, Dodge City. Perhaps more than any other frontier town, Dodge City—"The Cowboy Capital of the West," "The Sodom and Gomorrah of the Plains," "The Wickedest Town in the West"—has come to symbolize the American frontier. To this day, when gunfire erupts in some urban setting, witnesses are certain to tell a TV reporter that "It sounded like Dodge City."

Wyatt had the good fortune to be fired at the right time. In 1876, the Wichita cattle trade dropped off sharply; from then until the end of the cattle drive era, most trails would lead to Dodge City. Following the Bill Smith fracas, the Wichita City commission voted four to four on the question of reinstating Earp. One more yes vote would have kept Wyatt out of Dodge City at its peak. A couple of dozen movies and two of the most successful TV series of all time, "The Life and Legend of Wyatt Earp" and "Gunsmoke," would never have been made.

The year 1876 was a turning point for frontier legends. As Wyatt's was beginning, two others came to an end. Preparing for the country's Centennial, the county was shocked by news from the Little Big Horn region in Montana. On June 26, Lt. Col. George Armstrong Custer and more than 250 of his men were killed by Plains warriors led by Crazy Horse and Sitting Bull. A nation fixated on the romance of the Wild West was still numb when more bad news came from Deadwood, Dakota Territory: On August 2, Custer's friend, James Butler Hickok, holding the famous hand of aces and eights, was shot in the back of the head by a man named Jack McCall.

Custer's Last Stand and Hickok's last poker game eliminated two of the most famous men in the West. Within five years, Jesse James and Billy the Kid would also be dead. Of the best known figures of the Old West, only Wyatt Earp and Bat Masterson lived out the century. (Buffalo Bill Cody doesn't count in this context: He became famous as a showman, not a frontiersman.)

Wyatt was no legend when he rode into Dodge on May 19, but he was not unknown in the territory. He was immediately hired by the Dodge City police force under Marshal Larry Deger, an indication that whatever bad publicity lingered from the Bill Smith incident was secondary to Wyatt's reputation as a good, tough cop.

No cow town was more in need of one. Dodge had gone through several marshals by the time Earp arrived. A reporter from an Atchison paper wrote that "The arm of the law is palsied and hangs powerless by the side of Justice, who stands in the background like the statue of a forlorn exile." Prostitutes solicited drunks openly on city streets; daylight muggings were common. A century later historians and sociologists would produce statistics to prove that duels were more frequent in cities in the deep South and that murders were committed with far greater frequency in Chicago and New York, but this was true only after Dodge was lifted by the cattle boom from the level of buffalo camp. Dodge became civilized in a short time, and the civilizing agent was its extraordinary police force.

Residents of Dodge not only relished the their scarlet reputation, they embellished it. Sometime in 1883, for instance, an idea began circulating within Dodge's higher circles that there wasn't enough going on to attract business from other parts of the world, and a Mexican-style bullfight on the Fourth of July was proposed as the answer. When word got out, the U.S. Attorney's Office sent a telegram to city officials reminding them that bullfighting was illegal in the United States. Mayor A. B. Webster's reply would stand as the town's epitaph: "Hell, Dodge City isn't in the United States!" Just as often repeated was the story of the anonymous cowhand riding the Santa Fe who was asked his destination by the conductor. "Goin' to hell, most likely," replied the drover. "That'll be two dollars," said the conductor. "Get off at Dodge City."

Whether Dodge was heaven or hell depended on whether one's proper place was north or south of the Deadline. To the hoards of buffalo hunters and, later, cowhands who rode in after weeks on the Plains, Dodge's saloons, brothels, casinos, hotels, music halls, theaters, and restaurants, most of which were found south of the railroad tracks, were a young Texas male's idea of heaven. To the townsfolk and farmers, outnumbered and cowering in their wooden frame houses or hiding behind their farm wagons as the ground shook from the din of an arriving herd of steers and drovers, Dodge must have seemed like something else. Most citizens were northsiders.

Dodge began when astute buffalo hunters noticed that the area was the center of the herds' north-to-south migrations. The first buildings were mud-wall huts, which housed saloons and primitive general stores for the hunters. After the Civil War, another fact about Dodge's location became obvious: The town was close to the easiest and safest crossing of the Arkansas River for wagon trains headed west. The men who controlled the Atchison, Topeka, and Santa Fe Railroad soon realized this as well and made Dodge the site for a terminal carrying pioneers west and buffalo hides east. The other great Kansas cow towns of the 1870s—Abilene, Wichita, Caldwell, Hays—lacked these natural advantages. "There's room for only one Dodge City in Kansas," Dodgites boasted, "and God chose us."

If God favored Dodge, He used William Tecumseh Sherman as His instrument. While commander of the Southwest military district, Sherman ordered the construction of a fort a few miles west of the congregation of buffalo trading huts. The outpost—for it was little more than that—was named for a general, Grenville M. Dodge, whose nephew, Maj. Richard Irving Dodge, would be the fort's first commander. The purpose of Fort Dodge was to offer settlers protection from marauding Indians, but Dodge, like many other soldiers, understood that the best way to get rid of the Indians was to eliminate their year-round food supply. When a group of hunters asked Dodge what the Army's response would be if they killed buffalo on the forbidden Indian ranges south of the Arkansas, Dodge drolly replied, "Well, boys, if I was hunting buffalo I'd go where the buffalo are."

That's what the hunters did. In the spring of 1874, about the time Wyatt Earp was arriving in Wichita, a score of buffalo hunters, twenty-two-year-old Bat Masterson among them, invaded Indian territory near the tip of the Texas panhandle and sparked one of the last major confrontations between armed white civilians and Plains Indians. For three days and nights the hunters, barricaded in adobe huts, held off hundreds of Kiowa and Comanche warriors under the leadership of the legendary half-breed Chief Quanah Parker. The hunters finally made a break for the Kansas state line only to discover that the Indians had retreated during the night. They returned to Dodge as heroes, holding high a grisly collection of Indian scalps, severed heads, and bloodied lances as trophies. "The Battle of Adobe Walls" gave Dodge its first folk heroes. More would arrive shortly.

The Matt Dillon of "Gunsmoke," and for that matter, the Wyatt Earp of the television series, "The Life and Legend of Wyatt Earp," were composites based on all the legendary Dodge City peace officers of the mid-'70s, mostly Wyatt but also Bat, Jim, and Ed Masterson, Bill Tilghman, Charlie Bassett, and Neal Brown. Within a short time, their collective reputation spread through much of the West. In his 1903 memoir, *The Log of a Cowboy*, drover-turned-author Andy Adams wrote:

> I've been in Dodge City every summer since '77 . . . and I can give you boys some points. Dodge is one town where the average bad man of the West not only finds himself badly handicapped. The buffalo hunters and range men have protested against the iron rules of Dodge's peace officers, and nearly every protest has Cost human life. Don't ever get the impression that you can ride your horses into a saloon, or shoot out lights in Dodge; it may go somewhere else, but it don't go there. . . . Dodge's officers are as game a set of men as ever found danger.

Adams didn't single out any one of them; Dodge City's peace officers were known for acting as a team. That we remember Wyatt Earp today while the others are now mostly known only to western buffs is due largely to the melodramatic Stuart Lake. In his *Frontier Marshal*

Dodge's newly elected mayor, George Hoover, contacted Wyatt in Wichita:

> Hoover wrote Wyatt and asked him to come to Dodge City; after a few more experiences with the Texas Men he took to telegraphing.
> "You don't need me anymore," Wyatt told Mike Meagher, "I don't blame you," Mike answered somewhat enviously.
> On May 16th, 1876, Wyatt started for Dodge City.

This fib can't be put off entirely on Stuart Lake's imagination; Earp had told much the same story years earlier to John Flood. What was the truth? Well, if Mayor Hoover ever wrote to Wyatt in Wichita, there is no record of it. Still, there seems to be truth in Lake's exaggeration. Three decades after Earp was hired in Dodge, Bat Masterson would write that "In the spring of 1876 he was appointed assistant city marshal of Dodge City, Kansas. . . . Wyatt's reputation for courage and coolness was well known to many of the citizens of Dodge City—in fact, it was his reputation that secured him the appointment of assistant city marshal." Mayor Hoover probably did know of Wyatt before he came to Dodge City, and more than likely thought he would be the cure for the near-anarchic conditions there. Less than a month after the vote on his reinstatement in Wichita, Wyatt was an assistant city marshal in Dodge. Wyatt Earp wasn't hired to be the boss; he was hired to be the enforcer.

It seems deflating to Earp's legend that in Dodge he never attained the rank of city marshal granted to the fictional character he inspired. On the other hand, if he had been given the top job he would probably be unknown today. In the mid-1870s, city marshal in Dodge was largely an administrative position, which was fortunate for the administrator, Larry Deger, who weighed in the vicinity of 300 pounds and wasn't much use in any matters that involved being quick on his feet. Personally Wyatt got along with Deger but professionally regarded him as "a cipher." Wyatt claimed, or Lake claimed for him, that he was initially offered Deger's job, "but Hoover told me that for political reasons he wanted Deger to complete his year in office. He would pay me more money as chief deputy than Deger was drawing. I would have power to hire and fire deputies, could follow my own ideas about my job and be marshal in all but name. The marshal's pay was $100 a month, but Mayor Hoover said they would pay me $250 a month plus $2.50 for every arrest I made. . . . I was to appoint three new deputies at wages of $75 a month, each, and make my own arrangements with them about the bonus."

Everything in that statement is plausible except the figures. In fact, an item from the January 8, 1878, *Dodge City Times* would seem to refute them soundly. Charles E. Bassett's salary as Marshal is listed as $100 a month, while Assistant Marshal Earp's salary is listed as $75, the same as policemen James Masterson and John Brown. Either Earp's memory or Lake's imagination, must have invented that amazing $250 a month. On the other hand, Earp may well have been compensated by off-the-book funds. The same issue of the *Times* that listed the peace officers' salaries contained an article on gambling and prostitution ordinances that justified new, harsh laws and fines because, "The city was running heavily into debt, necessary to keep up a large police force"—presumably this meant a police force augmented by special officers when the cattle herds hit town. "It is wise and proper," wrote the editorialist, "that the class who entail this additional expense should meet it with their own contributions and thus afford themselves protection under the law." This sounds very much like a sin tax, designed to make the saloons, gambling houses, and brothels pay for the extra cops needed to keep order. It also suggests that other, let's say more respectable businessmen forked over their share for auxiliary police of the kind employed in Wichita. Whether or not he actually had the power to hire deputies, Wyatt Earp's recommendation certainly would have carried some weight, particularly concerning Bill Tilghman, Neal Brown, and others he knew from the buffalo camps.

Whoever hired him, Dodge had a new special policeman in the summer of 1876, one who walked with a limp. Bat Masterson had just returned from the Texas panhandle and the most dramatic gunfight of his life. In January, in Sweetwater, Texas, Bat had been romantically involved with a dance hall girl named Mollie Brennan. A disreputable soldier and gambler identified in most chronicles as Sergeant King kicked open Mollie's door in a jealous fit, gunning for Mollie or Bat or both. It's not clear whether King was a poor shot or if Mollie was trying to shield Bat; since King's bullet killed her, we'll be charitable and assume the latter. Bat took King's second bullet in the pelvis, but managed to draw and fire, killing Mollie's killer. He would walk with a limp for some time afterwards.

Bat was twenty-three, five years younger than Wyatt, when he rode into Dodge in the summer of 1876. He had already scouted for the Army, taken part in the Battle of Adobe Walls, and killed a man in a gunfight. He had watched his mistress die in his arms. At this point in their careers, Bat would seem to have had a head start on Wyatt Earp in the building of a legend. He was a good policeman; according to Wyatt he patrolled Front Street "with a walking stick for several weeks and used his cane to crack the heads of several wild men hunting trouble; even as a cripple he was a first-class peace officer." The cane gave rise to stories that he earned his nickname by "batting" cowboys. The stories were false, but Masterson became famous for his walking stick. The popular image of Bat carrying a cane and wearing a derby hat, expressed in the theme song to the 1950s Bat Masterson TV series, was just a couple of years away.

Wyatt and Bat would become the most famous of the Dodge City–Ford County peace officers. A photograph of them, taken in 1876, shows two splendid looking young men in the prime of life. The slender, blondish Earp is seated; Masterson, shorter and stockier, is standing, his right hand resting on his holster. They're wearing what appears to be a kind of uniform: white, loose-fitting shirts with billowing sleeves, dark trousers, and soft leather gun belts. There is an odd looking pin of some sort over Wyatt's left breast (in reverse-image tintypes it appears on the right). The pin seems to be a badge; if so, this is the only existing photo of the Old West's most prominent lawman wearing one. But it's not the famous five-point sheriff's star or star-in-a-circle of most Federal badges, just a pin that looks like a name tag at a convention. (Bat, who was probably just a special deputy at the time, wears no badge of any kind.) The white shirts and dark trousers were often supplemented with black Victorian frock coats of a style then worn in Eastern cities. The officers must have stood in stark contrast to the gaudily dressed cowhands, making it easy for them to quickly pick each other out of a crowded street or saloon.

Even the combined Dodge City force and Ford County Sheriff's Office was hard pressed to deal with hundreds and even thousands of rowdy cowhands, so teamwork was more important than individual courage. Consequently most of the Dodge officers were friends and used to both taking orders from and giving them to one another. They were a mix-and-match bunch. Wyatt began as an assistant city marshal and later, while in the same position, also did a stint as a deputy sheriff under Charlie Bassett, who would later be his boss as town marshal of Dodge. Bat Masterson was a deputy marshal in Dodge, later a county deputy sheriff, and, finally, a full sheriff. (Morgan served a stint as a Ford County deputy sheriff before Wyatt came to Dodge, and Virgil may have been a special deputy under Wyatt.) Kansas historians have made themselves dizzy trying to establish exactly who was serving in which position at what time—for instance, did Wyatt Earp serve two hitches as a Dodge City officer or three? When Hollywood retold the tale, Tilghman, Bassett, and Brown would be relegated to subordinate positions under Wyatt Earp, but in the mid and late 1870s their peacekeeping credits were at least as impressive as Wyatt's.

Bill Tilghman's career was probably the most impressive of the lot. Six years younger than Earp, Tilghman had dropped several thousand buffalo before his nineteenth birthday and served as a deputy sheriff under Charlie Bassett before his twenty-fifth, the beginning of a long career in lawing. Later, after Dodge, he moved to Oklahoma territory during the land rush, and, together with Chris Madsen and Heck Thomas, formed the famous Three Guardsmen of the territory. His greatest fame came in the 1890s when he hunted down the colorful Bill Doolin gang in Oklahoma, a group that featured such notables as George "Bitter Creek" Newcomb, Ray "Arkansas Tom" Daugherty, Charley "Tulsa Jack" Pierce, and Annie "Cattle Annie" McDougal.

In 1924, at age seventy-five, Tilghman was shot and killed by a drunken prohibition agent he was trying to disarm. He had been a lawman for nearly half a century, and though he remains largely undiscovered by Hollywood, a great many students of frontier history regard him as the premier law enforcement officer of the frontier.[1] George Bolds, a respected frontier marshal himself, told historian James D. Horan that of all the lawmen he had known,

> The man I consider it an honor to have known and to have ridden with was Bill Tilghman. It has always been a mystery to me why Wyatt Earp has been made into the great hero of the frontier. Personally, I think Bill Tilgh-

man's contributions were far more important to our history than Earp's. . . . Tilghman was a warm, kindly
man in contrast to Wyatt Earp, whose manner was cold
and impersonal. Wyatt Earp was a great Western marshal,
but to my mind, Bill Tilghman was greater, both in character and in deeds.

As a career evaluation this is undoubtedly true, but Wyatt's career as
a lawman was effectively over ten years before Tilghman's most famous exploits. In the late 1870s, at the peak of the cow town era,
Wyatt Earp, several years older and more experienced than either Bat
Masterson or Bill Tilghman, was the man the younger deputies
looked up to. "He had a quiet way," the *Dodge City Times* said in July
1877, "of taking the most desperate characters into custody which
invariably gave one the impression that the city was able to enforce or
mandate and preserve her dignity. It wasn't considered policy to
draw a gun on Wyatt unless you got the drop and meant to burn
powder without any preliminary talk."

What strikes an observer more than a century later is the lack of
powder the Dodge officers needed to burn in order to keep the peace.
Matt Dillon began each episode of "Gunsmoke" with a stand-up
gunfight; that's as many as all of Dodge's officers had in the four
years of Dodge's prime. As most of the Dodge City papers for 1876
are missing, there may have been shootings we don't know about, but
Wyatt Earp claimed there were none: "There were some killings in
personal quarrels," he told Stuart Lake, "but none by peace officers."
Wyatt himself almost managed to make it through four years in
Dodge without having to kill anyone.

The comparison with the pre–Earp-Masterson years is startling.
In 1872 alone, as Dodge was making the transition from glorified
buffalo camp to cow town, there may have been at least nine homicides, and Mayor Hoover placed the figure as high as fifteen. When
Earp, Tilghman, and the Mastersons came to town, the killings were
cut by half. "Hoover," Wyatt told Lake, "had hired me to cut down
the killings in Dodge, not increase them." However much Earp later
exaggerated his position in Dodge, he did exactly what he was hired
to do. In effect, after Wyatt Earp's arrival Dodge City ceased to be
Dodge City.

From its beginning as a cow town, Dodge City could be credited

with intelligent, one might say enlightened, organization of its vice
industry. When reading about the cattle towns of the era, one is
puzzled by the number of laws against gambling and prostitution—
how could such vices have existed, and so visibly, in the face of so
much effort to shut them down? The answer is that the vice laws
weren't meant to *abolish* sin but to *control* it. Gambling, which was
illegal, was permitted south of the tracks or "deadline"; prostitution,
which was illegal, was banned north of the line for licensed prostitutes and everywhere for unlicensed prostitutes. A favorite Dodge
story has a disgruntled gambler, after losing his pile, seeking out
Mayor Bob Wright (Hoover's predecessor) to complain that the
game he dropped his money in was held in violation of city law.
Wright, like Claude Rains's character in *Casablanca*, was shocked,
shocked, to find gambling in his town. He ordered the town marshal
to arrest the complainer and fine him for gambling in violation of
town ordinance.

Dodge's unofficial sin line was Front Street, which ran parallel
to the railroad tracks. Front Street was about 250 feet wide, with
false-front stores and saloons on both sides. Everything on the
street—the awnings, sidewalks, and hitching posts—was wooden;
all of Dodge City was wooden. Barrels, which had once held beer,
whiskey, water, and molasses, were spaced along the boardwalks as
a hedge against fire; for all their sin taxes, Dodge's residents never
taxed themselves for a fire department.

There were some hot spots north of the line: such as the Opera
House Saloon; the Alhambra, owned by future mayor Jim "Dog"
Kelly; and—fans of "Gunsmoke" will surely be happy to find out that
it really existed—the Long Branch Saloon, named for the New Jersey
resort that half-owner Will Harris had visited as a boy. (Chalk
Beeson, a lifelong friend and supporter of Earp, was the other
owner.) There were also famous gunfights north of the line: Earp's
friend Mysterious Dave Mather shot Tom Nixon in front of the
Opera House, and, in one of the West's most celebrated fights,
Cockeyed Frank Loving killed Levi Richardson inside the Long
Branch. The gaudy places were south of the deadline, on the wrong
side of the tracks,[2] including the Comique (pronounced "Comic-
Kew") Theater (named after Harrigan & Hart's famous vaudeville
theater in New York), the Lady Gay Saloon, the Alamo Saloon, and
the Lone Star Saloon (so named to attract Texan business). But there

were no churches north of the line. (The First Union Church, where Wyatt was a member, was two blocks north of the tracks. The area where officers wouldn't allow so much as public cursing began a block north of the tracks, where Military Avenue, after a quick right and left, led into Tinpot Alley. This is where the residential area started. Newcomers to Dodge were startled at the difference a single block made. As one resident put it, "It was only a few steps from the Long Branch to the Lady Gay, but every step was paved with bad intentions."

Wyatt Earp's life in Dodge City was lived on both sides of the tracks. The July 21, 1877 edition of *The Dodge City Times* ran an item about a minor altercation between a Miss Frankie Bell, thought to be a prostitute, and the "ex-officer" Earp (Wyatt was between lawing stints at the time). For some reason, Wyatt offended Ms. Bell, who "heaped epithets upon the offending head of Mr. Earp to such an extent as to provoke a slap." What provoked Earp wasn't noted; some sort of business disagreement between the real Marshal Dillon and Miss Kitty seems likely. Ms. Bell spent a night in jail and was fined $20; Wyatt drew the lowest fine possible, $1. The incident didn't prevent Wyatt from serving as a deacon for Reverend O. W. Wright's Union church; nor did it discourage the law firm of Sutton and Colburn from later presenting Wyatt with a Bible. "To Wyatt S. Earp," the inscription on the flyleaf read, "as a slight recognition of his many Christian virtues and steady following in the footsteps of the meek and lowly Jesus. Sutton & Colburn."

Wyatt Earp's double life rankled some. Many years later, Virgil Earp's widow, Allie, who did not like her brother-in-law, recalled that "One Sunday we went to church . . . and there was Wyatt, sanctimonious and God-fearin' as all get out, acting as a church deacon! . . . What got me was that Deacon Wyatt strutted up and down the aisle wearin' his gun on the outside of his coat. None of the others did. And it sure wasn't like the meek and lowly Jesus." The reader can decide later if Allie Earp's view of Wyatt is legitimate or even if her memoirs, *The Earp Brothers of Tombstone*, represents Allie's view. For now suffice it to say that Wyatt was less meek than most.[3] In a letter to the English researcher David Cruickshanks, a man named S. D. Allen related a story his father told him about Earp at work:

Well to get to Wyatt Earp. My father first mentioned
Earp when I gave him the book of Stuart Lake, *Wyatt
Earp Frontier Marshal.* I had read the book and found it
fascinating but unbelievable and passed it on to the old
man to read. As soon as he saw it he grinned and said, Oh
Yes I remember him . . .

I will conclude this letter by relating to you the only
story father ever told me which concerns Wyatt Earp as a
marshal in Dodge City. He told me the story about five
years ago and said it was a typical arrest.

My father and a group of friends were gathered around
a billiard table watching a game when Wyatt entered the
room and pointed at one of the number, saying that he
wanted him. The man approached Wyatt and they talked
for awhile and then Earp swung him around searched
him, taking a knife and a number of shotgun cartridges
from him. Earp then pushed him towards the door and
the cowboy spun about and returned the compliment
whereupon Earp punched him in the face and dragged
him towards the street, on the sidewalk the prisoner began
to struggle telling Earp to let go and cursing him loudly.
Soon they were fighting and Earp butted the man then
tripped him, sending him sprawling into the street. Before
he got up Earp cracked him over the head with his revolver, opening a deep gash. Once the battered drover was
in the city jail Earp and another policeman returned to the
billiard hall and searched everyone present including my
father, but found nothing. A doctor had to be called to
the jail to attend to the prisoners head and friends of the
cowboy, my father was one, complained to the mayor
about Earp's treatment of his prisoner but got the brush
off. . . .

I am not suggesting that Earp was a bully. He seems to
have been a very brave and intelligent man but I am
pointing out to you that the reason he lasted so long was
because he knew better than to allow his adversaries to get
the upperhand.

Clearly Wyatt Earp was a peace officer in a rough town, not a politician running for office. If there is a thread that runs through Earp's career as a lawman, it's his complete indifference to the personal consequences of enforcing the law. Though his name would later be dropped into twentieth century debates on law and order versus personal freedom, Earp, in his time, saw no reason for debate. On the frontier one had complete freedom regarding one's own life in all areas except where a handful of laws clearly and strictly prohibited something. In such matters the law did not negotiate.

Yet, most of the work done by cow town peace officers didn't involve bravery or intelligence. In fact, it was menial and boring. Officers were often called upon to repair sidewalks and to serve as "municipal sanitary inspectors," that is, to keep litter off the streets. Arresting drunks, which often meant dragging men covered in vomit off to jail, was no bargain, even at $2.50 per arrest. Some work was both menial and dangerous; Wyatt shot a great many more stray dogs suspected of carrying rabies than he did cowhands. Often, tough choices had to be made; at times the law must be enforced in defiance of those who hired officers to do the dirty work in the first place. Wyatt Earp, like his brother Virgil, had a code stricter than most. In his first summer in Dodge City, Wyatt made an arrest that jeopardized his career as a lawman.

Bob Wright, one of the founders of the Dodge City, emerged from the buffalo hunter's station. (He had already made a small fortune shipping buffalo hides in the early part of the decade.) Wright was also a very influential political figure, having served in the state legislature. On a summer night in 1876, according to Stuart Lake, Wright interfered, or tried to interfere, when Wyatt and Neal Brown arrested a wealthy Texas cattleman named Bob Rachal. Rachal was taking pot shots at a traveling musician on Front Street when, in Lake's words, "The twelve-inch barrel of the Buntline Special was laid alongside and just underneath the Rachal hat brim most effectively. The buffaloed cattleman dropped to the walk, unconscious." (Astute readers have noticed that another facet of the Earp legend—the famous long-barreled "Buntline Special" Colt—has made its first appearance in the story. We will come back to it later.)

An indignant Wright burst into the Marshal's office:

"Here, Earp; you can't lock up Bob Rachal," Wright said.

"What makes you think so?" Wyatt asked.

"Why, his business is worth half a million dollars a year to Dodge."

"I know that," Wyatt admitted, while Neal Brown sloshed water over the cattle king to hasten his return to consciousness. Wright's anger mounted as the marshal answered further protestations by heaving Rachal into jail. Emboldened possibly by the crowd which had gathered, Wright made open threats.

"You'll let him out if you know what's good for you," he warned the Marshal. Wyatt locked the calaboose door. Wright seized his arm.

"You let Rachal out or Dodge'll have a new marshal in twenty-four hours," he stormed.

"Take your hand off my arm," Wyatt said.

The upshot is that Wright ended up spending the night in the calaboose with Rachal—at least that was what Wyatt said. No surviving newspapers record the arrest, and Earp debunkers have had a field day picking at the story. In *Wild, Wooly, and Wicked*, author and Old West historian Harry Sinclair Drago was skeptical:

> We are asked to believe that Wright was in jail overnight. Larry Deger was still city marshal. He certainly had authority over his assistant marshal. Had he permitted this indignity to be suffered by his best friend, Robert Wright? Would Chalk Beeson, George Hoover, Charlie Bassett, and a dozen others, the big men of Dodge, have kept hands off? . . . Would he (Earp) have dared anything so rash? It passes belief. Would the *Dodge City Globe*, if not the *Times*, Bob Wright's staunchest supporter, have remained silent? There is only one answer; it never happened.

Other pieces of evidence would support Drago's contention. In his own autobiography, *Dodge City—The Cowboy Capital of the World*, Wright doesn't mention the incident. Moreover, Wright's name

headed the list of forty-five leading citizens of Dodge in the document sent to support Earp during the O.K. Corral Inquest in 1882.
Surely Wright would not have written so vigorously in defense of an
enemy.

But a simple answer is that Earp and Wright weren't enemies.
Wright simply crossed a line in interfering with a respected police
officer—he knew it, Mayor Hoover knew it, Wyatt's good friend
Chalk Beeson knew it, and certainly Marshal Deger, who had no
intention of interfering with one of Earp's arrests, knew it, too. Simply put: Yes, Wyatt Earp would have done something so politically
foolish as to arrest an important citizen, and he did it many times in
his career. Wright signed the O.K. Corral document testifying that
Earp was an "honorable citizen, ever vigilant in the discharge of his
duties" because it was the truth.

Earp's arrest of Wright, to say nothing of the arrest of Rachal, is
precisely the kind of story we know cow town papers avoided—such
news was not fit to print. In his 1907 *Human Life* profile on Earp,
Bat Masterson describes an incident where

> one of the aldermen of the city, presuming somewhat on
> the authority his position gave him over a police officer,
> ordered Wyatt one night to perform some official act that
> did not look exactly right to him, and Wyatt refused point
> blank to obey the order. The alderman, regarded as some-
> thing of a scrapper himself, walked up to Wyatt and at-
> tempted to tear his official shield from his vest front where
> it was pinned.
>
> When that alderman woke up he was a greatly changed
> man . . . Wyatt was never bothered any more while he
> lived in Dodge City by aldermen.

This could well have been the Wright incident, with Bat, thirty years
later, recalling Wright as an alderman. And once again, an eyewitness account supports an Earp story not mentioned in a contemporary paper.

Such intrusion of politics into street law must have given Wyatt
second thoughts about a career in "lawing." So must an incident that
happened to his old boss, Mike Megher, back in Wichita. Sometime
in January 1877, while sitting in an outhouse in back of a saloon,

Megher was shot in the leg by a cowhand with a grudge. Hitching up his trousers, Megher pursued and killed his attacker. Wyatt had now put in two years of service as a cow town peace officer, which is not a long time if your job is selling insurance, but is quite a long time to deal with armed drunks and not take a bullet. He had been in lawing long enough to see some of his old colleagues get shot, and he decided to spend the winter lull in the cattle trade considering more lucrative and less dangerous employment. Before spring he was exploring possibilities in the legendary gold mining boomtown Deadwood in the Dakota Territory, from which Wild Bill Hickok, aces and eights in hand, had recently departed.

Wyatt apparently went to Deadwood with no more thought than trying his luck in the gaming halls; unlike cattle towns, mining camps had a steady flow of cash all year around. Earp was always quick to adopt new ways to make a dollar. "I didn't gamble much that winter," he told Lake. "I delivered wood seven days a week and when night came I wanted to sleep. But I was young and tough, so were my horses, and we came through into spring in fine shape physically, with a profit of about $5,000."

That Earp made anything like that astonishing sum is unlikely, but in the Lake papers at the Huntington Library there is a note Stuart Lake apparently wrote to himself after a conversation with Wyatt. It reads, "76, Sept. 9. outfitted went to Deadwood, S.D., hauled wood. netted $120-$130 a day." This was good money, for the time, but wood hauling was a sometime thing and before long Wyatt was working at a job more suited to his talents.

Wyatt claimed to have ridden shotgun for the Wells Fargo gold shipments coming out of Deadwood in the winter of 1877. In his account, a man named Dunc Blackburn had found a spot in the hills from where he could monitor Wells Fargo shipments. During one robbery he and his gang killed a well-known driver named John Slaughter (not to be confused with the famous Texas John Slaughter we will meet later in Tombstone). All this changed when the local shipping company posted a bulletin, which read:

NOTICE TO BULLION SHIPPERS
The Spring Clean-up will leave for Cheyenne on the
Regular Stage at 7:00 A.M., next Monday.
Wyatt Earp of Dodge will ride shotgun.

The stage carried the breathtaking sum of $200,000. Wyatt, carrying
a pair of single-action Colt revolvers, a Winchester repeating rifle,
and a Wells Fargo regulation short-barreled shotgun, was the only
guard. About two miles from Deadwood, two groups of horsemen
were spotted keeping pace with the stage along the base of the hills,
which flanked both sides of the road. Wyatt fired several shots at
long range, apparently hitting a horse. The strangers retired, and the
shipment got through without further incident.

That's the story, and as James Garner's Wyatt Earp in *Sunset* is
fond of saying, it's true, give or take a lie or two. The biggest lie
seems to be that Earp rode shotgun for Wells Fargo at all: The
company had no overland stage out of Deadwood after 1870 and has
no record at all of Earp riding for them. This would seem to throw
out Earp's heroic Wells Fargo ride. But as is so often the case in the
Earp legend, a tale begins as truth, is later debunked, and then, on
further examination, appears to be true again—give or take a lie or
two.

In Stuart Lake's papers there is a note that reads, "77 June, rode
shotgun—Wells Fargo. $50." There was in fact a company hauling
gold out of Deadwood in 1877, the Cheyenne and Black Hills Stage
and Express. The company's records do reveal a problem with stage
robbers and the murder of a driver named John Slaughter. An obscure volume entitled *The Cheyenne and Black Hills Stage and Express
Routes* contains this passage: "Among the special shotgun messengers
who brought the shipment [of $200,000 in gold] through to Chey-
enne without mishap was Wyatt B. Earp, who was on his way back
to Kansas." Wyatt gave the name of the Wells Fargo agent as Gray,
which is all he could remember. The name of the express company
agent in Deadwood was in fact Isaac Gray. And so, the only part of
the story that doesn't jive is Wyatt's claim that he was working for
Wells Fargo. What he was probably doing was working *with* them.
Wells Fargo was subcontracting with the local Deadwood company,
an arrangement not apparent from records examined a century later.
No matter which company paid him, Wyatt Earp made the ride.

More significant than the ride itself is that it was Earp's first
association with Wells Fargo, the beginning of a shadowy arrangement that was instrumental in much of the controversy Wyatt would
be involved in later in Tombstone.

Oh, yes—note that the book passage says that Wyatt was "among the special shotgun messengers." On the frontier, was making a tall tale a bit taller the same as lying?

The July 7, 1877, *Dodge City Times* noted that Wyatt was back: "Wyatt Earp, who was on our City police force last summer, is in town again. We hope he will accept a position on the force once more." The *Times* wasn't just being polite. Dodge was now the world's biggest cattle shipping town, and July was the wildest month of the year. Good cops were in short supply, and in June, Bat Masterson had eliminated himself from consideration for an officer's job when he interfered with an arrest by Marshal Deger. The details are fuzzy, but apparently Masterson thought Deger was being hard on some visiting Texans—Bat tended to get along with the Texans better than some of the other Kansas officers—and Deger clubbed him over the head. The incident may have contributed to Dodge's dissatisfaction with the ineffectual Deger; at the end of the year he was fired and Bat's brother Ed given the job. Later, Bat would have the satisfaction of beating out Deger in the election for Ford County sheriff.

In July, Nicholas and Ginnie Ann Earp stopped briefly in Dodge, headed for California, this time for good. Virgil also passed through, on the way to Prescott, Arizona, with his new wife, the feisty, sharp-tongued little Irish girl named Alvira—the Allie of the primary Earp debunking book, *The Earp Brothers of Tombstone*, which we will see much more of later on. By the end of the summer, the Earp brothers would be scattered all over the West—Jim in Texas, Virgil in Arizona, Morgan in Montana, and Wyatt still trying to decide if there was a living to be made in Kansas.

If Wyatt was uncertain about his future, he at least knew his services were in demand; Lake claimed that Mayor Jim "Dog" Kelley wired Wyatt in Deadwood, asking him to return for the cattle season, and that may be true. Wyatt certainly could have had his assistant marshal's job back or even the city marshal's post if he had wanted it. He did some police work, almost certainly a stint as a special deputy, but there is no other record of Wyatt Earp's having served on the Dodge City police force in 1877.

In fact, for the rest of the year there is no record where Wyatt was or what he did. There are indications that he dropped in on the mining camp of Leadville, Colorado, and from there went to Fort

Worth, Texas, where James Earp was working as a bartender for a man named Bob Winders. (Winders would later be a mining partner of the Earp brothers in Tombstone.) The Earp sightings from Colorado to Texas would indicate that Wyatt was on a gambling circuit; he also did some bounty hunter's work for Wells Fargo or another express company, work for which gambling would have provided an excellent screen.

The first definite indication of Wyatt's whereabouts in 1878 comes on January 22 when the *Ford County Globe* in Kansas reported his location as Fort Clark, Texas. Five days earlier bandits had held up the train in Kinsley, about 40 miles from Dodge, and fled south. (Fans of the Billy the Kid movie, *Young Guns II*, will recognize one of the gang members, "Dirty" Dave Rudabaugh, as a future member of Billy's group in New Mexico.) The Santa Fe Railroad wired Earp, asking him to pursue the outlaws, which suggests that he kept someone in authority posted as to his traveling plans.

History and Kevin Costner's *Wyatt Earp* film have given Wyatt credit for capturing Dirty Dave, but it was Bat Masterson, the Ford County sheriff, who made the pinch early in February. (Dave apparently had the audacity to stick around Kansas to try for another train.) What brought Wyatt back to Dodge wasn't the arrest of an outlaw but the killing of an officer.

None of the town's three most legendary figures—Wyatt Earp, Bat Masterson, and Bill Tilghman—were involved in the town's most famous shootout. Instead, it was Dodge's most popular lawman, Bat's older brother Ed. In November 1877, in an incident that dismayed Wyatt and Bat, Ed was shot by a Texas cowhand named Bob Shaw. Shaw was in the process of shooting another cowpoke called Texas Dick when Ed laid the barrel of his Colt revolver on Shaw's head. He should have hit Shaw harder; for that matter, he would have been fully justified in shooting or even killing him. An angry Shaw then shot Masterson in the right breast; while on the floor, Ed made the "border shift," transferring his pistol from the right hand to the left and, returning the fire, he hit Shaw in the left arm and right leg. Then, bleeding profusely, he managed to pull himself up and drag Shaw off to jail.

Such courage endeared Ed to the Dodge City fathers—in December, they promoted him from assistant marshal to chief of police. Bat, though, had doubts about his brother. Years later, in a profile he wrote of Wyatt Earp, Bat would make a distinction between courage and nerve, the latter being the psychological toughness needed to keep a handle on such a nerve-wracking job. For one thing, Ed's lifting of the ban on carrying firearms could only lead to more trouble; it had already led to the gunfight with Shaw. Five months later it led to worse.

While attempting to disarm two Texas cowhands through use of diplomacy, Ed was shot at such close range that his shirt caught fire. Bat, who was in town on Sheriff's Office business, would later testify under oath that he was the one who killed the cowhands. Other accounts, though, have Ed, once again firing from the ground after having been wounded, killing both men. According to one witness, he got up and staggered a distance of a couple hundred feet and collapsed on the steps of his boarding house. About a half hour later, he died in his room. Ed Masterson was twenty-six.

Dodge City's citizens were shocked and angered. The Times' reporter praised the actions of Ed and his deputy Nat Heywood, but in a tone that suggested they might have been more forceful: "The officers were brave and cool though both were at a disadvantage, as neither desired to kill their whisky-crazed assailants." Nonetheless, now both cowhands were dead and with them the best-liked officer the city had ever had. The funeral, with its procession to Boot Hill cemetery, was the biggest Dodge had ever seen. A black-bordered editorial in the following day's Times contained an ominous note: "As we see the draped doors, the solemn faces, and the cold quiet air of remorse, we see depicted that steady determination to give no quarter to the ruthless invader of our lives, peace, and prosperity." In practical terms, "give no quarter" meant rehire Wyatt Earp.

On May 8 Wyatt was back from Texas and immediately given his old assistant marshal's job, this time under Charlie Bassett, Bat's former county undersheriff and now Dodge City marshal. Four years had passed since Wyatt first tried cattle town lawing, and at least four Kansas policemen he knew had been shot. Over the next five years Earp would try to get out of lawing, and in the process watch three more men who were close to him go down from gunfire.

"Dodge," wrote an editorialist in the September 1, 1877, issue of the *Dodge City Times,* has many characteristics which prevent its being classed as a town of strictly moral ideas and principles, notwithstanding it is supplied with a church, a court-house, and a jail. Other institutions counterbalance the good works supposed to emanate from the first mentioned. . . . Even the Mayor of the city indulges in the giddy dance with the girls and with his cigar in one corner of his mouth and his hat tilted to one side, he makes a charming looking officer.

Some things occur in Dodge that the world never knows of. Probably it is best so. Other things occur which leak out by degrees, notwithstanding the use of hush-money.

This was Wyatt Earp's Dodge at the peak of the cattle drive era. If one could be transported back in time to a town that would typify the American frontier, it would be Dodge City, Kansas, on a summer night during the cattle season of 1878. Dodge's handsome, spacious saloons with their oak paneled–front bars served cold lager twenty-four hours a day, and from late morning till midnight a passing cowhand was free to partake of lunch, which included pickles and several types of cheeses and sometimes even caviar. At night, gaslights reflected off the polished wood to give the saloons a sepia glow, and music from pianos and banjos wafted along Front Street. Not just the rowdier numbers; musicians who knew Stephen Foster's songs were often favored in the wee hours by sentimental cowhands. Peels of laughter could be heard from the Comique Theater, where comics of the caliber of Eddie Foy, the famed vaudevillian, were booked.

Dodge City in 1878 attracted all sorts of what the *Times* referred to as "fast men and women." One of them took out an ad in the June 8, 1878, *Times*: "Dentistry. J. H. Holliday, Dentist, very respectfully offers his professional services to the citizens of Dodge City and surrounding country for the summer. Office at room No. 24, Dodge House. Where satisfaction is not given money will be refunded." This was to be Doc Holliday's only mention in a Kansas newspaper during his stay.

The title of "Doc" influenced Hollywood's portrayals of him. He would later be played by actors such as Walter Huston, Kirk Douglas, and Jason Robards, Jr., in their middle-age, but John Henry

Holliday was just twenty-six when he rode into Dodge City during
the summer of 1878. He was tall, strikingly handsome, blond, and
slender—not yet the emaciated, ghostlike figure he would become in
a few years. His accent was soft and highborn Southern—the Hollidays had been walking in tall Georgia cotton before the Civil
War—and in his soft gray suits with his aristocratic manners, he
stood in vivid contrast to the hordes of rough-hewn, colorfully
dressed Southern cattle drovers. Even his favorite gun—with its off-
white ivory grips and gleaming, nickel-plated finish, often carried in
a cross-draw or in a shoulder holster—set him apart.

Wyatt met Doc Holliday while bounty hunting in the Texas panhandle at the establishment of John Shanssey, the former Irish
prizefighter he knew from the railroad camps. Holliday already had
what older men on the gambling circuit worked hard for: a reputation. Contrary to hundreds of westerns, reputations generally kept
trouble *away* and allowed gamblers to concentrate on their business.
He had killed men, they said, though no one was quite sure where.
(He was known to have had one famous gunfight in Dallas, more like
a duel, really, in which his opponent was merely wounded.) Wyatt
had heard of him. "Know him?" John Shanssey asked. "By reputation," said Earp, "and I wouldn't figure him to be friendly toward a
peace officer. He's the killer, isn't he?" Shanssey's reply is classic:
"He's killed some, but none around here." No one recalled ever seeing Doc Holliday kill someone. Doc's killings always seemed to happen somewhere else.

Doc Holliday was a loner, a fatalist with a sardonic wit made
sharper by the knowledge that he would soon die of tuberculosis.
(Legend had him making bets that he'd "die with his boots on"—
that is, in a fight rather than in bed.) That is, he was a loner except
for an attractive female companion with an accent, which few frontiersmen were qualified to identify as Hungarian. Her name was
Kate Harony, though at the time, for reasons that are convoluted,
she was known as either Kate Elder or Kate Fisher. Like Allie Earp,
she did not like Wyatt. One tradition had her involved in an affair with Earp back in Wichita, but the documentation for this is
dubious. Jealousy alone would suffice to explain her hostility; Kate
regarded Wyatt as a bad influence on Doc and thought Earp had
some unnatural hold over him.

Wyatt Earp *did* seem to have an influence over John Holliday; he was the only one who did. Holliday's history since his mysterious departure from Georgia had been a practically unbroken series of altercations—a shooting at a gambling table here, a knifing there, an arrest on some minor charge. But in wide-open Dodge City, where he might have been expected to explode, Doc's behavior was impeccable.

Bat Masterson, who did not like Doc—there was, perhaps, a touch of envy in his dislike—would become one of the principal builders of Holliday's legend, just as he was with Wyatt's. Most subsequent stories about Doc Holliday would refer to Masterson's 1907 *Human Life* profile. "Holliday," Bat wrote, "had a mean disposition and an ungovernable temper, and under the influence of liquor was a most dangerous man . . . he would no sooner be out of one scrape before he was in another, and the strange part of it is he was more often in the right than in the wrong." One might conclude that something about Doc Holliday brought out the worst in people. Some people, anyway: Miguel Antonio Otero, later governor of New Mexico, spread tales of Holliday's worst deeds but "met him several times and found him to be a likable fellow."

To the amazement of all who knew him by reputation, Doc behaved himself in Dodge. Masterson attributed that to Earp's influence: "His whole heart and soul were wrapped up in Wyatt Earp and he was always ready to stake his life in defense of any course in which Wyatt was interested. . . . Damon did no more for Pythias than Holliday did for Wyatt Earp." The last comment may have contained a touch of sarcasm, considering that Doc's rep became, in Tombstone, the main weapon Wyatt's enemies would use against him.

At that, Wyatt may have gotten a bargain. In August one of the biggest street rows in Dodge's cattle town years erupted in front of the Long Branch saloon on Front Street when Earp and Bat's brother Jim got themselves into a tight spot with some angry cowhands. Several drovers were buffaloed; the sight wasn't pretty. The *Dodge City Globe*, a Democratic paper indulging in an opportunity to take a jibe at two prominent Republican officers—Wyatt had helped to choose the delegates for the upcoming Kansas State Republican convention—wrote about the brawl as if the combatants were a dysfunctional family. "We . . . cannot help," said the editorial, "but regret the too ready use of pistols in all rows of such character and would like to see a greater of spirit of harmony exist between our officers and cattlemen." It was Wyatt's only bad press notice in Dodge City.

Wyatt Earp claimed to his dying days that Doc Holliday saved his life when a group of irate cowhands got the drop on him, but he never specified the date. This was probably the night. Doc had been playing faro with another notorious gambler and gunman, Cockeyed Frank Loving, when he heard shots fired in the street. Before Loving could move to Wyatt's aid, Holliday grabbed his nickel plated pistol and someone else's six gun from the "shooter rack" at the end of the bar and bolted through the door. This gave Wyatt the opportunity to draw his own weapon, bringing the affair to a nonfatal conclusion. A couple of weeks earlier Earp hadn't been so lucky.

The summer of 1878 started off well enough for Wyatt. On June 18 the *Globe* reported that "Wyatt Earp is doing his duty as Ass't Marshal in a very creditable manner—adding new laurels to his splendid record every day." Even when the cattle herds hit town, things were slow. According to an Earp family friend, Wyatt spent some time "down along the Arkansas River under the shade of towering cottonwoods," keeping Blue, a Missouri mule raised by his uncle Jonathan in Lamar, available in case gunfire erupted and he had to get quickly back to town.

Nothing of any consequence happened till the night of July 25. Some time around 3:00 A.M., Wyatt and Jim Masterson were on the south side of the tracks opposite the Long Branch listening to Dodge City's popular new attraction, Eddie Foy, perform at the Comique Theater. Inside, Bat Masterson and Doc Holliday, minding their own business, were playing Spanish monte. Suddenly, three Texas cowhands tore down the street, firing their revolvers and "hurrahing" the town. In his autobiography, Foy said he was impressed with the "instantaneous manner" in which the club patrons "flattened out like pancakes on the floor." The flatteners included both Masterson and Holliday, as well as Foy himself. Three years later, at the gunfight near the O.K. Corral, Holliday stood in front of Frank McLaury and virtually dared him to shoot; on this night in Dodge he wasn't quite ready to accept a bullet.

Earp and Jim Masterson drew their revolvers and sent "two or three volleys" after the Texans. The herders made for the Dodge toll bridge, which ran over the Arkansas and separated the town from the cattle grazing area; as they reached it, the Texan who had shot at Earp, a twenty-three year old named George Hoy—identified for a time as Hoyt—fell from his horse, a bullet in the back of his arm. Wyatt Earp had finally killed someone. Or at any rate he did after Hoy died a month later—if it was Wyatt who really shot him. The fatal bullet could have come from Jim Masterson's gun or even from one of the Dodgites who were reported to be firing away at the cowhands.[4] Wyatt Earp certainly *thought* he was the one who killed Hoy. When he spoke of the shooting in his 1896 interview with the *San Francisco Examiner* he didn't even mention Jim Masterson. Bat thought Wyatt had killed Hoy, too; when he wrote his 1907 profile of Wyatt, Bat didn't mention his brother and called the Hoy incident the only time "when he [Wyatt] shot to kill."

As the Kansas papers backed Wild Bill Hickok in the Phil Coe shooting, so they now backed Wyatt Earp in the killing of Hoy. Hoy, after all, exchanged shots with town marshals in full view of witnesses and then fled from the scene. Nonetheless, the shooting of Hoy shocked Dodge almost as much as Ed Masterson's death. It had been a long time since anyone could remember two shootings involving Dodge police within so short a span—the reputation of the town's officers had always been enough to ward off serious trouble. Now, three Texans and a city marshal had been killed in the space of four months, a trend that could prove to be disastrous for business. On August 23, a crowd of sullen Texans accompanied Hoy's coffin to Boot Hill.

That Wyatt, too, was shaken by the killing of Hoy is evident from the elaborate conspiracy theories he later concocted. Fifty years later Wyatt told Stuart Lake that Hoy was part of a plot to assassinate him, that a $1,000 bounty had been put on his head by cattle bosses—the inference was that this was a result of Earp's arrest of Bob Rachal. Earp told Lake that Hoy had confessed the plot before he died and that the *Globe* "verified and later published Hoyt's story."

No such story was ever printed and if such a conspiracy existed it has never been uncovered. That Wyatt did believe Hoy had been paid to kill him, though, is likely; he tried to question the young Texan about his motives right after the shooting, but Hoy was delirious. What Wyatt probably would have asked him is why, if Hoy was

simply hurrahing the town, did he shoot in the direction of a marshal? No one has ever satisfactorily answered that question.

If Wyatt was succumbing to paranoia with his conspiracy theory,
he was suffering from a syndrome common to lawmen who worked
too long in cow towns and mining camps. Even the great Hickok fell
prey to it; it was his undoing as a peace officer. "In time," wrote
Hickok's biographer Joseph G. Rosa, "the strain of being Abilene's
marshal began to tell (on Bill). He was constantly aware of the feeling against him among the Texans . . . and fearing assassination he
was ever on guard. Wild Bill always walked down the middle of the
street, and rarely used the sidewalk. Hickok avoided open doorways
and windows, and he always had a wall at his back. This all hints at
nervous tension—but with only three deputies to control an estimated five thousand Texans and others, Wild Bill had cause to
worry!" Let us remember that on the one famous occasion when
Wild Bill failed to keep the wall at his back, a man he had never met
put a bullet in his head.

The shooting of George Hoy increased Wyatt's anxieties. About a
week after Hoy died, Earp claimed that an unidentified horseman
took a shot at him and rode away over the toll bridge. Shortly after
that came the disturbance in front of the Long Branch in which Doc
Holliday intervened and which was probably a response to the young
cowhand's death. The messiness of the scuffle was an indication that
the Texas drovers versus Kansas buffalo hunters-turned-lawmen confrontation was about to escalate. In September, the *Dodge City Times*
reported "no less than half a dozen shooting scrapes" in a span of one
week—more shooting than Dodge had seen in a similar period in a
couple of years.

The most famous clash between Kansans and Texans in 1878
didn't involve a shooting. A great many Old West historians, including not a few Texans, deny it happened at all. Once again, the popular version of the story, the one repeated on television shows and in
coffee-table books and comics, started with Stuart Lake. This time
the protagonist was a junior-grade Ben Thompson named Clay Allison.

Tennessee-born Clay Allison is a good example of a once well-
known frontier figure now forgotten, his legend absorbed by Wyatt
Earp. In his own day Allison was much better known than Earp, but
despite a mild comeback in the 1950s as TV sheriff, his rep never

recovered from being faced down by Wyatt Earp, at least in the pages
of *Frontier Marshal*. Allison, described by British researcher Denis
McLoughlin as a "ranch owner, alcoholic, and a neurotic psychopath
of the worst order," was the certified killer of at least two marshals in
New Mexico. (He beat both raps on self-defense pleas.) One of the
more colorful stories about him concerns a dentist who pulled one of
Allison's teeth—the wrong one. Allison returned to the dentist's office, laid the barrel of his gun on his head, and proceeded to pull the
dentist's own teeth out with a forceps. (Fortunately for Allison, he
hadn't visited Doc Holliday.)

As Lake told it, and as many have retold it since, Allison was the
hired gun of Bob Rachal, the Texas cattleman, and Bob Wright, the
Dodge City businessman and politician that Earp busted along with
Rachal. Though warned of Allison's presence by Mayor Kelley,
Chalk Beeson, and others, Wyatt calmly shaved and breakfasted; "I
did not intend to give Clay the satisfaction of thinking he had hurried me."

In Lake's narrative, Allison stumbled across Wyatt leaning calmly
against the front wall of the Long Branch saloon.

> "Are you Wyatt Earp?" the killer demanded.
> "I am Wyatt Earp," the marshal replied.
> "I've been looking for you."
> "You've found me."
> "You're the fellow that killed that soldier the other
> night, aren't you?" Allison continued.
> "What business is it of yours if I am?" Wyatt coun-
> tered, although the charge implied was without founda-
> tion.
> "He was a friend of mine," Allison retorted.
> As Allison talked, he had stepped close, and was actu-
> ally leaning against Wyatt, thus shielding his right side
> and his right hand from the marshal's view.
> "Clay was working for his gun all the time," Wyatt
> said, "trying to get into a position that I couldn't see him
> start after it."
> "I'm making it my business right now," Allison snarled.

Allison goes for his gun; he gasps in amazement as he finds Wyatt's .45 jammed against his ribs. Allison wisely backs off. Mounting his horse, he shouts an insult at Wright for not backing his play—Wright claims not to know what Allison is talking about—and gallops toward Earp, who pulls his famous Buntline Special .45 from his holster. Just as he approaches firing range, Allison stops, reels around, and leaves town.

If the Allison-Earp confrontation is fiction, it originated with Earp himself. In his 1896 interview with the *San Francisco Examiner*, Wyatt gave a toned-down version of the encounter that sounds a great deal more plausible than Lake's. Bat Masterson, he told the *Examiner* reporter, was covering him with a shotgun from the district attorney's office—Earp and Masterson liked to place shotguns at key spots in town, just in case—watching for trouble not just from Allison but from any of his friends who might care to join in.

> "We greeted each other," said Wyatt, "with caution thinly veiled by insouciance, and as we spoke backed carelessly up against the wall, I on his right. There we stood, measuring each other with sideways glances. An onlooker across the street might have thought that we were old friends.
>
> "So," said Allison truculently, "you're the man that killed my friend Hoyt!"
>
> "Yes, I guess I'm the man you're looking for," I said.

That Allison mentioned Hoyt—that is, George Hoy—and not the unnamed "soldier" of Lake's narrative is the key to the story. Allison was probably liquored up and looking to appear as some kind of champion to the Texans. Wyatt says he faced Allison with "a firm grip on my six-shooter, and with my left I was ready to grab Allison's gun the moment he jerked it out." With Wyatt Earp in front of him and Bat Masterson covering him with a shotgun, Allison, who was no fool even when drunk, backed off. Lake's version sounds melodramatic, like something out of the Hollywood westerns it found its way into. The *Examiner*'s s version, on the other hand, is entirely plausible. Earp makes no personal boast; he's simply relating some sound police work and explaining how serious trouble was avoided. Since Clay Allison was known to be in Dodge at this time, there's no reason to believe that the famous confrontation, which was thought to have happened and then thought not to have happened didn't happen after all. Give or take a lie or two.

In *Frontier Marshal* Wyatt Earp halts Clay Allison with his legendary Buntline Special, the extra–long-barreled Colt .45 single-action revolver that would become, with the possible exception of Davy Crockett's long rifle Old Betsy, the most famous firearm of the American frontier. Earp did not mention the Buntline Special to the *Examiner*; in fact, no one recalls him having mentioned the gun at all. And so, the Buntline Special, reproduced by the thousands as a toy in the 1950s, was assigned by the next generation of western historians to the trash heap of debunked western myths. The consensus is that Lake, having created a virtuous western knight in the Arthurian mold, had to arm him with an oversized, mythical weapon. Other critics have suggested it was simply a phallic symbol.

Many old-timers do recall the gun; George Bolds, for instance, who knew Wyatt in Dodge City, said in his 1956 book *Across the Cimarron* that Wyatt "had a healthy respect for the barrel of his six-shooter, especially his Buntline. Facing that barrel was fearsome . . . a terrible blow administered with that barrel could demoralize any man and knock out his courage. For the marshal, it meant one less life taken."

A long-barreled Colt would have been ideal for a cow town peace officer, a weapon that could function as both sidearm and nightstick. The problem with accounts such as Bolds' is that they remember the Buntline Special *after* Stuart Lake wrote about it.

Oddly enough, Lake never claimed that Earp was the only possessor of a Buntline. Ned Buntline, a.k.a., E. Z. C. Judson, was the man who "created" Buffalo Bill Cody and who cashed in on the fame of Wild Bill Hickok after George Ward Nichols made him nationally famous. On a visit to Dodge, wrote Lake, Buntline obtained enough material from Wyatt Earp and his associates "for hundreds of frontier yarns, few authentic, but many the basis of fables still current as facts"—an interesting comment on one fablemaker about another.

> Buntline was so grateful to the Dodge City peace officers
> for the color they supplied that he set about arming them

as befitted their accomplishments. He sent to the Colt's factory for five special .45-caliber six-guns of regulation single-action style, but with barrels four inches longer than standard—a foot in length—making them eighteen inches overall. Each gun had a demountable walnut rifle stock, with a thumbscrew arrangement to fit the weapon for a shoulder piece in long-range shooting. A buckskin thong slung the stock to belt or saddle horn when not in use. The walnut butt of each gun had the word "Ned" carved deeply in the wood and each was accompanied by a hand-tooled holster modeled for the weapon. The author gave a "Buntline Special"—as he called the guns—to Wyatt Earp, Charlie Bassett, Bat Masterson, Bill Tilghman, and Neal Brown.

Bat Masterson and Bill Tilghman, Lake says, cut the barrels down to standard length (usually four and three-quarters inches). Earp, Bassett, and Brown kept them at the original length.

That's the legend. In fact, no one knows if the Buntline Special existed. The principal arguments against the existence of the gun, or guns, are (1) that there are no known surviving Buntlines, (2) there are no shipping records from Colt indicating such a purchase, and (3) no one before Stuart Lake mentioned the guns. Actually, there is another: There is no evidence that Ned Buntline ever went to Dodge City or ever met Wyatt Earp.

Because Buntline was a character in the 1950 Wyatt Earp television series, many assumed that the real Buntline "created" Earp the way he did Buffalo Bill and Hickok, but there are no surviving Buntline dime novels in which Earp and Masterson are mentioned. In his biography of Buntline, *The Great Rascal*, Jay Monaghan seems to confirm that Buntline met Earp and Masterson and did indeed travel to Dodge City. The problem is that the book's bibliography lists no other source for this or the Buntline special than Lake's *Frontier Marshal*.

Still, Buntline could well have visited Dodge City—many Eastern writers did—and if he had given the guns personally to the Dodge officers there would be no shipping records. (Jeff Morey suggests that he might have bought several long-barreled Colts at the Philadelphia Centennial Exposition in 1876, where they were known to be on display.) Colt did make .45 caliber peacemakers with 10- or 12-inch barrels. In Colt's files there is a letter from Wyatt's friend in Tombstone, the gunfighter Buckskin Frank Leslie, ordering a long-barreled Colt; evidently Buckskin Frank saw somebody in Tombstone carrying one.

The most solid evidence for the existence of the gun comes from the Spicer hearing after the O.K. Corral gunfight, in which a local butcher, A. Bauer, testified that "it (Earp's pistol) seemed to me an old pistol, pretty large, 14 to 16 inches long." This is specific—that's about the overall length of a Colt with 10- or 12-inch barrel from pistol grip to gunsite. The Colt .45 with a 7 1/2 inch long barrel, the standard army length revolver, was fairly common in Tombstone and would not have impressed Bauer so much. Wyatt obviously used an exceptionally long-barreled gun in the O.K. Corral gunfight.[5] Letters found in Lake's papers indicate that if the gun didn't exist, at least Lake didn't invent it. In one letter to an old acquaintance of Earp's he asks if anyone knows of the gun's whereabouts: "I want it as a keepsake. It is valueless as a weapon."[6] If Lake invented the Buntline Special, he went to extraordinary lengths to preserve the hoax after he was gone, writing fake letters and distributing them among his papers. Perhaps the question ought not to be "Did the Buntline Special exist?" but "Did Stuart Lake, former press agent, find a catchy nickname for Wyatt's long-barreled Colt?" If the Buntline Special existed, what became of it? Who knows? Where are any of the guns used in the most famous shootout in American history? Legends were often careless with these future museum pieces.

With or without Buntline Specials, Wyatt, Bat Masterson, Bill Tilghman, and Charlie Bassett came together in October 1878 to form the most famous posse in the history of the Kansas cow towns. James Kennedy, the son of a wealthy and influential cattleman, had received what he regarded as rude treatment in Mayor "Dog" Kelley's saloon. In retaliation Kennedy fired four shots through the bedroom window of Kelley's house. One of the .45 caliber bullets passed through the front door of the house, on through the plaster partition between the bedrooms—this gives you an idea of how solid most frontier homes were—and struck His Honor's house guest, Miss Dora Hand, killing her instantly.

"Dora Hand," Lake wrote in tribute,

was the most graciously beautiful woman to reach the camp in the heyday of its iniquity, and in no other community on earth is it probable that she could have occupied the anomalous position in which the cow town placed her. By night, she was Queen of the Fairy Belles, as old Dodge termed its dance hall women, entertaining drunken cowhands after all the fashions that her calling demanded. By day, she was Lady Bountiful of the prairie settlement, a demurely clad, intensely practical, generous, forceful woman, to whom no appeal for the succor of another's trouble would go unheeded.

Ms. Dora Hand, a.k.a. Fannie Keenan, was also a madam, the most respected in Dodge City. On Sunday she sang hymns in the same church in which Wyatt Earp and Bat Masterson served as deacons. It is not recorded that anyone in the congregation held her double life against her; it is not even clear that anyone regarded her life as double. As an unknown Dodgite phrased it, "The only thing anyone could hold against her was her profession, and, by God, she elevated that considerably." The rigid social divisions that would ostracize the Dora Hands of the West would come later, with civilization and respectability. The very fact that Dora Hand was in Kelley's house— the mayor and his wife were out of town—is a testament to her standing in the community.

Needless to say, the population was outraged by the killing, probably more so than if Kelley himself had been the victim. ("A cold-blooded assassin," the *Globe* called Kennedy, "a fiend in human form.") Wyatt is often given credit for leading the posse, but Bat Masterson, as Ford County sheriff, had jurisdiction. Wyatt, Tilghman, Bassett, Neal Brown, and a young deputy sheriff named Bill Duffy rounded out what the *Ford County Globe* labeled "as intrepid a posse as ever that pulled a trigger." Assuming that Kennedy was heading for the relative safety of the Indian nations to the south, the lawmen made a spectacular one-day, 75-mile ride to beat Kennedy to the border.

The plan worked. On the afternoon of October 5, Kennedy approached the posse's camp; he was recognized and told three times, according to the *Globe*, to halt. We should pause for a moment and applaud the officers for their patience. When Kennedy raised his quirt as if to strike his horse, the lawmen let loose a volley. Kennedy's horse was killed; he himself was wounded. Wyatt claimed to have shot the horse—"I hated to do it," he said, "Kennedy's horse was a beauty"—and credited Bat with dropping Kennedy.

"Did I kill him?' Kennedy said as the officers approached, meaning Mayor Kelley. When informed that he had instead killed Dora Hand, Kennedy turned on Bat: "You sonuvabitch, you ought to have made a better shot than you did." "Well," Masterson is said to have replied, "you murdering sonuvabitch, I did the best I could."

The stunning upshot to one of the most famous posse rides of the Old West is that Kennedy went free. Though everyone knew him to be guilty, no witnesses appeared. Wyatt never discovered who was behind the appalling miscarriage of justice, but it was obvious that Texas money and Kansas politics had come to a cozy agreement. The sensational capture earned posse members statewide publicity, but Wyatt, for one, was soured on lawing. "There was no one," he recalled bitterly, "to champion the cause of the victim, who was without money and influence." Seeing Kennedy go free must have accelerated Wyatt's growing disgust the profession of frontier law.

A few months before the killing of Dora Hand, the Dodge City papers, like those all over America, made note of a huge silver strike in a tiny camp near the Mexican border in Arizona territory. The camp had the unpromising name of Tombstone, but that didn't keep people from all over the continent from flocking there. In Prescott, Arizona, Virgil had been talking of going south. Here was an opportunity for the brothers to unite and pool their efforts.

An incident in May 1879 seemingly hurried Wyatt into retirement. Leading an unruly Missourian off to jail by the ear—one of his favorite methods of dealing with ruffians—Earp was nearly killed when the fellow's companion drew a concealed gun. Fortunately, Bat Masterson was on the scene and buffaloed the man. Young George Bolds recalls that Earp and Masterson beat the Missourian senseless: The men "were a terrible sight . . . their own mothers would have had a hard time picking out their own sons." One can assume that Earp's patience at this point was exhausted. He had had, in his own words, "a belly full of lawing."

There was something else. Dodge was, in Wyatt's words, "losing its snap." In times when it wasn't deadly, it was becoming deadly dull. Wyatt made just twelve arrests all year, more than any other officer but hardly enough to start building a ranch fund, even at $2.50 per pinch. Cattle shipping had dropped off in 1879 compared to the previous year, and the growth of railroads promised a time in the not too distant future when the long cattle drives would be obsolete. Already Kansas farmers were lobbying for placing the deadlines-farther away from the town sites; many believed that the Texas beef carried ticks that would infect their cows, but many others, who had no stake in the cattle trade, simply wanted the herds and herders pushed farther away from the settlements. Civilization was arriving.

Wyatt saw it coming—he always saw it coming. On September 9, wrote Stuart Lake, the *Globe* reported that "Wyatt Earp, the most efficient marshal Dodge City ever had, has resigned and is heading for Arizona." The *Globe* had actually said "one of the most efficient marshals Dodge City had ever seen." It was only a small exaggeration, the kind a press agent might make.

In recent years, the general assessment of Earp's record as a Kansas peace officer is that it was solid but unspectacular. It was unspectacular in the sense that there were no sensational eruptions such as the O.K. Corral gunfight or the subsequent Vendetta Ride. Of course, that there weren't any such occurrences in a town so volatile as Dodge City can be taken as an indication of how well Earp did his job. What else would a "spectacular" performance in the West's wildest cow town have looked like? There is no clear gauge of how well a policeman is performing when violence is under control; one can only point out that the violence is under control. It was only later, in the bloody aberration of Tombstone, that Wyatt Earp's competency as a peace officer would be called into question.

By the end of September, Dodge papers reported that the Earp party—consisting of Wyatt, his wife Mattie, his brother Jim and his wife, and fifteen thoroughbred horses—had reached Las Vegas, New Mexico. There they were joined by Doc Holliday and Kate for the trek to Prescott, Arizona. Did I neglect to mention that Wyatt had a wife named Mattie? That's because neither Wyatt nor anyone else in Dodge ever mentioned her, either. We shall catch up to her story soon.

Dodge City began its inevitable slide into a tourist town. Towns had a way of slowing down when Wyatt Earp left them.[7]

Notes

1. To my knowledge, Tilghman has been featured in just one movie, Lamont Johnson's superb but little-seen *Cattle Annie and Little Britches* (1980) starring Rod Steiger as Tilghman and Burt Lancaster as Bill Doolin and costarring Amanda Plummer, Scot Glenn, and John Savage. In the movie, Tilghman and Doolin are already legends through the writings of "dime" novelist Ned Bunt-line. Ironically, Lancaster had previously played Buntline in Robert Altman's *Buffalo Bill and the Indians* as well as Wyatt Earp in *Gunfight at the O.K. Corral.*

By the way, Tilghman did finally capture Bill Doolin, but he never "brought him to justice" as several popular frontier histories claim. In 1894 Doolin escaped from jail and rejoined his wife in Lanton, Oklahoma. Tilghman's colleague, Heck Thomas, knocked on their door one day; a few minutes later, he rushed into the house and the sound of a shotgun was heard. Doolin's pellet-ridden body was worth $5,000 to Thomas, but, as it was later revealed, he never killed Doolin. The old bandit died of consumption shortly before Thomas arrived. Thomas claimed the reward, then persuaded Doolin's widow to take the money. Thomas, like Bill Tilghman, had a grudging respect for Doolin and didn't want his wife to become destitute.

2. An old Kansas tradition says that the terms "Boot Hill" and "Red Light District" originated in Dodge. This has never been proved, but Dodge almost certainly is responsible for making those terms famous. Tradition also credits Dodge City for giving the world "The wrong side of the tracks," meaning anything north of Front Street and the railroad tracks. A couple of years ago when I interviewed the actor and director Dennis Hopper, he told me that growing up in Dodge, south of Front Street, it was common knowledge that the term originated there. Hopper also said having grown up amid tales of Wyatt Earp and Doc Holliday, he was "proud of the fact that I'm the only one to have played someone on both sides of the gunfight at the O.K. Corral. I played Billy Clanton [in *Gunfight At The O.K. Corral*] and Doc Holliday [in the Sam Elliot TV movie, *Wild Times*]. Actually, Hopper isn't the only actor to have done this. Jeff Morey points out that DeForest Kelly played Virgil Earp in *Gunfight at the O.K. Corral* and was a crew member of the Starship *Enterprise*—and hence one of the Clantons—in episode 56 of "Star Trek: Spectre of the Gun."

3. Something in Wyatt Earp touched off this nerve in a certain kind of woman. Kate Elder, like Allie, was adrift in the American frontier with her man, Doc Holliday. Like Allie, Kate blamed Wyatt for her man's misfortunes. Not enough has been written about

the fact that these two women of similar temperament and circumstance have supplied anti-Earpists with most of their material.

4. That so many people are surprised to find out that George Hoy is the only man Wyatt Earp killed before Tombstone is due in large part to the misinformation spread by Earp's own family. For instance, in a much quoted and anthologized piece from the December 1958 *Reader's Digest*, Wyatt's cousin, George Earp, described a trip to Dodge City made in the spring of 1879. George, age fourteen, wanted Wyatt to help him get a job as a cowboy–how he could have accomplished that was not explained. As the two walked from the train station to the Dodge House, Wyatt was attacked in front of the Alhambra Saloon by a mounted desperado known as Texas Jack. Wyatt draws his Buntline Special, and Jack "crumpled away from his horse and rolled in the dust of Front Street, a bullet through his head." That, says George, "was one of the eight men Wyatt had to kill in some 100 personal gun battles while serving as a peace officer in the Old West."

Obviously, George Earp had read Lake's *Frontier Marshal* and done a bit of embroidering. The story, by the way, won *Reader's Digest*'s prize for best "First Person" story.

5. Considering that the testimony following the O.K. Corral gunfight provided the only eyewitness account of Wyatt's long-barreled gun and considering how man movie Earps carried some variation of the Buntline Special, it seems odd that Kurt Russell in *Tombstone* is the only movie Earp ever to use the Buntline Special in the gunfight at the O.K. Corral (Hugh O'Brian used it in the fight on TV).

6. Bob Boze Bell, among other Earp researchers, thinks Lake was trying to pull a fast one in getting the gun for nothing, particularly in light of a California museum's purchase a few years back of a gun thought to be Earp's. The price—$250,000. A long-barreled Colt that could be proved to have been Earp's could easily net over $1 million at auction. But giving Stuart Lake the benefit of the doubt, *Frontier Marshal* had yet to be written, and Earp's fame was yet to be revived, so the gun, even if discovered, couldn't have been worth much at the time Lake tried to find it. The situation is somewhat analogous to a baseball historian in the mid-1960s hunting down former Negro League stars and asking for game balls and bats.

7. Actually, Dodge is a thriving city of 17,000 plus today, but, like all the cattle towns, it never made intelligent use of its enormous cattle profits to build up other industries. One industry that still does good business is the tourist trade in "Old Dodge" with its wax museum statues of Wyatt Earp, Bat Masterson, and Doc Holliday and its replication of Front street, which features a plaque with a quote from Zane Grey: "Along the two blocks known as

Front street was enacted more frontier history than anywhere else in the West," which would be true if not for Tombstone. Thousands of tourists visit Dodge every year, including the Griswold family in *National Lampoon's Vacation*. "That's a crummy Wyatt Earp," says the actor who plays Chevy Chase's son in the movie; "He was wearing track shoes." "Yeah, they all did back then, Rusty," says Chase.

German-born Nicholas Eggenhofer became enamored with the American West through Wild West shows and reproductions of Frederick Remington's and Charles M. Russell's work. This painting of the Gunfight at the O.K. Corral was on the 1955 reprint of Stuart Lake's *Frontier Marshal* and now hangs in the National Cowboy Hall of Fame in Oklahoma City. In the original version he did for the 1931 first edition of Lake's book, he forgot to include Doc Holliday (on the left, holding the shotgun).

✦ Wyatt Earp ✦
Probably taken in 1869, in
Missouri, which would make
Wyatt 21. Within a short
time he would be widowed
and get involved in a horse-
thieving incident.

✦ Wyatt and Bat Masterson ✦
Taken in Dodge City, probably
in 1876. Both were serving on
the Dodge City police force;
Wyatt may have had the authority to hire Bat. The pin on
Wyatt's shirt is a badge, the only
known photo of America's most
famous lawman wearing one.

✦ Virgil Earp ✦

✦ Wyatt – 1887 ✦

The most famous image of Wyatt Earp. Taken in San Diego during the economic boom of 1887.

✦ Morgan – 1881 ✦

✦ John Behan ✦

As county sheriff, Behan had reason to regard Wyatt Earp as a political rival. When Josephine Marcus left him for Wyatt, their feud became personal.

The first Wyatt Earp movie, released in 1932, made from a novel by W.R. Burnett.

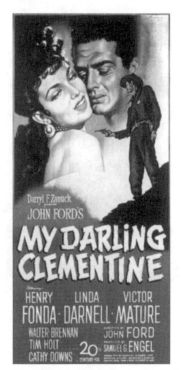

Released in 1946. John Ford knew Wyatt and claimed he told him the real story of the gunfight at the O.K. Corral. He didn't.

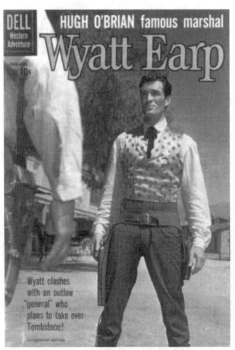

The Life and Legend of Wyatt Earp, starring Hugh O'Brian, was one of the most successful TV series of the 1950s.

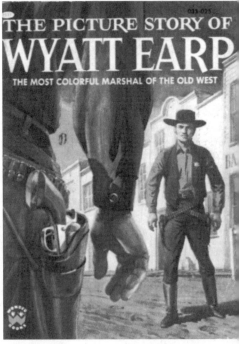

One of the numerous Earp books for kids that weren't part of the Stuart Lake Earp empire.

4

Tombstone: The Iliad

W alter Noble Burns, a prominent Chicago newspaperman with a passionate love of the Southwest, was the first journalist to try to capture the romance of Tombstone on paper. Burns first saw Tombstone as the scraggy, dust-covered near–ghost town it had become by the 1920s, but in his imagination Tombstone was once again "the magic city of the desert." A mining town in the heart of cattle country, he wrote in his once best-selling, now largely forgotten *Tombstone, An Iliad of the Southwest*

> It had the picturesqueness of a boom silver camp and the colour of a trail-end, cowboy capital. It was a town of lawlessness and law, saloons and schools, gambling halls and churches, lurid melodrama and business routine, red lights and altar candles. It was Hangtown of the rush-rush days of 'Forty-nine. It was San Francisco of the Stranglers. It was Virginia City, Alder Gulch, Poker Flat, and Deadwood. It was the Hays City and Abilene of Wild Bill Hickok, the San Antonio of Ben Thompson and King Fisher, the Dodge City of Bat Masterson. It was all the hectic, mad romance of the Old Western border, but in a stage setting of modern comforts and conveniences.

Burns was wrong about Tombstone being in "the heart of cattle country"—the area around Tombstone was too dry to support a ma-

jor cattle industry—but he was right about the rest of it. In popular
imagination Tombstone has merged with Dodge City because Wyatt
Earp was prominent in both.[1] If Dodge City was the archetypal
frontier town; Tombstone was a fabulous aberration. Situated in the
southeast corner of Arizona some 30 miles from the Mexican border,
the town sits on a small plateau, Goose Flats, which is surrounded by
mountains—the Dragoons to the northeast, the Mule to the southeast, the Huachucas to the southwest, and the Whetstones to the
northwest. The air is clear and dry and, because of Tombstone's
elevation, much cooler, especially at night, than the desert towns and
cities to the north. At dusk, the sky is a riot of pastels—blue, orange
and pink—and the air is fragrant with the odor of desert flowers and
creosote. The first recorded white man to see Goose Flats was a
Spanish Franciscan missionary, Fray Marcos de Niza, who, like a
priest out of Willa Cather's *Death Comes for the Archbishop,* came
there from Mexico on a donkey's back in the spring of 1539. Except
for the addition of "a hodgepodge of shacks, adobes, and tents,"
noted by Virgil's wife, Allie, it hadn't changed in 340 years. Allie,
who didn't want to go to Tombstone, was unimpressed. She didn't
have to wait long to see something more impressive; new structures
were going up, literally, while the Earps slept.[2] For instance, around
the corner from the shack the brothers rented on Allen Street, construction began on a new corral as they ate their first breakfast in
Tombstone. The world's most famous parking lot took its name from
the Democratic O.K. Club, an organization, according to H. L.
Mencken's *The American Language,* originally dedicated to the support of Martin Van Buren's second presidential term. O.K. was an
abbreviation of Old Kinderhook, an affectionate nickname for Van
Buren taken from the Hudson Valley village in New York where he
was born in 1782. Not far from the valley where young Martin grew
up, a Scotch-Irish family was taking roots whose descendants, Tom
and Frank McLaury, would help make the O. K. Corral famous.

     In later years some Tombstonians would say, "Silver made Tomb-
stone rich, but Wyatt Earp made it famous." But it is equally true
that Tombstone made Earp famous, and that southeast Arizona gave
Wyatt Earp the setting he needed to become a legend. As Arizona
folklorist Bob Boze Bell has remarked, the 22,000 odd square miles
which encompass Fort Sumner, New Mexico, where Billy the Kid
was killed, El Paso, Texas, and Tombstone, Arizona, is America's

Bermuda Triangle, a spawning ground of myth. Cochise, Geronimo, Billy the Kid, Pat Garrett, the Earps, Doc Holliday, Big-Nosed Kate, the Clantons, the McLaurys, Johnny Ringo, Tom Horn, Texas John Slaughter, John Wesley Hardin, and, later, Pancho Villa, all earned immortality in this region. Has any other area of the United States produced so much legend in so small a space?

Much of the romance of the southwest border territories had to do with their remoteness; in the 1870s scarcely any white men had seen many of their valleys and canyons. Tombstone itself, despite its natural beauty and mineral wealth, had two major drawbacks. One was a dearth of water. There was none at all on the mesa, and the nearest river was the San Pedro, 10 miles to the southwest, which would become the site of the mill nearest Tombstone. Tents and shacks that accumulated around the mill evolved into the town of Charleston, one of Tombstone's satellites.

The second drawback was Apaches. To counter them, in March 1877 a party of U.S. Cavalry and scouts from Fort Whipple near Prescott established another fort, eventually called Camp Huachuca, near the Mexican border. One of the scouts, Al Sieber, was a local legend; another, by the name of Ed Schieffelin, soon would be. According to one of Tombstone's most popular folk tales, Schieffelin began exploring the territory on his own. The cavalrymen warned him: "All you'll find in Apache country is your tombstone."

Schieffelin thought he could actually see something gleaming off rocks near the edge of the San Pedro valley: Was it a mirage, he wondered, or could it possibly be silver? Much silver and some gold had already been found in southeast Arizona, but snakes, scorpions, and tarantulas made the prospect of living in the region without shelter a formidable one, and unless he had mastered the art of building adobe huts, a prospector would be spending cold nights on open ground. No prospector could travel far from water without a string of mules, and heavy equipment was sometimes needed to extract the silver, so capital was a prerequisite for prospecting. Crowning these difficulties was the absence of law. The soldiers were of some help in deterring Apaches, but they could do nothing about the bandits, Anglo and Mexican, who preyed on lone travelers.

Ed Schieffelin's solution to the perils of prospecting, like Wyatt Earp's to buffalo hunting, was to prepare as well as he could and deal with the difficulties as they arose. During the summer of 1877

Schieffelin collected samples and, in the winter of '78, having made elaborate preparations, he returned to the San Pedro valley with his brother Al and another miner and assayer named Dick Gird. They arrived none too soon. Word had leaked of the richness of Schieffelin's ore samples, and prospectors began flocking to the region—the proximity of silver made snakes, thirst, and Apaches seem less daunting.

By rights Ed Schieffelin should have met the fate of numerous prospectors and miners before him, but he had sand, as westerners liked to say about someone with resolve, and he had luck. "Ed, you lucky cuss," said Dick Gird upon assaying Schieffelin's ore from a silver vein so rich that, as the story was later told, it left the imprint of a coin pressed against it. The ore, Gird estimated, was worth $15,000 a ton. One mine became the Lucky Cuss, while another claim turned out to be the Tough Nut, as in it was "a tough nut to crack." The mine would lend its name to the street that led to the red light district of the new town. To Schieffelin went the privilege of naming the town; the first name that popped into his head was what the soldiers told him he'd find there: Tombstone.

By spring, Tombstone was a cluster of adobe huts, tents, and a few shacks. A year later the population had grown to about 250, all men. When the Earps rolled into town in December, Tombstone had grown to perhaps twelve hundred.

By the time of the gunfight in October 1881, Tombstone, by one estimate, had ten thousand inhabitants; Burns actually thought it had fifteen thousand. Carl Chafin, a lifelong Tombstone researcher, places the peak population at about five or six thousand. Period estimates vary from six to eight thousand, though no one was ever entirely clear about what constituted a resident; in the boom years there must have been hundreds and perhaps thousands of prospectors, gamblers, salesmen, cattle dealers, and other transients in town.

Some historians feel that when Wyatt Earp left town in the spring of 1882, Tombstone was the on the verge of becoming the largest city between Kansas City and San Francisco, but it's doubtful that Tombstone was ever as big as Tucson, let alone Denver. Certainly, though, no other frontier town grew so sophisticated in so short a time. By '82 Tombstone had capital from Philadelphia, New York, Chicago, Boston, and Europe; with the money came a lifestyle some old pioneers thought odious. An Arizona travel guide from '82 re-

ferred to Tombstone as "that spasm of modernism." "Nobody hag-
gles," it read. "The most expensive of anything is what is most
wanted." Expensive is what Tombstonians got. By the end of 1882
the mining camp that four years earlier had consisted of canvas and
adobe had French restaurants, oyster bars, tennis courts, a bowling
alley, and ice cream parlors. (Wyatt Earp loved ice cream; his favorite
shop was on Fourth Street, a baseball's throw from the O.K. Corral.)
There was a New York–style cigar shop run by a Mr. Cohen. There
were also telephones, though their range was only from the mines to
the town.

In movie westerns, nobody orders anything but whisky. In Tombstone's sixty-odd saloons, at the town's peak, cowhands and miners
could cultivate tastes for champagne and other imported wines, as
well as mixed drinks (gin fizzies were particularly popular). Those
with more exotic desires would wander off the main street to Chinese
opium dens.

Tombstone's crown jewel was the elegant Bird Cage Theater,
which catered to small, intimate entertainments. Larger-scale productions played at Schieffelin Hall on Fremont—also just a baseball
throw from the O.K. Corral. (After 1882, everything in Tombstone
was identified by its proximity to the O.K. Corral.)

Gen. William Tecumseh Sherman, who had been so instrumental
in the creation of Dodge's prosperity, hated the southeastern portion
of the Arizona territory and suggested, perhaps not facetiously, that
the United States give it back to Mexico. (Sherman didn't consider
that to many Mexicans it never stopped being part of Mexico.) After
the Tombstone strike he would call the region "a permanent mine of
silver to the United States."

"Permanent" turned out to be about ten years. There was a lot of
legend to be crammed into three years, and Tombstonians wasted no
time in getting started.

Later, after the killings, Wyatt would be awarded the blame for
uprooting the brothers and their families and bringing them all to
that godforsaken corner of Arizona. No letters survive to shed light
on who influenced who. Stuart Lake claimed that Virgil had written
first to Wyatt about Tombstone. But Wyatt, after all, was supposed
to be the aggressive Earp, the brother constantly on the make, so it
had to have been Wyatt who brought everyone to Tombstone and

was thus responsible for the tragedies that ensued. Allie Earp blamed Wyatt, or so said Frank Waters when *The Earp Brothers of Tombstone* was published some eighty years later. She was furious over the thought of leaving Prescott for a boom silver camp, "Because we got a good home right here! . . . We're too busy cuttin' wood to be traipsin' round the country!"

Allie believed that Wyatt exercised a strange hold over Virgil just as Kate Elder thought Wyatt had an inexplicable influence on Doc Holliday. Indeed Wyatt did have an unusual influence over his two older brothers, James and Virgil, and he was the only man on earth to have any influence over John Holliday. Still, the likelihood is that all the Earp brothers, including James down in Texas and Morgan out in Montana, were ready to stop roaming and get together in a suitable town. (Holliday almost certainly would have made it to Tombstone anyway, just as he eventually showed up in just about every wide-open town.) Allie Earp and Kate Elder, both orphans, always resented what Frank Waters called the "silence, secrecy, and clannish solidarity of the Earps," which is easy enough to understand, though in fact the Earps were no more clannish than any brothers on the nineteenth century American frontier. The Mastersons, the James, the Youngers, the Thompsons, the Clantons, the McLaurys were all called "clannish" by someone. But Allie cared nothing about brotherly solidarity; all she had in the world was Virgil, and Wyatt was a rival for his attention. James, the oldest, was only peripherally involved in most of the brothers' decisions, and Morgan was too young to influence the others. To Allie's way of thinking, the blame for the bad decisions fell on Wyatt.

In Prescott, Virgil had worked as a stage driver, serving a route that included stops at towns and mining camps with names like TipTop, Humble, Bumblebee, and a tiny village called Phoenix. Later, he worked at a sawmill. More prone to manual labor than Wyatt, Virgil nonetheless found that making a living at his sawmill in a desert town was a tough go. He tried a second job in 1878, running for town constable, essentially a night watchman's position that paid $75 a month. The strain of working day and night proved too great, and before Christmas he gave up the sawmill. But lawing in Prescott would have its drawbacks as well. Deputized by the Prescott sheriff, Virgil grabbed a Henry repeating rifle and helped to pursue two fugitives, one a man named Vaughan who was wanted for a murder in Texas. After a short, sharp gun battle, both outlaws lay mortally wounded. Vaughan was shot in the head, probably by Virgil, and was found with a cigar clenched firmly between his teeth. It might have made Virgil feel better to find out that Vaughan, whose real name was Wilson, had an extensive criminal record. In addition to the murder in Texas, he had once been arrested in Wichita by Wyatt Earp.

Aside from the Wilson incident, Virgil found lawing in Prescott fairly tame. As the territorial capital it was more settled than most Arizona towns, particularly those to the south. Virgil had time to make contacts and made an important one. He became friendly with U.S. Marshal Crawley Dake, and like Wyatt in Dodge City, quickly learned the value of cooperation between different levels of law enforcement. Before leaving Prescott, Dake offered, and Virgil accepted, a position as a deputy U.S. marshal for the Tombstone area. Wyatt would later snag an even better if not bigger plum, a deputy sheriff's appointment. Wyatt's job carried a regular salary with it; Virgil's federal appointment paid on a per job basis. Wyatt would later claim that Crawley Dake "had heard of me and begged me so hard to take the [federal] deputyship in Tombstone that I finally consented." This sounds self-serving, but it's not wholly unlikely that Wyatt was offered the federal position before Virgil (and, as we will see, Wyatt would eventually accept the job). Wyatt was probably speaking the truth when he told Stuart Lake that he went to Tombstone with "no thought of a peace officer's job"; he would seek the deputy sheriff's job in Tombstone only after his first clash with the McLaury brothers.

But if Wyatt really had ruled out the possibility of any peace officer's job in Tombstone, he was being disingenuous. Both Virgil and Wyatt were fed up with the politics and danger of frontier law enforcement—not to mention having to shoot people—but neither was sure exactly what else he was qualified to do. Wyatt, for one, had done no other work besides gambling and hauling lumber since he quit hunting buffalo. The law positions were insurance, a safety net, as it were. Wyatt's was the better one in this respect. Pima County Sheriff Charlie Shibell, a Democrat, needed a good man in the growing Tombstone area to collect taxes, of which the deputy got to keep a percentage. It was easy and lucrative work, particularly since much of the tax revenue came from the Tombstone mining interests.

Wyatt probably regarded the post more as a glorified tax collector's and process server's job than a real law appointment. Wyatt should have known himself well enough to understand that he did not have the temperament of a process server.

Wyatt's announced reason for going to Tombstone was to open a stage line, though the string of thoroughbred horses he brought with him were more suited to racing than hauling. Whatever his long-term business plans, it's clear that Wyatt and Virgil planned to hold on to their badges at least until their interests were secure. The only problem was that the Earps, once they had badges, weren't content to look the other way when laws, even unpopular laws, were broken. It would have been better for the Earps if they had followed the example of John Behan.

Virgil had known Behan before Wyatt met him. The Behans, of Irish descent, had come to Prescott from the same part of Missouri inhabited by numerous Earps. Like so many children of immigrant Irish, John took to politics—Democratic politics, of course. He had held several elected positions, including serving two terms in the territorial legislature, and quickly developed a reputation as a glad-hander. He also gained a reputation as a lady's man; his wife sued him for divorce in 1875, a rare enough occurrence to raise eyebrows in Prescott. An incident in October 1879 raised them even more: "Hon. J. H. Behan," reported the *Prescott Miner*, "had occasion to call at the Chinese laundry this P.M., when a controversy arose, leading to some half dozen of the pig-tail race making an assault on him with clubs." Apparently Behan responded by pulling a gun that, luckily for him, misfired. Getting himself humiliated by a crowd of Chinese launders in public probably hastened Behan's departure to Tombstone.[3] On November 4, the Earp party departed for Tombstone, with Wyatt and Virgil leaving behind them considerably better reputations than John Behan's.[4] Meanwhile, Doc Holliday's reputation was on the decline. Doc and Kate had stayed behind in Prescott playing out a winning streak at the gaming tables, but while he played, reports of some nastiness Doc had gotten into back in New Mexico reached Arizona. Precisely what Holliday had done to earn such bad press in Las Vegas and Albuquerque papers isn't clear. Legend has him racking up as many as seven victims in gunfights between Dodge City and Prescott, though only two of the "kills," Las Vegas characters named Mike Gordon and Charly White, have any evidence to verify them, and one of those is questionable. By one account, Doc had an altercation with Gordon, a suspected outlaw, and invited him to step out into the street to settle matters in accepted frontier fashion. For once, the classic western stand-up fight was really that, with Holliday killing Gordon in the main street of Las Vegas.

What happened in the Charly White shooting isn't clear. Legend credits Doc with killing White, but no records survive to support the claims. White had known Doc in Dodge City and the two had a disagreement; Holliday apparently refrained from killing White there in order not to embarrass Earp. Doc was under no such restraints in New Mexico. As Holliday walked into a saloon, White saw him coming and drew; shots were exchanged, and a moment later White lay behind the bar with a head wound. But according to the reminiscences of Miguel Otero, later the New Mexico governor, White wasn't killed but merely stunned by the bullet and recovered, soon leaving the west for his home in Boston. Whatever happened, no newspaper or eyewitness account mentions the death of Charly White.

Numerous other shootings were tacked on to Doc's mythical rap-sheet in this period, including the murder of a couple of Mexicans on a trip to northern Mexico and two cowhands who were slain on Doc's first visit to Tombstone, supposedly shot over some gambling disagreement. As with so many of Holliday's kills, no one is quite sure when they happened or where; all the storytellers could agree on is that the shootings happened when they weren't around. However unjustified, Doc brought a bad reputation with him to Tombstone and it quickly attached itself to the Earps.

Later, in her memoirs, Kate would claim Doc received a letter from Wyatt in which he wrote that Tombstone was "very lively" and added that "Doc could do well there as there was no dentist." Before long, some people felt that Tombstone had one too many.

Wyatt's hopes of establishing a new stage line in Tombstone were dashed by the discovery that Tombstone already had several good ones. The brothers wasted no time in finding other ways to make money. Not long after arriving in town, Wyatt was approached by a gambler named Lou Rickabaugh about a local thug named Johnny Tyler who was chasing customers from the gaming tables at the

Oriental Saloon with threats and verbal abuse. With Tyler around, the elegant saloon had quickly gone from a sin palace to, in the words of George Parsons, "a regular slaughterhouse." For, say, a quarter interest, Rickabaugh wanted to know, would Wyatt be interested in dealing Mr. Tyler out? Indeed he would. One afternoon, as Tyler shouted at customers, Wyatt came up from behind, grabbed him by the ear lobe—a favorite Earp method of dealing with troublemakers—and led him through the front door. "I didn't know you had an interest in this place," Tyler moaned. "I have," Earp replied, "and you can tell your friends it's the fighting interest." (Stuart Lake adds that Doc Holliday, nickel-plated six gun on the ready, covered Wyatt from Tyler's confederates.)

Wyatt Earp never denied that he was "an adept hand at faro and monte." When police duties in Dodge became less demanding, he spent more time dealing for Luke Short at the Long Branch saloon than in rounding up drunken cowhands or fixing sidewalks. Tombstone offered something new. He could do more than merely supplement his salary through gambling, he could become a businessman by owning a piece of the action. Wyatt might have agreed with sentiments crime boss Frank Costello would voice seventy-five years later when he told a reporter, "I am not a gambler. My customers are gamblers. I am a businessman." On the late-nineteenth-century American frontier the possibilities existed for a man like Wyatt Earp to actually make the transition from gambler to businessman. Gambling was considered a legitimate profession on the frontier; Bat Masterson, on a visit to Dallas in the 1870s, observed that "gambling was not only the principal but the best-paying industry of the town . . . it was also reckoned among its most respectable." Billy Breakenridge, at one time John Behan's deputy, felt that most of the gamblers and dealers in Tombstone "were good citizens, and gambling was just as legitimate as dealing in merchandise or any other business." One Arizona editor thought of gamblers "as honorable as the members of any stock exchange in the world—and braver."

Like most newcomers to Goose Flats, they immediately filed mining claims. The Arizona Historical Society lists several claims filed by the brothers, both together and separately, one of them filed almost exactly one week after their arrival in Tombstone. One was named "Earp"; another was named for Wyatt Earp's second wife, Mattie Blaylock.

Who was she, and where had Wyatt met her? More than 110 years after her death not much has been added to Mattie Blaylock Earp's brief biographical sketch. Her given name was Celia Ann Blaylock, and her family was from Iowa. How she got the nickname of Mattie is a mystery. Some believe she and Wyatt met in Wichita and that he already regarded her as his common-law wife in the mid 1870s; this is unlikely if only because Wyatt was known to be rooming with Jimmy Cairns, a Wichita deputy marshal, at the time. Cairns never mentioned anything about Mattie; in fact, neither did Bat Masterson, John P. Clum, or any of Wyatt's companions or relatives. Her name never appeared in Lake's *Frontier Marshal* or Walter Noble Burns' *Tombstone*. Nor is she mentioned in early accounts of the Tombstone controversies by Wyatt's enemies such as Billy Breakenridge in *Helldorado*.

For that matter, none of these sources mentions Wyatt in connection with any woman up to and including Josephine Marcus. This seems odd in light of Wyatt's later reputation as a ladies' man, but then, almost all those claims were to appear after Wyatt "stole" the beautiful Josephine from John Behan in Tombstone. An old-timer from Dodge said that he never heard "so much as a suspicion that Wyatt had what you might call an entangling alliance in any South Side dance hall," which might indicate that Wyatt was simply going home to Mattie after work. But where did he meet her? In her memoir Kate Elder said that Mattie was with Wyatt when she and Doc met him in Fort Griffin, Texas. It seems strange that Wyatt would bring a woman along on such an arduous trek through the Texas panhandle, but it wouldn't be outside the realm of possibility. Doc and Kate traveled all over the West together, and later Wyatt and Josephine Marcus would show up at every mining camp and racetrack from Texas to Mexico to Alaska. If Mattie was with Wyatt in Fort Griffin in 1876, there is a good possibility that he met her in Texas. Why she was there and what she was doing is lost to history.

She might have been a prostitute; many have claimed she was, but most of those stories smack of the "Uncle Ned" history. We know Mattie wound up a prostitute, but we don't know how she started out. There are tales about her drug addiction; the coroner's report following her death in 1888 mentions laudanum several times, but we don't know when she began taking the drug. There is no record of Wyatt and Mattie having been married; that she was listed as his wife in the Tombstone 1880 census indicates that by then they considered their relationship a common-law marriage. This was the norm for couples who met on the frontier in the 1870s. The 1880 census gave her age as twenty-two, which would have made her ten years younger than Wyatt.

Some would later claim that Wyatt, while in Tombstone, tried to keep his marriage a secret, but there is no evidence of this; Wyatt named a mine after her, which is an odd way of keeping someone hidden. Wyatt never spoke to anyone on record about Mattie after Tombstone, but then, apart from the bare facts of Urilla's life and death, there is no record of his mentioning any of the women in his life to any interviewer or biographer.

Arizona historian Glenn G. Boyer has called Mattie a "dissatisfied and carping woman with a short temper" and maintains that Wyatt "stuck with her from pity rather than love." But the only descriptions we have of Wyatt and Mattie's domestic relations come from Allie Earp in *The Earp Brothers of Tombstone,* and those were written more than six decades after the fact. Allie makes much of her own and Mattie's resentment at being made to stay home and sew while Wyatt goes out on the town and has all the fun; one day Allie takes Mattie out on a wine tasting spree and the two get plastered. Wyatt throws a fit: "I told you to keep out of town and not to show your face on the streets," he shouts. The passage seems dubious; it grants a modern, liberated sensibility to Allie and a Victorian, sexist one to Wyatt. (One wonders why Allie didn't get her husband, Virgil, to escort her around town.)

What is likely is that Wyatt and Mattie were a bad match, that Mattie simply didn't have the kind of fire and spirit Wyatt needed in a companion. At least, that's the conclusion one draws from looking at the companion he was to spend nearly half a century with. Theirs does not appear to have been a happy marriage, but Wyatt made no more attempt to keep Mattie a "secret" in Tombstone than the other Earp brothers did their wives. There is virtually nothing written on the Earp wives in their time; letters and reminiscences came later. If not for the interest in the Earps stirred up by *Frontier Marshal* in the 1930s, we wouldn't know their names today.

We probably wouldn't know the name of Wyatt Earp today if the Texas Rangers hadn't been granted a legal carte blanche to clear out troublemakers from the West Texas plains. Chased out of the state, the rootless ex-cowhands and saddle tramps gravitated toward the small towns in southeastern Arizona, attracted to the climate and the relative lack of law enforcement on either side of the border. Almost all of them had backgrounds in cow theft. A few had once been legitimate cowhands in Texas and had driven herds to the great Kansas cow towns—more than one, apparently, had heard of Wyatt Earp before 1880. Others had ties to the Lincoln County war in New Mexico from which the Billy the Kid legend emerged and to which the coming troubles in Arizona bore not a small resemblance.[5] Still others, such as John Peters Ringo, had drifted west after garnering reputations as killers in the Mason County or "Hoodoo" war in Texas between the earlier English-speaking settlers and German immigrants. Their natural profession was trading in stolen livestock. By 1880 or so, they came to be referred to collectively as "cow-boys" or "Cowboys;" we refer to them as Cowboys for the rest of our story to distinguish the cattle rustlers and their colleagues from the general working-variety of cowhand who later came to be associated with the term.

The primary reason for their existence was that Arizona Territory as yet had no Rangers like those in Texas, and the Posse Comitatus Act forbade the army from being used to arrest civilian lawbreakers. The Army's intervention in the Lincoln County war in neighboring New Mexico had been so disastrous that most southwesterners were appalled at the idea of *any* government interference in the Arizona border conflict. Federal influence was confined to the overworked Crawley Dake in Prescott, who had a part-timer, Virgil Earp, as his only marshal in the region. Within a short time, the rustlers forged friendships and alliances with local ranchers Newman Haynes "Old Man" Clanton and the McLaury brothers, Frank and Tom.

The Cowboys were recognizable as a group—"vigorous, sinewy fellows," Stuart Lake called them, "all with a similarity of attire as marked as, but contrasting sharply with, that of the Earps," who generally dressed in clean white shirts with black coats and trousers whose legs covered their boots. The rustlers, Lake wrote, wore not the sideswept Stetson hats made familiar by thousands of Hollywood TV and movie westerns but instead favored "huge sand-hued sombreros, gaudy silk neckerchiefs, fancy woolen shirts, tight-fitting doeskin trousers tucked into forty-dollar half-boots—a getup so generally affected by Curly Bill followers that it was recognized as their uniform." The earliest and one of the best representatives of their dress in contrast to the Earps' was the painting, *The Gunfight at the O.K. Corral* by the German-born artist Nicholas Eggenhofer that first appeared on the cover of the 1931 and 1955 editions of *Frontier Marshal*, a picture that is nearly as famous from reproductions as the Anheiser-Busch–distributed *Custer's Last Fight*.[6] The term *cowboy* wasn't new, but it wasn't in wide use till the mid-1880s, with *cow-hand*, *drover*, or *stockman* being the most commonly used terms before that time. Some said John P. Clum's Tombstone Epitaph popularized it, intending "Cowboy" as a term of derision, rather as one might say "redneck" today. For a while, the term became almost synonymous with cattle rustlers. Some papers put quotes around the term, implying that the boys so named were not to be compared with *real* ranchers, men who made a living by the raising and selling of cattle. The Cowboys themselves seemed to embrace the term the way that, say, modern bikers rally to names such as Hell's Angels.

Curly Bill Brocius was generally regarded as a leader, if not the leader, of the rustlers; Billy Breakenridge thought so, and so, too, did George Parsons, the Samuel Pepys of Tombstone, a former San Francisco bank clerk whose diary would prove to be an invaluable source of information on Tombstone in its boom years. Breakenridge and Parsons knew Curly Bill well, but little about his background has ever been discovered. Though he would contribute much to town lore, except for a couple of memorable occasions, Curly Bill spent most of his time outside of Tombstone in the small satellite towns such as Galeyville.

Much more is known about John Ringo, though he, too, is so shrouded in myth as to seem enigmatic. Ringo, like Doc Holliday, brought with him to Arizona the reputation of having been a killer in Texas and, also as in Doc's case, no one is entirely certain how he earned it. There is at least one reliable story of Ringo giving an exhibition of fancy gun-handling, and one old Arizonian called him "the best pistol shot in the county," but the only recorded victim of his alcohol-induced mood swings in Arizona was a man named Lewis Hancock. Ringo shot Hancock in the neck, so the story goes, for refusing to drink whiskey with him. Contrary to the legend, Hancock didn't die, but the incident established Ringo as a man who would pull a trigger, which is exactly what it took to establish a reputation in that place and time.

The evolution of Ringo's legend is a study of Old West myth-mongering in microcosm. Walter Noble Burns was the first to resuscitate Ringo's story from the tales told to him by Arizona old-timers; if not for Burns, Ringo's minor cult would almost certainly have died out after Tombstone went bust. Ringo had been well thought of in Texas by John Wesley Hardin—not exactly the best character reference, as Hardin himself was a rabid racist, psychotic, liar, and murderer—but had few close friends in Arizona, where he mostly kept to himself. His past was supposed to have been tragic, and indeed what was learned of it proved to be. While Ringo was in his early teens his father was killed in a shotgun accident that nearly decapitated him.[7] By the time Ringo reached Arizona he was a brooding paradox, both a loner and a man with a reputation for fierce loyalty to his friends, most of whom, like him, stole cattle for a living. Both Burns and Billy Breakenridge (who was interviewed by Burns for *Tombstone*) thought Ringo to be an educated man with a shelf of classics in his cabin. (Fans of the movie *Tombstone*, which relied heavily on Burns's out-of-print volume, will recall the scene where Doc Holliday, played by Val Kilmer, and Ringo, played by Michael Biehn, insult each other in Latin.) Breakenridge went so far as to confer a college degree on Ringo, probably so he could compete in status with Doc Holliday.

Burns, who was remarkably nonjudgmental in such matters, concluded that Ringo was "an introspective, tragic figure, darkly handsome, splendidly brave, a man born for better things," in short, "a Hamlet among outlaws." In his 1987 book *John Ringo—The Gunfighter Who Never Was*, Jack Burrows studied Ringo's legend, from Gregory Peck's angst-ridden Jimmy Ringo in *The Gunfighter* to Lorne Greene's kitsch-hit 1960s recording "Ringo," and concluded, "He remains a western figure largely because of the mellifluous tonal quality of his name." Burrows was unable to find evidence of a single gunfight John Ringo had ever engaged in.[8] Decades later, Hollywood would award group leadership status to Ike Clanton after the death of Old Man Clanton, but most observers believed that Curly Bill and Ringo shared an unofficial cocaptaincy. Ringo would come to be called "The King of the Cowboys," though exactly who awarded him this crown and what he did to earn it is uncertain. Probably, Ringo's status grew after his death, as small ranchers saw him as a symbol of resistance to Wyatt Earp and the forces of liberalism, nineteenth-century-style, that he embodied. Whether Ringo ever actually led the Cowboys in any formal sense is doubtful. The Clantons didn't need to be led. The Cowboys needed places to keep cattle and other stolen stock, and the Clantons and McLaurys had working ranches, which gave them respectability in the community not enjoyed by many of the Cowboys they befriended. The Clantons had two ranches, one in the San Pedro Valley, the other in the Animas Valley, while the McLaurys had a place in Sulphur Springs Valley. Such locations were well placed for keeping stolen Mexican cattle, not to mention occasional army horses and mules.

Southeast Arizona was still too dry in 1879 to breed large herds of cattle. Most cows in the immediate area belonged to Mexican ranchers in Sonora, south of the border. The fast growing territorial American population as well as the Army bases and Indian reservations made cattle a valuable commodity, and it was much more profitable, and much faster, to steal cows and bring them north than fight nature by raising them.

Thus, cattle theft became the first profession in Old Man Clanton's life that he was any good at. A deserter from the Confederate Army in Texas, Clanton had bounced his family around the country almost as much as Nicholas Earp, and when California didn't pan out he started up again in Arizona. The McLaurys came by a different route, through Texas by way of New York State where the family's ancestors still live. Though Old Man Clanton would later be granted by legend a leadership role in the Cowboy gang, his family and the McLaurys were more likely the fences for the stolen Mexican cattle, which was just fine with the small legitimate ranchers who had no love for either the U.S. or the Mexican government and who liked cheap cattle.

Still, not all American ranchers of southern Democratic roots saw the Clantons and McLaurys as heroes. For instance, "Texas" John Slaughter, who would become a famous sheriff in the Tombstone area after the Earps left, knew the Clantons for what they were. Slaughter spent years building up his Arizona cattle business by moving stock from his holdings in Texas; several of the Cowboy faction probably came to Arizona with him on cattle drives. Shortly after buying a ranch from the McLaurys, Slaughter began losing stock. One day he came upon Ike Clanton on his property; according to Tombstone historian Ben Traywick, Slaughter threatened to kill Clanton if more cattle were lost. The cattle stopped getting lost. "We knew the Clantons, they were thieves," wrote John Slaughter's wife in her journal. But then, she added, most ranchers of that era were.

What Mrs. Slaughter probably meant was that the ranchers who weren't cattle thieves usually benefited from those who were. Thus, to many who lived outside Tombstone, the Cowboys took on a Robin Hood kind of aura, and many reminiscences later found in the Arizona Historical Society are similar in tone to Missourians of Confederate sympathies who rationalized the robberies of the James and Younger brothers. James Hancock, an Arizona justice of the peace and professional windbag who went by the title of "judge," wrote that the Cowboys "never molested the small ranchers," a fact which some historians attribute to their shared national, historic, and cultural backgrounds, but which was more likely due to the small ranchers having nothing to steal. Big ranchers such as New England born officer Henry Hooker—eventually an Earp ally—were not so lucky. Neither were big ranchers like Texas John Slaughter, who had exactly the national and cultural background as the rustlers.

Background and culture exacerbated what was already a huge sore spot all along the Mexican border and especially in remote Arizona territory. Bandits had been crossing the border both ways for years, but as the American population increased the problem worsened from north to south. There were several reasons for this, one being that the region's mineral wealth brought hundreds of well-armed Americans every month to Tombstone and surrounding towns like Charleston, Galeyville, and Bisbee. The big reason, though, is that Mexican ranchers had exactly what the Cowboys wanted and couldn't find enough of—cattle. It would be years before the cattle industry in Arizona would catch up with the demand for beef, a demand that by 1880 was increasing by the week.

And so, scores of heavily armed Cowboys, some former Confederates, some veterans of range wars in Texas and New Mexico, all with an intense dislike of the U.S. federal government and a contempt for Mexicans shared by their American friends and neighbors, converged in and around Tombstone as the decade of 1880 began. The Cowboys bitterly resented the law, which in this case was represented by brothers with Northern and Unionist backgrounds and federal associations, "towners," not ranchers, men conditioned to suffer no insolence from real Cowboys, let alone professional cattle thieves. That cast of characters that would take part in the most famous outbreak of violence in frontier history was assembled—or would be soon when young Morgan Earp, and, later, Doc Holliday arrived in Tombstone.

By February Tombstone was growing faster than anyone could keep track of. The population passed the two thousand mark, making it bigger than Wichita or Dodge City. Residents included Welsh and Irish miners, Mexican laborers, and perhaps two hundred Chinese. Tombstone now had a city marshal, a genial former Union Army veteran, Fred White, and Wells Fargo established an office in Tombstone with a man named Marshall Williams as agent. The town still had no courthouse or city hall, but soon it had a new saloon destined for legend, the Oriental, located at Fifth and Allen; a Major League outfielder could hit the entrance of the O.K. Corral from the Oriental on two bounces.

There was a new newspaper to join the *Daily Nugget*, which began publishing on October 2 of the previous year. John Phillip Clum, a former student at Rutgers University in New Jersey and later Indian agent, started a newspaper called the *Epitaph*. Ed Schieffelin got to name that, too; every tombstone, he told Clum, needs an epitaph. "But the epitaphs don't always tell the truth," Clum protested. "They tell the truth about as often as newspapers," Schieffelin shot back. There was a new restaurant, too: Ike Clanton opened a small lunch counter that must have been well stocked with beef.

Early in July, a man identifying himself as "King Pin" rode into the San Carlos Apache Reservation with a herd of cattle whose estimated value was about $2,000—on the open market, anyway. Mr. Pin and his companions, who included a Mr. Dutch George, tried to make a deal with the reservation contractor. Suspecting some sort of chicanery, he put the cattlemen off until they broke down and sold the herd for a fraction of its worth. King Pin and Dutch George were identified as Joe Hill and John Ringo; Ike Clanton was also spotted. Angry at their failure, the Cowboys left San Carlos reservation and followed the Gila River, shooting at houses as they passed, till they came to the small town of Safford, where they shot up a saloon and a general store.

Whether out of support for the Cowboys or simple fear of them, no charges were pressed. As they had broken no federal law, they avoided Virgil Earp's jurisdiction. A clash, though, was inevitable, and it came a couple of weeks later. On July 21, six mules were stolen from Camp Rucker, a small fort east of Tombstone built to contain Geronimo's Apaches. The thieves were never caught, but local rumor named Curly Bill Brocius and two Cowboys, Zwing Hunt and Sherman McMasters. The animals were then left at the McLaurys' ranch, and the brands changed so they could be fenced.

This was crime the locals, given their contempt for federal authority in general and the Army in particular, were willing to overlook, especially if some of them got cheap mules from the deal, and this made it precisely the sort of crime that Shibell's Sheriff's Office in Tucson was going to be lax in investigating. The deputy U.S. marshal in Tombstone didn't see it that way.

An officer from Camp Rucker, Lt. J. H. Hurst, led a platoon of cavalry into Tombstone looking for help. He rode out from Tombstone with U.S. Deputy Marshal Virgil Earp and his two newly deputized specials, Wyatt and Morgan Earp. The soldiers were forbidden to search civilian property, which is something the Cowboys must have counted on. But the theft of the mules was a federal offense. Virgil was the logical choice to conduct the search, and Wyatt and Morgan were his logical deputies.

In a more settled country, or even in a state rather than in a territory such as Arizona, the authority of a deputy to deputize others might have been disputed. In southeast Arizona, in 1880, Crawley Dake in faraway Prescott regarded anyone Virgil deputized as legitimate, and that was all that mattered. An angry Frank McLaury later said that the soldiers came to his ranch "accompanied by several citizens," implying that his rights were violated. Wyatt found a branding iron that read "D8," which had been used to cover the army's "U.S." brand; the case seemed cut and dried.

But Hurst, who understood that trouble with the local ranchers they were theoretically sent to protect would not reflect well on the army or on him, backed down. It was up to Hurst to press charges, so he told a disgusted Virgil and Wyatt that he'd work out "some kind of a compromise" with McLaury. The Earps returned to Tombstone, utterly unable to understand Hurst's theory of criminal justice. Whatever deal Hurst thought he was making with McLaury came apart, and nine days later he published a notice in the *Epitaph* promising rewards for the "arrest, trial, and conviction of the horse thieves." He also made it known that the mules were seen at the McLaurys' Babacomari ranch.

Unused to dealing with legal authority of any sort, McLaury exploded. Six days later he published a response in one of Tombstone's numerous papers, the *Daily Nugget*, calling Hurst a "coward, a vagabond, a rascal, and a malicious liar." His own name, McLaury said in tones of righteous indignation, "is well known in Arizona . . . and thank God this is the first time in my life that the name of dishonesty was ever attached to me," which, when one cuts through the bombast, was probably true. In fact, despite years of cattle theft and holdups, few of the Cowboys were ever arrested for anything. The last line of his statement was a call to the populace: "I am willing to let the people of Arizona decide who is right," an appeal McLaury knew he could not lose.

McLaury should have stuck to the papers. He pushed things further when he showed up at Virgil's office and proceeded to give his unwanted opinion of the whole affair. Virgil kept his temper, but let McLaury know his anger was not appreciated. Still, he and Wyatt must have been taken aback by the audacity of the Cowboy's attitude, first, in brazenly stealing government property, and, second, by even more brazenly defying the law in its recovery. It was now obvious to the brothers that they weren't dealing with an ordinary bunch of drunken cowherders but something far more organized and formidable. For McLaury's part, he must have understood something, too: As they would come to say in western movies, there was a new marshal in town. There was a new sheriff, too, or at least deputy sheriff: the day after the stolen mule incident, Wyatt Earp wired Charlie Shibell in Tucson and said he'd take that deputy's job after all. The timing was no coincidence.

Frank McLaury thought he had reason to be angry, not just with Hurst, whom he could bully with impunity, but with the Earps, whom he could not. What business was it of theirs if he took a few government mules? Why did the Earps stick their noses into his affairs? From McLaury's standpoint, the question was not an unreasonable one. Were the citizens of Pima County affected by the loss of some army mules? Why make a fuss? If the Earps simply wanted to get along, to get rich and get out, they could easily have come to some agreement with the local rustlers, as Behan himself was to do. Instead, they kept trying to enforce the law.

They did more than that. Through the summer and fall of 1880 it looked as if the Earps intended to stay in Tombstone. By early fall, all the brothers had built houses in town, and Wyatt became secretary of the first Tombstone Volunteer Fire Company (an outfit formed just in time—in June a fire had burned down two square blocks and destroyed more than sixty stores). The Earps were acquiring property—town lots, mines, and interests in gambling halls. Wyatt's first job on arriving in Tombstone was to ride shotgun on Wells Fargo shipments to Tucson, and, later, on shorter runs to a little town to the north, Benson, where the railroad had finally been extended. With the deputy sheriff's job and money coming in from other interests, Wyatt felt secure enough to give the shotgun rider's job to Morgan.

Before the Earps' stay in Tombstone was over, Wyatt, Virgil, and Morgan would all do work of some sort for Wells Fargo. The extent of that work has never been revealed. Wells Fargo was doing enormous business out of the Tombstone area and the company had no intention of trusting millions in silver shipments to the vagaries of town or county law. Help from the army was unwanted and, in any event, out of the question. Sometime before Christmas 1879, Wells Fargo planted a secret agent in Tombstone in the person of Fred Dodge. Dodge posed as a gambler and faro dealer while gathering information. Similarly, the Earps' involvement with the shipping company is a hazy one, partly because many of Wells Fargo's records no longer exist, having been destroyed in fires, but also because Wells Fargo often hired capable men in "unofficial" capacities to implement company policy. The most extreme policy would have been contract killings of known bandits, something that was whispered of but never proven. More likely, the company simply made use of men like the Earp brothers, men who had established reputations, in a rent-a-cop fashion, in the same way that the railroads in Missouri and Kansas employed the Pinkerton detectives against the James and Younger gangs. Records do survive that show Wyatt, Virgil, and Morgan were all paid by Wells Fargo to pursue bandits who had robbed their shipments, and there is solid evidence that the relationship went further. In 1882, for instance, Virgil gave an interview to the *San Francisco Daily Examiner* during which he displayed a large, gold five-pointed star, inscribed "V.W. Earp, With Compliments of Wells, Fargo & Co." An Arizona historian, Glenn G. Boyer, takes the Wells Fargo connection even further. Boyer claims that Wyatt was contacted by the company's chief detective, Jim Hume, after leaving Dodge City and was in Wells Fargo's employ when he arrived in Tombstone. If so, the question would arise as to how he and his brothers were paid, as there is no record of surviving Wells Fargo payrolls. For that matter, there's no record of Fred Dodge on Wells Fargo payrolls, though Marshall Williams, the company's oafish, alcoholic Tombstone agent, is listed on company payrolls. Yet, Dodge seemed much more aware of criminal activity against Wells Fargo than Williams.

In his autobiography, *Under Cover for Wells Fargo,* published thirty-one years after his death in 1938, matters were unclear.[9] What is clear is that Dodge was kept appraised of everything Wells Fargo was doing in Tombstone and that he had the utmost faith in Wyatt and Virgil Earp. Dodge claims to have made the connection between Wyatt and Wells Fargo, having written to company president John J. Valentine in response to Valentine's request that Dodge

> select someone to look after Wells Fargo and Co.'s interest— Run Shot Gun Messenger and Guard heavy shipments of Bullion and Money. I recommended Wyatt Earp, giving what I knew at that time of his past record, and advising Mr. Valentine that with this appointment, the Company would receive the cooperation of all the Brothers. Jim Hume Shortly come there and Made the Arrangements with Wyatt Earp—Wyatt did not know anything at that time about any connection I had had in this appointment. That my judgment was good in this Selection was proven in many ways by future Events.

If Wyatt at first didn't know that Dodge was working for Wells Fargo he must certainly have had his suspicions later when Dodge, a professional gambler, repeatedly volunteered for every posse ride involving the recovery of Wells Fargo shipments.

In October of 1880, it was Morgan Earp who rode shotgun on a fateful coach ride from Benson to Tombstone. Josephine Sarah Marcus took immediate notice of young Earp when she stepped off the train at Benson: "I don't hesitate," she would later recall, "to say I noticed him because he was a very handsome man. He greatly resembled Wyatt. In fact, they were sometimes mistaken for each other." This stage ride was remarkable, not because of a robbery or killings—that would begin shortly. It was significant because it marked Josephine's return to Tombstone. Josephine, "Josie" or "Sadie," Marcus managed to keep herself out of the Earp saga for nearly a century, which is an amazing accomplishment considering the importance of her role in the story. "The Helen of Troy of Tombstone," she has been called, and if she wasn't quite that she certainly did her part to make a mining camp near the Mexican border a legend.

She was Jewish, born of parents who came to New York from Germany in the early 1850s, part of the great migration of Germans and German Jews who settled in the area of the Lower East Side of Manhattan known as Kleindeutschland. Within a year, the immigrants crossed the river into the Williamsburg section of Brooklyn and beyond. When Josie was about seven, her father, Hyman, moved his wife and three daughters to San Francisco; no one has established the exact date of the journey, which was by way of the Isthmus of Panama and up the California coast to San Francisco, but it probably happened soon after the Civil War when the economy in the far west began to boom.

By the age of eighteen or nineteen—she said the former, but she may have shaved a year or two in the retelling—Josephine was high-spirited and stunningly beautiful. Bat Masterson told Stuart Lake that she was "the belle of the honky-tonks, the prettiest dame in three hundred or so of her kind," and compared her favorably to the famous New York actress Jeffreys Lewis, said to be one of the great beauties of her day. She joined a theatrical troupe run by a Miss Pauline Markham known as the English Opera Company; the opera was Gilbert and Sullivan's *H.M.S. Pinafore*, which went on the road billed as *Pinafore on Wheels*. Josie's role was that of the cabin boy in the "Hornpipe Dance," a routine she is said to have remembered well into her eighties.

In 1879 she ran away from home with the troupe, helping to bring culture to Tucson, Phoenix, and Prescott. In the last town she got something back for her efforts—the attention of a handsome deputy sheriff named John Behan, who was perhaps fifteen years her senior.

Josie also concocted a courtship where Behan came to San Francisco and asked for her hand from her parents in proper late-nine-teenth-century fashion. Actually, she was returning to Tombstone in 1880 to live as Behan's mistress, a fact she later fought hard to conceal from prying biographers such as Stuart Lake, which is one of the reasons the Earp story would be told for more than half a century without the glittering jewel that was its center.

The future was an exciting prospect for the lovely young girl who stepped off the stage in Tombstone in the fall of 1880. In a passage from *I Married Wyatt Earp* Josephine is quoted asking, "What was a strictly raised girl from a prosperous German-Jewish family doing in a place like this?" she asked. "I don't know where I got the adventure in my blood. Certainly not from my parents, who were the soul of middle-class respectability." She did know exactly what she wanted in a man: "I liked the traveling sort of man better than the kind that set back in one town all his life and wrote down little rows of figures all day or hustled dry goods or groceries and that sort of thing. I can see the need for solid citizens such as these, but they were never my type for a husband. My blood demanded excitement, variety and change."

The passage may be bogus, but the sentiment seem genuine. If she wanted excitement, variety, and change, she had come to the right town, and she would soon find the right man.

By the fall of 1880, Tombstone appeared ready to move beyond boomtown status and become a full-fledged city. In September, the Grand Hotel, Tombstone's finest, opened on the corner of Allen Street and Fremont. Camillus S. Fly thought Tombstone could sup-port a photography business; he built a studio on the back of the boarding house where Doc Holliday would soon be living with Kate Elder when Kate wasn't in Globe, Arizona, running her own board-ing house. About a year after Fly built the extension, the sound of some two dozen gunshots would echo off its walls.

Within Fly's studio was the equipment that would take two of the most famous photographs of the Old West. The first would show the McLaury brothers and Billy Clanton in their coffins, dressed in their Sunday best, awaiting a procession to Tombstone's Boot Hill. Five years after snapping the Cowboys' funeral picture, Fly would haul his cumbersome cameras out into the foothills and snap Geronimo's picture just before his surrender.

Through the summer and early fall of 1880 the Indians and the

Cowboys gave little cause for alarm. The Earps were lawing all over the county; Judge James Reilly's docket shows Wyatt arresting one E. L. Bradshaw shortly after the mule incident for killing a man in a drunken dispute over a shirt. A few weeks later Wyatt arrested his friend Buckskin Frank Leslie, a man he would later rank with Doc Holliday as one of the fastest and deadliest gunmen he had ever seen. Leslie shot and killed a man named Mike Killeen in a gunfight; he was acquitted on self-defense and later married Killeen's widow, over whom the fight had taken place. (Leslie would later go to prison for murder of a woman named Molly Williams.) Curiously, these arrests were not made by Town Marshal Fred White, but by County Deputy Sheriff Wyatt Earp. Wyatt had a working agreement with White, just as he had had with Charlie Bassett, Bat Masterson, and other peace officers back in Ford County, Kansas. Jurisdiction in law enforcement had not yet become a political issue.

In mid-August Virgil and Morgan were reported by the *Epitaph* as aiding a Fort Grant sheriff who was chasing a mule thief; the man surrendered "when a six-shooter was run under his nose by Morgan Earp." It's not apparent why Virgil, a U.S. marshal, was out chasing stolen private property The simplest answer is that the county sheriff wasn't doing his job. When it came to lawing the Earps' style was out of sync with the easygoing attitude of Pima County Sheriff Charlie Shibell's office in Tucson.

The Earps' to-the-letter approach to law didn't sit well with Tombstone's new justice of the peace, James Reilly, either. Reilly had been Buckskin Frank Leslie's counsel in the Killeen shooting, and there had been some speculation that Leslie hadn't pulled the trigger, that he was covering for a friend, George Perine. There was enough evidence to warrant an investigation, and again, it was Deputy Sheriff Wyatt Earp and not Town Marshal Fred White who made the arrest, finding Perine hiding next to George Parsons's house. ("Lively times," noted Parsons in his August 14 diary entry.)

Perine's lawyer, Harry Jones, reasonably suggested that Reilly should excuse himself from a case in which he had served as a counsel. Reilly lost his temper and ordered Jones from his courtroom; Jones refused, and Reilly ordered the court officers, including Wyatt, to arrest Jones. While the puzzled officers pondered their options, an enraged Reilly charged Jones, and Jones responded by pulling a gun. Strange as it seems, Jones would have been justified, according to the unwritten code of western self-defense, in killing the judge in his own courtroom. Fortunately for Reilly and Jones, Wyatt intervened and arrested them both. After escorting Jones to the stage depot for a trip to Tucson, Earp was tongue-lashed by Reilly for failing to carry out his initial arrest order. He then ordered Wyatt to appear in court the following day on contempt charges, after which Wyatt reminded him that he was due in Tucson the next day with Jones, whom Reilly had ordered him to arrest. Oh, yes, and by the way, Reilly was under arrest himself on assault charges. Despite a citizens' petition calling for Reilly's dismissal, the bizarre affair soon faded from memory. But once again, in the course of doing his job, Wyatt Earp created an enemy who would later have an opportunity for revenge.

Two more farcical incidents with repercussions for the Earps occurred in October and, predictably, both involved Doc Holliday. First, the thuggish Johnny Tyler appeared back in town. Holliday faced a whimpering Tyler down and ran him out of Tombstone. Wyatt could scarcely disapprove, since he had tossed Tyler out of the Oriental Saloon just a few months back. But after a fracas on October 11 at the Oriental, Wyatt must have reconsidered his wisdom in inviting Doc to join him in Tombstone. The saloon's owner, Milt Joyce, dressed Holliday down for creating a disturbance and a drunken Doc pressed the issue into a fight. Joyce got his thumb clipped by a bullet while his partner, a man named Parker, took a round in the foot. (It seems that Holliday was not trying to kill either man.) A bleeding Joyce creased Doc's skull with the barrel of his gun. Deputy Sheriff Wyatt Earp arrested Doc before matters could escalate. Surprisingly, Doc was fined only for assault and battery, not attempted murder, which probably indicates that some witnesses thought Joyce was baiting Holliday.[10]

None of this caused a ripple on the surface of life in Tombstone, but on October 28 a shooting occurred that would change the town forever. Around 12:30 A.M., near the corner of Sixth and Allen Street where the Bird Cage Theater would later stand, several Cowboys began to shoot at the moon and the occasional streetlamp. Nothing like this had happened for a while. Tombstone had been fairly quiet since the Earps arrived, and more so since Virgil had been appointed assistant marshal by Fred White. Anyone firing pistols in the streets knew they would have to deal not only with Fred White but with

Virgil and probably Wyatt and Morgan as well. Until October 28 no one had tried to shoot up the town.

Wyatt, off duty from his deputy sheriff's job, was dealing faro in Billy Owens's saloon. He was unarmed when the first shots rang out. Looking out the front door Wyatt saw the flash of a gun shot on Allen Street, and ran in the dark toward the sound of the firing. When Wyatt got to Sixth and Allen, he found Morgan and Fred Dodge, who shared a cabin, crouched behind a chimney in the dark trying to figure out what was going on. Wyatt asked to borrow Morgan's revolver; Morgan objected that he might be needing it himself. Instead, Wyatt was handed Fred Dodge's sidearm just as a volley of slugs ricocheted off the chimney. As he moved out of cover and toward White, Earp saw a Cowboy whose face he didn't recognize in the dark as Curly Bill Brocius's. "I am an officer," Wyatt heard White bark, "give me your pistol."

There are several versions of what happened next. The best known, told by Stuart Lake, was taken partly from Wyatt's recollections and partly from Fred Dodge's. Dodge said that White took Curly Bill's pistol by the barrel and the gun went off, hitting White in the left testicle. Wyatt reacted instantly, using Dodge's Colt to introduce Curly Bill's head to the venerable Kansas art of buffaloing. Wyatt then grabbed Curly Bill by the collar and told him to get up. Brocius was indignant. "What have I done?" he protested. "I have not done anything to be arrested for." One might pause here and consider that with a friend and fellow policeman lying shot on the ground, Wyatt Earp showed enormous restraint in not blowing off the back of Curly Bill's head.

Dodge, recalling the tragedy many years later to Lake, wrote:

> Wyatt's coolness and nerve never showed to better advantage than they did that night. When Morg and I reached him, Wyatt was squatted on his heels beside Curly Bill and Fred White. Curly Bill's friends were pot-shooting at him in the dark. The shooting was lively and slugs were hitting the chimney and cabin . . . in all of that racket, Wyatt's voice was even and quiet as usual.
>
> "Put out the fire in Fred's clothes," he said. White had been shot at such close range that his coat was burning.

White was carried to a doctor. The next day, he appeared to be recovering and gave a statement exonerating Curly Bill of attempted murder.[11] Overnight, White's condition worsened. He died the next day. Wyatt, in later testimony, claimed to have grabbed Curly Bill from behind as White approached him. According to Earp, White said, "Now, you goddamn son of a bitch, give up that pistol." Brocius never made it clear why he didn't simply drop his gun. If Curly Bull wasn't drunk or up to some mischief, it seems unlikely that he would have to be told twice by a town marshal to surrender his weapon. More confusion would be created by the fact that the gun that killed White had only one bullet discharged, the one that hit White. Did Curly Bill fire all his rounds in the shooting spree and then reload? If he wasn't shooting with the other Cowboys, why did White approach him? And if he hadn't been firing his gun, why did he have it drawn in the first place?

Whether the marshal's shooting was an accident or murder, the day after Fred White's death Virgil Earp was appointed town marshal and the Earps were plunged into the maelstrom of Tombstone politics.[12] White was scarcely dead before rumors arose that the shooting was connected to the town lot troubles. The town lot controversies began in the summer of 1879 when Mike Gray, a former Texas ranger, began selling rights to small plots of land in the city limits he didn't own. The problem for those who occupied the disputed lots was that Tombstone was not yet incorporated as a town, so it was difficult to establish who actually owned the lot. Gray used his son, Dixie, and several men with Cowboy associations as enforcers. Those who didn't buy their lots from Gray's company would find rough-looking fellows with revolvers on their hips waiting when they returned home to what they regarded as their lots. The town-lot connection would become even more apparent in the summer of 1881 when young Gray was killed with Old Man Clanton in the Guadalupe Canyon massacre.

This is a simplified account of a complex situation, but from a law and order perspective what it meant was that the election of White as the first marshal was a reaction to Gray's thuggish tactics in expelling townsfolk from lots he claimed title to. Several prominent citizens, particularly *Epitaph* editor John Clum, looked to White and Virgil Earp to lead the fight against Gray and his partner, James Clark. This they did quite effectively by running off numerous claim jumpers, but not before some Tombstonians contemplated vigilante action. "Model town," George Parsons noted in his diary on February 17, 1880. "Shooting this A.M., and two fellows in afternoon attempted to go for one another with guns and six-shooters, but friends intervened. . . . Mingled with the hardy miners tonight. Talk of killing indulged in again tonight. Everyone goes heeled (armed). Jumping claims great cause of trouble." On May 10 he wrote: "Bad state of feeling in town tonight and throughout day. Shooting and rows of various kinds. Lots being jumped the trouble."

Gray's appointment as justice of the peace exacerbated the problem by cloaking the gang's lot-jumping ambitions with respectability. On May 5, the town nearly exploded. Gray and his companions tried to eject one Dr. Henry Hatch from his lot; Parsons recorded that "a crowd gathered and sided with Hatch when Gray and party—after a flourish of pistols—retired." Thanks largely to the efforts of Virgil and Wyatt, White was able to make progress against Gray and the lot jumpers and tensions in Tombstone, duly incorporated as a legal town, began to ease. For a while, anyway. But the killing of White soon fired up talk of vigilante action, the first priority in the eyes of many being instant justice for Curly Bill Brocius. But no lynching had ever occurred in a town policed by Virgil or Wyatt. Heavily armed and making a show of it, they escorted Bill to Tucson, an act that put the Earps in the odd situation of guarding the perceived leader of their antagonists against several men they counted as their friends and supporters.

Nothing happened. Curly Bill's ride to Tucson wouldn't be the last time the Earps' icy professionalism discouraged potential vigilantes. But the question of intent in Curly Bill Brocius's shooting of Fred White was never satisfactorily answered. Fred White's deathbed testimony seemed to absolve Curly Bill of any crime more serious than manslaughter. And yet, suspicion that White's death was more than an accident came not from the Earps and their supporters but from witnesses favorable to the Cowboys.[13] John Pleasant Gray, for instance. Like John Clum, Gray was a college man, having come to Tombstone after graduation from the University of California at Berkeley. His affiliations, though, were on the Cowboy side; his father was Mike Gray of the town lot controversy, and his brother was Dixie. Gray thought that Brocius had filed off the safety catch on his single-action Colt so he could "fan" the gun by simply pulling back the hammer. (On a single-action revolver, the hammer had to be pulled back in a catch position before the trigger could be pulled.) Gray's implication must have been that Curly Bill planned for White to yank the gun away, with Curly Bill sliding his palm over the hammer as White tugged. This sounds farfetched. So does a similar story by John Behan's future deputy, Billy Breakenridge.

Billy Breakenridge, though insignificant in the history of Tombstone, is an important figure in the evolution of the Earp legend. Breakenridge, whom some Earp researchers think may have been gay—there is no strong evidence—was a perpetual Tombstone outsider who, like Fred Dodge, could always be trusted to come up with a version of a story a little stranger or wilder than other tellers'. For instance, the story of the "Curly Bill Spin." According to Billy's book, *Helldorado*, published in 1928,

> [Curly Bill] was a remarkable shot with a pistol, and would hit a rabbit every time when it was running thirty or forty yards away. He whirled his pistol on his forefinger, and cocked it as it came up. He told me never to let a man give his pistol butt end toward me, and showed me why. He handed me his gun that way, and as I reached to take it he whirled it on his finger, and it was cocked, staring me in the face, and ready to shoot. His advice was, that if I disarmed anyone, to make him throw his pistol down.[16]

So, Brocius certainly could have used "the Curly Bill Spin" to shoot the marshal. That Curly Bill Brocius murdered Fred White seems plausible for every reason but one: White was replaced, as could have been anticipated, by a much more formidable marshal who had backers and whose politics were diametrically opposed to those of the men who supported the Cowboys.

The Earps were unabashed Republicans in Democratic country; Lincoln admirers all. Most of the Earps' leading supporters, "boomers" who had just recently arrived in town, were Republicans. But it can not be said with any accuracy just how attitudes about law and order in Tombstone broke down along political lines. The Earps' opponents in Tombstone weren't representative Democrats; Mike Gray, John Behan, and other members of what would come to be referred to as the County Ring or Ten Per Cent Ring, so named because of the tax money they were supposed to be skimming, were simply corrupt politicians who hid behind the illusion of Democratic respectability. Though Wyatt and Virgil were ruthlessly apolitical in their enforcement of the law, their political and business affiliations constantly drew them into a partisan struggle.

For the Earps' part, what was on their mind as 1880 drew to a close was not the Cowboys or politics but making money. If the Earp brothers' mining interests hadn't made them rich, they were at least profitable, and Wyatt, Morgan, and James were all making good money dealing faro in the saloons. For the first time in their lives, the brothers owned property. They were settled. They were seemingly entrenched in important law enforcement positions. Then came the elections of November 12, 1880.

On November 9, Wyatt resigned his deputy sheriff's commission. The *Daily Nugget* lauded his performance, the last time it would give Wyatt a good notice. The paper would soon become a Democratic organ and Cowboy defender, in fact, the leading disseminator of anti-Earp propaganda in Wyatt's lifetime. The *Nugget* also spoke well of the man Charlie Shibell chose to replace him, John Behan. The choice could not have pleased Wyatt or Virgil since Behan was known as a politician with no law enforcement experience.

Then, on November 12, the election was held for White's town marshal position, which Virgil had been filling since October. Ben Sippy, described by Virgil's biographer Don Chaput as a "do-nothing, harmless, pleasant fellow," was the choice of Clum's law and order party and won the election, 311 votes to 259. Virgil's defeat seemed puzzling: Who in the world was Ben Sippy? This was the question everyone in Tombstone would ask in June 1881 when Sippy skipped town for good. Later, the election loss would be cited as evidence of the Earps' unpopularity in Tombstone, but in November 1880 the gunfight that would make them unpopular, or at least controversial, was a year away. Apparently Sippy won the election because he was the favorite candidate of the *Epitaph* and John Clum. Why a man with no reputation as a law officer would have been backed by a man who would become the Earps' staunchest supporter is the real mystery. A simple answer is that Clum, who knew politics, figured that Virgil was a fine marshal but a bad candidate. A simpler one is that Clum didn't yet know Virgil that well. Certainly if Clum had known Sippy better he wouldn't have backed him.

Wyatt's resignation has never been satisfactorily explained. In her study of the causes of the O.K. Corral gunfight. *And Die in the West* (1989), Paula Mitchell Marks has concluded that, "Wyatt may well have quit Democratic Sheriff Shibell's employ in order to throw his support to Republican Bob Paul for the office. However, Wyatt Earp wasn't the type to work on behalf of another man unless it provided a ready road to power for himself. . . . Wyatt was alliance-building with such prominent local Republicans as Clum and such prominent county Republicans as Paul." That's one way of viewing Earp's resignation; another would be that Wyatt was stuck between two friends and chose the one he respected more as a lawman. (That Wyatt didn't take part in either man's campaign suggests his neutrality.) Whatever the reason, Wyatt didn't resign his deputy sheriff's job till after the election, and then he resigned in disgust. He had good reason to be disgusted.

In the November election, Charlie Shibell edged out Bob Paul by just forty-two votes. The results revealed a new alliance between the Cowboys and the County Ring: John Ringo served as a precinct judge, Ike Clanton as a voting inspector, and Curly Bill, as a kind of ward boss, rounding up voters all over the San Simon Valley. For many of the rustlers, participation in the democratic process was new, and they took to it with a zest that warmed the hearts of Democratic bosses. The morning after the election, Curly Bill rode into Tombstone with the votes that tipped the election to the incumbent: 103 votes for Shibell, one for Paul. (One Cowboy was heard to say that he voted for Paul because he didn't want folks in town to think that people in San Simon were crooked.) Paul contested the election.

The Earps were surprisingly slow to see what would soon become obvious: Shibell, who seemed an honest enough law man in most respects, was the tool of dishonest politicians. Some of the Cowboys had proved useful to the County Ring in the town-lot evictions; now they were proving valuable in winning elections. In return, county law would be too busy to deal with the problem of cattle theft across the Mexican border: Who in Pima County felt that his life was any the worse for cattle stolen in Mexico? But if Shibell really thought that cattle thieves, once organized and sheltered from the law, would confine their illegal activities to Mexico, he was being naive. So were a great many others in Southeast Arizona.

Towners were concerned with a problem more immediate than cattle theft. Sometime in early November rumors began circulating that Mayor Alder Randall had made a secret alliance with Gray and Clark's Townsite Company. Randall received the patent for creating new lots in September; if he was in league with Gray, he could give Gray the town patent and with it the power to expel from their property anyone who had not bought it from Gray. On November 6 angry citizens demonstrated, forcing Randall to promise to heed the wishes of Tombstone's town council. To no one's surprise, Randall, as Tombstonians said, crawfished on his promise and handed the patent to Clark and Gray. An angry John Clum responded by forming the Tombstone Citizens League and sought an injunction against the Townsite Company.

Gray and Clark brazenly ignored their opposition. On December 5, escorted by several thugs, they actually dragged a small house sitting on disputed property into the street. Marshal Sippy, in one of the two finest moments of his brief and farcical law career, confronted them, and, according to one eyewitness, made a show of taking off his coat to demonstrate that he was ready to confront lot jumpers with his fists.

John Clum stopped the Townsite Company with a court injunction that came down on December 5. It isn't clear that Clum had prior political ambitions, but after halting Gray and his confederates at least temporarily, he was thrust into the center stage of Tombstone politics, a spot he would not relinquish until he left town. And he didn't shrink from the opportunity. Principled, arrogant, ambitious, and more than a bit pompous, Clum had, to that point, lived the most colorful life of any of Tombstone's colorful characters. He had attended Rutgers University (then College), though he did not graduate, as is often claimed. He played football, too, or what passed for football in 1869, though not, as he would later claim, in the first intercollegiate college football game (against Princeton) but in the second. The Dutch Reformed Church, which was much concerned with the plight of Indians in the late nineteenth century, was affiliated with Rutgers. The church hit upon the idea of canvassing the students to see if there was an idealist in their midst willing to undertake the guardianship of nearly a thousand Apaches in Arizona Territory.

"That some human experience," noted a historian, "as well as good will and piety, might be useful in such a labor, seems not to have entered into their calculations." No Rutgers senior volunteered, but within two years a zealous underclassman would come forward.[15] John Clum, like the McLaury boys, was the son of a New York farmer. His father, with several children to care for, couldn't keep John at Rutgers, so Clum, just turned twenty, applied for a job with the fledgling meteorological service, later to become the Weather Bureau. After reporting for duty in Santa Fe, New Mexico, he learned of the plight of the Apaches and found that the post of Indian Agent for San Carlos reservation was still open. He applied and was sent back to Washington where he learned that the Apaches were, as he would later write, "a nation, with laws, legends, and a history," that their land had been taken from them by whites, and that the real burden of protecting the Indians would fall on the Indian Office rather than the army, which was essentially an agent of extermination. In August of 1874 Clum reported for work at San Carlos. He was not quite twenty-three.

Clum's attitude toward the heathens was tempered by his own Dutch reform upbringing. In Washington, he was trained by an Office of Indian Affairs that was a great deal more liberal than the county as a whole regarding Indians. After the Civil War, a Quaker delegation approached President Grant with a plan to solve the "Indian Problem" that involved the settling of the tribes as farmers and the removal of the army in favor of civilian police. This is the philosophy Clum took west with him, and he practiced it as though it were an article of his religion.

It has been argued that, since the Indians had no say in creating the laws they lived by, agents such as John Clum were essentially benevolent white dictators. One might also argue that that is what the place, time, and situation called for. According to Geronimo's best biographer, Angie Debo, Clum liked the Apaches and treated them fairly, and they reciprocated. He was, Debo writes, "honorable, able and efficient; he had all of General Crook's (the then ranking military official) single-minded confidence that he could manage all the Apaches by himself if only the wicked rival service"—that is, the army—"would keep out of it." Clum established courts, formed a reliable Indian police, and created industry by encouraging the Apaches to farm and then by buying supplies from their little farms.

But 1875 saw the Indian Office begin its absurd policy of "concentration," which involved the uprooting of barely pacified Indians and removing them to agencies farther away from their original homeland. This left Clum with nearly four thousand Apaches to care for.

Many Apaches slipped away and became renegades, the most famous of whom was, of course, Geronimo. Clum became obsessed with his capture; he seemed to regard Geronimo as much of an enemy to his "happy family" (his words) of Apaches as General Crook. In April 1877 he succeeded, by a ruse, in capturing Geronimo—the only time that the great Apache warrior was ever captured. (Many years after his surrender many years later Geronimo would taunt the U.S. soldiers by saying, "You never caught me shooting.") Clum, with what Debo calls "typical arrogance," kept Geronimo's rifle and handed it down as a family heirloom.

Arrogance aside, Clum was a superb agent and organizer. During his three years at San Carlos, he consolidated five Indian agencies into one, saving the government more than $100,000. But in June 1877 he angered the War Department with a telegram, that read: "If Your Department Will Increase My Salary (?) Sufficiently and Equip Two More Companies of Indian Police For Me, I Will Volunteer To Take Care Of All Apaches In Arizona—And The Troops Can Be Removed." He might have been able to do just that. The problem wasn't just the army but local merchants who turned against him because of the loss of army business would have crippled them. After the inevitable rejection of his proposal, Clum resigned in July. The whole experience should have taught him that he was a fine crusader and a bad politician, but on December 29 he accepted the Republican nomination and, on January 4, became not, as he would later claim, Tombstone's first mayor but the first mayor of the newly incorporated City of Tombstone. The vote was overwhelming, 532 for Clum of 787 cast, the one-sidedness at least in part explained by public sympathy, as Clum's wife had died of a fever while in childbirth shortly before the elections. One of the citizens who came by to offer his sincerest condolences was John Behan, who would shortly be running for sheriff of the newly formed Cochise County, of which Tombstone would be the seat.

If Clum thought that Ben Sippy was the Marshal to implement his law and order program he was guilty of poor judgment. All through December there were random shootings in streets and saloons. On January 10, George Parsons wrote: "Shooting now about every night. Very lively town." And on January 22: "Shootists again on the rampage, 'Red Mike' shot last night and another man reported killed tonight. Heard shots. Things lively." Wyatt, with no law appointment on the county or city level, involved himself in none of the disturbances. Anyway, he had problems of his own to think about. One was the theft of his horse; another was the state of his marriage.

Sometime in late December Wyatt found his prize racehorse, Dick Naylor, was missing and was told by a Cowboy named Sherman McMasters that the horse was in the town of Charleston, in the possession of Billy Clanton. McMasters is one of the numerous shadowy figures in the Earp story. He would later be indicted in robberies committed by Cowboys or men associated with the Cowboys, and not long after that he'd ride with Wyatt's posse in open warfare against the Cowboys. McMasters was one of the several Tombstone figures with Cowboy affiliations who would turn coat and side with Wyatt—Josephine Marcus and Behan associate Henry Jones, the lawyer, were others—or he was, as some researchers have speculated, a Wells Fargo informant who had infiltrated the Cowboy ranks.

Acting on McMasters's tip, Wyatt asked Doc Holliday to ride with him to Charleston. They found the animal in a corral and confronted the strapping, six-foot, four-inch young Clanton on the spot. Hostilities with the Cowboys could well have broken out right there. Billy, who was eighteen at the time, had what we might today call an attitude. Horse theft was a serious matter on the frontier, and it's doubtful that Earp or Holliday could have been prosecuted had they killed Billy in a gunfight on that day. Clanton, though he backed down, was unapologetic and let Wyatt know in no uncertain terms that he had no regrets regarding the theft. After some sharp words, Wyatt stifled his anger and rode away on Dick Naylor.[16]

Wyatt's problems with Mattie would not be so easily resolved. Their marriage, or whatever they regarded their relationship as, must have begun to disintegrate around this time. It's not known exactly when Wyatt met Josephine Marcus; in *I Married Wyatt Earp* Josephine blandly says, "When Wyatt heard of my falling out with Johnny, he sought to court me for the first time. I knew he was married, but it was no secret that his marriage was on the rocks." The only other information offered is that her breakup with Behan was precipitated by a drunken assault he made on her, following which she ran to the house of Henry Jones (the lawyer Wyatt had arrested in Judge Reilly's courtroom) and his wife, Kitty, for protection. The episode is too neat and self-serving to suffice as an explanation for Josie's breakup with Behan. In light of later developments, her statement that "He [Behan] did me just one favor. Through him I met Wyatt Earp" might serve as the best explanation. The point about her "breakup" with Behan is also interesting, since Wyatt would later be accused of "stealing" Behan's girl. Apparently Josie, if she was telling the truth, was getting fed up with Behan before her involvement with Wyatt began.

If Wyatt and Josephine had become romantically involved by the beginning of 1881, no one else knew about it. John Behan didn't seem to suspect and by April 1881 the house he and Sadie were living in was rented to Dr. Goodfellow, so he may have broken up with her anyway. Indeed, Behan was probably giving Wyatt more attention than he gave Josephine. It was common knowledge that the sheriff's job for the newly formed Cochise County would be the prize law enforcement plum in southeastern Arizona; the sheriff's share of collected taxes alone would be enough to support a comfortable life. Wyatt was the obvious choice for the job, and since the only other serious candidate was John Behan, a Democrat, in a territory governed by a Republican, John Fremont, it was assumed that the territorial governor would appease his party by appointing Earp.

Billy Breakenridge estimated the annual income from the sheriff's position at about $40,000 a year, which is a staggering sum even by Tombstone's boomtown standards. Of course, this figured in the sheriff's 10 percent of collected tax money, much of that from the hugely profitable mining corporations. Wyatt convinced himself that all he wanted was a peaceful, lucrative job as tax collector and process server, but the County Ring politicians knew better: Wyatt, like Virgil, had a bad habit of enforcing the law to the limits of the job's authority, and occasionally testing those limits. If he had become Cochise County sheriff he certainly would have interfered with Cowboy activities as well as those of the county political bosses; by the end of 1880 he had already made enemies of the McLaurys, the Clantons, and Curly Bill Brocius, all the while holding no position higher than county deputy sheriff.

What happened between Wyatt Earp and John Behan depends on which of them the reader chooses to believe. In fact, most of one's interpretation of what happened in Tombstone through 1882 depends on which of the two one believes. Stuart Lake, using Wyatt's testimony from the O.K. Corral inquest, built a scenario highly favorable to Earp. "You telegraph your friends at Prescott to withdraw your name," Behan says in *Frontier Marshal*, "and I'll get the job, sure. I'll appoint you undersheriff. I'll run the civil business; you can run the criminal end and appoint your own deputies. We'll hire a clerk to handle all collections and split even. Somebody's going to earn this money and it might better be us than a stranger. Is it a deal?" The skeptical reader might notice that this sounds very much like what Wyatt told Lake he had been offered in Dodge City. But Behan admitted during the inquest hearing that he had offered Wyatt the job of undersheriff and that Wyatt told him that if Fremont made him sheriff he couldn't reciprocate with Behan because he had brothers to consider. This has a ring of truth; we recall that while on the Wichita police force Wyatt got into a brawl after being accused of trying to make jobs for his brothers.

In light of later developments one might ask what two men with such diametrically opposed idea of law enforcement were doing cutting deals with each other. One answer is that early in 1881 John Behan and Wyatt Earp didn't know how just how different they were. It's possible that Behan was sincere about offering Wyatt the job of undersheriff; Behan knew that he wasn't really a peace officer. Somebody had to handle the rough stuff. For Wyatt's part, he probably regarded Behan as a more amiable version of the ineffectual Larry Deger back in Dodge City. He saw no reason why he couldn't work for Behan if the circumstance should present itself. In Dodge Wyatt had learned the importance of cooperation between different levels of law enforcement and probably envisioned Virgil, as a deputy U.S. marshal and Tombstone deputy marshal, working with Behan and himself. Behan and Earp had political differences, but what of that? Wyatt had gotten along well with Charlie Shibell, a Democrat, who had given him the deputy sheriff's position.

Wyatt never got a chance to find out how he would get along with Sheriff Behan. On January 14, for reasons that were never made clear, Fremont chose Behan as sheriff of Cochise County. (It has been assumed that Fremont simply gave in to pressure from leading

Democrats, who represented the majority party in Arizona.) Behan promptly reneged on his promise to make Wyatt undersheriff, choosing instead Alabama-born Harry Woods, editor of the pro-Democratic and pro-Cowboy *Daily Nugget*. For Wyatt, this was offset partly by John Clum's resounding victory in the mayoral election of January 4.[17] With the Earps out of law enforcement, things began to get, as old Arizonians like to say, woolly. On January 8, celebrating Curly Bill's release from jail, the Cowboys shot up their own favorite town, Charleston, and broke up a religious service, making the preacher "dance" to their Colts. The next day, in the most brazen display since the shooting of Fred White three months earlier, several Cowboys shot up Tombstone, causing damage in the Alhambra Saloon.

Behan, meanwhile, settled into the comfortable life of a county sheriff in a booming country. Sometime in January he opened a faro table at a local saloon, hiring as his dealer a man named Freis. (This was probably the "German," called "Freeze," named later in the inquest following Morgan Earp's death.) The Earps, it seems, weren't the only law officers in Tombstone to have gambling interests.[18] Behan's table didn't last long, though: Wyatt broke his bank, putting Behan temporarily out of the gambling business. If Wyatt's relationship with Josephine still wasn't known to Behan, this act alone would have been enough to have forced open hostilities.

There were other reasons that would have caused the Earp-Behan split even if Josephine had never come to Tombstone. The most important was that Wyatt, more than anyone else, was responsible for getting the results of the Pima County sheriff's election overturned. Lake has Wyatt telling Bob Paul, "You demand a recount, and if I can make Curly Bill talk, you'll be sheriff," which is probably exactly what Earp said. Wyatt then rode to Charleston and confronted Curly Bill with the prospect of hanging for the shooting of White unless Brocius admitted that the San Simon election was rigged. This suggests that White's deathbed statement might have been a forgery cooked up later by Wyatt as part of a deal with Curly Bill. Whatever the details, the cold-bloodedness of the arrangement is mitigated only slightly by the fact that Bob Paul in the Pima County Sheriff's Office meant more to law and order in southeast Arizona than would Curly Bill Brocius in prison or on Boot Hill.

Several months later, John Behan would testify at the O.K. Corral inquest that in January 1881 he was out serving a subpoena to Ike Clanton relating to Bob Paul's contesting of the November election. According to Behan, two horsemen dashed by him on the road to Charleston; the first, he thought, was Virgil Earp, and the second Doc Holliday. Upon reaching Charleston he found not Virgil and Doc but Wyatt and Doc, looking for the horse Billy Clanton had stolen from Wyatt.

A few days later, Behan said, he saw Ike Clanton in Tucson. In his testimony, Behan claimed that Ike said "Earp had sent him [Ike] word that I [Behan] had taken a posse of nine men down there to attempt to arrest him . . . and then he told me he had armed his crowd and was not going to stand it." This was Behan's reason for reneging on his promise to make Wyatt undersheriff; he thought Wyatt was trying to stir up trouble between the Sheriff's Office and Ike Clanton. Behan never mentioned Billy Clanton's theft of Wyatt's horse; Wyatt never mentioned an encounter with Ike Clanton.[19]

What was incontestable was that Wyatt Earp had succeeded in overturning the election results for sheriff of Pima County. Bob Paul, a law and order man, was now in office, and Wyatt Earp had placed himself in the center of the Earp-Cowboy conflict. He would remain there till he rode out of Arizona a little more than a year later.

In between momentous events in Tombstone history a minor incident occurred that added a long footnote to Wyatt Earp's legend. On January 14, W. P. Schneider, an engineer living in Charleston, stepped into a restaurant to warm his hands. Johnny O'Rourke, an eighteen-year-old small-time gambler referred to as Johnny-Behind-the-Deuce, made some sort of sarcastic comment to the effect of "I thought you never get cold." Schneider dismissed the gambler with a chilly "I wasn't talking to you." Enraged, O'Rourke threatened to kill Schneider when the engineer went back outside. Johnny-Behind-the-Deuce was as good as his word, one of the few times he was according to those who knew him: He ambushed Schneider and murdered him.

No one knows what bad blood had passed between the two men that brought matters to such a conclusion, but the Deuce, who could properly be labeled as one of the tinhorn gambler element old Arizonians would later talk so much about, was immediately taken into custody. The local miners, among whom Schneider was popular, were outraged, and there was talk of a lynching. Charleston's Constable McKelvey was smart enough not to make a dash all the way to Tucson. He headed for Tombstone, but made about half the distance when he saw the mob of miners closing in on his wagon. It was McKelvey's good fortune, and certainly the Deuce's, that Virgil Earp was in the area exercising Dick Naylor. Virgil had O'Rourke swing onto the horse's back and rode straight to Vogano's Saloon, where James Earp was tending bar.

McKelvey had the presence of mind to telegraph Ben Sippy before leaving Charleston, so the marshal had several armed men waiting for the mob. But the ugly mood spread among Tombstone's miners, and soon a throng of townspeople, several of them armed, began to advance on the wagon Sippy was preparing for the trip to Tucson.

In the TV series and in some of the Earp movies, Wyatt, standing alone, backs down the Johnny-Behind-the-Deuce mob. (In Costner's *Wyatt Earp*, Wyatt, twin army Colts leveled, invites the "brave men" in the mob to try and take him and his prisoner, here inexplicably called "Tommy-Behind-the-Deuce.") In recent years, Stuart Lake is credited with inventing the story, or at least Wyatt's role in it, just as he had supposedly invented the Ben Thompson and Clay Allison stories in Kansas. According to Lake, who placed John Ringo in the mob, "five hundred blood-lusting frontiersmen" poured into Allen Street as Virgil and Morgan got Johnny-Behind-the-Deuce to safety. In *Frontier Marshal* Wyatt stands close to the curb, shotgun in the crook of his right arm. "Don't fool yourselves," he cautioned the front ranks. "That tinhorn's my prisoner and I'm not bluffing."

Lake put Wyatt out in front of the others: The Deuce is "my prisoner." But Wyatt wasn't the marshal, or an officer of any kind, and had no authority to take prisoners. Aside from embellishing Wyatt's credentials, Lake's account contains no undue histrionics. In fact, it contains a bit of psychology Wyatt just might have used. "Nice mob, you've got, Mr. Gird," Wyatt remarks in a casual tone, targeting the well-known mining man in the crowd. "Don't be a fool, Dick." This sounds like Wyatt Earp: By isolating one man in the mob, a well-known citizen, Wyatt got the attention of the other men and momentarily distracted them. By directly addressing Gird, he emphasized the fact that he knew some of them: Why are you fellows acting like this? Is this tinhorn really worth our killing ourselves over? Wyatt was emphasizing something else, too: He would kill—

he would kill them—if he had to, to uphold the law. By convincing the mob that he was prepared to kill, he prevented an outbreak of violence.

The only thing wrong with the story, say Earp debunkers, is that it never happened. They cite the January 27 issue of the *Epitaph*, which describes Ben Sippy as being "cool as an iceberg (as) he held the crowd in check." Sippy, John Behan, and Virgil Earp are singled out for praise, while Wyatt isn't mentioned. Nor was Wyatt mentioned in George Parsons's journal. Parsons, walking along Allen Street, came upon the mob, and that night recorded in his journal that

> The officers sought to protect him and swore in deputies—themselves gambling men—(the deputies that is) to help. Many of the miners armed themselves and tried to get at the murderer. Several times, yes a number of times rushes were made and rifles leveled causing Mr. Stanley and me to get behind the most available shelter. Terrible excitement. But the officers got through finally and out of town with their man bound for Tucson.

James Hancock went further and asserted that no extra officers—not Wyatt, Virgil, nor John Behan—were needed. There was no mob, "Just a band of 'rubber-necks'—I was one of them myself." Ben Sippy and the Deuce rode off "as quietly as if they were going on a picnic." That would seem to lay to rest the Wyatt Earp–Johnny-Behind-the-Deuce legend. Paula Mitchell Marks concludes that, "In truth, Officer Sippy and Behan, with former marshal Virgil Earp and a number of other deputies, had successfully insisted on upholding a system of law."

But once again, as we see over and over in the Wyatt Earp legend, something was said to have happened, was then debunked, and then, after close examination, appears to have happened after all. James Hancock's account is the easiest to dismiss; he never mentioned witnessing the incident until fifty years after the fact, and then his story doesn't square with anyone else's. But why doesn't the *Epitaph* or Parsons's journal mention Wyatt? Probably because Wyatt Earp wasn't an officer at the time. George Parsons mentions no officers by name but says they swore in deputies (Wyatt was almost certainly one of the deputies). The *Epitaph* probably left Wyatt's name out for the same reason: They were plugging their candidate, Ben Sippy.

As was so often the case in Kansas, the newspapers failed to document a story integral to the Earp legend, and, once again, eyewitnesses supported the Earp-Lake account. The backup for Earp's part in the Johnny-Behind-the-Deuce affair comes from the recollections of four people who were there: Fred Dodge, George Parsons, John Clum, and Billy Breakenridge. Dodge credited Wyatt with holding off the crowd, he also claimed Behan and Sippy stood off to the side and did nothing. Perhaps Dodge was myth-mongering, doing what many would later do—puffing up Wyatt's feats in order to sell books. John Clum, in his later recollections, also gave Wyatt the lion's share of the credit and criticizes Sippy, all but admitting that his newspaper had lied about the incident when it happened. Was Clum also suffering from late-life hero worship?

Then how to explain Billy Breakenridge's account? In his 1926 *Helldorado*, Breakenridge mentions Wyatt, *and only Wyatt,* at the Deuce standoff. "Wyatt," he wrote, "stood them off with a shotgun, and dared them to come and get him. It didn't look good to the mob." Breakenridge doesn't mention his boss, John Behan, at all.

Finally, George Parsons, in a story written for the *Los Angeles Mining Review*, gave Wyatt almost full credit for stopping the mob. One cannot accuse Parsons of riding a legend—the first nationally distributed profile of Earp, Bat Masterson's story for *Human Life* magazine, was still four years away and Wyatt was merely a local legend. One also cannot write it off as hero worship of an old man: Parsons was not yet fifty. Why, then isn't Wyatt mentioned in Parsons's journal? Probably because Parsons was not writing a biography of Wyatt Earp.

So, if Stuart Lake exaggerated Wyatt's role in the Deuce incident, he did not fabricate it. And once again we get a glimpse of the folk tale process at work: If Stuart Lake immortalized Wyatt Earp's courage and cold nerve saving the worthless tinhorn gambler Johnny O'Rourke, it was because everyone Lake talked to had vivid recollections of those qualities. So much so that in the retelling Wyatt Earp became the only one in the picture.

O'Rourke, by the way, escaped from the inept Charlie Shibell's Tucson jail. Some legends have him returning later to murder a sleeping Johnny Ringo, but no one really knows what really happened to him. Perhaps he was swallowed up in the void that seemed to take so many players in the Tombstone saga after they moved on.

If Wyatt felt surrounded by enemies during the winter of 1881, he must have relaxed in February when some old friends from Dodge City got off the Tucson stage. Bat Masterson and Luke Short, a diminutive, hair-triggered gambler with a reputation almost as scarlet as Doc Holliday's, came to Tombstone. Bat and Luke quickly obtained jobs as faro dealers. Short didn't wait long to get into trouble. On February 25, Bat tried to break up an altercation between Short and a drunken gunman and gambler named Charlie Storms. He failed; Storms challenged Short a second time, and Short killed him, directly in front of the Oriental Saloon. The Oriental seemed to be turning into a magnet for trouble. A week after the Luke Short–Charlie Storms gunfight, a two-armed gambler nicknamed One Armed Kelly was shot and killed by another gambler, also at the Oriental. "Oriental," Parsons wrote in his journal, "a regular slaughterhouse now."

This brand of random violence, however, was just a sideshow. In mid-March, bandits made a robbery attempt on the stage from Benson, and the real slaughter began. From March 15 to October 25, anywhere from nineteen to thirty-five men—no one was ever able to determine just how many—would die in incidents connected with the Cowboys and their associates. Relations between the United States and Mexico would turn ugly, martial law in Arizona Territory would be threatened, and the path to the O.K. Corral gunfight and its even bloodier aftermath would be inevitable.

Notes

1. In the 1976 film *Silver Streak*, Ned Beatty, playing a FBI agent, anticipates trouble when the train stops at Dodge City. "Kind of appropriate, don't you think," he says to Gene Wilder, "Gunsmoke at the O.K. Corral?"

2. *Tombstone* in 1994 was the first movie to portray the town with anything like historical accuracy. Some critics, particularly *Entertainment Weekly*'s Owen Glieberman, complained that "the town looks as if it was being built as the cast rode in"—without realizing that that was the point.

3. One of the many delightful bits of Earpiana in Kevin Jarre's script for *Tombstone* is John Behan's (Jon Tenney) proud pronouncement to Wyatt Earp (Kurt Russell) that he is "chairman of the nonpartisan Anti-Chinese League."

4. Though apparently not with everyone. A local tradition says that Virgil stiffed a local merchant by the name of Goldwater to the tune of about $300. Goldwater's grandson, Barry, contributed several documents on Earpiana to the Arizona Historical Society.

5. In the 1990 novel *Silver Light* by English-born writer and film critic David Thompson, the leader of the Arizona cattle rustlers, Curly Bill Brocius, is a friend and business partner of Billy the Kid and arrives from Tombstone to Fort Sumner on the night Billy is killed by Pat Garrett. Wyatt Earp is a sinister presence, skulking around the back of the book until he finally kills the amiable Curly Bill, as indeed the real Wyatt is thought to have killed the real Curly Bill.

6. Eggenhofer painted the gunfight for the cover of the original 1931 *Frontier Marshal*, but inexplicably left out Doc Holliday. In later reproductions, Doc is back in, though faint, partially obscured by gun smoke. Eggenhofer's attention to the details of the late-nineteenth-century Southwestern dress was a big influence on the movie *Tombstone*, the first Earp film to portray the characters in authentic costume. In the course of researching this book, I discovered that Eggenhofer lived in Milford, New Jersey, close to my own home in South Orange, until 1972, when he moved to Cody, Wyoming. According to his family, he became fascinated with the American West as a boy in Germany through Buffalo Bill's traveling Wild West show and through the art of western artist Charles M. Russell. He came to the United States at age thirteen and found work as an illustrator for western pulps; he died in 1985 at the age of eighty-seven.

Eggenhofer established a solid reputation as a painter of landscapes, but he remains best known for his western work. The original painting *Gunfight at the O.K. Corral* is on view at the National Cowboy Hall of Fame in Oklahoma City, Oklahoma.

7. Because Ringo was known to be related to a man named Coleman Younger, it was long believed that John was blood kin to Cole Younger of the James-Younger gang in Missouri. Coleman Younger was indeed the uncle of Cole, Bob, and James Younger. Most researchers now believe that the connection with Ringo was through marriage, not blood.

Nevertheless, there are some fascinating connections here. A few Missouri historians still believe that the Jameses and Youngers were distant cousins; even if they're not correct, there are links of blood, marriage, and gang association among an amazing number of the most notorious figures of the West from the 1860s to 1930s.

The Dalton brothers were related by blood to the Youngers; and Al Jennings, the Oklahoma bank robber of the 1890s, learned his trade from Bill Dalton and Bill Doolin. Cole Younger was the lover of Belle Shirley, who later went to Tucson, married Sam Starr, and became the infamous Belle Starr; out of gangs they spawned eventually came Vern Miller, best remembered for his part, along with Pretty Boy Floyd, in the Kansas City massacre of 1933.

Historian Paul Wellmann has traced this genealogy in his 1961 book, *A Dynasty of Western Outlaws.* Interesting enough, Wellmann never made the link between the Jameses, the Youngers, and John Ringo, and, through Ringo, the Clantons.

8. Burrows's superb, unsentimental study of a minor American legend, recently reprinted in paperback by the University of Arizona Press, has many admirers, including Paula Mitchell Marks, author of *And Die in the West.* It has also sparked a bizarre reaction among Cowboy apologists, for whom Ringo remains a viable symbol of resistance. Visitors to bookstores out West, such as Tombstone's own Territorial Book Trader, can now choose from four books about Ringo. The reader will either trust the author of this book and stick with Burrows or be subjected to hours of warped and convoluted writing.

9. *Undercover for Wells Fargo* was edited by Carolyn Lake, daughter of Stuart Lake. In a 1995 phone interview, Ms. Lake told me that she had never satisfactorily answered that question either.

10. Perhaps Joyce had read Mark Twain's *Roughing It* and agreed that "to be a saloonkeeper and kill a man was to be illustrious."

11. Most accounts of this incident say that, but in fact I have been unable to determine whether White's statement was made at the time or produced later at Curly Bill's hearing. The distinction is important, as we shall shortly see.

12. Fifty years later a rumor that Virgil had somehow been involved in the shooting began circulating. Though he wasn't present at the scene, Judge Hancock once again decided he knew what really happened. His source for implicating Virgil (and by extension, Wyatt and Morgan) was a couple of "old timers," who, if they could be identified today, would probably be named Uncle Ned. Hancock gave this opinion in a 1932 interview, in response to the nationwide interest in Wyatt Earp revived by Burns and Lake's best-sellers. It was the first mention of the Earp-White murder conspiracy theory; thirty-one years later it resurfaced in Ed Bartholomew's rabidly anti-Earp biography. Paula Mitchell Marks concluded, "Such a Machiavellian move on the part of the Earps seems unlikely." This is certainly true, but Marks gives the theory credibility simply by mentioning it. Like Hancock and Bartholo-

mew before her, she neglects to mention that Virgil wasn't there when White was shot.

13. It also came from Henry P. Walker, who studied the Tombstone town-lot controversy in a thirty-six–page article in *Arizona and the West—A Quarterly Journal of History*. In the spring 1979 issue Walker concluded that White's death "was the first killing in a vendetta of economic origin that some experts claim took the lives of twenty-seven men."

14. What is curious about this story is not the "Curly Bill spin" but the fact that Breakenridge is telling the story at all. Here, as in several other incidents, Billy comes off as something of an idiot. It doesn't seem to occur to him that he is building up the legend of a friend, Curly Bill, as a cold-blooded murderer.

15. Some of this information comes from a 1941 book by Flora Warren Seymour, *Indian Agents of the Old Frontier*. Mrs. Seymour, who served for six years in the United States Indian Service, was appointed by the president as the first female member of the Board of Indian Commissions. In the 1950s, she authored several books for young readers including *Daniel Boone, Pioneer; The Boy's Life of Kit Carson;* and *We Called Them Indians*—all of which were put by my bedside when I first learned to read. I would be curious to read one of her books, *A Boy's Life of Fremont*, to see if she dealt with the great pathfinder's mishandling of the Tombstone troubles in which John Clum figured so prominently.

16. In a scene cut from the 1994 film, *Tombstone*, scriptwriter Kevin Jarre managed to sneak in a bit of Wyatt's past while offering a possible explanation for Earp's lenience. "Look, Kid," he says, "I know what it's like, I was a kid, too. Even stole a horse once."

17. History also records an Earp defeat in January when Virgil was defeated for a second time in the marshal's race by Ben Sippy. History recorded that, but it never happened, because Virgil never ran for town marshal a second time. Certainly it would have made no sense for him to run against Sippy again just a few weeks after losing to him, especially since by January 1881 it was apparent that both Sippy and the Earps were friends and allies of John Clum. Why, then, did so many historians, including Paula Mitchell Marks, write about Virgil's defeat? Probably because that's what Frank Waters wrote in *The Earp Brothers of Tombstone*, which is the earliest mention of Virgil's unsuccessful campaign. Waters was pushing an anti-Earp agenda, and a second defeat for Virgil fit in by making the Earps seem both ambitious and unpopular.
Stuart Lake wrote that Sippy's opponent was "an exponent of Cowboy liberality" named Howard Lee. Nothing else is known about Lee, but he is the only opponent of Sippy mentioned in

surviving newspaper articles. Subsequent historians simply rejected Lake's account in favor of Waters's without checking sources.

18. This is significant largely because of the myth of the "tin-horn" gambler-criminal element that would later grow around Tombstone's boom years and the stories that the "Earp gang" was somehow at the center of it, as if Tombstone's honest citizens were somehow duped into gambling by the duplicitous Earps and the demonical Holliday. (In fact, the rumors would start up much later. Many can be traced to a book called *Gunsmoke—The True Story of Old Tombstone* by an Arizona woman named Grace McCool, published in 1954.) In 1881, no one thought much about the Earps' or anybody else's gambling. Billy Breakenridge, for instance, thought that "most of the gamblers and card dealers were good citizens, and gambling was just as legitimate as dealing in merchandise or any other business."

The Cowboys themselves wouldn't have known what to make of later historians who saw them as victims of a tinhorn gambling element. Ringo, the Clantons, and the McLaurys gambled frequently; Wes Fuller, a Cowboy associate, was a professional gambler. The Earps and Holliday, however, did have reputations as being better gamblers than most.

19. In *And Die in the West* Paula Marks places this incident shortly before the November elections. This makes no sense, as Behan could not have been serving a subpoena stemming from a contested election before the election.

5

"Three Men Hurled into Eternity"— The Streetfight in Tombstone

On March 15, the Tombstone stage en route to the small town of Benson some 30 miles away was attacked by bandits. Stage holdups had ceased for a brief time when Wyatt and Morgan rode shotgun, but on March 15, waiting for the court's decision on the November sheriff's election, it was Bob Paul who was earning a few hard dollars sitting to the left of driver Bud Philpot and cradling a Wells Fargo shotgun. That is, Paul started out sitting to the left, which is where shotgun guards traditionally rode. At 10:00 P.M., according to some passengers, Paul was sitting to the right of Philpot. Passengers later said Philpot had "cramps" in his bowels and asked Paul to drive. Another source had the two trading places so that Philpot could warm his hands; it was a cold night and an early light snow was still on the ground. Coming up a grade, the stage was intercepted by several masked men—at least four were counted, and one witness claimed he saw eight—one of whom shouted, "Whoa, boys." Paul was a fighter, and his immediate response was to shout back, "I hold for no one!" The highwayman let loose a volley of rifle shots, one of which killed one of the eight passengers, Peter Roerig, who was riding on the top of the coach. Another struck Bud Philpot in the heart, killing him instantly. Paul leveled his shotgun and fired; the bandits didn't seem prepared for such a response and retreated.

Why were the bandits disconcerted? Possibly because they thought they had killed the guard and expected no resistance from the driver. The robbers knew the stage route, and they certainly knew that Paul would be riding shotgun that night. Was the attack, then, an attempt to eliminate the new law and order sheriff of Pima County? If it was a robbery, the job was certainly bungled; the horses bolted, and Paul, retrieving the reins, finally brought the stage with its seven terrified passengers to the station. On board was a Wells Fargo shipment (by one account, $26,000, by another $80,000) intact. Astonishingly, the bandits did not pursue the stage.

George Parsons was playing chess with a friend when Tombstone's respected physician, Dr. George Goodfellow, rushed in and demanded a gun. Parsons's friend let him have one, "upon Doc's assurance he didn't want to kill anyone." Dr. Goodfellow's intention was to join the posse being assembled to pursue the Benson stage robbers, but on this night no amateurs would be needed. A posse was quickly assembled that rivaled the intrepid Dodge City group who caught Dora Hand's killer: Virgil, Wyatt, and Morgan Earp, Bat Masterson, and Bob Paul, as well as Wells Fargo agent Marshall Williams. Virgil commanded by the authority of his U.S. deputy marshal's badge; there had been U.S. mail on the stage. Dodge and Williams were along to look after Wells Fargo's interests. As Virgil's posse set out it was joined by a second group of lawmen led by John Behan, which included his undersheriff, Harry Woods, Billy Breakenridge, and Buckskin Frank Leslie. Perhaps two hours behind the holdup men, the combined posses rode to the site of the shootings; at the end of two days of hard riding they had followed the trail to a small ranch in the lower San Pedro Valley owned by a man named Len Redfield. (Masterson and Leslie, who had been scouts with the army, must have been particularly valuable on this ride.)

Wyatt and Morgan got ahead of the posse. As they approached Redfield's ranch, a man tried to escape by jumping a corral fence. Wyatt and Morgan caught him, and, using pre-Miranda forms of persuasion, found out that his name was Luther King. He was running away, he said, because he thought the riders were outlaws. Behan wanted to let him go, but Wyatt was suspicious, particularly since there were two spent horses in Redfield's corral. And why would a man go to milk a cow, as King claimed to be doing, with two revolvers in his belt?

According to the Glenn Boyer version of Josephine's memoirs, Wyatt and Bob Paul, trying to loosen King up, told him that the bandits had killed Doc Holliday's woman at the attempted holdup. Wyatt supposedly told Josie

> That scared hell out of him because he knew Doc would be coming after whoever did it. He looked pretty scared and spilled the beans. He wanted to be damn sure we told Doc he'd only held the horses. He admitted his pals were Harry Head, Billy Leonard, and Jim Crane.
>
> About that time Johnny [Behan] came up and smelled a rat. He wanted to know what we'd said. King told him and found out from what Johnny said how we'd actually trapped him. He tried to skin it back, but he'd already talked too much. Johnny still didn't want to run him in, so I told him I'd do it on a federal warrant for robbing the mail.

(In fairness, it should be mentioned that this account isn't found in Josephine's original attempt at a memoir, the Cason manuscript, and some Earp researchers are skeptical that certain Tombstone passages were written or dictated by Josephine.) This minor detail of Behan's attitude toward the suspects is important because the Earps returned to Tombstone to find that rumors that Doc Holliday was involved in the holdup. These were followed by a second, more fantastic wave of rumors that the Earps and Holliday had actually engineered the robbery and were putting on a show with the long posse ride.

How the stories about the Earps' involvement in the holdup got started isn't clear. Probably they had to do with suspicions some locals had as to why the Earps always seemed to know so much about Wells Fargo's comings and goings. No one at the time knew of the brothers' involvement with the company, or for that matter, Bob Paul's. The Holliday rumor, though, seemed much more credible: Wasn't Doc Holliday one of the most notorious and unprincipled killers in the West?

The likely source of the Holliday-Benson stage rumor was easier to pin down. Leonard, Head, and Crane, the men named in the holdup attempt and the murder of Philpot, all had cattle rustling pasts and Cowboy associations. In *I Married Wyatt Earp* Josie inferred that John Behan wanted to let Luther King go. Behan, Josie implied, was keeping his part of the bargain by screening the law, or at least as much of it as he controlled, from Cowboy activities in Cochise County. If this is true Behan got the idea of implicating Holliday when he heard Wyatt mention Doc to Luther King. In fact, there was a connection: Leonard, a fellow southerner, and, like Doc, a consumptive, had known Holliday in Las Vegas, New Mexico, in the summer of 1879 and was considered one of the few men who could call the former dentist a friend. Leonard, like Doc, had a checkered past; a letter in the *Tucson Citizen* identified him as a horse thief nicknamed Billy the Kid Leonard. (In the late 1870s and the 1880s, nearly every William in the southwest who had a scrape with the law was given that nickname.) Like Doc, Leonard was literate— John Pleasant Gray recalls Leonard reading a life of Wild Bill Hickok to a gathering of delighted Cowboys—and, like Doc, he had a trade, jeweler.

All of this, however, made for no criminal connection. If Doc had been a member of the holdup gang, why wasn't he named by King when the Earps rode him down at the Redfield ranch? Why hadn't Wyatt and Morgan cut down the fleeing King before he could implicate Holliday? Putting aside all other objections, why would a gang of three to seven men want the volatile and unpredictable Holliday along on a stage robbery?

Though not many took the accusation seriously, for Holliday, being implicated in the Benson stage holdup was a simple case of chickens coming home to roost. Doc had behaved himself quite well while in Dodge City, and in fact, except for the altercation with Joyce, had been on good behavior in Tombstone. But in the West, a reputation, especially that of a killer, sooner or later caught up with a man. The *Las Vegas Optic* would describe Doc as "a shiftless, bagged-legged character—a killer and professional cutthroat and not a whit too refined to rob stages or even steal sheep," though, like all papers that wrote of Holliday's notoriety, it failed to list crimes he was actually guilty of. More to the point, the *Optic* didn't mention any crimes he was rumored to have committed. Doc Holliday annoyed some people, usually people in authority.[1] The Earp brothers came to Tombstone with impeccable records as lawmen; their friend Doc Holliday's reputation was the only front on which their reputations were vulnerable.

Disappointing as the truth is to mythmakers, Doc Holliday's rap sheet up to 1881 wouldn't have disqualified him for political office.

No doubt Doc was guilty of some of the shootings legend has attached to his name, but all of them, on examination, were personal quarrels or gambling disagreements. The most serious crimes—in fact, the only crimes—charged against Holliday before 1881 were arrests in Fort Griffin, Texas, in 1875 for "gaming in a saloon" and "playing . . . at a game with cards in a house in which spirituous liquors were sold."[2]

Probably the strongest argument against Doc's involvement in the stage holdup is his solitary nature. An early biographer, Pat Jahns, who can not be counted among Doc's admirers, concluded that "nothing in the stereotyped pattern of Doc's behavior admits so violent a deviation from his usual behavior as engaging in a stage robbery," though Jahns thinks "it is quite possible that Doc was an accessory before the fact." Leonard, she writes, "knew Holliday and his code of loyalty. Possibly he told or hinted broadly about the planned robbery to Doc, knowing he would never tell anyone, not even his law officer crony, Wyatt Earp." Perhaps, but such an argument doesn't explain why Doc's loyalty to Wyatt Earp, whom he had known for at least five years and whose life he had saved in Dodge City, wouldn't have been stronger than whatever loyalty he felt toward Billy Leonard. It also doesn't explain why Leonard would feel compelled to test Doc's loyalty by telling him of the robbery plans.

There is one more strong argument against Holliday's involvement. As Doc is said to have said later, if he'd robbed the stage, "I'd have shot a horse and got the bullion."

Whatever Holliday's connection to the stage robbery, if any, nothing was made of it at the time King was captured. Behan and Breakenridge headed back to Tombstone with King in tow, accompanied by Wells Fargo agent Marshall Williams. (Williams's presence in this group may or may not have been significant, but let's record it for later reference.) Virgil Earp's posse stayed out for several days and nights, riding over 300 miles in pursuit of the holdup men before deciding that they had crossed the territorial line into New Mexico. When the posse returned to Tombstone they could at least console themselves that they had the link to the stage robberies in Luther King, or so they thought.[2] In his diary, George Parsons wrote, "King, the stage robber, escaped tonight early from H. Woods who had been previously notified of an attempt at release to be made. Some of our officials should be hanged, they're a bad lot."[3] Harry Jones agreed. Evidently he felt that the horse-selling transaction was a plot to get him out of the office; from that time on he counted himself an Earp partisan.

Amazingly, though, Wyatt and Virgil still didn't see what was happening in partisan terms. Both men were used to cooperation between the different branches of law enforcement and didn't seem to understand that Behan's County Sheriff's Office had been at cross-purposes with the town marshal and federal marshal from the beginning. Working on a rumor that Leonard, Head and Crane were headed for a cattle ranch used by the rustlers in the Cloverdale section of New Mexico, Virgil Earp's new posse cooperated with Behan's posse and they rode parallel paths out of Arizona into New Mexico in pursuit. This time the officers did a lot of riding—Virgil rode a horse into collapse—for nothing.

In fact, considerably less than nothing. While the Earps were away, the campaign against Doc Holliday intensified. The *Daily Nugget*, sticking to its claim that Luther King had implicated Doc, now printed a follow-up story with details about the fourth suspect in the robbery. The *Nugget* found a livery stable hand who claimed that an unnamed man had appeared at his corral armed with a revolver and a rifle—the rifle was specified as a Henry repeater—and asked for a horse. He might be back that night, the unknown fellow had said, but also might be gone for several days. (How the man could have rented a horse without leaving his name was not explained.) In fact, Holliday had ridden to Charleston the afternoon of the holdup attempt, to gamble, he said, an explanation that was generally accepted as gambling was known to be Holliday's trade. Several witnesses recalled seeing the former dentist back in Tombstone by about 6:30; researchers have also produced witnesses who claim that Holliday was riding hard toward Tombstone after the robbery attempt and that a "consensus of opinion" at Drew's station, where the stage was headed, had Holliday "at the bottom of it," that is, the robbery attempt.

The case against Holliday would probably have faded away if not for Kate Elder. Nearly three months after the attempted holdup, Doc and Kate had one of their periodic fallouts. Later chroniclers would record this as a brawl, giving birth to Hollywood's conception of Doc and Kate. Victor Mature, Kirk Douglas, and Dennis Quaid all used the actresses portraying Kate as punching bags. (One biographer even has Doc slamming his pistol barrel off her head, which would have been extremely difficult with the short-barreled "Gambler's Model" Colt Doc is said to have favored.) But in fact Kate never said that Doc hit her, and no contemporary account confirms physical abuse. Doc's verbal abuse was probably brutal enough, and after getting her fill on this night, Kate went on a bender and made her anger over Doc's behavior—and, probably, her dislike of Wyatt Earp and his influence over Doc—apparent to sympathetic listeners in the Oriental Saloon. One of the listeners was Doc's old enemy Milt Joyce, now a political figure and member of the County Ring.

The next thing anyone knew, John Behan had gotten Kate to sign an affidavit charging Doc with participation in the holdup. (In the court records she wrote her last name as Eder rather than Elder, which might be an indication her condition at the time.) On the strength of the affidavit, Behan arrested Doc; Wyatt posted $5,000 cash bond for his release. Wyatt produced several witnesses that Doc had been back in Tombstone before the holdup. Kate sobered up and recanted, and Doc was released. Lake has an embarrassed Holliday telling Wyatt, "You say the word and I'll leave Tombstone." "You send that damn fool woman away and I'll be satisfied," Earp replied. Supposedly Doc then peeled $1,000 from a roll he kept in Lou Rickabaugh's safe and gave it to Kate, who left for Globe. Wyatt thought Doc and Kate would never see each other again. He was wrong. Kate was back in Tombstone by October and even swore that she had witnessed the gunfight, a claim at least as dubious as the affidavit she signed for Behan. Kate outlived Doc and even Wyatt and wrote her memoirs, but she never mentioned the Benson stage robbery again.

Another anti-Holliday witness checked in many years later: Fred Dodge. About half a century after the holdup, Dodge wrote to Stuart Lake:

> Marshall Williams did do some tipping off, but Doc was a full-fledged member of the gang that Leonard was in with. I know who was present at the holdup at the time Bud Philpot was killed and I know who killed him. It was Bob Paul, though, they were after. If Wyatt has not told you, out of respect to his memory I will say nothing more about Doc Holliday . . ."

This is interesting and also a bit bizarre. Dodge's informant on Holliday was Marshall Williams, who was in the posse that escorted Luther King back to Tombstone. Williams—who, like King, later disappeared without a trace—is one of the shadier characters in the Earp story and could well have been playing on the Behan-Cowboy side – or playing both ends against the middle. Dodge contends that the point of the holdup was not to steal money, but to assassinate Bob Paul, which can't be proved but does fit the facts. If Dodge was right, why would Holliday have been involved? Why would Dodge think that Holliday would become a contract killer, particularly when the contract was on Wyatt Earp's friend, Bob Paul? One gets the impression that Dodge, like Billy Breakenridge, didn't want to get caught without a theory about anything that ever happened in Tombstone.

Mid-April brought more news Wyatt didn't want to hear. Bat Masterson was leaving Tombstone for Dodge City; his brother Jim was in trouble, and Bat was returning to see what he could do to help. A couple of weeks later Luke Short, the charges against him from the Charlie Storms killing dismissed, also left. This deprived the Earp faction of two formidable allies. If Bat alone had stayed, the history of Tombstone might have been different. Masterson would still make a contribution to the outcome of the Earp-Cowboy war, but that would be nearly a year later, in Colorado.

Marshal Ben Sippy must have sensed trouble coming. In the spring he had been granted a leave of absence and Virgil was made acting town marshal. On June 6 Sippy left Tombstone again, never to return. This time there was no special election, as there had been when Fred White was killed; Clum and the city council knew they had made the wrong choice in the fall of 1880 and rectified it by appointing Virgil full Town Marshal. Sippy joined Luther King before him and Marshall Williams after him as one of the key players in the Tombstone story who seemed to vanish after playing his role.[4]

Flipping through Stuart Lake's papers at the Huntington Library, Virgil Earp's biographer, Don Chaput, pieced together a street conversation between Wyatt and an unidentified city council member:

> "Virgil, want to put you on as City Marshal, going to buy Ben Sippy off."

"Wrong man." "Ain't you Virg?"
"No, Wyatt."

Apparently Tombstone's city fathers had run out of patience with Sippy's lethargic attitude and wanted a law and order man to replace him. They got one. One of Virgil's first acts was to arrest Wyatt for disturbing the peace after nearly causing a street brawl. Shortly afterward, Virgil arrested his boss, John Clum, for riding his buggy too fast in the city streets.

There would soon be more serious matters for the new marshal's attention. The lot-jumping problem, which had never ceased, intensified late in June when a fire that started in the Oriental Saloon wiped out more than sixty buildings. Ironically, the only serious injury was of town chronicler George Parsons, who was caught on the second floor of a collapsing building. Wyatt prevented another casualty by rescuing a young woman from a burning second floor; a small legend has grown up that it was Josephine Marcus, but if so she failed to mention it in her memoirs.

The fire left plenty of new lots to jump. Clark and Gray immediately took advantage of the situation by hiring men to put up tents on burned out sites. John Clum and the town council quickly met and assured the town marshal he had their backing to handle the situation as he thought best. In the words of Chaput, "The first act of Marshal Earp was to stroll down the smoke-filled streets. He walked slowly, all six-feet-one of him, with pistol at his side, and Winchester cradled in his arms, carrying the double authority of a deputy U.S. marshal and a city marshal." The Wyatt Earp of Tombstone that Stuart Lake would package for TV and movies in the 1950s was largely drawn from this image of Virgil Earp, whom history and Hollywood would relegate to the status of Wyatt's deputy. In the summer of 1881, however, Virgil Earp was in charge, and Wyatt was one of his special policeman; so were Morgan and Warren, the youngest Earp brother, who was giving southeast Arizona a look over. Fred Dodge was a frequent choice for deputy, as was Texas Jack Vermillion, who would later ride in Wyatt's vendetta posse to avenge the shootings of Virgil and Morgan. This was a hard group of men. As Dodge recorded it, they would ride to a claim jumper's tent, throw a rope over it, and yell, "Lot jumper, you *git.*" The lot jumpers got.

This was a crude method of dealing with the complex problem of who owned which lots—essentially, it just transferred the problem back to the courts—but it was popular with townsfolk who were tired of the public squabbles. True to his word, Clum supported the Earps in print: "This decisive and just action on the part of the marshal acted like oil upon troubled waters, and peace and order were restored." And it was. As Tombstone rebuilt itself after the fire, the lot-jumping activity slowed. No more did drunken cowhands hurrah the town; overall arrests went from sixty in the month of July to just twenty-two in August, three for use of "vulgar language." (One wonders was said.) By August 1 Virgil was confident enough to tell the city council: "The same peace and quietness now can be maintained with just two policeman," James Flynn and A. G. Bronk. It didn't hurt that Virgil had Wyatt around to back him when needed or that Wyatt had Doc Holliday.

Tombstone was quiet, but a few miles to the south, on the Mexican border, things were heating up. The fire would soon reach back to Tombstone.

If, as Wyatt Earp's enemies would later claim, the Earps and Holliday were plotting to get rid of Leonard, Head, and Crane, they didn't move fast enough. On or near June 6 Leonard and Head got themselves killed in the Hachita (or Hatchet) Mountains of New Mexico by two brothers named Hazlett. A story that remains unconfirmed but that is believed by many Earp researchers is that Tombstone Justice of the Peace Mike Gray—the same Mike Gray of the Town Lot troubles—had hired the two cattle rustlers and accused stage robbers to assassinate the Hazletts in a scheme to acquire their ranch, or at least that appears to be what the Hazletts believed.

The Hazletts didn't live long enough to confirm any of it; within a few days of their killing of Leonard and Head, the Hazletts themselves were murdered by a group of Cowboys including (the Earps believed) John Ringo, Curly Bill, and Jim Crane, the known surviving member of the Benson stage holdup gang. In August, Crane got himself eliminated from the story. Camping with seven other men associated with the Cowboys, Crane was caught in an ambush about one hundred miles from Tombstone in Guadalupe Canyon, which ran from Sonora on the Mexican side into Arizona and served as a natural trail for rustlers running cattle in either direction. The ambushers were Mexican soldiers, and this time they hadn't stopped on the Mexican side of the border. This marked an escalation in the ongoing conflict. In all five men were killed, including Dixie Gray, son of the Tombstone justice, and Old Man Clanton. It isn't clear what the senior Clanton's function was within the loosely knit Cowboy fraternity; with two ranches and three sons to help rustle stolen stock he was in a position to have substantial influence within the group. Whatever Clanton's role, the Cowboys as a group seemed to get more reckless and irresponsible after his death. Some students of the Earp saga see Clanton as a kind of Old West equivalent of an organized crime capo; others saw him a semirespectable rancher. Of course, anyone who thinks the two roles are incompatible doesn't know how much crime bosses strive for respectability.

The Guadalupe Canyon massacre brought a temporary halt to a cycle of violence that began with the murder of Bud Philpot in the Benson stage holdup. In between were the deaths of four other members of the Cowboy faction by Mexicans, the deaths of Leonard, Head, and the Hazlett brothers, and anywhere from four to nineteen Mexicans in a massacre in Skeleton Canyon, not far from Guadalupe Canyon. The border troubles were touched off on May 22, 1881, when, according to the *Tucson Weekly Citizen*, four Cowboys from "Cachise" County—the correct spelling of the Apache chief's name, misspelled when the county was formed and never corrected—were killed in a cattle raid on a hacienda 10 miles into the state of Sonora. The Cowboys, who included a butcher from Galeyville, attempted to make off with a herd estimated at from four to five hundred cattle before Mexican ranchers organized and caught up to them. Four Cowboys were killed, and at least one Mexican died.

About a week later the *Arizona Weekly Star* followed up on the story: About seventy Cowboys, the paper reported, were forming an irregular regiment to avenge the death of their friends (though the Mexicans, it appeared, were entirely in the right). Precisely where the *Star* got its information is not known, but the paper even went so far as to predict that Mexican Federales were on the lookout to confront them.

"The Cowboys," said the *Star*, "are reckless, daring fighters, good shots, ride good horses and don't place great deal of value on life. Should any damage be done to our Mexican neighbors, the United States will not be able to escape censure. This whole affair was organized on American soil and with an open and avowed purpose of murder, robbery, and outlawry."

The Cowboys' defenders scoffed at such claims, calling them the result of paranoia spread by John Clum, who, it must be admitted, never used black ink when purple would do. To some, particularly those who didn't much care what went on south of the border, the Cowboys were simply rebellious, essentially good-humored ruffians whose rustic ways were misunderstood by outsiders, particularly Yankee and Republican outsiders. As for cattle theft, the laissez-faire attitude was summed up by a modern Arizona journalist who said at an O.K. Corral symposium, "Cattle rustling wasn't such a big deal; everybody did it." In 1881, though, not every rancher saw rustling as such a harmless vice. One victim, a Mr. T. W. Ayles, wrote angrily to the *Epitaph* that

> I am not a growler or chronic grumbler, but I own stock, am a butcher and supply my immediate neighborhood beef, and to do so must keep cattle on hand, and try to and could do so always if I had not to divide with unknown and irresponsible partners, viz: "Cow Boys," or some other cattle thieves. Since my advent into the territory and more particularly on the San Pedro River, I have lost 50 head of cattle by cattle thieves. I am not the only sufferer from these marauders and cattle robbers on the on San Pedro, within the last six months. Aside from 50 head of good beef cattle that I have been robbed of, Judge Blair has lost his entire herd, P. McMinnimen has lost all of his finest fat steers. Dunbar at Tres Alamos, has lost a number of head. Burton of Huachuca, lost almost his entire herd, and others—and in fact all engaged in the stock business—have lost heavily from cattle thieves. And not always do these thieves confine themselves to cattle; horses and mules are gobbled up by these robbers, as well as cattle. Is there no way to stop this wholesale stealing of stock in this vicinity or in the county?

Local ranchers weren't the only ones to see the Cowboys as a growing menace. William Henry Bishop, a correspondent for *Harper's Weekly* whose work on the Southwest would later be collected under the title, *Old Mexico and Her Provinces,* visited New Mexico and Arizona in 1881. Not all "cow-boys," as Bishop called them, were "stealers of cattle." Some Arizona cow-boys were honest men, but most of

> The cow-boys frequenting Tombstone at this time were generally from ranches in the San Pedro and San Simon valleys. There were said to be strongholds in the San Simon valley for concealing stolen cattle, until rebranded and prepared for market, where no officer of the law ever ventured. The running off of stock from Mexico was possibly looked upon only as a more dashing form of smuggling, although it was marked by frequent tragedies on both sides.

Another correspondent who observed Tombstone and the surrounding area in 1881 was Clara Spalding Brown, a correspondent for the *San Diego Union* who moved to the silver camp in June 1880 with her husband, Theodore Brown, a mining entrepreneur. Brown was the best journalist to visit Tombstone in its glory period, and her exclusion from the numerous scholarly books on the southwest in this period is a mystery.[5] She was unmoved by Tombstone's scenic wonders: "In the clear, rarefied atmosphere of southern Arizona," she wrote in a short story after leaving Arizona, "the eye scanned in vain for a glimpse of beauty . . . bare, dust-colored mesa." But Tombstone's fluid and colorful social life fascinated her, and she wrote about it in a style that, she said, presented "a fair, candid statement of facts, avoiding that flowery verbosity . . . indulged in by some newspaper correspondents." After the gunfight near the O.K. Corral she would record that "he inhabitants of every house in town . . . were greatly startled by the sudden report of firearms about 3:00 P.M., discharged with such lightning rapidity that it could be compared only to the explosion of a bunch of firecrackers; and the aspect of affairs grew more portentous when, a few moments later, the whistles of the steam hoisting works sounded a shrill alarm. 'The cow-boys!' cried some, thinking that a party of those desperadoes were 'taking the town.' 'The Indians!' cried a few of the most excitable."

Brown saw the "cow-boys" in nonromantic terms. "One would suppose," she wrote in a dispatch, "that all peaceable, honest men would denounce and oppose the outlaws, for they are virtually such, but a large proportion of otherwise good citizens waste a surprising amount of sympathy on them, in the face of evidence against them which ought to be thoroughly convincing." One wonders what Brown would have thought of a generation of modern historians whose judgment of the Cowboys would be filtered through consideration of the social and economic forces they represented.

In truth, aside from the *Daily Nugget*, whose owner had strong ties to the them, it was hard to find any defenders of the Cowboys or their activities in the early 1880s. As the rumors of a raid on Fronteras grew, a Las Vegas, New Mexico, paper called the Cowboys "the most reckless gang of outlaws ever banded together." The assistance of U.S. troops, the paper reported, "will give the honest settlers assistance necessary to put down these lawless vagabonds, who are more of a disgrace to this country than the worst bandits were in Spain or Italy." General Sherman in Washington and Arizona Commander Willcox also thought U.S. soldiers were needed, but from the end of the Civil War there was strong resistance in the Democratic party in general and especially from Democrats in the Western states and territories to any kind of federal action in the Southwest. In 1878 Democrats attached a rider, the Posse Comitatus Act, to an army appropriations bill which barred the military from serving as posses involving civilian depredations. Though it often seemed as if it would be, and many insisted it should be, the act was never repealed.

Feeble as it was, federal resistance was the only kind the Cowboys encountered. In Tucson, Deputy U.S. Marshal Joe Evans did his best to monitor Cowboy activities and keep law enforcement officials informed. In the spring 1881 he wrote to Crawley Dake in Prescott that "the Cowboys number about 380. They are constantly raiding in Sonora bringing out stock and killing Mexicans when they interfere. A great many Mexicans have been killed by the Cowboys. In one instance the Mexicans retaliated by killing law-abiding American citizens." Evans's report wildly exaggerated the number of men who filled the Cowboy ranks; Virgil Earp put the number at about one hundred and he was probably inflating the figure, though it was difficult to give an actual count on the manpower available to the Cowboys since there must have been numerous part-timers who did real ranch work between raids. Evans's report was probably also responsible for Dake's own exaggeration a short time later when he wrote the Mexican governor in Sonora telling him that "From two hundred to three hundred" armed and organized rustlers were operating in Mexico. Since Dake was later found to be guilty of gross misappropriation of federal funds, he might have had more personal reasons for emphasizing the Cowboys' threat: The more Cowboys, the bigger the budget needed to curtail them.

Actually, all that would have been needed to curtail Cowboy activities was a tightening of law enforcement by the county most of them lived and operated in, but by 1881 the relationship between the rustlers and the Cochise County Sheriff's Office had become cozy indeed. John Behan's deputy, Billy Breakenridge, was capable of taking a clear-eyed view of the Cowboys: "They know no law but their own," he wrote in his 1928 book. "Nearly all Texas Cowboys whose feeling toward the Mexicans was so bitter that they had no compunction about stealing from them or shooting and robbing them whenever they got a opportunity . . . they confined their crimes to stealing stock and robbing Mexican smugglers who were bringing Mexican silver across the boundary line to buy goods. Most of the time they killed the smugglers."

Breakenridge identified the leaders as Ringo and Curly Bill Brocius, but that didn't stop him from hiring the latter as an assistant tax collector. In *Helldorado* he describes seeking out Brocius in a Galeyville saloon and asking him to assist in collecting from the Cowboys the county taxes owed on land and animals: "The idea of my asking the chief of all the cattle rustlers in that part of the country to help me collect taxes from them struck him as a good joke. He thought it over for a few moments and then, laughing, said, 'Yes, and we will make everyone of those blank-blank cow thieves pay his taxes.' Breakenridge then described a ride with Brocius through "blind canyons and hiding places where the rustlers had a lot of stolen Mexican cattle, and introduced me like this: 'Boys, this is the county assessor, and I am his deputy. We are all good, law-abiding citizens and we cannot run the county unless we pay our taxes'." Brocius was shrewd. He reminded his fellow thieves that "if any of them should get arrested, it would be an good thing for them to show that they were taxpayers in the county."

That using Curly Bill to collect taxes in Cochise County might be the equivalent of asking Al Capone (the most famous gangland figure in America the year Breakenridge's book was published) to col-

lect taxes in Chicago does not seem to have occurred to Breakenridge. Nor does it seem to have occurred to him that there might be
something a bit immoral to say nothing of illegal in building the
prosperity of his county on taxes generated from stolen foreign cattle,
cattle that Mexicans had been murdered for.

In his introduction to the 1992 reprint of *Helldorado*, historian
Richard Maxwell Brown wrote, "Breakenridge operated on a theory
of law enforcement that . . . played down violence. . . . Breakenridge's mode was to handle things in such a way as to avoid the
stand-one's-ground, no-duty-to-retreat confrontations that so often
resulted in death to one or both opponents." Brown expresses this
point of view as well as anyone has, and in doing so pinpoints one of
the major reasons why the Earps remain controversial to this day. For
all their gambling and mining interests, the Earps were active, aggressive lawmen who enforced laws without regard to politics or popularity and who had no compunction about stretching the power of
their federal appointments to do so. Breakenridge, while probably
not so corrupt as his boss, Behan, shared with him a live-and-let-live
attitude toward the enforcement of unpopular laws. To anyone who
doesn't share Breakenridge's philosophy of law enforcement—or at
least Richard Maxwell Brown's definition of Breakenridge's philosophy—the idea of ignoring one kind of lawbreaking in order to curb
another is to simply postpone disaster. Much of the violence that
occurred near Tombstone from the spring to the fall of 1881 was easy
for most Americans in Arizona and New Mexico territory to rationalize or simply ignore since it involved Mexican nationals and happened near or below the Mexican border. In retrospect it's hard to
believe that anyone could have thought it would never spread north.

Long before organized bands of Americans and Mexicans clashed in
the border canyons, Skeleton and Guadalupe had served as corridors
for smugglers and rustlers operating on both American and Mexican
sides of the border; before the smugglers these same canyons had
made splendid refuges for renegade Apaches. (Locals still debate the
exact site of Geronimo's final surrender to General Miles in Skeleton
Canyon in 1886.)

Walter Noble Burns was the first journalist to gather the legends and
stories surrounding the Skeleton Canyon massacre. *Tombstone, An*

Iliad of the Southwest was composed of stories still current in the mid 1920s. In Burns's book, a veteran smuggler named Don Miguel Garcia was leading a train of silver-laden mules—"small, lithe, clean-limbed, of ancient Andalusian stock, each with a jingling bell at its throat"—through the pass and on to Tucson. Coming around a bend, Don Miguel is confronted by a smiling Curly Bill Brocius, "one leg nonchalantly over the pommel of his saddle and, drawing a sack of tobacco and a package of yellow paper from his pocket, rolled a cigarette." "*Coma esta usted, señor?*" says Bill, his fluent, easy, Spanish drawing the Mexican out. Of course, this is the prelude to an ambush: "Death leaped upon the Mexicans in the canyon as a mountain lion springs from a tree upon the back of a deer . . . the mules, stampeding, swept over the bodies in a whirlwind of terror. . . . Throwing his hands aloft in wild death spasm, a bronzed horseman dived to the ground and rolled over in a somersault." Don Miguel dies with "knightly courage as well knightly courtesy. Staggering to his knees, he pointed his six-shooter in a weakly wobbling hand toward the heights of flaming death."

No one is sure how many were killed in the massacre; Burns gave the oft-quoted figure of nineteen, while another source said fourteen. Billy Breakenridge said nine, which is what the Mexican governor of Sonora, Luis Torres, would claim. Ed Bartholomew, a Texas-based western writer and Earp debunker of the 1950s and '60s, claimed that the massacre never happened at all, that the legend was an invention of the Earp faction to further discredit the Cowboys.

The Mexican government certainly believed something happened. Torres wrote to Arizona's territorial governor John Fremont (who was, characteristically, absent from Arizona), requesting immediate assistance from the United States in apprehending the killers. Given the endless debates in Washington on whether the problem should be handled by federal or local authority, and the unwillingness of either to allocate funds, no assistance was forthcoming. Torres couldn't have been too surprised; about two months earlier he had written to his friend, Joe Evans, the federal deputy in Tucson, about the "cow boys" intended invasion, but there was nothing Evans, with his meager resources, could do.

Wyatt Earp, at the O.K. Corral inquest, would state that he was "satisfied" that Frank and Tom McLaury were involved in the Skeleton Canyon killings, which seems plausible in Frank's case as he had earned a reputation as a terrific shot and gun handler (witnesses reported piles of empty cartridge casings in front of the McLaury ranch where Frank had taken practice). Members of the Earp faction claimed that rumors in Tombstone placed the McLaurys and the Clantons, as well as Curly Bill, there but where they got their information isn't clear. Sherman McMasters, who rode with the Cowboys and may have been a Wells Fargo informant, was a likely source. Whoever did the actual killing, James Hancock would later claim in his memoirs that Galeyville, the Cowboys' favorite stronghold, was "flooded with new Mexican silver dollars that looked as if they had just come out of the mint." Where they came from didn't seem to trouble Hancock or anyone else in Galeyville.

As for the Guadalupe Canyon reprisal, in which Jim Crane and Old Man Clanton were killed, Cowboy supporters later turned the incident into an act of Mexican aggression: the boys had just been on a cattle buying trip and had been caught at the wrong place at the wrong time. According to John Pleasant Gray, whose brother was killed in the fight, it was simple coincidence that the group ran into the angry Mexicans. In fact, said Gray, Crane, the last known Benson stage robber, was ready to turn himself in and reveal the Earps' involvement—if he had made it back to Tombstone. The implication was that Wyatt Earp had silenced the last witness against him. But according to a survivor, Harry Ernshaw, the shooters in Guadalupe were Mexican soldiers. The *Arizona Weekly Star* would even give the name of the commanding officer, Captain Carillo. This marked an escalation in the hostilities.

The Skeleton and Guadalupe Canyon massacres, occurring in such a short time, sent shock waves through the Governor's Office and all the way to Washington. In Tombstone, Billy Byers, a rancher who had escaped despite a bullet wound to the stomach, displayed a buckboard the party had taken with them into Mexico. The wagon was pierced by perhaps forty Mexican bullet holes and provoked locals into argument over who had killed who and why. George Parsons, for one, had no doubt: "This killing business by the Mexicans," he wrote in his journal, "in my mind, was perfectly justifiable as it was in retaliation for killing of several of them and their robbery by cow-boys recently, this same Crane being one of the number. Am glad they killed them." And: "As for the others—if not guilty of cattle stealings—they had no business to be found in bad company." Over the next few months, several more Cowboys and their associates would be found in bad company.

Did Wyatt Earp have anything to do with the death of Old Man Clanton and Jim Crane? In truth, the story seems to be one of the wilder tales in the Earp legend, but oddly enough it is believed today by both rabid Earp partisans and his debunkers. The story is that Wyatt, wanting to get rid of Jim Crane—the last man who could prove his involvement, along with Holliday, in the Benson stage holdup—rode into Guadalupe Canyon with Doc Holliday to rendez-vous with Mexican Federales. The pro-Earp version given by researchers such as Glenn G. Boyer and Michael Hickey, is surprisingly similar: Earp was working closely with Wells Fargo and the U.S. government, and, through their connections, the Mexican government, all of whom had good reason to want the Cowboys controlled or eliminated. In the absence of a coherent southwestern border policy, the U.S. government was leaving the job to Wells Fargo and Wyatt Earp.

In Boyer's telling, Wyatt and Doc trailed Joe Hill, a friend of Jim Crane's, to what Earp correctly guessed would be a meeting with Crane. The killings were an accident; Wyatt's purpose was to arrest Crane; when he called out to Clanton's party to surrender he had Sherman McMasters call out in Spanish in case there were Mexicans in the group. The Cowboys, hearing the Spanish, assumed that Mexican police or soldiers had found them and began firing, which precipitated the massacre.

As for the first version, one either believes that Wyatt Earp was a cold-blooded killer and the leader of a ring of stage robbers or one doesn't. As for the second, there is one other intriguing bit of near-evidence to support it: On the day of the O.K. Corral gunfight Doc Holliday was walking with an unexplained limp—remember that Doc met the Earp brothers in front of Hafford's saloon with a cane that he exchanged for Virgil's shotgun. Was Doc limping? Boyer claims that Holliday sustained a leg wound in the Guadalupe Canyon shootout, and that Wyatt's youngest brother, Warren, was also in the posse and took a bullet in the upper arm. Wyatt, according to Boyer, smuggled Doc and Warren out of Arizona by way of nearby Deming, New Mexico, and Holliday went home to recuperate in Georgia while Warren went home to Nick and Ginnie Ann in California. In fact, Doc and Warren Earp did drop out of the scene for a while.

Boyer's theory, if true, would at least explain the near-crazy behavior of Ike Clanton in the last hours before the gunfight, particularly if, as Boyer claims, Holliday goaded Ike by bragging that he had killed Ike's father. But there is simply no documentation available to outside historians to prove Wyatt Earp's involvement in Old Man Clanton's death. Wyatt never claimed responsibility for the death of Old Man Clanton, not to John Flood, Walter Burns, or Stuart Lake. For that matter, Doc, who despised Ike, went to his grave without claiming responsibility for the death.

What Wyatt did admit to all three writers was having made a deal with Ike Clanton. Sometime in June, before the death of Crane and Clanton senior in Guadalupe Canyon, Wyatt approached Ike Clanton. Billy Breakenridge, being either a troublemaker or simply his usual dimwitted self, had mentioned to Wyatt that Clanton had designs on a small ranch near the New Mexico border owned by Billy McLaury. (For a peace officer, Breakenridge seems to have been privy to a great deal of inside knowledge about Cowboy-related activities.) Ike must have figured that Leonard, on the run from the Benson stage holdup, wouldn't be needing the place, but Leonard returned and evicted Ike. Wyatt saw an opening. Or perhaps Ike saw one when reward posters went up around Tombstone for the capture of the suspected Benson stage robbers: Leonard, Head, and Crane. According to Stuart Lake, "On two or three occasions the outlaw sought to discuss the reward posters with the marshal, but Wyatt shut off the overtures. 'I let Ike itch a bit,' Wyatt said."

Ike, of course, later said that it was Wyatt who approached him. For once, Ike was probably telling the truth. Wyatt was shrewd enough to know that Ike had no qualms about turning on men who had been his associates. Clanton left for Sulphur Springs Valley; on June 6, he returned with Joe Hill and Frank McLaury. Hill had a perfectly intelligent question to ask: "Any strings on your offer?" To which Earp replied, "None." Ike Clanton, uncharacteristically, had an even more intelligent question: "The reward is offered for their arrest. Does that go, dead or alive?" Wyatt apparently hadn't considered that; he said he'd ask Marshall Williams to telegraph a message to his Wells Fargo superiors and find out. Williams said he later saw

Wyatt show the telegram to Hill, Clanton, and McLaury. The answer was affirmative: They could be taken dead or alive.[6]

One might stop here and ask precisely what every participant's motives were in this scheme. Later, testifying before Wells Spicer at the O.K. Corral inquest, Clanton would claim that Wyatt Earp told him that he wanted Leonard, Head, and Crane eliminated before they could connect the Earps with the Benson stage holdup. The story sounds fantastic; it's easier to believe that Wyatt Earp was ringleader of a stage robbery gang than that he'd reveal such a thing to Ike Clanton. (Ike also claimed that Hill and McLaury weren't party to the scheme.) What is clear is that Ike Clanton at least thought about taking the bait; the cash reward and a chance to grab Billy Leonard's ranch would be obvious motives. But what did Wyatt Earp want? Earp never made any secret of what he was after: "I wanted the glory," he later told Judge Wells Spicer. "I had an ambition to be sheriff of this county in the next election, and I thought it would be a great help to me with the people and businessmen if I could capture the man who killed Philpot."

What, then, of Wyatt's later claim that he had come to Tombstone with a "belly full" of lawing? It's entirely possible that he believed it, that he saw the sheriff's position not so much as a law enforcement job but as a simple way of making money (that's certainly the way Behan saw it). Probably, too, he now made the connection between John Behan and the Cowboys and figured that, without the political protection given by the Sheriff's Office, the Cowboys' rustling operation would simply drift away. In this, too, he was probably right. But no matter what he said he wanted, Earp's instincts were those of a lawman, and every step he took in 1881 brought him closer to a bloody clash with the Cowboy faction.

Early on September 8, the Sandy Bob stage traveling from Tombstone to Bisbee, the little copper mining town right near the Mexican border, was robbed by two masked men. This time Doc Holliday was off the hook; in fact, it was Johnny Behan who was squarely on it when one of the bandits was heard to refer to the stolen money as "sugar"—"Give up the sugar" and "Don't hide any sugar from us"— slang for money that everyone on board knew was used by Behan's deputy, Frank Stilwell. (Levy McDaniels, the driver, claimed to recognize Stilwell despite the bandit's mask.)

News of the holdup didn't get back to Tombstone until after nine in the morning. A posse including Wyatt and Morgan Earp, Fred Dodge, and Marshall Williams was soon formed. Behan, probably humiliated at the thought of having to track down his own deputy, did not go, but Billy Breakenridge and another sheriff's deputy, a respected lawman by the name of Dave Neagle, represented his office. The group followed the outlaw's trail to the Mule Mountains, south of Tombstone, where they found an imprint of a distinctive boot heel. (Later, both Wyatt and Billy Breakenridge would claim to have discovered this clue.) A fast and nifty bit of detective work located the bootmaker in Bisbee, who identified Stilwell as a recent customer; Fred Dodge soon located Stilwell and a Cowboy associate named Pete Spence at a Bisbee corral. Stilwell, it was quickly revealed, had new boot heels.

Back in Tombstone, Virgil hauled Stilwell in front of Judge Spicer, who released him on bail. Irritated, Virgil, in his capacity as deputy U.S. marshal—the Bisbee stage had been carrying U.S. mail—arrested him again and rode him to Tucson. Maddeningly, the charges against Stilwell and Spence could not be made to stick; both were released by the end of October and would be involved in acts of vengeance against the Earps after the gunfight.

But as October came around, the Earp brothers were more worried about vigilante action than Cowboy vengeance. The Bisbee holdup had angered the law and order advocates who were tired of inexplicable escapes from Tombstone jails and of suspected stage robbers who walked for lack of hard evidence. Vigilante action was something Wyatt and Virgil were no more anxious to see than they were to see the Cowboys, though John Clum all but called for it in the *Epitaph* when he wrote that, when law enforcement failed, "the people are justified in taking the law into their own hands and ridding themselves of dangerous characters who make murder and robbery their business." Just as he had done in the cow towns of Kansas, Wyatt was forced to act as a buffer between those he was paid to protect and those he was supposed to control.

Clearly the Cowboys were concerned about the threat of vigilantes, from whom Behan would be almost powerless to protect them. Clearly, too, the Cowboys misunderstood the Earps' role in Tombstone and saw them as potential vigilante leaders. While Wyatt and Virgil were in Tucson with Stilwell and Spence, a confrontation nearly occurred between Morgan and several Cowboys on busy Allen Street, in full view of onlookers. Stuart Lake identified the group as Ike and Billy Clanton, the McLaury brothers, Milt Hicks, Joe Hill, and, making a rare appearance in Tombstone, John Ringo. "I'm telling you Earps something," Frank McLaury is said to have said, "you may have arrested Pete Spence and Frank Stilwell, but don't get it into your heads that you can arrest me. If you ever lay hands on a McLaury, I'll kill you." "If the Earps ever have occasion to come after you," Morgan is supposed to have replied, "they'll get you."

This exchange was curious for several reasons. First, Morgan wasn't an officer at the time—Virgil made him a special officer on October 17, possibly in response to the Cowboy threats. Second, as all parties were unarmed, it's doubtful that the Cowboys were out to pick a fight. They might have been pressing to find the extent of the Earps' involvement with the vigilantes. (Frank McLaury, who was probably involved in the agreement to turn over Leonard, Head, and Crane, was using the opportunity to bluster in front of his friends in case word had gotten out that he was involved.) Shortly after the harangue with Morgan, McLaury confronted Virgil. In his standard no-nonsense way, Virgil assured him that the Earps were not part of the vigilantes, who were called "stranglers" for obvious reasons. McLaury either didn't believe him or continued to put on a show: "I'll never surrender my arms to you. I'd rather be fighting than be strangled." This was a fairly safe boast on Frank's part, since, in accordance with town laws, he was unarmed.

Around this time Virgil and Wyatt's tempers must have been on the verge of breaking. Starting with the death of Fred White, the brothers had to endure the lot-jumping controversies, election fraud, a near riot in the Johnny-Behind-the-Deuce affair, Bud Philpot's murder in the Benson stage robbery, and, now, the frustration of seeing Behan's deputy walk away from obvious participation in the Bisbee stage holdup. In addition to sharing these problems with Virgil, Wyatt had a few all to himself. With the deaths of Leonard, Head, and Crane he had been unable to entirely clear Doc Holliday's name in the wake of the *Nugget*'s attacks. His marriage, or whatever relationship he had with Mattie, had fallen apart; he scarcely saw Mattie anymore, taking every opportunity to serve as a deputy or special officer and go on long posse rides or to escort prisoners to Tucson. As his relationship with Josephine became more obvious, so did John Behan's hostility. Added to all of this was the simple physical threat of the Cowboys themselves, men who had now become brazen enough to rob stages just a few miles from Tombstone, men who threatened his brothers in the streets of Tombstone.

What was becoming increasingly clear to Wyatt was that the violence escalating around Tombstone would not be addressed by local law—Behan's office was in league with the cattle rustlers—nor by the law and order faction in town—vigilante action was clumsy and ineffective and likely to cause more violence than it prevented. Nor could the Earps expect help from the federal government in the form of soldiers or more U.S. deputies. To the extent that Washington chose to involve itself, the Earp brothers *were* the U.S. government's representatives in southeast Arizona. Or at least Virgil was, and Crawley Dake in Prescott continued to indicate that he regarded Wyatt and Morgan as "my deputies" as well.

If anything was going to be done about crime and violence in Cochise County, it would have to be done by the Earps; it was that or leave and start over somewhere else. James, Virgil, Wyatt, and Morgan had all made substantial investments in mines, gambling halls, and real estate. They had also risked their lives on numerous occasions and ridden hundreds of miles in pursuit of bandits and killers. The Earps would leave Tombstone, but it would not be without a fight.

On September 19, President James Garfield died from an assassin's bullet. In his diary, George Parsons reflected the feelings of many townsfolk in Tombstone: "Sad—sad news. Despite the prayers of a Christian world, one of the greatest men the world ever saw . . . died at 10:35 last night. . . . God help the stricken household and be with this country in the present crisis. Away out here on the frontier where politics are quite generally ignored and party lines very loosely drawn, the feeling is more profound than I imagined it would be." Parsons, with crepe across his saddle, helped carry the news to the sparsely populated areas around Tombstone.

The immediate effect of Garfield's death on Arizona was to postpone the efforts to force Fremont out as governor. But on October 15, Chester A. Arthur, Garfield's successor, announced Fremont's resignation and the appointment of John J. Gosper as acting governor. A few weeks earlier Gosper had visited Tombstone and talked to both John Behan and Virgil Earp about the continued threat of the Cowboys to Mexican-American relations. His subsequent letter to U.S. Secretary of State James Blaine reveals tensions about federal versus local authority that are relevant today:

> [Behan] represented to me that the deputy U.S. marshal, resident of Tombstone, and the city marshal for the same, and those who aided him seemed unwilling to heartily cooperate with him in capturing and bringing to justice these out-laws. In conversation with the deputy U.S. marshal, Mr. Earp, I found precisely the same spirit of complaint existing against Mr. Behan (the sheriff) and his deputies.

The "and his deputies" remark at the end of the letter showed how spectacularly uninformed Gosper was: He apparently did not know that one of Behan's deputies was currently residing in a Tucson jail, arrested by Virgil Earp a week earlier for the Bisbee stage robbery. Perhaps Gosper was enlightened by a letter he received on returning to Prescott from Tombstone. Written by Joseph Bowyer of the Texas Consolidated Mining Company, it read, in part,

> The gang who are known as 'Cowboys' are engaged in stock raiding in the valleys of San Simon and Cloverdale, in the South-eastern portion of Arizona, and from good authority I learn that the cattle, horses, and sheep, now controlled by said cow-boys had been stolen from the citizens of Sonora and Arizona and New Mexico. . . . The Cowboys frequently visit our town [Galeyville] and often salute us with an indiscriminate discharge of firearms, and after indulging in a few drinks at the saloons, practice shooting at the lamps, bottles, glasses, etc., sometimes going to the length of shooting the cigar out of one's mouth.

One wonders what Gosper's reaction would have been on discovering that the leader of the cigar shooters had been an assistant tax collector for Cochise County.

Early in October, Curly Bill Brocius would perform another service for the county: host. Following a rare uprising by the usually

docile White Mountains Apaches, about forty heavily armed Tombstonians took off in pursuit. The posse included Behan, Breakenridge, Virgil, Wyatt, and Morgan Earp, Marshall Williams, and,
surprisingly, John Clum and George Parsons. (Clum's presence on
the ride was never explained; the former Indian agent probably
wanted the story for his newspaper.) Nothing came of the posse
ride—indeed, nothing more came of the expected uprising except the
initial deaths of a handful of troopers—and after a couple of hundred
grueling miles the seventeen remaining posse members found themselves at a ranch Parsons later identified as belonging to "the McLor-
ing" brothers, Tom and Frank McLaury. Parsons didn't note whether
or not the owners were at home, but their friend, Curly Bill, "Arizona's most famous outlaw at the present time," as Parsons thought,
was there.

"To show how we do things in Arizona," Parsons wrote, "I will say
that our present marshal and said 'CBill' shook each other warmly by
the hand and hobnobbed together some time, when said 'CB'
mounted is horse with his two satellites [Tom and Frank McLaury?]
rode off." Parsons's next entry would be written on October 23.
"Nothing new in these parts," he said. "Rather monotonous. I hope
this state of things won't continue long."

As if in response to Parsons, two nights later, on October 25 at about
11:00 P.M., Ike Clanton and Tom McLaury rode a wagon loaded
with beef into town and parked at the West End Corral. They had
been on the range and trail for a long time and wasted no time in
sampling Tombstone's delights. Starting with drinks at the Grand
Hotel bar, the favorite Cowboy hangout, they separated to pursue
their preferred forms of gambling. Ike liked faro; Tom thought the
odds were better at poker.

About one o'clock in the morning Ike headed for the Alhambra
and lunch (meaning simply a light meal). There, he bumped into
Doc Holliday. A verbal battle began, with Doc drawing on his considerable education to shower Clanton with abuse. What prompted
the confrontation? No one knows. A few days earlier Ike had showed
up in town and accused Wyatt of having spoken of their deal to
Holliday; an apparently surprised Wyatt denied this and sent Morgan to Tucson to fetch Doc away from Kate and the gambling tables.
When Doc returned, on October 22, he angrily denied knowing

anything of a "deal" between Wyatt and Ike. Three days later Doc's temper hadn't cooled.

What was going on? Most students of the conflict are convinced that Ike was trying to weasel out of the agreement he had made with Wyatt; most are sure that Ike was also trying to provoke a fight. In retrospect it seems insane that he would have done so, but Clanton's behavior leading up to the fight was erratic and almost increasingly dictated by liquid courage.

Something else might have spurred him. Marshall Williams, the Wells Fargo agent, let slip after a couple of drinks that he knew about the deal between Ike and Wyatt. Wyatt could hardly have made a deal involving Wells Fargo money and not have told their agent, but Williams would have had to have been drunk, stupid, or duplicitous to let that knowledge slip to Ike Clanton. Remember that Williams rode back with Behan's posse before Luther King's escape; remember, too, that Williams would soon vanish from Tombstone with absconded funds. Williams's role in the Tombstone troubles may never be known, but in retrospect he seems to have sparked a confrontation between the Earps and the Cowboys by convincing Ike that Wyatt was going to make public the agreement to hand over the Benson stage robbers. Much of what followed might be explained by Ike's panic that his comrades might find him out.

Some researchers have theorized that the Cowboys, or at least Curly Bill, already knew that Ike was betraying Leonard, Head, and Crane. Ike's likely response to their questions was that he was trying to lure Wyatt Earp into a trap. One can also picture the response Curly Bill and John Behan must have had if they found out about the deal: "You made a deal with *Wyatt Earp?* One that might get him elected *sheriff of Cochise County?* What exactly were you thinking of?" Whatever Ike was thinking of when he made his agreement with Wyatt, it's apparent that on the night of October 25 what he had in mind was a fight.

Around one o'clock in the morning, though, Ike was fairly certain he didn't want to get into a fight with Holliday. According to Ike, Doc thought Clanton had threatened the Earps and stood with his "hand in his bosom," presumably on the butt of a pistol in a shoulder holster, calling him "a son of a bitch of a Cowboy" and told Ike to "go heel [arm] yourself." (One historian has Ike saying a variation of this to Doc: "Physician, heel thyself," a pun on Holliday's medical degree, but the joke was beyond Ike's ken.) Ike replied that he was unarmed, in accordance with town laws, but Holliday would certainly have been unarmed, too. So, probably was Wyatt, who Ike would claim was standing nearby with his hand on his pistol butt. Morgan was a special policeman and could legally carry a gun; Wyatt had been acting marshal when Virgil went to Tuscon for the Stilwell-Spence trial but it's not clear that he had any legal status at all on the night of October 25.

Actually, Wyatt tried to make peace, or at least preserve it. He called Morgan over from the Alhambra bar, telling him "You're an officer, you should do something about that." Morgan told Doc and Ike to desist, and Clanton left, mouthing threats. Hostilities once again threatened to break out but, fortunately for Ike, Virgil walked out of the Occidental Saloon and let Ike and Doc know in simple terms that he would stand for no more.

That broke up the antagonists—for a few minutes. Wyatt went back to the faro game he was dealing at the Eagle Brewery. A while later, on break, he was surprised to see Ike, who asked him to step around the back of the Eagle for a talk. Warily, Wyatt agreed. Clanton, obviously drunk, then proceeded to tell Wyatt that in the morning he would have him "man for man." Wyatt claimed that he tried to placate Ike, telling him that Doc didn't want to fight him but, in his own way, merely convince Clanton that he knew nothing about a deal he had made with Wyatt. Ike would have none of it. This provided Wyatt with an opportunity to get off two of his most famous lines: He wouldn't fight him, Wyatt told Clanton, "because there is no money in it." Ike continued to bluster. Wyatt looked Ike in the eye and said, "Go home, Ike, you talk too much for a fighting man."

This is Wyatt's account, of course. That Clanton would openly challenge Earp and Holliday to a showdown borders on the fantastic, and yet, in a few hours, Clanton would be making the same threats within earshot of dozens of townspeople. Whatever was said between Earp and Clanton, Wyatt left Ike and walked down Allen Street, where he met Doc Holliday and walked with him to Doc's room in the back of Fly's Photography Studio. In less than twenty-four hours they would make this walk again, this time with hundreds of people watching.

About a half hour later, in perhaps the most famous and certainly the strangest game in the history of poker, several of the leading characters in the following day's gunfight were gathered at the Occidental Saloon for an all-night session. One wonders what the new governor, John Gosper, might have thought. His report had stressed that the county sheriff and the town and deputy U.S. marshals couldn't get together; now John Behan, Virgil Earp, Ike Clanton and Tom McLaury sat in the Occidental for nearly five hours playing poker and watching each other. What was discussed? No one knows. In later testimony, the game wasn't even mentioned. That such natural enemies could have spent nearly five hours drinking and playing poker without trying to kill each other is practically impossible to believe.

Sometime around six in the morning the game broke up. No one knows who the big winner was. Ike followed Virgil out. According to Clanton he gave the town marshal an earful to the effect that Clanton knew "he stood in with those parties that tried to murder me on the night before. I told him if that was so, that I was in town." Presumably this meant: You were trying to work up a situation where you could kill me last night, and if you want more trouble, you know where I can be found. Virgil's version of the conversation is more in line with other statements Ike had been heard to make. Virgil said Ike wanted him to carry a message to Doc Holliday: "The damned son of a bitch has got to fight." To which Virgil replied: "Ike, I am an officer and I don't want to hear you talking that way, at all. I am going down home now, to go to bed. I don't want you to raise any disturbance while I am in bed." As Virgil walked away, Ike called to him: "You won't carry the message?" Virgil yelled back: "No, of course I won't."

Virgil returned to find Allie waiting up for him. Virgil related his efforts to keep Ike and Doc from killing each other. Allie was unimpressed. "Why didn't you let 'em go ahead? Neither one amounts to much."

Ike Clanton's behavior to this point seems inexplicable. If he thought the Earps were out to murder him, as he later claimed, why not simply leave town, or at least seek the protection of his friend, Sheriff Behan? Over and over again Ike not only tried to pick a fight, he tried to pick it alone.

Instead of going to the Grand Hotel for some sleep, Ike wandered the streets of Tombstone carrying a gun, in blatant violation of city ordinance. A bartender named Ned Boyle encountered him about 8:00 A.M., in front of the telegraph office. Boyle later testified that Ike said "As soon as the Earps and Doc Holliday showed themselves on the street, the ball would be opened—that they would have to fight."

Boyle immediately went to Wyatt's house and told him what he had seen and heard. For once, Wyatt Earp was unsure of what to do; the thought was now in his mind that Ike might have wired for help, probably to Galeyville for Curly Bill Brocius and John Ringo. Wyatt stayed in bed. Ike, meanwhile, wouldn't let it go. At Julius Kelly's saloon he began haranguing listeners about what he would do to the Earps and Holliday now that he was "heeled." Kelly "cautioned him against having any trouble, as I believed the other side would also fight." And about this time, A. G. Bronk, one of Virgil's two regular deputies, knocked on his door to tell him of Clanton's threats. Practically before a cock could crow on the morning of October 26, a sizable portion of Tombstone's population knew that Ike Clanton had not only threatened to kill Doc Holliday but the town marshal and his brothers.

By noon, Ike was at the saloon on Hafford's corner—from which the Earps, in about two and a half hours, would begin their fateful walk—waving a rifle (no one was certain where it had come from) and repeating his threats to the saloon's owner. Kate Elder would later claim that a short time later she was looking at some of Camillus Fly's photos in his studio in front of the boarding house where Doc Holliday was sleeping when a man with a rifle walked in. Kate went to tell Doc that Ike had been by looking for him. "If God will let me live long enough, he will see me," said Holliday as he rose.

Now, in the early afternoon, Wyatt and Virgil came out from their homes and into the bright, clear fall air. Both wore black; both were armed. Everywhere, people came to tell them of Ike's threats. James Earp, who had managed to keep himself apart from the entire business, found Morgan, and the two went to warn Wyatt and Virgil that Ike had a Winchester rifle and a Colt revolver. Harry Jones who had switched allegiance from Behan to the Earps, also brought a warning. Wyatt told him, "I will go down and find [Ike] and see what he wants." Wyatt, it appears, was still mildly puzzled by the vehemence of Ike's reaction to a deal gone sour.

Wyatt, Virgil, and Morgan began searching for Ike—Wyatt moving down Allen Street while Virgil and Morgan looked down Fremont Street, where the fight would soon take place. Virg and Morg found him first, walking toward Allen Street. Only minutes before Mayor Clum had seen Ike, rifle in hand, and asked, sarcastically, "Hello, Ike, any new war?" Apparently Clum had no idea of what was afoot. Virgil moved up quickly behind Ike, grabbed the Winchester with his left hand, and brought the barrel of his side arm across Clanton's crown. Ike fell to the wooden sidewalk. Were you looking for us? Virgil wanted to know. Yes, replied Ike, and "If I had seen you a second sooner I'd have killed you." A few stores away, Clum and former sheriff Charlie Shibell watched.

Wyatt showed up seconds later, and the three brothers herded the rustler off to the recorder's court less than a block away. Virgil went to fetch Judge A. O. Wallace, while Wyatt and Morgan sat staring at Ike, who held a bandanna over his bleeding head. R. J. Campbell, a county clerk, later testified that Wyatt lit into Ike verbally, stating that Clanton had threatened his life "two or three times"—actually, at this point, Ike had made six recorded threats against the Earps' lives—and that he had better stop. Campbell paraphrased Wyatt's next words: "You cattle thieving son-of-a-bitch, you've threatened my life enough, and you've got to fight." According to Campbell, Ike shot back, "Fight is my racket, and all I want is four feet of ground." (His detractors would later say he had it backward; he should have said "Racket is my fight.") Campbell also testified that Ike said to Morgan Earp, "If you fellows had been a second later, I would have furnished a coroner's inquest for the town."

What, besides a great deal of alcohol, had gotten into Ike Clanton? About an hour later he would earn immortality as the man who ran from the gunfight at the O.K. Corral—though in fact it would be more accurate to say that he ran through it, fleeing the fight. Yet, practically from the moment of his arrival in Tombstone on October 25, Ike not only made repeated threats against three men—four if you count Morgan Earp—who had established reputations as shootists, he had tried to carry out those threats all alone.

Whatever was motivating Ike, Wyatt had had enough of him. After Ike's threats at the recorder's court, Wyatt openly challenged Ike for the first time: "You damned dirty cow thief," he later testified to saying, "you have been threatening our lives, and I know it. I think I would be justified in shooting you down any place I should meet you. But if you are anxious to make a fight, I will go anywhere on earth to make a fight with you—even over to the San Simon, among your own crowd." Ike responded that if he had a six-shooter he would make a fight; Wyatt and Morgan both responded by offering him his own six-gun. He was stopped from accepting it by a deputy sheriff, also named Campbell.

Judge Wallace finally appeared and fined Clanton a hefty $25 plus court costs (apparently another $2.50) for carrying a concealed weapon. According to Campbell, Virgil then asked Ike where he wanted his guns left, to which Ike responded "Anywhere I can get them." Virgil left them at the bar at the Grand Hotel, where Ike was staying.

On leaving the courthouse, a still-steamed Wyatt confronted Tom McLaury, who had just heard of Ike's predicament. No one was close enough to see for sure if McLaury was armed. There were words. Wyatt said that Tom said, "If you want to make a fight, I will make a fight with you anywhere" and Wyatt responded, "All right, make a fight right here." Then: "Jerk your gun and use it." At the same time, he used one of his favorite tactics of intimidation: He slapped McLaury with his left hand and drew his gun with his right, cracking Tom across the head.

McLaury may have just been in the wrong place at the wrong time. Most townspeople who knew the Clanton and McLaury brothers seemed to regard Tom as the least belligerent of all the brothers, but Wyatt assumed that because Tom was a friend of Ike's and came into town with him that he was there to threaten the brothers and Doc Holliday. Probably, too, Wyatt was remembering the incident with the stolen army mules and was determined not to let the McLaurys off this time. The later testimony of some witnesses indicated that Earp overreacted; A. Bauer, a local butcher, said that Tom had protested, "I am not heeled, I have got nothing to do with anybody." It was then, said Bauer, that Wyatt struck him, after which McLaury "opened his eyes up large and tumbled all over." But, then, Bauer did a great deal of illegal beef business with Tom McLaury and may have felt pressured to present testimony favorable to the Cowboys.

A bookkeeper named J. H. Batcher told a story about halfway between Bauer and Earp's. Batcher said Tom told Wyatt, "That he had never done anything against him and was a friend of his," but "whenever he wanted to make a fight, he was with him." It's difficult to believe that Tom McLaury looked straight at Wyatt Earp and said he was a friend. It's also difficult to believe that he wasn't carrying a partially concealed gun at the time of the confrontation since a bartender named Andrew Mehan testified that Tom checked a pistol with him at the Capitol Saloon shortly afterward. If Tom McLaury was armed, some have asked, why didn't Earp run him in? Possibly because Wyatt hadn't seen Tom's gun, or, even if he did, he simply wanted the Clantons and McLaurys out of town and thought his message would suffice (Wyatt didn't arrest Ike Clanton the night before when he was carrying a pistol after his argument with Holliday).

It did not. About ten minutes later, Wyatt walked into Hafford's saloon to buy a cigar, then stepped outside. Frank McLaury and Billy Clanton walked by and glared at Wyatt. About twenty minutes earlier, Doc Holliday, crossing Allen Street, had walked up to Billy Clanton, and, in the manner of a true Southern gentleman, shook the hand of the man whose brother had been threatening his life for several hours. Neither Billy nor Frank knew about the pistol whipping of their brothers at that point. They were on their way to meet their brothers at Spangenberg's gunsmith shop, a red flag that the Earps could not ignore. Wyatt wasn't the only one who knew it—at least a dozen townsfolk had gathered out in front of the gun shop.

One of the McLaurys' horses must have been curious, too, stepping up on the sidewalk—in violation of city ordinance—and poking his head through the door. Once again, as he had done so often during the Tombstone troubles, Wyatt took the initiative. Not waiting for Virgil or Morgan to arrive, he boldly walked up to the horse in full view of the onlookers and the momentarily startled Cowboys and pulled it off the sidewalk. An angry Frank rushed out of Spangenberg's and grabbed the reins from Wyatt, leading his horse back into the street. When Virgil arrived, the Earps could see the Cowboys staring at them from the shop, putting cartridges into their guns. It was now apparent that a fight could not be avoided. Virgil walked down the street to the Wells Fargo office and borrowed one of their standard short-barreled shotguns.

By now it was almost two o'clock, and there were so many people watching the Earps and the Cowboys that it's almost possible to reconstruct a minute-by-minute account of the events leading up to the fight. Here's an approximation of what onlookers saw as they saw it:

About twenty minutes after walking into Spangenberg's, the Clantons and McLaurys walk back to Hafford's, presumably where they expect Wyatt and Virgil will be standing. The staring contest continues. The Earps have good reason to believe that all the Cowboys are now armed. They do not know that Mr. Spangenberg has refused to sell Ike Clanton a gun.

Representatives of the Citizens' Safety Committee now find the Earps at Hafford's corner. They offer assistance; armed civilians are the last thing Virgil wants right now, and he politely refuses this offer of aid.

The Cowboys walk west from the Dunbar Corral to the O.K. Corral. Their purpose is not certain. They stop for a few minutes to confer; this is when Mr. Sills, the man we met in our Preface, overhears them. Sills is alarmed and seeks out Virgil Earp to tell him of the Cowboy threats. Virgil then spots John Behan in the gathering crowd and asks him to take a quick drink at Hafford's. Virgil asks Behan to come with them and "disarm these parties." Behan refuses, saying there would be a fight if the Earps "went down there."

Virgil reassures them that there will be no trouble so long as the Cowboys stay in the O.K. Corral—it is not illegal to carry firearms in a livery stable. But, "if they come out on the street, I will take their arms off and arrest them." Which means if the Cowboys had stayed in the O.K. Corral, there would have been no gunfight at the O.K. Corral (which, of course, wasn't at the O.K. Corral).

While they are talking, a stockbroker named William Murray approaches Virgil and tells him he can get "twenty-five armed men at a moment's notice." Behan, apparently, understands that there is now a strong possibility of vigilante action. This spurs him. He goes off immediately to talk to the Clantons and McLaurys.

Behan would later testify that he told the Clantons and the McLaurys that "there was likely to be some trouble and I proposed to disarm everybody having arms." Frank McLaury, who appeared to set the tone for the Cowboys, refused, saying that "he did not intend to have any trouble" but that "he would not (give up his arms) without those other people being disarmed." That the town marshal and his deputies would have to give up their weapons to please Frank

McLaury should immediately have struck the county sheriff as ludicrous.

Then, probably at about 2:30, Doc Holliday, clad in a long overcoat, walks up the street to Hafford's. Doc has a cane in his left hand; no explanation for it has ever been offered. Doc asks where the brothers are going. "Down the street to make a fight," Wyatt responds. Doc volunteers to go along. "This is our fight," said Wyatt. "There's no call for you to mix in." Doc is indignant: "That's a hell of a thing for you to say to me."

It is not recorded that Virgil actually deputized Doc. Later, Virgil would come under much criticism for taking along so notorious a gunman. At the time, faced with an unknown number of armed Cowboys, taking Doc Holliday along seemed like an excellent idea.

Besides, Virgil and Morgan knew that Wyatt's words, "This is our fight," were patently false. Not only was Holliday the focus of Ike's threats, the Cowboys were, almost as Wyatt and Doc were speaking, waiting next to Doc's room in the lot in back of the O.K. Corral and next to Fly's Photography Studio. For what, exactly? It appears that a couple of the Cowboys wanted a crack at Holliday first. But who, besides Ike, wanted to fight? At this point the Cowboys seem divided and uncertain.

At about 2:45, Virgil hands Doc Holliday his shotgun and takes Doc's cane. His reasoning is that he will cause less of a disturbance if he walks to the lot without the weapon. (Holliday can conceal it under his coat.)

In the lot, the Cowboys are jumpy. William Cuddy, a theatrical manager, later testified he looked into the lot and that Billy Clanton, seeing him, "put his hand on his pistol, as if in fear of somebody."

The Earps and Holliday begin their walk—one that would be imitated by so many movie and TV actors that it has become a ritual of Hollywood westerns. On reaching the corner of Fremont, they turn left, west. A cold wind pulls back the flap of Holliday's coat, revealing the shotgun to an onlooker.

All four squint toward the lot next to Fly's: How many men are in there? As Virgil passes Bauer's meat market, he sees six; the Clantons and the McLaurys, Billy Claiborne, a Cowboy associate, and John Behan. They may have been told that Wes Fuller, another Cowboy associate, had been there a short time before.

Behan runs up to them and says, or so he later claimed, "I am the sheriff of this county, and I am not going to allow any trouble if I can help it." But he couldn't help it. "I am going down to disarm them," Virgil says. Wyatt later testified that Behan said, "I have disarmed them," and that on hearing this he took out his long-barreled pistol, "which I had in my hand, under my coat, and put it in my overcoat pocket." The Earp party brushes past Behan at a pace, a housewife in Bauer's butcher shop would later say, "as any gentleman would walk, not fast, or very slow." She hears someone on the street yell "Here they come!"

The Earps and Holliday turn the corner into the lot. Nine men and two horses are suddenly in a lot perhaps eighteen feet wide. The Cowboys, for all the warnings that the Earps were coming, still seem to be taken by surprise, as if they can not believe that the moment of confrontation they had been calling for for nearly two years is finally at hand.

Witnesses friendly to the Cowboys will testify that someone in the Earp party said, "You sons of bitches, you have been looking for a fight and you can have it." Everyone heard Virgil Earp say "Throw up your hands." John Behan added that Virgil also said, "I have come to disarm you." Whatever Virgil says is followed by a click-click sound, probably the sound of Frank McLaury and Billy Clanton pulling the hammers back on their single-action Colts. Tom McLaury has his hand on a Winchester rifle on his saddle. Billy Claiborne starts to run.

Then, to borrow the words of Ike Clanton, the ball opened. Wyatt Earp, the most famous gunfighter of the Old West, the very symbol of a "gunfighter nation," draws his gun in a fight for the first and only time in his life.

Two shots ring out so close together that they almost seem to be fired simultaneously. Then, there is a brief lull as the bark of the revolver shots echoes off the sides of nearby buildings. The first two shots immediately send a haze of gray smoke around the lot; the horses scream and try to bolt. Virgil switches the cane to his left hand and draws his gun. Then comes a torrent of bullets and two loads of buckshot, echoing around the town like a string of super loud firecrackers. Men groan in agony—first, Frank McLaury, a bullet in his stomach, then Billy Clanton.

Ike Clanton, stunned by the sudden turn of events, charges up to Wyatt Earp, screaming something; it appears that the man who tried so hard to instigate this fight is unarmed. Wyatt yells, "This fight has commenced, go to fighting, or get away." Ike elects to get away. Wyatt turns and resumes firing, calm as a man cracking off rounds at a target. Frank McLaury and Billy Clanton, severely wounded, resume the fight. Virgil Earp is hit in the calf and goes down. Somebody shoots at Morgan Earp and hits him across the shoulder blades—is it Tom McLaury firing over the saddle of his horse? In the noise and smoke and confusion, no one can tell. Wyatt moves over to Morgan and yells for him to stay down, moving in front to shield him.

Tom's horse bolts; the sound of a shotgun is added to the din. Tom is mortally wounded.

Wyatt and Virgil each take aim and hit Billy Clanton, who staggers back against a wall and collapses. Frank McLaury also staggers, but forward, into Fremont Street, still holding his horse's reins. He takes aim at Doc Holliday and grunts, "I have you now, you sonuvabich." Doc gets off perhaps the best line of his life. "Blaze away," he says, "you're a daisy if you do." (So much conversation in so short a fight!) Frank fires at Doc, and the bullet grazes his hip. Morgan and Doc both fire; Frank, it was later said, would have died from either bullet. He died in the middle of what is now U.S. Highway 80.

The fight is over. It has lasted perhaps thirty seconds. Everyone has been hit except Wyatt. The thick cloud of gun smoke hangs like fog in the cold air and, slowly, people come out to examine the wounded and dead.

A whistle goes off from the Vizina mine. Apparently the vigilantes have been organized the whole time. The whistle is a signal, and within a couple of minutes scores of armed men appear on the scene.

John Behan pokes his head out of Fly's studio, where he has spent the brief gunfight. He speaks not to Virgil, the Marshal, but to Wyatt: "I want to see you."

"I won't be arrested now," Wyatt replies.

Citizens who hadn't heard the gunshots or heard the shouting awoke the next morning to the headline in the *Tombstone Epitaph*: "Three Men Hurled into Eternity . . ." The rest of the country had to wait a day or so to get the news. Tombstone, as George Parsons noted in his diary, was the U.S. town farthest from New York by rail or telegraph. It took two days for news of the gunfight, or streetfight, as it came to be called, to reach New York City. *The New York Times* of October 28, 1881, gave the incident the middle of page two status (to illustrate how fixated the Northeast was with the Southwest, there were two other stories about Arizona on page two). The *Times* did a fairly good job of getting the facts right, except for calling Doc "Judge Holliday."

Back in Tombstone, it was as if a huge bomb had dropped. Townsfolk had always derived so much humor from their town "having a man for breakfast" image when they had to endure little more than the occasional shooting among drunken gamblers; even Curly Bill's shooting of Marshall White was seen in this light. After all, most of the real violence had occurred *around* Tombstone or just south of the border in Mexico. As a result, it was easy to rationalize the killings or to ignore them altogether. Now, because of twenty-seven seconds, Tombstone had lived up to its name and would be forever synonymous with frontier violence.

The storm was only beginning. By the summer of the following year, John Behan would be the only major player remaining in Tombstone, and Wyatt Earp and Doc Holliday the only other principals left alive and unmaimed.

Notes

1. Jeff Morey is of the opinion that Holliday earned his bad press in New Mexico by winning money from some influential people. Remember, too, he was credited with two gunfights there but arrested for neither.

2. Tombstone historian Ben Traywick adds that Doc is popularly credited with having killed a gambler and a soldier at Fort Griffin, but that there are no records of any kind to back up the stories.

3. In his 1928 book, *Helldorado*, Billy Breakenridge invents a bogus *Nugget* story about King's escape that finishes with the line "He [King] was an important witness against Holliday." A generation of Earp debunkers quoted the passage and built cases against Holliday without realizing that King's being an impotant witness against Doc was Billy's invention.

4. Ben Sippy's name did, however, pop up again, a little more

than one hundred years later, as the dime-store novel writer in Larry McMurtry's Billy the Kid novel, *Anything for Billy*.

5. Jeff Morey has collected most of Brown's *San Diego Union* columns as well as numerous tidbits on her life and career in a paper for the Arizona Historical Society. In addition to her newspaper stories, Brown wrote for *The Californian*, the San Francisco monthly magazine that helped establish the careers of Bret Harte and Mark Twain, and was a member of both the Los Angeles and New York press clubs. After the death of Theodore Brown, she married Edward S. Ellis, the author of numerous works for children, in 1900. Clara Brown outlived Wyatt Earp by six years, dying in Los Angeles in 1935.

6. The telegram was signed by a Wells Fargo official, L. F. Rowell, and is dated June 7. Modern readers will note that Wells Fargo was, in effect, putting a price on the head of a man who had yet to be convicted in a court of law.

6

Wyatt Earp on Trial

L ot 2, block 17, in back of the O.K. Corral fronting Fremont Street, was thick with gun smoke, dust, and the anguished cries of wounded men and animals. As the echoes of the gunshots faded, the sounds of running footsteps and slamming gates—Ike Clanton and Billy Claiborne fleeing the premises—were heard by citizens poking their heads out of windows and doors.

"What in hell did you let Ike Clanton get away like that for, Wyatt?" asked Doc Holliday.

"He wouldn't jerk his gun," replied Earp.

Morgan's shoulder wound was potentially serious but not severely painful; Virgil's calf wound was relatively insignificant but extremely painful. Wyatt saw that his brothers were cared for, and then, with Doc and Fred Dodge, made his way up Fremont.[1] As John Behan approached, "Wyatt," he announced, "I'm arresting you." "For what?" replied the indignant Earp. "For murder," said the sheriff.

"Behan," said Wyatt, "you threw us. You told us you had disarmed those rustlers. You lied to throw us off and get us murdered. *You* arrest *me*? Not today. Not tomorrow either."

It's a good speech, albeit one that Wyatt and/or Stuart Lake had nearly half a century to prepare. But if Wyatt's words weren't quite so scriptlike at the time, he did say something impressive. Ruben Coleman, who witnessed the exchange, remembered it as "I won't be arrested. You deceived me, Johnny, you told me they were not armed. I won't be arrested, but I am here to answer what I have done. I am not going to leave town." Fred Dodge recalled that, "Wyatt was cool and collected as usual, and was quietly giving directions for the removal of Morg and Virg to their home." When Behan threatened to arrest Earp, "Wyatt looked at him for two or three seconds and then told him—more forcibly than I had ever heard Wyatt talk before—that any decent officer could arrest him. But that Johnny Behan or any of his kind must not try it." At least one other bystander, Sylvestor B. Comstock, overheard the conversation and leapt to Wyatt's defense, saying, "There is no hurry in arresting this man. He done just right in killing them, and the people will uphold him." Well, some of the people would and some of them wouldn't.

What exactly had Behan been trying to do by telling the Earps that the Cowboys were unarmed? Perhaps Behan meant "I've been down there to disarm them," as in, "This is my jurisdiction, please, let me handle it." Whatever he was saying or trying to say, Behan wasn't being honest about his success in disarming the Cowboys. At least two of the group were armed, three if one counts Tom McLaury, who was seen to have had a Winchester rifle within reach of his horse. Behan probably wouldn't have minded seeing the Earps gunned down, but he certainly had an interest in preventing a fight where some of his allies could be killed. It's safe to surmise that contrary to Wyatt's understandable suspicions, the sheriff wasn't trying to set up an ambush.

No evidence has ever been discovered that reveals a criminal conspiracy between the sheriff and the Cowboys. It's obvious that Behan was a great deal friendlier with a group of known cattle thieves and stage robbers—remember his own deputy, Frank Stilwell—than even a glad-handing local politician need be. From a distance it would seem that Behan was simply one more local Democrat in southeastern Arizona who received support from the Cowboy faction in return for ignoring illegal activities, particularly illegal activities that much of the community was tolerant of. Also, we don't know how much Behan knew about Wyatt and Josephine and whether this might have fueled a desire for revenge. Whatever Behan's motives, Billy Allen, a friend of the Clantons and McLaurys, would later testify, perhaps with some irritation, that Behan "did not use any very great exertion" to keep the Earp party out of the lot.

It has been asked why, if the Earps thought Behan had disarmed the Cowboys, they continued their walk to the lot. The obvious reason is that they were the town law, and if Behan hadn't disarmed the Cowboys there was every reason for them to go, while if Behan had disarmed them, there was not reason not to. Whether they trusted Behan or not, the Earps were going to that lot. But it was Wyatt who went there with his hand on the butt of his gun.

From a distance, the quarrel between the Earps and John Behan seems like the result of the inherent confusion built in to the territorial system of law enforcement. Precisely who had jurisdiction on the afternoon of October 26, 1881, County Sheriff John Behan or Town Marshal Virgil Earp? If Behan, then did Virgil's position as deputy U.S. marshal give him authority over the county sheriff?

When the Cochise County troubles are looked at from our perspective, it's easy to conclude that both parties failed to communicate and cooperate, but it wasn't that simple. The Earps were accustomed to close cooperation with between levels of law enforcement—town, county, federal, even private companies such as Wells Fargo. John Behan was a politician, and on the afternoon of October 26 he was playing the angles. It has been argued that the Cowboys were in the process of leaving town when the Earps and Holliday came down Fremont, but it's difficult to maintain that argument in the face of numerous threats on the lives of the Earps that were overheard by several disinterested parties. Moreover, it has never been sufficiently explained just what the Cowboys were doing waiting so long next to the building where Doc Holliday lived and had, only a short time before, been sleeping. (It also hasn't been explained why, if they were leaving town, they didn't reclaim the guns the Earps had taken from them.)

Most likely, they were arguing as to what their next move would be, with Tom McLaury making the sensible suggestion that they get out quickly before trouble started. (Remember that Wyatt later claimed that Ike and Frank McLaury were in on the deal to deliver Leonard, Head, and Crane for the Wells Fargo reward money.) Billy Claiborne, the Cowboys' friend, was probably just sitting in on the conversation, though the Earps, hearing that Claiborne was in the lot, had no way of knowing what his role in the affair might be. For that matter, they could not be sure if Wes Fuller was armed and ready to fight for his pals.

One wishes to shout back through the decades and through the tangle of argument and debate and simply ask Behan, "Why did you not simply arrest the Cowboys, if not for carrying weapons in town in defiance of city ordinance then for threatening the lives of the town's peace officers?" Or, since the Clantons and McLaurys were obviously his allies, why not arrest them just to keep them out of trouble? Behan's actions in this moment of crisis illustrate how out of his depth he was in the office of sheriff. Later, fumbling for an excuse, he would claim that "At the time I left the McLaurys and Clantons. I considered the Clanton party under arrest, but I doubt whether they considered themselves under arrest or not, after I turned to meet the other party."

He doubted whether they considered themselves under arrest or not? He, the county sheriff, wasn't sure? But he was sure the Cowboys hadn't given their guns to him. They not only refused to do so, but, as Behan would later admit, Frank McLaury said he wouldn't give up his gun "without those other people," the Earps and Doc Holliday, "being disarmed." In light of what was to follow, this deserves careful consideration: Frank McLaury, carrying a gun in violation of town law, refused to surrender it to the county sheriff unless the town marshal gave up his gun first.

And, so, failing to disarm a group of armed cattle rustlers making threats on the life of the chief of police, Behan then "turned to meet the other party." The only result of Behan's actions was to deter the town's officers from doing their duty. That, and possibly to touch off the gunfight by causing the Earps to react when they saw that the Cowboys had guns after all.

If some Earp partisans are to be believed, Behan's actions against the brothers took a more direct form immediately after the fight. Some believe he seized a pistol belonging to Tom McLaury, the absence of which would allow the Cowboy faction to make the claim that the Earps and/or Holliday fired on an unarmed man. In any event, there was no pistol beside Tom when a crowd of people rushed out to tend to the wounded. It was then that a whistle went off; it was from the mine's hoisting works and signaled the town's vigilante group. Some of the vigilantes must have been in the party that approached Virgil before the fight and asked if they could help. Receiving a polite but firm no from the Marshal, they waited to see if they were needed. They were not, but Wyatt, his brothers, and Doc must have found their presence reassuring afterward, as they had expended nearly all their ammunition in the fight.

Frank McLaury lay dead in the street; the wound he received from Wyatt finished him, but the kill was a shot from either Morgan or Doc. Astonishingly, Billy Clanton and Tom McLaury were still alive. Camillus S. Fly ran from his photography studio and took the gun from the hand of the dying Billy. (It was probably Fly, who, in a few hours, would photograph Billy, along with Frank and Tom McLaury, rouged and tuxedoed, in their coffins. The photo would become one of the most famous images of the Wild West.) One account has the youngest Clanton gamely asking for "more car-tridges" while spitting up blood. Another has him crying to onlook-ers, "Take off my boots. I promised my mother I wouldn't die with by boots on" (that is, in a fight). *Tombstone Nugget* acting editor Richard Rule and Wes Fuller carried Billy into a nearby building where, according to the *Nugget*, "just before breathing his last, he said, 'Goodbye, boys, go away and let me die.' " This sounds too much like words Rule scripted for him. A local carpenter who helped a doctor inject morphine into Clanton said that "He kicked, screamed, and twisted horribly, saying 'They have murdered me, I have been murdered.' "

Tom McLaury was carried in and placed next to Billy. He died without a word. The coroner, Henry M. Matthews, found nearly $3,000 in cash, checks, and deposits on him. It's likely that some of that money had been picked up on a trip to Bauer's butcher shop just minutes before the gunfight and was given in return for Mexican cattle.

Kate Elder, writing some fifty years later, would claim that Doc went back to his room at Fly's boarding house where he sat on his bed and cried, "Oh, this is just awful—awful." He then pulled up his shirt to wash the wound, a red scrape about two inches long, on his hip. The part about the wound sounds real, but Doc crying on his bed over a man he just killed sounds like Kate trying to soften Doc's image for posterity.[2]

Finn Clanton, absent for much of the famous action around Tombstone, once again missed the show. He rode into town later, went to see Billy's body at the morgue, and checked into the jail to spend the night, under guard, with Ike.

On the evening of October 26, perhaps four hours after the streetfight, John Behan called on Virgil Earp at his home. As might be imagined, Virgil was testy, and sharp words were spoken. Behan would later make an amazing accusation: At that meeting, said Behan, Virgil accused him of trying to incite the vigilantes to hang the Earps. Later, Virgil denied making this statement, and none of the others present, including James and the wives of the four brothers, remembered hearing such a ridiculous charge. The vigilantes, of course, were vociferously pro-Earp, and Virgil's fear at this point was not that they would turn on him and his brothers but that he couldn't continue to keep them on a short leash.

John Behan was trying to instigate something, and in a short time, he would succeed.

The morning of October 27, 1881, started out well for Wyatt Earp and Doc Holliday. The *Epitaph*'s feature story was headlined "Three Men Hurled into Eternity in the Duration of a Moment." John Clum either wrote or edited an account in which "Wyatt Earp stood up and fired in rapid succession, as cool as a cucumber, and was not hit. Doc Holliday was as calm as though at target practice and fired rapidly."

Amazingly, Tombstone's other major paper, the *Nugget*, also printed an account favorable to the Earps: "The 26th of October, 1881, will always be marked as one of the crimson days in the annals of Tombstone, a day when blood flowed as water, and human life was held as a shuttlecock, a day always to be remembered as witnessing the bloodiest and deadliest streetfight that has ever occurred in this place, or probably in the Territory." Apparently the *Epitaph* wasn't the only Tombstone paper given to purple prose. The story went on:

> It was now about two o'clock, and at this time Sheriff Behan appeared upon the scene and told Marshal Earp that if he disarmed his posse, composed of Morgan and Wyatt Earp, and Doc Holliday, he would go down to the O.K. Corral, where Ike and Billy Clanton and Frank and Tom McLowry were and disarm them. The marshal did not desire to do this until assured that there was no danger of an attack from the other party.
>
> The sheriff went to the corral and told the Cowboys that they must put their arms away and not have any

trouble. Ike Clanton and Tom McLowry said they were not armed, and Frank McLowry said he would not lay his aside. In the meantime the marshal had concluded to go and, if possible, end the matter by disarming them, and as he and his posse came down Fremont Street towards the corral, the sheriff stepped out and said: "Hold up boys, don't go down there or there will be trouble; I have been down there to disarm them." But they passed on, and when within a few feet of them the marshal said to the Clantons and McLowrys: "Throw up your hands boys, I intend to disarm you."

As he spoke Frank McLowry made a motion to draw his revolver, when Wyatt Earp pulled his and shot him, the ball striking on the right side of his abdomen. About the same time Doc Holliday shot Tom McLowry in the right side, using a short shotgun, such as is carried by Wells-Fargo & Co.'s messengers. In the meantime Billy Clanton had shot at Morgan Earp, the ball passing through the left shoulder blade across his back, just grazing the backbone and coming out at the shoulder, the ball remaining inside of his shirt. He fell to the ground but in an instant gathered himself, and raising in a sitting position fired at Frank McLowry as he crossed Fremont Street, and at the same instant Doc Holliday shot at him, both balls taking effect, either of which would have proved fatal, as one struck him in the right temple and the other in the left breast. As he started across the street, however, he pulled his gun on Holliday saying, "I've got you now." "Blaze away! You're a daisy if you do," replied Doc. This shot of McLowry's passed through Holliday's pocket, just grazing the skin.

While this was going on Billy Clanton had shot Virgil Earp in the right leg, the ball passing through the calf, inflicting a severe flesh wound. In turn he had been shot by Morgan Earp in the right side of the abdomen, and twice by Virgil Earp, once in the right wrist and once in the left breast. Soon after the shooting commenced Ike Clanton ran through the O.K. Corral, across Allen Street into Kellogg's saloon, and thence into Toughnut Street,

where he was arrested and taken to the county jail. The
firing altogether didn't occupy more than twenty-five seconds, during which time thirty shots were fired.

This is a balanced and fairly accurate account of what happened from
the moment the Earps left Hafford's saloon. What is startling about
it is that it was published in the *Nugget*, the paper that supported
Behan and the Cowboys. The story not only corroborates most of
the Earps' later testimony, it vindicates the Earps and Holliday completely. Yet, this important document was lost for nearly one hundred
years and was not referenced by any Earp chronicler until recently.[3]
    Why would the anti-Earp *Nugget* have printed such an account,
and from whom did they get their information? The answer to the
second question is simple: John Behan. Harry Woods was out of
town at the time, and the story was probably written by Richard
Rule, a future *Nugget* editor, who could not have written the story
without Behan's firsthand knowledge of what happened. Why would
Behan give an account so favorable to the Earps? Because it was the
truth as he saw it, and because he hadn't had time to formulate
another account. As soon as they did have time to make a plan,
however, Harry Woods and Behan printed a new story.

There was no time at which the majority of Tombstonians were not
behind the Earps, but a shift in at least a segment of the citizenry
could be detected the day after the gunfight when the bodies of Billy
Clanton and the McLaury Brothers were on display at Ritter and
Ream's Undertakers. The bodies were propped up in the window
beneath a sign that said, Murdered in the Streets of Tombstone. A
few townsmen did business with the Cowboys, and some of them
were particularly fond of Tom McLaury, by far the most amiable of
the bunch. Had the slain Cowboys been, say, Curly Bill Brocius, the
killer of Marshal Fred White, or John Ringo, whose reputation was
as unsavory as Doc Holliday's, there might have been no repercussions in the community. But Billy Clanton and the McLaurys owned
property and, hence, a modicum of respectability, and they made
money for the town. More importantly, they were allied with Harry
Woods, the *Nugget*, and John Behan.
    Thousands turned out for the funeral, which, according to the
Nugget, "was the largest ever witnessed in Tombstone." It probably

was, surpassing the two thousand or so who came to Fred White's funeral. Clara Brown, writing a dispatch for the *San Diego Tribune*, thought much of the sentiment misplaced: "No one could witness this sight without realizing the solemnity of the occasion, but such a public manifestation of sympathy from so large a portion of residents of the camp seemed reprehensible when it is remembered that the deceased were nothing more or less than thieves."

The town's brass band led the procession, which was two blocks long. The funeral march ended at Tombstone's celebrated Boot Hill, where Clanton was placed in a solitary grave while the McLaurys were buried together. Tombstone had always had an attitude of black humor toward its own image, an attitude that as best expressed on some of its headstones. One of the most quoted read:

> Here lies Lester Moore,
> Four slugs from a forty-four,
> No less, no more.

There was nothing humorous, however, about this funeral. George Parsons, as usual, caught the mood in his journal: "A bad time yesterday when Wyatt, Virgil, and Morgan Earp with Doc Holliday had a streetfight. Bad blood has been brewing for some time, and I was not surprised at the outbreak. It is only a wonder it has not happened before." Parsons noted that some townsfolk feared a raid by the Cowboys in reprisal, but this was unlikely considering how many vigilantes were armed and ready and in no apologetic mood for what had happened in back of the O.K. Corral. Still, thought Parsons, "The worst is not yet over, some think."

Clara Brown, too, saw public opinion as divided "as to the justification of the killing. You may meet one man who will support the Earps, and declare that no other cause was possible to save their own lives, and the next man is just as likely to assert that there was no occasion whatever for bloodshed, and that this will be a warm place for the Earps hereafter."

Parsons and Brown's intuitions were deadly accurate. Wyatt Earp was in a similar position to the one he had been in after the shooting of George Hoy in Dodge City three years earlier: The members of the community who should have supported him wholeheartedly were afraid that the shootout was bad for business. Who would now want to come all the way to this sprawling mining camp in the mountains near the Mexican border in Apache country and invest their Eastern money? Clara Brown even wrote home about an Eastern business-man who had just missed being shot by a stray bullet: "He left for home on the next train, and will probably convey the impression that the notorious camp is a den of cutthroats, when in reality, a man had not been shot for many months prior to this tragedy." Mrs. Brown might have added that the shock of Marshall White's death and the killing of Bud Philpot perhaps 20 miles outside of town were still fresh in the minds of many.

There was one substantial difference between Wyatt's situation in Tombstone and the one in Dodge after Hoy was shot. In Kansas, Earp was surrounded by sympathetic supporters and was part of a police force so formidable that any kind of organized reprisal was unlikely. The situation in Tombstone was admirably summed up in one of Clara Brown's dispatches:

> While there are many people of the highest order sojourn-ing here [in Tombstone], whose business is honorable and whose voices are always heard on the side of law and or-der, there yet remains a large element of unscrupulous personages, some outwardly regardless of restraining in-fluences, and others [more than one would suspect] se-cretly in sympathy with the "Cowboys," acting in collu-sion with them. Even the officers of the law have not escaped the stigma of shielding these outlaws, some of them being believed to have accepted bribes to insure their silence.

No journalist covered Tombstone with greater clarity than Clara Brown, but the irony is that her dispatches on Arizona were read in California and in other Western towns whose papers reprinted them, but not in Tombstone or anywhere else in Arizona. Decades later, researchers digging in libraries and museums would find copies of the *Epitaph* and the *Nugget*, but none of them carried Brown's work. The observations of the finest journalist in Tombstone went unregarded by historians for more than a century.[4]

*   *   *

The coroner's inquest into the streetfight in Tombstone began on October 28. In the two days since the fight, Sheriff Behan had remembered all sorts of thing he had neglected to disclose to the newspaper owned by his friend and undersheriff. Behan now claimed to have heard Billy Clanton yell out, "Don't shoot me, I don't want to fight" when the Earp party began shooting and that Tom McLaury screamed, "I have got nothing" and pulled open his blouse to reveal that he was unarmed. This was tantamount to a charge of murder, and since everyone knew Virgil Earp had entered the lot with a cane in his hand, the charge was directed, partly, at Morgan Earp, but mostly at Behan's political and romantic rival, Wyatt.

Behan also claimed that when he confronted Virgil Earp at Hafford's Corner he had asked him what all the excitement was about and Virgil replied that there "was a lot of (I think sons-of-bitches) who wanted to make a fight.' I said to Virgil, 'It is your duty as a peace officer to stop this thing, and I want you to do it. I am going to try.' I said, 'I am going down to arrest and disarm the Cowboys.'" Behan was now relinquishing, his jurisdictional authority by telling Virgil that "It is *your* duty phasis mine] to stop this thing." Behan, the county sheriff, was calling this a town matter. Saying he would attempt to stop the trouble only if the Earps would not. According to Behan, Virgil refused; Behan, if he is to be believed, attempted to disarm the Cowboys only after Virgil refused. According to Behan, then, Virgil wanted a fight.

Is it possible Behan misinterpreted Virgil Earp's words and actions, or was he simply lying? Subsequent events suggest the latter. Virgil did refrain from arresting the Cowboys while they were in the O.K. Corral, since it was not illegal to carry firearms there, where one might be preparing to leave town. He acted only when it was apparent that the Cowboys, at least two of whom were armed and a third with a rifle at arm's length, were loitering by the boarding house where Doc Holliday lived and had no intention of leaving town. Virgil's reasoning was sound: If the Cowboys were leaving, as Ike Clanton and his friends would later claim, why hadn't they retrieved the weapons they had checked upon entering town? To leave town without one's arms would have been unthinkable. Further, once Virgil did decide to act, he took pains not to provoke the Cowboys. He had Doc Holliday (whose primary function was to watch for an ambush) carry the shotgun, while he entered the lot with a cane, not a gun, in his hand and everyone heard him say "I've come to disarm you" or something close to it.

Ike Clanton testified next. He and his brother Billy and the McLaurys, he said, were on their way out of town and attending to some important business (business so important that both Ike and Tom forgot to reclaim their guns). When the Earps appeared, "Frank McLaury and Billy Clanton threw up (their hands); Tom McLaury threw open his coat and said he had nothing; they said you sons of bitches have come here to make a fight. At the same instant Doc Holliday and Morgan Earp shot." This was much like Behan's own testimony, and, considering that the two would later hire a lawyer together, it's likely that they had done a bit of rehearsing.

Up to now, Ike was doing fine, but he kept on talking and thus began to undo the Cowboys' case. He admitted problems with the Earps—this certainly meant the busted deal over Leonard, Head, and Crane, his run-in with Virgil, and probably the one with Doc, too—but that there "was nothing between the Earps and the boys that were killed. The Earps and myself had a transaction which made them down on me"—meaning Leonard, Head, and Crane—"they don't like me." Ike was telling the truth about the deal going awry and the Earps not liking him (though *contempt* might have been more accurate than dislike), but he was being disingenuous about the Earps having no problems with the "boys" who were killed. Billy Clanton had stolen Wyatt's horse; Frank and Tom McLaury had stolen army mules and had the temerity to threaten Virgil, a U.S. deputy marshal, for investigating the theft; and the McLaurys had also had a run in with Morgan following the mule incident. They were known friends of Curly Bill Brocius, the man who had killed the Earps' friend, Marshall White—recall that Bill was staying at their place when an Earp posse had stopped at the McLaury ranch. The Earps had good reason to believe that they had participated in the election fraud aimed at keeping their friend, Pima County Sheriff Bob Paul, out of office, and, since the Clantons and McLaurys clearly had been receiving stolen Mexican cattle, the Earps had every reason to believe that they had participated in killing Mexicans across the border. And, obviously, Ike and possibly Frank were friendly with the stagecoach robbers Leonard, Head, and Crane. The Earps also knew that they had been wearing guns, threatening their lives, and waiting outside of Doc Holliday's boarding house the day of the shootout. What Ike didn't explain—in fact, never explained—was why, if the Earps' animosity was directed solely at him, they didn't simply kill him [Ike] and have done with it.

Billy Claiborne's testimony was much the same as Behan and Clanton's. In his testimony, the only surprise was that he had caught a bullet through the pants leg and his most damaging against the Earps was that Doc Holliday fired the first shot "with a nickel-plated six-shooter"—Doc was well known for his nickel-plated revolver. (Behan had been saying he did not know who in the Earp crowd carried a nickel-plated gun, but he as being disingenuous—everyone knew.)

From the remaining witnesses, there were numerous curious comments. R. F. Coleman, a mining man, testified that he had warned Sheriff Behan to "disarm those men, I thought they meant mischief." He also said that he was not in position to see if the Cowboys threw up their hands when ordered, "except Billy Clanton," whose hand "was on his left hip," as if in the act of drawing. "This was after the first two shots were fired." P. H. Fellehy, a laundry owner, made a statement that was potentially far more damaging to the Earps than Behan or Clanton's because he was supposedly neutral: Virgil Earp, he said, told Behan that "Those men (the Cowboys) have made their threats. I will not arrest them but will kill them on sight." This pretty much corroborates Behan's testimony. Yet, incredibly, Fellehy was not called later, before Judge Wells Spicer, to repeat the charge later. The only explanation would seem to be that Fellehy changed his mind or that the prosecution, after interviewing him, did not consider him a reliable enough witness. His testimony accusing Virgil of saying he would kill the Cowboys on sight would seem to be in direct contradiction to Virgil's actions, since, as nearly everyone agreed, Virgil's first action on entering the lot was to announce that he was there to disarm the Clantons and the McLaurys.

Martha J. King, a housewife, was in Bauer's butcher shop when the Earp party passed on the way to the lot. Mrs. King heard someone say "There they come," meaning the Earps and Holliday, then heard one of the Earps say "Let them have it!" Mrs. King testified that Doc Holliday, the only one in the group she knew, said "All right." Much has been made of these comments over the years. Some students of the fight are convinced that the first speaker was Morgan Earp, but there is no evidence to support that. If Morgan Earp said something to incite Holliday, Virgil Earp would certainly have admonished him and reminded him who was in charge. Morgan might have said it, but it was likely part of a longer conversation, only part of which Mrs. King heard—something along the lines of "If they make a move for their guns, or to seek cover, *let them have it.*" If this was the case, it was probably Virgil Earp who said "Let them have it," as he was the one who gave Holliday the shotgun.

All of these statements come from the coroner's inquest. Since it was highly irregular to hold an inquest on a shooting without consulting the policemen involved, some have speculated as to why none of the Earps were called. The simplest answer is that the following day Ike Clanton filed murder charges, and further testimony gathering from the coroner was irrelevant.

On October 31, Wyatt Earp began the bitterest legal fight of his life.

Everyone around the world with an interest in the American West has heard of the gunfight at the O.K. Corral. But until recent years the accounts of what happened were tainted with partisan interest or by outright fraud. This is largely due to the handiwork of Billy Breakenridge, John Behan's on-and-off deputy in 1880–81, whom all chroniclers of the Earp story relied upon before Stuart Lake's *Frontier Marshal* was published in 1931. Lake's version of the gunfight was accepted till the great wave of Earp debunking began around 1960; subsequent historians then rejected Lake and returned to the views of Breakenridge. Three years of research have led me, to my surprise, to the conclusion that Lake's account of what happened is more accurate than those of all the Earp debunkers that followed. Lake was a professional journalist and, rather than relying on "Uncle Ned" history, he sought primary documents as sources. He found that the transcript for the O.K. Corral inquest, along with contemporary newspaper reports from the *Epitaph* and *Nugget* are the source of all we know about what actually occurred in the West's most famous gunfight.

When he began *Frontier Marshal*, Lake asked Earp where he could find some primary documents. Earp told him that much was destroyed in the fire of 1882 but that "The old 'dobe courthouse (in Tombstone) wasn't burned in '82. A load of prisoners brought a load of papers and stuff over here and dumped 'em into a storeroom out back that's been shut for years. What's in there no one knows. If you don't mind dirt, you could find out." After a week's investigation Lake found a treasure trove of hundreds of handwritten documents, ledgers, and, at the bottom of the pile, the court reporter's transcript of what Lake dubbed "Organized Outlawry vs. Wyatt Earp."

Lake took voluminous notes from the transcript, then made the mistake that many Earp researchers would repeat over the next decades: He handed it to an authority without having a copy made. The transcript went to the clerk of the Superior Court of Cochise County, where it eventually fell into the possession of a man named Hal Hayhurst, characterized by Lake as "an itinerant newspaper reporter, minor political job-holder, and occasional political press agent of questionable ability, habit, and integrity." (As Lake had been a press agent himself for Teddy Roosevelt, one wonders why his remarks about Hayhurst were so disparaging.) According to Lake, Hayhurst, who was working for the Federal Writers Project begun by FDR's administration, mutilated the original text, adding peripheral footnotes and editorial comments and deleting and distorting much else. It was Lake's belief that Wyatt's testimony, the best-remembered and most influential at the inquest, suffered particular and deliberate damage at Hayhurst's hand. We don't know what Hayhurst's prejudices were, though we do know that he exchanged several friendly letters with John Behan's son, Albert. When Hayhurst died in 1951, his personal effects were destroyed, and the court transcript was probably among them.

Nearly three decades later a nonpartisan researcher, Alford Turner, published the Hayhurst manuscript with Hayhurst's footnotes deleted and Turner's more accurate and informative comments in their place. Turner thought Hayhurst to be "thoroughly anti-Earp in his viewpoint," which, unfortunately, without the original transcript, no amount of scholarship or research can correct.

So, consider that what follows is based on an imperfect method of frontier court reporting, which is left to sit in a dusty back room for forty years, then discarded for a version rewritten by a man who seems to have resented the most famous participant in the inquest. Consider, too, that it involved witnesses whose credibility we can't be sure of, witnesses whose view of the gunfight was obscured by the gun smoke and dust—when they weren't ducking to avoid stray bullets.

* * *

After calling just nine witnesses, Coroner Henry M. Matthews made his report: "William Clanton, Frank and Thomas McLaury, came to their deaths in the town of Tombstone on October 26, 1881, from the effects of pistol and gunshot wounds inflicted by Virgil Earp, Morgan Earp, Wyatt Earp, and one—Holliday, commonly called 'Doc' Holliday." On October 30 the *Nugget*, under a headline that read "Glad to Know," reported that "The people of this community are deeply indebted to the twelve intelligent men who composed the coroner jury for the valuable information that the three persons who were killed last Wednesday were shot. We might have thought they had been struck by lightning or stung to death by hornets."

Earp support began to erode, from the barrage of negative publicity and the fact that none of the Earps had a chance to testify in his own defense. The city council suspended Virgil Earp as chief of police pending the outcome of the investigation, though, to be fair, Virgil's calf wound made it impossible for him to carry out his duties.

Two days later George Parsons, still a staunch law-and-order man, wrote in his journal that Wyatt Earp "took me in to see Virgil. He's getting along well. Morgan too. Looks bad for them all thus far." On the night of October 31, it began. James Earp opened the door at Virgil's house to see a "veiled visitor," who appeared to be a man dressed as a woman. The visitor quickly left, leaving the family to consider that he might have been an assassin looking for Virgil, Wyatt, or Morgan. The Earp women—Virgil's Allie, Morgan's Louisa, and Wyatt's Mattie (whom he now scarcely saw at all)—moved into the Cosmopolitan Hotel, where they could more easily be watched over.

It was Ike Clanton, not Sheriff John Behan, who filed murder charges against the Earps and Holliday. In light of the damage Ike did to the Cowboy case, one wonders why, particularly Clanton and Behan were, for all intents, partners. As a ranch owner, Ike did have a certain respectability, but not so much that it could survive too much probing. (For instance, he had no registered brand in either Pima or Cochise County: One needed a brand to raise one's own cattle.) The only value Ike brought to the Cowboy case was as a witness to the fight, but only the part of it he saw before he ran. John Behan would have made a far more credible witness, except he, too, had skeletons—the nature of his association with the Cowboys, his reneging on the deal with Wyatt, his personal animosity over Wyatt's relationship with Josephine, his own ineptness as a peace officer—that he probably didn't want aired. He did succeed in keeping some of these matters hidden during the inquest, and for most of his lifetime, but despite this the gunfight and subsequent inquest would finish him as a power in southeast Arizona as surely as it did Wyatt Earp.

The day after the charges were filed, Wyatt and Doc Holliday were brought before Judge Wells Spicer. Spicer would later be accused by Earp debunkers of being an Earp partisan. Not on this day: Bail was fixed at $10,000 for each, including Virgil and Morgan. Wyatt had no trouble raising the money, most of which came from local mining men appreciative of the Earps' work in their behalf. Wyatt's attorney, Tom Fitch, gave him $10,000. Fred Dodge contributed $500, and probably passed on more from Wells Fargo. Wyatt himself had considerable capital from his Tombstone holdings and business interests.

On November 1, the Cowboy assault began, and it was clear that the testimony Behan, Clanton and Billy Claiborne had given at the coroner's inquest was just a warm-up. Now, they had their story prepared. According to Billy Allen, a friend of the Clantons and McLaurys, Tom McLaury had not reached for a Winchester on his horse's saddle but instead held up his hands, saying "I ain't got no arms." Billy Clanton had not thrown his right hand across his left hip to reach for the Colt revolver in a cross-draw holster but instead yelled, "I do not want to fight." Doc Holliday had fired the first shot; the second had come from the Earps.

Behan testified on November 2. This time, after thinking it over, he thought it was Wyatt who yelled, "You sons-of-bitches have been looking for a fight." The first time Behan discussed the fight with the *Nugget*, it was Frank McLaury who started things off by reaching for his gun, but, testifying before the coroner, Behan said it was someone in the Earp party who began the show with a "nickel-plated pistol": "My impression *at the* time [emphasis mine was that Doc Holliday had the nickel-plated pistol." He would not say for certain that it was Holliday, but it was someone in the Earp party. "These nickel-plated pistols I speak of were in the hands of the Earp party." Behan had become obsessed with nickel-plated pistols; at the moment Billy Clanton said, "I don't want to fight," Behan said, "My attention was directed just at that moment to a nickel-plated pistol, the nickel-plated pistol was the first to fire." Doc Holliday started the fight.

The current of opinion in southeast Arizona changed after Behan's testimony. The same *Arizona Star* that had only months before been calling for army intervention now editorialized that "It now appears, after the smoke of the Tombstone bloody street affray has passed away, that but one side of the tale has been told." The only side that had been told up to now was the Cowboys'. But, "If under the color of authority they wreaked their vengeance on these victims, as set forth, then let the law claim its due, no matter what the consequences." The "as set forth" referred to the testimony of Billy Allen and John Behan, both Cowboy allies. The "victims" were members of a gang that the *Star* had been screaming for federal action against for months. Now that they got the action, like many law-and-order Tombstonians, they weren't so sure they approved of the shape it took.

Wyatt's lawyers, Tom Fitch and T. J. Drum, perceived that the prosecution would find nothing in the records of Virgil, Wyatt, and Morgan as lawmen that could be attacked, so they would chose to go after Doc Holliday. To counter the "nickel-plated gun" theory they asked a question that has never been satisfactorily answered: If Holliday had a shotgun in his hands, why did he draw his revolver? Many researchers have subsequently countered with the argument that Doc did not like shotguns and would have preferred his own six-gun in a fight; this is true, but he accepted the shotgun from Virgil, and there is no question that he carried it into the lot and that he used it.

But no one claimed to have heard a shotgun at the beginning of the fight, so the only way the Cowboys' lawyers could incriminate Holliday was by claiming that he drew and fired his revolver first. In that case, what did he do with the shotgun? Did he stop at the beginning of the fight and lay it on the ground? No one saw him do this. We do know that Holliday did eventually use the shotgun (on Tom McLaury). What, then, did he do with the pistol? That he would have stopped in them middle of the fight to holster the pistol in order to fire the shotgun seems even more unlikely.

Alford Turner, the researcher who edited the O.K. Corral transcript into book form, offers this scenario: "It was no trick for the ambidextrous Holliday to whip up the shotgun as an attention getter with his left arm and immediately follow with a shot from his nickel-plated pistol held in his right hand." Paula Mitchell Marks, author of the 1989 study of the gunfight, seems to subscribe to this theory. "The confusion over Doc's shooting of the McLaurys," she writes, "stems from the fact that he apparently shot both within the first few seconds of the melee, first firing the nickel-plated pistol at Frank, then, after Morgan fired, swinging the shotgun up and hitting Tom with a load of buckshot." Both Turner and Marks are students of the gunfight and their opinions cannot be easily discounted. Yet, there are glaring holes in what we'll call "The Nickel-Plated Gun Theory." Holliday may have been ambidextrous with six-guns, but no one short of Arnold Schwarzenegger's Terminator could be ambidextrous with a pistol and a shotgun.

Let's consult an expert on the subject of frontier ambidexterity: "If a man carried two weapons, one usually served as a backup; the ambidextrous fellow with two six-guns blazing is primarily a creature of myth." The author of that passage is Paula Mitchell Marks. If, as Marks concludes, the two six-gun man is a creature of myth, so too must be the six-gun/shotgun man. Yet, Marks has this mythical creature in the lot, blazing away at the McLaurys with pistol and shotgun.

According to Turner and Marks, Doc, the murderous hothead, walked into the lot holding a shotgun, then started the fight by drawing his pistol because he didn't like the shotgun; then he proceeded to shoot Frank McLaury, after which, deciding that he didn't mind the shotgun after all, holstered the pistol and used the shotgun to kill Tom McLaury; then he threw the shotgun down and re-drew his handgun to shoot Frank McLaury a second time. To anyone familiar with firearms such a sequence is incredible. You have a shotgun, you intend to use it, you use it—you do not fire another weapon first, holster it, then go back to the shotgun. Since no one contends that Holliday began the fight by firing the shotgun—and this is one of the most important facts—the only scenario that could have Holliday initiating the fight would be one in which Doc holds the shotgun and the revolver at the same time, firing the pistol first and then the shotgun. This would mean that Holliday fired both barrels, and scored two hits, while holding the Wells Fargo gun with one hand. Ambidextrous or no, this would seem beyond the powers of even the man Wyatt Earp called "the fastest, deadliest man with a gun I have ever seen."

In the files of the Arizona Historical Society there is a paper by Earp researcher Jeff Morey entitled "Equivocation at the O.K. Corral" that humorously critiques the different gunfight theories. If Holliday began the fight, Morey contends, he must have walked into the lot with both hands on the shotgun, then twirled it around with one finger on his left hand and whirled it into the air, and, while it spun over his head, drew this revolver with his right hand and shot Frank McLaury, spun the revolver into the air, caught the shotgun, then caught the revolver as it came down—being ambidextrous he could have done this with either hand, of course—then proceeded to finish off Frank McLaury. Morey's scenario is only slightly more improbable than Turner's or Marks's.

Fitch sought to undermine Behan's testimony by implying that the sheriff had both personal and professional reasons for seeing Wyatt Earp brought up on a murder charge.

> (Q) Were not you and Wyatt Earp both applicants to General Fremont for the appointment of sheriff of Cochise County, and did not Wyatt Earp withdraw his application upon your promise to divide the profits of the office and did not you subsequently refuse to comply with your part of the contract?
> [Objected to by the prosecution; overruled.]
> (A) In the first place we were both applicants for the office. I was, and I understood Mr. Earp was. When I became satisfied that I would get the appointment, I went to Mr. Earp and told him that I knew I would get the appointment of sheriff, and that I would like to have him in the office with me. I also told him that I did not want him to cease his efforts to get the office if he could. I told him I was sure I could get it and that if I did, I would take him in, that in case he got the office, I did not want anything to do with it. He said it was very kind of me, that if he got the office he had his brothers to provide for, and could not return the compliment if he got it. I said I asked nothing if he got it, but in case I got it, and I was

certain of it, I would like to have him in the office with me. I said, "Let this talk me no difference with you in your efforts to get the office." Something afterwards transpired that I did not take him into the office.

The "something that afterwards transpired," might have been Earp's support of Bob Paul for Pima County sheriff; it might also have been Josephine Marcus. Behan and Earp would in this instance act like Victorian gentlemen; her name was never mentioned in the inquest. Fitch did, however, press home the fact that John Behan and Wyatt Earp had had a falling out over the issue of the sheriff's election.

> (Q) On your cross-examination you stated that you promised Wyatt Earp a position in your office, and that something subsequently occurred that caused you not to do it. Please state what that some-thing was.
> (A) It was this: Shortly after I had the conversation with Wyatt Earp, I received a telegram from Charles A. Shibell, sheriff of Pima County to subpoena Ike Clanton. . . . I hitched up a team and started to Charleston. I had gotten about halfway to Charleston, and a man dashed by me on horseback, on the run; and about five minutes after-wards another passed me on the run. I got to Charleston and found a man going out to Clanton's place. I gave him the dispatch and told him to hand it to Ike Clanton, and stayed around Charleston an hour or so, and met Wyatt Earp and Doc Holliday. I think I asked them what they were doing or what they were on. Wyatt Earp told me he was down after a horse that had been stolen from him sometime before.

This is strange testimony. Behan digresses without ever addressing the question of why this incident caused a rift between himself and Wyatt Earp. A moment later Behan testified that Ike Clanton told him that Earp threatened to have "a posse of nine men" come and arrest him and that they would be sent by the sheriff. Behan contended that "He [Clanton] had armed his crowd and was not going to stand it." Why did Behan bother to relate this seemingly irrelevant story? Behan's implication must have been that Earp caused trouble for him by threatening Ike Clanton with the power of the Sheriff's Office without informing Behan first. He was also implying that this somehow interfered with the summons Behan was delivering to Ike. Judge Spicer took note of this story and how its odd parts didn't fit together; it would come back later to damage Behan.

Behan's story is all double-talk. First, Wyatt's problem wasn't with Ike, but with Billy Clanton, who had stolen his horse. Earp simply took it back. If either Ike or Billy thought Wyatt had violated some law in doing so, they were free to file charges with Behan, but they didn't. Second, it's improbable that Wyatt had told Ike that "nine armed men" (why nine?) were going to arrest him; after recovering the horse, Wyatt was free to press charges but instead chose to forget the matter. Third, Behan or one of his deputies would have had no trouble delivering the summons if he really wanted it delivered. If the subpoena was for Clanton's role in the election fraud intended to keep Bob Paul out of office, both Behan and Clanton would have been quite happy if Earp had interfered in its delivery.

Wes Fuller, a local gambler and another Cowboy associate, was standing in back of Fly's when the fight commenced. He also testified that Billy Clanton threw up his hands on Virgil Earp's command and said "Don't shoot me, I don't want to fight," that the first two shots came from the Earp party, and that the fight was started by Doc Holliday and Morgan Earp. Billy Claiborne, who was so close to the Cowboys that the Earps might have assumed he would fight with the Clantons and McLaurys if it came to a shootout, gave almost identical testimony: Billy, Ike and Tom all threw up their hands—it was becoming a litany—and Doc Holliday and Morgan Earp fired first. Morgan, the youngest and least experienced of the Earp lawmen, was an easier target than Virgil or Wyatt.[5]

In all, Spicer heard the testimony of some twenty-nine witnesses. One, John Behan, was Wyatt's political and romantic rival; one, Ike Clanton, was a known cattle rustler whose brother had been killed by the Earps and who had been involved in a clash with Earp much to Ike's detriment; and three, Billy Claiborne, Billy Allen, and Wes Fuller, were all friends of the slain Cowboys. Allen and Claiborne were even suspected by some of having taken a potshot at the Earps during the fight. All five were lucky or brave enough, considering the number of stray bullets, to have witnessed most or all of the battle.

No other witnesses but these five identified Doc Holliday or Morgan Earp as the instigators of the fight.

After hearing Wes Fuller's testimony, Judge Spicer was convinced that there was sufficient evidence to hold the Earps and Doc Holliday over for trial on the charge of murder. On November 7, Behan's undersheriff, Harry Woods, arrested Wyatt and Doc and took them to a makeshift jail on Sixth Street where they would spend the next sixteen days. As a show of strength, Earp supporters placed more than a dozen armed guards in front of the jail just in case Clanton and McLaury supporters had ideas of revenge. At least one of them did, but for now Will McLaury, brother of the dead rustlers, chose legal recourse.

William R. McLaury was the oldest, most respectable, and certainly the smartest of the McLaury brothers. In background and outlook he had much more in common with the Earps than with his dead brother's friends—Will was raised in Iowa and his family was solidly Republican—but he did not know this. He had been working as a lawyer in Texas, a place not naturally disposed to sympathy for Northern lawmen such as the Earps, when he heard news of the gunfight. When McLaury went to Tombstone, he found, as he wrote to his brother-in-law in Iowa, that "With the exception of about thirty or forty men here whose business is gambling and stealing among whom are the Earp brothers and one J. H. Holliday, my brothers were universally esteemed as honorable, personable, and brave citizens." Actually, several of his brothers friends, who had already testified against the Earps, particularly Wes Fuller, Billy Allen, and Billy Claiborne, to say nothing of John Behan, were also full- or part-time gamblers, but Will McLaury didn't make that distinction. He did not seem to know that his brothers were cattle and livestock thieves or that they had been accused of stealing federal property. He talked to some locals and found out what he wanted to know: "It was as cold-blooded and foul a murder as has been recorded," he wrote to his law partner in Texas. "It will not bring my brothers back to prosecute these men but I regard it as my duty to myself and family to see that these brutes do not go unwhipped of justice. I think I can hang them."

McLaury immediately joined the prosecution team, which featured Lyttleton Price (who was the district attorney) and Ben Goodrich, a former Confederate infantry officer. McLaury did a lot of glad-handing around town and bought drinks as if he was running for office; he gave himself the credit for getting Wyatt and Doc thrown in jail, at which point his spirits must have been high. But the Cowboy case was a house of cards, and on November 9 a joker named Ike Clanton began to bring it down.

Like his friends, Ike claimed that Doc and Morgan had started the fight. He, Ike, had not pleaded for his life; on the contrary, he charged Wyatt Earp and tried to take him out of the battle. After grappling with him briefly he gave up and ran toward Fly's. To reinforce the notion that the gunfight was essentially an attempt to eliminate him because of his knowledge of the Leonard, Head, and Crane deal, Ike claimed "one or two bullets" passed right by his head. Why men involved in a desperate fight for their lives would turn away from men with guns to shoot at a fleeing and unarmed man was not explained.

Had you at any time threatened the Earps? asked the defense before dismissing Ike. The man who had spent the night and morning before the gunfight threatening Wyatt, Virgil and Doc humbly answered, "No, sir."

Two days later—Ike asked for some time off to be treated for the headaches caused by the barrel of Virgil's revolver—the defense went to work. Didn't Ike say, in the Oriental Saloon on the day of the gunfight: "The Earp crowd and Holliday insulted me the night before when I was unarmed. I have fixed or healed myself now, and they have got to fight"? Ike thought it over for a moment and admitted that, well, he had. So, then, that was one threat.

Then, finally, it was time to discuss the Leonard, Head, and Crane deal. Ike admitted that he had talked the deal over with Wyatt, but decided not to take it, though promising Wyatt he would never tell anyone about it. Ike should then have kept his mouth shut; instead, almost as if he were drunk, he went on to expound on a version of the deal and its aftermath that had people in the courtroom shaking their heads in wonder.

Clanton said that he met Wyatt "in the Eagle Brewery Saloon one night and he asked me to take a drink with him"—though Wyatt did not drink—"and while they were mixing our drinks he told me he wanted a long private talk with me." From here, the testimony goes on:

> Virgil told me to tell Bill Leonard at one time, not to
> think he was trying to catch him when they were running
> him, and told me to tell Billy that he [had] thrown Paul
> and the posse that was after him off of his track, the time
> he left Helm's ranch at the foot of the Dragoon Moun-
> tains, and that he had done all he could for him.

From a historical perspective, this is one of the crucial points in all
the testimony, for deciding what happened in the Benson stage
holdup, the murder of Bud Philpot, and the O.K. Corral gunfight
depends on whether one believes Wyatt Earp or Ike Clanton was
telling the truth. What Ike was saying was nothing less than that all
the Earps were involved in a scheme to steal money from the stage;
that Doc Holliday was their instrument and the man who killed the
stage driver, Philpot; and that Virgil had deliberately misled the
posse in its pursuit of Leonard. This was Ike's explanation for the
events that led up to the gunfight. The gunfight, then, was an attempt by the Earps and Holliday to get rid of Clanton before he
could tell the story.

One either believes the Earps were a stage-robbing gang—stealing
from the same company, Wells Fargo, that was using them as special
agents—or one doesn't, but aside from the fact that Wells Fargo
reported no money missing from the Benson stage holdup, the most
rabid anti-Earp partisan must be dumbfounded at the thought that
Wyatt and Virgil Earp, two men well known as close-mouthed,
would confide their holdup plan and their intention to use Holliday
to "pipe-off" the money to someone like Ike Clanton. Why did Ike
think that the Earps confided in him? His only explanation was that
"Before they told me, I made a sacred promise not to tell it and never
would," if he hadn't been put on the witness stand.

If Ike had been visiting a saloon or an opium den before testifying—he did, after all, ask to be excused for a day because of headaches—he must have been in the same condition the next day.
According to Ike, not only Wyatt and Virgil Earp had sought his
confidence but Doc Holliday as well—like Nick Carraway in *The
Great Gatsby*, Ike was privy to the secrets of wild, unknown men.
When Doc started to volunteer information about the holdup and the
killing, Clanton claimed he told him "not to take me into his confidence, that I did not wish to know any more about it." Still, nothing

could keep the deadly dentist from pouring out his heart to the cattle thief: "Doc Holliday told me he was there at the killing of Bud Philpot. He told me that he shot Bud Philpot through the heart."

As Clanton's mouth motored on, the prosecution's case started to come undone. Fitch and Drum decided to press the attack. Did not, the defense asked, "Marshall Williams, the agent of the express camping out at Tombstone, state to you that he was personally concerned in the attempted stage robbery and the murder of Philpot?" At this, Ike must have wondered what was going on. "Did not James Earp," Wyatt's lawyer continued, "also confess to you that he was personally concerned in the attempted stage robbery and the murder of Philpot?" By now, even Ike caught the sarcasm. Judge Spicer sustained the prosecution's objection, but clearly the point was made.

It was Wyatt Earp, cool and deliberate, who destroyed the Cowboy case.

After answering the obligatory questions about his name, age (thirty-two years and nine months), and residency in Tombstone, Wyatt gave his occupation as "saloon keeper at present. Also have been deputy sheriff and also a detective." This is a curious testimony. Wyatt wasn't licensed for any saloon in Tombstone, nor had he ever "kept" a saloon in the strict sense, though he certainly had gambling interests in more than one. Also, he did not say "deputy marshal," though he had spent far more time as one in Kansas than he had as a deputy sheriff in Arizona. "Detective"? Wyatt was almost certainly alluding to his work for Wells Fargo.

Then, to the surprise of the prosecution, Wyatt began reading from a prepared statement. This brought howls from Clantons' attorneys and continues to bring howls from anti-Earpists to this day. But territorial law did allow a defendant in a preliminary hearing, which is what this was, to make a statement without facing cross-examination. Spicer ruled in Earp's favor; he couldn't see why it made any difference whether the statement was oral or written.[6]

Wyatt began with a list of grievances he and his brothers had against the McLaurys, beginning with the theft of the army mules a year before; he also made it clear that Captain Hurst, who led the soldiers in pursuit of the mules, had conveyed threats against the Earps from the McLaurys. A month or so later, Earp said, they had made the threats in person when Wyatt was in Charleston. Then

came an interesting admission: After Bud Philpot was murdered in
the attempted holdup, Wyatt, working "as a detective," helped "trace
the matter up, and I was satisfied that these men (Leonard, Head,
and Crane) were in that robbery. I knew that Leonard, Head, and
Crane were friends and associates of the Clantons and McLaurys
and often stopped at their ranches." Wyatt's statement continued:

> It was generally understood among officers and those who
> have information about criminals, that Ike Clanton was
> sort of chief among the Cowboys; that the Clantons and
> McLaurys were cattle thieves and generally in the secret
> of the stage robbery, and that the Clanton and McLaury
> ranches were meeting places of shelter for the gang. I had
> an ambition to be sheriff of this county at the next elec-
> tion, and I thought it would be a great help to me with the
> people and businessmen if I could capture the men who
> killed Philpot. There were rewards offered of about
> $1,200 each for the capture of the robbers. Altogether
> there was about $3,600 offered for their capture. I thought
> this sum might tempt Ike Clanton and Frank McLaury to
> give away Leonard, Head, and Crane, so I went to Ike
> Clanton, Frank McLaury, and Joe Hill when they came to
> town. I had an interview with them in the back yard of
> the Oriental Saloon. I told them what I wanted. I told
> them I wanted the glory of capturing Leonard, Head, and
> Crane and if I could do it, it would help me make the race
> for sheriff at the next election. I told them if they would
> put me on the track of Leonard, Head, and Crane, and
> tell me where those men were hid, I would give them all
> the reward and would never let anyone know where I got
> the information.

If one accepts Wyatt's working as a detective for Wells Fargo, the
rest of his story fits the known facts. Using his Wells Fargo connection to do some detective work—this probably meant offering bribe
money in order to obtain information—Wyatt became satisfied that
the stage robbers knew the Clantons and McLaurys and some of
their Cowboy associates regarded Ike as "sort of a chief among the
Cowboys." In making that assumption, Wyatt would, with Holly-

wood's help, confuse the issue of Cowboy leadership for the next century. To the degree that the loose association of stock thieves and occasional bandits known as "Cowboys" had a leader, it was, after Old Man Clanton's death, probably Curly Bill Brocius or John Ringo; what Wyatt's informants were probably telling him was that the property-owning Clanton brothers were the geographical focus of the cattle stealing business in the area. Or perhaps Ike was inheriting the reputation his father had before the old man was killed by Mexicans.

Wyatt's information that Ike was intimate with the Benson stage holdup men was obviously true, or Ike wouldn't have thought about making the deal. Earp was candid about his reason for wanting to make the deal: "I had an ambition to be sheriff of this county" and he thought that capture of the stage robbers would help him get elected. By using his Wells Fargo connections he could get reward money for the informer who would help him capture the three suspects. (If Wyatt had no Wells Fargo connections, from where would the thousands in reward money have come from?) Moreover, Wyatt maintained that he had talked to Joe Hill and Frank McLaury as well and that they were in the deal with Ike.

More threats had been made against the Earps by the Cowboys, said Wyatt, weeks before the gunfight when Frank McLaury abused Morgan Earp for chasing Pete Spence and Frank Stilwell after the Bisbee stage robbery. According to Wyatt, Frank had told Morgan, "If you ever come after me, you will never take me." Morgan replied that if he ever had occasion to go after him, he would arrest him. McLaury's last words were "I have threatened you boys' lives, and a few days later I had taken it back, but since the arrest [of Spence and Stilwell] it still goes."

In addition, said Earp, at least seven other locals, any one of whom could be called on for corroboration, had heard death threats made against the Earps by the Clantons, the McLaurys, Joe Hill, and John Ringo. "I know of the McLaurys stealing six government mules, and also cattle, and when the owners went after them, finding their stock on the McLaurys' ranch, that he was drove off and told if he ever said anything about it, he would be killed." This wasn't the last time locals would maintain that a Cowboy had threatened their lives if they called on the law.

Wyatt added: "I heard of John Ringo shooting a man down in

cold blood near Camp Thomas. I was satisfied that Frank and Tom McLaury killed and robbed Mexicans in Skeleton Canyon." In this, it's possible that Wyatt was projecting too much into the McLaurys' activities, though from his perspective it may well have seemed as if all Cowboys were equally guilty. Still, if half the threats or shootings or illegal activities attributed to the Clantons and McLaurys were true, Wyatt had good reason to be wary and "not intend that any of the gang should get the drop on me if I could help it."

Wyatt then went on to present his version of the fight. In case there was anyone present who questioned his record or reputation in Kansas, the defense presented petitions signed by sixty-two prominent citizens from Dodge and Wichita. The Dodge petition was signed by old friends like Chalk Beeson and Wells Fargo agent John McGinnis, as well as Bob Wright and others with whom Wyatt had had unpleasant run-ins. It read, in part: "We do not believe that he would wantonly take the life of his fellow man" and that "As marshal of our city he was ever vigilant in the discharge of his duties, and while kind and courteous to all, he was brave, unflinching, and on all occasions proved himself the right man in the right place." The word *marshal* was used twice, indicating that the citizens of Dodge did not regard Wyatt as a deputy marshal or assistant marshal, regardless of what his job description said. So much for debunkers who would later claim that Wyatt padded his resume. In their eyes, after just a few short years, Wyatt was remembered by friends and enemies as marshal of Dodge, just as in years to come he would be remembered as marshal of Tombstone.

The Wichita petition claimed that Wyatt was on the police force of their city "in the years A.D. 1874, 1875, and part of the year 1876. We further certify that the said Wyatt Earp was a good and efficient officer and was well known for his honesty and integrity, that his character while here was one of the best, and no fault was ever found with him as an officer or as a man." The brawl which led to his firing clearly left no hard feelings.

Charles Holton, the notary public, added this: "I hereby certify that I knew personally Wyatt S. Earp during his residence in the city of Wichita. That I served four years as city attorney of said city and have known personally all of the officers of said city for the past ten years. I take great pleasure in saying that Wyatt S. Earp was one of the most efficient officers that Wichita ever had and I can safely testify that Mr. Earp is in every sense reliable and a trustworthy gentleman."

The petition was a pretty strong character reference. The signees included not only Wyatt's close friends but city officials with whom he had clashed. There were even a few Texas cattlemen, an indication that Kansans weren't the only ones grateful for the law and order Earp had maintained. In the face of the petition and of Wyatt's strong testimony, the Cowboy case began to melt away. Will McLaury, though, did not think so. Concerning Wyatt's testimony, he wrote to his sister that "One of their principal witnesses have been on the stand today and they feel bad his evidence is much stronger for us than it is for them. I think the scoundrel feared to act his role. I do not think that by perjury these men shall escape." Will McLaury seems to have been a respectable man—he is not known to have had a criminal record—and perhaps he couldn't accept the fact that his brothers were in league with a man like Ike Clanton.

Virgil Earp followed Wyatt. He did not read his testimony, like Wyatt, and he was cross-examined. Virgil rolled back the prosecution's case even further as he was the town marshal and a respected one; even those who accused Wyatt of being involved in crooked behavior were hesitant to include Virgil. He carefully related the proceedings that led up to the fight with emphasis on the Cowboy threats. Upon entering the lot, he said "Boys, throw up your hands, I want your guns, or arms." With that, he said, Frank McLaury and Billy Clanton proceeded to thumb their six-shooters—he could hear the click-click as they pulled back the hammers of the single-action revolvers.

"At that I said, throwing up both hands, with the cane in my right hand, 'Hold, I don't want that.' As I said that, Billy Clanton threw his six-shooter down full-cocked" (that is, he drew and pointed his gun). Two pistols went off, Virgil said, one of them Billy's. Tom McLaury had had his hand on a Winchester rifle on his horse's saddle; at the first shot the horse jumped to one side, and Tom failed to grab the Winchester. He then got around behind the horse, "making him a kind of breastwork, and fired once, if not twice, over the horse's back." There was one hole in Virgil's testimony, and the prosecution, curiously, did not exploit it: If Tom had a handgun (presumably concealed under his shirt) why would he have reached for the rifle? But, then, maybe he wasn't reaching for the rifle but grabbing at the saddle trying to position himself behind the horse.[7]

The question as to whether or not Tom McLaury was armed, aside from the rifle, has never been answered, but at least one neutral witness, an army doctor named J. B. W. Gardner, thought he was. Gardner "saw no pistol but supposed at the time on seeing the right-hand pocket of his pants extending outwards that he had got his pistol." The doctor told hotel keeper Albert Billickie "that I was sorry to see Tom McLaury had gotten his pistol"—meaning, presumably, that he was sorry to see that trouble was now bound to ensue. This does raise the question as to why, if McLaury was leaving town and unarmed, he hadn't been down to retrieve the gun he had checked at a saloon after Wyatt pistol-whipped him.

The most important testimony after Wyatt's came from the gentleman we met at the beginning of this book, the railroad engineer, H. F. Sills. Being impartial, Sills's story did more than any other to exonerate the Earps. It indicated that Virgil and Wyatt and probably Morgan and Doc, too, acted prudently. On the afternoon of October 26, he saw a party of five men standing in front of the O.K. Corral. They had threatened to kill "the whole party of the Earps" on sight. Sills's testimony was important in at least one other respect: He corroborated Wyatt's testimony that the fight started when Wyatt and Billy Clanton fired, at nearly the same time.

Sills's testimony severely weakened the Cowboy case. Prior to Sills, Spicer had refused to allow testimony as to what prompted the shootout; now, a neutral witness had verified the threats the four had made publicly against the Earps and also supported Wyatt Earp's story about how the fight itself had begun. Spicer now allowed testimony from barkeepers Julius Kelly and Ned Boyle, and both told of Ike's bluster and belligerence in the hours before the gunfight. Then, the testimony of newly appointed Assistant District Attorney Winfield Scott Williams dropped a minor bombshell. When John Behan had visited Virgil Earp in bed after the fight, said Williams, Behan told the marshal that "I then met you and your party [on the way to the lot] and spoke to you. You did not answer. I heard you say, 'Boys, throw up your hands, I have come to disarm you.' One of the McLaury boys said, 'We will' and the shooting commenced." That, Williams concluded, "is as I remember it." Williams's account of what Behan told Virgil matches the *Nugget*'s account, which had to have come from John Behan.

Albert Billickie of the Cosmopolitan Hotel then chipped away at the prosecution's contention that Tom McLaury was unarmed: "When he (Tom) went into the butcher shop his right-hand pants pocket was flat. When he came out his pants pocket protruded as if there was a revolver therein." Why, the prosecution asked, was Billickie watching McLaury's pants so closely? "Every good citizen in this city was watching all them Cowboys very closely on the day the affray occurred." The Cowboy defenders' caustic reply was: "Did you know every good citizen in Tombstone, or did you on that day?" "I know not all of them but a great many," Billickie replied.

This left just one more important witness. Addie Bourland, a dressmaker, lived almost directly across from Fly's Photography Studio. Her testimony stunned both prosecution and defense. She saw the Earp party walk up to the Cowboys, and Doc Holliday push a pistol into the chest of one of the men and then step back—Holliday started the fight after all! Not quite: The defense asked if the pistol was nickel-plated, as Behan, Ike Clanton, Billy Allen, and Billy Claiborne said it was. No, replied Bourland, it was "dark bronze." It took everyone a moment to realize that Bourland had almost certainly mistaken the short- barreled shotgun for a pistol or else she would have remarked that Holliday was carrying something in his other hand as well. She saw only one gun with a strange "dark bronze" barrel. The defense relaxed; she meant the shotgun.

More importantly, Bourland testified that she did not see the Cowboys with their hands up and that she did not see who fired first. She saw Holliday walk up to one of the Cowboys and point a gun at him, she did not see him fire it, which meant that Doc did not initiate the fight.

Bourland may not have known a pistol from a shotgun, but her view of the fight was better than that of any other neutral witness. Judge Wells Spicer took exceptional care to get her story straight: He visited Bourland at her house, discussed the gunfight, then recalled her to the stand. This time, Spicer himself would ask the questions. Understandably, the prosecution objected to such an unprecedented move, but Spicer ruled in his own favor and began the questioning.

Did Bourland see anyone hold up their hands? "I did not see

anyone hold up their hands," Bourland said. "They all seemed to be
firing in general on both sides."

The prosecution grilled Bourland about what Spicer had asked
during his house call. "He asked me one or two questions," she
replied, "in regard to seeing the difficulty, and if they had thrown up
their hands whether I would have seen it, and I told him I thought I
would have seen it." That was what Spicer wanted to know. There
were no more questions about the dark bronze gun.

Wyatt's lawyers called one more witness; the prosecution, led by
McLaury and Price, called one more. Nothing of consequence was
said.

When Judge Wells Spicer retired to make his decision, he had no
idea it would be the only legal opinion of his career that would still
be debated more than a century later.

Spicer returned to the courtroom at 2:00 P.M. on November 30. He
began by announcing that he had considered only facts on which
some kind of consensus could be established—which meant that testimony regarding the Cowboys having their hands in the air, which
was disputed by the Earps and unsupported by neutral testimony,
would not be considered. Spicer recounted Ike Clanton's constant
threats to the Earps, as well as Wyatt's brief and brutal clash with
Tom McLaury. But this was a lead-in to a censure of Virgil's actions:

> In view of these controversies between Wyatt Earp and
> Isaac Clanton and Thomas McLaury, and in further view
> of this quarrel the night before between Isaac Clanton and
> J. H. Holliday, I am of the opinion that the defendant,
> Virgil Earp, as chief of police, subsequently calling upon
> Wyatt Earp and J. H. Holliday to assist him in arresting
> and disarming the Clantons and McLaurys—committed
> an injudicious and censurable act, and although in this he
> acted incautiously and without due circumspection, yet
> when we consider the conditions of affairs incident to a
> frontier country; the lawlessness and disregard for human
> life; the existence of a law-defying element in [our] midst;
> the fear and feeling of insecurity that has existed; the sup-
> posed prevalence of bad, desperate, and reckless men who
> have been a terror to the country and kept away capital

and enterprise; and consider the many threats that have been made against the Earps, I can attach no criminality to his unwise act. In fact, as the result plainly proves, he needed the assistance and support of staunch and true friends, upon whose courage, coolness and fidelity he could depend, in case of an emergency.

Well, at least it began as a censure: The last sentence seemed to cancel out the first. Virgil "committed an injudicious and censurable act" in deputizing Doc Holliday, yet "as the result plainly proves," he needed him. Moreover, he needed "staunch and true friends, upon whose courage, coolness, and fidelity he could depend." In other words, the people he chose—Wyatt, Morgan, and, yes, Doc—had exhibited those qualities. This was an odd censure. It was evident that after considering the evidence and testimony, Spicer was convinced that Holliday had not begun the fight and had in fact done precisely what Virgil had ordered him to do: take the shotgun, watch the flank, see that they didn't get ambushed. At this, the prosecution must have known that their case had collapsed.

Spicer went on to say that the Cowboys' purpose in leaving the O.K. Corral and going on to Fremont "will probably never be known," but that to his mind Virgil Earp "honestly believed that their purpose was, if not to attempt the deaths of himself and his brothers, at least to resist with force and arms any attempt on his part to perform his duty as a peace officer." He might as well have said that if they refused to surrender their weapons to the sheriff, it was reasonable for the Earps to assume that the Cowboys intended to resist the town marshal. Spicer indicated that he put a great deal of stock in the testimony of H. F. Sills, a man who "had arrived in town only the day before and totally unacquainted [with] any person in town, or the state of affairs existing here."

What, then, was Virgil Earp supposed to do when "several citizens and a committee of citizens insisted he should perform his duty as such officer and arrest and disarm the Cowboys, as they termed the Clantons and McLaurys."

Was it for Virgil Earp as chief of police to abandon his clear duty as an officer because its performance was likely to be fraught with danger? Or was it not his duty that as such officer he owed to the peaceable and law-abiding citizens of the city, who looked to him to preserve peace and order, and their protection and security, to at once call to his aid sufficient assistance and persons to arrest and disarm these men?

There can be but one answer to these questions, and that answer is such as will divest the subsequent approach of the defendants toward the deceased of all presumption of malice or of illegality.

That was it; Spicer had ruled for the Earps. But the judge was far from through: "When, therefore, the defendants, regularly or specially appointed officers, marched down Fremont Street to the scene of the subsequent homicide, they were going where it was their right and duty to go; and they were doing what it was their right and duty to do; and they were armed, as it was their right and duty to be armed, when approaching men they believed to be armed and contemplating resistance."

Subtly, Spicer revealed that he had ignored the pro-Cowboy testimony; "Witnesses of credibility," he said—with perhaps a touch of sarcasm, since he meant those affiliated with the Cowboys—testified that each of the deceased "or at least two of them" yielded to a demand to surrender, "and that the discharge of firearms from both sides was almost instantaneous." But, "other witnesses of equal credibility testified that William Clanton and Frank McLaury met the demand for surrender by drawing their pistols, and that the discharge of firearms from both sides was almost instantaneous." That was the crux of the matter. One set of partisan witnesses, Behan and the friends of the Cowboys, all said one thing, and another set of witnesses, Wyatt and Virgil Earp, said another, but all nonpartisan witnesses agreed with the Earps. As to whether or not Tom McLaury was armed except for his Winchester, "I will not consider this question because it is not of controlling importance if Thomas McLaury was one of a party who were thus armed and were making felonious resistance to an arrest, and in the melee that followed was shot, the fact of his being unarmed, if it be a fact, could not of itself criminate the defendants, if they were not otherwise criminated."

As to those who testified otherwise, "I must give as much weight to the testimony of persons unacquainted with the deceased or the defendants, as to the testimony of persons who were companions or acquaintances, if not partisans of the deceased." What Judge Spicer seemed to be saying was that the testimony of witnesses who were not friends of the slain Cowboys was a great deal different from the testimony of those who were. "Considering all testimony together," the judge went on, "I am of the opinion that the weight of evidence sustains and corroborates the testimony of Wyatt Earp." Then, to Ike Clanton's thesis that the whole fight was a plot to get him because of his knowledge about the Benson stage holdup: "Issac Clanton was not injured at all, and could have been killed first and easiest, if it was the object of the attack to kill him. He would have been the first to fall; but, as it was, he was known or believed to be unarmed, and was suffered and, as Wyatt Earp testified, told to go away, and was not harmed." A charitable way to say Ike Clanton was a bald-faced liar.

About John Behan, Spicer was a bit more sly:

> I also give great weight in this matter to the testimony of Sheriff Behan, who said that on one occasion a short time ago Isaac Clanton told him that he, Clanton, had been informed that the sheriff was coming to arrest him and that he, Clanton, armed his crowd with guns and was determined not to be arrested by the sheriff—or words to that effect. And Sheriff Behan further testified that a few minutes before the Earps came to them, that he as sheriff had demanded of the Clantons and McLaurys that they give up their arms, and that they "demurred," as he said, and did not do it, and that Frank McLaury refused and gave as a reason that he was not ready to leave town just then and would not give up his arms unless the Earps were disarmed—that is, that the chief of police and his assistants should be disarmed.

Spicer, in the first sentence, could only have been referring to the aftermath of Billy Clanton's theft of Wyatt Earp's horse. A great many unpleasant things about Ike and Billy Clanton and Behan were revealed in this testimony: that Billy Clanton was a horse thief, that Ike was threatening a peace officer who had merely come to retrieve his property in as nonviolent a manner as possible, and, perhaps most significant of all, that the county sheriff, Behan, instead of arresting Ike and Billy Clanton, had turned his indignation on Wyatt Earp. And all of this was revealed voluntarily by Behan himself. Behan had established that a bond existed between himself and the man he had come to subpoena.

Closing his statement, Spicer noted the existence in Cochise County of "reckless and lawless men in our midst, banded together for mutual support and living by felonious and predatory pursuits, regarding neither life nor property in their career, and at the same time for men to parade the streets armed with repeating rifles and six-shooters and demand that the chief of police and his assistants should be disarmed in a proposition both monstrous and startling!"

Finally, the judge said, "I conclude the performance of this duty imposed on me by saying in the language of the statute: There being no sufficient cause to believe the within named Wyatt S. Earp and John H. Holliday guilty of the offense mentioned within. I order them to be released."

Will McLaury stayed on after the decision hoping that the grand jury would take up the Clanton case, but on December 16 the jury upheld Spicer's decision that there would be no murder trial. Many people in Tombstone, and more in the surrounding rural areas where Cowboy influence was greatest, were angered by the decision. "There being two strong parties in the camp," wrote Clara Brown to her San Diego paper, "of course this verdict is satisfactory to but one of them. The other accepts it with a very bad grace, and a smoldering fire exists, which is liable to burst forth at some unexpected moment. If the Earps were not men of great courage, they would hardly remain in Tombstone."

The gunfight in the lot behind the O.K. Corral is the most controversial single incident of violence in the American West. Based on the facts we have, it does not deserve to be. Paula Mitchell Marks, whose exhaustive and well-intentioned *And Die in the West* has done more to muddle the issues involved in the gunfight than any other single text, is of the opinion that Judge Spicer's "political and socioeconomic interests were bound up with those of Tombstone's law-and-order businessmen, but he appears to have brought a fair degree of objectivity to the hearings." Marks sees the Earps and the Cowboys mostly as representatives of their respective social classes and orders and interprets their behavior accordingly; her remarks about Judge Spicer's "political and socioeconomic interests" is a polite way of saying that he was prejudiced for the Earps from the outset. This is undoubtedly so: What would a community where a judge did not have more in common with the town lawmen than with cattle rustlers be like?

The Earps represented the town and federal law, and prior to the fight had done so in an exemplary manner. It was for the Cowboys to make a case otherwise. Marks is implying something else, namely that Spicer, however fair he may have tried to be, was prejudiced toward the Earps not because they were the law but because they were of the same social class or, stated from a Marxist perspective, that their social class was the law. So, too, were the so-called impartial witnesses: city folk, businessman and women inclined to look down on the crude and rural Cowboys, representatives, as Marks terms it, of "Southern Democratic values." The Earps cannot win in such an argument: Since all witnesses without Cowboy affiliations saw things happen the way the Earps saw them, the pro-Earp testimony automatically becomes slanted simply by dint of the fact that it's pro-Earp. The Cowboys' testimony, then, must be given weight simply because it supposedly represents the point of view of a different socioeconomic class from that of the townspeople. Viewed as symbols, not as men, the Cowboys as a class aren't guilty of crimes; they were simply resisting the encroachment of the civilization that the Earps represented.

Is an unbiased interpretation of the conflict possible? Yes, if one agrees that the Cowboys were, by and large, thieves, and that the Earps were respected lawmen. The first is difficult to do from a modern legal perspective, as none of the most prominent members associated with the Cowboys were ever convicted of anything more than misdemeanors. Most newcomers to the Earp-Cowboy conflict are surprised to find this out; but, then, people are equally surprised to discover that Jesse and Frank James, Dutch Schultz, and Al Capone, to name just four of America's most illustrious criminals, were not convicted of major crimes either. (They got Capone for income tax evasion.) The evidence history has used to convict these men is circumstantial, and I submit that there is more circumstantial evidence to convict the prominent Cowboys than Jesse James, Schultz, or Capone.

The second part is easy. Judged by the standards of their place and time, the Earps had sterling records as lawmen. All of the stories about shady deals and racketeering arose after the O.K. Corral shootout, and all stem from the charges made by Ike Clanton at the inquest. Wyatt Earp was indirectly responsible for many of the strange stories; he was a taciturn, secretive man, hardened by the frontier and by personal tragedy, and, except for a small group of friends and family who led lives as adventurous as his own, he kept to himself, inspiring all manner of tales about his doings with such men as Buckskin Frank Leslie, Bat Masterson, Luke Short, and Doc Holliday. Regarding the accusation of a stagecoach robbery gang run by the Earps, there is not a shred of evidence, nor, in fact, is there anything to suggest that Doc Holliday was involved in such activities. To believe Doc was a stage robber is to believe Wyatt knew about it—how, as a Wells Fargo operative, could he not?—and that he would shield Doc to the point of risking his brothers' lives. Or perhaps Wyatt and Doc were in league to rob stages, which must mean that Virgil and Morgan were involved with them, which is to believe that Wells Fargo, who had a secret agent in Tombstone in the person of Fred Dodge, would have paid Wyatt and Virgil to rob them and continue to then employ them years after Tombstone. Finally, it's difficult to believe that Doc Holliday, who had never been anything but a solitary gambler since arriving in the West, would suddenly turn to violent crime and require confederates such as Leonard, Head, Crane, and King. That the Earps would have continued to protect him to the point of risking their lives and everything they'd worked for in Tombstone is equally hard to believe.

It is far easier to believe that the whole story was exactly what it appears to be: the desperate and ridiculous attempt by a cattle rustler and associate of bank robbers to save his skin by deflecting his own act of treachery onto others.

A strong case against the Earps and Holliday at the O.K. Corral cannot be made with facts: There is simply no nonpartisan evidence that they were doing anything but their duty. Whether or not Josephine Marcus made the statement attributed to her in *I Married Wyatt Earp*, the sentiment is accurate: "If a similar shootout had occurred elsewhere in the West, where the sheriff wasn't violently prejudiced, the matter wouldn't have gone beyond a brief preliminary hearing."

But if Wyatt Earp the lawman can't be condemned by the facts of the O.K. Corral shootout, Wyatt Earp the symbol has proved to be quite vulnerable to academics who have reinvented him, along with Wild Bill Hickok, as an "incorporation gunfighter." The phrase was originally used by Richard Maxwell Brown in his widely quoted 1991 book, *No Duty to Retreat—Violence and Values in American History and Society*. Brown, a Beekman Professor Emeritus at the University of Oregon, made a study of the O.K. Corral gunfight, which became the centerpiece for his study of the evolution of American law from its English common law origins.

Brown begins with a simple analysis of English law: The right to kill is reserved for the Crown, and private citizens faced with the prospect of having to take life, even in their own defense, have a "duty to retreat" first before attempting to fight back. American law, Brown notes, has largely rejected this unwritten rule, particularly in the West, as symbolized by the gunfighters of legend. "At the core of both the myth and reality of the American as gunfighter," Brown writes, "is the theme of no duty to retreat as an energizer of violent behavior." Or, put another way, the dictate that one doesn't have to back down from a confrontation causes more violence than it prevents.

Brown's analysis of the Cochise County war is, like Paula Mitchell Marks's, neo-Marxist. "The key to understanding Wyatt Earp," says Brown "is to see his Tombstone triumph in the context of Arizona's 1881–82 Cochise County conflict—one of many such struggles in the decades-long Western Civil War of incorporation. The use of his gunfighting skill in the interest of lawfully gained wealth and property gained him the admiration and the patronage of his moneyed Republican friends in Tombstone." This, of course, is true. But by reducing Wyatt to a symbol, a great deal more truth is left out—was not Earp's "gunfighting skill" equally in the interest of Democrats or apolitical citizens who might also be grateful for and benefit financially from the law and order he helped provide?[8]

The "value system" of mining-oriented Tombstone, Brown argues, "placed a heavy emphasis on law and order as the basis for social stability and economic progress." This is certainly true, but one wonders what community, what "value system," does not place "heavy emphasis on law and order as the basis for social stability and economic progress." The Earps and Holliday, he further argues, were "violent point-men for the incorporating social and economic values represented by urban, industrial, Northern, capitalistic Tombstone.

(Doc Holliday, raised on a Georgia plantation and the son of a Confederate officer, might not have appreciated being called a point man for Northern capitalism.) The Clantons and McLaurys, then—supported by their criminal allies John Ringo, Curly Bill Brocius, and others—were equally violent protagonists of the resistant rural, pastoral, Southern Cowboy coalition of Cochise County."9 (The word *pastoral* is used so frequently by modern western historians in describing the Cowboys of this period that it's impossible not to summon up an image of Ike Clanton reclining on a hillside beside a flock of sheep playing a flute.) It comes as no surprise, then, that Brown concludes that Judge Wells Spicer's ruling on the O.K. Corral gunfight "was squarely in the context of the new American legal tradition of no duty to retreat that allowed one to stand one's ground and kill in self-defense."

The idea that a citizen had a duty to retreat before killing in self-defense was traced by Sir William Blackstone to the centuries-old common law tradition that held "the idea of all homicides" to be "public wrongs." Someone who killed in self-defense was considered guilty of murder until two essential points were proved: first, that retreat was not possible and that a "reasonable determination of necessity" was apparent. Brown's theory is that "The centuries-old English legal severity against homicide was replaced in our country by a proud, new tolerance for killing in situations where it might have been avoided by obeying a legal duty to retreat." This, for Brown, is symbolized by the gunfight at the O.K. Corral, and the gunfight, of course, is symbolized by Wyatt Earp. And so a man who had been involved in perhaps one street shooting prior to Tombstone, a peace officer renowned for his ability to avoid shooting scrapes, was transformed for ideological purposes into a symbol of the perversion of the American legal tradition.

Whatever the strengths of *No Duty to Retreat*, there is a serious weakness at the heart of Brown's conclusion about the gunfight: It was the Earps who had the jurisdiction, not the Cowboys, and not merely the town but federal authority as well. To extend the analysis back to Blackstone, it was the Earps who represented the authority of the Crown, therefore it was the duty of the Cowboys to retreat. (Ike Clanton, who may or may not have been up on his Blackstone, was the only one to obey this law.) To imply that the Earps should also have retreated would be to answer yes to the rhetorical question

✦ Old Man Clanton ✦

✦ Ike Clanton ✦

✦ Tom McLaury ✦

✦ Frank McLaury ✦

None of the Clantons was ever convicted of a serious crime, but the Old Man, Billy, and Ike all died violently at the hands of Lawmen. Finn spent a lot of time in jail. The McLaury Brothers may not have been bad fellows for cattle thieves.

John Ringo ✦ Like Doc Holliday, he had a fearsome reputation, though no one was sure why. One writer thought him "a Hamlet among outlaws." No one knows who put the final bullet in his head.

McLaury Brothers and Billy Clanton in their coffins ✦ The losers in the O.K. Corral gunfight. One of the most famous photos taken in the Old West; widely believed to have been taken by C.S. Fly.

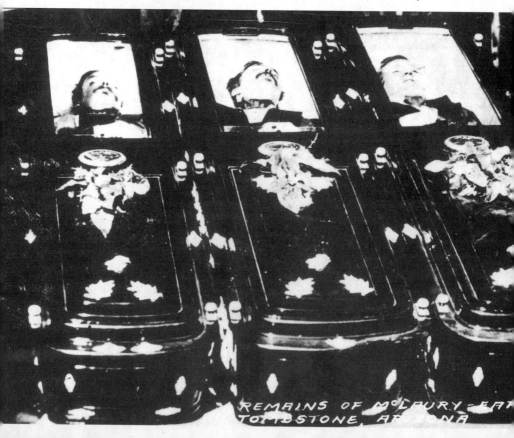

REMAINS OF M^CLAURY — EAR
TOMBSTONE, ARIZONA

Wyatt ✦ Old age portrait, late '20s.

Wyatt looking across the
Colorado River, 1925.

Mattie Blaylock Earp ✦ No one knows where Wyatt met her; they were apparently never married. She died of a drug overdose. The town where she was buried has disappeared from the map.

Disputed Josephine Marcus Earp ✦ Earp historians are divided as to whether or not this is the middle class Jewish girl from New York who became Wyatt's mate for 47 years. Few doubt she would have posed for it.

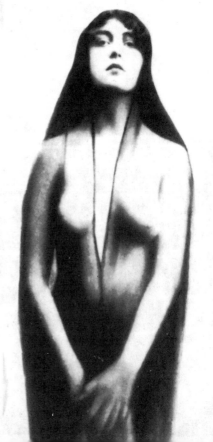

Bat Masterson wearing derby ✦
Buffalo hunter, Indian fighter,
Kansas peace officer, New York
sportswriter, life-long friend of
Wyatt Earp. He was an inspira-
tion for Damon Runyan's Sky
Masterson.

Doc Holliday ✦ Tubercular
son of a Confederate officer
from Georgia, he had a
degree in dental surgery
from a Philadelphia college.
Wyatt Earp was the only
man to whom he ever
showed devotion. On his
deathbed, he said, "This is
funny."

Tombstone – **O.K. Corral walk** ✦ *Left to right:* Val Kilmer, Sam Elliott, Kurt Russell, Bill Paxton

Tombstone – **Kurt Russell and Val Kilmer** ✦ Screenwriter Kevin Jarre paid meticulous attention to detail in clothing, hats, mustaches, guns, and period speech. Russell and Kilmer were the first movie "Wyatt" and "Doc" close to the originals in age at the time of the O.K. Corral shootout; Kilmer was the first movie "Doc" with a Southern accent.

✦ *Wyatt Earp* – Dennis Quaid and Kevin Costner ✦

Gunfight at the O.K. Corral – **Burt Lancaster, Kirk Douglas** ✦ The most popular Earp movie of all time.

Pall bearers at Wyatt Earp's funeral ✦ *Left to right:* W.J. Hunsaker (Wyatt's attorney in Tombstone), George Parsons, John Clum, William S. Hart, Wilson Mizner, and Tom Mix. Adela Rogers St. Johns said that Tom Mix wept.

Wyatt and Josephine are buried in a Jewish cemetery at Colma, California, which led some historians to speculate that Wyatt had converted to Judaism. "Hero of the Oy K Corral?" said one wag.

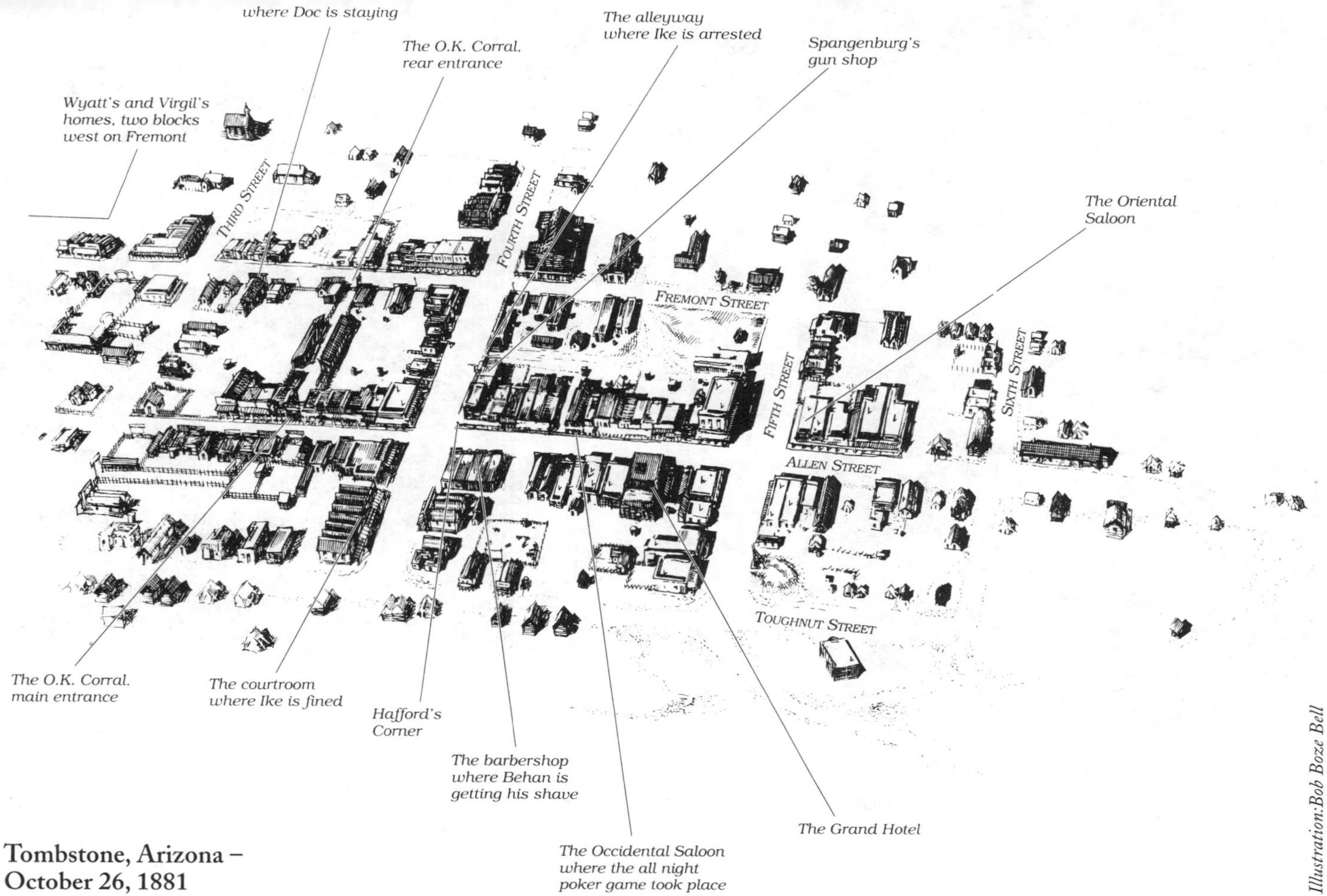

**Tombstone, Arizona –
October 26, 1881**

Illustration: Bob Boze Bell

Labels on the illustration:

- The Oriental Saloon
- Spangenburg's gun shop
- SIXTH STREET
- FIFTH STREET
- FREMONT STREET
- FOURTH STREET
- THIRD STREET
- ALLEN STREET
- TOUGHNUT STREET
- The Grand Hotel
- The alleyway where Ike is arrested
- The O.K. Corral, rear entrance
- where Doc is staying
- Wyatt's and Virgil's homes, two blocks west on Fremont
- The O.K. Corral, main entrance
- The courtroom where Ike is fined
- Hafford's Corner
- The barbershop where Behan is getting his shave
- The Occidental Saloon where the all night poker game took place

All-night poker game before the O.K. Corral ✦ The night before the most famous gunfight of the Old West, several of the participants played poker, a fact that has never been explained.

San Francisco Examiner **headline** ✦ Wyatt received more publicity from the Sharkey-Fitzsimmons fight than anything he did after Tombstone, all of it bad.

The Examiner.

"SHARKEY WINS BY A FOUL," SAID REFEREE EARP

Although Declared the Victor He Was Writhing on the Floor When the Decision Was Given in His Favor.

WYATT EARP, WHOSE DECISION MEANT $10,000.

✦ Northern Saloon ✦
Most researchers believe that the woman on the left is Josephine.

George Parsons ✦ George Parsons' Tombstone diary was a gold mine for historians. The church was founded by Endicott Peabody, later a tutor to Franklin D. Roosevelt at Groton School. Peabody built it with Wyatt Earp's winnings at the poker table.

Dodge City Peace Commission ✦ Taken in Dodge City, 1883, made famous by reprints in *The Police Gazette*. Bat Masterson is second from the right, standing; Wyatt is second from the left, sitting.

Buntline Special Colt .45 ✦ Wyatt probably had a long-barrelled Colt, but there is no proof that it was given to him by "dime" novelist Ned Buntline.

✦ **Doc Holliday's Saloon** ✦

On Avenue A, New York City. Doc Holliday might have visited saloons in this area as a dental student.

Painting: Bob Boze Bell

Wyatt and Josie ✦
They were together for nearly half a century. There is no record they were ever married.

New York Times **account of the gunfight ✦**
The *Times* got most of it right, except for "Judge" Holliday.

Post Office at this place was entered by burglars last night. A small amount of money was taken, but no Government property or registered mail was molested.

TOMBSTONE, Arizona, Oct. 27.—Four cowboys, Ike and Bill Clandon and Frank and Tom McLowery, have been parading the town for several days, drinking hard and making themselves obnoxious. City Marshal Earp arrested Ike Clandon. Soon after his release the four cowboys met the City Marshal, his brothers Morgan and Wyatt Earp, and City Judge Halliday. The Marshal ordered them to give up their weapons, when a fight was begun, about 30 shots being rapidly fired. Both of the McLowery boys were killed; Bill Clandon was mortally wounded, and died soon after. Ike Clandon was slightly wounded in the shoulder, and Wyatt Earp was also slightly wounded. The others were unhurt.

ALBANY, Oct. 27.—Dr. Vanderpoel has recovered all but four of the diamonds stolen from his residence.

UTICA, N. Y., Oct. 27.—William Henry Ostrander, who killed his brother, George Lyman

John Clum asked in the *Epitaph* after the gunfight: "Was the police force of Tombstone to be bullied and cowed?" For the Cowboys to demand that the police be unarmed was found by Judge Spicer to be "a proposition both monstrous and frightening"; a sentiment hardly confined to the American frontier in the 1880s. Is there any time and place in history where authority should have allowed armed citizens to decide when the police should be unarmed? How should policemen respond to repeated threats to their lives, when commands of "Throw up your hands" are ignored? Would modern policemen respond differently? Should they? These and similar questions keep the gunfight at the O.K. Corral at the center of debates on the limits of the use of force by police.

Regardless of what symbols one wishes to impose on the gunfight, the only way to condemn the Earps as aggressors on October 26, 1881, is to ignore all objective testimony in the O.K. Corral inquest. In the eyes of modern historians, the Earps' real crime wasn't firing on unarmed men but in being "violent point-men for the incorporating social and economic values represented by urban, industrial, Northern, capitalistic Tombstone," or, simply, in having "moneyed Republican friends." The Earps, especially Wyatt, went from being heroes in the 1940s and '50s to villains in our time because, after 1960, they were on the wrong side of history.

Is it possible, then, to sift through the reams of academic controversy, back through the partisan politics of the Arizona Territory in 1881 and determine precisely what did happen, and why? Probably not, but what follows is my attempt at a reasonable scenario that fits all the known facts.

The Earp brothers are tough, hard policemen, raised on law-and-order principles in a culture that reveres Unionist sympathies. They had learned frontier life as buffalo hunters, freight haulers, shotgun guards, gamblers, and cattle town peace officers. In these towns they kept the peace with rare recourse to their guns except to use them as billyclubs; they ruled by intimidation and nerve. After both Wyatt and Virgil were forced to kill in the line of duty, they began to sour on law enforcement. They come to Tombstone to make their fortune outside lawing. But their chosen activities—gambling, detective work and riding shotgun for Wells Fargo—inevitably pull them back into law enforcement positions on the federal, county, and town levels, and this brings them into repeated conflict with the local criminal element, a group loosely referred to as the Cowboys, mostly former Texans who made their living by rustling livestock from across the Mexican border. The Cowboys and their associates include everyone from semilegitimate ranchers (who serve as holders and fences for stolen cattle) to occasional holdup men. Some of them are killers; many Mexican vaqueros and federales are murdered in the cattle raids. Some Cowboys rent themselves out as strong-arm men in political disputes (such as the Tombstone town-lot troubles) and in election campaigns where ballot stuffing, usually against Republican candidates, is useful to Territorial Democrats. They are also useful, as Behan's deputy, Billy Breakenridge, later reveals, in helping the Sheriff's Office collect taxes from stubborn ranchers (among the "southern Democratic values" common to the early settlers was an antipathy to taxes in any form).

These talents were useful to local politicians who wanted to gain a foothold in the new, booming corner of the territory, so arrangements are made. John Behan, a corrupt, small-time politico with no experience as a peace officer is backed for the office of county sheriff, and he agrees to look the other way at illegal Cowboy activities, which are good business for many small local ranchers. The most profitable Cowboy activity is Mexican cattle rustling, which many locals, having a deep and abiding contempt for Mexicans, do not regard as a crime.

The Earps are law-and-order officers par excellence, which suits the town's businessmen, most of whom are from the East and who are anxious to expand their interests. From their point of view, cattle rustling contributes to the instability of the area's economy and social order. Besides, those making a living stealing cattle are eventually going to steal something else, and when the cattle business goes soft Wells Fargo's silver money shipments are a handy target. But the Earps are stymied in their efforts to sew up the plum law jobs in the newly formed Cochise County, where John Behan reneges on a deal to make Wyatt his undersheriff—in Earp's hands the second-in-command position of undersheriff would have been that of an "enforcer," roughly the equivalent of his Assistant City Marshal status in Dodge City. But Behan has no intention of giving Wyatt a job that would allow him to curtail Cowboy activities, so the Earps are left with Virgil's U.S. deputy marshal's badge, and, later, when their friend Town Marshal Fred White is killed, the town marshal's badge.

Since the U.S. government has no mechanism to curtail "Cowboy depredations"—requests for federal troops meet with deaf ears in Congress, particularly among Democrats—the Earps are the sole representatives of federal authority in southeastern Arizona and as such are resented by the Cowboys and many of their supporters who are disdainful of any kind of law, particularly that coming from a government many of them had fought against in the previous decade.

For a while, both factions pursue a policy of accommodation. The Earps, with Wyatt's notorious gunfighting friend Doc Holliday and Dodge City cronies Bat Masterson and Luke Short in town, are simply too formidable to confront in open combat. Then, Wyatt gets a county deputy sheriff's position, which threatens Cowboy activities more than both of Virgil's jobs combined. It looks as if the Earps and the law-and-order advocates will have a lock on lawing in and around Tombstone. But Virgil loses the marshal election to Ben Sippy—an amiable cipher who will desert Tombstone in a few months—and Wyatt resigns the deputy sheriff job to support his friend Bob Paul, a candidate for sheriff in nearby Pima County (though he counts on later becoming either sheriff or undersheriff in his own county). Then, Masterson returns to Kansas to aid his own brother and Short leaves Tombstone after killing a man in a gunfight. Now, the balance of power had shifted, and southeastern Arizona waits for a bloody confrontation.

Two new developments come into play at this time. The first affects the Cowboys. The Mexican government steps up its federal police force, building posts along the border and curtailing Cowboy cattle thefts. No longer held in check by the Earps and unanswerable to any form of federal or county control on the U.S. side, violence increases dramatically. Between May and July 1881 there are at least three confrontations between Cowboys and Mexican vaqueros and federales, with the collective death toll as high as two dozen. Mexico is no longer a free ride, so the Cowboys turn to the few large cattle ranches on the Arizona side of the border and to Wells Fargo shipments for their plunder. Stages are now robbed with increasing brazenness; a former deputy of John Behan's is involved in one robbery. On March 15 the Benson stage is held up, and the driver, Bud Philpot, is killed. Some believe the Cowboys' intention was to murder Pima County law-and-order sheriff, Bob Paul, who is riding shotgun guard. A suspect, Luther King, names three men—Leonard,

Crane and Head—as the holdup men. Then, King conveniently escapes from Behan's jail. A rumor then starts that Doc Holliday was
in the holdup gang and may have been the one who killed Philpot.

The second factor is Josephine Sarah Marcus. "Josie" or "Sadie" as
she will come to be called, a beautiful Jewish girl from New York,
who arrives in Tombstone with an acting troop and becomes John
Behan's mistress. Before long, she and Wyatt meet; Wyatt's relationship with his wife, Mattie, is deteriorating, and Josie and Wyatt
begin a clandestine relationship, giving John Behan yet another reason to fear and hate Wyatt Earp.

In June, Town Marshal Ben Sippy inexplicably leaves town, and
Virgil Earp is given his old office back. Wyatt determines to run for
Cochise County sheriff against Behan. The forces are now in motion
that lead to the shootout.

Wyatt, who is also working as a detective for Wells Fargo, determines that Leonard, Head, and Crane have ties to Ike Clanton.
Correctly sizing up Ike for a shiftless back-stabber, Wyatt extends a
substantial cash offer for the three stage robbers; Wyatt will also later
claim that Frank McLaury was in on the offer. Wyatt's intention is
clearly stated: He wants "the glory" of capturing the robbers and
thinks it can help him win the election. Not incidentally, it will get
Doc Holliday and the Earps off the hook from nasty rumors that
they had been involved in the Benson stage holdup. Ike wants to
know if the offer for the stage robbers covered dead as well as alive,
which, of course, means he is thinking of killing the three and getting the reward from Earp under the table so other Cowboys won't
find out about his treachery. Wyatt says he will ask Wells Fargo if the
reward also means dead; he inquires through the company's local
agent, Marshall Williams, a shady character who may have been
playing both sides against each other—he was nearby when King
escaped from Behan's jail. Williams blows the deal by getting drunk
and blabbing to Ike, who then accuses Wyatt of breaking their agreement of confidentiality—the last thing Ike wants is for word to leak
that he sold out his friends for money, and in the process helped
Wyatt Earp become county sheriff. He accuses Wyatt of telling Doc
Holliday; Wyatt denies this. Holliday does not take the accusations
lightly and threatens to kill Ike Clanton. Exactly why Ike goes ber-
serk at the thought of Holliday knowing the plan is never disclosed;
perhaps Ike feels that Doc, who plays the same gambling circuit as

Cowboy associates like Wes Fuller and Billy Allen, will let matters slip during a late-night card game.

Ike is now in a state of panic. If they have heard about it, John Behan and the Cowboy leaders, particularly Curly Bill Brocius, who has already had a run-in with Wyatt after Marshall White's death, cannot be happy with Ike's scheme. The day before and on the day of the gunfight Ike gets in one scrape after another with the Earp party; at one point, Virgil clunks him over the head and drags him into court after catching him wandering around Tombstone with a Winchester rifle and a six-gun. Not only is Ike carrying the guns in blatant defiance of city ordinance, he is heard by numerous people making death threats against the Earps. The reason for this irrational behavior is unknown. Ike seems to keep provoking a fight in which he would surely be killed, and then backing down. Considering his public threats, the Earps, by the standard of behavior in the Old West, would have been fully justified in shooting him on sight even if they weren't policemen.

At one point, Wyatt ran into Tom McLaury, who makes some form of mild protest such as "Why are you picking on Ike?" Wyatt has had enough—he bashes Tom over the head with his gun barrel and clubs him to the ground in the streets of Tombstone: It's the same method for intimidating troublemakers that Wyatt had found to be effective in Kansas. It doesn't work this time. Goaded on by Ike—and possibly by Frank McLaury, who, if Wyatt was telling the truth, was also in on the Benson stage reward deal—the Cowboys make a show of going into Spangenberg's gun shop. This can have no purpose but to provoke the Earps and show them they are prepared to fight. Now it is the Cowboys' turn to find out that Wyatt Earp is not intimidated. Alone, Wyatt walks over to Frank McLaury's horse, which is on the sidewalk, a violation of town ordinance, and leads the animal back out into the street. The McLaurys simmer but hold their tempers. Why doesn't Wyatt arrest them at this point for carrying guns? Probably because he simply wanted them to leave town; if the Cowboys back down, the Earps will have succeeded in their purpose. (Wyatt didn't arrest Ike the night before when he was carrying a gun, probably for the same reason.)

But the Cowboys don't leave. With at least two of their number wearing guns and leading horses with repeating rifles on the saddles, they mill around in front of the O.K. Corral, where they are overheard making threats against the police chief and his brothers. They walk through the Corral to a back lot and loiter next to Fly's Photography Studio, in the back of which Holliday rooms. They are there long enough for several townspeople to inform the Earps, who are standing a block and a half away in front of Hafford's saloon. Private citizens give the marshal an offer of aid; Virgil turns them down. The Earps are professionals and have never allowed citizen interference in their procedure.

To complicate matters, Doc Holliday comes on the scene. Apparently neither Wyatt nor Virgil wants him along, but they defer for the simple reason that if Doc is with them they at least know where he is and have a chance of controlling him. Virgil finally decides it's time to go. He takes Doc Holliday's cane—why Doc was using a cane has never been established—and gives Doc his Wells Fargo short-barreled shotgun. Virgil's purpose is probably twofold; first, Doc can conceal it under his long coat until they are at close range, and, second, Doc can also keep an eye on anyone attempting to turn their flank. (Billy Claiborne, Billy Allen, and Wes Fuller, all known Cowboy associates, have been spotted nearby, and the Earps have no way of knowing what they'll do if a fight breaks out.)

The Earps and Holliday begin the walk that will be re-created some two dozen times by Hollywood. As they turn left on Fourth Street and walk swiftly up Fremont, John Behan, who has failed miserably in his attempt to disarm the Cowboys, runs up and says something like, "I've been down there to disarm them." The Earps go right on by him into the lot next to Fly's.

What happens next? I submit that the simplest answer to that question, the one that fits best with the testimony of the nonpartisan witnesses, is Wyatt Earp's account in the Spicer hearing:

> We came up on them close; Frank McLaury, Tom Mc-Laury, and Billy Clanton standing in a row against the east side of the building on the opposite side of the vacant space west of Fly's photograph gallery. Ike Clanton and Billy Claiborne and a man I don't know were standing in the vacant space about halfway between the photograph gallery and the next building west.
>
> I saw that Billy Clanton and Frank and Tom McLaury had their hands by their sides, Frank McLaury and Billy

Clanton's six-shooters were in plain sight. Virgil said, "Throw up your hands, I have come to disarm you!" Billy Clanton and Frank McLaury laid their hands on their six-shooters. Virgil said, "Hold, I don't mean that! I have come to disarm you!" Then Billy Clanton and Frank McLaury commenced to draw their pistols. At the same time, Tom McLaury throwed his hand to his right hip, throwing his coat open like this, [showing how] and jumped behind his horse. [Actually it was Billy Clanton's horse.]

I had my pistol in my overcoat pocket, where I had put it when Behan told us he had disarmed the other parties. When I saw Billy Clanton and Frank McLaury draw their pistols, I drew my pistol. Billy Clanton leveled his pistol at me, but I did not aim at him. I knew that Frank McLaury had the reputation of being a good shot and a dangerous man, and I aimed at Frank McLaury. The first two shots were fired by Billy Clanton and myself, he shooting at me, and I shooting at Frank McLaury. I don't know which was fired first. We fired almost together. The fight then became general.

No neutral witness saw Doc Holliday begin the fight; no neutral witness heard the Earps approach the Cowboys with their hands up. None of the nonpartisan testimony contradicts Wyatt's. Among modern researchers, Paula Mitchell Marks crystallizes an argument many have made in dismissing Wyatt's version of the fight:

Wyatt Earp was nervy and good with a gun. Nobody was that good with a gun. Weapons authorities have established that the reaction time of even the most skilled gunman will make him the loser if his reasonably swift opponent has even started to draw first. As testimony would show, Billy Clanton and Frank McLaury were both considered swift, efficient shooters. If they were already standing there with their pistols cocked, intending to shoot, Wyatt Earp could not have drawn and fired almost simultaneously with one of them.

I do not know which weapons authorities Marks contacted in her research. Jim Dunham, a prize-winning Cowboy shooter and gun-handler who was hired to work on *Tombstone*, assures me that there is no particular reason why a good gun handler such as Wyatt Earp couldn't beat another good gunman to a draw even if the latter started first:

> First of all, the reaction time of one gunfighter responding to the moves of another is about the same as a hitter in baseball trying to get around on, say, a 98-plus mile-per-hour fastball. It's not easy, but it's done regularly. But there are a lot of other factors involved. Clanton or McLaury might have telegraphed their intentions with their eyes, or one or both of them might have failed to make a clean jerk of the gun from the holster. Remember, Billy Clanton was wearing a cross-draw rig, so he had to pull the gun to the right, across his body. And remember one thing—Wyatt Earp was expecting trouble. He already had his hand on his gun.

Dunham makes a very important point: Wyatt was anticipating trouble and already had his hand on his gun. The gunfight in the lot in back of the O.K. Corral was not an athletic contest or a duel; it was an attempted arrest gone bad. From a policeman's point of view what is so dangerous about such situations is that he cannot fire first—even if the subject is armed, the officer must wait for a response to his command before he can take action. H. F. Sills, a nonpartisan witness, said that the Cowboys did not raise their hands on Virgil's command and that Billy Clanton and Wyatt Earp fired first, which is what Wyatt said. Earp did not call it a fast-draw contest: He didn't say he beat Clanton or Frank McLaury to the draw. Billy might have shot at Wyatt a split-second before Wyatt's gun was in position. If so, he missed, and Wyatt shot at the man everyone considered the more dangerous gunman, Frank McLaury. He hit him. After that, the fight became "general."

No witness thought that Doc Holliday began the fight with a shotgun blast. According to Wyatt Earp and the *Nugget*, the fight began when Frank McLaury went for his gun. Then everyone heard two shots, fired almost simultaneously from the guns of Billy

Clanton and Wyatt Earp. That's what Wyatt said; that's what H. F. Sills said; and nothing in the testimony of any nonpartisan witness contradicts it. That is most likely what happened.

Wyatt was released on December 1 and immediately registered to vote in Cochise County. This sent a public message that he had no intention of leaving Tombstone. The rest of the Earp family wasn't sure this was a good idea. "Virge's leg began to heal up," Allie Earp is quoted as saying.[10] "And I knew it was time for us to be gettin' out of town. Tombstone wasn't the same after the O.K. Corral. There was a feelin' in the air. You couldn't put your finger on it, but it was bad just the same. I told Virge we'd better be movin' on. He didn't say anything, but I know he felt like that, too. But we kept puttin' it off." Simply, "We didn't get out while the gettin' was good."

Josephine Marcus did, either late in 1881 or early the next year, just as hostilities were breaking into open warfare. We do not know how she and Wyatt remained in touch after the gunfight; presumably they had little contact for the next few months as Wyatt was either in jail or surrounded by supporters and allies everywhere he went. In March 1882 the *Arizona Daily Star* reported that Behan traveled to San Francisco; it's a good guess that he was making a last attempt at getting Josephine back.

By Christmas, most of the Earps were in the Cosmopolitan Hotel with armed supporters on guard night and day; across the street, at the Grand, armed Cowboy supporters kept watch. In the midst of the tension, Doc Holliday started off Tombstone's new year with a bang. Ever the scamp, Doc snuffed out a lamplight with a shot from his revolver, and hundreds of townsfolk came running in anticipation of a battle. "Great excitement," wrote George Parsons in his journal. "Done for devilment."

Back home in the little town of Colton in San Bernardino County, Nicholas Earp, after some serious drinking, got into an angry brawl with a local lawyer. No one knows what the fight was about, but it was news enough to be printed in the *Los Angeles Herald*, an indicator that the scrape in Tombstone had made the Earp name famous. In a short time, Wyatt Earp would make the family name legendary.

Notes

1. Josephine Marcus was almost certainly within earshot of the fight and may have come running up as Behan approached Wyatt. This scene worked so well in the movie *Tombstone* that one wants it to be true. Unfortunately, it's out of *I Married Wyatt Earp* and not to be found in Josephine's original recollections. Here's more:

> I almost swooned when I saw Wyatt's tall figure very much alive, starting up Fremont with Doc and Fred Dodge. He spotted me, and all of them came across the street. Like a feather-brained girl my only thought was, "My God, I haven't got a bonnet on." But you can imagine my real relief at seeing my love alive. I was simply a little hysterical. Can you blame me?

No, particularly when the sentiments seem to fit Josie perfectly. But this reads suspiciously like a novelist trying to get inside Josephine's head. The reader must take this text, like much of *I Married Wyatt Earp*, for what he or she thinks it might be worth.

2. It has been suggested that Doc's sorrow might have been due to Morgan Earp's wound, which might have looked fatal on the street. Doc was fond of Morgan and knew that he was Wyatt's favorite brother.

3. The credit for discovering this important document goes once again to Bob Palmquist, who found it reprinted in the *Tucson Citizen*, or perhaps rediscovered it is a better word, since the *Nugget*'s account of the fight was referred to by researchers in the 1950s. Then, somehow, knowledge of it seemed to disappear until recently; perhaps in an era when Earp debunking was the fashion, no one was interested in evidence that made Wyatt look good. There is no mention of it in *I Married Wyatt Earp*, edited by Glenn Boyer, *The O.K. Corral Inquest* by Alford Turner, or in Paula Mitchell Marks's exhaustive study of the gunfight, *And Die in the West*.

4. Incredibly, neither Earp partisans such as Glenn Boyer nor debunkers Frank Waters or Ed Bartholomew show the slightest awareness of Clara Brown's writing on Tombstone. Paula Mitchell Marks, probably the best known academic to write about Tombstone, fails to mention her at all. Brown would also have escaped the attention of the author of this book if not for Bob Palmquist and Jeff Morey.

5. Later Earp debunkers would jump on the fact that at least one "pro-Earp" witness also identified Doc and Morgan as the instigators of the gunfight: Josephine Marcus. From *I Married Wyatt Earp*: "It's clear that at the hearing in court Wyatt and Virg both said what was necessary to protect Morg and Doc." And: "You can bet though that Wyatt and Virg were hot under the collar, especially at Doc, but almost equally at Morg." She also refers to Morgan as "the hothead" of the Earp family. There are several problems with this, starting with the fact that nowhere in *I Married Wyatt Earp* does it say that Josephine actually witnessed the gunfight. The text reads: " *Later* I discovered exactly what happened"—meaning, of course, that Wyatt told her.

This leads to a bigger problem. As Tucson lawyer and researcher Bob Palmquist points out, the above quoted passages aren't in Josephine's memoirs but were added later when *I Married Wyatt Earp* was assembled. No one has ever discovered those words written in Josephine's hand, therefore there is every reason to believe they are bogus.

For that matter, at no time in Josephine's actual memoirs does she refer to Morgan Earp as a "hothead," which is an important point since all subsequent books and articles that give Morgan a share of the blame for starting the fight refer to remarks attributed to her in *I Married Wyatt Earp*. This appears to be the imaginative invention of someone other than Josephine. In fact, no one has ever uncovered any reference to Morgan Earp being called a hothead anywhere before the gunfight; on the contrary, in every tense situation he found himself in Morgan seems to have acted with the characteristic Earp coolness and deliberation.

6. In *And Die in the West*, Paula Marks concludes that Spicer's "biggest lapse involved not his reasoning in the [final] decision but his allowing Wyatt Earp to read a prepared statement and escape cross-examination, that cornerstone of the fair legal process." In truth, that conclusion is one of Mark's biggest lapses. Bob Palmquist found this passage in the *Compiled Laws of Arizona Territory* (1877):

> When the examination of witnesses on the part on the part of the territory is closed, the magistrate shall distinctly inform the defendant that it is his right to make a statement in relation to the charges against him (stating to him the nature thereof), that the statement is designed to enable him, if he see fit, to answer the charge, and to explain the fact alleged against him, that he is at liberty to waive making a statement and that his waiver cannot be used against him on the trial.

Palmquist points out that the initial objection from the prosecution stemmed from the fact that they had never seen anyone read from a written statement before. Palmquist also feels that later researchers have made more of this than Clanton's lawyers; after the initial objection the matter was not raised again.

7. Mrs. J. C. Collier was visiting from the East and was apparently standing on the corner of Fourth and Fremont when the fight broke out. The Earp party "approached the Cowboys," she told the Kansas City paper, "and told them to hold up their hands. The Cowboys opened fire on them, and you never saw such shooting as followed. One of the Cowboys after he had been shot three times raised himself on his elbow and shot one of the officers and fell back dead." Collier apparently had no idea that her testimony might be important; she waited two months before telling it to a journalist.

8. "The good reputation that Wyatt enjoyed in Dodge," writes Paula Marks in *And Die in the West*, "resulted at least in part from the fact that he did the dirty work for the town's God-fearing law-abiding citizens." One might argue that the good reputation Wyatt enjoyed in Dodge resulted entirely from the fact that he did the dirty work for the town's God-fearing, law-abiding citizens and further remark that that is a pretty good definition of a good policeman in just about any time and place.

9. John Mack Farager used almost identical language in an article on Earp for a 1995 issue of *American Heritage* magazine: "The trouble in Tombstone was just one episode in a series of local wars that pitted men with traditional rural values and Southern sympathies against mostly Yankee capitalist modernizers. As the hired guns of the businessmen in town, the Earps became the enemies of the Clantons." By Mr. Farager's definition, one fears that the only lawmen of the Old West who wouldn't carry the taint of a "hired gun" label are corrupt lawmen such as John Behan.

10. The reader will have ascertained by now that I regard *The Earp Brothers of Tombstone* as fraudulent, and though its origin is Allie Earp's jealousy and dislike of Wyatt, there is no telling where Allie's comments end and those of Frank Waters, who was certainly pushing an anti-Earp agenda, begin. Still, in the interest of presenting varying points of view, I feel compelled to include some passages from Waters's book.

7

Wyatt Earp Unleashed: The Vendetta Ride

On December 28, close to midnight, the Wednesday after Christmas and three days before the town marshal's election, Deputy U.S. Marshal Virgil Earp walked from the Earps' main hangout at the Oriental Saloon to the Cosmopolitan Hotel. As he crossed Fifth Street, the roar of shotgun blasts filled the streets—even those in noisy saloons came running. How many shotgun blasts isn't known. Virgil thought it was three, but George Parsons, who was nearby, claimed to have heard four, which probably meant two men, both with double-barreled shotguns. All others could make out was that the shots came from a nearby construction site.

Virgil was hit by two of the loads. Incredibly, he was only hit in the arm and small of the back. Virgil stopped back at the Oriental, looking for Wyatt. He found him and collapsed. Wyatt and some friends carried Virgil to the Cosmopolitan Hotel where Doctors Matthews and Goodfellow were called in. George Parsons went to see Virgil and found the "hotel well guarded, so much so that I had trouble to get to the Earps' room. . . . Told him I was sorry for him. 'It's Hell, isn't it!' Said he. His wife was troubled. 'Never mind, I've got one good arm to hold you with,' he said." Virgil was right. Most of the damage had been to his left elbow. The doctors' report called the wound "a longitudinal fracture of the humerus, a bone between the shoulder and elbow," and they debated as to whether or not they should amputate; they settled for more than five inches of bone.

Virgil would some day serve as a lawman again, but his days as a fighting man were over.

Three men had been spotted running from the scene of the shooting. The night after, George Parsons speculated that the potential assassins were Ike Clanton, Curly Bill Brocius, and Will McLaury. "Bad state of affairs here," he wrote. "Something will have to be done." Something would be.

On March 18 of the following year Wyatt, Morgan, and John Clum took in *Stolen Kisses* at Schieffelin Hall, Tombstone's "big" theater named for the man who founded the town. (The "small" Bird Cage Variety, "Tombstone's Gem," had opened just before Christmas.) All three carried concealed .45 Colts. After the show, the brothers walked to Campbell and Hatch's saloon for some pool, a game Morgan loved. They were accompanied by a friend, Dan Tipton, and by Sherman McMasters, former Cowboy associate, suspected stage bandit, and possible Wells Fargo informant.

As Morgan leaned forward to make a shot, at least two bullets ripped through the door in the back of the saloon. One struck the wall above Wyatt's head; the second hit Morgan in the back, shattering his spine. It passed through his body and stopped in the thigh of George Berry, a bystander. Morgan fell on the table, then collapsed to the floor. He lived for an hour. Clara Brown, in her dispatch to the *San Diego Tribune*, wrote that "the man was surrounded by his brothers and their wives, whose grief was intense. He whispered some words to Wyatt, which have not been give to the public, but spoke aloud only once when his companions endeavored to raise him to his feet: 'Don't, boys,' he said, 'I can't stand it. I have played my last game of pool.'"

At the saloon door, a hound raised by the brothers howled and moaned. The *Nugget*, in a rare moment of sentimentality, reported that "when the body was taken to the hotel, no sadder heart followed than that of the faithful dog."

Morgan's last words have been the subject of much speculation. In *I Married Wyatt Earp*, Josephine Marcus says they were, "They got me, Wyatt, you be careful, don't let them get you" and "Father, mother." The most popular version is the one in *Frontier Marshal*. Apparently Morgan had been reading a book on people who had had near death experiences with supposed glimpses of heaven. He got

Wyatt to read it, too, and one night, camped on the desert, they talked themselves to sleep discussing it. Wyatt was, characteristically, skeptical. The brothers made a pact: Whichever one went first would try to give the other an idea of what he saw. Wyatt forgot the pact; Morgan didn't. As he was dying he asked Wyatt to bend close. "I guess you were right, Wyatt," he whispered. "I can't see a damn thing."

Nearly forty years after Morgan's death, Wyatt would tell another biographer of another final exchange: "Do you know who did it?" asked Morgan.. "Yes," Wyatt replied, "and I'll get them." "That's all I'll ask," Morgan whispered. "But Wyatt," he pleaded, "be careful."

Whether or not Wyatt spoke the words, he had made the promise in his heart. He had had enough. He had held back when the Cowboys had stolen his horse and army mules and endured their threats; he had held his temper when Marshal White was killed, even though he would have been entirely justified in killing Curly Bill on the spot; he had simmered when Ike Clanton, of all people, accused him and his brothers of fronting a stage robbery ring; and he had withheld his revenge when his older brother was crippled for life and his friend John Clum was nearly assassinated. All his mature life he had been a lawman, perhaps too strict and unbending a lawman, one who followed the law when politics would have served him better. Now, Morgan was dead, murdered after Wyatt had made a peace offering to their enemies. He saw the powerlessness of the law in this time and place. Now, he would settle matters himself.

The Wyatt Earp of the Vendetta Ride, or "Ride of Vengeance," is the Wyatt Earp who lives most vividly in western legend and controversy. It's also the Wyatt Earp that Hollywood, in making a world-famous legend from a pale reflection of the original man, would choose to omit.

We have no record at all of Wyatt's home life during the last difficult months before Morgan's death. We know that he was seeing Josephine, but we don't know when or where. "We all knew about it," said the Allie Earp of *The Earp Brothers of Tombstone,*

and we knew Mattie did too. That's why we never said anything to her. We didn't have to. We could see her with her eyes all red from cryin', thinkin' of Wyatt's carryin'-

on. I didn't have to peek out at night to see if the light was still burnin' at daylight when I got up.

Everything Wyatt did stuck the knife deeper into Mattie's heart. Polishin' his boots so he could prance into a fancy restaurant with Sadie.[1] Cleanin' his guns to show off to Sadie. You never saw his hair combed so proper or his long, slim hands so beautiful clean and soft.

There's a good chance that Wyatt was "carryin'-on" with Sadie, though the part about Wyatt cleaning his guns to show her seems a bit much. (Like everyone else in the Old West who handled guns, Wyatt probably cleaned them every other day just out of habit.) The problem here is that, like Sadie's alleged account, *I Married Wyatt Earp*, *The Earp Brothers of Tombstone* is highly suspect. We can be reasonably sure that the author, Frank Waters, spent some time with Allie, though apparently very little. (It's likely that Stuart Lake spent more time with Wyatt while working on the discredited *Frontier Marshal*.) The original notes or tape recordings either don't exist or are in the hands of private collectors. The result is a book that one wag called *I Married Virgil Earp—But I Hated Wyatt Even More than I Loved Virgil*. In fact, Allie herself rejected what she saw of Waters's finished book. Even the rare parts of the book that were developed out of something Allie actually said are largely the rantings of an octogenarian who blamed Wyatt Earp for poisoning her husband's mind, getting him crippled, and then becoming the more famous after death.[2]

The Allie of *Earp Brothers* would later claim that Wyatt kept Sadie "hidden in the Earp closet," but in fact all the Earp women were pretty much kept penned up in their homes in the frontier Victorian fashion of the times. (Oddly enough, it was Wyatt who would break this mold, later dashing all over the western half of the continent with Josephine.) It seems doubtful that Wyatt ever tried to impress Josephine by showing her his guns, particularly since Wyatt was unarmed for most of the time he spent in Tombstone. It's even less likely that Wyatt pranced into any fancy restaurants with Josie, since there is no public record of the two of them together in Tombstone, not in John Clum's memoirs nor in Fred Dodge's. One might remark that these were Victorian times and that gentlemen practiced discretion in public, but not even the private journal of George Parsons mentions Josie. Tombstone was huge for a mining camp, but it wasn't big enough for a man as well known as Wyatt Earp to meet a beautiful woman in public without someone noticing.

Allie certainly knew of Josephine and saw her. "Sadie's charms," wrote Waters, "were undeniable. She had a small, trim body and a *meneo* of the hips that kept her full, flounced skirts bouncing. Certainly her strange accent, brought with her from New York to San Francisco, carried a music new to the ears of a Western gambler and gunman." This description predates *I Married Wyatt Earp*, when Josie's existence was scarcely known to researchers; the description could only have come from someone who was there, almost certainly Allie. The question is how much of the description of Josie and Wyatt was Allie's and how much was Waters's invention.[3] At one point in the book, Allie and Mattie "was makin' a patchwork quilt to keep her mind off things" when "there, just before us, I saw her flounce out of the stationery store. I knew right off it was Sadie. Nobody but a strumpet would be dressed up that early in the mornin' in a silk dress with practically a bare bosom covered only by a peek-a-boo little shawl just to be tantalizin'!"

Mattie winces, watching Sadie "flounce around the corner"—presumably Josephine learned flouncing in her acting troupe—and "all them mad, hurt, jealous, and sad feelin's was boilin' inside her like a teakettle." Allie, distraught, runs home where she reflects that "Wyatt doin' that to her made me more suspicious of what I had got into. And when Virge didn't come home, I got scairt." (Seems like near every time Allie got scairt it was Wyatt's fault.) She runs to her dresser and reads an eight-line poem from Virgil that ends, "I long for thee and weep." There is no other recorded instance of Virgil's taste in poetry. One wonders if there wasn't just a touch of anti-Semitism in Allie's reaction to "Sadie."[4] One thing is for sure: Josie turned heads, and if she had been seeing a lot of Wyatt in public more people would have noticed.

What is likely is that Wyatt, a taciturn man to outsiders, was smitten not merely with Josie's beauty but with her adventurous spirit, while she sensed a strength in him she did not feel in John Behan. Wyatt and Josie may have been lovers in Tombstone, but given the Victorian temper that still prevailed in middle-class society on the frontier, probably not. Although they must have talked and made some kind of pact to meet outside Arizona later.

From December 1881 until his departure from Tombstone, Wyatt had a great many other matters to occupy his time. One December 14, as a prelude to the assassination attempts on Morgan and Virgil, the Benson stage was attacked by unknown assailants. What was notable about this holdup was that John Clum was aboard and that the bandits blasted away before the passengers were given a chance to surrender. The stage lurched ahead and outdistanced the attackers, though one passenger and one horse were wounded. When the stage stopped further down the road, the driver decided to get everyone out and walk to the station. Clum, carrying two .45 Colts for protection, stumbled out on his own into the desert night, convinced that the shooters were after him and would make another try.

The Nugget, predictably, snickered at such a notion. "The prevailing opinion," said an editorial on the next day, "is that he is still running." Clum's penchant for melodrama may have led him to overplay his own importance in this instance, but the facts are that the attackers did not attempt to rob the stage after the initial volley and Clum did not invent the wounds to passenger and horse. The callousness with which armed assault was now being accepted in Tombstone was alarming. Acting Governor John J. Gosper asked the secretary of the interior to urge Congress to repeal the Posse Comitatus Act and allow federal troops into Cochise County. But too many congressmen recalled the mess that the army had made in Lincoln County, New Mexico, just three years earlier in the trouble that spawned Billy the Kid. No federal help would be forthcoming.

Four days after the stage attack, the *Epitaph* printed an anonymous letter addressed to Judge Wells Spicer: "Sir, if you take my advice you will take your departure for a more genial clime, as I don't think this one healthy for you much longer. As you are liable to get a hole through your coat at any moment. If such sons of bitches as you are allowed to dispense justice in this territory, the sooner you depart from us the better." Gary Roberts, a Georgia-based academic and researcher, has studied the syntax carefully and concluded that the letter was probably written by an educated man trying to sound illiterate; Will McLaury makes a handsome suspect.

Spicer revealed in the *Epitaph* that he had received "similar threats" and that if his enemies wanted him "I will say that I will be here just where they can find me should they want me." This brought an old Earp foe into the fray. On December 21, James Reilly, the judge Wyatt had arrested the previous year, wrote the first of several crackpot letters that brought some unintentional amusement to an otherwise tense scene. Reilly, no longer a judge, blasted the *Epitaph* for giving so much ink to threats to Spicer but not taking seriously threats made by the Earp faction to Milt Joyce and to "many others who have denounced the killing of the McLaurys." (Joyce had gotten into a shouting match on December 17 with Wyatt and Doc before being arrested by John Behan, who finally found someone he could disarm.) Precisely what those threats were and to whom they were made was not specified.

The nuttier Reilly's letters got, the more they were taken to heart by some of the more virulent anti-Earpists. In Reilly's view, the Earps, Clum, and the entire Citizens League had instigated "a systematic attempt to inaugurate a state of terrorism in Tombstone." Reilly was "convinced that seven of ten of the stage robberies committed in Arizona for the last fifteen years have been put up and engineered by the trusted agents of the post office, of Wells Fargo & Co.'s agents, and agents of the stage companies." Reilly saw the government, big business, and law enforcement all in league to rob the stages and see that the Cowboys were discredited.

Unwittingly, though, Reilly may have hit on something when he mentioned "Wells Fargo & Co.'s agents," at least in regard to Marshall Williams, who had been suspiciously close to two disasters— the escape of Leonard, Head, and Crane and Ike Clanton's rampage before the gunfight—and who may have been in league with some of the stage robbers. Oddly enough, Reilly also charged that the murder of Bud Philpot in the Benson stage holdup was a scheme "to kill Bob Paul, whose known honesty, energy and bravery was dangerous to the clique that had hoped by a monopoly of gambling, stage robbing and dead-fall keeping to control the politics and business of Tombstone." He may have been right, only it was the Cowboys, particularly Ike Clanton, Curly Bill, and John Ringo, who had tried to rig the election to keep Paul out of office, and they did it in the interests of the newspaper that Reilly was writing for.

John Clum was visiting family in the east and also, perhaps, office-hunting in Washington, but while he was away the *Epitaph* continued to hammer at the Democratic tax-skimming Ten Per Cent Ring. Finally, though, the election would not be about politics but about the Earps and the postgunfight controversy. The *Nugget* attacked the

Earps and anyone associated with them unmercifully, going so far in one instance as to reprint an obviously erroneous story from the *Las Vegas Optic* that claimed that Wyatt had been killed "and has been planted for worm feed. He was previously a policeman at Dodge City under Bat Masterson and had something to do with Fort Worth, before coming to Las Vegas." Such was the state of frontier journalism in 1882.

On election day the *Nugget* swept the boards. John Carr, their candidate for mayor, handily beat (830 votes to 298) a lumberyard owner named Lewis W. Blinn, who had the *Epitaph*'s endorsement. Dave Neagle, who had gained a solid reputation as Behan's deputy, beat Jim Flynn, 590 to 434. (Reilly, who was probably too nutty for even the Nugget to back, lost his bid for city recorder.) "Exeunt Earps!" was the *Nugget*'s headline on January 4. "The honest masses of people were jubilant at the complete discomfiture of the open and insidious enemies of the prosperity of our city, and the Strangler's organ." Stranglers, of course, were vigilantes, and their organ was the *Epitaph*. The *Nugget* had apparently succeeded in convincing more than a few residents that the Earps were the heads of a potential mob (though on at least two occasions Virgil and Wyatt had made heroic stands in keeping lynch mobs from accused killers).

"There need be no fears of turbulence or violence on the part of the lawless elements," the *Nugget* crowed. "Our mayor-elect is a man of considerable adipore [sic] tissue and he will suppress 'em. He will set down on 'em, as he did on one Mr. Blinn yesterday." If Carr and the *Nugget* thought they were capable of controlling the forces they had set in motion, they were in for a shock.

Ike Clanton's hat, which had his name in it, was found near the scene of Virgil's shooting. That couldn't be taken as evidence in courts that he was involved, but there were few people in Tombstone who doubted that Ike was in on it. It was later determined that Will McLaury had left for Fort Worth two days before the ambush, so he was off the hook. Nearly eighty years later a letter McLaury wrote to his father in Iowa was discovered. "My experience out there," McLaury wrote, "has been very unfortunate—as to my health and badly injured me as to money matters—and none of the results have been satisfactory—the only result is the death of Morgan and the crippling of Virgil Earp." Modern students have taken this as an admission that McLaury engineered the assassination attempts, possibly paying the shooters himself. They are doing McLaury an injustice. Will McLaury was a civilized man, a lawyer, and determined though he was to see the Earps punished by legal means there is no reason to suspect that he'd have resorted to murder. If anything, his letter seems to imply disgust with the way things turned out. For their part, the Cowboys needed no one to pay them to kill the Earps. Both Ike and Curly Bill had grudges to settle with the brothers, and Ike was certainly capable of shooting someone in the back, especially when supported by friends.

On December 29, Wyatt sent a wire to Crawley Dake, the U.S. marshal for Arizona Territory in Phoenix: "Virgil was shot by concealed assassins last night. His wounds are fatal. Telegraph me appointment with power to appoint deputies. Local authorities are doing nothing. The lives of other citizens are threatened." Virgil's wounds proved not to be fatal, but Wyatt's course was now fixed. Dake immediately wired back, telling Wyatt he now had federal authority and could appoint deputies.

Wyatt sold his gambling and other business interests and lived off the proceeds. With federal funds from Dake and, probably, from Wells Fargo, he began to form a posse. He was now a full-time deputy U.S. marshal, though he did briefly work in one freelance job. On January 4, a mining tycoon from California named George Hearst visited Tombstone amid rumors of a kidnapping. Through a friend of mining interests, Wyatt met him and took a job as his bodyguard. It was a connection that had wider ramifications than Wyatt could possibly have imagined. Before the century was out, Wyatt would become friendly with Hearst's son, William Randolph, whose publications would help create the Earp legend.

But the thought of future fame was undoubtedly light years from Wyatt Earp's mind in January as he tried to deal with the sudden outburst of robberies in Cochise County. On January 6, the stage traveling from the village of Hereford to Bisbee, the copper mining town in the mountains near the Mexican border, was fired on. The stage driver tried to double back to Hereford, but the bandits caught up, stopped the stage, and relieved the strong box of $6,500.00 (The location of the robbery, by the way, was just a short distance from the Clanton ranch.) The driver was threatened with death should he reveal the identity of one of the gunmen, which indicates that he was

well known in the area. If a follow-up report in the *Los Angeles Times*
was correct, he certainly was known: it was John Ringo. Oddly
enough, the Tombstone papers failed to mention Ringo. (Or perhaps
they did since modern files are incomplete. But no mention has yet
been found.) In February, Ringo posted an $8,000 bail; it would be
interesting to know who put it up. In fact, it would be interesting to
know why he needed to make bail. It has always been assumed that
he was in trouble because of a holdup of a poker game, but $8,000
seems like a lot of money to put up because of a drunken altercation
at a card game. Papers and other records from this period are missing, but it's a good bet that the bail followed an arrest on suspicion of
robbery. It is known that Ringo was tried before a territorial court,
which failed to convict him, probably because the stage driver refused
to talk. Where, then, did the *Los Angeles Times* get the information
to name Ringo? Probably from a Wells Fargo informant, possibly
Wyatt Earp or Fred Dodge.

Wells Fargo was increasingly concerned about the Cochise County
outlawry and sent one of their best agents out to investigate firsthand. Jim Hume couldn't have asked for a better introduction to the
Tombstone troubles: On January 7, the Benson stage was once again
held up, and Hume, riding the stage to Tombstone, surrendered his
money and two revolvers to robbers. (There has been speculation as
to why Hume didn't open fire—a gunfight might have gotten passengers killed, which would been bad publicity for Wells Fargo.)

Common sense indicated that Cochise County was more in need
of a law-and-order party than ever. But, rumors were now rampant
that the Earps (despite the crippling of Virgil's arm) were sneaking
out of town and engineering the holdups. If that was the case, Wells
Fargo, with three other operatives in the area, either had the worst
intelligence unit in the West or one that was in league with the
Earps.

As John Ringo and Doc Holliday were both suspected stage robbers, they must have had a great deal to talk about when they came
face to face on January 17 in Tombstone. George Parsons recorded
that "Ringo and Doc came nearly having it with pistols. . . . I
passed both not knowing what was up. One with hand in breast
pocket and the other probably ready. Earps just beyond. Crowded
street and looked like another battle. Police vigilant for once, and
both disarmed."

Parsons didn't say it, but he must have been rooting for Doc to perforate Ringo's reputation. Six days later, Parsons nearly got a chance himself. In the wee hours, he was awakened and asked to join a posse riding to Charleston to arrest Ringo. (It's not clear whether this was for the Bisbee stage holdup or a poker game where Ringo had walked off with some other players' cash.) Ringo came in peaceably, but Parsons was still ecstatic: "The Earps are out on U.S. business and lively times are anticipated." As usual, he was right, but he would prove wrong when he prophesied that: "At last the national government is taking a hand in the matter of our trouble and by private information I know that no money nor trouble will be spared to cower the lawless element. Our solution is nearer at hand. It looks like business now when the U.S. Marshal Dake takes a hand under special orders."

What special information Parsons thought he was privy to isn't known. The federal government did little to increase the U.S. marshal's resources in southeastern Arizona, and Dake's increased funds probably came from Wells Fargo. In practice, U.S. government policy in the area was enforced by Wyatt, Morgan, and, now, just in from California, the youngest of the Earp brothers, Warren. (James remained out of the picture.) Doc Holliday, of course, was always in the mix. Near the end of January, Wyatt, Morgan, Warren, Doc, and perhaps five other deputies made a show of arming themselves with rifles, shotguns, and pistols as the residents of Tombstone gawked and wondered what the fuss was about. Wyatt had obtained warrants for Ike and Finn Clanton and a Cowboy hanger-on called Pony Deal; this was tantamount to a declaration of war against the Cowboys. According to the *Arizona Star*, a few hours after the Earp posse rode out, a boy rode to town with a story that perhaps twenty Cowboys were out in pursuit of the Earps. Everyone waited for news of a battle, but the two groups never made contact. For all their bluster and that of the paper, the *Nugget*, that supported them, the Cowboys never would catch up to Wyatt. He would catch up with them.

Wyatt went straight to Charleston, the Cowboys' favorite hangout, but, apparently tipped off by a friend in Tombstone, there were no Cowboys around when he arrived. Parsons, who spotted Earp's posse while passing through Charleston on the way to Tombstone, wrote that the town looked "almost like a deserted village and as though having undergone a siege." The *Nugget* printed a telegram, supposedly sent by a terrified resident of Charleston, begging Sheriff Behan to rescue their town from "Doc Holliday, the Earps, and almost forty or fifty more of the filth of Tombstone." But there were no fights of any kind in Charleston while the Earp posse was there, and the likelihood is that the *Nugget* simply invented the telegram. The *Nugget*, meanwhile, railed against the "pestiferous posse with federal authority."

The Clantons fled, waiting for their lawyer to prepare a defense. Ringo, meanwhile, had ridden into Tombstone to have Judge William Stilwell (no relation to Behan's former deputy) review his bond. There was a mix-up; Ringo rode out of town thinking he was free, and James Earp, for once getting involved in his younger brother's business, swore out an affidavit against Ringo. Headed by a man named John Henry Jackson, the posse (which George Parsons joined) rode in pursuit. They found Ringo in Charleston; to avoid trouble, Jackson agreed to give Ringo a chance to come in to Tombstone voluntarily, which he did, trailing the posse by about an hour.

The comings and goings of large groups of determined men unnerved Tombstone's Mayor Carr. Crawley Dake rode to Tombstone to ask for the assistance of Tombstonians in rounding up the criminal element, and Carr responded by asking citizens to cooperate with the federal marshal's pursuit of Clanton and another Cowboy, Pony Deal. Coming so soon after an election in which it had crowed loudly over the defeat of the Earp faction, the *Nugget* must have found the presence of a territorial U.S. marshal in their town to be galling. The paper claimed to support Carr while continuing to criticize the Earps, leaving some citizens wondering just how the mayor's request could be carried out if not by the Earp brothers.

This tangle of animosities, deceits, and conflicting loyalties had to be resolved somehow, and late in the winter of 1882, Wyatt tried to find legal solutions. The Clantons finally surrendered—not to Wyatt, because Ike didn't want to accede to federal authority—and found out to their chagrin that the charge was not for the robbery of the U.S. mails but for the attempted murder of Virgil Earp. This triggered the strongest and least understood incident of Wyatt Earp's stay in Tombstone.

On February 2, a headline in the *Epitaph* startled residents: "Draw Your Own Inference/Resignation of Virgil W. Earp and Wyatt S. Earp as Deputy Marshals." Virgil's, of course, was no surprise, as he had barely survived the shotgun attack and could scarcely use his left arm, but Wyatt's resignation was stunning. The *Epitaph* printed his letter of resignation, which read, in part:

Major C. P. Dake, United States Marshal, Grand Hotel, Tombstone—Dear Sir: In exercizing [sic] our official functions as deputy United States marshals in this territory, we have endeavored always unflinchingly to perform the duties intrusted [sic] to us. These duties have been exacting and perilous in their character, having to be performed in a community where turbulence and violence could almost any moment be organized to thwart and resist the enforcement of the processes of the court issued to bring criminals to justice. And while we have a deep sense of obligation to many of the citizens for their hearty cooperation in aiding us to suppress lawlessness, and their faith in our honesty of purpose, we realize that notwithstanding our best efforts and judgment in everything which we have been required to perform, there has arisen so much harsh criticism in relation to our operations, as such a persistent effort having been made to misrepresent and misinterpret our acts, we are led to the conclusion that, in order to convince the public that it is our sincere purpose to promote the public welfare, independent of any personal emolument or advantages to ourselves, it is our duty to place our resignations as deputy United States marshals in your hands, which we now do, thanking you for your continued courtesy and confidence in our integrity, and shall remain subject to your orders in the performance of any duties which may be assigned to us, only until our successors are appointed.

This is an extraordinary document that, like everything which carried Wyatt Earp's signature, revealed a man who was direct and dignified. (Like his statement at the O.K. Corral hearing, this letter was probably written in part by Wyatt's lawyer, Tom Fitch, and it's a good bet that Doc Holliday touched it up in spots.) The sentiments expressed in the resignation were something no one could have guessed. The reference to "harsh criticism" shows how much the unrelenting attacks on his character by the *Nugget* meant to a man who was used to basking in the good will of those he was protecting. Wyatt Earp wasn't a man who responded openly to public criticism—no newspaper in Dodge or Tombstone contains a letter from him on any public controversy before his resignation—but this letter, obviously written for the public as well as Crawley Dake, indicates that he was very much aware of what people were saying.

The *Epitaph* wasn't the only paper out on February 2 with extraordinary Earp news. As locals were passing around copies of Wyatt's resignation letter, the *Nugget* was circulating a story that claimed Earp had contacted Ike Clanton in jail. Apparently, Wyatt put out a peace feeler, saying "he wished to interview with him [Ike] with a view of reconciling their differences and obliterating the animosity that now exists between them." Ike declined, "emphatically," to speak with Wyatt.

Why had Wyatt made the offer? Probably because he understood that it was the last chance he had to reconcile matters before a war broke out. Wyatt was tired of conflict. The killing of Marshal Fred White, the killing of Billy Clanton and the McLaury brothers, the shooting of Virgil, the grueling posse rides, the constant pressure of possible ambush, the relentless criticism from the *Nugget*, the dissolution of his marriage—this was not what he had come to Tombstone for. He would make one more attempt at a peaceable solution if Ike Clanton would listen to reason.

There was another factor. The next day, February 3, it was announced that the *Nugget* had been sold, and that the paper's backer was a Democratic political boss from Prescott named Hugo Richards. Harry Woods was relieved as editor and faded out of the Tombstone story. Richard Rule became the new editor; he was the reporter who had written the *Nugget*'s account of the gunfight, thus proving that whatever his politics, he was a journalist. The *Nugget* didn't change its political stripe or change sides in the Earp-Behan feud, but from that date the reporting and editorials on the Earps became less strident.

What was happening? Several things at once. Because Wyatt Earp's name survived the Tombstone debacle to become world famous, historians have focused on the fact that the controversy following the O.K. gunfight damaged Earp's reputation. What isn't obvious from more than a century's remove is that John Behan's

reputation was badly damaged, too. Not as quickly as the Earps',
because Behan wasn't as well known and he hadn't taken a direct part
in the gunfight. But slowly and surely Behan's reputation slipped,
and as it did, his support from the state's political backers began to
fade.

Behan had gotten away with a great deal: His deputy had been
accused of stage robbery, key suspects in another robbery had simply
walked out of his and Harry Woods's jail, and his association with
Ike Clanton was now undeniable. Under his watch, and often with
his aid, the Cowboys had grown into a gang that threatened U.S.
relations with Mexico. Perhaps worse was the rash of shootings and
stage robbings in his own Cochise County, violence that Behan
seemed powerless to control. The Arizona political bosses who had
found the Cowboys useful in such matters as stuffing ballot boxes
now found that they couldn't keep them in check. Wells Fargo had
threatened to close its operations in Tombstone if effective law wasn't
established, which might have been a bluff but was a possibility no
one with an interest in Tombstone and Cochise County wanted to
face. As stage drivers and passengers were being shot at and sometimes hit, it was no longer possible for the *Nugget* or anyone else to
pass off the thefts and shootings with rumors of a shadowy criminal
empire run by the Earps and Doc Holliday (particularly when the
holdups increased as Virgil Earp was in bed fighting for his life).

Wyatt's letter to Ike was a peace feeler to the *Nugget* as well, a
signal that Wyatt was tired of being a political pawn. Rule and his
bosses must have been seeing diminishing returns in backing Behan
unconditionally while bashing the Earps, and the paper's tone light-
ened from that point on.

Something else was reported on February 3. Though it made no
headlines and in fact was scarcely noticed by most residents, Wells
Fargo agent Marshall Williams skipped town. Or, as the *Arizona
Star* in Tucson put it, he "skinned out of Tombstone . . . headed
toward the Orient . . . and had a sport with him." No one knows
what the remark about "toward the Orient" meant; "sport" was slang
for prostitutes. What was known was that he left behind several
thousand in debts, some of it owed to Wells Fargo. From here, Williams vanishes from the story, his full role in the Tombstone turbulence not yet uncovered. Forty-seven years later, in a letter to Stuart
Lake, Fred Dodge revealed that "Marshall Williams did do some

tipping off," which meant that he was giving inside information to
stage robbers, and meant as well that he knew who the stage robbers
were and that he was almost certainly responsible, along with Behan
and Woods, for the escape of the suspects after the Benson stage
holdup.

Wyatt's peace offer to Ike was the result of wishful thinking. Alibi
Ike didn't need to bargain. There were no eyewitnesses to tie Ike to
the shooting of Virgil, and he could not be convicted on the only
piece of physical evidence—his hat being found at the scene of the
shooting. The same day that news of Wyatt's letter appeared in the
Nugget, Ike and Finn Clanton were released. Crawley Dake refused
Wyatt's resignation as U.S. Marshal, and Wyatt decided to keep the
badge.

On February 9, Ike took the legal offensive, filing a second murder
charge against the Earps and Doc Holliday in Contention City,
about half a day's ride from Tombstone. Ike had no new evidence to
present, and it's doubtful that Wyatt really worried about the case
going to trial. Still, it was one more legal expense for the Earps and it
kept U.S. Deputy Marshal Wyatt Earp out of the field, which might
have been the point. The next day Wyatt mortgaged his house, presumably to get money to pay legal fees, listing Mattie as his wife on
the document. On February 14, John Behan, without a single deputy, set out to take Wyatt and Morgan to Contention City. Wyatt
later told a would-be biographer, Forrestine Hooker, that he anticipated an ambush on the road to Contention. He refused to surrender
his guns as Behan asked; wisely, the sheriff did not press the issue.
Moreover, twelve of Wyatt's friends, including his lawyer William
Herring, all armed with revolvers and rifles, showed up to ride shotgun. Herring reportedly walked into the courtroom and bellowed,
"Your honor, we came here for law, but we will fight—if we have to."
He did succeed in getting the proceedings moved to Tombstone.

After much legal wrangling, it was apparent to even Ike Clanton
that he would have to show some new evidence of murder in order to
keep the show going. He had nothing; Wyatt, Morgan, and Doc
were released. As if to make his point that such tricks were not going
to slow him down, Wyatt was down near the Sonora-Arizona border
leading another posse—this one including Morgan, Doc, Sherman
McMasters, and the youngest brother, Warren—looking for the suspects in Virgil's shooting.

On February 18, George Parsons wrote in his journal of "another killing by Indians, this one at Antelope Springs." But there was no more organized Indian resistance in the area to disturb the peace, and in Tombstone it began to look as if the fireworks that seemed so imminent after Virgil's shooting would not go off. "There being a lull in Cowboy criminality," reported Clara Brown to home, "and the Indians apparently having left the Dragoons, Tombstone people have been obliged to look to other causes of excitement."

Then, a couple of weeks later, Wyatt and Morgan Earp went to shoot pool at Hatch's.

There is no telling how different Wyatt Earp's life might have been after age thirty-four had he not spotted Frank Stilwell at the train station in Tucson on March 19. In Tombstone, the wife of one of the Cowboy associates had been talking, so everyone knew that it was John Behan's former deputy, Frank Stilwell, who had pulled the trigger on the fatal rifle shot that killed Morgan. Parsons wrote in his journal: "Another assassination last night about eleven o'clock. I heard the shots, two in number, but hearing so many after dark was not particularly startled . . . the second shot was fired apparently at Wyatt Earp. . . . Murderers got away of course, but it was and is quite evident who committed the deed. The man was Stilwell in all probability. . . . Bad times ahead now."

Much of Tombstone had heard rumors that Stilwell was the killer, and the word had no doubt reached Wyatt only a short time after the shots were fired. Wyatt had a long time to consider this information. After leading the funeral procession to the Benson train station, he left James with the coffin and returned to Tombstone to pick up Virgil and the remaining Earps. They left for Tucson, accompanied by Doc Holliday, and two Earp allies, Sherman McMasters and Turkey Creek Jack Johnson. From there, James, Virgil, and the Earp wives would ride with Morgan's body to Colton, California, where Nicholas and Virginia Ann awaited them.

Some would later claim that Frank Stilwell couldn't possibly have murdered Morgan Earp as he had been seen in Tucson early in the morning of March 19, impossible if he had been in Tombstone the previous night. But if Stilwell had shot Morgan Earp in Tombstone, he certainly could have prepared an alibi in Tucson. In any event, he was there on the March 20 when he and Wyatt Earp spotted each other.

The best explanation for what happened next was probably given by Virgil Earp in a newspaper interview a couple of months after the incident. Virgil said that the Earp party had dispatches from Tucson warning that Stilwell and a party of friends were watching all the railroad trains passing that way, and they were going through the cars in search of Earps and their friends, "carrying short [sawed-off] shotguns under their overcoats and promising to kill on sight." If this was true, it could be said that Wyatt headed for Tucson with the idea of confrontation; it might also be said that he had no choice, as the train that would carry his family West left from Tucson and he had to protect them.

If Stilwell didn't know that Wyatt Earp was coming to Tucson, he was one of the few people at the train station who didn't. A railroad employee named David Gibson later testified that a newsboy told him "there will be hell here tonight" because "the Earps and Holliday were aboard and are going to stop here as they had told him that the man who killed Morgan Earp was in Tucson." It was later said that Stilwell was in Tucson to meet a deputy from Charleston who was to testify at his trial for the Bisbee stage robbery. One might think that Stilwell—and Ike Clanton, for that matter—knowing that Wyatt Earp thought Stilwell responsible for Morgan's death, might find Mexico a safer place to be and let someone else pick up the deputy. Whatever the reason, about 7:00 P.M., near the train Virgil and Allie were to ride on, Wyatt Earp and Frank Stilwell saw each other, and Stilwell suddenly decided he would leave Tucson after all. He was too late.

In the dark, Wyatt, who never doubted for a moment why Stilwell was in Tucson, chased him across the railroad tracks. According to Stuart Lake's account, about fifteen feet away, Stilwell halted as if to put up a fight. Wyatt kept coming; at a distance of three feet, Stilwell, instead of going for his own gun, lunged for Wyatt's Wells Fargo shotgun. Wyatt later said:

> I've never forgotten the look in Frank Stilwell's eyes, or
> the expression that came over his face as he struggled for
> that gun. I forced the gun down until the muzzle of the
> right barrel was just underneath Stilwell's heart. I had not

spoke to him, and did not at any time. But Stilwell found his voice. You'd guess a million times wrong, without guessing what he said. I'll tell you, and you can make what you care to out of it.

"Morg!" he said, and then a second time, "Morg!" I've often wondered what made him say that.

A sudden moment of remorse, perhaps? Maybe in the smoky moonlight of the train yard, staring into Wyatt's double-barreled shotgun, terror seized of Stilwell and he thought he was looking at the ghost of Morgan. Wyatt then "let him have it. The muzzle of one barrel . . . was just below his heart. He got the second before he hit the ground."

That was Wyatt's account. Skeptics would later question why Stilwell didn't draw his gun; perhaps staring into a shotgun took his nerve away. Whatever the reason, he didn't draw.

Wyatt claimed to have run alongside the train that was carrying Virgil to California and held up one finger. "It's all right, Virgil," he shouted. "One for Morg!"

No one is quite sure why, but Stilwell's body wasn't found until the next morning. The coroner's report confirmed Wyatt's first shot: Buckshot, fired at close range, had passed through the liver and stomach. It was also noticed that Stilwell's body had been riddled with bullets. A reasonable explanation would be that Doc Holliday, in a moment of solidarity, decided to stake his claim for the killing of Frank Stilwell. He probably didn't suspect that later he would be the only one arrested for it.

Of Ike Clanton, who once again fled, there was no sign. Wyatt also swore he had seen another Cowboy, Hank Swilling, at the station, dressed in street rather than range clothes, but after Stilwell's death he was nowhere to be found either.

A witness later said that shortly after the shooting he walked past "four men dressed in dark clothes and carrying guns": Wyatt, Doc, and perhaps Turkey Creek Jack or Warren Earp or another associate of Wyatt's, Texas Jack Vermillion. Just southeast of Tucson, at the Papago station, Wyatt and his men hopped a train to Contention City, where they had apparently left horses. Before dinner on March 21 Wyatt was back at the Cosmopolitan Hotel in Tombstone. None of the residents who saw him, and many did, could have suspected that what Wyatt Earp had done in the previous two years would make their mining camp world famous. Nor could they have realized that in another couple of hours he would be riding out of Tombstone for the last time.

The Arizona papers were electrified by the killing of Stilwell, and their accounts were quoted and paraphrased by papers all over the West. The headline in the *Arizona Star*, a staunchly Democratic paper in Tucson, read "Murder in Cold Blood . . . The Shadow of Tombstone's Bloody Feud Reaches Tucson." The subsequent story never suggested the likelihood that Frank Stilwell and Ike Clanton, prime suspects in the shootings of Virgil and Morgan Earp, might have been in Tucson to take a shot at the surviving Earp brothers. It scarcely mentioned Morgan Earp's murder at all.

The rest of the country got a different story. "One thing is certain," Virgil Earp told the *San Francisco Examiner*, "if I had been without an escort they would have killed me." Other papers made much of the murder and stage robbery charges against Stilwell, the Star simply noted that Stilwell had never been convicted.

A couple of days later, anti-Earp papers were given an opportunity to deny even more circumstantial evidence against Stilwell. Back in Tombstone, Marietta Spencer, wife of Pete Spencer, referred to as "Spence" so regularly that people thought that was his name, testified before the coroner's inquest on the murder of Morgan Earp. Marietta, who was Mexican, said that her husband with Frank Stilwell, a man called Indian Charlie, and another man named "Freeze"—a German, she thought—were conspirators in the murder of Morgan. Apparently, her marriage to Spencer was not happy; on the day of the shooting they had a quarrel in which Spence struck both Marietta and her mother. Later that night, she and her mother heard shots and then Stilwell and Indian Charlie appeared at the Spencer house (which was directly across from where the Earps lived). Thirty to forty-five minutes later Spencer and two other men arrived. "Spence didn't tell me so, but I knew he killed Morgan Earp; I think he did it because he arrived at the house all of a tremble . . . Spence's teeth were chattering when he came in . . . I judged they had been doing wrong from the condition, white and trembling, in which they arrived." She also remembered an incident a few days earlier when Morgan Earp had passed by and Spencer had said to an Indian, presumably Indian Charlie, "That's him."

Even assassin's henchmen have home lives, and Mrs. Spencer's testimony offers a rare glimpse into a gunman's reaction to a moment of violence. In all probability Pete Spencer wasn't guilty of Morgan's murder, but he was an accomplice and he came home shaking. Hatch's saloon and pool hall was perhaps two blocks from Spencer's house on Fremont, in fact, it was only a hundred feet or so from the lot where the gunfight had taken place in October. (Virgil and Allie's house was on the opposite side of Fremont as the lot, less than a stone's throw from Fly's Photography Studio.) Stilwell and Spencer and whoever was with them had to take off into the back alleys to avoid detection, since people were about in all hours in Tombstone. This means that somebody would probably have been playing look-out at the alley entrance and that after the shots were fired they could retreat north in a hurry, toward Fremont Street and away from Hatch's. But according to Mrs. Spencer, the assassins showed up at the house in two groups, at least a half-hour apart. Aside from the possibility of being seen by townsfolk, there was the chance that one of the Cowboy gang would be spotted by someone in the Earp house as they snuck back to Spencer's, so the Cowboys must have split up and first gone to a saloon or house where friends could help establish an alibi.

The question is why Stilwell and the others went to Spence's house at all and why they talked so freely in front of Marietta Spencer, instead of retreating across the Mexican border. Once again, the Cowboy killers, protected by the law and secure in the knowledge that they would all have alibis, displayed a sloppiness born of arrogance and left a trail absurdly easy to follow. Which is why Pete Spencer was shaking when he returned home that night. It might have occurred to him that this time Wyatt Earp might not leave matters to the legal system. Luckily for Pete Spencer, Wyatt Earp had already come to the conclusion that whatever part Pete Spencer might have played in the affair, he had not killed Morgan.

If Marietta Spencer is to be believed, or if she correctly understood what was going on, it was Morgan, not Wyatt, the assassins were after at Hatch's—but, then, since the brothers looked so much alike, it might well have been Wyatt they were referring to when she overheard Spence say to Indian Charlie, "That's him." Then again,

an incident from *I Married Wyatt Earp* on the subject of John Behan
might be genuine:

> We were arguing there on the front porch when Morg
> stepped out. Johnny's attitude had put Morg into one of
> his rages. With-out saying a word, he hit my former
> sweetheart in the mouth and knocked him off the porch.
> When the stunned man got up, Morg hit him in the
> stomach, doubling him over and causing him to fall again.
> I was terrified, but somehow got between them anyhow. I
> suppose there were still some tender feelings in my heart
> for Johnny. He left bleeding from the mouth, but without
> saying a word. Later, Doc, who heard the whole story,
> made the fatal mistake of giving Johnny the "ha-ha" about
> it in public. I think this public mockery is what sealed
> Morgan's fate. In any case, the whole episode is certainly
> worth relating, for it reveals both extremes of Morg's per-
> sonality, the sweet and the violent.

The Morgan Earp–John Behan clash isn't in Josephine's actual
memoirs and therefore, like all the Tombstone passages in *I Married
Wyatt Earp*, is suspect. Still, it can't be discounted. Would Behan
have been foolish enough to seek open revenge against the Earps this
way, leaving a trail that could lead back to him? Given the artful way
Behan distanced himself from Cowboy violence, the answer would
seem to be no. But Stilwell was John Behan's deputy, and despite the
accusations that continued to pile up against him, Behan never denounced him, though he did not fire him after the arrest.

Whoever was the intended target of Stilwell's rifle, Wyatt no
doubt knew everything the inquest would reveal before he set out for
Tucson. Wyatt almost certainly grilled Marietta Spencer before he
left, and Wyatt and Fred Dodge had their own sources of information as well. It appears that Wyatt did know that Stilwell would be in
Tucson, but it's a reach to say that he went there to kill him. He
would have gone to Tucson to guard Virgil and James in any event;
knowing that Stilwell was there no doubt caused him to move a little
faster.

In Arizona, public reaction to Frank Stilwell's death wasn't tempered by news of the inquest. Most people didn't find out about the

inquest or understand its implications when they did. The mostly Democratic papers of the territory, none of whom, outside of Cochise County, had never heard the name of Frank Stilwell before Wyatt Earp killed him, practically turned Stilwell into a martyr. In Tombstone, the reaction of those who knew him by reputation was best summed up by George Parsons in his diary: "A quick vengeance and a bad character sent to Hell where he will be the chief attraction until a few more accompany him."

About 8:00 P.M. on March 21, Sheriff John Behan was given a telegram informing him that Wyatt Earp and his party were wanted for the killing of his former deputy, Frank Stilwell. The Earps had already been in Tombstone for several hours; the manager of the telegraph office delayed delivery of the message to give Wyatt a chance to make his preparations for leaving town.

A few minutes after eight, as Wyatt, Doc, Sherman McMasters, Turkey Creek Johnson, Texas Jack Vermillion, and Dan Tipton mounted their horses for departure, they were confronted by John Behan and perhaps two deputies. As this was Wyatt's last moment in Tombstone, and since the exchange has taken on the dimensions of legend, it's worth examining the different versions of what was said.

According to the *Nugget*, Behan ordered Earp to stop; Wyatt and his group drew their guns on the sheriff and then rode away. The *Epitaph* did a better job, quoting eyewitnesses who said that the Earp party had not raised them. In this account, "The sheriff said to him, 'Wyatt, I want to see you.' Wyatt replied, 'You can't see me; you have seen me once too often,' or words to that effect." Then, he said, "I will see Paul," which meant Bob Paul. Earp was saying that what happened in Tucson at the train station had happened in Paul's county and was no business of Behan's. He was also saying, "I will see a real law man."

In Billy Breakenridge's book, *Helldorado*, he claimed that Behan told him and Dave Neagle—there were no other deputies around— to go get their shotguns. The six members of the Earp party, though, stopped them at gunpoint. Three years after *Helldorado*, Stuart Lake would claim in *Frontier Marshal* that Earp's party confronted Breakenridge, Behan, Neagle, and "eight heavily armed deputies."

Both versions are probably false. "Heavily armed" implies more than sidearms, and it's doubtful Behan had a full complement of deputies waiting around with shotguns and rifles for Earp to ride into town. And it's just as unlikely that Wyatt would have pulled a gun on Behan or Breakenridge and certainly not on Neagle. There was no need to, in none of these accounts does Behan present Wyatt with a warrant or tell him he's under arrest. Clearly John Behan did not want a confrontation with Wyatt Earp. (Breakenridge never explained why, if Earp was under arrest, the sidearms he and Neagle and probably Behan were carrying weren't sufficient to at least attempt to uphold the law.)

Bat Masterson's 1907 profile of Wyatt for the Hearst publication *Human Life* introduced the incident to many thousands of readers around the country outside the West. Bat's friend and editor, Alfred Henry Lewis, himself a popular writer of western fiction, may have polished Wyatt's response to a fine point: To Behan's "Wyatt, I want to see you," Earp responds "Johnny, you may see me once too often." Bat, or Lewis, also had Wyatt telling Behan, "And remember, I'm going to get that hound you are protecting in jail when I come back, if I have to tear the jail down to do it." This probably refers to Pete Spencer, who had put himself in Behan's custody, but it is unlikely that Wyatt said this. Wyatt wasn't given to that sort of bluster; if he were going to go after Spencer while he was in Behan's custody, he would have done it right then and there. Besides, at this point it's doubtful that Wyatt knew Spencer was in Behan's custody or he might have gone after him.

When John Clum wrote his memoirs, *It All Happened in Tombstone*, some two decades after Bat's profile of Wyatt, the exchange had been shortened to, "Wyatt, I want to see you," with Earp responding, "You will see me once too often." Finally, by 1931, Stuart Lake honed it to the lines that would be repeated in hundreds of articles, books, and anthologies:

> "Wyatt," the sheriff called, "I want to see you."
> "Behan," the marshal shot back so sharply that the sheriff stopped short, "if you're not careful, you'll see me once too often."

Then, H. Solomon, a prominent banker and an Earp supporter who had put up money for Wyatt's bail after the October gunfight, rushed up and said "Good luck, Wyatt" and presented Doc Holliday with a sawed-off shotgun and a belt of shells. As if to refute the claims of later debunkers that Wyatt Earp "fled" Tombstone, Lake presents Earp as calmly sitting on his horse while the others rode out, looking down at Behan and his deputies, lighting a cigar, wheeling his horse around, and trotting out of town.

Whatever Wyatt Earp's last words were to John Behan, they must have been memorable, because so many people repeated them in one form or another. Having said them, he left Tombstone, forever.

From Tombstone, Wyatt and his posse rode to a camp in the hills about two miles north. Though Wyatt was finished with the town, he still had loyal friends there, one of whom brought him a copy of the final coroner's report which listed Frank Stilwell, Pete Spencer (called Spence in the report), "John Doe" Fries, Hank Swilling, and Florentin Cruz, a.k.a. Indian Charlie, as chief suspects in the murder of Morgan Earp.

Turning south to the Dragoon Mountains, Wyatt rode his men to Spencer's wood camp where they inquired as to the whereabouts of Spence and Cruz. Spence, they were told, was in Behan's custody; Cruz was just beyond the camp rounding up loose stock. Wyatt and the group rode off; a few moments later, perhaps ten shots were heard. As in the case of Frank Stilwell, Florentin Cruz's bullet-riddled body wasn't discovered until the next day.

No one has ever fit the pieces of this killing together, though that didn't stop every chronicler in the Southwest from being sure of their story. The facts are sketchy. Theodore Judah, a local teamster, later testified at the coroner's inquest that Wyatt came riding over the hill with Doc, McMasters, Texas Jack, and, apparently, Warren Earp behind him. Judah and a Mexican named Acosto, who were looking for some straying mules, were asked questions by Wyatt. Judah then watched as the riders quickly turned in the direction of Tombstone. A short time later Judah and Acosto heard the shots. Judah did not see the killing but somehow Acosto did, or said he did. (How Judah could have missed seeing what his companion remembered in detail was not explained.) According to Acosto the pursuers spread out and chased Cruz. A man named Vegas who was chopping wood on a nearby hill gave a similar account, claiming that eight men, three men more than Judah or Acosto saw, did the shooting. "I saw him [Cruz] fall," said Vegas. "They were about from 1,000 to 2,000 yards

from me." There is simply no telling what Vegas could have meant; it
is improbable that he could have seen anything in detail at 1,000 feet,
let alone yards.

According to Lake, as Cruz fled, Wyatt ordered Sherman Mc-
Masters to bring him down with a rifle shot in the leg. Then Wyatt,
using McMasters as an interpreter, interrogated the half-breed: Ike
Clanton, Frank Stilwell, Curly Bill, John Ringo, Billy Claiborne,
Hank Swilling, and Finn Clanton had led the plot to assassinate
Mayor Clum; Frank Stilwell and Ike Clanton had twice made plans
to ambush Doc Holliday; and Ike, Stilwell, Swilling, and Ringo had
fired four or five shots at Virgil. Anti-Earpists would later claim that
all of this was hogwash, that Wyatt never extracted a confession out
of Cruz. But nothing Wyatt told Stuart Lake was particularly shock-
ing: Virgil, after all, was shot and Clum had been shot at. Billy
Breakenridge would later offer corroboration of sorts by revealing
that he believed he had inadvertently stumbled on one of Stilwell's
attempts to kill Doc and thus saved Holliday's life.

Theodore Judah would later claim that mere seconds had passed
from the time Wyatt left him to the time he heard the shots that
killed Cruz—he, Judah, had traveled but twenty feet back towards
the direction Earp took when he heard the firing—so that Earp
couldn't possibly have had time to question Cruz. But in the time
it took Judah to travel just 20 feet there wasn't nearly enough time
for Wyatt to find and reach Cruz, so more than a few seconds must
have passed. (It may or may not be relevant that Judah admitted
under oath to being a friend of Pete Spencer and Frank Stilwell's
and had almost certainly heard of the latter's death at the hands of
Wyatt Earp.) In any event, unless one simply believes at this point
that Wyatt Earp had become a crazed killer, the question arises as
to why Earp would have killed Cruz without good reason.

The reason, however unjustifiable it may have appeared in the eyes
of Wyatt's detractors, was probably exactly what Earp said it was.
From Cruz, Wyatt learned that Curly Bill, Ringo, Stilwell, and Ike
Clanton had met at the Clanton ranch where they plotted to kill
Wyatt and Morgan. Pete Spence had then taken Cruz, or Indian
Charlie as he was called in Tombstone, to Allen Street to point out
Morgan Earp. (Cruz said he already knew Wyatt on sight.) On the
night of Morgan's murder, Cruz, Stilwell, Swilling, and Spencer had
met Curly Bill and Ringo at the rear of the courthouse, near the

theater the brothers had gone to. Several people came and went with messages, Cruz said. He told Curly Bill it was foolish to have so many people know of their plans and was told by Bill to shut up.

Someone got something wrong: Wyatt Earp, they said, had gone to bed and Morgan was playing pool at Hatch's. Curly Bill and Stilwell decided to go ahead and get Morgan. The German, Fries, must have been a messenger; his job to let the Cowboys know if the situation changed. It did. Fries brought word that Wyatt Earp was back and had walked into Hatch's. Then, Curly Bill, Stilwell, and Swilling went into the alley; moments later there was shooting, and everyone ran. Later, when they met at a ranch owned by a Cowboy associate named Frank Patterson, Cruz claimed to have heard Stilwell admit to killing Morgan, and Curly Bill and Swilling admit they shot but missed. He also heard Stilwell claim that he'd killed one Earp and put another, Virgil, "out of business." Then the Cowboy assassins rode to Tucson to fix an alibi. If this is true, it discounts the claim that would later be made that Stilwell couldn't have killed Morgan as he had checked into a Tucson hotel too early in the morning to have been in Tombstone the previous night. It also meant Wyatt would have been right when he claimed to have seen Swilling in the Tucson station. Whatever Florentin Cruz said, Wyatt Earp had come for information and was now satisfied he had it. Lake suggested that Wyatt was about to let Cruz go, thinking he might prove useful later when, unfortunately for Cruz, Wyatt had a parting thought. "Neither of my brothers nor I ever harmed you did we?" "No," said Cruz. "Then what made you help kill my brother?" Curly Bill, Ringo, Clanton, and Stilwell were all his friends, Cruz replied. Curly Bill gave him $25 to stand watch. "That twenty-five-dollar business," Earp told Stuart Lake nearly half a century later, "just about burned me up."

Lake gave Indian Charlie a dramatic farewell. Wyatt, through McMasters, told Charlie he could draw any time he liked and that he, Wyatt, wouldn't draw till the count of three. At "*tres!*"—charitably, Wyatt counted in Spanish so Cruz wouldn't be at a disadvantage—Cruz had his gun out, but "the Buntline Special flashed from the holster and roared three times." According to the inquest, Cruz was found lying "face downwards, with this right arm resting on his head."

Dr. George Goodfellow, George Parsons's roommate, later identified four hits by bullets. One, a wound in the left thigh, could be the rifle shot that Wyatt ordered McMasters to make. Another was a shot to the temple that was "sufficient to cause death." But there were two more wounds. Either Wyatt kept on shooting or, as might have happened with Stilwell, others—perhaps Doc Holliday and Warren Earp—joined in for a show of solidarity.

The killing of Frank Stilwell by Wyatt Earp at the Tucson station seems defensible to modern interpreters, even if it didn't to the Democratic newspapers in Arizona back in 1882. Stilwell probably did shoot Virgil and Morgan, and Wyatt had very good reason to believe he was in Tucson to threaten him and his family again. Cruz, or Indian Charlie, was a threat to neither Wyatt nor his family. In killing him for any other reason than self-defense—and to be entirely fair, we don't know for sure that Cruz wasn't armed and didn't go for a gun—Wyatt Earp crossed the line from lawman to vigilante. It was a line, as he well knew, that could never be crossed back over. In pulling the trigger on Cruz, Wyatt was serving notice that he would no longer be bound by the limitations of law, that he would fight his enemies' way. ("You called down the thunder," Kurt Russell's Wyatt tells Stephen Lang's Ike Clanton in *Tombstone*, "Well, now you've got it."[5])

In the spring of 1882, not everyone in southeast Arizona was against Wyatt Earp. On March 23, George Parsons, who no doubt spoke for many who had followed the story from the beginning, wrote in his journal: "More killing by the Earp party. Hope they'll keep it up." Parsons also noted that Pima County Sheriff Bob Paul was in Tombstone, but refused to join a posse Behan was forming. "If the truth were known," felt Parsons, "he would be glad to see the Earp party get away with all of these murderous outfits."

The posse was Behan's reaction to the public criticism over letting Wyatt Earp ride out of Tombstone. Even the *Nugget* joined in the carping: "The action of Sheriff Behan in attempting the arrest before completing his preparations to enforce it . . . was strongly censured last night by many of our citizens. The sheriff certainly has as good cause as any in this community to know the desperate character of the man with whom he had to deal, and it is possible he was a little hasty in the authority vested in him."

This was a polite way of saying that Behan's performance in letting Wyatt Earp ride away proved that he wasn't man enough for the job. Behan certainly did have good cause to know the character of Wyatt Earp and Doc Holliday, and wisely he didn't try to stop them. Even more wisely, he never told them they were under arrest, since he knew that he would then have to back it up. Behan waited until the Earps were safely on their way to Pete Spencer's wood camp before he began to form a posse. His selection of deputies was made from a roster of Arizona's most accomplished cattle thieves and stage robbery suspects, including Ike and Finn Clanton, and John Ringo. Some Tombstonians were shocked; apparently many had forgotten that two-time stage robbery suspect and coroner's report murder suspect Frank Stilwell had once been Behan's deputy.

Bob Paul, meanwhile, was caught between duty and principle. As Paul was highly respected by most Arizona papers of all political affiliations, a bizarre war of words ensued with different papers quoting him in wildly contradictory ways. The *Rocky Mountain News* had him defending Behan's choice of deputies, saying that Doc Holliday was "one of the leaders" of "the so-called Earp gang, or faction if you please," a group "composed entirely of gamblers who preyed on the Cowboys, and at the same time in order to keep up a show of having a legitimate calling, was organized into a kind of vigilante committee, and some of them, including Holliday, had United States marshal's commissions." This sounds very much like a partisan editor putting words in Paul's mouth; in any event, it contradicted sentiments expressed elsewhere in the interview when he supposedly said that Holliday "was always decently peaceable, though his power when engaged in following his ostensible calling, furthering the ends of justice, made him a terror to the criminal class of Arizona." One moment Doc was a member of a predatory class that "preyed" upon unfortunate Cowboys, the next, his calling (albeit an ostensible one) was "furthering the ends of justice" which made him a "terror" among the same class he was just accused of preying upon. With text like this to draw from, it's no wonder so many writers on Holliday and Earp seem schizophrenic.

An interview with the *Epitaph* probably more accurately gauged Paul's feelings: "I'll let Wyatt know I want him, and he'll come in." (Actually, it would have been interesting to see what Earp's reaction would have been had Paul called him in.) "He [Behan] persists in cloaking the most notorious outlaws and murderers in Arizona with

the authority of the law. I will have nothing to do with such a gang."
Paul would probably have never made so blatantly partisan a statement, but the *Epitaph* had as much right to put words in his mouth
as anyone. Ironically, in 1898, Paul would tell the *Tucson Citizen* that
he would have ridden with Behan, but that the latter left while Paul
was sleeping—Behan had no use for due process at this point and
thus no intention of bringing Paul along.

Meanwhile, Florentin Cruz was garnering much more sympathy
in death than he ever had in life. Gone was the memory of an arrest
for that second most reviled of western crimes: horse theft. Forgotten, too, was the fact that he was listed in the coroner's report as a
suspect in the murder of Morgan Earp. Suddenly, the papers
sprouted with testimonials to his good character and explanations
that Cruz was nowhere near the scene of the murder and even claims
that Indian Charlie and Florentin Cruz weren't the same person. It
seemed that no one Wyatt Earp had a warrant for was ever anywhere
near the scene of a crime. Earp's detractors would forever claim that
he simply rode into Pete Spence's woods camp and murdered an
innocent man.

But something Cruz said to Earp at the camp changed Wyatt
Earp. Wyatt left the camp, "very leisurely," according to Judah, with
a clearer picture of who was behind the shootings of his brothers.
Forty-five years later he would reveal to a journalist that he was
convinced Pete Spencer "had nothing to do with the assassination of
Morgan, although he was against us." So Spence was safe from Wyatt's vengeance. His brief conversation with Cruz had convinced him
of something else: He was wasting time hunting down the small fry.
The man he would now go after was the man who had engineered
the Earps' misfortune, the acknowledged Cowboy leader, Curly Bill
Brocius

The day after Cruz was killed, Wyatt, accompanied by Doc Holliday, Sherman McMasters, Turkey Creek Jack Johnson, and Texas
Jack Vermillion, rode to Iron Springs, a water hole about nine miles
north of Tombstone. Behan's posse of twelve or more men was in
slow pursuit. As they came upon the water hole there was an explosion of bullets from the opposite bank.

Curly Bill had seen Wyatt first. Brocius, Pony Deal and perhaps
eight or nine Cowboys began firing on the posse, scoring at least one

hit when Texas Jack's horse went down, temporarily pinning him. Earp felt that he had nowhere to go but forward. Dismounting, Wyatt threw his bridle over his arm as his horse tried to pull away from the noise and smoke. Giving a quick look in back of him, he found, to his surprise, Doc Holliday and the others were headed for cover, no doubt expecting that Wyatt would do the same.

Wyatt had no thought of retreating: This is what he had come for, this was the whole game right here. "From the instant I laid eyes on Curly Bill," he would say years later, "I was seeing and thinking clearly. Nothing that went on in that gully escaped me. . . . I can see Curly Bill's left eye squinting shut and his right eye sighting over the shotgun to this day"—Earp even recognized the gun as having a Wells Fargo label, perhaps one of the guns taken from Jim Hume in the robbery—"and I remember thinking, as I felt my coat jerk with his fire, 'He missed me; I can't miss him, but I'll give him both barrels to make sure.'" Wyatt hit the Cowboy leader squarely in the chest, nearly cutting him in two. Pony Deal and the others, too frantic to shoot straight, continued to put holes in Wyatt's long coat while he stepped behind his horse to reach for his Winchester. The animal was tugging too violently on the reins for Earp to reach it— one recalls the similar fruitless action by Tom McLaury at the O.K. Corral gunfight—so he reached for his Buntline Special only to find it wasn't there. (Debunkers, of course, claimed it never was.) He reached for another pistol and returned the Cowboy fire, scoring two hits, perhaps three. Then, with some exertion he pulled himself onto his horse as a bullet struck his saddle horn. Pulling his rifle, he fired twice to cover his retreat then wheeled and rode away as a bullet struck his boot, numbing his leg.

This, basically, is Lake's account, pieced together from Wyatt's letters but mostly from Wyatt's own earlier versions in the *San Francisco Examiner* and his aborted biographies. How much of it is true? None of it contradicts the known facts. The problem is that there are so few known facts.

More than any other incident in his life, more, even, than the October gunfight in Tombstone, the shootout with Curly Bill was the foundation of Wyatt Earp's early fame. Either Wyatt killed Curly Bill, in which case he revenged his brothers and won the war against the Cowboys, or he didn't, in which case he is indeed a colossal fraud as all his detractors maintain. Considering the enduring controversy that surrounds Earp, it is fitting that the last and most important gunfight of his life would take place in some obscure foothills miles from Tombstone with no impartial witness.

What are the known facts? First, no one doubts there was a fight. The first rumors filtered into Tombstone the next day: There had been a clash between Wyatt Earp's posse and Curly Bill's Cowboys, and four of the Earp party had been killed. Before long, both major Tombstone papers had the story. Where did the *Nugget* get its information? Possibly from an Earp ally who was sent to town to pick up money for Wyatt's posse, either from Crawley Dake's federal funds, Wells Fargo, or a personal loan from a mining friend. (Wyatt had left Warren at a rendezvous point to watch for the messenger's return with the cash; why he missed the Curly Bill shootout isn't obvious, unless Wyatt simply wanted to keep him out of danger.) Wyatt's messengers, a local named Dick Wright and an Austrian immigrant named Tony Kraker, missed connecting with Earp's group but came across some of the Cowboys. Wright, talking fast, made up a story about chasing lost mules, and the Cowboys insisted the pair sit down and eat with them, the Cowboys never suspected that they were carrying sacks of cash for Wyatt Earp.

During the meal the Cowboys told Wright and Kraker what they knew of the fight, and on their way back, the pair met a *Nugget* reporter. Just as the *Nugget* had done after the O.K. Corral gunfight, the paper printed a version of the shootout essentially supportive to Wyatt Earp's own. The *Epitaph* had a field day: "Like a thunderbolt from the hand of Jove, the six desperate men charged their assailants like the light brigade at Balaklava." The remaining Cowboys fled toward their refuge in Charleston "as if the King of Terrors was at their heels in hot pursuit."

None of the Earp party was hit, with the exception of Texas Jack's horse. At least one other Cowboy was shot: Johnny Barnes would later die from a wound inflicted by Wyatt's Colt. But what of Curly Bill? Fred Dodge would later claim that Barnes, before he died, revealed that Wyatt had indeed killed Bill and that the remaining Cowboys took the body and buried it at Frank Patterson's ranch. This might have been true, and it might also have been a case of a worshipful Fred Dodge going out of his way to place himself at the heart of Earp's story.[6]

In truth, no one knows what happened to Curly Bill. The *Nugget* contemptuously offered $100 to anyone who could give conclusive evidence that Curly Bill had been killed; all they did was set themselves up for a counter offer from the *Epitaph*—$2,000, to a worthy charity if Curly Bill would put in a live appearance in Tombstone. The money remains uncollected.

Cowboy supporters responded to the stories of Curly Bill's death by simply refusing to believe them. Their descendants still don't believe it. Judge Hancock, the garrulous gasbag whose memoirs have livened up many a western's academic's pages, wrote to the *Epitaph* that Wyatt Earp "never arrested Curly Bill" and certainly did not kill him. The first statement displayed Hancock's ignorance of Tombstone history prior to his arrival in 1880, as everybody knew that Wyatt Earp buffaloed Curly Bill after Brocius killed Marshal Fred White. He was probably wrong about his second point, too, because somebody killed Curly Bill, and it was Wyatt Earp who went looking for him.

The easiest way for Wyatt's enemies to deny him the credit for killing Brocius was simply to claim that Curly Bill wasn't at the Iron Springs fight in the first place. Many years later, when dictating his memoirs, Daniel Chisholm claimed to have bumped into John Ringo in the San Pedro Valley shortly after the Iron Springs incident. Ringo said he had a message from "a friend," Curly Bill. When Chisholm expressed surprise, because he had heard of Wyatt Earp's killing Bill, Ringo replied: " 'Killed, hell!' Ringo laughed and said: 'That old "curly lobo" wasn't even within a day's ride of Wyatt Earp and his gang when that fight was supposed to have taken place.' " Chisholm and Ringo then head to Galeyville where, of all people, Curly Bill himself is waiting. Ringo shows Bill the *Epitaph*'s account of his demise; all have a good laugh. But Brocius decides that since the Earps are "pulling out," too, it might be a good time to find new "stomping grounds." (One might think that since the Earps were leaving it would be a good time for Curly Bill to stay, but let that pass.) He sells Chisholm his heavy freight wagon for $3,000 cash, on the spot, and leaves for the quiet life in Mexico. (But not before Ringo confesses to Chisholm that he and Brocius were the ones who ambushed both Virgil and Morgan Earp.)

This isn't the silliest of the Curly Bill stories. Judge Hancock claimed to have bumped into Bill up in Montana where he had quit his wild ways and become a character known to the locals as "Old

Cack," a colorful and benevolent fellow who loved giving candy to children. Billy Breakenridge had no one Curly Bill story that ridiculous, but he takes the prize for spreading the most silly stories. One was that a "reliable merchant and rancher" (though unnamed) told the sometime deputy that two weeks after the fight Curly Bill, back from a trip to Mexico, showed up at the man's house. Curly Bill had had enough of the outlaw life and was leaving for Wyoming to lead a "decent life, as he was tired of being on the dodge all the time. The merchant gave him a good saddle horse to ride away on." (What happened to Bill's own horse and why the merchant was so generous with his own horses is not explained.) But if Curly Bill really wasn't an outlaw, as Earp's critics maintain, what was he on the dodge from?

Breakenridge also identified a "Mr. Vaughan, now living in Tombstone"—now meant 1927, when *Helldorado* was written—who said that ten years after the fight Curly Bill passed through Benson on a Texas-bound train and said hello to old pals. At least no one gave him a free horse in this tale.

Most of the "Curly Bill Lived" stories end with Arizona's most famous cattle rustler either leaving for Mexico or for the northern territories (Ed Bartholomew, the most virulent anti-Earp historian, had him returning to Texas well before the Iron Springs fight). But all have one thing in common: Curly Bill, like Billy the Kid before him and Jesse James and Butch Cassidy after him, led a peaceful life and never clashed with the law again. For the skeptical among us, it's easier to believe that they were never outlaws at all than to believe that they changed from outlaws to citizens.

Breakenridge was one who never thought of Curly Bill as an outlaw in the first place: "I never heard of Curly Bill being accused of any crimes except cattle-stealing, and I never knew of any warrant being issued for him. I most certainly should have heard of it if there had been any, as all warrants for any of the rustlers were given to me to serve." Breakenridge was right about one thing: He did hear of warrants against cattle rustlers, he just never served any of them. And one might think that a deputy sheriff would show a little less reverence toward a cattle thief and suspected bushwhacker and highwayman who killed a Tombstone town marshal by shooting him in the testicles.

Breakenridge is responsible for spreading if not actually inventing the most bizarre story to come out of the Earp-Cowboy clash. This one, of course, started with the *Nugget* story that ran after the Iron Springs fight, and, like many of the old Arizona stories about Earp, it has the tone of a warped folk tale. It seems that two minor Cowboys, Pink Truly and Alex Arnold, had a clash with Earp at Mescal Springs. (It's not clear if the telling of this is intended as the "real" story of what happened at Iron Springs or a different gun battle. Anyway, Curly Bill wasn't at this fight, having been, of course, in Mexico when it happened.) Leaving his group, Earp dismounted and charged Truly and Arnold, who found Wyatt's bright white shirt to be a splendid target. They opened fire; one bullet tipped the horn off Wyatt's saddle, another turned Earp around and staggered him—a direct hit and no kill. Wyatt Earp, the Cowboys concluded, had a kind of steel vest on under his shirt. Breakenridge allegedly found a corroboration of sorts from a deputy of Behan's who was hiding in a granary at a ranch where the Earp posse stopped. Someone supposedly said to Wyatt, "The steel saved you this time."

There are other stories about Wyatt's "steel vest," all inspired by the failure of several excited Cowboys to hit a target that was firing at them. The steel vest stories never explain or even speculate about where this steel shirt came from or how any so-called steel vest that could be made in southeast Arizona in 1882 could deflect .45 caliber bullets at close range. Was it supposed to be some early form of bulletproof vest or an actual cast-iron shield of the kind later worn by the Australian bandit Ned Kelly? No explanation is ever offered.

The implication of the steel vest is that Wyatt was somehow cheating by shielding himself from the Cowboy bullets—it wasn't a fair fight (like, presumably, the ones where Virgil and Morgan were shot). Ironically, the steel vest stories served to make Wyatt seem superhuman. Anyone who had ever ridden the rugged foothills around Tombstone while battling heat, dust, and fatigue, must have wondered what kind of man would choose to travel such terrain wearing a heavy steel vest under a shirt and long coat.

The funny thing is that in Wyatt's telling of the story—and it stayed the same from his 1896 *Examiner* profile to his early attempts at biography and, finally, through Stuart Lake—he comes off as human and almost a bit ridiculous. In Wyatt's telling, he loosened his gunbelt as his posse approached the water hole. The fight broke out, and moments later, after killing Curly Bill, Wyatt tried to swing back on his horse, but his belt had slipped down on his thighs and he could not mount. It was at that moment that a rustler's bullet ripped into the saddle horn in front of his face. The combination of the hot lead and old leather produced a distinctive smell. "If you get my position," he said, "you'll understand that my nose was almost touching the tip of the saddle horn. I thought someone had struck a match on the end of it—my nose, I mean—and I smelled a very rotten egg." These details have the ring of truth about them. A man who is inventing a tale to puff up his own legend does not stop insert an anecdote about his gunbelt falling down around his knees. The very thought of the most famous legend of the American West being in this ridiculous posture in the defining moment of his career seems so ludicrous that you would think a debunker had come up with it.

After Wyatt made his stand, Holliday, Texas Jack, and Turkey Creek rallied to his aid. Moments later, when the shooting stopped, Doc inspected Wyatt's tattered coat. "Why, you're shot all to pieces," he exclaimed. But, incredibly, the bullets and buckshot hadn't touched Earp himself. Lifting the boot on his still numb leg, he found a bullet embedded in the heel.

Was there no one at all to corroborate the most storied moment of Wyatt Earp's life? In fact, there was. Two months after the Iron Springs fight, Doc Holliday was interviewed by the *Denver Republican*.[7] Here's Doc's account:

> We were out one day after a party of outlaws, and about 3 o'clock on a warm day after a long and dry ride from the San Pedro river, we approached a spring which was situated in a hollow. As we did so eight rustlers rose up from behind the bank and poured from thirty-five to forty shots into us. Our escape was miraculous. The shots cut our clothes and saddles and killed one horse, but did not hit us. I think we would have been all killed if God Almighty wasn't on our side. Wyatt Earp turned loose with a shotgun and killed Curly Bill.

This is so similar to the Stuart Lake account that one at first suspects that Lake developed his version out of it. But there is no indication in Lake's notes that he ever saw the Holliday interview; and, anyway, by 1929 Wyatt had already given substantially the same story to three other writers. What, then, to make of Doc's story? Is it possible that Earp and Holliday rehearsed the tale, so both would be in sync when grilled by future historians? This is hardly likely. So, then, it appears that Wyatt's story has a creditable corroborating witness. The strongest reason, though, for believing Earp's account of the Curly Bill fight is precisely the one rejected by modern historians: Wyatt Earp said it. If Earp claimed to have killed Curly Bill only to have him appear in public a month later, he would have been a mockery in Arizona for the rest of his life, something a man of Wyatt's pride could never have lived with.

Unless one simply chooses to believe that Curly Bill quit his outlaw ways and moved to Montana, Wyoming, or Mexico, where he handed out candy to children, it would seem that Wyatt Earp, standing upright through a hail of bullets—whether in spite of or because of a loose gunbelt—essentially ended the Cowboy war by killing Curly Bill Brocius.

That's the way Wyatt Earp said it happened, and, as with his O.K. Corral testimony, that's most likely the way it did happen.

In medieval Europe, a knight who vanquished another knight won his horse and armor. On the American frontier, it worked pretty much the same way: Vanquish your enemy and you absorb his reputation. Wyatt Earp killed Curly Bill, the leader of the Arizona Cowboys, who was then relegated to the back pages of western pulp magazines. Fair or no, Curly Bill joined the ranks of men who had fearsome reputations in their own time and are today no more than sidebars to the Earp legend. It took sixty-three years for Hollywood to resurrect Curly Bill.[8]

There may have been other shootouts on the Vendetta Ride. Wyatt implied this in his 1896 interview with the *San Francisco Examiner*. In Colorado, newspapers would report "six dead Cowboys" or "thirteen slain Cowboys," but no names. Bat Masterson's first biographer, Richard O'Connor, claimed a dozen victims for Earp and his men, but never cited his source. In all probability there were other fights— Warren Earp may have taken a bullet in the leg in one of them—but if Wyatt killed any more Cowboys he took care not to leave bodies to be found, and the Cowboys, of course, were not anxious to give Earp and Holliday credit for more kills. Some stories had Cowboys leaving

Arizona rather than face the possibility of running into Earp. Whatever the truth, with Curly Bill gone, the Cowboys, always a loosely
knit group, unraveled. Only two major figures among the cattle rustlers remained: Ike Clanton and John Ringo, and one of them didn't
have long to live.[9]

Wyatt's run in Arizona was nearly played out. There was time for
just one more act, and it was a farce.

On March 23 Wyatt and his posse arrived at the ranch of Henry
Clay Hooker, about 60 miles north of Tombstone, seeking rest and
refreshment. Hooker appears late in the Earp story, but he had an
important role. Hooker was from New England, and like many of
the key Tombstone figures—the Earp brothers, Josephine Marcus,
Old Man Clanton, George Parsons, Clara Brown, John Ringo—he
had gone West to California first and then backtracked to Arizona.
He saw the area as a paradise without enough water and set about
correcting that flaw, locating the best water sources in the county and
building the legendary Sierra Bonita ranch next to them.

The Sierra Bonita was—is, actually, since it is not only well preserved but is still a working ranch—a Mexican hacienda–style dwelling that was partly a fortress built to withstand attack from Apaches
and bandits. It was already famous in the early 1880s; by 1889 the
Sierra Bonita had been sketched and recreated on the Broadway
stage in the melodrama *Arizona* by Augustus Thomas. By that time,
Hooker had built it into a Ponderosa-like industry that took up more
than 700 square miles and maintained perhaps 10,000 cattle, most of
them pure-bred. In 1882, when Earp rode in, Hooker's ranch, despite a determined force of loyal stockmen, had been hit hard by
Cowboy rustling raids. Hooker had no trouble in making a decision
to side with the Earps.

Wyatt relaxed at the Sierra Bonita and took a drink of hard liquor,
perhaps his first since Urilla Sutherland had died. The ride had been
grueling and all the men, especially, one assumes, the tubercular
Holliday, were exhausted. No sooner had they rested and eaten than
Behan's posse appeared on the horizon. Hooker offered to let Earp
make his fight at the Sierra Bonita: The ranch's walls and the combination of Wyatt's posse and Hooker's tough cowhands would certainly have caused Behan to think twice about forcing a fight. Wyatt,
as he had always done, refused to involve citizens in what he still

regarded as a lawman's job. Gathering the posse, he retreated to a large hill a couple of miles north of the ranch, where riders approaching from any side could easily be seen.

The old buffalo hunter in Wyatt must have been itching for Behan to lead a charge up the slope and into the sights of his rifle, but the battle never happened. Behan, as usual, had been prudent in his hunt for Wyatt, though by this time anyone in Tombstone with decent hearing knew where he was as the sounds of gunshots had been echoing through the surrounding hills since the previous day. George Parsons thought the shots were prearranged signals between the Earp party and friends in the town who were bringing them food and supplies. "I went out several times to see what was up," he wrote after hearing the volleys. "Discovered nothing."

While John Behan was out pretending to look for Wyatt Earp, Tombstone itself had descended into near chaos, which must have made many yearn for the placid days of Virgil Earp's tenure. George Parsons wrote of "fourteen murders and assassinations in ten days"— this seems exaggerated, but the available records do suggest an epidemic of violence. In a particularly senseless murder, a man named Martin Peel, son of a local judge, was robbed and shot at the Tombstone Milling and Mining Company. The killers were thought to be two Cowboys, Zwing Hunt and Billy Grounds, the latter a protégé of Curly Bill's. Billy Breakenridge, left on his own by Behan, earned his stripes. Carrying warrants for the two on robbery charges, he tracked them to a ranch a few miles outside Tombstone and laid siege. (Breakenridge may have been spurred to act by the local citizen's committee, which was outraged by the murder and prepared to act if he didn't.) In the ensuing shootout, three deputies were shot, one of whom died. Grounds and Hunt were both shot. Grounds died from his wounds, and Hunt, recovering in a hospital, joined the swelling ranks of Cowboys who simply slipped out of Behan's custody.

Meanwhile, back at the Sierra Bonita ranch, Behan was not pleased with his reception from Hooker. Harry Woods, the former *Nugget* editor, was, once again, Behan's undersheriff, and the *Nugget* would later note that "Woods speaks in the highest terms of the treatment of the posse by the citizens of both Cochise and Graham counties with the single exception . . . [of] Mr. H. C. Hooker of the Sierra Bonita ranch, a man whom from the large property interest he has in the country, would naturally be supposed to be in favor of upholding the constitutional authorities and the preservation of law and order."

The *Nugget*'s hypocrisy was staggering, as the very posse that Behan and Woods were riding in was made up of numerous men who, for some time, had been stealing that property. When Behan asked Hooker for Earp's whereabouts—this may have been for form's sake, as everyone knew that Earp was waiting at the top of a hill just a couple of miles away—Hooker replied that he did not know and that, if he did, he would not tell. According to an *Epitaph* report, Behan then said, "You must be upholding murderers and outlaws then," and Hooker replied, "No, sir, I am not. I know the Earps and I know you and I know they have always treated me like gentlemen; damn such laws and damn you and damn your posse. They are a set of horse thieves and outlaws." Behan, said Hooker, should be ashamed to be found in such company, much less leading it.

Things got nasty when one of the Cowboys riding with Behan said, "Damn the son of a bitch, he knows where they are and let us make him tell." Hooker's foreman, Billy Whelan, pulled a Winchester and told the Cowboy, "You can't come here into a gentleman's yard and call him a son of a bitch. Now skin it back. If you are looking for a fight . . . You can get it right here."

Behan's posse was in no mood for a fight, and neither was Behan. He tried to calm things by telling Hooker, "They are not our associates; they are only here on this occasion with us." (Behan must have forgotten that Ike Clanton was in his posse.) "Well," Hooker responded, "if they are not your associates I will set an extra table for you and set them by themselves." The meal was uneventful. Hooker later claimed that Behan told him, "If I can catch the Earp party it will help me at the next election." It's doubtful that this was said; Behan was subtler than to say such a thing to a friend of Wyatt's. Besides, everyone already knew it.

Hooker also said that he finally did tell Behan where Wyatt was, though it was hardly necessary as all anyone had to do to was to look on the conical hill a half hour's ride to the north to see the most logical place for Earp's posse to retreat to. Behan, probably as Hooker anticipated, decided to go south or, as Hooker phrased it, "Any direction except where the Earps were waiting for them." When Behan returned to Tombstone after ten days out with his posse, he charged the County of Cochise $13,000 for his "expenses." Hooker was never reimbursed for feeding Behan's gang, which numbered more than two dozen.

A story would later grow around Earp's visit to the Hooker ranch that Wyatt had shown up with a severed head in a sack—the head of Curly Bill, he claimed—demanding a cash reward of $1,000 that Hooker, the head of the Arizona Cattlegrowers Association, had offered. Hooked laughed in his face, the story goes. Actually, Hooker had put up a $1,000 bounty on Curly Bill, but he later claimed that Wyatt refused it, saying, "I don't want any reward for carrying out my promise to Morgan." Messengers from Tombstone soon arrived with money from friends and from Wells Fargo.

Though the Behan posse contained such hard cases as Pony Deal, Ike Clanton, and John Ringo, it doesn't appear that the sheriff made any further effort to track the Earp party. At one point he rode to Fort Grant to get army permission to use Apache scouts. The commanding officer, Col. James Biddle, was contemptuous, telling Behan, "Hooker said he didn't know and would not tell you if he did? Hooker said that, did he? Well, if he did, you can't get any scouts here." When this hit the newspapers Arizona Democrats had one more reason to be resentful of the federal government. They would have another a couple of weeks later when Deputy U.S. Marshal Earp strolled into Fort Grant to mail some documents, including deeds to property he was willing to his sister in California. Colonel Biddle indicated he would have to arrest Wyatt, then invited him to stay for lunch. After eating, Biddle excused himself, and Wyatt and his companions rode back to Hooker's.

That was about it for Wyatt and the territory of Arizona. There were still people Wyatt suspected of complicity in the shooting of Virgil and Morgan, particularly Ike Clanton and John Ringo, since Wyatt seems to have decided that Hank Swilling, like Pete Spencer, was just a hanger-on, but there was no point staying around Hooker's ranch waiting for them to show up. Whatever his plans at this point, he would need a new base of operation.

Before Wyatt and his men left the Sierra Bonita, a letter was printed in the *Epitaph* that responded to Harry Woods's allegations in the *Nugget*. Postmarked from Wilcox, perhaps 70 miles from Tucson and close to the New Mexico border. It read, in part:

Editor, *Epitaph* – In reply to the article in the *Nugget* of March 31, relating to the Earp party and some of the citizens of Graham and Cochise counties, I would like to give you the facts in the case during our trip. . . . Leaving Tombstone on Saturday evening, March 25, we went into camp some six miles north of town. . . .

From here we continued our journey on the wagon road to Henderson's ranch where we had refreshments for ourselves and horses. Here we were informed that a gentlemanly deputy sheriff of Cochise county, Mr. Frank Hereford (for whom we have the greatest respect as a gentleman and officer) was at the ranch at the time of our arrival and departure and have since learned the reason for not presenting himself was fears for his safety, which we assure him were groundless. Leaving this ranch we went into camp in good grass one mile north. At seven next morning we saddled and went north to Mr. H. C. Hooker's Ranch in Graham County where we met Mr. Hooker and asked for refreshments for ourselves and stock, which he kindly granted us with the same hospitality that was tendered us by the ranchers of Cochise County. As regards to Mr. Hooker outfitting us with supplies and fresh horses as was mentioned in the *Nugget*, it is false and without foundation, as we are riding the same horses we left Tombstone on. . . .

Leaving Hooker's ranch on the evening of that day we journeyed north to within five miles of Eureka Springs. . . . Next morning, not being in a hurry to break camp, our stay was long enough to notice the movements of Sheriff Behan and his posse of honest ranchers, with whom, if they had possessed the trailing abilities of an average Arizona ranchman, we might have had trouble, which we are not seeking. . . .

At Cottonwood we remained overnight and here picked up the trail of the Lost Charley Ross. . . . We are confident that our trailing abilities will soon enable us to turn over to the "gentlemen" the fruits of our efforts so that they may not again return to Tombstone empty-handed. Yours respectfully.

The letter was signed "One of them." The author was never revealed, but it contained enough detail about the posse's movements to indicate it was written by one or by several of the Earp party. The directness suggests Wyatt; the sarcasm, such as references to Sheriff Behan's "posse of honest ranchers" and their not possessing "the thinking abilities of an average Arizona ranchman" suggests Doc Holliday's college educated pen. ("Lost Charley Ross" was a boy who was kidnapped in Philadelphia in 1874 and subsequently seen all over the United States, sort of the Judge Crater of his day. The case fascinated America for more than half a century; the gangster chief "Lucky" Luciano used to sign "Charlie Ross" on his hotel bills.)

The letter was an elegant parting shot, written in seeming defiance of later historians who would claim that Wyatt Earp "fled" Arizona.

On March 27 the *San Francisco Exchange* would write, on hearing of Curly Bill's death, that "this makes the fourth the Earp party has scored to the Cowboys' one. We are beginning to doubt the courage and invincibility of that much-talked of class, and are willing to give long odds on the murderous superiority of the Earp crowd." Much of the western half of the United States was following the Vendetta Ride, but perhaps not viewing the results with the same sentiments as Arizona's predominantly Democratic papers.

Some were even enjoying it. On April 24, the same *San Francisco Exchange* would print, that "It was renowned that the Earp brothers would arrive in Oakland and the light cavalry was immediately put under arms. That gallant and well-trained body resolved that if the two Earps came to Oakland and showed the least disposition to attack them, every man would bite the dust before those redoubtable bandits were allowed to run the town."

Oakland was safe. By April 24, the Earp brothers and their companions had been in New Mexico for more than ten days. The Arizona adventure was over. Or perhaps not. One last killing that may or may not have involved Wyatt Earp neatly wrapped up the story.

On July 13, exactly three months after the Earps left Arizona, John Ringo, "King of the Cowboys"—"A Hamlet among Outlaws," as Walter Noble Burns called him—was found not far from Rustlers' Park, West Turkey Creek Canyon, a few miles from Tombstone, sitting against a large black oak tree. In his right hand was a standard

Colt .45 single-action revolver, and in his temple a bullet from that or a similar gun. One round had been discharged from Ringo's pistol, or so it was said. The coroner's report didn't make clear whether the pistol contained one empty *chamber*—remember Wyatt Earp's dictum that experienced gun handlers always left the hammer resting on an empty chamber—or a chamber with one empty shell casing. That was merely the start of a tangled web of confusion over Ringo's death that still spurs arguments in Tombstone saloons to this day.

The facts surrounding Ringo's death, all derived from interviews with nearby ranchers who were summoned to the scene or from the coroner's report, are vague, seemingly contradictory, and endlessly intriguing. Ringo, who may have been dead for a day when found by a wood hauler named John Yoast, was wearing a cartridge belt for a Winchester rifle (which was propped up against the tree) as well as an ammunition belt for a Colt pistol, which was odd: Who would go to the trouble to kill a man and not take his revolver and repeating rifle? But the cartridge belt suggested an even more curious scenario: It was on upside down. Ringo's boots were missing; so was his horse, which had wandered nearly two miles before it was found. Around Ringo's feet were torn-up strips of what someone assumed to be an undershirt. There was also, as if to thoroughly confuse matters, a kind of scalp wound on "a small portion of the forehead and part of the hair."

The simplest method of dealing with all these different facts is to round up the suspects, usual and unusual, and consider the arguments for and against their having pulled the trigger.

The theory that the murder as committed by Apaches can't be discounted. Though there was little in the way of organized Apache resistance during the late 1870s and early '80s, there were always reports of renegades about. (We have already seen George Parsons's mention of a killing by an Apache.) Some say this might account for the partial scalp wound—the Apache who killed Ringo was in the act of scalping him when someone passed near by. This would also account for why Ringo's guns weren't taken.

The arguments against this theory, however, are equally sound. It's doubtful that a lone Apache or small group of Apaches would be marauding an area frequented by so many well-armed white men. (Teamsters frequently traveled the vicinity where Ringo was found, which is why John Yoast found him.) Also, it seems a bit melodramatic for an Apache in 1882 to take the scalp of an unknown white man. And, simply, no one had seen any sign of Apaches in the area.

Perhaps the murderer was our old friend Johnny O'Rourke, a.k.a. Johnny-Behind-the-Deuce, whom Wyatt and Virgil, and possibly Morgan, saved from a lynch mob after he senselessly shot a mining engineer. For years, this was the most popular theory of Ringo's death, and as near as can be determined, it was first advanced by Fred Dodge in his *Undercover for Wells Fargo*, edited by Stuart Lake's daughter, Carolyn. The motive was supposed to be that Ringo was in the mob that tried to lynch the Deuce, and that O'Rourke, coming upon Ringo sleeping off a drunken binge, shot him.

Ringo had apparently been bingeing, but the rest of the story once again appears to be a case of Dodge creating interesting tales just to show off some supposedly "inside" information. O'Rourke disappeared after the Earps saved him and wasn't seen in Tombstone before or after his salvation. Nor does anyone remember seeing Ringo at the Deuce's near-lynching. Also, using Johnny-Behind-the-Deuce as the killer doesn't explain any of the other strange things like the gunbelt being upside down or the scalp wound.

Or was it Buckskin Frank Leslie? He makes a more interesting candidate. The Leslie theory was advanced by a Tombstone bartender, Billy King, who dictated a book in which Leslie and a drunken Ringo got into a shouting match in Tombstone, after which Ringo rode out of town and was never seen alive again. Presumably he stopped for a rest and placed his boots on his horse, which wandered while Ringo slept. Leslie found him and put a bullet in his head. Billy Breakenridge, who favored the suicide theory, added, "We all know that Leslie would not care to tackle him even when he was drunk."

But many thought Leslie to be at least Ringo's equal as a shootist; Wyatt Earp considered Leslie to be, along with Doc Holliday, the best he had ever seen. Leslie thought nothing of engaging in a shouting match with Ringo while John was sloshed, so he certainly wasn't afraid of him. But why would he want to kill Ringo? Breakenridge said that Frank killed Ringo to "curry favor with the Earp sympathizers," but though Frank was a friend of Earp's he was rather neutral on the subject of Earp and the Cowboys—he rode in none of Earp's posses. And most of Wyatt's supporters weren't in a position of power at the time Ringo was killed.

Doc Holliday was a man with motives aplenty. There were stories about Kate and Ringo (which we'll examine in the next chapter), which may have been true; Wyatt Earp, whom Ringo threatened, was Doc's best friend; and Ringo and Doc came very close to shooting it out just a couple of months earlier.

For years, Doc was, in some circles, second only to Johnny O'Rourke as a candidate for Ringo's killer. This was due to magazine articles and a book by a man named Wayne Montgomery, who claimed to be the grandson of John Montgomery, a Tombstonian who, like George Parsons, saw much of the action firsthand. Wayne Montgomery's book, *Forty Years on the Wild Frontier—Authentic Tales of Wyatt Earp, Doc Holliday and Their Cronies*, was cowritten with Carl Breihan and published in 1985. Supposedly assembled from the diaries of John Montgomery, who owned the O.K. Corral, the book was worshipful in its view of Holliday. One story, which made its way into the western pulps, had Doc taking pity on a street urchin in Denver and, after explaining to him "the importance of education"—just look what it did for Holliday—making arrangements with a local banker to give the boy a sum of money every month (where this money came from is not explained). As for Ringo, according to Montgomery,

Doc had an insane desire to kill Ringo, whom he hated with an uncontrollable passion. So he decided to return to the Tombstone area and kill him. He knew full well that if he was discovered in Arizona he would be hanged to the nearest tree or post, yet he took that chance. Getting killed didn't bother Doc to any great extent, for he had an incurable disease that would sooner or later claim his life anyway. . . .

Soon he saw Buckskin Frank ride off, leaving Ringo alone. Ringo removed his boots and stretched out under a tree to sleep it off. Doc mounted and rode toward the sleeping man, surveying the area to make certain no one was about. When he reached the tree Ringo opened his eyes and said, "You dirty S.O.B.," and reached for his gun. Doc killed him. He sat and watched him expire, then rode back to the house to get his things and was soon on his way to Pueblo again.

That Buckskin Frank was out for a ride with Ringo seems odd. And it certainly couldn't have taken Doc long to watch Ringo expire, as he was shot in the temple.

As you might guess, as a score of writers and editors should have guessed, *Forty Years on the Wild Frontier* was proven in a court case to be a fraud. That doesn't mean that Doc wasn't involved in Ringo's death, but that family of friendly Mexicans he lived with while waiting for Ringo to show up stretches the imagination.

Wyatt Earp: No shady motives need be advanced here. Wells Fargo wanted Ringo, the last potential Cowboy leader, dead. Wyatt had good reason to believe Ringo had had a role in the shootings of Virgil and Morgan. Wyatt would have had as much financial and logistical support from Wells Fargo (including an informant in Tombstone in the person of Fred Dodge) to help him keep tack of Ringo's movements. Wyatt had reliable gunhands available in Doc Holliday, Sherman McMasters, Texas Jack, Turkey Creek Jack, and even Warren Earp; for that matter, Buckskin Frank could well have been bribed into keeping an eye on Ringo when he was in town.

There is at least one reason for believing that Wyatt Earp killed Ringo: he said he did. Or at least, in some extant versions of his two early attempts at biography, the writers who worked with him said he did. There are plenty of reasons why Wyatt would have publicly denied killing Ringo, from wanting to avoid murder charges to not wanting to implicate people still living in Arizona. But it's difficult to imagine why his biographers, who got most of their information from Wyatt, would have made a claim for him that he never made for himself.

Could he have done it? The logistics of travel from Colorado, which is where Wyatt was when Ringo was shot, are tough, but researchers have determined that it could have been possible—unlikely, but by making exact train connections, possible. (More so if, say, Ringo hadn't been dead for twenty-four hours but for, say, just ten or twelve.[10])

Jack Burrows, in his book *John Ringo—The Gunfighter Who Never Was* has made the most intelligent study of Ringo's death and concludes, "I think Wyatt Earp was quite capable of trying to do just that," traveling all the way back to southeast Arizona and hunting Ringo down, but "I do not think he did it." Burrows argues persuasively that Ringo was depressed by "the death of his outlaw friends, the rejection by his sisters" (whom he had often written to in California), and the feeling that, finally, there was "no place, now, for Johnny to run, no escape from himself." Ringo, Burrows says, "truly marched to a different drummer, and the beat was a dirge." Ringo, Burrows believes, killed himself. The last minor legend of Tombstone may have gone out with a whimper and a bang.

Jack Burrows puts no great importance on the missing boots—perhaps, he says, he simply wanted to die with his boots off—and suggests that the scalp wound was made by an animal after Ringo was dead. This theory is as plausible, which is to say as plausible as anything else in the whole implausible story. But is it plausible that Ringo held a Colt .45 with a 7 ½ inch army-length barrel to his temple, fired it, and continued to grip it in death? Burrows notes that many suicides are found holding their guns, which is true, but the overwhelming number of suicides use short barreled weapons and many put the barrel in their mouths. A long-barreled pistol held at such a precarious angle might fly right out of the shooter's hands. As to the lack of powder burns on Ringo's head, I do not know black powder weapons well enough to know if one would still leave powder if pressed against the object it was firing into. Perhaps some obliging editor from *Guns and Ammo* will someday run a test on this and enlighten us. And, finally, there is that gunbelt. I simply refuse to believe that anyone could get so drunk as not to know their gunbelt was on upside down.

Having said that, I don't think Ringo was killed by Apaches, Johnny-Behind-the-Deuce O'Rourke, Wyatt Earp, Doc Holliday, Buckskin Frank, or one of Henry Hooker's real Cowboys. There are simply too many holes in all the theories. Perhaps Big Nose Kate Elder tracked Ringo down and killed him to save Doc the effort.

No one will ever know the truth; the kill will always be claimed by Wyatt Earp's supporters for him, with Ringo's fans split between those not wanting to give "credit" to Earp and those who don't want to admit their man cashed in his own chips.

Ringo's name left a tinny echo down a hundred small corridors, surfacing here as John Wayne's Ringo Kid in *Stagecoach* and there in the Gregory Peck film *The Gunfighter*, where he is Jimmy Ringo, a gunfighter trying to escape from his past but who nonetheless brags about having beaten up Wyatt Earp. The Lone Ranger himself once posed as a border bandit named Juan Ringo. In a late '60s TV show,

Ringo was a sheriff, played by Don Durant, with a theme song that included the words,

> Ringo, Johnny Ringo,
> His fears were never shown.
> The fastest gun in all the West,
> The quickest ever known.[11]

In 1970, Ringo's legend had perhaps its last gasp in the Lorne Green hit single, "Ringo." "They can't explain," says Green in the first verse, "the tarnished star, over the name of Ringo." No more than they can justify why the real one ever got to wear a star in the first place.

Walter Noble Burns wrote that "the heroic age of Tombstone" ended with Curly Bill's death, but that could more properly be said of the death of John Ringo. There would be more gunfights. After years of trying, Billy the Kid Claiborne succeeded in getting himself killed, the instrument being Buckskin Frank Leslie. They got into a row at the Oriental, with some old Tombstonians claiming that Claiborne had accused Leslie of killing Ringo. Claiborne went outside for a Winchester rifle; Leslie, according to George Parsons, "rolled a cigarette, jammed it between his lips, and lit it before he picked up his pistol and walked into the street. Claiborne fired once and missed; Leslie fired and hit." Parsons also noted that "Frank didn't lose the light on his cigarette." The fight caught Claiborne at the tail end of a losing stretch. Not long before, he had threatened the town's Episcopal minister, Rev. Endicott Peabody, because the latter had preached a sermon on "the evil of the cattle-stealing rustlers and the drinking and carousing Cowboys." Peabody responded by letting everyone know that he would be preaching a similar sermon and that Claiborne was welcome to attend.[12] The Kid declined. If Claiborne wasn't ready to tackle the good reverend, he certainly should have left Buckskin Frank alone.

But there was an autumnal flavor to the gunfight. By that time, most of the major figures in the Tombstone saga—Old Man Clanton, his youngest son Billy, the McLaury brothers, Marshal Fred White, Frank Stilwell, Curly Bill Brocius, Johnny Ringo, and Morgan Earp—had all given their lives for tourism. Most of the rest—including Virgil Earp, Bat Masterson, Luke Short, Marshall Williams, Sherman McMasters, Texas Jack Vermilion, Turkey Creek

Jack Johnson, and, of course, "The Lion of Tombstone" (in Burns's words), Wyatt Earp—had moved on. John Clum was back East, though he would eventually see Wyatt again in Alaska and California, as would George Parsons. Josephine Marcus returned to San Francisco. Clara Brown would soon be back in San Diego. Harry Woods, whose vicious and slanted reporting had done much to cause the Tombstone troubles, would soon disappear from history.

Geronimo, who had no part in the Tombstone adventures, but whose presence always seemed to be felt by whites in southeastern Arizona, held out till 1886 before surrendering with perhaps two dozen of his warriors. He always maintained that this was his only real surrender; the one to John Clum didn't count because he had been "tricked." Camillus S. Fly lugged his camera equipment down from Tombstone to snap a picture of Geronimo holding a rifle that would become as famous as his shot of Billy Clanton and the McLaurys in their coffins. It is the only known photo of an American Indian taken while he was still at war with the United States.

After the death of her first husband, Theodore Brown, Clara Brown remarried and eventually moved to Montclair, New Jersey, where she died in 1935, outliving Wyatt Earp by six years. She is buried in Mount Hebron Cemetery in Montclair, perhaps five miles from my home, where this book was written.

John J. Gosper, the acting governor of Arizona Territory and champion of the Earps during the Tombstone troubles, joined the Arizonian exodus to Los Angeles in the later 1880s and early 1990s. He died in L.A. in 1913 at the county hospital. According to the *Los Angeles Times*, the once wealthy mining operator was "unattended by relatives or friends and penniless."

The bartender and part owner of the Oriental Saloon, Irish born Milt Joyce—or Colonel Joyce, as he was described in his obit in the *San Francisco Examiner*—who was for a while a business partner of Wyatt's before joining the Behan faction, also died in California in 1889. Concerning his ugly fight with a drunken Doc Holliday, Joyce told a San Francisco reporter that he had seen Doc after Tombstone: "Only once," in Denver, "and then I made a blanked fool of myself." In a Denver saloon, Joyce responded to what he regarded as a provocation from Holliday by brushing up against Doc and walking back and forth in from of him "to remove any idea he might have that I wanted to run away." Holliday said nothing; he may not have recognized Joyce. "I have thought of it lots of times since then, and have thought how foolish I was to go back," he told the reporter, "but the impulse struck me to do it and I couldn't help it."

Judge Wells Spicer, whose decision on the O.K. Corral gunfight is still revered as a model of balanced judgment and fine prose, would eventually disappear somewhere in the Arizona desert. No hint of foul play was ever attached to his disappearance.

John Behan saw his political ambitions collapse. He sought re-nomination as sheriff, but the Democrats would not support him. (A man named Larkin Carr eventually won the nomination, only to be beaten by a Republican, Jerome Ward.) Behan drank and became warden of the prison at Yuma; George Parsons would write that he should have been on the other side of the bars. In 1883 he would be indicted for illegal collection of taxes. Behan's son, Albert, would remain a lifelong friend to Josie Earp and was friendly to Wyatt as well.

Billy Breakenridge was fired by Behan in August 1882 and ran against his former boss, unsuccessfully, for the Democratic nomina-tion. Like Clum and Parsons, he would see Wyatt Earp again, in Los Angeles. Curiously, Breakenridge never mentioned his falling out with Behan in *Helldorado*.

Crawley Dake, the U.S. marshal who supported Virgil and Wyatt, came under investigation because of the money spent on the posse's ride. The investigation was eventually dropped, though Dake had almost certainly pocketed funds that he claimed had gone to Earp. Sherman McMasters would work for the U.S. Army during the cam-paign against the Spanish in the Philippines; Texas Jack Vermillion would move to Virginia and become a preacher.

Those who stayed in Tombstone witnessed the slow death of a boomtown. Water began to seep into the silver mine shafts, and, slowly, production dropped off. Tombstone had never managed to bring in the railroad,, and now it was too late. In 1886 a fire de-stroyed the Continental Hotel and several other landmarks. Luckily, neither the Bird Cage Theater or Schieffelin Hall was touched. Ed Schieffelin, who was born the same year as Wyatt, lived the high life in California for years after leaving Arizona. But, like Wyatt, what he really wanted to do was prospect. In 1898 he went out to Oregon looking for gold; he died alone in a cabin of a heart attack, with several samples of high-grade gold ore around him. He was buried back in Tombstone. Tourists approaching the town he founded from the west will see the Schieffelin Monument at the town limits.

In 1887, Ike Clanton, after having received numerous felony indictments, was shot and killed by a detective named J. V. Brighton. Brighton had received his license from a correspondence school. Wyatt Earp never spoke about why he had not hunted Ike down; most likely he didn't hold him as high on the Cowboy totem pole as Hollywood would in later years. Shortly after Ike's death, Doc Holliday finally succumbed to tuberculosis in Glenwood Springs, Colorado. It isn't clear whether or not Kate Elder was with him; shortly afterward, she would be running a boarding house in Globe, Arizona.

A short time before he died, Doc met with Wyatt and Josie in Denver. It was obvious from his appearance that Doc had only a short time to live. "Isn't it strange," Wyatt told him, "that if not for you, I wouldn't be alive today. Yet you must go first." As they parted, Doc threw his arm over Wyatt's shoulder. "Good-bye, old friend," he said. "It will be a long time before we meet again." Josie said that Wyatt cried; it was the only time that anyone recalled seeing Wyatt cry.

We can only wonder what Wyatt's reaction was eight months later when he heard of the death of Celia Ann "Mattie" Blaylock Earp— she kept the name till she died—in Pinal, Arizona. The unfortunate Mattie had drifted into prostitution and died from an overdose of laudanum after having told a friend that she was "tired of life." A coroner's witness, T. J. Flannery, testified that Mattie blamed Wyatt for wrecking her life. The town Mattie died and was buried in doesn't exist today; beyond the coroner's report there is no record of her death and virtually none of her ever having lived.

As regards legend, Tombstone experienced a kind of Silver Age, though the silver mines were shut down following an 1887 earthquake, when Texas John Slaughter became Cochise County sheriff. But by the end of 1882 the era that the world would remember had passed, and by the end of the century Tombstone, "the town too tough to die," had nearly become a ghost town. "Once it was a Romance," wrote Walter Noble Burns, after visiting in 1926. "Now, it's just a town."

Just a town, perhaps, but America's Brigadoon, a town that would be revived again and again, first by writers and journalists and then by Hollywood as a metaphor for the failings of law or the dangers of lawlessness, depending on the eye of the beholder and the temper of the times.

Notes

1. Sadie appears to have been Josephine's nickname later in life. It's not clear that anyone called her by this in Tombstone, though she is constantly referred to by this name in Waters's book.

2. It's interesting to note how subsequent Earp researchers have made liberal use of *The Earp Brothers of Tombstone* without subjecting it to the same scrutiny as Stuart Lake's book. Paula Mitchell Marks, for instance writes that, "I believe that many of the statements [in *The Earp Brothers*] reflect Allie's perceptions of events better than she was willing to acknowledge." First, one wonders precisely how Marks knows what statements in the book were actually made by Allie Earp, since no one else does. Second, one also wonders by what mysterious process Marks perceives the truth of Mrs. Earp's remarks more clearly than she herself did. Ms. Marks, it can be said, wants the book to be true.

3. Waters, not Allie, was the originator of stories that Josie had been "on the line," or a prostitute, for a while in Tombstone. His source was a woman who, in 1960, was "the oldest living resident of Tombstone"—she had to have been at least one hundred years old to have remembered Josephine—and another elderly Tombstone woman, dead by the time Waters's book was published. This story may be filed, literally, under the category of old wives' tales.

4. In a taped interview in 1995, Waters, discussing the possible anti-Semitic feelings Allie might have harbored toward Josephine, admitted to this author that he "tried to play that element down," but wasn't precise about how "that element revealed itself" or how he played it down.

5. In Quentin Tarantino's script for the film *True Romance*, a hired killer says, "The first time you got to kill someone it's hard, I don't care if you're Jack the Ripper or Wyatt fuckin' Earp. The second one's no day at the beach, either. After that, it's easy."

6. In a letter Dodge wrote to Stuart Lake during the writing of *Frontier Marshal*, Dodge also claimed that a Charleston saloon keeper named J. P. Ayers was also a Wells Fargo informant and that several Cowboys who came into his place talked freely about Earp's killing of Brocius. Dodge also claimed that Ike Clanton admitted as much to him. This seems unlikely to me, if only be-

cause I can't see any reason why Ike Clanton would confide in Fred Dodge, but it's an interesting variation on Ike's tales in which Wyatt Earp and Doc Holliday confided in him.

7. This article, and all subsequent newspaper references to Holliday in Colorado were gathered by a researcher named Emma Walling from Snowmass, Colorado, who herself credited one of Doc's Georgia descendants, Susan McKey Thomas. Amazingly, all this valuable material was sitting in the vaults of Colorado libraries and historical societies waiting to be picked through.

8. It took Hollywood sixty-three years to resurrect Curly Bill. He put in a minor appearance in 1941 in Richard Dix's *Tombstone—The Town Too Tough to Die* played by a surprisingly menacing Edgar Buchanan. Curly Bill was also a semiregular character on the TV series "The Life and Legend of Wyatt Earp" in the 1950s, played by various character actors. By 1967, eighty-five years after Wyatt killed him, he graduated to the role of Ike Clanton's (Robert Ryan) underling in *Hour of the Gun*, played by Jon Voight in one of his first movie roles. (He's killed by James Garner's Wyatt Earp just as he's about to draw on Jason Robards's Doc Holliday.) Finally, in *Tombstone* (1994), Curly Bill got his due, played by a demonic-looking Powers Boothe and restored to his rightful role as Cowboy leader. Later that year, in Kevin Costner's *Wyatt Earp*, Bill had been demoted back to the status of gang member.

Curly Bill's name hasn't resonated in American popular culture like that of his pal, John Ringo. But in a 1991 sports news segment on ESPN, Chris Berman referred to the New York Yankees third baseman as Scott "Curly Bill" Brosius.

9. Among the Earp papers at the University of Virginia is a letter by Jas. A. Zabriskie, U.S. attorney, to U.S. Attorney General Benjamin Harris, dated January 21, 1885. In it Zabriskie tries to defend U.S. Marshal Crawley Dake's use of funds during the Earp-Cowboy war. Zabriskie writes that "Deputy Marshal Earp and his band killed quite a number of these cow-boys, and a regular vendetta war ensued between the marshal and his posse." Unless Zabriskie was exaggerating, this would indicate more killings than the newspapers recorded.

10. Many books, including Paula Mitchell Marks's *And Die in the West* have quoted freely from *I Married Wyatt Earp* in support of the logistical possibilities. But there's no indication that Josephine actually said any of this, as these passages are not in her original manuscript. They appear to have been added by a later writer trying to impose his theories on Josephine's story.

11. I once saw the plastic Johnny Ringo TV gun at a toy rack at the supermarket where my mother shopped. It had two barrels—

the lower one was supposedly for firing shotgun shells. I could kick myself for not having bought it.

12. Peabody's lovely Episcopal church, the first Protestant church built in Tombstone, is as beautifully preserved as the Bird Cage Theater. It's located a half block off Fremont, about a baseball's throw from where the famous gunfight took place.

8

Putting Clothes on a Ghost: The Life and Legend of Doc Holliday

Doc Holliday's life has only recently begun to come out of the shadows. As the most enigmatic of the movie Doc Hollidays, Val Kilmer, expressed it in an interview with this writer, "Trying to flesh out his character is like trying to put clothes on a ghost."

Aside from the fact of his having contracted tuberculosis as a teenager—and no discussion of Doc's character or behavior should fail to take this into account—most of what was considered true about him up until a couple of decades ago is now known to be false. Most of the Sunday supplement stories, taking their lead from entries in Old West encyclopedias printed before 1970, feature these "facts" about him: Doc was born in Valdosta, Georgia, in 1850, the son of a wealthy man who served as a colonel in the Confederate Army; he attended dental college in Baltimore, where he contracted tuberculosis; he killed several blacks or Union soldiers in an incident at the family swimming hole back in Georgia; out West he took up with a prostitute named Kate Fisher; he killed a gambler named Ed Bailey in a knife fight in Texas before fleeing to Dodge City, Kansas, where he became friends with Wyatt Earp; in the silver boomtown of Tombstone, Arizona, he participated in the Gunfight at the O.K. Corral; he died in a Glenwood Springs, Colorado, sanitarium in 1887. And, of course, that he killed eight or twelve or twenty-one men, depending on whose account you give credence to.

Except for the tuberculosis, every "fact" on that list is now either suspect or known to be wrong. Doc wasn't born in Valdosta, where he spent much of his time growing up, but in nearby Spalding County. His father, whose ancestors were not Anglo Saxon but Northern Irish, was a major in the Confederate Army, not a colonel as he was usually identified (probably because nearly every ex-Confederate above the rank of corporal was granted the honorary status of "Colonel"). Doc's family wasn't particularly wealthy; the Holliday home in Valdosta was modest by the standards of Southern aristocracy. (Actually, it's no more impressive than the house Wyatt Earp was born in.) It's now known that he went to dental college in Philadelphia, not Baltimore.[1]

We know that Kate's name was Harony and later Elder, though she apparently used the alias Fisher at one time, probably adopting the name of a man she had taken up with. It's not certain that anyone was killed in the notorious water hole shooting incident of Doc's youth, or that he actually killed the gambler Ed Bailey. Most western historians now agree that Doc was friendly if not actually friends with Wyatt Earp before Kansas. Of course, we know that The Gunfight at the O.K. Corral wasn't actually in the corral. And Doc died at the Glenwood Hotel in Colorado, not the sanitarium, which didn't exist in 1887.

Though the birth record is lost to us (burned with other property, said one family historian, by passing Union troops), the descendants of Holliday in Georgia believe he was born, not in 1850, but on August 14, 1851, as recorded in the family Bible, in which someone finally thought to look. No one is certain how or where he contracted tuberculosis. His decision to leave postwar Georgia for the frontier was long thought to be based on reasons romantic and mysterious, such as a murder or a doomed love affair or a rejection of his father for remarrying so soon after his mother's death. More mundane possibilities are the Southwest's drier climate and the need to make a living—patients lack confidence in dentists who burst into fits of coughing while their hands are in the patient's mouth. Whatever the reason, Doc, a gentleman untrained for any other profession, drifted into the one best suited to wayward members of his social class—gambling.

The identification of Kate simply as "prostitute" seems hard. We wouldn't even know the name of Doc Holliday today if Kate hadn't saved Doc's life after the Ed Bailey incident—if, that is, the incident actually occurred.

In his best-selling 1989 western travel book, *The Great Plains*, Ian Frazier went looking for Ed Bailey's grave in Fort Griffin, Texas, without success, most of the graves being simple heaps of stones with no markers. A reason why Frazier didn't find Bailey's grave is that it probably isn't in Fort Griffin. Most researchers now believe that Holliday simply stabbed Bailey with a penknife and left him bleeding. Apparently Doc's mercy didn't prevent Bailey's friends from threatening revenge. The story Wyatt Earp heard and repeated to Stuart Lake, that Kate set fire to a livery stable and sprung Doc in the confusion, may well be true. (It's certainly a more likely scenario than the one in *Gunfight at the O.K. Corral*, where Burt Lancaster's Wyatt slips Doc away as the town battles the diversionary fire set by Jo Van Fleet's Kate.[2]) Fort Griffin had no newspapers, so there's no evidence to support popular tradition that Doc and Kate were running from something when they left Texas.[3] By the time Doc arrived in Dodge City he had what every frontier gambler wanted, a reputation.

Dodge, with its hordes of newly paid cowhands, would probably have drawn a professional gambler like Doc anyway—in the *San Francisco Examiner* account Wyatt says that when he met Doc in Texas "Holliday asked me a good many questions about Dodge City and seemed inclined to go there"—and Dodge had special advantages for Doc. For one thing, no one in Kansas was going to bother him about some trouble in Texas. Second, the combination of his now unsavory reputation and his friendship with such a formidable policeman as Earp would allow him to ply his trade in peace, under the protection of the law.

It wasn't Doc Holliday's reputation that attracted trouble—contrary to movie westerns, a reputation as a killer repelled trouble, rather than attracting it—but his temper, which was bad when sober and worse when drunk. In either condition, the real Holliday, like all fabled gunfighters, is now known to have fewer "kills" than his mythical counterpart. This has gained him no favor with Earp debunkers, who invariably take the same approach with Doc as they do with Wyatt: If he killed a lot of men then he was a cold-blooded murderer (though hot-blooded murderer would seem to fit Doc better) and, if he didn't, he was a fraud. Wyatt Earp was quoted by Stuart Lake as calling Doc, along with Buckskin Frank Leslie, "the fastest, deadliest man with a gun I have ever seen," but, without doubting Wyatt's word, it would be interesting to know exactly when he saw Doc shoot. There was the streetfight in Tombstone, of course, but Wyatt had his own business to take care of there and wasn't paying too much attention to Doc. It's possible that Doc had a hand in the vendetta killings of Frank Stilwell and Indian Charlie, or even that he killed them himself; these are the only times we know of for certain. It's also possible that there were other killings during the Vendetta Ride that Earp never talked about. More than likely the two spent a lot of time practicing together. Wyatt told Lake that Doc "set out to master the fine points of draw-and-shoot as cold-bloodedly as he did everything. He practiced with a Colt for hours at a time." Practicing where people could see would not only have honed their skills but spread their reputations.

In one of the most famous passages in *Frontier Marshal*, Holliday saves Earp's life by facing down perhaps as many as fifty angry Texas cowhands, an incident that, Wyatt says, cemented their friendship. Debunkers in the 1950s seized on the fact that town records at Dodge revealed no multiple killings or even arrests that would substantiate such a story, but arrest records for Dodge City are now known to be incomplete.

Whatever story Wyatt told him, Lake embellished it, and he wasn't the first to do so. In 1896 Wyatt told an *Examiner* reporter that Doc "saw a man draw on me behind my back. 'Look out, Wyatt!' he shouted, but while the words were coming out of his mouth he had jerked his pistol out of his pocket and shot the other fellow before the latter could fire." This story sounds more plausible—it's one man and not fifty—but there is no record, either verbal or written, of Doc having shot anyone in Dodge. Wyatt could have been feeding a tall tale to a gullible big city reporter, but given the distortions and inaccuracies in the rest of the interview it's more likely that Robert Chambers, *Examiner* reporter (and later, potboiler novelist), did just what Stuart Lake was to do later, which is to take what Wyatt really said and build it into a better story.

What did Wyatt really say that Doc did for him? At the O.K. Corral inquest he said that his friendship with Holliday stemmed from Doc's having saved his life in Dodge City. Not that he stood off fifty men or even five, or shot anyone, just that he saved his life. In his book on the O.K. Corral inquest, Alford Turner suggests that the story was a fabrication of Wyatt's lawyer to explain why a lawman

would be friends with such a notorious character as Holliday. Perhaps, but that doesn't explain why Earp told the same story fourteen
years after to a reporter when such a fabrication would no longer be
needed. There is, surely, no reason not to believe Wyatt Earp when
he said that Holliday saved his life in Dodge City, and no reason to
assume that Doc did it for any other reason than that he chose to.

   Much of Doc Holliday's reputation as a killer was hokum, perpe-
trated, no doubt, by Doc himself. As we've seen, this reputation
backfired against him—and against Wyatt—at the O.K. Corral inquest, where a great many people who only knew him by his press
were ready to believe he started the fight by killing Tom McLaury.

Nearly every account of Doc Holliday the killer begins with a version
of the infamous water hole shooting incident of his youth, and the
origin of all the stories is Bat Masterson's profile for *Human Life*.
Here's Masterson's account:

> Near the little town in which Holliday was raised, there
> flowed a small river in which the white boys of the village,
> as well as the black ones, used to go in swimming to-
> gether. The white boys finally decided that the Negroes
> would have to find a swimming place elsewhere, and noti-
> fied them to that effect . . . which they promptly re-
> fused to do and told the whites that if they didn't like
> existing conditions, that they themselves would have to
> hunt up a new swimming hole.
>
>   As might have been expected in those days in the
> South, the defiant attitude taken by the Negroes caused
> the white boys to instantly go upon the war path. . . .
> One beautiful Sunday afternoon at the point of dispute,
> Holliday appeared on the river bank with a double-bar-
> reled shotgun in his hands, and, pointing in the direction
> of the swimmers, ordered them from the river.
>
>   "Get out, and be quick about it," was the peremptory
> command. . . . Holliday waited until he got a bunch of
> them together, and then turned loose with both barrels,
> killing two outright, and wounding several others.
>
>   The shooting, as a matter of course, was entirely unjus-
> tifiable, as the Negroes were on the run when killed; but

the authorities evidently though otherwise, for nothing
was ever done about the matter. . . . His family, however, thought it would be best for him to go away for a
while and allow the thing to die out; so he accordingly
pulled up stakes and went to Dallas, Texas.

There are several things wrong with this story. First, why would such
a frail young man—a photograph as he probably looked around this
time, taken around the age of eighteen while in college in Philadelphia, shows him to be nearly as thin as in the Tombstone years when
he was thought to weigh about 130 pounds—be carrying such a
difficult to handle weapon as a double-barreled shotgun? (Wyatt
Earp claimed that Doc hated shotguns and that until Virgil handed
him one before the streetfight in Tombstone, he never saw one in
Doc's hands. Doc would have scoffed at the oil portrait by a Japanese
artist that hangs in the Lowndes County Museum in Valdosta,
which shows him with a double-barreled shotgun.) And just who
were the "authorities" who thought Holliday's deed justified? And if
"the authorities" didn't pursue the matter, why did Doc "flee" to
Texas?

Masterson says that "Holliday never boasted about the killing of
the Negroes down in Georgia, [but] he was nevertheless regarded by
his new-made Texas acquaintances who knew about the occurrence
as a man with a record; and a man with a record of having killed
someone in those days, even though the victim was only a 'nigger,'
was looked upon as something more than the ordinary mortal." But
there is no indication that Holliday's Texas acquaintances had heard
of any such deed. If they had, no one has ever found mention of it.

The only reputation John Holliday seemed to have had when he
arrived in Dallas, where he hung out his shingle, was that of a pretty
good dentist. The first record of drinking and shooting incidents
came much later, and the first "notch" in Doc's rep, Ed Bailey, came
after he had been in Texas nearly three years.

If Holliday didn't boast about the water hole killings, how did Bat
find out about them? No newspaper in Georgia or Texas mentions
them; neither do Doc's obituaries. There is nothing about the incident in the Flood manuscripts or in Stuart Lake's papers. Josephine
Marcus never speaks of it. Surely Billy Breakenridge would have
been happy to discredit Holliday, but the water hole incident does

not appear in *Helldorado*. For that matter, both John Clum and Fred Dodge, who disliked Holliday and related other unpleasant stories about him—Dodge is the only real source for Doc's implication in the Benson stage robbery—say nothing of the water hole shooting. The story seems to have arisen only years after Holliday died.

In *In Search of the Hollidays*, published in Valdosta in 1973, two of Doc's descendants, Albert S. Pendleton and Susan McKey Thomas, relate a version slightly different from Masterson's. It seems young John Henry was out buggy riding with his Uncle Thomas when they came upon some black youths swimming in a part of the With-lacoochee River that had been cleared to be used for a family swimming hole (there are no white boys in this narrative). For some unexplained reason, Holliday became enraged and pulled a pistol—a much more plausible weapon for Doc than a shotgun—and, in the words of his Uncle Thomas (as passed on by his daughters), began shooting over the boys' heads. The uncle, the only one who ever claimed to have been a witness, never said anyone was killed.[4]   If this is the mother of all Holliday water hole shooting stories, one wonders why it survived since scarcely anything that happened is worth remembering. No one *outside* the Holliday family mentions it until the family published their pamphlet in 1973, and even then it seems to originate ten years after Doc's death. Perhaps not coincidentally, this is exactly the time when John Wesley Hardin's self-serving autobiography was published. Hardin, a psychopathic racist, bragged of numerous killings of blacks and found many sympathetic readers in the old Confederate South. Masterson, a proud Republican from Illinois who did not like Holliday, may well have taken whatever version of Doc's water hole story he heard and embellished it with killings of the kind Hardin boasted of.

To paraphrase the reporter in *The Man Who Shot Liberty Valance*, when there's no facts at all, print whatever legend you like.

Another gunfighter who got his legend printed before the facts were known was John Peters Ringo. For years, Ringo was widely believed to have been a college graduate and the black sheep of a proud Southern family, or at least that's the way magazine and coffee table book writers wrote about him after 1930. The only sources for those claims were Walter Noble Burns's *Tombstone* and Billy Breakenridge's *Helldorado*. Burns's book came out first but owed much to

Breakenridge's recollections. From them, the legend of John Ringo, frontier scholar, the gunfighter who kept classics in his saddlebags, was born. It is entirely possible that the brooding, seemingly tormented Ringo wasn't properly stimulated by hanging out with the likes of Ike Clanton and did dip into a few books. One researcher has tracked down copies of Xenophon's *Anabasis*, Bunyan's *Pilgrim's Progress*, Dickens's *The Pickwick Papers*, and other classics that John probably inherited from Missouri kinsmen. A dropped Latin schoolbook phrase or two could easily have helped him pass as an intellectual in the Arizona of the early 1880s. That Ringo had anything like Holliday's education, though, is unlikely. Doc almost certainly was schooled in Latin and the classics before entering college, in the manner of a young Southern gentleman of the Victorian era; we do know that fluent Latin was a requirement for a degree in dentistry. But as more stories were told about Doc and Ringo and they were compared and contrasted, the more educated and more Southern John Ringo became.

Like Doc, Ringo was supposed to have had a "death wish," though, unlike Doc's TB, the source of Ringo's angst has never been named. (TB could well have been the source of it; John's mother and younger brother died from the disease.) To some western writers this has only served to make him more fascinating. (In *Tombstone*, Val Kilmer tells Kurt Russell that Ringo "wants revenge." "For what?" asks Russell. "For bein' born," Kilmer replies.) Ringo, like Holliday, had an unidentified woman in his life from whom he received letters. (This is true, actually; Doc corresponded with his cousin in Georgia, while Ringo exchanged letters with his family, mostly with his sister, in California.) His past was also clouded with mystery; it was said that he could never return to his family (it turns out that they were simply ashamed of him). Like Doc, he was believed to have been involved in numerous killings, most of them in Texas and he probably was, in at least two. In other words, as the years went by, Ringo appeared more and more to be a smudged, carbon copy version of Doc.

As representatives of their particular factions, Doc and Ringo were such natural antagonists that some versions of the Earp saga have Doc killing Ringo at the O.K. Corral shootout—Kirk Douglas, for instance, gunning down John Ireland (who earlier had played Billy Clanton in *My Darling Clementine*) in *Gunfight at the O.K. Corral*. In fact, Ringo and Doc did come perilously close to a confrontation. According to Walter Noble Burns, shortly before the O.K. Corral fight, Ringo tried to call out the Earps. In full view of the Clantons and the McLaury brothers, he accosted the Earp party in front of the Grand Hotel on Allen Street:

> "Wyatt Earp," he said, "I'll make you a proposition. We hate you and you hate us. If this feeling keeps up, there's going to be a battle some day, and a lot of men'll be killed. You and I can settle this whole thing. Just the two of us. Come out in the middle of the street with me, and we'll step off ten paces and shoot it out, fair and square, man to man."
>   Wyatt Earp looked at Ringo for a moment in amazement. "Ringo," he says, "I'm not given to makin' sucker plays. If you're drunk or crazy, I'm neither one nor the other. I'd be a fine simpleton—a peace officer and a candidate for sheriff—to fight a duel with you in the street. Go and sleep it off."

Then, according to Burns, Wyatt turned and walked inside a saloon.
    As we've seen, something like this did happen, but it happened after the famous streetfight and it was noted by George Parsons in his diary. Burns must have gotten the story from some old Tombstonians some forty-odd years after the fact, because the near-confrontation happened long after Wyatt tried for the sheriff's job. The Earps, probably unarmed and already up to their necks in trouble, had no intention of engaging in another streetfight. Holliday, on the other hand, was ready to go. According to Burns, Ringo

> drew a handkerchief from the breast pocket of his coat and flipped a corner of it toward Holliday.
>   "They say you're the gamest man in the Earp crowd, Doc," Ringo said. "I don't need but three feet to do my fighting. Here's my handkerchief. Take hold." Holliday took a quick step toward him.
>   "I'm your huckleberry, Ringo," replied the cheerful doctor. "That's just my game."
>   Holliday put out a hand and grasped the handkerchief.

Both men reached for their six-shooters.

(This is the only mention anywhere of Doc Holliday being "cheer-ful.") In every account, including those in the *Epitaph* and the *Tucson Weekly Citizen* (which carried the *Nugget's* account)—none of which mentions the handkerchief by the way—friends or officials intervene before we find out who would have won. Tombstone's do-gooding bystanders not only deprived us of a classic stand-up gunfight, they probably ensured that Cochise County would be in for a lot more violence in months to come.

The story is interesting for another reason. Doc is often identified as the "hothead" who pulled the first trigger in the O.K. Corral fight. Yet, on the occasion of his near fight with Ringo, he was content to engage Ringo in some sort of duel, or at any rate, didn't simply leap into the fray shooting. (Neither, it should be noted, did Ringo. Both were careful when sober and in public to observe the unwritten code of the duel.) One hesitates to write such behavior off to some kind of Southern chivalric code, especially in light of the times Doc did pick up a pistol and start firing (most of these when drunk). Doc some-times displayed, for a hotheaded gunfighter, an odd propensity—again, when sober—for letting the other fellow draw or perhaps even fire first.

The O.K. Corral fight furnishes an intriguing example. "I've got you now, you sonabitch," grunts a gut-shot Frank McLaury. Hol-liday replies, "Blaze away, you're a daisy if you do." Why in the world is Doc stopping in the middle of a gunfight to have a conversation? Was he giving Frank McLaury a sporting chance to shoot first? After all, if you have time to crank off a couple of sentences, however pithy, you have time to cock and fire. The story adds a dash of credence to the notion that the real reason Doc went West was to die in a gunfight rather than letting TB get him "with his boots off." (By exquisite coincidence, John Ringo also died with his boots off.)

Most of what has been written about Doc, either material currently in print or available only through collectors' editions, is nonsense. Bob Boze Bell's *The Illustrated Life and Times of Doc Holliday*, a 1994 book available in most Phoenix and Tucson bookstores, is the only book available that can walk the general reader through Doc's story with historical accuracy. Nearly everything else with the name "Doc Holliday" on it should be regarded with suspicion.

For instance, *An Illustrated Life of Doc Holliday* (not to be confused with Bob Bell's book), a much-quoted sixty-four-page 1966 pamphlet by longtime Earp researcher Glenn Boyer, is in such demand that it sells for $100 or more in collectors' book shops. It contains a wealth of information on Holliday, and also a great deal of nonsense, such as the story that after leaving Arizona Doc and Wyatt teamed up to hunt down and kill Johnny Tyler, an old Tombstone nemesis in Colorado. Near the end of the pamphlet Boyer reveals that much of the material was actually taken from "Doc's letters which are extant in the possession of parties who are not willing to be identified with Doc," and that "in due time this material will probably be made available to some historical society." Thirty years later, the letters have yet to show up.[5]

Boyer, at least, admits his Doc Holliday book was bogus; it would have been better for this field of study if some other writers had done the same a long time ago. One book that unfortunately came back in print after the success of the movie *Tombstone* was *The Frontier World of Doc Holliday* by a California writer named Pat Jahns. Originally published in 1957, it's much favored by debunkers of the Wyatt Earp–Doc Holliday myth—the Texas writer Ramon Adams, in his study of Western histories, *Burrs Under the Saddle*, thought it the best book written about Doc—but it's not so much a biography as a lurid novel with footnotes. In this passage, for instance, Doc addresses Wyatt after the revenge shootings of Virgil and Morgan:

> Now, Wyatt, see what your ambition and your pride have done. Morg is dead. Morg. You stomped all over the feelings of others; now you know how they felt. Now you are going to react in the same way they did, and make your own revenge in this lawless country. You saw the men who shot Virg go unpunished. You know the murderers of Morg will escape the law, too. So you are going after them as marshal, jury, judge and executioner—and by this revenge become as mean and cowardly as your enemies, and as human.

Clearly Jahns's purpose wasn't to write a book about Doc Holliday but to trash the Wyatt Earp who was popular on TV and in the movies at the time Jahns wrote. Jahns's point of view is at least unusual; most observers saw Doc as a bad influence on Wyatt, whereas Jahns sees Wyatt as the evil one and Doc as worthy of at least a modicum of sympathy. " He would force the sick heart numb," she writes, "by concentrating on the cards, the opium of his days." And: "He had to go to bed before his customary dawn. It wasn't that his consumption was worse; it was the black depths of depression that made him feel as if he were losing his mind. . . . He lay on his bed staring at hell from the empty blackness of space, it seemed; alone, alone, alone"

Not so alone—Jahns is in his head with him. And in bed with Doc and Kate:

Doc arose in his wrath and a long white night shirt. . . . He clobbered her one aside the head with nearly three pounds of .45 caliber Colt . . . and rather put his heart in it.

Kate came to feeling sober and sorry and very fragile . . . and lying in Doc's bed with a wet towel on her head . . . Kate snuggled down in bed and grinned at Doc. He stood by the lamp for a long minute looking down at her and then swiftly bent over and blew out the light . . .

The ellipsis at the end was put there by Jahns. Presumably some things about Doc's life will be left to our imagination.

That so many Old West scholars would prefer Jahns's Holliday book to John Myers's 1955 book, *Doc Holliday*, is indicative of how partisan the study of Earp and those around him has become. Myers, who was born on Long Island and died in Tempe, Arizona, was one of several Eastern or Midwestern journalists (Burns, who wrote about the Capone mob in Chicago, and James D. Horan, a New Jersey–based journalist, were other examples) who saw the lawlessness of the West in terms of American organized crime, a point of view that offended many western writers (particularly Texans, since the books the Easterners wrote tended to place Texans at the center of the most criminal activity).

Myers's book, recently reprinted by the University of Nebraska press, was the basis for most of the information about Doc used in the movies *Gunfight at the O.K. Corral, Tombstone,* and *Wyatt Earp.* He had already written about the Tombstone wars in a 1950 book, *The Last Chance,* recently reprinted under the title *The Tombstone Story,* and his Doc Holliday followed a similar bent: The Earps represented the law and the Cowboys and John Behan were the forces of lawlessness and corruption. Myers, like Lake and Burns before him, got a lot of the facts wrong, and the book would have benefited greatly from being written twenty years later when Myers could have used the information now made available in the Holliday family booklet. But Myers was the first writer to consider Doc as more than a mere appendage to Wyatt's story, and is refreshingly nonjudgmental.

Doc, he wrote,

> was good at keeping faith with such friends as he saw fit to make. He was good both at keeping his own counsel and respecting the privacy of others. He was good at accepting facts without flinching. He was good at facing death, both as an ever-present to a victim of consumption and a special menace in the many gun-and-knife fights in which he engaged.
>
> By contrast, he was not good at winning the regard of society's moral leaders, where found.

Would that Myers had cut similar slack for poor Kate. Myers, like Jahns, cites no evidence concerning Kate's prodigious sexual appetites, but "they can, however, be easily imagined by anyone who has ever observed a lusty tart saturated with booze and self-pity." But where is the evidence for all the booze and self-pity?

The real Kate seems to have been a tough, practical frontier immigrant who, her nickname aside, was supposed to have been a very attractive woman when young. (The most commonly reproduced photograph of her, used in scores of coffee table western books, shows her as stout and plain. The photo has now been proved to be bogus.) No one knows just how or why she got her famous nickname. It wouldn't have been necessary for her to have had a big nose; most western nicknames had nothing to do with the people who acquired them. Wild Bill Hickok wasn't wild; he wasn't even a Bill (his real name was James Butler). Billy the Kid was a kid, but he wasn't a Billy (his name was Henry McCarty). Black Bart wasn't black; "Dirty" Dave Rudabaugh was no dirtier than most of his friends; Hurricane Bill Martin was mostly hot air; Indian Charlie wasn't an Indian; Mysterious Dave Mather wasn't mysterious; Buffalo Bill didn't kill any more buffalo than a couple of hundred other men; and Wyatt Earp's friend, Texas Jack Vermillion, when asked why he was called Texas Jack, said, "'Cause I'm from Virginia." All one can say for certain about frontier nicknames is that once acquired, they stuck for life, and in some cases considerably longer. Shrewd and resourceful, the real Kate ran a boarding house after Doc's demise and traded on the legend she had earned a piece of, though her attempt to write a book failed. One thinks she would have been amused to find herself as the mother of John Wayne and Dean Martin in 1966's *The Sons of Katie Elder*, the implication of which was that Doc was the dad of Duke and Dino.

Which leads to the intriguing question of Doc's ambiguous sex appeal. In virtually all descriptions of Doc Holliday we hear he is "slender," "boyish," "handsome," and, later, near the end, "handsome but nearly emaciated." One Tombstone woman found Doc and Wyatt "the handsomest men I have ever seen." Women who Doc took the effort to ingratiate himself with were invariably charmed by his accent and courtly manners, and perhaps excited by his terrible reputation. No other figure of the Old West, even Billy the Kid, suggests such a glamorous combination of vulnerability and menace.[6] Doc's TB, far from detracting from his appeal, may actually have been a prime source of it. As Susan Sontag points out in *Illness as a Metaphor*, TB victims were widely believed to be possessed with remarkable sexual powers—witness the wild tales attributed to legendary country music star Jimmy Rogers, who died of TB at nearly the same age as Holliday.

In retrospect, it seems inevitable that someone would have suggested a homosexual relationship or at least attraction between Wyatt Earp and Doc Holliday. What's amazing is that it took till 1971 to find its way into a movie. In the original version of Frank Perry's *Doc*, from a script by Pete Hamill, Wyatt (Harris Yulin) tells Doc (Stacey Keach) over a campfire that "maybe men love each other better than men love women, and vice-a-versa. . . . And maybe you an' me ought to keep on goin'. Just keep goin'. Pull up stakes. Go out to California." (Which is where Wyatt would end up, with Josephine.) The prairie-wise Kate (Faye Dunaway) knows what Wyatt really wants: "I seen your kind in a dozen towns, Marshal. Walkin' around, swingin' your eggs like you wanted to use them. But nothin' happens. The pistol stays locked up in the holster, don't it, Wyatt? Until you see a man you like. A nice, beautiful man. A poor skinny death-sick man. Ain't that what's the matter with you, Marshal? Ain't it?" (Hamill's script must have been one of the last ones made in Hollywood where homosexuality indicated that something was "the matter.")

If the real Kate had such suspicions she never voiced them, but she did mistrust Wyatt—probably out of jealousy of Doc's loyalty to him—and considered Wyatt a bad influence on Doc. In earlier Earp-Holliday pictures, actors such as Caesar Romero, Kent Taylor, and Harry Carey, Sr., had portrayed Doc as a roustabout with a hair-trigger temper who could only be restrained by Wyatt's severe righteousness. But as America's suspicion of authority grew in the late 1950s and '60s, the civilized and more cultured Doc, who lived outside the respectable life, metamorphosed into a moral check on the darker side of Wyatt Earp's nature. In *Gunfight at the O.K. Corral* Kirk Douglas begs Burt Lancaster not to throw away "a lifetime of being a lawman" after James, the youngest Earp (the real James was actually the oldest) is murdered. (Wyatt had put in perhaps four years as a constable, assistant marshal, and deputy sheriff at the time Morgan was killed.) By the time we get to Jason Robards, Jr., in *Hour of the Gun* (1966) Doc has practically become a frontier philosopher, dispensing cautionary nuggets of cracker-barrel wisdom between gunfights. James Garner's Wyatt Earp gets so irritated he actually strikes him—the only time in an Earp movie Wyatt loses his temper with Doc. By 1971, Doc has the high moral ground and actually loses his temper with Wyatt, pulling a gun on him when Earp roughs up a fictitious Cowboy called "the Kid"—an obvious Billy the Kid stand-in.

The first movie Doc to behave in a manner that fits most of the facts is Val Kilmer's Doc in *Tombstone*. While on the Vendetta Ride to avenge Virgil and Morgan, Doc is asked by another member of the posse why he's out killing Earp's enemies instead of in bed; he replies, "Wyatt Earp is my friend," which is exactly what a late-nineteenth-century Southern gentleman would have said.

In fact, since so much of Doc's character is explained by his southernness, one wonders why, in a dozen previous movies, Doc Holliday was never portrayed as a Southerner. Kirk Douglas, Jason Robards, and Stacey Keach were all given Southern pasts, but not the accent or mindset. Victor Mature's surgeon-turned-gunfighter in *My Darling Clementine*, looking about as tubercular as a Kodiak bear, was actually made to play Doc as from Boston. The reason might have been that Ford didn't want the Doc Holliday of *My Darling Clementine* confused with an earlier Ford character based on Doc, John Carradine's Gatewood, the gaunt, gentleman gambler and defender of Southern womanhood in *Stagecoach*, who is clearly a variation of the Holliday legend. In fact, Carradine is probably the most historically accurate character modeled on Holliday before Kilmer. (The least accurate was fifty-plus-year-old Willie Nelson, who played Doc Holliday in a dreadful 1986 TV remake of *Stagecoach*. Absurdly, the character of Gatewood was left in the story, making this the only film with two Doc Hollidays.)

No matter what their accent, all movie Doc Hollidays are spiritual kin. Their past is never too carefully explained, the reason for their exile never made clear. (In *Stagecoach*, Carradine's Gatewood, mortally wounded, tells the other passengers, "If you ever see the Judge"—his father—"tell him that his son . . ." then expires.) All movie Docs come from a more refined background than the frontiersmen they encounter in gambling halls, and there's always a woman in their past who symbolizes a life they can never return to. (Kirk Douglas's Doc looks mournfully at a picture in a pocketwatch.) All movie Docs are alcoholics; they drink to ease the pain of their memories—for Doc Holliday, memory is pain. Doc has a past he can't forget, and, as the fire in his lungs reminds him, he also has no future. He has an edge over any gunfighter or gambler he encounters, since in any situation he might just as well play for keeps. (This may have been one of the reasons for the real Doc's admiration for Wyatt Earp: he saw someone who had everything to lose and still played for keeps.)

The reason why the movie Docs never explain their exile in the West is because the real Doc never talked about it. Albert Pendleton and Susan McKey Thomas believe that John Henry and his father

did communicate from time to time but that the letters were misplaced or destroyed. An 1885 item in a Valdosta paper indicates that
Major Holliday met his son in New Orleans and begged him, without success, to return home; if true, this would support the conclusion of some descendants that Doc never forgave his father for
marrying so soon after his mother died. If he did see his father in
New Orleans, Doc certainly didn't go back to Georgia with him. He
went West again, this time with the knowledge that he would die
soon.

Doc spent the last few months of his life in Glenwood Springs,
drawn by the reputation of the miraculous curing power of its sulfu-
rous vapors. We now know enough about tuberculosis to know that
this was ill advised; the caustic fumes probably dissolved the last
remaining shreds of lung tissue. Doc left his deathbed in the Glenwood Hotel only twice in his last two months. The nearness of death
changed his character for the better; an undated clipping in the Colorado Historical Society said that his "gentlemanly demeanor" over
the last few weeks earned him several friends who brought food and
otherwise cared for him.

On Tuesday, November 8, 1887, sometime before noon, Doc
opened his eyes and asked for a shot of whiskey. Some accounts have
Doc looking down at his feet and muttering "I'll be damned"—he
was to die, after all, with his boots off. Just before he died he smiled
and said, "This is funny." He was just thirty-six, but his hair had
turned silver gray.

Holliday's hated enemy Ike Clanton had been killed five months
earlier. If Doc knew about Ike's death, it must have cheered him.
The most famous dental student ever to come out of Philadelphia,
the frail-looking gentleman who came West with only a few years
left, had lived longer than Billy Clanton, Frank and Tom McLaury,
Curly Bill Brocius, John Ringo, and Morgan Earp, not to mention
Jesse James, Billy the Kid, Butch Cassidy, and the Sundance Kid.
Alone on that list, Doc Holliday died in bed.

In a Glenwood Springs cemetery, surrounded by yellow weeds,
there's a weathered headstone that reads "This memorial dedicated to
Doc Holliday who is buried someplace in this cemetery." The headstone is decorated with crossed six-guns and a poker hand holding
four aces. Holliday's descendants in Valdosta sought to have the remains shipped back to Georgia, but no one knew exactly where the

burial site was, the original headstone having been moved to thwart thieves and curiosity seekers. John Henry Holliday remains an exile.

We do know the identity of the mysterious woman in Doc's life. Her name was Mary Melanie Holliday, and she was Doc's cousin, the daughter of his uncle, Robert Kennedy Holliday, who he played with as a child in the halcyon days before the Civil War. She later became a Catholic nun and was revered by many, particularly Margaret Mitchell, who made her the model for Melanie in *Gone With the Wind*. What exactly was the nature of Doc's personal relationship with Melanie? In *Tombstone*, Val Kilmer's Doc, on his deathbed, tells Kurt Russell's Wyatt that an affair with his cousin caused her to enter a convent and him to leave home in disgrace. This theory at least has the virtue of tying up matters in a grand, romantic knot. The speculation of a thwarted romance began with Pat Jahns's book and picked up steam with Glenn Boyer's *The Illustrated Life of Doc Holliday*. But there is no evidence for it. Melanie didn't enter the convent till 1883, so it's not likely she forsook the world as a direct result of an affair with Doc, though that doesn't mean that such an affair never happened. In fact, Sister Melanie did tell members of her family that had she not destroyed some of Doc's letters, "The world would have known a different man from the one of Western fame." So why did she destroy the letters? A packet of letters sent by Doc to Melanie that might have illuminated their relationship was discovered by a nun after Sister Melanie's death in 1939 and was promptly destroyed.

So, apparently, were letters from Doc to Melanie that were in the possession of Holliday family members. The next generation of Holliday relatives can tell us only that oral tradition says the letters were full of interesting descriptions of the frontier and that they gave evidence of Doc's classical education. Why were Doc's letters disposed of? The most logical explanation is that they contained something that nuns and family members thought improper to the memory of Sister Melanie.

Perhaps any further packets of Doc's letters still out there are best kept hidden. We'd be less interested in Doc if we knew why he left home forever, just as we would lose interest in Bogart's Rick Blaine in *Casablanca*, if we knew why he could never return to America.

Viewed from a distance, Doc has the quality of one of Conrad's outcasts, and his loyalty to Wyatt Earp is an act of nobility through

which he redeemed some deep personal crime or disgrace. Why were
Wyatt Earp and Doc Holliday friends in the first place? That Doc
had saved Wyatt's life doesn't suffice as an explanation. Such an act
might have made Wyatt grateful, but it wouldn't have made him and
Doc friends. Doc was, Wyatt told Lake, "a philosopher whom life
had made a caustic wit." Doc's dark, sardonic humor appealed to
Wyatt. Doc saw humor, however bitter, in everything. The reason
screenwriter Kevin Jarre gave Kurt Russell's Wyatt for liking Val
Kilmer's Doc in *Tombstone* can probably stand for all time: "He
makes me laugh." One thing is certain: Wyatt Earp remained loyal to
Doc even when distancing himself would have served him and his
brothers much better.

Perhaps the best summation of Doc's life is found in the work of
Alfred Henry Lewis, a one-time Kansas cowhand and later New
York journalist who became famous around the turn of the century
for his Wolfville novels (and who also edited Bat Masterson's *Human
Life* profiles). In his most famous work, *The Sunset Trail*, published
in 1905, a character named Doc Holliday explains his checkered life
to Bat Masterson: "I mixed up in everything that came along. It was
the only way I could forget myself." The line may well have come to
Lewis from Doc himself, through Bat Masterson. Mixed up in everything he did, but he never seemed to be able to forget himself.
The longer he lived, the more he gave himself to remember.

When we look back at Wyatt Earp now he appears as one of the
first representatives of the modern industrial society that would come
to incorporate the frontier into the America of Manifest Destiny. It
makes sense that he would die in Los Angeles in 1929, after working
as an advisor on the movie westerns his image would come to dominate. But Doc Holliday appears to us as the avatar of a past still
strongly felt but only dimly remembered, the eternal wild card in the
deck of the Old West's most enduring legend.

Notes

1. Specifically, from the Pennsylvania College of Dental Surgery. Dr. Milton Asbell of Haddonfield, New Jersey, who collects
information on the University of Pennsylvania Dental School,
which absorbed Doc's college, speculates that it was common in the
1870s for students to take weekend train excursions to New York.

Doc probably did, too. Perhaps he visited a restaurant or bar near 141 Avenue A, the current site of Doc Holliday's Grill.

2. Tombstone historian Ben Traywick claims that Shackleford County put out a warrant for Kate on the charge of arson. Traywick couldn't locate it, but he talked to people in Texas who claimed to have seen it. Curiously, no warrant for Doc's arrest on any charge in Texas has surfaced.

3. In her 1995 novel, *Doc Holliday's Woman*, western poet and historian Jane Candia Coleman has Kate setting a fire that practically burns down Fort Griffin, and since Coleman's narrative is based on the memoirs the real Mary Kate Harony wrote while at the Pioneer's Home in Prescott, Arizona, the story can't be disregarded. Replying to those who claim that Doc and Kate could never have made the torturous ride from the Texas panhandle to Dodge City, Kansas, Coleman, the Thor Heyerdahl of the American West, made the ride herself upon her Appaloosa, Jefe.

4. There are other, even less substantiated versions of the incident that suggest it was a federal soldier who was shot (or shot at) by Holliday. This is probably one of the myths that Glenn Boyer helped to perpetrate in his *An Illustrated Life of Doc Holliday* pamphlet; Boyer even adds the novelist touch of making one of the Yankee soldiers "a bully boy from a Bowery regiment." But there is no record of a Union soldier—white, black, or from the Bowery—killed in that part of occupied Georgia during that period. The federal government tends to keep records of such things.

5. Boyer managed to take in a lot of people with this booklet, including Paula Mitchell Marks, who cited the Tyler killing and *An Illustrated Life of Doc Holliday* in her bibliography for *And Die in the West–The Story of the O.K. Corral Gunfight*. Boyer admitted to me in a letter that the book was a hoax, claiming that he wrote it to trap historians who didn't check their sources. The point of this escapes me, as Boyer has long claimed to be the primary source for information on Earp and Holliday.

6. Western researcher Chuck Hornung is fairly certain that Doc and Billy the Kid played cards in Las Vegas, New Mexico, in 1879. There is no record of who won.

9

The Lion in Autumn

On April 15, 1882, a Mr. John Smith and a Mr. Bill Snooks checked their horses into the Elephant Corral in Silver City, New Mexico. The stable owner was curious; cursory examination proved that one of the gentlemen was Wyatt Earp, the other a member of his group, presumably Doc Holliday. Papers all over the West had been guessing where the party would surface—there had been half a dozen false sitings in Arizona—and now they knew. By the time editors in the Western states and territories got the news, though, Wyatt's group had sold their horses and arrived in Albuquerque.

So far in 1882, Wyatt hadn't paid much attention to public relations, but in Albuquerque he made a smart move. He went to the office of both local papers, one Democratic in leaning, the other Republican, and offered interviews. In return he asked that the papers not report his whereabouts or his men's until they were safely away. Three weeks later the *Albuquerque Evening Review* reported that "The party, while in Albuquerque, deported themselves very sensibly, performing no acts of rowdyism, and this way gained not a few friends in their side of the fight." Wyatt would need all the public support he could muster in the next couple of weeks. Doc would need more than that. If not for Bat Masterson, he might have got his wish of not dying in bed.

Wyatt left a firestorm of controversy behind in Arizona, typified by an editorial in the *Tucson Star*. The worst feature of present-day outlaws, said the paper, "is that they are deputy U.S. marshals. . . . What a comment on the U.S. government, that a band of so-called officials with a high hand rove over the country murdering human beings out of a spirit of revenge." The question, the *Star* concluded, was "law or no law: which shall prevail? The people say the former must." But the people didn't specify which laws it wanted obeyed, or who it was that would enforce them, or what course was left open when the law failed to work. Wyatt Earp's name was at the center of that debate and would remain there for more than a century whenever issues of law enforcement broke out into public controversy.

Once again, as in Tombstone, the main instrument Wyatt's enemies used against him was Doc Holliday's reputation. In Albuquerque, Wyatt and Doc had a quarrel, the only recorded falling out between them. No one knew for sure what caused it; Wyatt never mentioned it, and Doc, when questioned later, said, "We had a little misunderstanding, but it didn't amount to much"—an indication that whatever offensive behavior he was guilty of had occurred in public, or how would a reporter have known of it? (It was probably an incident referred to in the *Albuquerque Review*, which reported that Doc "became intoxicated and indiscreet in his remarks, which offended Wyatt."

Now, life was about to pull the group in different directions. Wyatt and Warren lingered around the town of Trinidad, and Doc, without other means of support, went to Pueblo, New Mexico, to gamble. (Wyatt's PR campaign was paying off; the local papers said that Earp's men were all " 'way up' boys—gentlemen of the first order.") A probable reason why Wyatt chose Trinidad was that Bat Masterson had become the local sheriff, which freed Wyatt from worry of Cowboy reprisals. Doc should have been so prudent. Instead, he chose to gamble in Denver, where he had become a celebrity. On May 15, a man named Perry Mallen stepped up to Doc on the street, pulled a gun, and announced "I have you now."

It would be hard to single out one incident in Holliday's life as the most bizarre, but this one ranks high. Mallen claimed to be a sheriff from, of all places, Los Angeles, and provided the local constabulary with telegrams calling for Holliday's arrest for the killings of Frank Stilwell, Billy Clanton, and, of all people, Curly Bill Brocius (a railroad conductor, unarmed, was also mentioned). At the Sheriff's Office, Mallen again pointed a gun at Doc, who calmly replied, "Oh, you can drop that. Nobody is going to try and get away from you. I have no weapons." "No," Mallen said, "you won't get away from me again. You killed my partner, you bloodthirsty coward, and I would have taken you in Pueblo if the man I had with me had stood by me."

No one, least of all Holliday, had the slightest notion of what Mallen was talking about, but an idea glimmered in Doc's head. "I can show who that man is," he told the handful of men who assembled in the hall, one of them a reporter for the *Denver Tribune*. "I can prove that he is not the sheriff, and, in fact, no officer of Cochise County. I can show you his reason for bringing me here." Doc had realized that Mallen was a bounty hunter, almost certainly hired by Behan or someone associated with him in Arizona.[1] But he would have to explain all that later in jail.

Just as things promised to get ugly, Bat Masterson arrived from Trinidad. Exactly how he had found out Doc was being held in Pueblo isn't known, but if Bat knew, then Wyatt knew, too. Many years later, writing about Doc for *Human Life*, Bat said, "I assisted him [Doc] substantially on several occasions . . . not because I liked him any too well, but on account of my friendship for Wyatt Earp, who did." We can assume Wyatt got Bat to wire the town marshal in Pueblo for a warrant to arrest Doc. The charge Masterson used was swindling a man in Pueblo of $150; it was fake, but since the alleged crime was in Colorado it would have changed the jurisdiction. Pueblo Marshal Henry Jameson showed up to claim the prisoner but the sheriff of Arapahoe County, Mike Spangler, said he wouldn't release Holliday until officers arrived from Arizona.

Playing politics artfully, Bat told the *Denver Republican* that "All this talk is wrong about Holliday. I know him well. He is a dentist and a good one . . . in Dodge . . . he was known as en enemy of the lawless element." Bat wasn't stretching the truth; Doc was a good dentist, and he had behaved himself in Dodge. Bat also faced down Mallen at the Sheriff's Office, forcing him to admit he was wrong about some of Doc's alleged misdeeds.

Back in Tombstone, Behan was making plans to travel to Denver and extradite the Earps and Holliday when Pima County officials interceded: Wasn't Frank Stilwell killed in Tucson, and didn't that make this Pima County business? Bob Paul eventually made the trip. Paul's disposition, if one went by the partisan press, was either virulently pro- or anti-Earp—it depended on the political affiliation of the paper you read. It's also possible that Paul was giving out contradictory statements in order to disguise his intentions. Paul dawdled, allowing himself to get tangled in red tape, while Bat Masterson met with Colorado governor Frederick Pitkin to ask him to deny extradition. It's likely that Paul and Masterson were working in concert, since the day before the hearing Pitkin issued a statement that he was refusing Arizona's request for Holliday. Paul rode with Holliday back to Pueblo where Doc was freed on bail; when asked why he didn't go to pursue the Earps at this point, Paul replied that he had to stay in Denver to keep an eye on Holliday. That essentially ended the political farce of the attempted extraditions: Governor Frederick Tritle, who had replaced Fremont in Arizona, never pursued the issue, and Governor Pitkin in Colorado said no more about it. Perry Mallen faded away, and no more bounty hunters appeared.

What is remarkable about the incident is the amount of bombast it stirred in Western newspapers. A reporter for the *Denver Republican* wrote that, "Doc Holliday . . . is one of the most noted desperadoes of the West. In comparison, Billy the Kid or any other of the many Western desperadoes who have recently met their fate, fade into insignificance. The murders committed by him are counted by the scores and his other crimes are legion." Of course, not a single crime or murder was specified. "In the Southwest," the story ended, "his name is a terror." The *Daily Chieftain* in Pueblo, where Doc had done no one any harm, reported that he had "killed over fifty men, and that Jesse James is a saint compared with him." This was tempered with the closing remark that "The article in question has caused much amusement among Holladay's [sic] friends." His friends, perhaps, but any family member reading this news back in Georgia couldn't have been happy.

The *Denver Republican* continued to run Holliday stories, each one more bizarre than the previous one. Doc got his nickname "because of a peculiar dexterity he possesses in the care and cure of gunshot wounds"; his "form" was "Herculean in activity in strength"—Doc weighed about 130 pounds—with a "sort of dashing, independent air, which"—and this was probably as true a statement about Doc Holliday as ever appeared in a newspaper—arouses in the mind of a beholder feelings of the deepest resentment."

The Republican story illustrates how factually unreliable frontier newspapers could be. In this version, Doc was the leader of the Cowboys, not one of the group hunting them, and "his record of shameless murders and robbery during the time throws the deeds of Jesse James, Billy the Kid or any other desperado entirely in the shade." In this version, "six bullets from Holloday's [sic] pistol perforated [Perry] Mallen's body, yet he did not despair." After seven years of perseverance, Mallen tracked "Holloday" down. "No cry of anguish or suffering deterred him [Doc] from his purpose," Mallen told the Denver paper, "and like a savage wild he gloried in his deeds of blood!"

Four years later, when Doc was arrested on a misdemeanor, the *Denver Tribune-Republican* made this hash out of the story: "Doc Holladay"—they still hadn't gotten the name right—"has the reputation of a 'killer.' He gained his notoriety as an Arizona rustler in 1881–83. He was a member of the noted Earp Brothers gang, who are reported to have killed a dozen or more men in those bloody days of Arizona's history." Now the Earps and Holliday were the rustlers!

By the time Doc died in 1887, they at least had his name right. The *Aspen Daily News* claimed that "few men of his character had more friends or stronger champions"—perhaps the "of his character" was the operative phrase. "He represented a class of men who are fast disappearing in the New West. . . . He had been well known to all the States and Territories west of Kentucky." The *Ute Chief* had him "sheriff in one of the counties of Arizona during the troublesome times. . . . Of him, it can be said that he represented law and order at all times and places." The *Denver Republican*, having learned of its earlier factual errors, set out to make new ones: "The best authorities . . . say he [Doc] had killed sixteen" men. In Dodge City, he "formed an acquaintance and friendship with the Earp boys, who are said to have been a pretty bad gang even in those days: At that time it is said that 'Bat' Masterson, who is almost as well known a Western character as 'Doc' Holliday was, was city marshal. Bat was 'running the town' after the most approved frontier manner and 'Doc' Holliday and the Earp boys were helping him." And, in Arizona, "a deadly feud existed between the 'rustlers,' which was the general name of the crowd to which the Earps and 'Doc' Holliday belonged, and the Cowboys. . . . 'Doc' Holliday used to say that his crowd killed thirteen Cowboys at that time."

And so on. Part of the confusion was no doubt caused by the

changing definition of terms. The Cowboys were, of course, the rustlers, but by 1887 the term had gained usage and was used in referring to "real" Cowboys, cowhands not criminals, the way we might use it today. And so, the seeds for more than a century of pulp westerns were sown—as if the truth wasn't bloody enough. Anyone who wanted to could find newspaper documentation that "the Earp boys" and Doc Holliday were thieves and "rustlers" who killed a dozen or more innocent Cowboys. Each paper would repeat nonsense from a previous paper, embellishing it in turn, grafting new stories onto old ones.

This brief period, lasting from about the early 1880s to roughly the middle of the next decade—some might date it precisely to August 1895, when John Wesley Hardin was killed, while some would extend it to about 1902 when Butch Cassidy and the Sundance Kid left the West for New York and then for South America—might be called the neoclassical era of Western legend-making. It was too early for any but a few journalists to know the facts about what had happened with Wild Bill Hickok in Abilene; with Billy the Kid in Lincoln, New Mexico; the Earps and Doc Holliday and John Ringo in Tombstone, the Jameses and Youngers in Northfield, Minnesota; or the Daltons in Coffeyville, Kansas. But by the early 1880s people were conscious that a short and remarkable period was coming to an end. The mythmaking had begun: Doc Holliday held the lead followed closely by Bat Masterson, "almost as well known a Western character," followed by the Earp boys, who owed much of their notoriety to their friendship with so famous a killer as Doc Holliday. Doc and Bat and the Earps were either as "notorious" as Billy the Kid and Jesse James or as noble as Wild Bill Hickok, depending on the principles and politics of the paper running the story.

An interview Virgil Earp gave to the *San Francisco Examiner* soon after leaving Arizona would prove to be accurate: "The press dispatches that have been sent here have been very unfair to us. . . . I am sorry to see the thing taken into politics as a personal measure, because the true aspect of the trouble will be lost." It wasn't lost entirely, but it would stay hopelessly muddled for a long time.

In the autumn of 1882, Wyatt and Warren lingered in the small town of Gunnison, waiting for—what? Perhaps for an indication that hostilities were over and that they could go back to Tombstone and dispose of some property at a profit. If so, this was wishful thinking. All remaining Earp holdings were sold off for taxes and the investment of more than two years lost. Finally, they left, not to join Mattie, who was with the rest of the Earps in Colton, but to join Virgil in San Francisco. We know nothing of what Wyatt's parting with Mattie was like; there are no letters, diaries, or known documents that shed light on their relationship and on whether it was a marriage. (Mattie, not Wyatt, called herself "Mrs. Earp," and he had named one of their mines the "Mattie Blaylock," not the "Mattie Earp." All other documents that indicate they were married, such as the mortgage on their home, might have been for convenience sake.) It would seem that they were not happy; certainly Wyatt was not happy, the evidence doesn't prove that Wyatt left Mattie for Josie—it just confirms that he left Mattie.

By the end of 1882 Virgil, Wyatt, and Warren were sharing an apartment in San Francisco. This was an odd arrangement, if only because Virgil was married and apparently not with Allie, a subject not broached in *The Earp Brothers of Tombstone*. It must have been at this time, around or before Christmas, that Wyatt and Josie began to see each other again. Josephine is of no help on this question; her memoirs skip from Tombstone to San Diego. The likely explanation is that she simply couldn't find a way to deal with the problem of Mattie, who haunted their relationship and who she managed to keep out of any book on Wyatt's life until her own death in 1944. It's a shame that there is no account of this period; one would love to know the reaction of a respectable middle-class Jewish couple from Germany by way of New York who find that their precocious daughter has taken up with a former buffalo hunter turned gambler and peace officer whose gun battles had dominated the Western papers for nearly a year.

Early in 1883, Wyatt and Josephine left San Francisco. They would be together for the next forty-six years.

Wyatt had a piece of a faro game waiting for him in Gunnison. Believing that the Cowboy war was over or that it could no longer reach him in Colorado, he and Josie went back. Then came a call from an old friend, and Wyatt found himself in a town he never expected to see again—Dodge City, Kansas.

The entire episode was rather uneventful although it filled many western pulp magazine pages. Luke Short, a Texan by birth, had established a successful gambling business in the old Long Branch Saloon, catering to his fellow Texans. Mayor Ab Webster, who owned the Alamo Saloon, didn't like the competition. Dodge hadn't yet become a backwater, but because of the railroads the heyday of the cattle drives was over. There was less business to go around, and the scramble for what was left brought politics into play.

Larry Deger, the town marshal who had done little to earn Wyatt Earp's respect in the glory years of Dodge, now ran for mayor. Times had changed, and Deger was elected on a reform ticket—the trick was how to reform and not hurt the interests of his friend and patron, Ab Webster. The obvious solution was to put a crimp in Short's business by enacting laws against vagrancy and prostitution and enforcing them selectively. So, three women, all "singers" as they were listed in the court records, were arrested in the Long Branch.

This led to the only shooting in the whole affair. Short walked to the city jail to get his girls; a deputy saw him coming, recalled some of Short's press clippings, and opened fire. Short fired back; the deputy tripped and fell. Short, making the perfectly reasonable assumption that he had just killed a deputy marshal, ran to the Long Branch, grabbed a shotgun, and barricaded the doors. Short was talked into surrendering on the promise that he'd only be charged with disturbing the peace. Instead, he was arrested on assault charges, given a stiff fine, charged $2,000 bail, then released, only to be re-arrested as an "undesirable." He was put on a train and run out of Dodge.

Short went to Bat Masterson in Colorado for help. By the time Bat was enlisted, Dodge was having a reunion of its old police force: Bat, Wyatt, Charlie Bassett, and Neal Brown were there, and two of Wyatt's Arizona associates, Texas Jack Vermillion and Dan Tipton, to name just a few, were also along for the ride. The group, traveling from different points, converged on Dodge. The anticipated shootout never happened; instead of bullets, telegrams flew, with various officials zipping back and forth, and petitions being sent to Kansas Governor George Glick, who was inclined to take Short's side in the dispute. A Kansas paper caught wind and ran a story that "Wyatt Earp, the former marshal of Dodge," was on the way "but, worse than all is another ex-citizen and officer of Dodge, the famous Doc Holliday." Both men were killers: Holliday was, "Among the desperate men of the West . . . looked upon with respect born of awe, for he killed in single combat no less than eight desperadoes." Wyatt Earp "is equally famous in the cheerful business of depopulating the country. He has killed within our personal knowledge six men"—actually, had killed or helped to kill at least seven—"and he is popularly credited with relegating to the dust no less than ten of his fellow men." By this time in 1883, with the exception of Bill Cody, who was doing his Wild West show, Doc, Wyatt, and Bat were the most famous living men on the rapidly shrinking frontier, even if most of what was written about them was nonsense (such as Doc's arriving in Dodge City for the Luke Short business; he remained in Denver the whole time).

In truth, Wyatt probably prevented a major battle from breaking out. After some difficulty, he got Bat to shake hands with Ab Webster, Sheriff George Hinkle, and with their old boss, Larry Deger. Earp still commanded enough respect in Dodge to act as a peacemaker—the leading citizens, after all, had sent a petition in his favor to the O.K. Corral inquest—and an amicable solution was reached. But only because Webster, Hinkle, and Deger knew Wyatt well enough to know he wasn't bluffing. On June 5, Luke Short's lawyer wired the Kansas attorney general that "Everything here has been settled. Parties have shook hands across the bloody chasm." The greatest irony of Wyatt Earp's life is that he is remembered for the one gunfight he couldn't get out of, not the dozen or so he prevented.

Before the band of brothers disbanded, eight of them sat for a picture that became so widely distributed that many thought it was taken at the height of Dodge City's fame. The group came to be known, perhaps facetiously, as "The Dodge City Peace Commission." A woodcut of the photo was nationally distributed in the *Police Gazette*, with the following information about Bat and Wyatt:

> Bat Masterson, of whom so much has been written, arrived from the West prepared for any emergency and with a shotgun under his arm, on the next train after Short had returned. His record of having killed 26 men and being 27 [sic] years of age, is rather exaggerated. . . .
> Wyatt Earp, of California, is the celebrity who about two years ago went on the warpath at Tombstone, Ari-

zona, against a mob of desperadoes who had assassinated his brother, Morgan Earp. In the terrible encounter which ensued he killed not less than eight [sic] of the assassins. Wyatt has been marshal of Dodge City, Kan., and Tombstone, Ariz., and other frontier towns.[2]

Wyatt must have read the *Police Gazette* with dismay. Just when it seemed he had managed to live down Tombstone, it was being dredged up again—and not because he had killed anyone, but because he had helped a friend. That was just the beginning. At the same time as the *Police Gazette* story, *Harper's* magazine was running a series of articles on the American Southwest by a correspondent named W. H. Bishop. In the spring of 1883, Bishop visited Tombstone. Here is his account of the streetfight in Tombstone:

City Marshal Earp, with his two brothers and one "Doc" Holliday, a gambler, came down the street armed with rifles and opened fire on the two Clanton brothers and the two McLowry brothers. The latter party had been practically disarmed by the sheriff, who had feared such a meeting, and meant to disarm others as well. Three of them fell, and died on the spot. "Ike" Clanton alone escaped. The slayers were imprisoned, but released on bail. . . . It was rumored that the town party, for such were the Earps, would be able to command sufficient influence to go free of indictment.

So now, laid out for the Eastern intelligentsia, it was official: The Earps had walked into the lot with rifles and murdered the "cowboys," then flexed their political muscle to beat the murder rap. Who had Bishop gotten this story from? Most likely from those left behind, particularly John Behan. John Clum was no longer there, and the *Epitaph* had been sold to an anti-Earp, Republican faction, so there were no journalists to stand up for the Earps. The problem was exacerbated over the years: The worse Tombstone's economy got, the more of Wyatt's friends and supporters would leave, which meant that when journalists came to Tombstone for the "real" story they were more likely to get the "real" story from Earp's enemies or the neighbors and friends of their enemies.

In 1885, Bishop's *Harper's* stories were published in book form under the title, *Old Mexico and Her Lost Provinces.* By this time Wyatt had found that he couldn't go far enough west to escape Tombstone.

The next good Wyatt Earp story is told by Bat Masterson, and it occurred in 1883 in Gunnison. Wyatt was running a gambling concession, and while he was away a man named Ike Morris, a gambler with a reputation as a local tough guy, tried to run a scam by claiming he had been cheated. Wyatt's dealer told Morris to wait till Mr. Earp returned and take the complaint to him.

Morris did; apparently the claim of cheating was a set-up to provoke a confrontation. Wyatt heard Morris's complaint, then talked to his dealer, who assured him that Morris had lost fair and square. By this time a small crowd had gathered in anticipation of a showdown. They got one, but not the kind they expected. Wyatt took the initiative, walking to where Morris was standing and telling the gambler, politely, that he had indeed been cheated. He felt as if he ought to return Morris's money, but on second thought he would not. "You are looked upon in this part of the country as a bad man, and if I was to give you back your money you would say as soon as I left town, that you made me do it, and for that reason I will keep the money."

Morris was dumbfounded; he had no response. It isn't clear what Morris was trying to do; he might have been trying to provoke Wyatt to see if he could get the drop on him, or, more likely, he was testing the mettle of a rival to see what the response would be. Of course, there was always the chance that Wyatt would wish to avoid trouble and return the money. What he was not expecting was for Wyatt to admit that his dealer had cheated Morris—since he hadn't—and for Wyatt to refuse to return the money because it would bring him bad publicity. Wyatt was willing to risk a fight with Morris in order not to let word get out that he could be pushed. This told Morris everything he needed to know about Earp. He invited him to smoke a cigar with him, then rode out of town.

Wyatt and Josephine toured the western mining circuit. In 1884 they traveled to northern Idaho where James Earp was exploiting the Coeur d'Alene gold rush. Spending more than $2,000 for a circus tent, they started a dance hall and saloon, the White Elephant. Here, in Eagle City, Idaho, Wyatt began to pursue what would become the dominant interest of the last forty-five years of his life: not gambling, but prospecting. He also encountered legal troubles common in the mining business when a man named A. J. Pritchard sued and won on the charge of claim jumping. In the western pulp magazines, this would later be added to Wyatt's list of felonies, but charges of claim jumping were a daily occurrence in mining camps of the time since no one was ever sure exactly where the boundaries began or ended. Shortly after Pritchard won his suit, a man named William Payne also sued Earp and was awarded $25; later Payne and Earp sued another man. Then Wyatt and Jim won a jumped claim case.

None of the claims ever paid off; the White Elephant was the nearest thing Wyatt had to a gold mine. The brief stay, though, gave Wyatt one more tale to add to his legend. When a town-lot dispute broke out into open warfare, Wyatt and James walked, literally, into the middle of the fight. "With characteristic coolness," read an account in the *Spokane Falls Review*, "they stood where the bullets from both parties flew about them, joked with the participants upon their poor marksmanship . . . and used their best endeavor to stop the shooting." One man was slightly wounded, and the Earps were praised by the paper as peacemakers. When trouble came again for Wyatt, this was not the clipping his enemies would resurrect.

The first official listing of Wyatt Earp in San Diego is in the city directory of 1887, but Wyatt and Josephine had probably been living there for two years by that time. They had first traveled to the city with Bat Masterson, Virgil, and Allie and found both the climate and boomtown atmosphere irresistible. The directory recorded Wyatt as "capitalist, res. Schmitt Block"—imagine Wild Bill Hickok, Jesse James, or Billy the Kid being listed as capitalists. Wyatt's first San Diego apartment, probably not by coincidence, was next door to the local Wells Fargo office.

San Diego was bigger than all the other boomtowns Wyatt had seen put together. When Wyatt and Josephine arrived, there was a population of around five thousand; within two years, it was thirty thousand. Wyatt didn't seem so much interested in making money as in constantly finding new ways to make money. He bought and sold property with abandon, including saloons and gambling halls (of which he may have owned four at one time), owned racehorses, and refereed boxing matches, bull fights, and cock fights, the latter, usually, across the Mexican border in Tijuana. When not working, he took time to become a good citizen. One San Diego old-timer, reminiscing for the Historical Society, recalled sitting under the palm trees and chatting with his next-door neighbor, Wyatt Earp. Another, summoning up childhood memories for the *San Diego Tribune*, remembered being fascinated by a gun Wyatt wore to breakfast at a hotel. Always fond of children, he dumped the cartridges on the table and let the eight year old play with the revolver.

Wyatt liked children, but he loved horses. Josephine called horses "the love of his life." Earp is known to have bought only one car in his life; Josephine recalled it as "an expensive make" that Wyatt learned to drive "in an indifferent manner." He took little pleasure in the car compared to his horses. "This love of horseflesh," she recalled, "coupled with his susceptibility to the wiles of Lady Luck, formed a combination that made it almost inevitable that at some time during his career the horse-racing game should claim him." At the San Diego racetracks, Wyatt met another sporting man destined to be a lifelong friend, E. B. "Lucky" Baldwin. Like Wyatt, Lucky didn't drink; his interests were horses and gambling. Both men had picked the right town. San Diego in the mid and late 1880s combined the climate of Hawaii and the licentiousness of the Barbary Coast.

Josephine was as much of an adventurer as Wyatt, but she acquired his lust for gambling without acquiring any of his skill. Sometime around 1887 she began losing heavily:

> I fell into the habit of placing bets with more recklessness than wisdom, on horses that I picked to win. To cover my losses on several occasions I borrowed money from Lucky Baldwin, insisting that he take a piece of jewelry as security. I hoped to retrieve my jewels before Wyatt should learn of it but each time he found out and redeemed them for me. Finally, his patience was exhausted.
>
> "You're not a smart gambler," he said, "And you have no business risking money that way. After this, I'm not going to redeem any of your jewelry."
>
> He told Lucky not to let me have any more money. "You'll just have jewelry on your hands if you do," he said, "I won't be responsible."

Considering the company she had been keeping since 1880—John
Behan, Doc Holliday, Bat Masterson, Lucky Baldwin, Wilson Mizner, and her own husband—it's surprising she hadn't been bitten by
the gambling bug sooner. It was a fast life. When the Wild West
show came to town, Josephine got to meet the most famous man in
America, Buffalo Bill Cody, whom Wyatt had met on the buffalo
killing fields about fifteen years earlier—fifteen years was another
lifetime to Earp and Cody. Cody, thought Josephine, was "a pin-
checked man in a white mustache and goatee and flowing hair. He
always rode a beautiful pony as straight and agile as a boy." Not long
after, she saw Chicago for the first time, traveling with Wyatt to join
Lucky Baldwin for the Chicago derby.

For Josephine, the San Diego years were like a cool, endless summer. She had Wyatt and she loved the horse racing life:

> The years that Wyatt spent in racing form a kaleidoscope
> in my memory. I have but to shut my eyes and call them
> to mind to see again the gay sights and hear the merry
> sounds of those full years—Santa Rosa, Chicago, Tanfo-
> ran, Cincinnati, St. Louis, Kansas City, Santa Anita, and
> many other tracks with jockeys in their bright colors and
> horses, bay, brown, sorrel and black, the flying legs, the
> roaring crowds, the bright banners, bold trumpets, gay
> parties, lovely women, special trains, horsey smells, music,
> laughter—and Wyatt coming home to me. A winner with
> the light of triumph or a loser with a gleam of hope for a
> better showing next time.

They made money, they lost it, they made more. Wyatt was philo-
sophical. "Someone must lose every race," he told his wife, "and a
fellow who wants to stay with racing might as well make up his mind
to take his turn at losing along with the rest and be cheerful about
it." But Wyatt was never entirely cheerful; throughout the remainder
of his life, just when it seemed that Tombstone had faded, some
national publication would revive it again. In 1887 it was the *Police
Gazette*, based in New York but read with interest by people in Wyatt's West Coast sporting circles. "Wyatt S. Earp," read the January
20 issue of the Gazette, "is one of the most famous Western characters living. . . .

Probably no man has a wider reputation throughout the Western territories than Wyatt S. Earp, of the famous Earp Brothers, who created such a sensation a few years since at Tombstone, Arizona, by completely exterminating a whole band of outlawed cutthroats." Compared to many of Wyatt's post-Tombstone press notices, this one was favorable. But for Wyatt, who craved privacy, any press, particularly national press, was odious.

What Wyatt never understood was that there was a built-in contradiction between his desire for anonymity and the high-profile life he led. In her memoirs, Josephine relates that in 1894 Wyatt was asked (presumably by Wells Fargo) to help guard a special "pay train" that was traveling from California to El Paso, Texas, carrying several hundred thousand dollars in cash. Numerous stops were to be made in small Arizona and New Mexico towns—all opportunities for holdups. Josephine was alarmed: " 'Don't go,' I warned him, 'Let them get someone else.' He laughed at my fears. 'There's practically no danger at all,' he said. 'I've been in tighter places than this hundreds of times.' " Nothing did happen, but one wonders why Wyatt took such risk so deep into middle age. In a disputed passage of *I Married Wyatt Earp* not found in her memoirs, Josephine mentions a time when Bat Masterson passed through San Diego working as a U.S. deputy marshal. He was picking up a prisoner, an army deserter in Esenada, and asked Wyatt to accompany him. It didn't seem a dangerous trip, so Josephine also went along. There were numerous short-term law enforcement stints in Wyatt's post-Tombstone years, both public and private, some involving across-the-border activities such as prisoner extradition, in which the Los Angeles or San Diego police or Wells Fargo didn't want its name dropped. Wyatt never stopped being a cop, or a gambler.

In 1888 the San Diego boom ended abruptly when the economy collapsed. Real estate prices plummeted and thousands left the city within a year. Public works came to a halt. Wyatt always had a great sense of how to make money and a terrible sense of what to do with it; he should have either sold his property quickly or held on past the mid-1890s, as it was obvious that any city as beautiful and ideally situated as San Diego would make a comeback. As it was, the Earps wound up with little to show for all the money made and invested. They complained not a whit about their change in luck—a fellow

who stays with racing makes up his mind to take his turn at losing—
and moved on to San Francisco.

By 1896, Wyatt Earp was a full-time "sporting man." The Earps
settled in San Francisco because the city was near Josephine's family,
but also because it was home to one of the country's most rabid
sporting crowds. Wyatt Earp and San Francisco in the Gay Nineties
were a perfect match; as in San Diego, the city directory from the
period lists him as a "capitalist," the capital being a string of race
horses he trained and managed.

After New York, San Francisco in the 1890s could lay claim to
being the boxing capital of the country. The Bay Area was home to
several of the greatest American fighters of the day, including such
heavyweights as the Jewish hero Joe Choynski and the Irish idol
Gentleman Jim Corbett. When the latter won the heavyweight title
from John L. Sullivan in 1892, in the first title fight fought under
Marquis of Queensberry rules, boxing interest in the Bay Area
boomed—despite the fact that, new rules or no, boxing was illegal.

The boxing world revolved around Corbett, but Gentleman Jim's
first love was the vaudeville stage, where he spent the three years
after winning the title. The variety circuit was not only safer than
boxing, it was much more profitable—you couldn't lose a side bet on
a stage. So long as Corbett didn't step into a ring, he could still bill
himself as "Heavyweight Champion of the World" and get lucrative
personal appearance offers, which was where the money was. Finally,
in 1896, he decided that a billing of "ex" champion would be just as
profitable. After Peter Maher KO'd Steve O'Donnel in 1896, Corbett stepped in the ring and announced, "I give the title to you." But
Maher declined; he didn't want it unless a lucrative bout with Corbett came with it. Maher's refusal left boxing without a heavyweight
champion, an intolerable state of affairs, so a match was arranged
between the two men many regarded as the best heavyweights in the
world: the stocky, powerful native Irishman, "Sailor" Tom Sharkey,
and Robert "Ruby Bob" Fitzsimmons, native of Cornwall, citizen of
Australia, a spindly-legged, 170-pound former blacksmith with
enormous upper body strength. Boxing had no governing bodies in
1896, but when Sharkey and Fitzsimmons were finally matched for
the Mechanics Pavilion for December 3, many regarded it as a bout
for the vacated heavyweight title.

Getting the local police to look the other way was not difficult; the problem was in finding a referee acceptable to both sides. Even in boxing-wise San Francisco referees experienced in the new Marquis of Queensberry rules were scarce. Curiously, Sharkey's camp nixed several candidates. A friend of Earp's from the prestigious National Athletic Club (of which Jim Corbett had been a member) spotted him at Ingleside Track the day of the fight and asked him if he would consider the job. Earp wavered, then decided to accept. "I don't know," he said afterward, "but what it will be a little bit of tone to referee a fight of this kind." The National Athletic Club representatives beamed, one of them bragging that they had found "the bravest fighter, the squarest gambler, best friend, and worst enemy ever known on the frontier" to officiate their bout. Though afterward tangled reports of a fix were heard, no one spoke up before the opening bell. Certainly none of the local cognoscenti had an inkling of the debacle that was to follow.

The crowd of ten thousand that packed Mechanics Pavilion on fight night was unlike anything the sports world had seen. For one thing, women were allowed to attend, the first time most of the San Francisco sporting crowd had heard of such a thing and the surest sign that the event transcended boxing. For another, ticket prices for the best seats near ringside were jacked up to an astonishing $10, while even the so-called cheap seats went for an eyebrow-raising $2. Fans grumbled, but the price must have been right as there were no empty seats at fight time.

In the moments before the opening bell, two strange things happened. First, Fitzsimmons's manager, Martin Julian, declared that he and his fighter were dead set against Earp as a choice for referee, partly because Sharkey's people approved of him, but also because Earp was inexperienced with the new rules. This was true. Wyatt had refereed only bouts fought under London Prize Ring rules, where all sorts of mayhem from biting to eye-gouging was allowed, if not condoned. That Sharkey's corner okayed Wyatt and nixed all other candidates indicates that they had some mischief planned and wanted an inexperienced official. Wyatt volunteered to step down, but the National Athletic Club, which had been charged with finding a referee, stuck to its decision.

Earp was given a hurried explanation of the rules, with the emphasis on the primary difference between the old and the new: under the old London Prize Ring rules, a round lasted until one fighter slipped, fell, or was knocked down; under Queensberry, a round was three minutes long. Fighters wore gloves, which weren't added for humane reasons but to turn the hand into a more potent weapon (bare-knuckled fighters were often reluctant to throw punches to the head for fear of hurting their hands). Punches below the belt were punishable by disqualification. In retrospect, the latter point may have been overemphasized.

Wyatt's bad night began as he stepped into the ring. A surprised police captain noticed a bulge under Earp's coat and asked him if he was carrying a gun. He was, and thus, for the first and only time in boxing history, as a local journalist later noted, "it became necessary to disarm the referee." Stuart Lake later identified the gun Earp was carrying as the legendary Buntline Special—another Buntline sighting! The gun was most likely the more modern "Double Action" Colt revolver that was popular with policemen in the late 1890s.

What western and sports historians truly puzzled over is not which gun Earp carried into the ring but why he carried one at all when he had so often walked the streets of Tombstone unarmed. The reason was that San Francisco in 1896 was a much more dangerous town than the Tombstone of 1881, especially the sporting areas. He had come to the Mechanics Pavilion directly from Ingleside Track carrying a sizable amount of cash and couldn't depend on just his reputation to frighten away would-be stick-up men.

The following day, newspaper cartoonists would have a field day with the "Wild West" marshal who carried his six-gun into the boxing ring. Wyatt saw his caricature, replete with walrus-sized mustache, in every paper in the Bay Area.

Wyatt was partly to blame for this. Aside from the misdemeanor of carrying a gun into the ring, five months earlier he had granted an interview to a *San Francisco Examiner* reporter for the purpose of three long articles dealing with his exploits. The stories were widely circulated and brought Wyatt the kind of attention he had shied away from for years. Why did he do it? An obvious answer is that he needed the money. Almost all of the Earps' San Diego real estate had been sold at a loss, and the couple didn't have the capital to live in San Francisco at anything like the level they had known in San Diego. Also, for Wyatt, the stories were an opportunity to right what he considered a blatant wrong and to correct the errors written about him and his brothers. William Randolph Hearst was repaying some of the kindness Wyatt had shown his father in Tombstone. Neither Earp nor Hearst could guess the ramifications of the Bay Area newspaper politics.

The result, supposedly written by Wyatt, sounded nothing at all like him. "It may be," the first story began, "that the trail of blood will seem to lie too thickly over the pages that I write." What was too thick was the reporter's verbiage; the story was so thoroughly overwritten that Wyatt, for the first time in his life, came off sounding pompous. For example: "And so I marshal my characters. My stalwart brothers, Virgil and Morgan, shall stand on the right of the stage with my dear old comrade, Doc Holliday," and so on. Nor did Wyatt check the finished copy, which identifies his dear old comrade Doc as hailing from Virginia, not Georgia, carefully. Simply put, Wyatt, like a modern athlete putting his name on a ghostwritten autobiography, was misquoted in his own story.

The stories made Wyatt a local celebrity; they also made him a target for Hearst's legion of enemies. The rash of caricatures and cartoons that followed the gun-toting incident, cartoons largely in reaction to Earp's puffed-up image in the *Examiner* stories, were the nastiest press Wyatt had received since the *Nugget*'s attacks fourteen years earlier. Not so malicious, perhaps—no one accused him of murder—but, the at least *Nugget* hadn't ridiculed him.

Earp must have been happy to finally see the fight begin. When it did, the taller, quicker, Ruby Bob Fitzsimmons dominated the slower Sharkey from the opening bell. In the seventh round Fitzsimmons seemed to observers to be on the verge of stopping Sharkey, but the Sailor, who was later to go the distance on two occasions with the great James J. Jefferies, held on. In the eighth, Fitz struck with his most powerful weapon, the "solar plexus punch," an uppercut directly under the heart that literally took an opponent's breath away and rendered him temporarily helpless. No boxer before or after Fitzsimmons would so master the art of body punching; a year later the solar plexus punch would put Jim Corbett on the canvas and make Fitz the undisputed heavyweight champion of the world.

But on this night, Tom Sharkey found a foolproof defense. Clutching his groin and rolling on the canvas, the Irishman screamed that he had been fouled. Wyatt, who may or may not have been in a position to get a clear view of the punch, walked over to examine

Sharkey. A few minutes later a stunned crowd saw Earp climb through the ropes and head for the exit. Slowly, the buzz traveled through the vast crowd that Earp, who was solely in charge of the decision, had awarded the victory to Sharkey by foul. Some spectators agreed with Earp; W. W. Naughton, covering the bout for the *Examiner*, talked to spectators who claimed that Fitzsimmons had kneed Sharkey in the groin. But then, it would be said, Naughton worked for the "pro-Earp" paper owned by Wyatt's champion, William Randolph Hearst. The majority of paying customers weren't in a position to see much of anything and only knew that they had paid a hefty sum to have the popular betting favorite lose on a foul they didn't see. Most of the people at the Mechanics Pavilion that night had never seen a prizefight stopped on a foul before; for that matter, most had never seen a Marquis of Queensberry bout before.

Fitzsimmons fueled the fire by telling any reporter who would listen that "I was simply robbed out of $10,000," and, what's more, "I knew I was going to be robbed before I entered the ring." Ruby Bob was referring to the Sharkey camp's rejection of several more experienced referees before the fight. He had a point. Experienced referees weren't easy to find, but right up until fight time Sharkey's corner turned down the few officials who were. When Sharkey refused to be examined by the official medical examiner for the National Athletic Club, the controversy broke into a full-fledged scandal.

Wyatt was adamant. He had simply called the fight as he saw it and that was that. His job was to render a fair decision, not a popular one. Who was winning at the time of the foul was irrelevant. Fitzsimmons had indeed fouled Sharkey, he insisted, not once, but several times. He had given Fitz several opportunities to get his punches up. He even told a reporter for the *Examiner* that his longtime friend, Bat Masterson, a friend of Fitzsimmons, had lost money on the fight. Masterson, in his newspaper column in New York, sided with Wyatt.

But Earp was caught in the middle of a political war as vicious in its way as the one he had left in Arizona fourteen years earlier. The *Examiner* was constantly feuding with its rival, the *San Francisco Call*, and the upstart paper didn't miss the chance to pillory Hearst any way it could. Within two weeks after the fight the *Call* had found "witnesses" to connect Earp with virtually every crime or murder the West had known since the James Gang had robbed their first train. The ghosts of Tom and Frank McLaury and Billy Clanton had risen from Boot Hill again.

Fitzsimmons and his manager took court action against Sharkey and the National Athletic Club. It was Wyatt Earp's reputation that was really on trial and no court ruling could ever completely restore that. Wyatt's decision in the Fitzsimmons-Sharkey fight and the subsequent trial got Earp more national attention than the shootout in Tombstone—indeed, it had the unpleasant effect of reviving discussion of the gunfight and its controversial aftermath. Wasn't Wyatt Earp still wanted on a murder charge somewhere? Alfred Henry Lewis of the *New York Journal* sat in on Earp's testimony and found him to be "grim, game, and deadly . . . but he doesn't kill as he used to. Many wounds have brought him caution." Years later, through his association with Bat Masterson, Lewis would reverse his opinion of Earp, but not before his first stories had been circulated and quoted all over the country. In later years Earp debunkers such as Ed Bartholomew would use Lewis's sharp anti-Earp sentiments without knowing or caring that Lewis came to regret them. (The final irony was that in 1907 Lewis would edit Bat Masterson's laudatory profile of Wyatt for *Human Life*.)

The court's decision, rendered a week before Christmas, was simply to remove itself from the dispute. A judge named Sanderson ruled that by engaging in a prizefight the combatants were "committing an offense against the law" and thus it was "not the sort of case for a court to consider." The $10,000 purse and unofficial title of heavyweight champion were Sharkey's to collect, by default. Many observers were quick to ask why, if that was the case, the court took up nearly two weeks of the city's time and money on a matter that could have been thrown out at the start; Wyatt Earp, at least, handed down his decision quickly.

The decision set a precedent, now one hundred years old, of the law courts' noninterference in boxing matters, and boxing remains the least regulated of sports. Subsequent western historians who wrote about the fight knew little of boxing history and made the mistake of treating the controversy as an isolated incident, when it was in fact just the first in a long line of referee's controversial decisions right up to the Riddick Bowe–Andrew Golota fight in 1997. Dave Barry in the 1927 Dempsey-Tunney "Long Count," Jersey Joe Walcott in the Ali-Liston "Phantom Punch" fight in 1965, and

Richard Steele in the 1990 Caesar Chavez–Meldrick Taylor fight—
all vastly more experienced referees—were as damned in their own
time as was Wyatt Earp in 1896.

Ironically, the next great foul controversy of the gloved era involved Tom Sharkey's namesake: Jack Sharkey, whose surname was
Zukauskas, grew up idolizing the Irish fighter and changed his name
in Sharkey's honor. In 1927, fighting Jack Dempsey for a shot at
Gene Tunney's title, Sharkey claimed to have been hit in the groin by
the former champ. But another "celebrity" referee, Jim Crowley of
Notre Dame "Four Horsemen" fame, had his back to Sharkey, and
when the fighter turned to complain Dempsey leveled him with a left
hook. Three years later, fighting Max Schmeling for the vacated title,
Sharkey unleashed what seemed to many to be a low blow; Schmeling fell to the canvas clutching his groin and was awarded the heavyweight title when his manager, Joe Jacobs, returned from the locker
room holding a protective cup with a dent in it. In each of these
controversies, the referee's decision stood, just as Wyatt Earp's had in
1896.

Until his death, Wyatt always maintained that he had simply
called the Sharkey-Fitzsimmons fight as he had seen it. Aside from
occasional smokers he never refereed a boxing match again, but his
association with the sport didn't end. Less than a year after the
Sharkey-Fitzsimmons fight, Wyatt and Bat Masterson were hired as
special policemen at the Fitzsimmons–Jim Corbett title fight in
Reno, Nevada. Jack Dempsey claimed to remember Earp and Bat
Masterson collecting weapons from the crowd at his championship
fight with Jess Willard in Toledo, Ohio, in 1919. Dempsey's memory
may have been faulty: Wyatt was seventy-one in 1919 and it's doubtful he would have traveled 2,500 miles for a prizefight. Dempsey
knew of Wyatt, whom he had almost certainly heard about from the
promoter, Tex Rickard, who loved to tell barroom stories about Earp
and other cronies from his Alaska days.

Earp never completely lived down the controversy of the 1896
fight, on which no further light has ever been shed. If there was a
scam, it certainly wouldn't have been uncommon for the boxing
game of those days—in truth, given the shady nature of the fight
game in the 1890s, it wouldn't have been uncommon for all of the
participants to have been in on it. (Why didn't the Fitzsimmons
camp, which represented the older, more popular fighter, simply re-

fuse to fight unless Fitz had referee approval?) But in the absence of any other proof, the final judgment had to be that the Sharkey camp got away with one. If a fix was on, it isn't likely the referee would have been chosen just hours before the fight. However, the most convincing argument against Wyatt's involvement in a swindle is that the fight wasn't stopped till the eighth round. If Earp was in on the fix, why would he have waited until the eighth round and given the harder punching Fitzsimmons numerous chances to win by a knockout? Everyone agreed that Fitzsimmons was giving Sharkey a pummeling and most of those at ringside thought Sharkey was ready to go down in the seventh round. A fix that would allow such possibilities for failure isn't much of a fix. Whatever happened on that night, Wyatt was so disgusted and discouraged that he made up his mind to quit San Francisco forever. It must have occurred to him that America was running out of places where he could escape controversy.

Notes

1. On May 22, 1882, the *Denver Republican* printed an interview with Doc in which he said he had previously met Mallen in Pueblo and that Mallen told him he had ridden in on the train with "Josh Stilwell, brother of Frank." Frank Stilwell did have a brother named Jack, and he could well have been the man who hired Mallen. It's significant that no one associated directly with Behan or the Cowboys tried to capture Doc themselves.

2. Credit for resurrecting this important example of the frontier mythmaking process goes to Tucson lawyer Bob Palmquist, who also ascertained that the title "Dodge City Peace Commission" wasn't used at the time the photo was taken, but more than a month afterward. This suggests it was used as a kind of joke by the participants after they saw the photo.

10

Hollywood Gunfighter

The 1897 gold rush in the Yukon was in many ways similar to the 1879 silver rush in Tombstone—the Earps even met several old Arizona friends there. The big difference this time was that Wyatt had no intention of getting involved in law enforcement. If Nome had a city directory in 1897, Wyatt's entry would have read the same as the ones in San Diego and San Francisco: capitalist. "Capitalist" to Wyatt meant saloon keeper, horse breeder, gambler, and, when he found the time to pursue his new passion, prospector. After two years, the *Examiner* back in San Francisco was able to report that Wyatt was "making money perhaps faster than he has ever made it before," and that with another good year "he will be able to retire with all the money he desires." But the more money Wyatt made the more he gave to friends or invested in oddball schemes. Wyatt may have been a capitalist, but he was never a businessman. The company Wyatt and Josie kept reflected their lifestyle. Among the notables who dropped by Wyatt's Dexter saloon were Lucky Baldwin (like the Earps, finding another boom town after the San Diego bust); the playwright and raconteur Wilson Mizner, best known for *Alias, Jimmy Valentine*; the gambler and fight promoter names G. L. "Tex" Rickard, who would soon become famous—and wealthy—staging "million dollar gate" boxing matches for Jack Johnson and Jack Dempsey; Doc Kearns, later to be famous as Dempsey's trainer and manager; and a couple of aspiring novelists, Jack London and Rex Beach. The former was just a few years away from *The Sea Wolf* and

329

The Call of the Wild, and only a few more from suicide. Beach is forgotten today. His books are out of print, but his legacy lives on in the film version of his novel, *The Spoilers*, starring John Wayne and Randolph Scott. A young mining engineer named Herbert Hoover also frequented the Dexter. For the most part, the Earps' lives were fun and uneventful. There were exceptions. Wyatt and Josephine's brother, Nathan, got in the way of the arrest of a couple of drunks in Nome. Wyatt was arrested for interfering with an officer but pleaded that he was only attempting to assist the marshals. It doesn't seem possible that Wyatt Earp's intentions to help an officer could be misconstrued, but it seems just as unlikely that Wyatt would have tried to keep an officer from doing his duty. The charges were dropped. Wyatt risked more serious trouble by helping out Lucky Baldwin when he closed his saloon and returned to California. Lucky's partner, David Unruh, was to ship the equipment back, but found that the city was holding their property for reasons not specified and demanding $20,000 in gold dust to release it. Unruh went to Earp, who came up with the gold—where Wyatt got that much was not explained—and redeemed the equipment, which they resold for nearly three times the $20,000. According to Unruh, Wyatt "refused a cent of pay for his accommodation." Once again, one sees the code of the frontier gambler at work. Wyatt hung around with gamblers and con men most of his life and may have been involved in some of their schemes, but he wouldn't take money from a friend. In 1900, while Wyatt gambled and prospected in the Alaskan summer, bad news worked its way up to Nome. Warren Earp had been shot and killed in Wilcox, Arizona. By the time Wyatt heard of the incident Warren had been buried, so there was no point in returning to Arizona or California.[1]

Warren's death touched off all manner of strange stories. The *Seattle Post-Intelligencer* reported that Virgil Earp had been killed, printing a version of the events that credited Wyatt with killing "ten men, one of them his own brother-in-law"—some reporter had gotten it into his head that Wyatt's sister and had come to Tombstone and married Ike Clanton. (Had that been true, Wyatt probably would have shot Ike.) According to the Seattle paper, there were two factions in Tombstone, the stage robbers—the Earps, Doc Holliday, and a man named Curly Bill—and the rustlers—led by Sheriff John Behan, Ike Clanton, and Jack Ringo. The stage robbing methods of

Wyatt and his brothers were explained in great detail. The famous gunfight supposedly came about as the result of a spat at the Bird Cage Theater—twelve men were killed or wounded. The story described Wyatt as "grim, game, and deadly. . . . But he doesn't kill as he used to. Age has cooled his blood; many wounds have brought him caution."

The *New York Tribune* topped the Seattle paper with a story on its front page headlined, "Wyatt Earp Shot at Nome; The Arizona 'Bad Man' Not Quick Enough with His Gun." The story claimed that Earp "bullied everyone," implying that the fatal shot came from a customer whom Wyatt had pushed too far. Newspaper stories about Earp became even more outlandish. In one, Wyatt was knocked out in Dawson, Alaska, by a Royal Canadian Mountie—a midget, no less. Uncharacteristically, Wyatt raised a ruckus over that one and got the paper to print a retraction. Later, when Wyatt was visiting from Alaska, the *San Francisco Call* printed a story about a barroom brawl in which "Tom Mulqueen, the well-known racehorse man" knocked Earp "down and out." Was it true? The *Call* was a bitter enemy of Hearst, and, therefore, of Earp—no paper so vilified or caricatured him after the 1896 prizefight—and no one else ever mentioned the incident. Earp may have replied to the *Call* and been refused a forum; more than likely he decided not to stir up more controversy in a town that still remembered the Fitzsimmons-Sharkey fiasco. By this time, Wyatt Earp was fair game for any newsman in the country with a grudge or a vivid imagination. Being in Alaska for nearly three years hadn't diminished his capacity for creating controversy, it had stimulated it.

On August 30, 1900, Wyatt sat through an evening and part of the night reminiscing with John Clum, the new U.S. postmaster general for Alaska, and George Parsons. Parsons's diary entries for this night show a more introspective and melancholy Earp than anyone has revealed.[2] Together with Clum and Earp, Parsons had "a regular old Arizona time, and Wyatt unlimbered for several hours and seemed glad to talk to us who knew the past. It was a very memorable evening. He went home with us." It isn't revealed that Wyatt Earp ever "unlimbered" himself with anyone else, not even with his three would-be biographers: Forrestine Hooker, John Flood, and Stuart Lake. We would give much to know what was discussed, but all Parsons tells us is that "We had such a séance last night. That evening with Wyatt Earp would have been worth $1,000 to the newspapers." *Séance* implies that they raised the dead with this conversation. Who? Did Wyatt confess to the killing of John Ringo? Did he mourn Morgan and Warren or did he regret leaving Mattie? What did Wyatt say that would been of such interest to the newspapers? Parsons, of course, was writing for himself, not for us. We can only hope that there's another volume to his journal in some old family trunk. Ten days later the two men got together again: "Wyatt Earp and I had a little confab today. The reputed badman from Arizona is straight and fearless and I believe is a good friend of mine and respects me and I him." Parsons writes as though he was trying to convince himself, not of their mutual respect, of which he seems assured, but that they were close enough to be lasting friends. Wyatt made many loyal friends in his life, but the only men he ever seemed to be intimate with were Doc Holliday and Bat Masterson. But by 1900, Doc was long gone and Bat was getting ready to enjoy the life of celebrity journalist in New York. That Wyatt Earp would seek out George Parsons, whom he had never known well in Tombstone, indicates an uncharacteristic nostalgia or melancholy. It isn't hard to see what triggered it, probably a combination of middle age, the death of Warren, and the barrage of newspapers stories in which he saw his life constantly reinvented according to the prejudices or politics or whims of journalists all over the country. It was around this time that Wyatt began drinking again, and the results were similar to those of three decades earlier. On September 12, two days after the last George Parsons entry, the *Nome Daily News* reported that "Wyatt Earp, N. Marcus, and Walter Sunmers" were the principals in a "fracas." We don't know who Sunmers was, but Nathan, Josephine's brother, is starting to look like a dubious influence. Apparently Nathan and Wyatt assaulted a patrolman who was attempting to arrest Sunmers for disorderly conduct. How the case came out isn't known, but this roughhousing stands out from all the other contemporary newspaper accounts, which either were exaggerated or downright fictitious. This time Wyatt not only interfered with an officer of the law, he struck him, the only known instance of such behavior.[3] Wyatt was beginning to act like some of his clippings.

Despite the brawl and the news of Warren's death, Alaska had been another lark for the Earps, who left Alaska in 1901 with the astonishing sum of $80,000. It would stake them for a few years while they looked around for a new frontier. None of the money was invested wisely. When gold was discovered in Nevada in 1901, Earp joined the rush, becoming a part-time prospector at a time in life when most men with $80,000 might be thinking about how pleasant it would be to leave a mining camp. In January 1902 Wyatt and Josephine departed from Los Angeles not in an automobile but in a horse-drawn wagon filled with camping equipment and supplies to embark on the last major gold strike in U.S. history. In February they were in Tonopah, where he found old acquaintances from Tombstone and Alaska. As usual, Wyatt opened up a saloon, and as usual it did good business. Mostly, a friend named Al Martin ran it while Wyatt and Josephine prospected. The pickings were lean; Wyatt took time out for freelance jobs once again, swearing out as a deputy U.S. marshal for a brief period. Apparently there were no shooting incidents during his stint. He also did some rent-a-cop work for a re-nowned mining engineer of the period, John Hayes Hammond. In a 1926 article for *Scribner's* magazine, Hammond revealed that he hired Earp to lead a private force to dissuade claim jumpers. On hiring him he told Wyatt that, "You will not shoot except in self-defense." Earp must have been mildly miffed at this. "O.K.," he told Hammond, "but I must be the judge when the self-defense starts." Hammond concurred. There were no shooting incidents; Wyatt's reputation and tact prevented violence, as Hammond must have supposed it would when he hired Earp. Once again, as it had every few years since he left Arizona, Tombstone flared up just when Wyatt thought it had been forgotten. This time it was a Los Angeles paper, the *Herald*, in an article now lost to us. We can judge its contents only by the replies that were made to it. On September 9 a letter from a furious Wyatt appeared in the *Herald*. According to Wyatt, the story related

to an experience I was reported to have had in Dawson City, in which I was said to have attempted to "shoot up the town" and to have been subdued by one of the Cana-dian Mounted Police. . . .
(This must have been the old "Midget Mountie" story.) The falsity of the article is shown by the fact that I never was within 1,000 miles of Dawson City. . . . I wish to say that neither I nor my brothers were ever "bad men," in

the sense that term is used, nor did we ever indulge in the practice of "shooting up" towns. We have been officers of the law and have had our experiences in preserving the law, but we are not, and never have been professional bad men. In justice to me and my friends and relatives I would like to have you make this statement. The next day, George Parsons leapt to Wyatt's defense:

As an old Tombstoner and one who knew the Earps in the stormy days of the early '80s, I wish, in simple justice to the family in general and Wyatt Earp in particular, to confirm his statement in yesterday's *Herald* that they were not "bad men" in the common acceptation of the term, but were ever ready to discharge their duty as officers of the law, and did it so effectively that they incurred the enmity of the rustlers and desperadoes congregated in that lively town and section of the country and were always on the side of law and order.

There was one exception. When their brother Morgan was assassinated, Virgil Earp shot and Wyatt Earp's life attempted, then they took the law into their own hands and did what most anyone would have done under the peculiar circumstances existing at the time, and what anyone reading *The Virginian* would consider their right to do. . . .

I state this in justice to a much maligned man who, as a public character, was a benefit and a protection to the community he once lived in.

That Parsons's letter appeared the day after Earp's and referred to it can only mean that Wyatt had shown him a copy in advance. It's significant that Parsons came to Wyatt's defense without white-washing him: Wyatt was "always on the side of law and order" with one exception, the Vendetta Ride. Even in that circumstance he had only done "what most anyone would have done under the peculiar circumstances"—meaning anyone with the courage. The reference to *The Virginian* is interesting, as Owen Wister's popular novel proba-bly did much to shape the country's attitudes toward revenge and violence in the West. Wister had been inspired by the actions of

Wyatt Earp and men like him; now Parsons used *The Virginian* to justify Earp's actions. The *Herald*'s attack was all the more surprising because Wyatt's press in L.A. had been favorable until then, as typified in an interview with the *Los Angeles Times* two years earlier. "Wyatt Earp," the story read,

> the well-known sporting authority, passed the day in Los Angeles with his wife. He has just returned from Nome, where He has mining properties sufficient to make him financially comfortable for the remainder of his life. . . . He states that he intends to enjoy the roped arena and other characteristic sports for some time yet, although the criticism he received from his decision in the Sharkey-Fitzsimmons fight was unfair, he alleges. . . .
>
> "I easily can explain the attack of certain newspapers," said Mr. Earp. "I had been doing work for the *Examiner* for three months previous to the fight. At that time both the *Call* and *Chronicle* were bitterly fighting the *Examiner*, and when I refereed the mill, I was their chance to get back at their rival over me. However, a referee is always open to the attacks of newspapers, friends of either fighter and to incompetent sporting editors who have exalted opinions of themselves."

Wyatt's comments, direct and to the point, are a lucid explanation of what had happened in San Francisco and seemed to explain why he had been vilified following the Sharkey-Fitzsimmons fight. But it couldn't begin to explain why journalists in other parts of the country persisted in reviving the name of Wyatt Earp, much against the wishes of the man who owned it, and reinventing his story, pumping it full of outlandish distortions. It was a process that, much to his bewilderment, would continue to the end of his life, then beyond. What Wyatt couldn't understand, couldn't begin to understand, was that he had become the representative figure of an era that Americans would always look to when questions of the influence of the frontier on our national character or the relation of force to law would arise. Thirty-odd years before Wyatt began building a legend on the buffalo covered prairies, a legend shaped by oral tradition. Now, early in the twentieth century, the story was being reshaped with dramatic suddenness in newspapers, magazines, and books. And in less time than it took Wyatt to get from the buffalo hunting grounds of Kansas to twentieth-century Los Angeles, his story would be picked up again by new media and retold over and over, finally distorted beyond anything he or anyone else in his time could have imagined.

In the summer of 1904 Virgil and Allie left Colton to join Wyatt and Josephine in Goldfield, Nevada. Wyatt and Josephine happily continued their prospecting. None of the family ever found much gold, but no one complained: They were adventurers and loved the lives they were leading. Virgil, though he had the use of only one arm, served a stint as a deputy sheriff with duties none too taxing. The *Tonapah Sun* reported that "Verge Earp, a brother of Wyatt and one of the famous family of gunologists . . . was a mild individual and to outward view presents none of the characteristics that have made that family name a familiar one in the west and in all the bonanza camps of the country from Mexico to Alaska." If she read this, Allie must have bristled upon seeing her "Verge" identified as "a brother of Wyatt." Her opportunity to set the record straight would not come for a half a century. In October 1905, Virgil caught pneumonia. Allie took him to the miner's hospital. He asked her to get him a cigar. She did. Then he asked her to put a letter from his grandniece under his pillow, to light his cigar, "and stay here and hold my hand." He died shortly afterward. The *Arizona Daily Journal-Miner* gave him a respectful sendoff: "A great many harsh things have been said and written about the 'Earp gang,' but nevertheless it is a fact that a more charitable man never lived than Virgil Earp, especially when he had the means to render assistance. Every desperate act ever known to have been committed by him was clothed with the authority of law, and he was ever known to avoid personal encounters except when invested with legal authority and in the discharge of this duty."

Virgil got the kind words, Wyatt would get the fame. In 1907, Bat Masterson would repay Wyatt's generous praise in his 1896 *Examiner* articles by introducing him to a new generation in the pages of *Human Life*. Wyatt appreciated the sentiment but deplored the publicity. He probably wouldn't have minded, though, if he could have found a way to make it pay off. With nothing left from the San Diego investments or the small fortune they brought home from the

Klondike—and little chance of collecting the large sums Wyatt had paid out in loans and stakes to others—the Earps entered a period of genteel poverty sometimes alleviated by money from members of Josie's family. Exactly what Wyatt did for a living during this period isn't known; if a family friend named Arthur King is to be believed, Wyatt sometimes did a little freelance work for the Los Angeles Police Department. Much of it, apparently, had to do with the illegal extradition of fugitives from Mexico, dangerous work that must have taken a great deal of exertion for a man in his sixties. King went along on these missions as Wyatt's special deputy, or at least he claimed he did. King knew Earp and offered some interesting observations. By around 1910, Wyatt had become "an artist at swearing, and he took to drinking pretty heavily when he reached fifty," King told an interviewer. (Wyatt reached fifty in 1898, and there's no evidence that King knew him till years later.) King found Wyatt to be "a very quiet fellow—a fine man, one of the coolest I've ever seen. He was afraid of nothing. When he'd get angry the corner of his right eye would twitch just a little. He loved to gamble, too. Faro, or Bucking the Tiger, was his choice.[4] At least one of King's remarks seems genuine: "He was a prospector at heart. He loved being around miners." Unfortunately some of King's recollections are suspect, as they were all told to interviewers (one of them at the *Sacramento Bee*) nearly half a century after the fact when the Wyatt Earp vogue was in full swing. (All of King's comments about Wyatt's exploits in Kansas and Arizona sound as if they were lifted secondhand from *Frontier Marshal*.) For instance, King relates a story about Earp leading a party of men into mountains near San Bernardino to remove several miners holding illegal claims. Wyatt's men come face to face with another organized party led by a federal officer who pointed a revolver at them. King recalled that "Wyatt grabbed that gun and threw it down in the dirt, swearing with as much color as any pirate. . . . He said he hadn't had his breakfast yet and didn't want no gun in his empty belly." The story seems exaggerated, if only because it's hard to picture Wyatt confronting a federal officer in this way. On the other hand, Earp's behavior in facing the man down certainly fits a known pattern, and we know that the expedition occurred because George Parsons was there to record it in his journal. (Parsons claimed he was the initial choice by the LAPD to lead the men but a bad ankle forced him to decline.) However heroic these stories sound in the telling, there is a pathetic quality to them, as if Wyatt could find nothing to do in this period but imitate his younger days. In his sixties, Wyatt was hiring out as a special cop, doing jobs for police departments as a bounty hunter, just as he had started out in the Kansas cow towns nearly forty years earlier working as an auxiliary. He found himself lost in the modern world, where prospecting was no longer possible and gambling was frowned on. If Wyatt didn't know this before July 21, 1911, he certainly knew it afterward. The *Los Angeles Herald*, which had taken a cheap-shot at Wyatt in 1903, now had a field day. Their headline read "Detectives Trap Wyatt Earp, 'Gun Man,' in Swindle," and called Wyatt, the "survivor of the famous Earp-Clanton feud" and a man who "devoted his time to fleecing the unwary." The *Herald* identified him as the man who "conceived the plot" to swindle a Los Angeles real estate man, J. Y. Peterson. Peterson alerted police to what he called a rigged faro game that was being held in a room at the Auditorium Hotel. The hotel was run by another ex-Tombstonian, Albert Billickie, Wyatt's friend from the Cosmopolitan Hotel. This suggests that Billickie had knowledge of the game and indicates that he was getting a cut of the action, but his name never came up in court. The story Peterson gave was that three men attempted to "lure" him into their game, where he was to purchase $2,500 in chips in order to win $4,000. Then, apparently, the money was to be split among Peterson and the other three. The point of the scam, the three men said, was to get back at the syndicate in San Francisco, which was scandalously underpaying the three for running the L.A. faro game. But for some reason never stated, Peterson thought the men were trying to get his $2,500 and called the cops. The police then booked an E. Dunn, a Walter Scott, and a W. W. Stapp. Stapp was Wyatt, who was recognized by someone at the station house. The *Los Angeles Times* didn't think much of the story and placed it on page two, identifying Wyatt only as "a prominent figure here during the days when racing thrived." But the *Herald*'s headline blew the story wide open. Since the cops busted the game before it started, no conclusion can de drawn from the evidence. We can't be sure who was the intended mark, Peterson or the syndicate. Who was Peterson, and why was he trying to get into an illegal faro game in the first place? What was Wyatt's role, if any, beyond dealing faro? Wyatt was indignant over the arrest, calling on several prominent Californians, including former governor Henry Gage, as character witnesses. He granted an interview to the friendly *Los Angeles Examiner* and said: "I was told a faro game was in operation in the hotel where Scott and Dunn had apartments. I like faro and went to the hotel to play. I know absolutely nothing else of what transpired." Wyatt was probably lying: If some kind of con was on, he was the dealer. What is doubtful is that he was behind it. Dunn and Scott needed Wyatt or some skillful dealer; if Wyatt had had the capital to run a game he wouldn't have needed them. A likely scenario is that Billickie, the hotel owner, was one of the architects of the game or the scam or whatever was taking place in his own hotel. He had given Wyatt a handout by letting him deal the game, and Wyatt wasn't going to betray him. Wyatt was charged with the misdemeanor of conspiracy to violate gambling laws, which charge was dismissed for lack of evidence. Whatever Wyatt's involvement, the incident seemed to do him good. He had eighteen more years to live, and there were no more stories about roughhousing or strong arm work or brushes with the law. Adela Rogers St. Johns, visiting Wyatt and Josephine at their Los Angeles bungalow, reported that Earp had taken to reading Shakespeare; he and Tom Mix, St. Johns wrote, were reading Shakespeare as a "joint educational enterprise." Wyatt reckoned "That feller Hamlet was a talkative man. He wouldn't have lasted long in Kansas." Henry Fonda, who played Earp in *My Darling Clementine*, told television producer Melvin Shestack that an old man once complimented him on his portrayal of Earp. The old man said he had met Earp several times as a child "at his family's Passover seders in San Francisco." Perhaps this is what gave rise to the stories that Wyatt Earp, sometime before his death, converted to the religion of his third wife. In 1928 Wyatt got out of a sick bed to vote for Al Smith, the first Roman Catholic to run for president. Smith was promising to repeal Prohibition—a sensible proposition, Wyatt felt, as Prohibition had only helped organized crime to flourish.

Nick Earp had passed away in 1907 in the Soldier's Home at Sawtelle, California, two years after Virgil's death. The *Los Angeles Times* obit called him " 'Old Judge' Earp, frontier justice and father of the noted 'Earp boys.' " James lived till 1928; his shoulder wound from the Civil War contributed to his decline. Half-brother Newton died in 1926. His youngest son, Virgil, won $32,000 on "The $64,000 Question" in 1957. Virgil told a number of whoppers to the

nationwide audience, particularly how he had been his uncle's deputy
in Tombstone. Virgil was five the year Wyatt rode out of Arizona.
The death that probably struck Wyatt hardest occurred on October
25, 1921, when Bat Masterson had a heart attack at his desk at the
New York Morning Telegraph. It had been a hell of a life. Bat had
spent the last fifteen or so years as a nationally known sports columnist, a friend to both the famous, such as Teddy Roosevelt, and the
infamous, such as gambler and gangster financier Arnold Rothstein,
who counted among his apprentices such luminaries as Legs Dia-
mond, Dutch Schultz, Lucky Luciano, and Meyer Lansky. Tradition
has it that a young reporter from Colorado, Damon Runyan, was so
taken with the stories told by the middle-aged ex-gunfighter that he
modeled the character of Sky Masterson after him.

Stuart Lake liked to tell stories about collectors who offered Bat
big money for the gun he had used to kill twenty-two or twenty-
three or twenty-six men. Bat would send an office boy to a pawnshop
to pick up a working revolver, then carve some notches before selling
it. The last words Masterson typed on the sheet in his typewriter
were: "There are those who would say it all breaks even because the
rich get ice in the summer while the poor get it in the winter . . ."
Early on Sunday, January 13, 1929, Wyatt Earp died quietly of
chronic cystitis aggravated by a bout of flu at his Los Angeles home.
He was nine weeks short of his eighty-first birthday. Like Doc Holliday, legend has given him an enigmatic last utterance: "Suppose
. . ." he is supposed to have said. Some say he was thinking of how
different his life would have been if not for the bloody chapter in
Tombstone, or, as some family members suggested, how he might
have saved the life of his favorite brother. In Josephine's memoirs,
she speculated that he was referring to Tombstone, as in "Suppose we
could back and do it over . . ." Or perhaps he had a premonition of
his incredible second life to come. Wyatt's funeral, like Bat Masterson's eight years earlier, drew its share of celebrities. Bat's were from
the world of sports and journalism, while most of Wyatt's famous
mourners were from Hollywood. Tom Mix and William S. Hart, the
two most popular western stars of their day, were pallbearers. Adella
Rogers St. John noted that Tom Mix wept. Josephine was too grief-
stricken to attend. Wyatt's body was cremated; several months after
the cremation, Josephine brought the ashes to the family plot in the
Hills of Eternity Cemetery in Colma, not far from San Francisco.

They had been together since the end of 1882; no record of a marriage certificate has ever been found. The whereabouts of Wyatt's final resting place would be a mystery until, in 1957, some joy-riding youths found the headstone, stole it, and then dumped it by the side of the road when chased by police. The discovery that Wyatt Earp had been buried in a Jewish cemetery led to endless speculation, never quelled, that America's most famous lawman converted to Judaism. ("Hero of the Oy K Coral?" read the headline of a UPI story.) Mix's reaction suggests the small but significant impact that Wyatt had on the movie colony, or at least the part of it that made westerns. Whether or not Wyatt was actually famous in Hollywood is debatable; to call him a cult figure might be more appropriate. Earp had spent years on movie sets and racetracks with Jack London, Wilson Mizner, John Ford, Harry Carey, Sr., Hart, Mix, and others. Raoul Walsh's recollection of Charlie Chaplin's comment on meeting Earp—"You're the bloke from Arizona, aren't you? Tamed the baddies, huh?"—suggests that in Hollywood Wyatt was something of a local celebrity. The greatest director of westerns, some say the best of all American directors, claimed the greatest of all western legends as a personal friend, but John Ford told so many tales about Wyatt Earp that it has now become impossible to separate fact from fiction. In a 1979 interview Ford's son, Patrick, recalled that, "my dad was real friendly with Wyatt Earp, and as a little boy I remember him. . . . But I was too young to grasp what Wyatt Earp was saying. I only remember him saying one thing: The only way to be a successful marshal in those days was to carry a double barrel 12-gauge and don't shoot until you know you can't miss." It's a wonder that line never made it into an Earp movie. In an interview taped for the 1964 TV special "John Ford's West," Ford claimed to have met Wyatt through Harry Carey, Sr. (who, in 1932, would play the first movie Doc Holliday). In Peter Bogdonovich's 1970 book on the director, Ford said he met Earp while working as a prop boy—he'd bring him coffee and get him to tell stories about Dodge and Tombstone. This sounds questionable; most people who knew Wyatt in his old age say he could be coaxed to tell stories about people he had known such as Bat Masterson and Doc Holliday, but was very reluctant to discuss specifics about his own exploits. Raoul Walsh said that at dinner one evening with Earp and Jack London he tried to "draw both men out about their doings," but that "neither wanted to talk about himself."

(They wanted to hear about Walsh's adventures with Pancho Villa.) Ford began making two-reelers in 1917 but as far as is known Wyatt never worked on a Ford film. The most enduring symbol of the American West made an inauspicious movie debut in a now-forgotten William S. Hart silent, *Wild Bill Hickok*, in 1923. No one has been able to track down the name of the first actor to play Wyatt Earp, a tall, blond, mustached man in a white shirt, black tie, and long black coat whose image survives in a sepia-toned still from the film. Why there was even a Wyatt Earp character named in Hart's *Wild Bill Hickok* isn't clear. The best guess is that Wyatt, who had been spending time as an advisor on the sets of Hart's and Tom Mix's westerns, was made a character in the film as tribute. Thus, Wyatt may have been only a few feet away when the picture was taken, watching the birth of his own screen legend. The next Wyatt Earp was Walter Huston, who played him (actually a character based on him) in 1932's *Law and Order*. The frequency with which Wyatt showed up on Hollywood movie sets before and after World War I inspired numerous strange tales and at least one bad movie, Blake Edwards's 1985 *Sunset*, in which Wyatt, played by James Garner,[5] and Tom Mix, played by Bruce Willis, get mixed up with gangsters while running around Hollywood. Researchers are still debating whether or not Wyatt was in a movie during this period. Allan Dwan insists that he was. In his autobiography Dwan wrote that Earp

> was a visitor to the set when I was directing Douglas Fairbanks in *The Half-Breed*. As was the custom in those days, he was invited to join the party and mingle with our background action. I think there was a trial of some kind. A group of people demanded that the half-breed be sent out of town. In that group was Earp. He only stood there and nodded his head. Earp was a one-eyed old man in 1915, but he had been a real marshal in Tombstone, Arizona and he was as crooked as a three dollar bill. He and his brothers were racketeers. All of them. They shook people down. They did everything they could to get dough. . . . They won all the gunfights simply by shooting the man before he was told he was arrested. . . . When I knew him, he was no longer a marshal and there was no longer a West, and he couldn't be the symbol he

had been. . . . I think he was timid about being photo-
graphed, about acting and pretending. He knew inside
himself that he wasn't an actor. . . . I remember he saw
Fairbanks bouncing around in the trees and said, "Oh, no,
I'd not like to do that." And I think, for that reason, he
took one last look and left.

Where Dwan got his information about Wyatt and his brothers being racketeers and "shooting the man before he was told he was
arrested" is not known; for that matter, where he got the idea that
Wyatt was "one-eyed" is a mystery. In a virtuoso bit of detective
work, Jeff Morey tracked down *The Half-Breed*, and the scene Dwan
described, reprinted in Bob Boze Bell's *The Illustrated Life and Times
of Wyatt Earp*. There is an extra who is an old man with a white
mustache sitting in the crowd, but it doesn't look like Earp. It appears to be the legendary Texas John Slaughter, who was at least as
well known out West in 1915 as Wyatt Earp and who also had
friends working in western movies. The whole episode is a minor
mystery that will never be unraveled. Nearly a quarter of a century
later, Dwan would direct Randolph Scott as the first Wyatt Earp
character named Wyatt Earp in *Frontier Marshal*. It was high time,
since characters based on Wyatt's had been making appearances in
films for years under aliases. The first, *Law and Order*, was directed
by Edward L. Cahn. Earp was played by the great Walter Huston,
who, at age forty-eight, began the tradition of actors much older
than Wyatt was during the Tombstone years being cast to play him.
(Eight years later Huston would play Doc Holliday in Howard
Hughes's *The Outlaw*, thus giving him the distinction of being the
only actor to have played Wyatt and Doc.) The scriptwriter was the
son of the star, a twenty-six year old rookie named John Huston.
Law and Order was taken from a novel called *Saint Johnson* by W. R.
Burnett, who, though forgotten today, wrote four of the most popular crime novels (*Little Caesar, Scarface, The Asphalt Jungle,* and *High
Sierra*) of all time. Like Walter Noble Burns (whose *Tombstone* had
inspired him), Burnett saw the Tombstone conflict in the context of
the 1920s Eastern crime wave. He once told an interviewer that
"Dillinger and Roy Earle"—the character from *High Sierra* who
would later be played on screen by Humphrey Bogart—"are not
gangsters. . . . They were a reversion to the western bandit." Oddly

enough, considering that so much of America's mythology has come out of the West, crime novels of the type Burnett and Dashiell Hammett were writing were seen by a great many critics as genuine literature, while the Old West, as the Argentinean writer Jorge Luis Borges once noted, wasn't seen by Americans as a fit subject for serious writers.[6] Burnett told film critic Pat McGilligan, "Everybody said to me, 'Burnett, are you out of your mind? Let Zane Grey write the westerns for chrissakes!'" Burnett ignored them and traveled to Tombstone, which, despite its annual "Helldorado" festival and re-creations of the gunfight, had not yet become the tourist mecca that movies like *Law and Order* would soon make it. Burnett sought out old-timers who claimed to have known the Earps and the Clantons, and, one drunken night, stumbled out with them onto old Fremont Street to re-create the gunfight at the O.K. Corral. Over the next few decades countless American, German, English, French, Italian, Japanese, and other foreign tourists would have the same impulse. A possible reason why Burnett didn't use Earp's name for his protagonist is that he didn't want to make his debt to Burns's *Tombstone* too obvious. With the success of *Tombstone* and then, in 1931, Lake's *Frontier Marshal*, Universal Studios would have loved to use Earp's name, but Josephine Marcus Earp killed that hope by storming the movie lot to protest the film version. Burnett intercepted her, and the two spent an afternoon drinking tea and talking and becoming absolutely charmed with each other. It isn't clear in other situations with writers and filmmakers whether Josephine was acting out of monetary or protective interests, but in this instance she left no doubt in Burnett's mind that she was out to see that Wyatt's image wasn't tarnished. After assuring her that Wyatt, or Saint Johnson, was his hero, too, Burnett and Josephine got along. *Law and Order* isn't a bad film, and the action, particularly the final shootout at the O.K. Barn—presumably Burnett didn't want to make his debt to Lake too obvious—was surprisingly brutal for its day. Universal got the most out of its investment, remaking it twice: first in 1940 with Johnny Mack Brown. Brown, who played Billy the Kid in the 1930 King Vidor film based on Burns's book, is the only actor to have played Billy the Kid and Wyatt Earp. The second was an absolutely forgettable 1953 version with Ronald Reagan, making Reagan, as of this writing, the only American president to play a character based on Wyatt Earp.[7] Meanwhile, Stuart Lake was cranking up the engine that would turn Wyatt Earp into a multimillion-dollar industry. Shortly after the success of his book, Lake sold *Frontier Marshal* to Fox for just $7,500; he split the money with Josephine, who was still not resigned either to Lake's book or to the use of her husband's name in a movie. And so, George O'Brien, the hero of *Frontier Marshal* (1934), was named Michael Wyatt (an actor named Alan Edwards played Wyatt's friend, Doc Warren). Though neither film did terrific box office, the Hollywood western mill had now decided, half a century after the actual events, that the Earp-cowboy feud in Tombstone was the classic story of the Old West. In quick succession after *Frontier Marshal* were King Vidor's *The Arizonian* (1935) starring Richard Dix, *Law for Tombstone* (1937) with Buck Jones, *In Early Arizona* (1938) with Bill Elliott, Dwan's *Frontier Marshal* (1939) with Randolph Scott, *Dodge City* (1939) (sort of a super-projection of Earp, Masterson, and all the Dodge City officers), and *Tombstone—The Town too Tough to Die* (1942). Each film picked and chose what it wanted from the Earp story, often using elements that weren't in or were only hinted at in the books by Breakenridge, Burns, and Lake. In *Law for Tombstone,* for instance, Buck Jones plays not a lawman but a Wells Fargo agent; Earp's name is not used, for legal reasons, but the agent's friend is Doc Holliday (played by an actor named Harvey Clark). In *The Arizonian* (which had a screenplay by Dudley Nichols, who won an Oscar for John Ford's *The Informer* and who later wrote *Stagecoach*), the trouble in Silver City is touched off by the rivalry between a reluctant ex-lawman (Richard Dix) and a crooked sheriff (Louis Calhern) for the affections of a show girl (Margot Grahame). No one knows how Nichols hit on one of the specific causes of the Earp-Behan hostilities that no one else caught; perhaps one of the old Arizonians who hung around the western movie sets took to gossiping. Clearly Nichols cribbed some things from Lake's *Frontier Marshal*: Wyatt's arrest of Ben Thompson is restaged in "Silver City," and Nichols had to have taken it from Lake's book since no other account of the Earp-Thompson incident has been found. Why didn't Lake sue? The only logical reason is that Lake claimed the story was historical fact and thus had no exclusive right to it.

Lake finally cashed in on Earp's movie potential with *Frontier Marshal.* The movie was awful, but it was a hit, largely because it was released at a time when the production of A-budget westerns was beginning to crest. For many moviegoers Randolph Scott became the first clear image of Wyatt Earp (some of Wyatt's family thought that Scott was the movie actor who most resembled Wyatt, even though Scott was clean-shaven). Not everyone was thrilled. Virgil's widow, Allie, thought the film was a pack of "sugar-coated" lies, and Josephine, angrier over *Frontier Marshal* than she had been over *Law and Order* seven years earlier, sued Fox for $50,000. Allan Dwan met with her, as W. R. Burnett had done, and talked her out of the suit— perhaps showing her that the Wyatt Earp of the movie was even more of an antiseptic hero than the one in Lake's book. Years later Allan Dwan told his own biographer, Peter Bogdonavich, that "We never meant it to be Wyatt Earp. We were just making *Frontier Marshal* and that could have been any frontier marshal." This shows how serviceable Wyatt's story, or at least some facets of Wyatt's story, had become. It also shows how far Stuart Lake (who had constructed his Wyatt Earp from parts of Wyatt, Bat Masterson, Wild Bill Hickok, Bill Tilghman, Virgil Earp, and others), was willing to bend his own "historical" record to suit the movies. The success of *Frontier Marshal* and the increasing popularity of westerns set studios to looking for Earp material other than Lake's book. Someone remembered Burns's *Tombstone—An Iliad of the Southwest,* perhaps remembering too that Burns' books had supplied material for two successful westerns, King Vidor's *Billy the Kid* (1930) and the legend of the Mexican bandit Joaquin Murieta, *Robin Hood of El Dorado* (1936). Also, Burns was long dead by 1942 therefore was not around to object to how his work was distorted. This was fortunate, since about the only bit of history that survived from book to film was that Doc Holliday (Kent Taylor) was once more a dentist (for reasons never quite explained Doc had been a Boston surgeon named Halliday in *Frontier Marshal,* and for reasons even more inexplicable John Ford, who knew better, repeated this error in *My Darling Clementine*). Richard Dix, at age forty-eight, was nearly a generation older than Wyatt had been in Tombstone. The problem with *Tombstone,* though, wasn't historical accuracy but the lack of vision from the director, William McGann. The next major Earp film would prove that conclusively. Josephine Earp would not live to protest this one. Josie, after having her last years enlivened by visits from Hollywood luminaries such as Cecil B. DeMille and Gary Cooper, died peacefully in December 1944. She missed by two years the most renowned of Wyatt Earp movies and one of the most highly regarded films in the history of American cinema. It's doubtful that even Josephine would had found anything to fault in Henry Fonda's portrayal of Wyatt Earp in *My Darling Clementine*.

Later, after *My Darling Clementine* was an acknowledged classic, John Ford would give interviews telling the "real" story of how the film had come about. In *Focus on Film* in 1971, Ford claimed that "He [Wyatt] told me the story of the fight at the O.K. Corral. And that was exactly the way it was done, except that Doc Holliday was not killed." In the film, Wyatt (Henry Fonda), his brother Morgan (played by Ward Bond, who is physically much more like Virgil), and Doc (Victor Mature, weighing perhaps twice as much as the real Doc Holliday) confront the Clantons sans McLaurys. The rustlers are led by Old Man Clanton (who was killed before the gunfight) and bolstered by the presence of Finn. Wyatt may or may not have talked to Ford about the gunfight—it seems doubtful that he would have told a movie director what he held back from his own biographers—but he never told him it happened like that. Nor, really, did Ford think that it did. Ford knew pretty much what had happened at the gunfight, and if he didn't, Stuart Lake's bestseller was there to tell him. (For that matter, Stuart Lake was there to tell him.) John Ford and Stuart Lake simply took what they liked best from Earp's story and invented the rest. Ford was famous for answering charges of fictionalizing history with statements like, "Do you want good history or a good movie?" This was one case where good history would have made at least an equally good story, but Ford wasn't interested in the politics and economics of Wyatt's time in Tombstone. (He wasn't even interested in the locale; the film was shot not in the south, in the mountains, but in the north of Arizona in Monument Valley.) There is no John Behan, no conflict between different levels of law enforcement, and no town factions. There is no Josephine to cause a rift between Earp and Behan, no townsfolk or ranchers to take the side of the cowboy rustlers. It's not even clear that anyone considers Wyatt and his brothers to be outsiders—they make their entrance into Tombstone driving a herd of cattle, thus making them more legitimate "cowboys" than the Clantons. Ford wasn't interested in dialectics. He was presenting a clash between good and evil in a primeval setting (Many critics have praised the scene where a church social takes place before the skeletal wooden framework of the future church, placed in stark contrast to the rugged, eternal mountains in the background.) Fonda's Wyatt Earp is a faultless human being—noble, brave, selfless, and able to win at poker without making enemies. Only Doc Holliday seems irritated by his presence: Has Wyatt Earp, he asks at their first meeting, "come to deliver us from all evil?" In fact, Walter Brennan's Old Man Clanton seems to like Wyatt better than Holliday does. For Earp aficionados, the most unsatisfactory part of *My Darling Clementine* is precisely the Earp-Holliday relationship; the two never seem to become real friends, and at one point, incredibly, engage in a shootout. Wyatt wins, shooting the gun out of Doc's hand at a distance of about fifty feet. (It's a good thing Wyatt doesn't miss, as the stagecoach horses are directly in back of Doc.) The Wyatt Earp of John Ford and Henry Fonda wasn't so much a lie as a highly selective half-truth. The church sequence is not so historically ludicrous as some Earp debunkers would later claim; Wyatt, after all, was a church deacon in Dodge City and had helped to build St. Paul's Church in Tombstone for the Reverend Endicott Peabody with his poker winnings. In fairness to Ford and Dudley Nichols, they were also honest about Wyatt's gambling. "I sure do love this game," says Fonda, sweeping his poker winnings into this hat. However compelling the Earp story is when stripped down to such essentials, those who know something about Tombstone in 1881 will always find *My Darling Clementine* a disappointment, if only because what actually happened was so much richer and more complex than Ford's movie hints at. Ford claimed that his conception of the film was not so simplistic as the studio's. The release print of the movie showed Wyatt Earp riding away to his destiny. Years later Ford claimed that "The finish of the picture was not done by me. That isn't the way I wanted to finish it. . . . I wanted Wyatt to stay there and become permanent marshal—which he did. And that was the true story. Instead of that, he had to ride away." But in truth Wyatt did ride away from Tombstone, because of circumstances Ford never touches on. The Wyatt in the existing version of *My Darling Clementine* has no murder warrant for Frank Stilwell's death hanging over him. Ford had to know that he was creating a grand romantic fantasy, but in all the interviews he gave in later years he vehemently insisted on the historical veracity of his Earp movie.[9] What Ford was being true to, of course, was his own passionate vision of how he wanted things to have been, and though the credits for *My Darling Clementine* list Stuart Lake's *Frontier Marshal* as the source, the final film bore little resemblance to even that already bowdlerized version. The principal change in the Earp story made by Ford and Lake was to take the gunfight near the O.K. Corral, the revenge shootings of Virgil and Morgan, and Wyatt's subsequent Vendetta Ride and turn them completely around. The gunfight provided a neat, politics-free denouement to the story, so in *My Darling Clementine* the shootings of Wyatt's younger brothers (for some reason James and Virgil Earp are the younger brothers) becomes the reason for the gunfight—the gunfight, in effect, becomes Wyatt's vendetta. (This was also the plot line for the most successful Earp film, *Gunfight at the O.K. Corral*, which Stuart Lake, though uncredited, had a hand in.) This had the unintentional effect of squeezing out the most colorful Cowboys in the Earp saga, Curly Bill Brocius and Johnny Ringo—since the movies ended with the gunfight, there was no room for the Vendetta Ride or Cowboys for Wyatt to take vengeance on. Curly Bill and Ringo, the Cowboys leaders, were now relegated to "guest" appearances in the Earp story while the Clantons, mainly Ike, took center stage. In *Gunfight at the O.K. Corral*, Ringo was the "hired gun" of the Clantons; in *Hour of the Gun* (1966), Curly Bill, played by Jon Voight, is around just long enough to get himself killed by James Garner's Wyatt Earp. Lake would continue to manipulate the large and small screen images of Wyatt Earp for another decade and a half after *My Darling Clementine*, but his overly simplified version of the story had already begun to stir up a legion of angry Earp debunkers. John Ford would outlive Stuart Lake, just long enough to join the debunkers.

The best, in fact the only good Earp film between *My Darling Clementine* and *Gunfight at the O.K. Corral* was *Wichita*, directed by French-born Jacques Tourneur, best known for his noir classic, *Out of the Past*—for which Stuart Lake served as advisor. Joel McCrea, much older than Earp at the time of his peace officer exploits, was cast in the lead. At fifty, McCrea was exactly twice as old as Wyatt had been when he arrived in Wichita. McCrea's problems start when he encounters cattle rustlers on the outskirts of town; they realize almost immediately that this fellow is going to cause them trouble because he carries an extra-long barreled gun. Actually, it's the standard 7 1/2 inch army-length Colt single action revolver, but for some reason everyone else carries the short-barreled model and agrees to pretend that Earp's gun is extraordinary. As historian John Mack Faragher pointed out in a 1996 broadcast of *Wichita* on the History Channel, the movie is awarding Wyatt the Buntline Special that he was given later in Dodge City—if indeed he was given the gun at all—even before he reached Wichita. The film confers on Wyatt a reputation (to say nothing of a full marshal's badge) in Wichita that he probably didn't have until Tombstone. The best scenes in *Wichita* are of McCrea controlling a large crowd of rowdy cowhands by sheer force of personality. These are fairly close to the descriptions of him in action that Wyatt's friends described in letters to Stuart Lake. *Wichita* was a moderate hit and was one of McCrea's last feature films. (His last two were *Gunfight at Dodge City* in 1959, in which he played a variation of Earp, and Sam Peckinpah's classic, *Ride the High Country*, 1962, which costarred Randolph Scott, the first western to star two former movie Earps.) McCrea enjoyed playing Earp so much that four years after "Wichita" was released, he starred in NBC's TV series based on the film, *Wichita Town*, playing a cow town marshal named Mike Dunbar. Earp's name couldn't be used, since he was already the star of the enormously popular "The Life and Legend of Wyatt Earp" on ABC. Thus, Stuart Lake, working in an advisory capacity, had two versions of Wyatt on TV at the same time. In fact, if one counts Matt Dillon of "Gunsmoke," who was a composite of Earp, Bat Masterson, Bill Tilghman, and other Dodge City peace officers, Wyatt Earp, in 1959, was the star of westerns on all three major TV networks.[9]

Actually, Wyatt's TV debut preceded "Gunsmoke." Early in 1952 CBS broadcast an episode of the pseudo-documentary series "You Are There," narrated by Walter Cronkite and starring Robert Bray as Wyatt. The episode appears to be lost to posterity, but its inspiration lives on in the superb 1972 telecast, "David S. Wolper Presents: Appointment with Destiny," narrated by Lorne Greene and actually filmed in Tombstone on the site of the gunfight. That the Gunfight at the O.K. Corral was reenacted on the same series that re-created the assassination of Lincoln and the signing of the Declaration of Independence shows how ingrained Wyatt Earp had become in American folklore by the early 1950s. What finally made Wyatt a household name was getting beamed into millions of households. "The Life and Legend of Wyatt Earp," one of the most successful

TV series of the so-called golden age of television, made its debut on
September 6,1955. Loosely based on Lake's *Frontier Marshal*, with
Lake as an advisor, the show starred a strikingly handsome young
actor named Hugh O'Brian, whom Lake approved for "the firm slant
of his jaw and those narrow hips." "The Life and Legend of Wyatt
Earp" ran for an amazing 226 thirty minute episodes over six years—
or about the same length of time Wyatt actually spent as a lawman.
The show's popularity with adults crested at the height of the western phase of TV and feature films, but it also had an enormous
attraction for children. Of all the real-life frontier legends portrayed
on '50s television, only Davy Crockett was as marketable with children as Wyatt Earp. Lake's Wyatt Earp Enterprises churned out
lunch boxes, coloring books, puzzles, Little Golden Books, cap guns,
tin badges, and even a Buntline Special plastic model assembly kit.
There was a Hartland Plastics statue of O'Brian as Earp mounted on
a horse; today, a Hartland Earp in good shape might sell for $300 or
more. Hartland made statues of numerous other western heroes, including Richard Boone as Paladin from "Have Gun, Will Travel,"
James Arness from "Gunsmoke." Clayton Moore as "The Lone
Ranger," and Roy Rogers. The Earp statue is distinctive in that it
portrays an actual historical figure. Or at least a version of a real,
historical figure: The Hartland Earp is clean-shaven, like Hugh
O'Brian, like all the TV and movie Earps of the Eisenhower era. He
is also wearing a fancy, gold-and-black vest of the kind Wyatt probably did wear—when he was dealing faro: America's most famous
western TV lawman in a gambler's outfit. Someone in the wardrobe
department probably just thought it looked distinctive.[10] As TV,
"The Life and Legend of Wyatt Earp," at least for the first couple of
seasons, was first-rate. There was a genuine period flavor and flavor
attention to detail, rare for an era when production design on westerns (especially those on fledging network ABC) were fairly shoddy.
The refrain from the a capella version of the theme song—"Wyatt
Earp, Wyatt Earp. Brave, courageous and bold"—went directly into
American lexicon. The Earp series inspired a sort of spin-off—"Bat
Masterson" starring Gene Barry. Bat had put in numerous appear-
ances in the Kansas-based episodes of "The Life and Legend of
Wyatt Earp," played by Mason Dinehart. By 1957, Masterson—who
had kicked off the Earp legend in the twentieth century with his
Earp profile and by inspiring Stuart Lake—finally earned his own

show, taken largely from a best-selling biography by New York journalist Richard O'Connor.[11] But popular as the show was, Bat never
caught on like Wyatt. There was a 1954 movie, *Masterson of Kansas*,
with George Montgomery as Bat and Bruce Cowling as Wyatt, but
it seemed as if no one was interested in Bat's story alone. Far better
known when he died in 1921 than was Wyatt at his death in 1929,
Bat remained an appendage of the Wyatt Earp legend, despite the
success of "Bat Masterson." The success of "The Life and Legend of
Wyatt Earp" inspired the second biggest success in the pantheon of
Earp movies, *Gunfight at the O.K. Corral*. Released in 1957, directed
by John Sturges with a screenplay from novelist Leon Uris, *Gunfight
at the O.K. Corral* was one of the most successful westerns of the
decade, with a theme song by Frankie Lane that became, along with
Tex Ritter's "High Noon," one of the best known western movie
anthems. In the 1990s, through constant rotation on TBS network,
Gunfight has become the Wyatt Earp film most familiar to Americans. This is despite Burt Lancaster's Wyatt Earp, who, as scripted
by Uris, is the dullest Earp in all the major films, interesting only
when contrasted with Kirk Douglas's Doc Holliday. Some references
are made to Wyatt's wild early life, but the Earp we see on the screen
is even more of a straight arrow than Fonda's in *My Darling Clementine*—at least he enjoyed poker. The fault is not in Lancaster's performance but in the script's limitations. After the release of *Tombstone* and *Wyatt Earp* in 1994, several critics, referring to the
attention getting performances of Val Kilmer and Dennis Quaid,
remarked that Doc Holliday always steals a Wyatt Earp movie. But
in truth, *Gunfight at the O.K. Corral* was the first movie that this
could be said of (no one accused Victor Mature of stealing scenes
from Henry Fonda). Leon Uris's script contrasted Kirk Douglas's
gambler-gunfighter Doc with Lancaster's Wyatt, who is generally
dressed in drab black like a frontier minister (Doc repeatedly taunts
Wyatt by calling him "preacher"). Though the real Wyatt and Doc
were friends because they had so much in common, the movie poster
for *Gunfight* played off the differences between them: "The strangest
alliance this side of heaven and hell." As Wyatt came more and more
to symbolize America's frontier lawmen, his screen image became
lighter and Doc Holliday's became darker and seamier. This is an
interesting contrast to Billy the Kid movies where the Kid and Pat
Garrett, who were in reality quite different, are made to seem rather

alike. The gunfight, in the film, takes up more than five minutes of screen time—lasting about ten times longer than the original—and took place on a cluttered lot that seems to take up more space than the outfield in Yankee Stadium. After the fight, Wyatt urges Doc to visit a sanatorium in Colorado and then leaves for California to meet up with a gorgeous lady gambler, played by Rhonda Fleming and modeled as a combination of Dora Hand, the madam who was murdered in Dodge City, the famous female gambler Lottie Deno, and possibly a bit of Josephine Marcus. Some critics insisted on seeing a homosexual attraction between Wyatt and Doc—this was a preoccupation of critics in the 1950s in almost any A-movie western with two male leads—but *Gunfight at the O.K. Corral* was the first Earp movie to give Wyatt a vital, independent-minded female partner. As "The Life and Legend of Wyatt Earp" was out of syndication until 2005, John Sturges can be credited with creating the image of Wyatt Earp that would be most visible from World War II into the 1990s. Like John Ford, John Sturges would live just long enough to become one of Earp's debunkers.

Gunfight at the O.K. Corral was far and away the most successful Earp film of the 1950s, but its popularity didn't so much contribute to Wyatt's fame as confirm it: It was the evidence that Wyatt had found a place in American folklore. Television and movies in the 1950s and early '60s were littered with Wyatt Earps. In 1954 an actor named Bruce Cowling played Wyatt in the movie *Masterson of Kansas*, letting Wyatt horn in on Bat's only real shot at cinematic glory. Oddly enough, considering his influence on the Earp story, Bat scarcely put in an appearance in an Earp movie till Tom Sizemore played him in Lawrence Kasdan's *Wyatt Earp* in 1994. In 1958 they were given equal status for the first and only time on the screen in a B-movie called *Badman's Country*. George Montgomery plays Pat Garrett, passing through an Arizona town on the way back from killing Billy the Kid in Fort Sumner, New Mexico. (Someone must have given Garrett bad directions, as Arizona is west of New Mexico.) The town is terrorized by the Sundance Kid, who actually operated a couple hundred miles to the north about twenty years later. Garrett captures the Kid with the help of Buffalo Bill (who must have been on vacation as there were no buffalo left in Arizona) and then sends for his good pals Wyatt and Bat to help out when Butch Cassidy's Wild Bunch shows up to try and free Sundance. Then—

well, suffice to say there's a happy ending. *Badman's Country*, awful as it is, is fascinating in its Cuisineart approach to Old West legends. In B-movie heaven, all western legends exist at the same time and in the same space; Wyatt Earp is virtually interchangeable with Pat Garrett and Bat Masterson, the Sundance Kid with Billy the Kid. A year later in the Bob Hope vehicle *Alias Jesse James* Hugh O'Brian's Wyatt puts in a cameo as one of several TV western heroes who come to Hope's aid in a shootout with the James gang. (Fess Parker's Davy Crockett is the only other character based on an actual historic frontiersman.) Wyatt Earp now stood in the street of a western town with a fictional character, Matt Dillon, who had been inspired by Earp. By 1963, Earp's name was so well known internationally that Guy Madison played someone called Wyatt Earp in an absurd Italian-French produced western called *Jennie Lee's Ha Una Nuova Pistola*, which had nothing to do with Earp. The film's producers thought that the name Wyatt Earp was good for international business.

By the 1960s, the character Wyatt Earp had become a stock figure in TV and movie westerns, often appearing in them whether he had a plot function or not. Actor Bill Camfield played him in a 1963 Three Stooges movie, *The Outlaws Is Coming*, and Med Flory played him as a darker, more sinister version of James Garner's gambler-gunfighter on TV's "Maverick." Character actor Steve Forrest also played a darker projection of Earp on a short-lived mid-sixties TV series called "Cimarron Strip." The series is now forgotten, but the fact of its existence makes it a curious cultural artifact, reflecting America's growing schizophrenia about one of its national heroes. As the Vietnam War loomed, America did not know how it wanted its national icons to be presented, and in keeping with this ambivalence, TV and movies served up both positive and negative versions of the same person, sometimes in the same feature. In "Cimarron Strip," Stuart Whitman played Marshal Jim Crown, king of the frontier lawmen, clearly a superprojection of Earp that surpassed even Hugh O'Brian's TV portrayal. (Whitman even dressed like O'Brian in a golden gambler's vest and black hat.) Forrest played Wylie Harp, a shady con man and killer, Crown's evil twin. Audiences could pick their preferred Earp image. In 1962 Sam Peckinpah had used the same formula to produce one of the most underrated westerns of the decade, *Ride the High Country* (also known as *Guns in the Afternoon*), the first film to feature two former Wyatt Earps, Randolph Scott from *Frontier Marshal* and Joel McCrea from *Wichita* and the TV series, "Wichita Town." McCrea is a stolid, principled lawman, Scott a veteran frontier marshal turned cynic. In the end, they must combine forces to get the job done—but the better of the two, McCrea, dies. Peckinpah tips his hand that he's borrowing on the Earp legend at the beginning of the film when McCrea tells Scott, "I hear you been runnin' around Dodge City with those Earp boys"—it's left hanging as to whether McCrea means that Scott picked up bad habits from them or was run out of town by them. Edward Dmytryk's *Warlock* (1959), starring Henry Fonda and Anthony Quinn, might be called the first Earp debunking movie. Made from a novel by Oakley Hall, *Warlock* borrowed freely from the Earp story without the use of actual names, which probably accounts for the fact that it alone, of all the anti-Earp movies, was a hit: Audiences didn't recognize it as an anti-Earp movie. Fonda (who had played both a positive and negative Earp figure) plays a professional gunman named Clay Blaisdell, a man with a reputation as a "town-tamer." What needs to be tamed in Warlock is the cattle rustlers who live in the San Simon valley (as did the cowboys of Earp's time), who are led by a stalwart group of character actors that included DeForrest Kelly, who only two years earlier played Morgan Earp in *Gunfight at the O.K. Corral*. *Warlock* is laden with Earp symbolism. Blaisdell is famous for his "gold-plated Colts," stand-ins for the Buntline Special, and his assistant, Tom (Quinn), supposedly a deadlier killer than Blaisdell, is club-footed rather then TB-impaired. They do "clean up" the town in a gunfight similar to the O.K. Corral shootout, done in a way that makes it clear that some cowboys didn't want to fight. Afterward, Blaisdell finds that there is no place in the community for a professional killer—though one would have thought he had learned that lesson many years earlier—and is forced to kill Tom, who, out of love for Clay, goads him into a gunfight so everyone in town can see that Clay is still the deadliest gun in the West. On the screen this looked very much like a homosexual attraction of Quinn's character for Fonda's, though Dmytryk vehemently denied it.. (A hint of homosexuality in a '50s "adult western" is generally what made it "adult.") Oakley Hall's novel was essentially a cautionary tale about the danger of turning a law enforcement figure into an icon. This wasn't fair to Earp, who was no icon while he was a peace officer and only became one as his story was retold and retold until it congealed into legend. The impact of Waters's book, *The Earp Brothers of Tombstone*, on Earp's movie image was dramatic. A self-contained Earp segment in John Ford's 1964 film *Cheyenne Autumn* features James Stewart as a puffed-up, white-suited Earp with Arthur Kennedy as a pipe-smoking, bowler hat-wearing Doc Holliday. (Doc would have shot the man who tried to place such a hat on him; in Tombstone he would often tip bowler hats off the heads of townsfolk pretentious enough to wear them in public.) Both actors were too old for the roles, which makes them appear even more ludicrous. Stewart, with Ford's approval, plays Earp as a narcissist and a bully (he shoots an offensive cowhand in the foot with a Derringer). Stewart's was the nastiest screen Earp up to that time, a harsher image even than Henry Fonda's killer in *Warlock*, who at least has some dignity. It isn't clear if Ford bought Waters's version of Earp (as he had once bought Lake's) or whether he was simply going with the times. Two years before *Cheyenne Autumn* Ford had made the most critically acclaimed western debunking film of its time, *The Man Who Shot Liberty Valance*, which included the most famous line to come out of a Ford western: "This is the West, sir. When the legend becomes fact, print the legend." Now, Ford had disregarded the facts (such as he had available to him) on two occasions and printed two legends, both of them false. Much the same thing happened with John Sturges, whose *Gunfight at the O.K. Corral* was one of his biggest successes. Five years after that film (and two years after Waters's book was published), Sturges told an interviewer, "I'm a westerner myself, and I can tell you I don't go for that Stuart Lake baloney"—though that Stuart Lake baloney had served him well when Lake had been an advisor on Sturges's film. Five years after the interview Sturges sought to rectify matters with *Hour of the Gun* (1967), starring a surprisingly effective James Garner as Earp and a much too old Jason Robards, Jr., as Doc. This was the darkest Earp feature to date, a more disturbing image than *Warlock* because it openly identified itself as a Wyatt Earp movie. ("Wyatt Earp," asked the bold caption at the top of the movie poster, "Hero with a badge or cold-blooded killer?") The film begins with the words "This Is the Way It Actually Happened"—compared to previous Earp films at least, this is true. The story begins where Sturges's first Earp movie ended, with the gunfight, which, except for taking place in the O.K. Corral, is reasonably accurate. The rest of the film is about what Sturges left out of *Gunfight at the O.K. Corral*—the inquest and the Vendetta Ride. Garner, lean and tanned, played the least romantic Earp figure up to that time. As the film progresses, his ideals are stripped away one by one until he can no longer deny that his purpose is anything but vengeance. Though Sturges set out to tell what he saw as the real story, the Wyatt Earp of *Hour of the Gun* is far closer to Stuart Lake's *Frontier Marshal* than to Frank Waters's depiction. For instance, in the scene where he kills the Florentino Cruz character, Wyatt gives him a count of three before he draws his own gun. This didn't ring true when Lake wrote it thirty-seven years earlier. Not only are several key incidents retold from Lake's book, the idea of Earp the archetypal peace officer turned avenger is also from *Frontier Marshal*. Garner's Earp isn't more idealized than the Earp of Lake's book: He *is* the Earp of Lake's book, undiluted by Lake for the movies. *Hour of the Gun* is a petty good western, but at the box office it was hard put to overcome two popular images: Wyatt Earp as a western knight—still the prevalent image of Earp as late as 1967—and Garner's own image as the sly, amiable Maverick on TV. As history, it failed in at least one important way: In the curious tradition of Earp debunkers from Breakenridge to Waters, it doesn't diminish Earp's role in the Tombstone war; it inflates it. Once again, Wyatt, not Virgil, is the marshal of Tombstone, and he's given more status in town and in Arizona territorial politics than the real Wyatt ever claimed for himself (and for all the talk of historical fidelity, Sturges couldn't resist having his Earp track Robert Ryan's Ike Clanton across the Mexican border and killing him). As with every film or book that tries to take Earp's legend down a peg, it first pushes him up two pegs to make him seem worth taking down. The next major Earp film took Wyatt's image as low as it's possible to go. *Doc*, directed by Frank Perry from a script by journalist Pete Hamill, was one of the first anti-westerns to trace America's involvement in Vietnam to our frontier myths. As *The New Yorker*'s Pauline Kael pointed out, the Cheyenne Indians slaughtered in *Little Big Man* were clearly meant to suggest the Vietnamese in the My Lai massacres. In the preface to the published script, Hamill made it clear that he saw Earp as the symbol of a predatory America whose armies were currently bogged down in Southeast Asia:

> We [Hamill and Frank Perry] talked a little about Wyatt
> Earp, and how I felt that Lyndon Johnson was some dis-
> torted version of Earp. . . . We knew from the sketchy
> history that Wyatt was nothing at all like the legend he
> later made up. He was a politician, a bully, a man who
> had hustled towns and moved on with the railhead. . . .
> The more we looked at the evidence, the clearer it became
> that the whole myth of the West, the whole legend of its
> heroes, all of that was a lie. And that was something im-
> portant to deal with and attempt to correct: If the country
> had gotten into trouble because it had tried to digest one
> lie too many, then perhaps we could make a film that
> would try to tell some truth.

One might think that these were awfully big truths to glean from a
sketchy history, but this was a time when a great many intellectuals
were simply prepared to believe a priori that America's western past
was a giant mistake from which we needed to be rescued. Some
would argue we are not yet past that point. And so, Wyatt Earp,
whose family was staunchly behind Lincoln and the Union, and who
in his time represented the forces of liberalism that were sweeping
into the West, was used a century later as the symbol of reaction.[12]

Played by Harris Yulin, the Wyatt Earp of *Doc* is a compost heap
of every nasty story ever told about Wyatt Earp and some new ones
that even Earp's most vehement detractors had not thought up. Gore
Vidal, whose Billy the Kid play, *The Left-Handed Gun*, was the basis
for Arthur Penn's 1958 movie, clearly intended for the dime-store
novel writers who followed Billy around to be seen as homosexual.[13]

In this retelling, Wyatt is inept with his fists; when pushed by Ike
Clanton into a man to man confrontation, Earp gets the stuffing beat
out of him. The script (the only one in an Earp movie to feature the
Benson stage robbery as a plot device) suggests that the reason for
the O.K. Corral shootout was Wyatt's desire for revenge on Ike.
That's Earp's personal motivation; politically, in Hamill's Tombstone, Earp is Lyndon Johnson and the U.S. Army, while Clanton
and the cowboys are the Viet Cong. After visiting Vietnam during
Johnson's seventeen-day journalists' junket of the Far East, Hamill
was convinced that, as he wrote in the introduction to the screenplay,
in the president's eyes, "Indochina was Dodge City and the Ameri-

cans were some collective version of Wyatt Earp." Hamill determined to write about the power this western myth had on American minds, but found that the West could not be "dealt with by the mere accumulation of facts. Vietnam had already taught me that the 'facts' often had nothing to do with the truth."

Wyatt became the town marshal of Tombstone—once again elevating him in the process of trying to debunk him—and Virgil and Morgan are made into bumpkins who embarrass Wyatt in public (in one scene they are shown wrestling in the dirt like Lil' Abner's brothers in Dogpatch). John Clum (played by writer Dan Greenburg), Wyatt's lifelong friend and supporter, is now suspicious and skeptical. The editor of what appears to be the only paper in town, he prints the truth that topples Wyatt from power even after their "victory" at the O.K. Corral. In other words, Clum is a stand-in for Hamill and all the other liberal journalists who had the guts to take a stand against the war.[14] At the O.K. Corral, the Earps, with their superior fire power, walk in and blow the Clantons and the McLaurys away, though Morgan Earp is killed in the process. This gives Wyatt a chance to make a pompous speech in front of the town about how, out of his brother's death, will come a "better Tombstone."

Wyatt Earp, in his afterlife, had now gone through three distinct phases: as police and the FBI-battled gangsters and gunmen in the 1930s, Earp emerged as an inspiration for a return to frontier justice; after World War II and Korea, he represented the Cold Warriors who held the line against the enemies of Democracy; and now, by 1970, he was seen as a point man for the military-industrial complex.

After the box office failure of *Doc*, Wyatt went through a slow period. Between *Doc* in 1970 and the James Garner (as Earp) and Bruce Willis (as Tom Mix) comedy, *Sunset*, in 1988, the only Earp feature was a 1985 TV movie, "I Married Wyatt Earp" with Bruce Boxleitner as Wyatt and, in one of the truly horrendous casting decisions in the history of Earp films, Marie Osmond as Josephine. Loosely based on the book *I Married Wyatt Earp*, which was supposedly the memoirs of Josephine Marcus, the movie had Josie save Wyatt at the O.K. Corral by grabbing a rifle and, in the tradition of Grace Kelly in *High Noon*, surprising two members of the Clanton gang who were about to ambush the Earps from Fly's Photography Studio. (Well, Wyatt did say he heard a shot from that direction.)

Though Wyatt took a hiatus from feature films, his hold on the American imagination remained strong. In 1972 "David S. Wolper Presents: Appointment with Destiny" aired, and, through repeated showings on such cable outlets as the Discovery Channel and the History Channel, has gained a solid reputation as one of the most intelligent and historically accurate Earp features ever made. Narrated by Lorne Greene and actually filmed in a slightly reconstructed Tombstone (including the lot where the gunfight took place), "Appointment with Destiny" was shot in a pseudo-documentary style that probably owed much to Walter Cronkite's "You Are There" series of the early 1950s. No previous version of the Earp story had paid such attention to detail in costuming and historical accuracy— Josephine is mentioned for the first time in any Wyatt Earp film— and if the script had a strong, anti-Earp tinge, it still seemed a model of fairness compared to the excesses of *Doc* and of Frank Waters's book. (For that matter, it remains a model of fairness compared to the A&E's two volume "Wyatt Earp—Justice at the O.K. Corral," which first aired in 1994. The program was billed as "a showdown with the truth about history's most infamous U.S. marshal.")

In vivid contrast to the sober this-is-how-it-really-happened approach of the Wolper production was episode 58 of the TV series "Star Trek," "Spectre of the Gun," which first aired on October 25, 1968. "Spectre of the Gun" is one of the shoddiest portrayals of the Earp legend, a perfect example of an artistically and historically worthless production having remarkable value as a cultural artifact. For one thing, it was seen by more people than any Earp program ever broadcast on TV. The show's importance, though, is that it shows how deeply the Earp story and the gunfight in back of the O.K. Corral had become ingrained in the imagination of the American people.

The show begins with Captain Kirk (William Shatner), Mr. Spock (Leonard Nimoy) and the crew landing on a seemingly deserted planet—deserted except for the city of Tombstone, Arizona, in 1881. Though they wander around in their space-age uniforms, everyone keeps mistaking them for the Clantons, McLaurys, and Billy Claiborne. They soon have their first clash with the dreaded Earps, who hold the entire town in fear. ("There's Morgan Earp," they're warned, "the man who kills on sight.") None of the crew has a clue as to what is happening. At one point, a puzzled Spock stares at a Colt

.45 in the palm of his hand. "Careful, Spock," Kirk warns, "at close range those things can be as deadly as phasors."

Gradually, the Treksters discover what their audience knew from the beginning, that Kirk and the crew are being manipulated by a powerful being who controls the planet. Wishing to determine the intention of the earth visitors, the being probes the subconscious of their leader, Kirk, to find some incident relating to violence. Since Kirk's ancestors settled in Arizona late in the nineteenth century, the first thing the being finds floating around in his head is the gunfight at the O.K. Corral. The being then places the crew of the *Enterprise* in the center of a re-creation of that incident to test their response. The Earps are depicted as bullies who goad the Clantons and McLaurys into the fight.

"Star Trek" revealed that Wyatt Earp and the O.K. Corral had worked their way into America's collective unconscious. It's possible that if Kirk had been from Chicago the space being would have probed his psyche and found the St. Valentine's Day Massacre, and a Texan's would probably have been imprinted with the Alamo, but for most Americans the gunfight at the O.K. Corral had become the single most symbolic act of violence in American history.

Oddly enough, the "Star Trek" episode was not the first Wyatt Earp foray into science fiction. Ken Leibowitz, a New York collector of Earpiana, located a 1966 videotape of an episode of the British series "Dr. Who" entitled "Dr. Who and the Gunfighters." For those unfamiliar with the show (which was syndicated in the United States for several years), Dr. Who is a time traveler and historical investigator, somewhat in the manner of Dr. Peabody and Sherman of the old "Rocky and Bullwinkle" cartoon show. His stop in Tombstone, 1881, is an accident; returning to England in 1966 from somewhere in the past, he's suddenly overcome by a toothache and lands his time travel ship next to the O.K. Corral to look for a dentist. Doc Holliday (who was raised in Alabama) is trying to settle down and open up a respectable dental practice, but Johnny Ringo and the Clantons are after him because he killed the youngest Clanton brother, Reuben. Bat Masterson, the sheriff of Tombstone, and Wyatt Earp, the marshal of Tombstone, try to keep Doc and the Clantons apart while Dr. Who gets his tooth fixed. The doctor gets his tooth fixed and there's an ineptly staged shootout. What's fascinating about this atrociously acted and produced show—the production values make the "Star Trek" episode seem like *Titanic*—is that it was put together by people who seem to be unaware of the revelations in the Frank Waters's book or the negative images of Earp that were starting to crop up in American television and movies. What could the writer's sources have been? A tip-off is that Warren Earp shows up in Tombstone, in his first appearance in an Earp production, and his only one until Lawrence Kasdan's *Wyatt Earp* in 1994. The writer must have dipped into an old copy of *Frontier Marshal*, which was enormously popular in Britain, or more likely, one of the volumes on Earp for young readers that Stuart Lake put out in the 1950s as a companion to the Hugh O'Brian television series.

A more ambivalent attitude toward Earp is expressed in an episode from the Japanese cult cartoon series "Adventures of the Galaxy Rangers," written by American pop culture critic Henry Beck, which aired in 1987. The Rangers are a space version of Old West U.S. marshals, "bringing law to the new frontier." The Rangers' friend, a space prospector named Wildfire Cody Carson, is found in space, delirious from a virus that causes him to identify the Rangers' medical expert as "Doc Holliday" and threaten to shoot "any varmits named Clanton." "Doc Holliday?" says another Ranger, "who was that?" "I think he was a nineteenth-century American myth," the other replies. "Didn't they make a movie about him?" says another. "I think it starred Kirk Lancaster." "Naaw," comes a reply, "It was Henry Mature."

The Rangers' computer does a search and finds an aerial map of Tombstone in 1881. "There was a famous gunfight there," says a Ranger, "that involved the Earp brothers, the Clantons, and the McLaurys. It isn't clear who were the good guys and who were the bad guys." The Rangers' computer must have been searching in Captain Kirk's subconscious.

The Rangers and Wildfire Cody Carson finally prevail after a shootout in an intergalactic parking lot called, of course, the O.K. Corral. It would be interesting to see what Robert Warshow might have written about the relationship between Westerns and science fiction.

Ever since King Vidor's *Billy the Kid* in 1930 and *Law and Order* in 1932, Wyatt Earp movies seem to follow Billy the Kid movies, and

vice versa, almost if in response to what the previous film has had to
say about America's notions of freedom versus law and responsibility
to community versus loyalty to kin and clan. Howard Hughes's *The
Outlaw*, with Jack Beutel and Walter Huston, was made in 1943
(though released years later, due to the controversy over Jane Russell's cleavage), followed by *My Darling Clementine* in 1945. Earp
dominated the 1950s, hitting his peak of box office popularity with
Gunfight at the O.K. Corral in 1957, only to be followed by Arthur
Penn's quirky but compelling Billy saga, *The Left-Handed Gun*,
which featured Paul Newman in a role that might have been played
by James Dean had he not died in a car crash three years earlier.
Whatever its faults, Penn's film undermined the staid complacency
of Sturges's view of law and order with a Billy who responded to the
theme of revenge with uncontrollable neuroses and anarchic vicious-
ness. In early Earp movies, after the O.K. Corral there was a feeling
of triumph; in *The Left-Handed Gun*, when Pat Garrett shoots Billy,
an empty feeling akin to defeat is left behind. Lawmen like Earp,
Penn seems to be saying, may be able to bring law to a community,
but they can't create order.

Following *Hour of the Gun* (1967) and *Doc* (1970), Billy made a
comeback in *Dirty Little Billy* (1971) with Michael J. Pollard and
Sam Peckinpah's *Pat Garrett and Billy the Kid* (1973), which featured
a soundtrack by the ultimate counterculture icon, Bob Dylan (who
also had a part in the film). A line from one of Dylan's songs states
the film's point of view: "Billy, they don't want you to be so free." In
Peckinpah's film, "they" are the government and newly arrived businessmen, whose forces combine to impose law on a community
whether it wants it or not. The leading symbol of that law, dressed in
Wyatt Earp–black with a string tie and Earp's flat-brimmed sombrero, is James Coburn's Pat Garrett.

The 1980s was a quiet decade for Wyatt, but while Hollywood
made only a few Earp features, the hold he exercised on America's
collective movie imagination was as strong as ever. For instance,
David Mamet's script for *The Untouchables* (1989) has little to do
with the real Eliot Ness and everything to do with Wyatt Earp
movies. The real Ness played a minor part in Capone's downfall, but
in Brian DePalma's film he seems to be the only law enforcement
officer in the country out to get Capone. Like Earp, Ness is a federal
man and thus resented by the local constabulary. And like Earp,

Ness is eventually forced to take the law into his own hands– "I have become what I beheld and I am content that I have done right," says Costner. Kurt Russell in *Tombstone* says it a bit more forcibly: "You tell 'em the law is coming," he tells Ike Clanton, "You tell 'em *I'm* comin.' And hell's comin' with me." Think of Chicago as Tombstone, Ness as Earp, Sean Connery as Virgil, and Andy Garcia's ace shooter, Stone, as Doc Holliday. Illegal booze for cattle, the Canadian border for the Mexican border, the Mounties for Mexican police, Al Capone for Old Man Clanton or Curly Bill, the corrupt Irish police chief for John Behan, Frank Nitty for Johnny Ringo, the ambush of two of the Ness's deputies, played by Sean Connery and Charles Martin Smith, for the shootings of Virgil and Morgan, and the shootout at the train station for the gunfight at the O.K. Corral, and you practically have the plot to *Tombstone*. Ness's "posse" even rides horses in a clash with Capone's men near the Canadian border.

Incidentally, there are a number of curious parallels between Ness and Earp. Both became world famous through books that had their name on them but that were largely written by others, both were stars of hugely successful TV series; both were given credit for destroying enemies they didn't destroy; and both were played in movies by Kevin Costner. Curiously, *Frontier Marshal* is much closer to the historical facts than *The Untouchables*, but Ness has never come under the scrutiny of debunkers and remains a national hero.

At the end of the eighties, it was Billy's turn again to have the first word with *Young Guns* (1988) and an equally successful sequel, *Young Guns Two* (1990), starring Emilio Estevez and Keifer Sutherland. The "brat pack" approach to the Billy saga was in keeping with the times. In 1990 Hollywood remade the Lucky LucianoñMeyer Lansky story with *Mobsters*—some wags called it *Young Tommy Guns*—starring Christian Slater (who had also starred in the *Young Guns* films). A more thoughtful if somewhat duller treatment of the Billy the Kid legend, was rewritten in 1990 for TV by Gore Vidal, whose play had been the basis of the Paul Newman film in 1958. Val Kilmer, with specially fitted back teeth, gave what most aficionados regard as the ultimate Billy portrayal. Kilmer (who grew up in Arizona and New Mexico) would soon do the same for Doc Holliday. In 1993, Hollywood was ready for another go around with Wyatt Earp. Fueled, perhaps, by the national debates on law and order that followed in the wake of Rodney King's beating and the L.A. riots,

Hollywood reexamined the Earp story with two major movies, a TV film, and three documentaries. The films are of the most interest, as they were essentially the first big budget attempts to tell the real story and to try and deal with the seemingly contradictory facts of Wyatt Earp's life.

Dan Gordon, the scriptwriter for Michael Landon's "Highway to Heaven" TV series, wrote a lengthy script based heavily on the work of Glenn G. Boyer, the editor of the University of Arizona Press' version of Josephine's memoirs, *I Married Wyatt Earp*. (Whatever else may be said for the authenticity of the book, Boyer's work in getting Josephine's name out to the public was one of the major spurs in the Earp revival; from here on, Josephine's place would be next to Wyatt at the center of the Tombstone story.)

Gordon approached Kevin Costner with the script, and Costner, who had previously played such icons as Eliot Ness and Robin Hood, was interested. The initial idea was to do the script as a six-hour miniseries, which, given that the story took Wyatt from boyhood in Iowa to prospecting in Alaska, seemed a sensible idea. Meanwhile, Kevin Jarre, the talented screenwriter of the Civil War epic *Glory*, sold a script called *Tombstone* to Universal. (Jarre had contacted Costner with his script, but Costner was already developing the Gordon script.) Costner, it was widely reported, suggested to Universal that Jarre's script should be put in "turnaround" until he had completed the film *Water World* and could begin his own Earp movie. Since no one was likely to do another Earp movie after Kevin Costner had done one, this all but killed Jarre's movie. Jarre was not shy about complaining to the press about dirty tactics, and he was determined to go ahead with his movie with a new studio.

The Hollywood press was filled with tales that C.A.F., the powerful talent agency that Costner is affiliated with, shut out several actors sought by Jarre, and that costume companies couldn't take orders from Jarre's production because they were booked for the other Earp film. Regardless, Cinergi Productions (which distributes films through Disney Studio's adult division) picked up on the deal, and *Tombstone* lived again.

Jarre (who hired Jeff Morey as historical advisor) researched the period extensively and achieved unparalleled accuracy of detail in mustaches, clothes, guns (including long-barreled and nickel-plated weapons), and, especially, hats (which had a distinctively southwest-

ern flavor, particularly in the cavalier-style sombreros worn by Wyatt
and Doc). Some purists objected to putting Wild Bill Hickok-type
red sashes around the Cowboys, but this was surely an acceptable
exaggeration. (Stuart Lake, for one, described Cowboy garb almost
as a "uniform.") *Tombstone* looked and sounded like an independent
film. Jarre also became a student of the Earp legend, drawing not just
from Lake's *Frontier Marshal* but from such disparate sources as
Burns's *Tombstone* and Breakenridge's *Helldorado*, as well as numerous revealing newspaper accounts (such as the *Nugget's* account of
the gunfight) supplied by Morey and Bob Palmquist.

Jarre also assembled a sensational cast, perhaps the best ever for an
Earp movie, including Kurt Russell (whose father, Bing, a veteran
character actor, had played a bartender in *Gunfight at the O.K. Corral*) as Wyatt, Val Kilmer as Doc Holliday, Sam Elliott as Virgil, Bill
Paxton as Morgan, Powers Boothe as Curly Bill, Michael Biehn as
Ringo, Dana Delaney as Josephine, Terry O'Quinn as John Clum,
Stephen Lang as Ike Clanton, Jason Priestly as Billy Breakenridge,
and Charlton Heston as Henry Hooker. The result was a huge,
colorful, and exciting package that was wholly impractical as a two-
hour movie. Jarre was fired after six weeks by the producers for falling behind schedule. Action movie director George Cosmatos
(*Rambo*) was brought in to direct, though rumors had it that Russell
directed a few minutes of footage before Cosmatos arrived.

Tombstone's opening scene was supposed to have been the Skeleton
Canyon massacre with Robert Mitchum, as Old Man Clanton, leading the cowboys. Perhaps a half-hour into the film, Mitchum was
scheduled to die in a Mexican reprisal. Keeping old Man Clanton in
the film would have necessitated several additional scenes at an enormous cost, so Clanton Pere was written out. (Robert Mitchum survived as the narrator at the beginning and the end of the film.) The
opening scene was rewritten as a massacre of Mexican police with
Curly Bill as the leader. Several key characters found their parts
shortened or cut altogether, and Wyatt's Vendetta Ride was turned
into an orgy of slaughter with numerous faceless cowboys (by one
count, twenty-two) hitting the Arizona turf.

Many scenes cut from *Tombstone* popped up on TV cable specials
or on laser disc versions of the film and gave an indication of the epic
intentions of Jarre's concept. For instance, there were allusions to
previous Earp movies. Such as Kilmer's Doc Holliday leaving Joanna

Pacula's Kate to join Wyatt on the Vendetta Ride. "Well, dahlin'," he drawls, "have you no kind word to say before I ride away?" The line, of course, is from Frankie Lane's theme song from *Gunfight at the O.K. Corral*. In another scene, a wagon train led by Hugh O'Brian offers Russell and Kilmer food and shelter while they hunt Curly Bill.

While lamenting what didn't make it into *Tombstone*, it's worth noting how much did. *Tombstone* is the first and only Earp movie to be shot in the country where the events took place, the first movie to use young, vigorous actors as the principals, and the first to make Tombstone itself look exciting. *Tombstone* has about as much Earpiana as is possible to crame into a two-hour film: Doc Holliday's fight with Ed Bailey (which actually happened, if it happened, not in Arizona in 1879 but a couple of years earlier in Texas); lovely, meticulous re-creations of the Oriental Saloon and Bird Cage Theater (though the latter opened a couple of years after the scene in the film); and the best O.K. Corral walk to date (at one point, the four, all dressed in black, are outlined against a burning building, as if they had just walked out of hell). The gunfight, though longer and noisier than the historical one, incorporates such historical detail as Virgil waving his cane and saying "That's not what I want" and Ike Clanton fleeing from the fight. Jarre's period dialogue is distinctive and idiomatic. When an unarmed Wyatt faces down Johnny Tyler (Billy Bob Thornton) in the Oriental Saloon, he dares him to "Skin that smoke wagon"—go for that gun—"and see what happens." Puffing on a cigar, Wyatt calmly taunts Tyler: "No need to go heeled [armed] to get the bulge [edge] on a dub like you."

Jarre's was the first script to pair off Tombstone's natural enemies, Wyatt with Curly Bill and Doc with Ringo and in doing so he restored Curly Bill and John Ringo to their rightful places in the cowboy hierarchy. (In the Oriental a snickering Boothe tells Stephen Lang's Ike Clanton to "shut up" while he sizes up Wyatt.) Actually, Jarre gives them more than their due; following the old stories about Ringo ("a Hamlet among outlaws") from Burns, Ringo is given a classical education, and in one scene engages in dueling insults with Doc Holliday—in Latin.

At the heart of the film are Wyatt's relationships with Josephine and Doc, two rather important aspects of Earp's life that previous films left unexplored. Dana Delaney's Josephine is immediately established as the liberating influence on Russell's Wyatt, who up to that point in the film is convinced that he wants to live a normal family life ("It doesn't suit you," Delaney says). When she tells him her idea of paradise is "room service," a light seems to go on behind Russell's eyes. Wyatt also reveals his bond with Doc early in the film. He doesn't say, "He saved my life," which is the usual reason offered for their friendship. He says, "He makes me laugh." For his part, Doc has sworn lifelong fealty to Earp because, as Kilmer tells Buck Taylor's Turkey Creek Jack during a pause in the Vendetta Ride, "Wyatt Earp is my friend." "I've got a lot of friends," says Jack. "I don't," replies Doc.

Thin, pale, and red-eyed, Kilmer's Holliday seems to be sweating alcohol through his pores; he looks as if he has no soul left to trade with the devil. With his coat hanging over one shoulder like a cape, a cigarette hanging from his lower lip, Kilmer's Doc is a decadent cavalier. He goads his doppelganger, Johnny Ringo (Michael Biehn) with, "I'm ya huckleberry." To of Kilmer's most quoted lines from *Tombstone*— "I'm ya huckleberry" and "You're a daisy if you do"— were actually said by him. In Jarre's script, the word *daisy* becomes a skeleton key to understanding Doc.

Jarrre's Doc has one fear: that he'll die "with his boots off"—in bed. So he searches for the only death fitting for a cavalier, a fight. But his vanity won't let him lose a fight, so he's looking for his "daisy," someone who can beat him. "You're a daisy if you do," in this context, means "If you're good enough to do it, you're the one I've been searching for."

In the dramatic duel between Doc and Ringo, Doc outdraws Ringo, shoots him in the head, twirls his gun, and holsters it without losing his cigarette. Then he implores his foe to get off one last shot. "C'mon, Johnny, c'mon." In a dying spasm, Ringo manages one more pull of the trigger, misses, then collapse against an oak tree. "You're no daisy," hisses a disgusted Kilmer. "You're no daisy a'tall." A moment later, he's remorseful, not for killing Ringo but for making him party to his torment. "Ahm afraid the strain was moah than he could bayuh."

Word of mouth, particularly about Kilmer, helped make *Tombstone* a surprise hit with a rabid cult following. President Clinton asked to have it screened at the White House and praised it; basketball star Karl Malone enjoyed Kilmer's performance so much he sent him season tickets to Utah Jazz games.

Though Kilmer got most of the attention in *Tombstone*, the film's real revelation is Russell's portrayal of Wyatt Earp. For the first time in some two dozen features, Wyatt emerges as an interesting, fully faceted person. The range of Russell's performance is amazing. In his first scene he's livid with barely restrained rage at a railroad baggage handler who mistreats his horse; a moment later he's vacillating and weak with Mattie, unable to deal with or even comprehend her drug problem. (Russell is the first actor to dare show weakness behind Wyatt's icy façade.) With strangers and enemies, he's foreboding; with Doc and Bill Paxton's Morgan, he's relaxed and open. He's shrewd, too, allowing himself a half smile in the Oriental when a faro player asks him for his autograph. Russell's Wyatt doesn't mind a bit of celebrity if it brings customers to the faro table.

Kurt Russell and Val Kilmer, in their Edwardian frock coats and perfect period mustaches, fit the description of Wyatt and Doc by a Tombstone woman (quoted by John Myers in his 1950 book, *Tombstone, The Last Chance*) as "the two handsomest men I've ever seen."

Kevin Costner looks handsome, too, in *Wyatt Earp*" but he never seems to completely inhabit the role. At its best, *Tombstone* showed you why all of these characters become legends and why Wyatt Earp emerged as the most legendary of all. But *Wyatt Earp* piles so much history into three hours that there's never enough time to stop and explore the characters. Costner's Earp, almost driven mad in the first half hour by the loss of Urilla and their child, spends the next two and a half hours shutting people out of his life. The film leads one to wonder what makes Wyatt Earp tick instead of showing us. Even his relationships with Josephine (played by the stunning Joanna Going) and Doc (an emaciated Dennis Quaid, who lost forty pounds to play the role) barely effect his demeanor. Nothing much around him changes, either. When we get to Tombstone, about halfway through the film, it looks as if the set designers simply transplanted the same wooden shacks from Dodge into the southwest corner of Arizona. (The film was actually shot in flatter, more arid New Mexico.)

Wyatt Earp was a financial failure in the United States, despite grossing over $40 million. (Production costs were about three times that much.) But it was a substantial hit in Britain and other foreign markets, and as time passed it has accumulated defenders.

Historically, at least, it deserves high marks for fidelity. In 1923 Wyatt Earp had written to William S. Hart that "many wrong impressions of the early days in Tombstone and myself have been created by writers who are not informed correctly, and this has caused me a concern which I feel deeply." Wyatt would have had to admit that Gordon and Kasdan got much of the record straight in *Wyatt Earp*.

Wyatt was shrewd enough to realize that movies, rather than the printed word, would create a lasting impression of the kind he wanted to leave behind. "The screen," he wrote to Hart, "could do all this, I know, with yourself as the mastermind." Though it didn't happen in time for him to see his screen image, Wyatt Earp would have little cause, outside of historical accuracy, to complain about most of his screen depictions. Film critics, historians, and social critics would criticize Hollywood for more than sixty years for glossing over Wyatt Earp's story, but on the whole Hollywood got something right that writers would all too often get wrong: The movies, however much they oversimplified the story, didn't lose sight of who the good guys and bad guys were.

Notes

1. Numerous bizarre stories about Wyatt returning to Arizona and hunting down Warren's killer, a man named Boyett, have all taken their lead from the restyled version of Josephine's memoir *I Married Wyatt Earp*. But the story isn't in Josephine's original memoirs, and in any event it seems impossible for Wyatt to have traveled back to Arizona in the time specified. The story sounds too much like a weak version of the Ringo killing, and until a corroborating source is found, must be considered fiction.

2. Credit for transcribing all this fascinating material goes to a California researcher, Carl Chafin. For years, only Parsons's Tombstone journals were thought to be of interest in following Earp's life and career, but Chafin, who is self-publishing the later journals, has uncovered a wealth of information essential to the study of Wyatt's life.

3. Robert Palmquist suggests that this may not be an ordinary case, as the officer, a Patrolman Vanslow, was described in the newspaper story as a soldier not a policeman. Why a soldier was being used in a civilian peacekeeping situation isn't known, but it's possible that Wyatt and Nathan thought that Vanslow was over-

stepping his bounds in enforcing a D&D charge against a civilian in their saloon.

4. It's not clear what King meant here since the term "Bucking the Tiger" referred to faro, so called because the trademark of the company that made the cards was a tiger. "Only suckers buck the Tiger's odds," says Val Kilmer's Doc Holliday in *Tombstone*, "They're all on the house."

5. Jeff Morey points out that Garner is the only actor to have played a character named Wyatt Earp in two films; sticklers might also point out James Stewart played Earp in *Cheyenne Autumn* (1964) and a cartoon version of same as the "Law Dog" Wylie Burp in *An American Tale* (1992). Purists credit Richard Dix with three Earps, one "real" one in *Tombstone* (1942) and two in films loosely based on Earp. Real purists might insist that Hugh O'Brian takes the cake for having played Earp six times: in the 1950s TV series, in a cameo in the 1959 Bob Hope vehicle *Alias Jesse James*, in the early '90s TV series "Paradise," in the 1992 Kenny Rogers TV movie "The Gambler," and in the 1994 TV movie "Return to Tombstone" which featured footage from the '50s TV series. In the last one, O'Brian costarred with Bruce Boxleitner, who played Wyatt Earp in the 1983 TV movie "I Married Wyatt Earp."

6. From Borges's *An Introduction to American Literature*: "In contrast to the 'poesia gauchesco' (South American literature of the gaucho) which came into existence shortly after the revolution of 1810, the North American Western is a tardy and subordinate genre. One must admit, however, that it is a branch of the epic and that the brave and noble cowboy has become a worldwide symbol." The failure of the American western novel to rise above genre status, says Borges, is due to "the ethical preoccupation of North Americans, based on Protestantism, (which) has led them to present in the cowboy the triumph of good over evil. The gaucho of literary tradition is usually a man of cunning; the cowboy may well be a sheriff or a rancher. Both characters are now legendary. The motion picture has spread the myth of the cowboy throughout the world; oddly enough, Italy and Japan have taken up the production of western movies, which are quite alien to their history and culture." Joseph Campbell, for one, might dispute that the American westerner is alien to the history and culture of other nations; since every nation has had a frontier, one might argue that, contrary to Frederick Jackson Turner's famous essay on the significance of the frontier in American history, what is really different about America's frontier experience is that it happened last among the nations of the earth. Considered from this perspective, the universal popularity of the North American western figure could well be due to the fact that other nations see their own mythic past reflected in him. The only American writer of westerns Borges mentions is Zane Grey; one would be interested to know what he thought of

such nongeneric westerns as Thomas Berger's *Little Big Man*
(which deals with Custer and Crazy Horse, among others); Charles
Portis's *True Grit*; Ron Hansen's novel about Jesse James, *The As-
sassination of Jesse James by the Coward Robert Ford*; the Bill Doolin-
Dalton gang novel, *Desperadoes*; Pete Dexter's account of Wild Bill
Hickok's last days, *Deadwood*; Larry McMurtry's *Lonesome Dove*;
Cormac McCarthy's trilogy; or Michael Ondaatje's book-length
poem *The Collected Works of Billy the Kid*, which was inspired by
Walter Noble Burns's *The Saga of Billy the Kid*. For that matter, one
would like to know what Borges would think of Jack Schaefer's
Shane, a book much darker and finely shaded than the hugely pop-
ular film made from it. Borges, though, may have hit on the essential reason why Wyatt Earp, arguably the most famous of western
legends, has never been the subject of such highbrow attention by
American writers as Jesse James, Wild Bill Hickok, and Billy the
Kid. (William Burnett's *Law and Order* in 1931, though long out
of print, is probably the closest Wyatt's life has come to literature.)
If North American writers see the western primarily as a contest
between good and evil, they never truly have been able to decide
which side Wyatt Earp is on. Like the South American gaucho,
Wyatt Earp, at least when seen from a distance, appears primarily
as a man of cunning.

    7. Jeff Morey points out the peculiar movie connection between
movie Wyatt Earps and movie politicians. Walter Huston, the first
Earp, played Abraham Lincoln in D. W. Griffith's film bio, and,
later, the U.S. ambassador to Russia in *Mission to Moscow* (1943);
James Garner, who played Earp twice, was a fictitious U.S. president in *My Fellow Americans* (1996); Henry Fonda, who played
Earp in *My Darling Clementine* starred in *Young Mr. Lincoln*, also a
John Ford film, as well as a fictitious president in *Fail Safe* and a
presidential candidate in *The Best Man*; and James Stewart, Earp in
John Ford's *Cheyenne Autumn*, was a senator in *The Man Who Shot
Liberty Valance* and *Mr. Smith Goes to Washington*. Surprising as it
seems, Burt Lancaster never played an American politician, but he
did play Shimon Peres in *Victory at Entebbe* (1976). Gene Hack-
man, who played Wyatt's father, Nicholas, in the Kevin Costner
Wyatt Earp, played the president of the United States in Clint
Eastwood's *Absolute Power* (1997).

    8. Interestingly enough, those who worked with Ford were not
taken with the Earp myth, at least if we believe Ford's biographers.
Andrew Sinclair, for instance, quotes Ford's editor, Leon Selditz,
as saying "Ford would bend history. He would take an incident
and glorify it. Wyatt Earp wasn't the great hero Ford made him
out to be, and Holliday was never at the O.K. Corral. There were
only two Earps there and three Clantons. I once talked to the old
Tombstone guys who said there was no pistol shooting, only shotguns." One wonders whom "the old Tombstone guys" were; it's a
fair bet their names were all Uncle Ned. Pete Hamill must have

talked to the same old Tombstone guys—in his script for Frank
Perry's *Doc* (1971), the Earps and Holliday all walk down to the
corral armed with shotguns. Another Ford biographer, Tag Gallagher, must have bumped into the same old Tombstone crowd. In
his 1986 book, *John Ford—The Man and His Films*, Gallagher
writes: "Actually, Earp, Holliday and the Clantons were leagued in
a holdup racket; disagreements led to the O.K. Corral incident,
which was a massacre, not a battle; afterward, Wyatt and Holliday
quit town and the Clantons' bodies were left hanging in a butcher
shop." Compared to Gallagher's account, *My Darling Clementine* is
a model of historical accuracy.

9. Actually, four if one counts "Tombstone Territory," which
featured weekly stories that had been told in a newspaper, the
Tombstone Epitaph. Lake also had two Wyatt Earp comic book
series going at the same time, one which was published by Dell and
featured Hugh O'Brian on the cover and billed itself as the "Autho-
rized Edition." The other Earp comic was published by Charlton
Comics and was also a part of Lake's Wyatt Earp Enterprises. Of
the two, the Dell comic often drew upon Lake's *Frontier Marshal*
for material and thus had a shred of authenticity. The Charlton
Earp stories were much raunchier and wilder and bore roughly the
same resemblance to the Wyatt Earp of Walter Noble Burns and
Stuart Lake as Walt Disney's *Hercules* does to *Bullfinch's Mythology*.

10. Wyatt Earp Halloween outfits included black, flat-brimmed
sombreros—indistinguishable from the ones in the Zorro Halloween suits—a badge, and a fancy vest. When eight or nine I wore
one while trick or treating, and as I left a neighbor's front door I
heard an older woman in the house say, "My goodness, that boy is
dressed like a pimp." It took me years to figure out what she meant.

11. I have been unable to find out much about Richard
O'Connor, though his name popped up constantly in the research
for this book. Like many popular New York journalists of the 1940s
and '50s—James D. Horan, for instance, who wrote about Wyatt
Earp in several popular coffee table books in the late 1950s and
early '60s—O'Connor was a Civil War devotee. His biography of
Union general Phil Sheridan is currently in print in the Barnes and
Noble reprint series. I've also found a '50s reprint of a bio he wrote
of Wild Bill Hickok, but neither of these books carries any biographical information.

12. The caption for the movie poster read, "On a good day, he
might pistol-whip a drunk, shoot an unarmed man, bribe a politician, and get paid off by an outlaw. He was a U.S. marshal." It's
worth noting that *Doc*'s screenwriter is one of America's best
known liberal journalists, but his sentiments about U.S. marshals
would probably be echoed by the most rabid right-wing militia
member.

13. As far as I know, this is the first blatant use of a homosexual character in a Hollywood film about a legendary figure of the Old West. The next year, in *Warlock*, the Doc Holliday figure played by Anthony Quinn has secret yearnings for Fonda's character. But *Doc* is unique in indicating that Wyatt was homosexual and that his sexual frustration is what made him a sadistic, cold-blooded killer. One recalls Larry McMurtry's quip that the problem with cowboys is not that they're suppressed homosexuals but that they're "suppressed heterosexuals."

14. Loren Estelman used Clum in the same way in his 1987 novel *Bloody Season*. Any student of the Earp-Cowboy conflict quickly discovers that, whatever his excesses and shortcomings, Clum was a real journalist while Harry Woods of the *Nugget* was a shill for Johnny Behan and the Democratic party bosses. So, if Earp is to be exposed, Clum, the legitimate journalist, must be transformed into his enemy.

11

"When the Legend Becomes Fact, Print the Legend."

One night, not long after my search for traces of the Earp legend in my hometown, my daughter and I were at the final repository of American folk heroes, Toys R Us. With her help, I found two Earp-related items. First, a 120-piece O.K. Corral playset with which, presumably, six year olds can re-create the most famous gunfight in American history using whichever version of the battle suits them (perhaps a simplified version of the O.K. Corral inquest is included). The set, with parts manufactured in the United States, China, and Mexico, comes with a Texas flag—Texas stands for all of the American West. A dark-haired, mustachioed, two-gunned Wyatt is pictured on the box. Other playsets in the series feature legendary characters Paul Bunyan and Johnny Appleseed. I wonder if the people who created the toy thought Wyatt was a mythical character or that Johnny Appleseed and Paul Bunyan were real.

The other Earp item is a sinister looking doll in a long black coat and black, flat-brimmed sombrero. It's from a Frontier Heroes series, which also included Jesse James, Sitting Bull, Billy the Kid, Custer, Buffalo Bill, and Geronimo; there's also a deluxe set with Wyatt and his black horse, Dollar (I have found no mention of Dollar in my research). This Wyatt doll looks like a Sicilian bandit, not at all like the sandy-haired, clean shaven Hartland statue, purchased in 1960, that stood on a bookshelf in my father's library for years. (The statue is now worth about $300 even without its long-lost Buntline Special.) The darker, more threatening appearance reflects the change in Earp's image over the last forty years.

On the front of the box there's a picture of Wyatt and Buffalo Bill about to capture Billy the Kid, who, with a bandanna pulled over his face, is trying to make off with a bag that has "Bank" written on it. Here, finally, at Toys R Us in Livingston, New Jersey, the two most storied legends of the American Southwest meet at last. Wyatt Earp is capturing Billy the Kid—who never robbed a bank in his short life, by the way—with, of all things, a lasso, and with Buffalo Bill's help.

We found the Billy the Kid figure behind some Batman toys. The text on the back of the box proclaims Billy was "not so bad as history has taught." It seems he was "driven to criminality" by the Lincoln County war, which "consumed many lives." In the text on his box, Wyatt gets raked over the coals: "He served as a policeman in Dodge City, Kansas, where he became friends with two men: Doc Holliday and Bat Masterson. They formed the Earp gang and acquired a very bad reputation in Dodge City. . . . At the O.K. Corral, in Tombstone, Arizona Territory, he helped to kill three men, some witness call it murder. His brothers were shot in retaliation, and then, riding with Doc Holliday, he avenged them by taking the law into his own hands."

I decided I had to know who wrote this and where they got their information. I decided I had to know. I bought the figure (and, after thinking it over, the O.K. Corral playset).

The fractured rhythm of the text on the package suggested that its author either translated something from another language into English or wrote it himself trying to synthesize sources from popular books or Sunday supplement articles on the Old West—probably modern ones, judging from the negative tone, because almost everything written before the 1960s about Earp was positive, with the exception of a few texts available only to specialists. Was the trail to the writer still warm?

The print on the box said that the toy was manufactured in 1991 by a Canadian firm and, apparently, made in China. The company wasn't listed in the Ontario phone directory, but a letter to the area chamber of commerce produced the phone number. I called. A person with a French accent said hello. I asked her, "Could you help me, I'm trying to locate the guy, he's probably Chinese, who wrote the text on the back of your Legends of The West series . . ." I thought

I sounded like an idiot, but to my surprise the woman dug through the company's files and found the number to their Taiwanese supplier.

I had no idea what time it was in Taiwan, but I took my chances and called. Knowing no Chinese, I was mentally prepared for everything except what I got: a cheerful, talkative fellow named, I think, if I heard him right, Wang Tzu. It took me only a few seconds to identify the toy and just a few more to establish Mr. Tzu as the author of the text on the box. "I veddy great enthusiast of Amellican West," was the way it came to me through the static. (I regret that it sounds as if I am using Mr. Tzu's accent for comic effect; what I'm trying to convey is how difficult it was for me to make sense of what he was saying from seven thousand miles away on a bad connection.) But, he said, he had become "disarusioned with Wyuh Earp and Doc Horriday" as he grew older and read a book on the subject that told the truth. "What book," I asked, "disillusioned you?" A book, he replied, by the great "Austree-an writer, Thomas Keneree." This is as much as I could make out. We spoke pleasantly for a few more minutes, then I thanked him and said good-bye.

Thomas Keneree. Austrian. I did have a copy of a biography of Earp by a German author; could this possibly be the book that disillusioned Mr. Tzu? If so, the trail had gone cold: The book was written in German.

Three weeks later I saw a poster which advertised a reading from *Schindler's List* at Temple Beth-El in Livingston, about twenty minutes from my home, by its author, Thomas Keneally. While waiting for him to begin, I flipped through my copy of *Schindler's List* and saw, under Other Books by Thomas Keneally, a volume titled *The Place Where Souls Are Born—A Journey into the American Southwest*, a 1992 travel book. A light bulb went on: Could Mr. Tzu have said Australian Thomas Keneally?

After Keneally's reading, I waited around and asked him to autograph my copy of *Schindler's List*, and, by the way, did he know where I might obtain a copy of *The Places Where Souls Are Born*? "I'm working on a book about Wyatt Earp," I said, "and I'd like to get your impressions of Arizona." Keneally's eyebrows arched. "You're going to have fun with that fellow," he said. "You know, he wasn't what he seemed to be." I told him I'd already found that out. "I'll tell you what," he said, "I'll send you a copy of my book if you'll send me

some of your research. I'd love to know more about the fellow." It
was an easy deal to make. Two weeks later I received a copy of *The
Places Where Souls Are Born* and flipped to the entry on Tombstone.
Keneally wrote:

> Venal Wyatt Earp would later portray what happened at
> the O.K. Corral into a national reputation as the quintes-
> sential marshal, the unblinking avatar of order. In fact,
> when Wyatt with his two brothers and Doc Holliday en-
> countered the Clantons and McLourys near the O.K.
> Corral in late October 1881, Wyatt was merely deputy
> city marshal to his brother Virgil.
>
> Both parties to the shootout had earlier thrown accusa-
> tions of stagecoach robbery at each other, and both camps
> had a talk of grievances. The Clantons, for example, knew
> that Wyatt Earp had deliberately seduced their friend
> Sheriff John Behan's mistress. . . .
>
> There was a trial of the Earps and an acquittal, and
> there were reprisals. Virgil was crippled in one am-
> bush. . . . Morgan was shot dead in another. . . . In
> riposte, the Earps and Holliday shot two men they sus-
> pected of killing Morgan. But at last they were forced out
> of town by civic outrage and the force of firepower arrayed
> against them.

No wonder Mr. Tzu was disillusioned. I wasn't surprised even so
careful a writer as Thomas Keneally had garbled the facts of Wyatt
Earp's life, since nearly every book he would have had access to had
already garbled them. I was, however, curious to know the sources of
Keneally's account.

There was no bibliography in *The Place Where Souls Are Born*, but
in the book's acknowledgments, Frank Waters's *The Book of the Hopi*
was listed, so there was a clue. I called Keneally at the California
college where was teaching, and once again he was kind and full of
enthusiasm. Waters, he said, had indeed been the source for his
information on the Earps, though he neglected to mention the book
he had used in the acknowledgments. The book was *The Colorado*,
published in 1948, which contained the genesis of what would, in
1960, become *The Earp Brothers of Tombstone*. A book of dubious
credibility is read by an Australian author traveling through the

American Southwest; his book is used by a man in Taiwan writing text for the box of a toy manufactured by a Canadian firm to be bought by an unsuspecting child in a Livingston, New Jersey shopping mall.

Stories, facts, lies, rumors—all work their way into the great mainstream of legend by trails and back roads long forgotten by history. For instance, an important link in the Wyatt Earp legend begins with a remark Bat Masterson made sometime between 1905 and 1910. There are several versions of this anecdote, so we'll stick with the most colorful: Teddy Roosevelt and Bat were discussing one of their favorite subjects, the Old West, when Teddy remarked, "Bat, your own life has been so eventful. Why don't you put it down on paper?" The versions differ, but Bat's response is always the same, "Mr. President, the real story of the Old West can never be told unless Wyatt Earp will tell what he knows, and Wyatt will not talk."

Actually, it was Bat who wouldn't talk, at least about himself. God knows Bat Masterson had an autobiography to write. Masterson had done most of the things Wyatt had done and some that he hadn't. Bat fought Indians: He was a survivor of the harrowing Battle of Adobe Walls in the Texas panhandle, and helped to hold off hundreds of Commanche and Kiowa warriors, and had been an Indian scout under Gen. Nelson A. Miles. Bat had been a sheriff (of Ford County, Kansas), not a deputy like Wyatt. In his middle years Bat went East to New York and became a sports columnist. He wasn't a bad writer; his profiles of Wyatt Earp, Doc Holliday, Ben Thompson, Bill Tilghman, and other well-known frontier figures prompted the conversation with Roosevelt. If Bat Masterson had been of another mind in that legendary exchange with Roosevelt, our perception of the Old West would be transformed. At the very least, a couple of dozen Western movies would have had different titles. But Bat Masterson did what a great many people who knew Wyatt Earp did: He bowed to him.

This would prove to be ironic, since Bat contributed more to Wyatt Earp's legend than his famous profile. Bat couldn't know it at the time, but through a man named Stuart Lake Bat would lend a major part of his own story to Wyatt's. Bat Masterson was Wyatt Earp, that is, a part of Bat became a part of the legendary figure we now know as Wyatt Earp. When *Wyatt Earp, Frontier Marshal* was published in 1931, two years after Earp's death, many of the significant passages were either paraphrases of things Bat had written or exaggerations of things he had said about his own life. Much of the first-person information on buffalo hunting, gunfighting techniques, and the difficult craft of "lawing" that the book attributed to Wyatt originated with Bat Masterson.

In 1921, when Bat died of a heart attack while sitting in front of his typewriter, he was one of the most famous men in America, much more famous than Wyatt. Roosevelt had liked Masterson enormously; he and other Old West lawmen such as Bill Tilghman and Billy the Kid's slayer, Pat Garrett, had visited the presidential mansion so often they were referred to collectively as the White House gunfighters. Forty years after his death, Bat Masterson had become a footnote to the legend of Wyatt Earp. By the 1950s, Earp's name recognition outstripped Bat's by at least two to one. Today, it's probably closer to ten to one. Because Bat Masterson himself thought Wyatt Earp's story was more worthy of immortality than his own.

No one knows whether or not Bat actually said that "The real story of the Old West can never be told unless Wyatt Earp tells what he knows," but evidently he said something very much like it, and Stuart Nathaniel Lake heard it. Lake was to invent a great many stories about Wyatt Earp, but it's doubtful he invented the quote from Bat. Stuart Lake wasn't a liar, he was a press agent.

Born in Rome, New York, and a graduate of Cornell University, Lake was, like many writers of best-selling books on the West from 1920 to '70, a veteran of Eastern newspapers (in his case the *New York Morning Herald*). Lake knew Bat Masterson well, and it was probably through him that Lake came to know Teddy Roosevelt, for whom he served as press agent during the 1916 Preparedness campaign. Later, he sustained a leg injury in the First World War and never fully recovered. After the war, looking for an occupation less strenuous than beat reporter, Lake moved to southern California. Sometime in the mid-twenties, Lake, by way of the Arizona Historical Society, succeeded in tracking Wyatt down and asked him if he'd be interested in a book on his life. Lake found that, as Bat had said, Earp would not talk. No matter; when the time came, Stuart Lake would talk for him.

In 1931, nearly half a century after what would come to be called the Gunfight at the O.K. Corral, *Wyatt Earp, Frontier Marshal* was published. The book was an immediate best-seller as well as a critical success. Reviewer Florence Finch Kelly wrote in *The New York Times* that the "situation [Earp faced in Tombstone appears to have been not unlike Chicago's predicament, to say nothing of New York's, and what both those cities need seems to be a few Wyatt Earps." *Frontier Marshal* received enormous national attention through serialization in the *Saturday Evening Post*. Whether or not Lake wrote Frontier Marshal with Hollywood in mind, the book was made to order for a western movie industry that was played out on outlaws such as Jesse James and Billy the Kid. The era of the bootlegger with its machine gun battles in big city streets had taken the glamour out of outlaws for many Americans; but, as early as 1925, some intellectuals, such as John Hays Hammond in Scribner's, were wondering if the FBI wasn't in need of some "Strong Men of the West" such as "Wyatt Earp and Wild Bill Hickok." Hollywood had an opening, as it were, for a lawman. There wasn't much in Wild Bill's record as a lawman to draw on, and no popular biographies of the great frontier peace officers such as Bill Tilghman and Oklahoma lawman Chris Madsen. Lake's book came along at just the right time to fill a need.

Wyatt Earp's story began just as the West of Hickok and Bill Cody, the West of frontiersmen and buffalo-covered plains, was giving way to that of the gunfighter and cattle towns. The movie audience was hungry for some new heroes. Lake gave westerns a modern hero, one who dressed not in buckskins but in white shirts and long black coats—not like a frontier cavalier, but more like a banker. Movie audiences looked to Wild Bill Hickok with his long flowing locks and red sash and two ivory-handled Colts and idolized him, but they could never fantasize being him. Wyatt Earp looked like someone who the average man, at the right time or under the right circumstances, could conceivably have been.

Stuart Lake, it has been said many times over the last half century, did a lot for Wyatt Earp. That is debatable, and Wyatt Earp, had he known what was to come, would have been the first to debate it. Earp has been branded as an opportunist and a self-publicist for allowing Lake to write the book that became *Frontier Marshal*, an odd criticism when one considers that nearly every important figure of the Old West, including Davy Crockett, William Cody, Wild Bill Hickok, George Armstrong Custer, Pat Garrett, Tom Horn, Elfago

Baca, former outlaws John Wesley Hardin, Emmitt Dalton, Frank James, and Cole Younger, and even Geronimo had either written books or lent their names to ghosted autobiographies. The criticism is even stranger when put beside the fact that his enemies had already published their accounts of the controversies in which Earp had been involved.

Earp had tried on two previous occasions to put his story into print. The first, early in 1920, involved Forrestine Hooker, the daughter-in-law of the Arizona rancher, Henry Hooker, who be-friended Wyatt during his war with cattle rustlers in 1882. The book was begun and abandoned. Why it was abandoned isn't known, but a good guess can be made as to why it was begun: The surviving manuscript pages are practically a line-for-line response to articles in the *Saturday Evening Post* by Frederick R. Bechdolt in which Wyatt and his brother were portrayed as the instigators of much of the Tombstone trouble of the early 1880s. (Bechdolt's primary source of information was William Breakenridge.) It wasn't Bechdolt's inten-tion to defame Earp; he merely related the only version of the story that surviving Tombstonians were giving. Still, Bechdolt's stories in-furiated Wyatt—once again he thought he had outlived the gunfight only to see it rise up again for all to see—and he wanted to reach the public with his version of the story.

A couple of years later Wyatt tried again with a friend and confi-dante named John Flood. Flood served Wyatt and his wife for years as an unpaid social secretary; he was a mining engineer by trade and a terrible writer. Despite the aid of Wyatt's good friend, William S. Hart, the most popular western film star of the silent era, the Flood manuscript never saw print.

A close reading of the Hooker and Flood texts suggests that Wyatt simply was not the right kind of man to be attempting an autobiogra-phy; he revealed almost nothing about his personal life and failed to correct even basic errors about his family and background. Earp wasn't seeking fame from an autobiography (though he certainly wouldn't have minded fortune). He wanted vindication, what he regarded as justice—the facts as he remembered them permanently recorded.

John Flood had one advantage not granted to Stuart Lake: Wy-att's cooperation. If Earp wasn't talkative, he at least gave Flood firsthand information. When Lake first approached Wyatt in 1928,

Earp put him off, telling him that he owed his loyalty to John Flood; he stayed loyal until it was obvious that Flood's manuscript would never sell. But Earp was no more willing to talk with Lake about many of the key people and events of his life in 1928 than he had been years earlier with John Flood, and, at now seventy-nine, he was unable to remember important facts and dates. In a letter written ten years after the publication of *Frontier Marshal* Lake admitted, "As a matter of cold fact, Wyatt never dictated a word to me. I spent hours and days and weeks with him—and I wish you could see my notes! I had to pump him for all the details. He knew information, but none of which he handed out in any sort of narrative form."

So much for the extensive quotes from Wyatt that comprise about a third of the book's content. "Possibly it was a form of cheating," Lake would later admit, more than a little disingenuously, "but when I came to the task I decided to employ the direct quotation form sufficiently often to achieve my purpose. I've often wondered if I did not overdo in this respect."

In his defense, Lake had spent time with Wyatt, interviewed him, and took good conversational notes. He made judicious use of Forrestine Hooker's and John Flood's manuscripts as well as a wealth of tall tales and legends he had heard over the years from Bat Masterson. He also did more firsthand research than he has been given credit for, contacting scores of people who knew Wyatt in Wichita, Dodge City, and Tombstone. Several months after Wyatt's death, Lake attended a reunion of old-timers in Dodge City where he picked up notebooks full of old stories. One of the most important, which he repeated in a letter to Josephine, was that "Wyatt Earp was one peace officer who could not be swayed from any course he thought was right." This became one of the recurring themes of *Frontier Marshal.*

When Stuart Lake first spoke to Wyatt about a collaboration, he promised that his intention was not to write a "blood-and-thunder yarn; I am turning out history, one man's contribution to the development of our frontier." But hampered by limited cooperation from Wyatt, and, after his death, unrelenting harassment from Josephine (who feared revelations about Mattie Earp and about her relationship with John Behan), Lake became, in effect, a novelist. He projected Wyatt in the heroic mold of Wild Bill Hickok (whose own story had also been overblown, in the manner of Davy Crockett before him), making Earp the heir to Hickok's title of Prince of the Pistoleers. To flesh out Wyatt's years in buffalo camps and cow towns he grafted what he knew of Bat Masterson's life—and he had more firsthand knowledge of Masterson's than of Earp's—and possibly the life of Wyatt and Bat's friend and Dodge City colleague Bill Tilghman, who lived until 1924 and who Lake knew through both Bat and Teddy Roosevelt. He probably added some color from the life of Pat Garrett, who, like Bat, corresponded with Teddy Roosevelt. The result was less a biography of Wyatt Earp than a mythic projection of Wyatt Earp, one that has practically come to symbolize, to the average American and, finally, to the rest of the world, the West itself. ("The real story of the Old West cannot be told unless Wyatt Earp tells it . . .")

Stuart Lake could not have done Wyatt Earp's legend more good; he could not have done the man more harm. Sixty-six years later historians are still judging Wyatt Earp not by his own achievements or by the standards of lawmen in his own time and place but by the absurdly unrealistic ideals of the saintly Hollywood characters derived from Lake's book: Henry Fonda in *My Darling Clementine*, Burt Lancaster in *Gunfight at the O.K. Corral*, and Hugh O'Brian in "The Life and Legend of Wyatt Earp"—to name just the three most popular incarnations of the Wyatt Earp that owe their existence to Stuart Lake.

That the historic Wyatt Earp has fallen short of people's expectations has hurt not only Wyatt's reputation but Stuart Lake's as well, which is a shame, because in some ways Lake the reporter did a good job. For instance, Lake, or John Flood through Lake, is almost our only source of knowledge about Wyatt's early years in the railroad and buffalo camps—there were no newspapers—as well as his early stint as a lawman in Wichita, Kansas. Lake discovered a great deal of information and used much of it, albeit in a garbled form, since primary sources were often contradictory or unreliable. And, of course, where the fact had become legend, he printed the legend.

Stuart Lake knew there was more to certain aspects of Wyatt Earp's story than Wyatt and Josephine wanted to tell, most of it concerning Wyatt's women, particularly "Tombstone's Helen of Troy," the cause of hostility between Wyatt Earp and Sheriff John Behan. Lake, concluding his research in 1930, actually thought Josie to be in the center: "Johnny Behan," he wrote his editor, "was a notorious 'chaser' and a free spender making lots of money. He persuaded the beautiful Sadie to leave the honky-tonk and set her up as his 'girl,' after which she was known as Sadie Behan." And: "In back of all the fighting, the killing, and even Wyatt's duty as a peace officer, the impelling force of his destiny was the nature of his acquisition and association in the case of John Behan's girl. That relationship is the key to the whole yarn of Tombstone. Should I or should I not leave that key unturned?" Lake decided, mostly because Josie threatened to sue, to leave it unturned. Josephine succeeded in keeping herself (and Mattie) out of Wyatt's story—for a couple of decades, at least.

Josephine Marcus's importance to this story extends beyond her personal charms. Her memoirs, unpublished in her own lifetime, are one of the most important sources we have on Wyatt's private life. Without them, it's likely that interest in Wyatt Earp would have faded by the 1960s. Josephine's story is what spurred the new Earp movies in the 1990s; not only is she a fascinating new character in what was thought to be an old story, her presence adds a much-needed human element to Wyatt's character. The difficulty—that is, the difficulty beyond Josie's bias—is that we can't be absolutely sure which memoir best represents what Josephine Earp really saw and remembered. *I Married Wyatt Earp—The Recollections of Josephine Sarah Marcus Earp*, currently in print from the University of Arizona Press, is the text quoted in virtually everything written on Wyatt Earp in the last two decades—Paula Mitchell Marks's *And Die in the West* relies heavily on it—but it varies widely from the so-called Cason manuscript, the raw text of which Josie worked on from 1936 to her death in 1944 with two of Wyatt's relatives, sisters Mabel Earp Cason and Vinolia Earp Ackerman. (The Cason manuscript isn't available in a library, but numerous collectors can be found who will loan copies.)

In the afterward to *I Married Wyatt Earp*, Glenn Boyer, who edited the book, says he spent years "merging" the Cason manuscript with an earlier manuscript that Josie had begun with the aid of John P. Clum in Tombstone at the start of the silver boom (the public has no access to this manuscript, which is in a private collection). The two manuscripts, Boyer says, "contained vastly different materials presented in widely varying styles. . . . To establish a conversational standard for the combined first person narrative, I interviewed and corresponded with many people who were intimately associated in life with Wyatt and Josie. . . . From directions and clues picked up from such informants, I was able to arrive at a vocabulary and syntax that closely approximated the speech of the living Earps."

Without questioning Boyer's dedication, the researcher who wants to come fresh to the task of weaving through this maze can't help but wish that for access to the first manuscript. Boyer has greatly confused matters by claiming at one time or another that Jack London and even Dashiell Hammett worked on the manuscript, and while this book was in preparation he told a reporter for he *Tucson Star* that the original manuscripts were lost in "a messy divorce settlement." In lieu of further evidence, what we have in *I Married Wyatt Earp* is a novel with footnotes and with vocabulary and syntax altered to fit Boyer's conception, however informed, of what Josephine, Wyatt, and others might have said.

Fortunately, we have less muddled versions of numerous other important sources. John P. Clum's *It All Happened in Tombstone*, was published during his lifetime and, thanks to the work of Douglas Martin in the 1950s and the more recent research of Jeff Morey, Bob Palmquist, and Carl Chafin, we have a reasonably complete collection of the Epitaph issues printed by Clum. Some of the diary of George Parsons, the most important and objective Tombstone observer, was printed while he was still alive, and Carl Chafin has done yeoman work in transcribing the remaining volumes. We also have the newspaper dispatches of Clara Brown, who has been curiously ignored by modern historians who might be expected to include an educated woman's perspective on Old Tombstone. But then, that woman's perspective is decidedly pro-Earp, unlike that of most historians of the last two decades.

Clara Brown, John Clum, Josephine Marcus, George Parsons, and, to a lesser extent, the rancher Henry Hooker could all be called pro-Earp witnesses, as their view of what happened in Tombstone pretty much agreed with Wyatt's. Weighed against them we have the existing newspaper files of the *Tombstone Daily Nugget*, the leading "anti" Earp paper of Tombstone, and the so-called O.K. Corral inquest, or at least those parts of the testimony given by John Behan, Ike Clanton, and other Earp enemies. Modern readers familiar with the largely critical image of Wyatt Earp and his brothers may be surprised to find, as was the author of this book, that the *Nugget* files and the O.K. Corral inquest provide virtually the only sources of anti-Earp material to be written until the controversial events of 1882. In fact, if we go back to before the gunfight in October 1881, the only existing source of anti-Earp material is the *Nugget*. All other anti-Earp accounts, Billy Breakenridge's *Helldorado*, the memoirs of Judge Hancock, the alleged memoirs of Allie Earp—come forty-seven or more years after the actual events. It can, and has, been argued that any or all of Earp's witnesses might be biased, but it must be asked if Earp's friends and supporters are less credible than John Behan and Harry Woods, who controlled the Nugget, or Ike Clanton.

Modern readers may also be surprised to find that there is so much documentation concerning a man who is now generally regarded as having been relatively unknown in his own lifetime. How famous was Wyatt Earp until *Frontier Marshal* was published in 1931? Did Stuart Lake "create" him? In his chapter for the 1991 book, *Past Imperfect—History According to the Movies*, John Mack Faragher pretty much sums up the prevailing opinion among current historians: "Earp, unlike other frontier legends in their own time, was a minor figure until a popular writer named Stuart Lake concocted a legend for him. In 1931, Lake published *Wyatt Earp, Frontier Marshal*, which featured a hero who single-handedly cleaned up the worst frontier hellholes. This book subsequently became the authority for nearly all the film portraits of Earp."

Faragher, as we have seen, is correct that Lake (and possibly Wyatt himself) exaggerated Earp's cow town exploits. But the now popular idea that Earp was virtual unknown till a "popular writer named Stuart Lake" chose to write about doesn't hold up to scrutiny. Lake didn't create Wyatt's fame, he revived it, and he wasn't the first to try. There had already been two widely discussed books on Earp in the few years before *Frontier Marshal*: Walter Noble Burns's *Tombstone*, published in 1927, and Billy Breakenridge's *Helldorado*, published in 1928, both, ironically, written with Earp's cooperation. As we have noted, *Helldorado* is a strange book in that it is generally regarded as an anti-Earp tract but nonetheless has served as one of the building blocks of Wyatt's legend. The best evidence of Earp's fame, though, is the very fact of the book's having been: Why debunk a legend if it's not a legend?[1]

Both *Helldorado* and *Tombstone* confirm that Wyatt Earp was very well known in the years in which he was a law man and for quite a while afterward. Earp wasn't famous in 1879, when he came to Tombstone, but he had a reputation. John Clum wrote that "The Earp brothers—tall, gaunt, intrepid—caused considerable comment when they first arrived, particularly because of Wyatt's reputation as a peace officer in Dodge City, Kansas. All the cattle rustlers in Kansas, Colorado, New Mexico, and western Texas knew—and feared— Wyatt Earp." Corroboration for this, as we have seen, comes from the Texas cowboy Andy Adams, whose 1903 book confirms how respected the Kansas officers were. The subsequent events in Tombstone were written about in papers from coast to coast: *The New York Times* gave the "Streetfight in Tombstone" (as the gunfight at the O.K. Corral was then called) feature status in its October 28, 1881, issue. As we've seen, Wyatt's Vendetta Ride to avenge the shootings of his brothers was covered eagerly by newspapers all over the West and parts of the East. *Harper's Weekly, the Police Gazette, The Saturday Evening Post,* and *Scribner's* magazine featured stories on Earp, not all of them favorable, and Clara Brown's dispatches on Tombstone had been run in many West Coast newspapers.

In 1896, Wyatt sat for an interview for a reporter from the *San Francisco Examiner* that was printed by all the major western papers and some in the East. Later that year he received much unwanted publicity by ending the Ruby Bob Fitzsimmons—Tom Sharkey fight on a foul call. Numerous papers printed cartoons and caricatures of the gun totin' marshal from Arizona: Unknowns don't get caricatured. Of course, there was Bat Masterson's profile, a piece that gained a wider audience when reprinted in the book *Famous Gunfighters of the Western Frontier.*

Tom Mix and William S. Hart knew Wyatt well; so did Jack London, John Ford, and Raoul Walsh. In his autobiography, Jack Dempsey swears that he recalls Wyatt and Bat in the crowd at one of his fights. When Wyatt's father, Nicholas, died in 1907, the *Los Angeles Times* referred to him as "father of the noted 'Earp boys'." When Wyatt Earp died in Los Angeles in 1929, his obituary appeared in The New York Times.

In truth, the trail from fact to legend to myth was no different for Wyatt Earp than for any frontier legend. What is different about Earp's case is that the attainment of legendary status came later than it did for the others—Wyatt Earp could be called the last of the frontier legends. And since it came so late, we actually have a chance to see the process of mythmaking at work.

In his recent study of Wild Bill Hickok's legend, *Wild Bill—The Man and the Myth*, British historian Joseph G. Rosa notes that prior to a highly colored 1867 profile in *Harper's New Monthly* magazine,

> Hickok had spent much of the period between 1861 and 1866 in parts of Missouri and Arkansas. He was well known in Rolla and Springfield as a wagonmaster and government scout. Some folks remembered him because of a recent gunfight, while others, particularly those who worked with him during the war, remembered his exploits behind enemy lines. And there were some who were appalled that his deeds should receive national attention. . . .
>
> Initial reaction from the press was very mixed. On February 11, the *Atchison Champion* recalled that "Bill was formerly a driver on the Overland Stage Line, and is well known to many old residents of this city. Few, however, would recognize him in the romantic picture Nichols draws.

This wasn't terribly dissimilar to the evolution of Wyatt's legend. Hickok was well known in the border states where most of his Civil War and Indian fighting exploits took place, just as Wyatt Earp would later be in the Southwest. Most people who knew him in his own time didn't think of Hickok as a candidate for immortality, but to his peers, to many of the hunters and scouts Nichols spoke to, Hickok fit the picture of the ideal frontiersman: "Whenever I had met an officer or soldier who had served in the Southwest," Nichols wrote in *Harper's*, "I heard of Wild Bill and his exploits, until the stories became so frequent and of such an extraordinary character as quite to outstrip personal knowledge of adventure by camp and field; and the hero of these strange tales took shape in my mind as did Jack the Giant Killer or Sinbad the Sailor in childhood's day." Nichols exaggerated and possibly invented much about Hickok; the people who Nichols talked to probably exaggerated their stories, too. But all of them saw in Hickok's deeds something worth exaggerating. The only essential difference between what Nichols (and to a lesser ex-

tent, Ned Buntline) did for Hickok's legend and what Stuart Lake
did for Earp's is that Lake did it sixty-four years later. Or stated
another way, all frontier legends were minor figures—or local heroes,
if you will—until some writer pulled their legend together and made
them famous.

Viewed from a modern perspective, the argument could be made
that Earp's legend was built on more solid ground than any of his
contemporaries'. Hickok, for instance, hadn't been featured in any
books or national magazines before Nichols made him famous. Wyatt Earp, on the other hand, was riding a wave that was starting to
crest years before Stuart Lake began work on *Frontier Marshal.* In
1927, Walter Noble Burns wrote the second most important book, in
some ways the most important, in the Earp pantheon. *Tombstone—
An Iliad of the Southwest* gathered together all the existing legends
and stories about Wyatt and Virgil Earp, Doc Holliday, the Clanton
and McLaury brothers, and John Ringo, for the first time placing all
the major characters in the Tombstone drama right in the center of
the Old West mythology, a position they have occupied ever since.

Tombstone has been out of print for decades, and Burns is forgotten today, though in his own time he was one of America's most
respected crime reporters. (His last book, *The One-Way Ride*, was
about Jake Lingle, the Chicago reporter killed by the Capone mob.)
His name survives in revivals of the classic Ben Hecht—Charles
MacArthur newspaper comedy, *The Front Page.* Burns's obit in the
Chicago Tribune suggests that the character of the unscrupulous
newspaper editor Walter Burns was a composite of Chicago Tribune
editor Walter Howey and Walter Noble Burns.

Burns was apparently a bit unscrupulous. In 1926 he approached
Earp about collaborating on an autobiography, but was turned down
because Wyatt was working with John Flood. Burns then asked Earp
for an interview, claiming to be writing a book about Doc Holliday.
After talking to Wyatt several times—he may have spent more time
interviewing Earp than did either John Flood or Stuart Lake—and
spending several months in Arizona poking through old newspapers
and talking to old pioneers, Burns produced *Tombstone*, a book which
chronicled the town's legends up to the 1890s but which was dominated by Wyatt Earp. We don't know what Burns' real intentions
were because we don't have most of his papers; it's a well-known tale
among Earp researchers that several boxes of Burns's papers were

stolen from the special collections of the University of Arizona and are now in the hands of a private collector. If Burns did start out to write a book on Holliday, he soon found out what every writer before and since discovered about the glory years of Tombstone, which is that such stories inevitably tilt in the direction of Wyatt Earp.

Walter Burns was no stranger to the Old West. Two years before *Tombstone* he had written one of the most influential western books of all time, *The Saga of Billy the Kid*, which rekindled interest in a man who, like Wyatt Earp, had suffered through a period of neglect. Billy, thanks to hundreds of silly dime-store novels written after his death in 1881, had been more famous before the turn of the century than Wyatt. But the Kid had been largely forgotten by the 1920s, so much so that in 1925, Harvey Ferguson, writing for H. L. Mencken's *American Mercury* magazine, began an essay with: "Who remembers Billy the Kid?" Many still did, but mostly southwesterners. In about two decades, Billy's status had dropped from national to local hero, back to where it had been about the time of the Lincoln County wars that spawned him. Burns went to New Mexico to seek out the old-timers and record their stories about Billy. *The Saga of Billy the Kid* has since been knocked full of holes as history, but as a work of American folklore it has had enormous impact, serving as the inspiration for a score of movies, a play (*The Left-Handed Gun*) by Gore Vidal, a ballet by Aaron Copeland, and even a book-length poem by novelist Michael Ondaatje.

That the legends of Billy the Kid and Wyatt Earp should be revived by the same man is fitting, since the stories of Billy and Wyatt are the two great parallel legends of the American West, sometimes reflecting on each other, sometimes contrasting, often threatening to meet but never quite doing so. (Wyatt and Billy might have crossed paths in Wichita, Kansas, when Billy was a young boy and Wyatt beginning his career as a lawman; Billy also worked briefly for Wyatt's friend Henry Hooker in Arizona.) There are many similarities between the Lincoln County war of New Mexico and the Earp-cowboy feud in Arizona, which was going on at the same time, the principal one being the tenacity of the blood feuds that developed out of a tangle of economic and political interests. Both legends involved revenge killings; Earp's image was forever tarnished by vengeance, while Billy's was enhanced by it. The bullet from Pat Garrett's gun made Billy immortal; Wyatt Earp's mythical power has derived in part from never having been hit by a bullet. Despite numerous revisions by creditable historians like Robert Utley and Frederick Nolan, Burns's original view of Billy still has enormous power.

For American intellectuals, Billy will always remain the "wronged outlaw"—a "resistance gunfighter" in the words of modern historian Richard Maxwell Brown—driven to misdeeds by the forces of civilization (that is, capitalism) that had been closing in on him all of his young life. To Billy's sympathizers, particularly intellectuals, lawmen like Wyatt Earp will always signify the corrupt (or at least compromised) hired guns who hunted down the Billy the Kids—Wyatt was an "incorporation gunfighter," in Brown's term. As poet Charles Olsen phrased it in one of his Billy the Kid poems, "Wyatt Earp . . . was . . . nothing but a company cop." Gradually, in the eyes of Earp's critics and debunkers, the Arizona cattle rustlers Earp feuded with—the Clantons, the McLaurys, Billy Claiborne, Johnny Ringo, Curly Bill Brocius, and the rest—have assumed the same heroic wronged-outlaw status as Billy. (The Kid was considered a hero by the Arizona cowboys. Billy Claiborne even called himself Billy the Kid, some say after the one in New Mexico.)

The idea of using Billy and Wyatt as symbols of opposing economic forces on the frontier derives from Walter Noble Burns, but Burns's books are important for at least one other reason: He was the first writer to see Earp and Holliday and Billy the Kid, the figures of the Old West we are most interested in today, as part of a new American mythology. (As his subtitle, *An Iliad of the Southwest*, suggests, he peppered his work with classical allusions.) He was much less judgmental than the generation of writers that followed him. Burns didn't take sides with Wyatt in his struggle against the Clantons, Curly Bill, and John Ringo, nor with Billy in his attempt to evade Pat Garrett. What Burns wanted was for people to see all the participants in the Southwest struggle, even such a minor legend as John Ringo, as heroic. Today Burns is often lumped together with Stuart Lake as a writer of fiction who glorified Wyatt Earp, but this charge is made by writers who haven't read Tombstone. Here is Burns's farewell to "the lion of Tombstone" as he rides out of Tombstone for the last time:

So hail and farewell to the lion of Tombstone. Strong, bold, forceful, picturesque was this fighter of the old frontier. Some-thing epic in him. Fashioned in Homeric mould. In his way, a hero. Whatever else he may have been, he was brave. Not even his enemies have sought to deny his splendid courage. The problems of his dangerous and difficult situation, he solved, whether wisely or foolishly, with largeness of soul and utter fearlessness. No halo is for this rugged, storm-beaten head.

The epitaph is, by today's standards, overwritten but in seventy-one years no one has bettered it. Wyatt himself was enraged when Burns' book came out, as it would hurt his chances of getting the Flood manuscript published, but one wonders what he secretly thought of this passage.

By 1931 Wyatt Earp had been dead for two years and his life had already been re-invented several times. Audiences in the 1920s and '30s wanted heroes, especially western heroes, who wore halos. Stuart Lake gave them one, and so won the sweepstakes as the creator of the Wyatt Earp story.[2]

Wyatt Earp lived long enough to see his life reinvented several times in print. One wonders what he'd have thought of Stuart Lake's incarnation; one really wonders what his reaction would have been to what Hollywood would so to his story.

Notes

1. Wyatt was particularly miffed at *Helldorado* because he had generously given his time to Breakenridge in recalling names, dates, and details of events. Why Wyatt would have helped Breakenridge in the first place remains a mystery, but he seems to have been happy just to see another old Arizonian around. Albert Behan, John's son, was disgusted with his dad's former deputy: "Breakenridge and I don't have any trouble," Josephine quotes him as saying, "but I've always known that he was two-faced." We may assume this is true, because Josephine would not have quoted Albert in her memoirs without his knowledge and permission. "Poor Billy Breakenridge," Josephine wrote, "should I condemn him for the character flaws that nature gave him? Should one be held responsible for one's inherent weakness?" Presumably, Josephine meant Billy's

weakness in not standing up to Behan and the Cowboys in Tombstone.

"I just can't understand him," Earp wrote to Stuart Lake after the publication of *Helldorado*. "As he always of late years seemed friendly towards me." Earp thought Billy had nursed a grudge because when "Behan and his so-called brave men came to arrest me, I just laughed at them and told them to just run away. And he held that against me." Breakenridge, of course, had been one of Behan's "brave men."

Earp was so upset that he wrote to Breakenridge's cowriter, William McCloud Raine. Raine replied to Earp that he hadn't researched the story himself, he just took Breakenridge's word as true. The same could be said for many subsequent historians.

Jeff Morey, my chief historical consultant, suggests that I expand on three other sources of anti-Earp literature. Eugene Cunningham's *Triggernometry-A Gallery of Gunfighters* first published in 1941 and still in print, is an entertaining and informative debunking book when it deals with numerous western outlaws and lawmen. The material on Wyatt Earp, however, all supplied by Billy Breakenridge (and swallowed whole by Cunningham) is mostly the product of the sometimes deputy sheriff's fertile imagination. Many of the points about Earp made by Breakenridge were things he told to other researchers or wrote about himself, and I've dealt with all the important ones.

Ed Bartholomew's two part biography, *Wyatt Earp The Untold Story* (1963) and *The Man and The Myth* (1964) are best summed up by historian Paul Hutton, who commented, "Bartholomew exposed an almost pathological hatred of his subject. Why anyone would spend years researching and writing a biography of someone they so intensely despised is perhaps worthy of psychological exploration . . ." That's the way Wyatt Earp affects some people. I find Bartholomew's books miserably written and Bartholomew's reputation as a researcher to be vastly overrated. Bartholomew did find a lot of important newspaper items and documents, but when he found them he didn't always know what to make of them and was often downright misleading in his interpretation. On several occasions, when I was able to locate his primary sources, I did not at all come to the same conclusion as as he did (particularly when he uses his own magazine articles as sources). Bartholomew is the spiritual father of the "grudge" books on Earp one sees on sale in Tombstone bookstores.

And, then, there is the Earp section of Ramon F. Adams' Old West debunking book, *Burrs Under The Saddle*, the follow-up to his *Six Guns and Saddle Leather*, books that have had much more influence than Cunningham's and Bartholomew's because they are still being consulted in libraries all across the country. Like his friend, Ed Bartholomew, Adams has a reputation as a researcher that, at least as it relates to Earp, is undeserved. For all I know his comments on the veracity of books on Jesse James and Butch Cassidy may be entirely accurate, but on the subject of Wyatt Earp, Mr.

Adams was either a liar or very dense. It is one thing to denounce Stuart Lake's excesses, but it's quite another to call the O.K. Corral fight "a case of murder, the shooting of men while their hands were up." Adams surely read the O.K. Corral transcript and knows that not a single non-partisan witness said the Earps shot the Cowboys while their hands were up, so all I can conclude is that Ramon Adams had an agenda concerning Wyatt Earp that he didn't let evidence get in the way of. The rest of his comments on Earp are of a piece with the item quoted.

2. Walter Noble Burns made a significant contribution to American culture with *The Saga of Billy the Kid, Tombstone,* and *Robin Hood of El Dorado,* yet I have been able to find out almost nothing about his life; all his personal notes and letters vanished with the papers stolen from the Arizona Historical Society. None of the many reprints of his books carry any biographical information. A *Who's Who of American Writers* published in 1932 indicates that he worked for papers in several states, most notably St. Louis and Chicago, and that he lived in Texas for a few years. His *Chicago Tribune* obit suggests that he knew Ben Hecht, but little else. Burns's life and how he came to write his most popular books would be a great subject for some enterprising literary detective.

It's possible, even likely, that Burns would have made a comeback had he not died in 1932, a year after *Frontier Marshal* was published. His enormously popular *Robin Hood of El Dorado* was published posthumously in 1932 and later made into a film starring Warren Baxter. Burns did much to keep the memory of the California bandit alive and may have inspired the Nobel Prizewinning Chilean poet Pablo Neruda's *The Splendor and Death of Joaquin Murieta* as Burns's earlier Billy the Kid book inspired Michael Ondaatje. Murieta still lives; in the popular 1998 film *The Mask of Zorro,* Murieta is slain by Capt. Harrison Love. The American ranger who is reputed to have killed Murieta and displayed his head in a jar was a California ranger named Capt. Harry Love and his brother goes on to become the next Zorro, thus uniting the two great heroes of old Hispanic California.

Burns appears to have gotten most of his ideas for books from Frederick R. Bechdolt, whose *Saturday Evening Post* stories, as we've noted, angered Wyatt so much that he decided to attempt an autobiography. Bechdolt wasn't much of a writer, but his 1922 collection of magazine pieces, *When the West Was Young,* contains chapters on Joaquin Murieta, Wyatt Earp, John Ringo, and Texas John Slaughter, as well as some passing mention of Billy the Kid, all of whom were to appear later in books by Burns. In his acknowledgments, Bechdolt credits "Colonel William Breakenridge," which is probably where Burns saw his name for the first time.

12

Wyatt Redux

You're a legend a lot longer than you're fact.

—CLYDE EDGERTON

A sk an American, ask anyone around the world, to name a real
person from the Old West, and the overwhelming odds are they
would answer, "Wyatt Earp." Might that change someday? No one
can say, of course. But Wyatt Earp has already been a household
word for quite a while. For the sake of argument, let's say that Earp
has only been famous, nationally famous, since Stuart Lake's book
was published in 1931. How many Americans who were famous in
1931 are as well known today as Wyatt Earp? Babe Ruth, of course,
and maybe Lou Gehrig. Al Capone, Charles Lindbergh, and Charlie
Chaplin have kept their fame, but not many others. Jack Dempsey
was certainly one of the best known Americans in 1931; Herbert
Hoover was president. Do more American now know the name Wyatt Earp than Jack Dempsey or Herbert Hoover? I'd bet on Wyatt
Earp.

Try the question another way: How many Americans who came to
prominence after the Civil War were as famous in the 1930s as
Wyatt Earp? Teddy Roosevelt, certainly, and Mark Twain, but not
too many more. Whatever the future holds for Wyatt Earp, his fame
is still fairy solid nearly 150 years after his birth.

Why did the myth-making process single out Wyatt Earp? Why
does he continue to be the one legend of the American frontier who
is constantly discussed, debunked, and revived? And why does he
remain contemporary when his peers, more famous in their own

time, have slipped back to the status of regional heroes or been forgotten altogether?

The most obvious answer is that everyone knows his name because of the television series and the dozens of movies in which he
has been portrayed in some form. Since World War II, he has been
portrayed more times than any other frontier figure, and, thanks to
cable TV, Wyatt Earp is practically ubiquitous. Scarcely a week goes
by without a Wyatt Earp popping up on TV—in a movie, TV movie,
or some documentary or biography. No doubt the success of *Tombstone* in 1994 and the wide distribution of Kevin Costner's *Wyatt
Earp* later the same year did much to revive interest in Earp, but by
the time those films were released there hadn't been a feature film
about Wyatt in more than a quarter century, (I'm excluding *Sunset*,
the 1988 comedy about Earp in Hollywood), and before *Tombstone*
the last popular Earp movie was *Gunfight at the O.K. Corral* in 1957.
More time has passed from that film to now than passed between the
first Earp movie, *Law and Order* (1932) and *Gunfight at the O.K.
Corral*. There have been numerous Earp films and TV shows between 1957 and *Tombstone*, but they merely reflected Wyatt's legend
rather than adding to it.

Still, the plethora of movies and TV shows about Wyatt Earp
doesn't answer the original question: Why keep making movies
about Wyatt Earp? Why not revive some other Old West legend?

Many would say that Earp's fame is due to his genius as a self-
promoter, referring to *Wyatt Earp, Frontier Marshal*, the biggest selling biography of an Old West legend ever printed. But every frontier
legend wrote a book or lent their name to one, and most of them had
more to do with their books than Wyatt Earp did. Well, his critics
would say, if it wasn't Wyatt Earp who made Wyatt Earp immortal,
it was Stuart Lake. There is something to this; including the 1995
Pocket Books edition, *Frontier Marshal* has now gone through seven
hard cover and nine paperback reprints and may have sold as many as
7 million copies worldwide. But this gives Stuart Lake all the credit
for Earp's legend when, as we have seen, Wyatt was already featured
in several books and national magazine articles (including a book by
one of his enemies) before the huge success of *Frontier Marshal* in
1931. Besides, the most recent films and articles about Earp are
largely concerned with aspects of Earp's story that Lake missed in his
colorful book.

Still others would say that the reason for Wyatt Earp's enduring fame is that he lived so long into the twentieth century, outlasting his friends and enemies. But Wyatt didn't outlive all his enemies, not Billy Breakenridge or Allie Earp, both of whom damaged his reputation but had no effect at all on his fame. Besides, longevity is no guarantee of immortality. Frank James and Cole Younger were as famous, or as infamous, as Jesse James in their train-robbing days. Frank and Cole outlived Jesse by more than thirty years, wrote best-selling books, and influenced the subsequent movies on their lives. They even hosted a touring Wild West carnival. Frank James and Cole Younger were among the most famous men in America when they died during World War I, yet, today, Jesse is the one everyone remembers.

It has been said that Wyatt Earp was the first real-life Western figure to be portrayed in a great and popular film. This is probably true. John Ford gave Wyatt's story a definitive boost with *My Darling Clementine*; no other notable figure of the Old West, not even Wild Bill Hickok, got such a break. But Wyatt had already been the star of several films when *My Darling Clementine* was released in 1946; Ford's film wasn't the first—in fact, at least part of it was remade from the *Frontier Marshal* script—just the best. And Burns and Lake's books had already been read by millions before any films were made.

Maybe, some have argued, it's some quality in the sound of his name: Wy-ut Erp. It sounds like a lawman's name, much more so than, say, Bill Tilghman, or even Virgil Earp. It's hard to imagine the theme song from the 1950s TV series reshaped for Virgil; "Virgil Earp, Vir-gil Earp . . ." No, it doesn't work. But Wild Bill Hickok and Bat Masterson do work, and Wyatt's fame, in our time, has eclipsed theirs.

In recent years it has become fashionable to say that the gunfight at the O.K. Corral made Wyatt Earp famous. This can't be denied. As the silly "Star Trek" episode, "Spectre of the Gun" illustrated, the streetfight in Tombstone touched something in America's collective unconscious. Whenever showdowns or confrontations are thought to be epic, Americans will always refer to the gunfight at the O.K. Corral and Wyatt Earp. O.K. Corral—you hear it once, you don't forget it. But, as we've seen, the gunfight wasn't at the corral but in back of it, and the clash didn't become regularly identified as the

Gunfight At The O.K. Corral until the 1950s. "Gunfight At The O.K. Corral" doesn't appear at all in early Earp literature—it's usually called "the streetfight in Tombstone." The fight didn't become legend because of a catchy name; the catchy name finally attached itself to the fight several decades after it became legend. *Law and Order* holds the fight at the "O.K. Barn," which sounds like something out of a comedy routine. In the 1941 *Tombstone*, the fight erupts in the street outside the corral. Finally, in 1946, Walter Brennan's Old Man Clanton in *My Darling Clementine* challenges Henry Fonda's Wyatt Earp: "We'll be waitin' for you, Marshal, down at the O.K. Corral." But it wasn't till *Gunfight at the O.K. Corral*, in 1957, that a film identifies the gunfight, absolutely, as the Gunfight At The O.K. Corral. And by then Wyatt Earp had been a household name for a quarter of a century.

Consideration, of course, must be given to Wyatt's own prowess as a peace officer. Wyatt Earp was a first-rate lawman in two of the West's most celebrated cattle towns, Wichita and Dodge City, in their heydays. But he was one of several fine lawmen in Dodge, and only western buffs remember the names of the others today. Wyatt also served as a lawman in the most fabled of mining camps, Tombstone, Arizona, but it was his brother Virgil who was town marshal there.

No doubt, too, that Wyatt's personal characteristics added to his legend. At a time and place where cold courage counted for much, everyone conceded that Wyatt Earp stood out. "Thirty-five years ago," wrote Bat Masterson in one of the most florid passages in his 1907 profile, "that immense stretch of territory extending from the Missouri River west to the Pacific Ocean, and from the Brazos River in Texas north to the Red Cloud agency in Dakota, knew no braver or desperate man than Wyatt Earp." Bat regarded him as "absolutely destitute of physical fear," which a close reading of the record supports. But the same could be said for some other well-known figures of the frontier. The great Oklahoma lawmen Chris Madsen and Heck Thomas were both exceptionally courageous men, and no one has ever made a movie about their lives.

For instance, Billy the Kid's conqueror, Pat Garrett, is one of several frontier lawmen who have been advanced by Old West historians as a candidate for the position Wyatt occupies. Some of Garrett's biographers, particularly the popular historian Leon Metz, have all declared Garrett to be an honest lawman and a first-rate sheriff, while dismissing Earp simply as a gambler and adventurer. Garrett (who was also a gambler, by the way) had a career in lawing much longer than Earp's, but aside from the bloody aftermath of New Mexico's Lincoln County war, Garrett isn't of much interest to us today. Some believe that the bad feeling directed to Garrett for killing the Kid kept him from getting his due, and there is much to this. The same hostility was directed at Earp for killing Arizona "cowboys." But Wyatt Earp is still controversial, while scarcely anyone today really holds Billy the Kid's "murder" against Pat Garrett, as many did during his lifetime, and, thanks to Hollywood, for some time afterward. (Some time in the 1950s, John Nance Garner, vice president under Franklin D. Roosevelt, wrote to Garrett's son, Oscar, that "your father was an honest, patriotic American. When the movies slander him, they slander their betters.") But though Pat Garrett added much to the color of the turbulent New Mexico years, he is not compelling apart from Billy. In the early 1960s Garrett (played by Barry Sullivan) was the star of his own TV series, "The Tall Man." In 1973, Sam Peckinpah gave him equal billing with Billy the Kid in *Pat Garrett and Billy the Kid*. Pat Garrett had his shot, and he didn't stick, except as part of the legend of the man he killed. Wyatt Earp, in contrast, dominates all the characters in his story. We remember them today primarily because of their association with Wyatt Earp.

If fame was awarded on the basis of merit alone, Bill Tilghman would be first in line. A buffalo hunting companion of Wyatt's youth and his colleague on the Dodge City (Ford County) police force, Tilghman had a long and distinguished career in lawing long after Earp quit the ranks. His pursuit of and eventual destruction of Bill Doolin and the Dalton gang is a classic chapter of American folklore, celebrated in movies and in music by the rock group, the Eagles. But Tilghman's name is almost unknown today except to readers of *True West* magazine. Younger than Earp, he missed most of the action in Wichita and Dodge and never made it to the great mining camps such as Deadwood and Tombstone that might have made him famous. Bill Tilghman's problem is that he didn't become truly interesting till after the classic period of the West had passed.

What of the larger satellites in the Wyatt Earp legend? Do they deserve elevation? Every few years someone puts forth a new argument that Virgil Earp, Doc Holliday, or Bat Masterson is more worthy of our attention than Wyatt. Doc Holliday certainly was more flamboyant than Wyatt, and closer to the classic western gun- fighter mold. But though Doc wasn't guilty of most of the sins his accusers have pinned on him, his legend just doesn't clean up well enough to replace Wyatt's. There are too many senseless fights and shooting scrapes—Doc seems to have been too close to crossing over to the wrong side of the law. And no matter how important he was to the events in Tombstone, the most interesting thing about Doc Holliday is that he was a man who didn't care if he lived or died but nonetheless felt a near fanatical loyalty to Wyatt Earp. This is really why we remember Doc's name today, and to realize this makes us think less about Doc and more about what kind of man Wyatt Earp was to inspire such loyalty.

Deciding why history chose Wyatt over his older brother Virgil is a little tougher. After all, it was Virgil, not Wyatt, who came to town wearing the U.S. deputy marshal's badge. As Virgil's biographer, Don Chaput, has pointed out, it was Virgil who made most of the decisions on the fateful afternoon of October 26, 1881. Allie Earp had reason to hold a grudge: In movies and on TV it's Wyatt who runs the show, while her husband, Virgil, is Wyatt's deputy, and in every movie, even the ones that debunk Wyatt, he gets to lead the procession down to the O.K. Corral. Wyatt's legend has absorbed Virgil.

Yet, while giving Virgil his due, Wyatt is by far the more interest- ing figure. Wyatt went to Tombstone with a reputation acquired in the Kansas cow towns; it was Wyatt who was in the fabled posse that rode down the killer of Dora Hand; It was Wyatt, always Wyatt, who was the focus of cowboy hostility in Arizona—they saw him as the truly dangerous one. (Remember that Billy Breakenridge made Wyatt the focal point of the Tombstone war three years before Lake wrote *Frontier Marshal*, and the purpose of Breakenridge's book was to attack Wyatt.) Wyatt was the one the beautiful Josephine Marcus left John Behan for. Wyatt was the only participant to emerge un- scathed from the O.K. Corral fight. Was that entirely luck? In truth, Virgil seems a bit comical walking into the most famous gunfight in history waving a cane. (Wyatt had his right hand where it should have been: on his gun butt.) And it was Wyatt who, rightly or wrongly, made the Vendetta Ride after Virgil was crippled and Morgan was murdered.

What of Bat Masterson, who contributed so much to Earp's legend, who could have had the fame Wyatt now enjoys? The truth is that Bat didn't want it; he deferred to Wyatt Earp. If Bat Masterson had stayed in Tombstone a little longer, he might have qualified for Wyatt's status anyway. But Bat made the mistake of leaving Tombstone, the place where legends were being made, and then leaving the West altogether for the life of a New York celebrity. (If he had stayed in Tombstone longer, the Earps' position might have been too strong; hostilities would never have broken out.) Bat chose the East. Americans do not look East for their frontier heroes.

The greatest irony of Wyatt Earp's afterlife is that it was his enemies who kept him famous. The postwar symbol of American law and order played by Henry Fonda, Ronald Reagan, Hugh O'Brian, George Montgomery, Joel McCrea, and Burt Lancaster was ultimately too one-dimensional to have survived. Wyatt's debunkers made him much more interesting, placing him at the center of controversies that, in their modern manifestations, are as lively today as they were 120 years ago. Many frontier heroes, from Davy Crockett to General Custer, were debunked in the iconoclastic 1960s, but only Wyatt Earp came under fire from both the right and left. Frank Waters's *The Earp Brothers of Tombstone* in 1960 set the standard for the left. Waters saw Earp as a symbol of "the juggernaut of conquest"—slaughtering buffalo, spoiling the Plains, "creating a materialistic ideology utterly opposed to the indigenously American and original Indian concept that all matter has a spiritual essence." Waters sought to expose what he saw as the lie of the heart of America's frontier myth by exposing the "lie" of Wyatt Earp. It never occurred to him that in doing so he was adding to Earp's stature by placing him at the center of the myth.

On the right, two Texas historians, Ed Bartholomew and Ramon Adams, regarded with abhorrence everything they saw the Earps as representing. With their federal badges, mining interests, and Wells Fargo association—not to mention their fondness for gun control—the Earp brothers were symbols of the Republican Eastern industrialists who some westerners have always seen as their nemesis. It was primarily from these three men, with an assist from Billy Breakenridge, that the Wyatt Earp bogeyman—bully, sadist, hypocrite, stage robber, bigamist, pimp, homosexual, predator, and killer—grew. Authors as diverse as Pete Hamill and science fiction writer Lee Cronin carried the negative image of Wyatt Earp to larger audiences. And, since no hero can ever live up to his legend, to many the repudiated image will always be truer than the original. As the years passed, of course, it became increasingly difficult to say what the original image was.

In time, after Tombstone's decline, the friends and allies of the Earps were gone, leaving only the descendants of the small local ranchers to tell the story. In their eyes, the ranchers-rustlers took on the aspect of heroes—almost of freedom fighters, as Jesse and Frank James were and are still seen by many Missourians. Historians irritated by the romantic excesses of Stuart Lake's Wyatt Earp are more and more willing to extend sympathy to common cattle thieves such as the Clantons and McLaurys and John Ringo while the Earps, "point-men" for the forces of exploitation, are subjected to modern standards in legal ethics, class, and sexual behavior.

This was especially true after the 1960s. Prior to that time, most academic Western historians followed the lead of Frederick Jackson Turner, who, in his hugely influential speech delivered at the World's Columbian Exposition (Chicago World's Fair of 1893), expounded on "The Significance of the Frontier in American History." Turner's thesis can be gleaned from the essay's title: He believed the existence of the frontier to be the most important element in the shaping of the American character. Most historians today reject Turner's thesis, though it is still a hotly debated question. But one aspect of Turner's thesis that became increasingly repellent to historians in the 1960s was his stress on the importance of the rugged frontier individualist over that of the group or community in shaping the West. Old-fashioned pioneer individualism was increasingly seen as the source of racism, sexism, and violence in modern American life.

The Wyatt Earp reinvented by Stuart Lake was the ideal target for debunking. In 1931 a literary scholar named Percy Boynton pinpointed America's growing fascination with the West in his book, *The Rediscovery of the Frontier.* Many writers, said Boynton, "were world weary and war weary, turning to the West to celebrate the passage of a heroic age and applauding in that remote setting men and events that could be duplicated in very dramatic detail by the gangsters of the nearest big city." The depression, thought Boynton, ushered in an era of cultural nationalism, and with it, a flood of popular books on the Old West. The most popular such book on the Old West in 1931 was Stuart Lake's *Frontier Marshal*.

When the reaction to the heroic view of the West became the dominant theme—the title of Patricia Nelson Limerick's influential 1987 book, *The Legacy of Conquest*, is a blatant example—Wyatt Earp was reinvented again as a symbol of what had gone wrong in the shaping of our national character.

Among those who didn't hold a progressive view of America's past, there was an equally convenient symbol of Wyatt Earp to despise. The never-ending quarrel over who had legal jurisdiction in Tombstone—John Behan's County Sheriff's Office or Virgil Earp's combination of town marshal and federal badges—echoes in the recent phenomenon of Western counties declaring sovereignty over federal lands. This debate may be new, but it is powered by sentiments that go back to a time when the Western states were still territories. As an anti-Earp historian said to me on an Arizona radio show, "You can draw a straight line from the Earps' walk to the O.K. Corral to the FBI's storming of the Branch Davidian compound." (I don't know that the historian's remarks were pro-Branch Davidian, but I'm pretty sure they were anti-FBI.) The Earps would have been surprised to find they had become the symbols of anything, and more astonished to find that Wyatt was the leading symbol.

In the end, it's not important that all the heroic exploits of Wyatt Earp actually happened—though many of them did. What is important is that Wyatt Earp was the man with the right qualities in the right age in the right time to become the stuff of legends. Looking back on his story, both supporters and debunkers would see elements of tragedy both American (family loyalty, innocence, ambition) and classical (pride, blood feuds, revenge). The worshipful TV shows and movies, and the heroic children books of my own youth, were like the idealized ballads and poems that were written for heroes of earlier ages—and surely those heroes, had we known their real stories, would now seem flawed to us as well.

The Wyatt Earp who survives in our cultural memory today is a composite character assembled from the biographies of Bat Masterson, Virgil Earp, Wild Bill Hickok, and others, but the core of the Wyatt Earp legend is Wyatt himself. On their own, none of the other characters in the Earp story command our attention for long. Placed alongside Wyatt Earp, they seem endlessly interesting.

The brief interlude between savagery and civilization on the Western Plains that continues to fascinate us lasted roughly from the end of the Civil War to perhaps the surrender of Geronimo in 1887. This is precisely the period of Wyatt's prime years, and the environment called for the talents and characteristics—courage, loyalty, nerve—that, in the eyes of his contemporaries, Wyatt possessed in abundance. They are not necessarily qualities that are called for, and hence not best appreciated, in more settled times and places, but those who possessed them are the ones we look back to in moments of national stress, either for inspiration or circumspection.

History and Hollywood have had plenty of time to seek other symbols of America's frontier past to mold into icons, to debunk, to read their ideological assumptions into: They keep coming back to Wyatt Earp. He rides on the eternally unsettled territory of our national consciousness, as if still on his Vendetta Ride looking for Curly Bill and Johnny Ringo. When another eruption of violence fuels our ongoing debate over law and order, he will be back, reinvented in exactly what way, as enforcer of the law or avenger, we cannot now say. But he will be back.

Bibliography

A note on some of the materials referred to in this book:

Printed material on Wyatt Earp, if brought together, would fill a small library. Unfortunately, many of the most important documents are either out of print or in the hands of private collectors. While Earp remains the focus of much debate, such important documents as the memoirs of Josephine Marcus and Wyatt's first attempts at telling his story, the Hooker and Flood manuscripts, are unavailable to the interested reader even in annotated university press editions.

Unfortunately, much of what is in print about Earp is either bogus or highly questionable. One of the purposes of this book is to steer the general interest reader through the swamp of misinformation which continues to surround Earp and his associates, which means coming to terms with the work of Glenn G. Boyer. After four years of consideration, my conclusion is that the major works of Boyer, *I Married Wyatt Earp* and *Wyatt Earp's Tombstone Vendetta* (Talei Publisher, Inc. 1993) are historically worthless. I say this despite the fact that I am in close agreement with most of Boyer's opinions regarding Earp's life and legend. But this isn't a question of agreement of opinion, it's a question of historical veracity. Boyer's Earp books are supposedly based on legitimate historical documents, but those documents have never been examined by nonpartisan researchers and in recent years have been more and more questioned by researchers all over the country. This means, by extension, that I regard the works which rely heavily on Boyer's material, such as Paula Mitchell Marks' *And Die In The West: The Story of the O.K. Corral Gunfight*, and the recently published *Doc Holliday: A Family Portrait* by Karen Holliday Tanner (University of Oklahoma, 1998) to be—there is no other word to use here—tainted.

As work on this book was being completed, Boyer told a Tucson journalist that the document which could legitimatize *I Married Wyatt Earp*, the so-called Colyn manuscript mentioned in the University of Arizona Press edition, had been lost years ago in "a bitter divorce settlement." This contradicts numerous remarks Boyer has made about the existence of the document (or documents), which he "merged" with the Cason manuscript to produce his book. After two years of trying, I have yet to find anyone who has seen this manuscript or documents, including the staff at the University of Arizona Press, which originally published (and currently publishes) *I Married Wyatt Earp*. That the University of Arizona Press continues to print this book as valid history without having verified its sources makes for dubious credibility at best.

Boyer's other recent Earp book, *Wyatt Earp's Tombstone Vendetta*, has been called by its author "a non-fiction novel" which purports to tell the inside story of what happened in Tombstone, but nonfiction novels such as Truman Capote's *In Cold Blood* are derived from documents which are a matter of public record. The "mountain of previously unknown facts" about Earp promised in the book's foreword were provided by "informants who placed restraints on what I could say, and in some cases forbade quoting them by name." In that case, Boyer's book must forfeit all claims to history and must simply be considered another novel.

An example of the mischief caused by this kind of I-have-better-primary-sources-than-you-but-I-can't-reveal-them approach to history is the dilemma posed by Ms. Tanner's *Doc Holliday: A Family Portrait*. Ms. Tanner, in a phone interview, told me that she had rejected the Cason manuscript as a source because she thought Josephine Marcus Earp to be an unreliable historical witness. This may be true to an extent, but Josephine Marcus' memoirs are surely no more questionable a historical source than numerous other sources, particularly Billy Breakenridge's or Frank Waters' books and the memoirs of Judge Hancock and John Pleasant Gray, which are listed among her sources. Ms. Tanner, like many who have been influenced by Boyer, has painted herself into a corner: since it's difficult to reconcile the Cason manuscript with *I Married Wyatt Earp*, the historian has to make a decision as to which he or she will put faith in. Ms. Tanner has chosen *I Married Wyatt Earp*, presumably because it contains material on Doc's adventures in Tombstone, whereas the entire Tombstone section of the Cason manuscript is either missing or was never written. But by relying so much on a source that is doubtful at best, she has undermined the creditability of her own work.

All of this being said, I have reluctantly chosen to quote some passages from *I Married Wyatt Earp* in my book. My subject is the evolution of a legend, and Boyer has had a great deal of access to family members and friends of Earp, and some of the stories he had put into the mouth of Josephine Earp *might* be as true as the ones Stuart Lake put into Wyatt Earp's. I present the passages for what they are worth in the context of the story, and in the interests of including diverse points of view. As the late, great Satchell Paige said, you pays your money and you takes your choice.

Books

Adams, Andy. *The Log of a Cowboy.* Boston: Houghton Mifflin Co., 1903.

Bartholomew, Ed. *Wyatt Earp, 1848 to 1880, the Untold Story.* Toyahville: Frontier Book Co., 1963.

Bechdolt, Frederick R. *When the West Was Young.* New York: The Century Co., 1922.

Boyer, Glenn G. *An Illustrated Life of Doc Holliday.* Glenwood Springs: The Reminder Publishing Co., 1966.

————. compiler and editor, *I Married Wyatt Earp: The Recollections of Josephine Sarah Marcus Earp.* Tucson: University of Arizona Press, 1976.

————. *The Suppressed Murder of Wyatt Earp.* San Antonio: Naylor Co., 1976.

Brown, Richard Maxwell. *No Duty To Retreat—Violence and Values in American History and Society.* New York: Oxford University Press, 1991.

Breakenridge, William M. (ghostwritten by William MacLeod Raine). *Helldorado: Bringing Law to the Mesquite.* Boston: Houghton Mifflin Co., 1928.

Burns, Walter Noble. *Tombstone: An Iliad of the Southwest.* New York: Doubleday, 1927.

Burrows, Jack. *John Ringo, The Gunfighter Who Never Was.* Tucson: University of Arizona Press, 1987.

Chaput, Don. *Virgil Earp: Western Peace Officer.* Encampment: Affiliated Writers of America, Inc., 1994.

———. *The Earp Papers.* Encampment: Affiliated Writers of America, Inc, 1994.

Cunningham, Eugene. *Triggernometry: A Gallery of Gunfighters.* New York: The Press of the Pioneers, 1934.

DeArment, Robert K. *Bat Masterson: The Man and the Legend.* Norman: University of Oklahoma Press, 1979.

DeMattos, Jack. *The Earp Decision.* College Station: Creative Publishing, 1989.

Dykstra, Robert R. *The Cattle Towns.* New York: Knopf, 1968.

Earp, Wyatt. *Wyatt Earp: His Autobiography.* privately printed, 1981.

Erwin, Richard. *The Truth About Wyatt Earp.* Carpenteria: The O.K. Press, 1992.

Faulk, Odie B. *Tombstone: Myth and Reality.* New York: Oxford University Press, 1972.

Foy, Eddie, and Alvin F. Harlow. *Clowning Through Life.* New York: E.P. Dutton & Co., 1928.

Jahns, Pat. *The Frontier World of Doc Holliday: Faro Dealer from Dallas to Deadwood.* Lincoln: University of Nebraska Press, 1979 ed.

Glasscock, C.B. *Lucky Baldwin, The Story of an Unconventional Success.* Indianapolis: Bobbs-Merrill, 1933.

Kintop, Jeffrey M., and Guy Louis Rocha. *The Earps' Last Frontier.* Reno: Great Basin Press, 1989.

Lake, Carolyn. *Undercover for Wells Fargo: The Unvarnished Recollections of Fred Dodge.* Boston: Houghton Mifflin Co., 1969.

Lake, Stuart Nathaniel. *Wyatt Earp: Frontier Marshal.* Boston: Houghton Mifflin Co., 1931.

Lamar, Howard R., ed. *The Reader's Encyclopedia of the American West.* New York: Harper & Row, 1977.

Lyon, William H. *Those Old Yellow Dog Days: Frontier Journalism in Arizona 1859-1912.* Tucson: Arizona Historical Society, 1994.

Martin, Douglas. *Tombstone's Epitaph,* rev. ed. Albuquerque: University of New Mexico Press, 1959.

Marks, Paula Mitchell. *And Die In The West—The Story of the O.K. Corral Gunfight.* New York: Morrow, 1989.

Masterson, Bart, and Jack DeMattos. *Famous Gunfighters of the Western Frontier.* Monroe: R.M. Weatherford, 1982.

McGilligan, Pat. *Backstory: Interviews with Screenwriters of Hollywood's Golden Age.* Berkeley: University of California Press, 1986.

Miller, Nyle H., and Joseph W. Snell. *Why the West Was Wild.* Topeka: Kansas State Historical Society, 1963.

Miner, H. Craig. *Wichita: The Early Years, 1865-80.* Lincoln: University of Nebraska Press, 1982.

Myers, John M. *Doc Holliday.* Boston: Little, Brown & Co., 1955.

———. *The Last Chance: Tombstone's Early Years.* Lincoln: University of Nebraska Press, 1973 ed.

O'Connor, Richard. *Bat Masterson.* New York: Doubleday & Company, 1957.

O'Neal, Bill. *Encyclopedia of Western Gunfighters.* Norman: University of Oklahoma Press, 1979.

Pendleton, Albert S., Jr., and Susan McKey Thomas. *In Search of the Hollidays.* Valdosta: Little River Press, 1973.

Rosa, Joseph. *The Gunfighter: Man or Myth?* Norman: University of Oklahoma Press, 1969.

———. *They Called Him Wild Bill.* Norman: University of Oklahoma Press, 1987.

Slotkin, Richard. *The Myth of The Frontier In Twentieth Century America.* New York: Atheneum, 1992.

Sonnichsen, C.L. *Billy King's Tombstone: The Private Life of an Arizona Boom Town.* Tucson: University of Arizona Press, 1972.

Trimble, Marshall. *A Panoramic History of a Frontier State.* New York: Doubleday & Company, 1977.

Turner, Alford E., ed. *The Earps Talk.* College Station: Creative Publishing Company, 1982 ed.

Walsh, Raoul. *Each Man in His Time: The Life Story of a Director.* New York: Farrar, Straus & Giroux, 1974.

Waters, Frank. *The Earp Brothers of Tombstone.* New York: Clarkson N. Potter, 1960.

Wright, Robert M. *Dodge City The Cowboy Capital and the Great Southwest.* Wichita: Wichita Eagle Press, 1913.

Manuscripts and Archival Sources

Clum, John P. Papers in Special Collections. University of Arizona Library, Tucson.

Cowboy Depredations File. Special Collections. University of Arizona Library, Tucson.

Earp Family Papers. Arizona Historical Society Collection, Tucson.

Earp, Josephine, Mabel Earp Cason, and Vinnolia Earp Ackerman. "She Married Wyatt Earp: The Recollections of Josephine Earp." Copy of typescript in the C. Lee Simmons Collection, Sonoita, Arizona.

Flood, John Henry Jr. "Wyatt Earp"; Chafin Collection. Culver City, Ca., 1926.

Gray, John Pleasant. "When All Roads Led To Tombstone" typescript at the Arizona Historical Society, undated.

412 INVENTING WYATT EARP

Halliwell, Hildreth (grandniece of Allie Earp). September 21, 1971. recorded interview. University of Arizona Library.

Hancock, James C. Papers in Arizona Historical Society Collection, Tucson.

[Hayhurst, Pat]; Summary/Transcript of Documents 45 and 94, District Court of the First Judicial District, Cochise County, in Arizona Department of Library. Archives and Public Records, Phoenix.

Hooker, Forrestine Cooper. "An Arizona Vendetta: The Truth About Wyatt Earp and Some Others." Typescript at the Southwestern Museum, Los Angeles. Undated, believed to be about 1920.

Lake, Stuart Nathaniel. Collection in Huntington Library. San Marino, California.

McLaury, Will. Letters; New York Historical Society. New York City.

Palmquist, Bob. "Election Fraud 1880: the Case of Paul v. Shibell." Seminar Paper. University of Arizona, 1986. Copy from Palmquist Collection.

———. "A Man for Breakfast Every Morning: Homicide and the Law in Tombstone." Seminar Paper. University of Arizona, 1991. Copy from Palmquist Collection.

———. "The Fight for the Tombstone Townsite," Seminar paper. University of Arizona, 1988. Copy from Palmquist Collection.

Parsons, George W. and Carl Chafin. "The West of George Whitwell Parsons, 1880-1910." Copies of Parsons' diary entries provided by Carl Chafin, who is transcribing fifty years of the diary.

Ringo, John; Ringo Ephemera File. Arizona Historical Society, Tucson

Trittle, Frederick. Scrapbooks in Arizona Historical Society Collection, Tucson.

Index

Abilene, Kansas, Hickok in, 39–41, 79
Ackerman, Vinolia Earp, 385
Across the Cimarron, 82
Adams, Ramon, 296, 402
"Adventures of the Galaxy Rangers,"
  362
Alamo Saloon, Dodge City, 63, 313
Albuquerque Evening Review, 306
Alhambra Saloon
  Dodge City, 63
  Tombstone, 129, 164, 165
Ali-Liston "Phantom Punch," fight,
  referee controversies, 326
Alias Jesse James (movie), 354
Alias, Jimmy Valentine, 329
Allen, Billy, 179
  trial testimony, 194–195
Allen, S. D., 64–65
Allison, Clay, 79–82
America's Bermuda Triangle, myth
  creation, 92–93
An Illustrated Life of Doc Holliday, 296,
  303
Anabasis, 293
*And Die in the West, The Story of the
  Gunfight at the O.K. Corral*, 10, 122,
  214–215
Antrim, William "Billy the Kid," 37,
  55, 103, 391–392
  movies about, 362–364
Apaches, 93, 164, 274–275

Appleseed, Johnny, 375
Arizona Cattlegrowers Association, 271
Arizona Daily Journal-Miner, V. Earp,
  336
Arizona Weekly Star, 149, 156, 195,
  227, 241, 245
Arizonian, The (movie), 345
Arness, James, 351
Arnold, Alex, 265
Arthur, Chester A., 162
Aspen Daily News, Holliday, 310
Atchison, Topeka, and Santa Fe
  Railroad, 36

Baba Comari, McLaury ranch, 110
Badman's Country (movie), 353–354
Bailey, Ed, 287–288
Baldwin, E. B. "Lucky," 318, 329, 330
Banning, Phineas, 25
Barry, Dave, referee controversies, 326
Barry, Gene, 351
Bartholomew, Ed, debunker, 34n.4–5,
  155, 326, 394n.1, 402
Bassett, Charlie, Dodge marshal, 13,
  32, 59, 61, 73, 313
"Bat Masterson," 351–352
Batcher, J. H., bookkeeper, 170
"Battle of Adobe Walls, The," 57
Bauer, A., butcher, 170
Beach, Rex, 329–330
Beck, Henry, 362

Beeson, Chalk, 80, 206
Behan, John
  attempt to capture Earp, 268–273, 308
  Earp/Holliday trial, 193–195, 197–199, 213
  Earp's departure, 253–255
  Gunfight aftermath, 178–183, 185, 245, 246, 252, 258–260, 281
  inquest testimony, 188
  Lake view of, 384–385
  O.K. Corral analysis, 220–222, 224–225
  Tombstone deputy sheriff, 12, 98, 101, 114, 121, 127–130, 132, 163, 167, 173–176
Bell, Bob Boze, 16, 92–93, 295, 343
Benson stage coach robbery, 139–146, 236, 240
  O.K. Corral analysis, 221–222
Berry, George, 232
Biddle, James, 271
Biehn, Michael, 366
"Big hunt," 21
Bill Doolin gang, 61, 88n.1
Billickie, Albert, Earp/Holliday trial, 209, 338
Billy the Kid (movie), 346, 352, 362
Billy the Kid. See Antrim
Bird Cage Theater, 95, 331, 367
Bishop, William Henry, 315–316
  on cowboys, 150–151
Black, Doc, hotel owner, 49
Blackburn, Dunc, outlaw, 69
Blackstone, William, 218
"Bleeding Kansas," 36, 41
Blind Cage Theater, 95, 281
Blinn, Lewis W., 238
Bolds, George, marshal, 61, 82
Boone, Richard, 351
"Boot Hill," 78, 88n.2, 114, 186
Boothe, Powers, 366
"Border shift," 72
Borges, Jorge Luis, 344
Bourland, Addie, Earp/Holliday trial, 209–210
Bowe-Golota fight, referee controversies, 326
Bowyer, Joseph, on cowboys, 163
Boxing, 321–328
  Earp early interest in, 26–27
  referee controversies in, 326–327

Boyer, Glenn G.
  on Doc Holliday, 296, 303
  Josephine "Sadie" Marcus Earp manuscript, 385–386
  on Mattie Earp, 102
  on Wells Fargo, 112, 140–141, 157–158
Boyle, Ned, Tombstone bartender, 168, 208
Boynton, Percy, 403–404
Branch Davidians, Wyatt Earp and, 404
Bray, Robert, as Wyatt Earp, 350
Breakenridge, William "Billy," 12, 100, 104–105, 120, 127–128, 133, 140, 153, 154, 191, 253, 264–265, 269, 281, 387, 402
Breihan, Carl, 276
Brennan, Mollie, dance hall girl, 59–60
Bridger, Jim, 24
Brighton, J. V., 282
Brocius, Curly Billy
  Iron Springs, 260–267
  Tombstone, 103, 104, 105, 109, 117–120, 122, 129–130, 153–154, 163
Bronk, A. G., Tombstone deputy, 168
Brown, Clara Spalding, journalist, 186, 187, 214, 232, 247, 280, 386, 388
  on cowboys, 151–152
Brown, Hendry, 32
Brown, John, 36
Brown, Johnny Mack, as Wyatt Earp, 344
Brown, Neal, 13, 32, 66–67, 313
Brown, Richard Maxwell, historian, 154, 217, 392
Buchanan, Pat, 6
Buel, J. W., dime novelists, 39
Buffalo Bill, folk figures, 10
Buffalo camps, 31–33
Buffalo hunting, Dodge city origins, 56–57
"Buffaloed," 6–7, 52n.3, 117, 263
Bullfighting, Dodge City, 55
Buntline, Ned, dime novelists, 39, 82–84
"Buntline Special" colt, 66, 82–84, 350
Bunyan, Paul, 375
Burnett, W. R., 343–344
Burns, Walter Noble, 12, 91, 154–155, 279, 283, 390–393, 395n.2

Ringo legend, 105, 274, 292–294, 392
Burrows, Jack, on Ringo legend, 105, 277–278
Burrs Under the Saddle, 296

Cairns, Jimmy, 50, 101
Call of the Wild, The, 330
Camfield, Bill, as Wyatt Earp, 354
Camp Huachuca, Arizona, 93
Camp Rucker, stolen mules, 109–110
Campbell, R. J., Tombstone county clerk, 169
Carr, John, mayor, 238, 242
Carrey, Harry Sr., 341
Cason, Mabel Earp, 385
Cason manuscript, 385
Cattle rustling, cowboys and, 150–151, 156–157
Cattle-shipping industry, 36–37, 87
Chafin, Carl, 94, 386
Chaput, Don, 15, 121, 146–147, 401
Chavez-Taylor fight, referee controversies, 327
Cheyenne and Black Hills Stage and Express Routes, 70
Cheyenne Autumn (movie), 5, 356
Cheyenne Indians, 57
Chisholm, Daniel, 263
Choynski, Joe, 321
Chrisman, Charles, 25
"Cimarron Strip," 354
Citizens' Safety Committee, Tombstone, 172
City of Tombstone, 125
Civil War
  Earp Unionist sympathies, 11, 22
  frontier and, 405
  impact on Earp family, 22
Claiborne, William "Billy the Kid"
  death of, 279
  funeral of, 185–186
  Gunfight aftermath, 178, 180
  inquest testimony, 1–2, 190
  O.K. Corral analysis, 173, 174, 224
Clanton, Billy
  cowboys, 106, 126, 171, 173–175
  inquest testimony, 1, 3
  O.K. Corral analysis, 224–225
Clanton, Finn, 182, 241, 242, 246
Clanton, Isaac "Ike," 105, 107, 108,

122, 130, 158–159, 164–170, 173–175, 238–239, 241–242
  death of, 282
  Earp/Holliday trial, 193, 201–203, 210–211, 213
  inquest testimony, 1, 189–190
  Gunfight aftermath, 178, 182
  O.K. Corral analysis, 222–223, 224
Clanton, Newman Haynes "Old Man," cowboys, 103, 106, 118, 158
Clum, John Philip, 104, 108, 119, 121–125, 129, 147–148, 160, 164, 169, 232, 236–237, 331, 359, 385, 386, 388
Cochise County, 125, 127, 129, 153–154, 239–247
Coe, Phil, drover, 40–41
Coleman, R.F., inquest testimony, 190
Colorado, The, 378
Comique Kew Theater, Dodge City, 63, 74, 77
Comstock, Sylvester B., Gunfight aftermath, 179
Confederacy, fomer soldiers of, 41
Conspiracy theory, western lawmen and, 78–79
"Constable," 28
Contention City, Arizona, 246
Coogan's Bluff (movie), 5
Cooksey, Virginia Anne, 20
Corbett, Gentleman Jim, 321, 324
Cosmopolitan Hotel, 193, 209, 227, 231, 249, 338
Costner, Kevin, 369
County Ring, Tombstone, 121–122, 127, 145
Cowboy Capital of the World- The Sage of Dodge City, 34–35n.8
"Cowboy depravations," 221
Cowboys, 2, 7, 103–108, 116, 122, 129, 148–154, 163, 187, 188, 215, 279–280
  Earp/Holliday trial, 193–194, 204–205, 208, 212
  O.K. Corral analysis, 220, 221–224
  O.K. Corral fight, 165, 173, 179–181
Cowhand, 104
Cowling, Bruce, as Wyatt Earp, 352, 353
Cramer, Effie Earp, 20
Crane, Jim, cowboy, 157

Crazy Horse, 54
Crockett, Davy, folk figures, 10
Cronin, Lee, 403
Cronkite, Walter, 350, 360
Crowley, Jim, referee controversies, 327
Cruickshanks, David, 64
Cruz, Florentin, death of, 255–258, 260
Cuddy, William, theatrical manager, 173
"Curly Bill Lived," stories, 264
"Curly Bill Spin," 120
Custer, George Armstrong, 54
Custer's Last Fight (painting), 104

Daily Chieftain, Holliday, 309
Dake, Crawley, 97, 103, 109, 152, 162, 239, 242, 244, 246, 281
Daugherty, Ray "Arkansas Tom," 61
"David S. Wolper Presents: Appointment with Destiny," 350, 360
"Deadline," 63
Deadwood, Dakota Territory, 55, 69–70
Deal, Pony, 241, 260
Debo, Angie, 124–125
Debunkers
  Earp legend, 10, 34n.4–5, 392
  John "Doc" Holliday, 289
Deger, Larry, Dodge City marshal, 55, 58, 71, 313–314
Delaney, Dana, 366, 367–368
Democrat, meaning of, 6
Democratic O.K. Club, 92
Democratic party
  Cowboys association with, 6, 9, 11, 121, 152, 179, 271
  Tombstone, 244, 273
Dempsey, Jack, 327
Dempsey-Tunney "Long Count" fight, referee controversies, 326
Dempsey-Willard fight, 327
Deno, Lottie, 353
Denver Republican, Holliday, 308, 309, 310
Denver Tribune-Republican, Holliday, 310
DePalma, Brian, 6
DeVoto, Bernard, historian, 43
Dexter saloon, 329, 330
Dick Naylor, racehorse, 126, 131

Dinehart, Mason, 351
Dirty Little Billy (movie), 363
Dix, Richard, as Wyatt Earp, 346
Dixon, Billy, on Wyatt Earp's character, 32–33
Doc (movie), 7, 357, 358–359, 363
Doc Holliday (movie), 16, 297–298
Dodge City Globe
  anti-Earp, 76–77, 78
  Earp praise, 87
  Hand assassination, 85
Dodge City, Kansas, 54, 55–57, 62–63, 73–74, 86–87
"Dodge City Peace Commission, The" (photograph), 314
Dodge City police force, 11
Dodge City - The Cowboy Capital of the World, 67
Dodge City Times
  Dodge City police salaries, 59
  on Dodge City, 73–74, 79
  Wyatt Earp's return, 71
Dodge, Fred, Wells Fargo agent, 111, 112, 140, 216, 262, 275
  on Doc Holliday, 145–146, 178–179
Dodge, Greenville M., 56
Dodge petition, 206
Dodge, Richard Irving, 56
Donovan, Mike, 27
"Dr. Who and the Gunfighters," 361–362
Drago, Harry Sinclair, historian, 67
Drover, 104
Drum, T. J., Earp attorney, 195, 203
Dunham, Jim, 226
Dwan, Allan, 342–343, 346
Dykstra, Robert, historian, 42
Dylan, Bob, 363

Eagle Brewery, 166, 201
Eagle City, Idaho, Wyatt Earp in, 316–317
Earp, Abigail Storm (grandmother), 20
Earp, Adelia (sister), 20, 26
Earp, Alvira Allie (sister-in-law), 64, 71, 92, 96, 102, 167, 227, 233–235, 336, 346, 387
Earp, Bessy, 50–51, 53n.6
Earp brothers
  John Philip Clum on, 288
  O.K. Corral analysis, 219–227
Earp Brothers of Tombstone, The, 5, 49,

64, 71, 96, 102, 230fn.10, 233–235, 312, 356, 402
Earp, Celia Mattie Blaylock, wife of Wyatt, 8, 51, 87, 100–102, 126, 161, 246, 282, 312
Earp family, background of, 20
Earp, James (brother), 242
  Coeur d'Alene, 316
  death of, 339
  early years, 20, 22
  Texas, 71, 72
Earp, Josiah, 20
Earp, Lorenzo Dow, 20–21
Earp, Martha (sister), 20
Earp, Morgan (brother)
  early years, 20, 26
  Gunfight aftermath, 178–182, 186
  inquest testimony, 2–3
  Montana, 71
  murder of, 232–233, 255, 257
  O.K. Corral fight, 166–170, 173, 175, 216
  Tombstone, 109, 111–113, 117, 140, 160–162, 164
  trial of, 193–203, 210–214,
Earp, Newton Jasper (halfbrother), early years, 20, 22, 28
  death of, 339
Earp, Nicholas Porter (father), 20–26, 28, 72, 227
  death of, 339, 388
"Earp papers," 11
Earp Papers, The - In a Brother's Image, 15
Earp, Sally, 51, 53n.6
Earp, Thomas, 20
Earp, Virgil (brother)
  Arizona, 71, 96–97
  attempted murder of, 231–232
  death of, 336
  early years, 20, 22, 25
  Gunfight aftermath, 178–183, 186
  inquest testimony, 1–3
  O.K. Corral fight, 166–175, 216
  reputation of, 401
  Tombstone, 109–112, 115, 118, 140, 143, 146–148, 160–162, 164
  Tombstone marshal, 97, 103
  trial of, 193–203, 207, 210–214,
  U.S. deputy marshal, 11, 13, 14
Earp, Virginia Ann (sister), 20
Earp, Walter (grandfather), 20, 21

Earp, Warren (brother), 242, 247
  death of, 330
  early years, 20, 26
  Guadalupe massacre, 157–158
Earp, Wyatt
  autobiographical efforts, 382
  boxing referee, 322–328
  buffalo camp, 11, 31–33
  burial place, 341
  character of, 32–33, 50
  constable, 28–29
  Deadwood, Dakota territory, 69–70
  death of, 340, 388
  death of Cruz, 255–258
  death of Stilwell, 247–249
  departure from Tombstone, 253–255
  Dodge City police officer, 55, 58–62, 64–69, 71, 73, 87
  Dodge City revisited, 312–316
  early years, 20–33
  federal officer, 11–12
  Gunfight aftermath, 178–182, 186
  on Hickok, 43
  as icon, 5, 404–405
  inquest testimony, 2–3, 289–290
  Kansas police officer, 11
  legends about, 12–15
  letter of resignation, 243–244
  movie interpretations of, 7–9, 342–370, 402
  occupations of, 14, 25, 28–29
  O.K. Corral fight, 166–171, 173–175, 216
  physical description of, 31, 60
  police tactics of, 42, 47–48, 62
  railroad work, 11
  Ringo and, 277
  in San Francisco, 312, 321, 335
  Tombstone deputy sheriff , 97–98
  Tombstone police officer, 109–112, 115–117, 122, 128–129, 140, 160–162, 164
  in Tonopah, Nevada, 333
  trial of, 193–206, 210–214,
  Wichita police officer, 38, 45–51
  in Yukon, Alaska, 329–333
Earp's Last Frontier, The - Wyatt and Virgil in the Nevada Mining Camps, 15
Earps Talk, The, 15
Eastwood, Clint, Earp legend and, 5
Easy Rider (movie), 6

Elder, Kate, 101, 287–288, 298–299.
  See also Harony, Kate
  Benson stage coach robbery, 144–145
  Tombstone, 114, 168, 182, 282
Elliott, Sam, 366
Ellsworth, Kansas, 38–39, 42, 44, 45
Emancipation Proclamation, 22
"Equivocation at the O. K. Corral," 197
Ernshaw, Harry, cowboy, 156
Estevez, Emilio, 364

Famous Gunfighters of the Western Frontier, 388
Faragher, John Mack
  on Lake's Frontier Marshal, 387
  on Wyatt Earp, 7–10, 350, 387
Faro, 100, 121, 134, 164, 337–338
"Federal abuse of power," on Earp, 12
Fellehy, P. H., inquest testimony, 190
Fievel Goes West, 5
"Fighting Earp," 30
Fitch, Tom, Earp attorney, 194, 195, 198, 203
Fitzsimmons -Corbett fight, 327
Fitzsimmons, Robert "Ruby Bob," 321, 324–326, 327–328
Fleming, Rhonda, 353
Flood, John, 10, 382–383
  manuscript of, 19, 45, 46, 58, 382, 384, 393
Flory, Med, as Wyatt Earp, 354
Fly, Camillus S., Tombstone
  photographer, 114–115, 182, 224, 280
Fly Photograph Studio, 114, 166, 173, 175, 224
Focus on Film (1971), 347
Fonda, Henry, 355, 356, 384, 402
Fonda, Peter, 6
Ford Country Globe
  Hand assassin posse, 85
  Wyatt Earp, 72
Ford, John, 341–342, 346, 347–349, 388
Fort Clark, Texas, Wyatt Earp in, 72
Fort Grant, 271
Fort Worth, Texas, Wyatt Earp in, 71–72
Forty Years on the Wild Frontier-

Authentic Tales of Wyatt Earp, Doc
  Holliday and Their Cronies, 276, 277
Foy, Eddie, vaudevillian, 74, 77
Frontier, description of, 8
Frontier Marshal (movie), 343, 345–346, 355
Frontier World of Doc Holliday, The, 296
Fugitive, The (movie), 12
Fuller, Wes, 173, 180, 182
  Earp/Holliday trial, 199–200

Gage, Henry, California governor, 338–339
"Gambler's Model" Colt, 145
Gambling
  Dodge City, 63
  Josephine "Sadie," Marcus, 318–319
  profession of, 100
  Tombsone, 99–100, 129, 134, 138n.18
  Wyatt's, 8, 72, 99–100, 330, 337
Gardner, J. B. W., Earp/Holliday trial, 208
Garfield, James, assassination of, 162
Garner, James, as Wyatt Earp, 342, 356–357
Garrett, Pat, 380, 391, 399–400
Geronimo, 124, 125, 280, 405
Glenwood Hotel, Doc Holliday and, 287, 302
Glick, George, Kansas governor, 313
Going, Joanna, 369
Gold rush
  Nevada, 333
  Yukon, 329
Gone With the Wind, 303
Goodfellow, George, 140, 231, 257–258
Goodrich, Ben, prosecuter, 200
Gordon, Dan, 365, 370
Gordon, Mike, 98–99
Gosper, John J., governor, 162–163, 167, 236, 280
Grand Hotel, Tombstone, 114, 164, 170, 227
Gray, Dixie, 120, 149
Gray, Isaac, Wells Fargo agent, 70
Gray, John Pleasant, 119–120, 142, 156
Gray, Mike, Tombstone lot
  controversy, 118–120

Great Rascal, The, 83
Greene, Lorne, 350, 360
Grounds, Billy, 269
Guadalupe Canyon massacre, 118,
    148–149, 156–157
Gunfight at O.K. Corral, The
    analysis of events, 219–227
    contemporary accounts, 8
    folklore and, 6
Gunfight at the O.K. Corral, The
    (painting), 104
Gunfight at The O.K. Corral (movie), 7,
    288, 293, 298, 300, 349, 352–353,
    363, 384, 397, 399
"Gunfighter nation," 14
*Gunfighter Nation - The Myth of the
    Frontier in Twentieth-Century
    America*, 9
"Gunfighting skill," 217
Gunnison, Colorado, 311, 312, 316
Guns and Ammo, 278
"Gunsmoke," 57, 62, 350, 351

"Had a man for breakfast," 1, 176
Hafford's Saloon, Tombstone, 171–173
Half-Breed, The (movie), 342–343, 343
Hall, Oakley, 355
Hamill, Pete, 7, 357–359, 403
Hammett, Dashiell, 344
Hammond, John Hayes, 333, 381
Hancock, James
    on cowboys, 156
    on Deuce affair, 132–133
    on the Cowboys, 107
Hancock, Lewis, 104
Hancock, William Box, cowhand, 45
Hand, Dora, 8, 84–85, 353, 401
Hardin, John Wesley, 93, 105, 311
Harony, Kate, 75, 98, 287. *See also*
    Elder, Kate
Harper's New Month, Wild Bill
    Hickok, 40, 389
Harper's Weekly, Earp coverage, 9, 388
Hart, William S., 9, 340, 341, 342,
    370, 388
Hartland Plastics, 351
Hatton, Charles, on Wyatt Earp's
    character, 50
"Have Gun, Will Travel," 351
Hayhurst, Hal, 192
Hearst, George, 239
Hearst, William Randolph, 324, 325

"Helen of Troy of Tombstone, The,"
    113, 384
Helldorado, 12, 120, 133, 153, 154,
    264, 281, 292, 387–388, 393–394n.1
"Helldorado Festival," 344
"Heroes of the West," 4
"Heroic age of Tombstone, The," 279
Herring, William, 246
Heston, Charlton, 366
Heywood, Nat, deputy marshal, 73
Hickok, James Butler "Wild Bill"
    death of, 55
    folk figures, 10, 13
    Illinois background, 19
    reputation of, 39–41, 42, 389–390
Higgenbottom gang, 37–38
High Noon (movie), 359
"High Noon," 352
High Sierra (movie), 343
Hill, Joe, cowboy, 108, 157–159, 205
Hinkle, George, Dodge City sheriff,
    314
Holliday, John "Doc," 74–75
    background, 286–287, 290–293
    Benson stage coach robbery, 141–
    146
    death of, 282
    Dodge City, 288–289
    Guadalupe massacre, 157–158
    Gunfight aftermath, 178, 181–182,
    186, 288, 295
    inquest testimony, 2–3
    interpretation of, 296–304
    Iron Springs, 260, 266
    O.K. Corral analysis, 224, 225, 226–
    227
    O.K. Corral fight, 164–168, 171,
    173–175, 216, 295
    relationship with Earp, 75–77, 79,
    288, 289–290
    reputation of, 13, 98–99, 142–143,
    288, 290–291, 292–295, 307, 309–
    311, 401
    Ringo and, 275–277
    Tombstone, 114, 116, 126
    trial of, 193, 195–203, 210–214
Holliday, Mary Melanie, 303
Holton, Charles, 206–207
Homicides, English law and, 218
Homosexuality, issue of, 7, 300, 355,
    358
"Hoodoo" war, 103

Hooker, Forrestine, 246, 382–383
Hooker, Henry Clay, 268–273, 386
Hoover, George, mayor of Dodge, 58, 59, 62
Hoover, Herbert, 330
Hopper, Dennis, 6
Horan, James D., historian, 61
Horse racing, Wyatt Earp in, 319
Horse stealing, accusation of, 29–30
Horses, Wyatt Earp's interest in, 318
Hour of the Gun (movie), 300, 349, 356–357, 363
Hoy, George, killing of, 78–79, 81, 187
Human Life, Bat Masterson profile of Earp, 11, 68, 133, 254, 336
Hume, Jim, Wells Fargo agent, 112, 240
Hunt, Zwing, cowboy, 109, 269
Hurst, J. H., Camp Rucker, 109–110
Huston, John, 343
Huston, Walter, as Wyatt Earp, 9, 342, 343

I Married Wyatt Earp (movie), 359
I Married Wyatt Earp- The Recollections of Josephine Sarah Marcus Earp, 114, 126, 141, 232, 234, 252, 320, 359, 365, 386
  analysis of, 385–386
Illness as a Metaphor, 299
Illustrated Life and Times of Doc Holliday, 295
Illustrated Life and Times of Wyatt Earp, The, 16, 343
In Early Arizona (movie), 445
In Search of the Hollidays, 292
"Incorporation gunfighter," 217, 392
Indian Charlie. *See* Cruz, Florentin
Ingraham, Prentice, dime novelists, 39
Inside Out (movie), 12
Iron Springs, gunfight at, 260–267
Irvine, Esther L., 20
It All Happened in Tombstone, 254, 386

Jacobs, Joe, referee controversies, 327
Jahns, Pat, on Doc Holliday, 296–297, 303
James, Frank, 41, 403
James, Jesse, 41, 55, 403
Jameson, Henry, Pueblo marshal, 308
Jarre, Kevin, 14, 16, 365–368

Jefferies, James J., 324
Jennie Lee's Ha Una Nuova Pistola (movie), 354
"John Ford's west," 341
John Ringo - The Gunfighter Who Never Was, 105, 277–278
Johnny-Behind-the-Deuce affair, 130–134, 275
Johnson-Dempsey match, 329
Johnson, Turkey Creek, 253–255, 260, 266
Joyce, Milt, Tombstone, 114, 145, 280–281
Judah, Theodore, 255, 256, 260
Julian, Martin, Fitzsimmon's manager, 322

Kael, Pauline, 357
Kasdan, Lawrence, 362, 370
Kearns, Doc, 329
Keenan, Fannie. *See* Hand, Dora
Kelley, Jim "Dog," mayor of Dodge, 71, 84
Kelly, Florence Finch, *Frontier Marshal* review, 381
Kelly, Grace, 359
Keneally, Thomas, 377
Kennedy, Edward, 29–30
Kennedy, James, posses to capture, 84–86
Kilmer, Val, 7, 300, 303, 304, 352, 364, 366, 368–369
King, Arthur, 337
King, Luther, Benson stage coach robbery, 140, 143
King, Martha J., inquest testimony, 190–191
"King of the Cowboys, The," 105, 274
"King Pin," 108
Kintop, Jeffrey M., 15
Kiowa Indians, 57
Kraker, Tony, 262

Lady Gay Saloon, Dodge City, 63, 64
Lake, Stuart Nathaniel, legend builder, 5, 9, 10–15, 39, 42, 43, 46, 47, 57, 79, 84, 128, 131, 133–134, 161, 253, 256, 257, 261, 265–267, 323, 344–345, 387–388, 393, 397, 403–404
  life of, 380
Lamar, Missouri, Earp family, 28–29

Lancaster, Burt, as Wyatt Earp, 45,
   352, 384, 402
Lang, Stephen, 366, 367
Lansky, Meyer, friend of B.
   Masterson, 340
Las Vegas Optic
   on Doc Holliday, 142
   Wyatt Earp, 238
Last Story, The, 298
Laudanum, use of, 101, 282
Law and Order (movie), 9, 342, 343,
   344, 362, 397
Law for Tombstone (movie), 445
Leadville, Colorado, Wyatt Earp in,
   71
Leahy, Dave, newspaper man, 38, 47
   on Wyatt Earp's character, 50
Left-Handed Gun, The (movie), 358,
   363
Legacy of Conquest, The, 404
Leibowitz, Ken, 361
Leonard, Billy, jeweler, 142–144, 158–
   159
Leslie, Buckskin Frank, 84, 115, 140,
   275–276, 279
Lewis, Alfred Henry, 326
   on Doc Holliday, 304
"Life and Legend of Wyatt Earp,
   The," 57, 350–351–353, 384
Limerick, Patricia Nelson, 404
Lincoln County war, 103, 400
"Lion of Tombstone, The," 13, 280,
   392–393
Little Big Horn, 54
Little Big Man, 357
Log of a Cowboy, The, 57
London, Jack, 329, 341
London Prize Ring rules, 26, 322–323
"Lone Ranger, The," 351
Lone Star Saloon, Dodge City, 63
Long Branch Saloon, Dodge City, 63,
   64, 76, 77, 79, 80, 100, 313
Los Angeles Examiner, W. Earp
   interview, 261, 339
Los Angeles Herald, W. Earp, 333–334,
   335, 338
Los Angeles Mining Review, Earp
   coverage, 133
Los Angeles Police Department, Wyatt
   Earp's relation with, 337
Los Angeles Times, 335, 240
   Gosper death, 280

Nicholas Earp, 339, 388
Loving, Cockeyed Frank, 77
Lucky Cuss mine, 94

Madsen, Chris, 61, 399
Mallen, Perry, bounty hunter, 307–
   308, 309, 321
Mamet, David, 6, 363
Man Who Shot Liberty Valence, The,
   292, 356
Manifest Destiny, 21
Marcus, Josephine "Sadie"
   background of, 5, 15
   Ben Thompson story, 45
   death of, 346
   O.K. Corral analysis, 222
   role of, 384–385, 401
   in San Francisco, 321
   in Tombstone, 101, 113–114, 126–
   127, 141, 227, 233–235
   in Tonopah, Nevada, 333
   view of Wyatt's film image, 344–
   345, 346–347
   on Wyatt's gambling, 8
   in Yukon, Alaska, 329–333
Marcus, Nathan, 330, 332
Marks, Paula Mitchell, 10, 122, 132,
   196, 214–215, 225–226
Marquis of Queensberry rules, boxing,
   321, 322, 323, 325
Martin, Al, 333
Martin, Douglas, 386
Mason County war, 103
Masterson, Bat, 8, 11, 13, 57, 59–60,
   146, 313, 379–380, 402
   death of, 340, 380
   Illinois background, 19
   on John "Doc" Holliday, 76, 290–
   291, 308
   on Josephine "Sadie" Marcus, 113
   on Wyatt Earp, 27–28, 31, 254,
   388, 399
Masterson, Ed, 71, 72–73
Masterson, Jim, 76, 77–78
Masterson of Kansas (movie), 352, 353
Matthews, Henry M, coroner, 182,
   231
"Maverick," 354
McCall, Jack, 55
McCrea, Joel, as Wyatt Earp, 45, 349–
   350, 355, 402
McDougal, Annie "Cattle Annie," 61

McLaury, Frank, 103, 106, 109–110, 155–156, 158–159 171–175
funeral of, 185–186
Gunfight aftermath, 182
inquest testimony, 1
O.K. Corral analysis, 223, 224–225
O.K. Corral fight, 171–175, 181
McLaury, Tom, 103, 106, 155–156, 164, 167, 170–171, 173, 175
funeral of, 185–186
Gunfight aftermath, 179, 180, 181, 182
inquest testimony, 1
O.K. Corral analysis, 223, 224–225
McLaury, William R., Earp/Holliday trial, 200–201, 207, 214
McLoughlin, Denis, historian, 80
McMasters, Sherman, cowboy, 109, 126, 156, 232, 253, 260, 281
Mechanics Pavilion, 321, 322, 323
Megher, Mike, marshal, 50, 68–69
Mehan, Andrew, inquest testimony, 171
Metz, Leon, historian, 40, 399–400
"Million dollar gate," 329
Mining claims, Earp, 100
Mix, Tom, 339, 340, 341, 342, 388
Mizner, Wilson, 329, 341
Monaghan, Jay, Buntline biographer, 83
Monmouth, Illinois, Earp family, 19, 20, 21
Monte, card game, 100
Montgomery, George, 352, 353, 402
Moore, Clayton, 351
Morey, Jeff, 6, 197, 343, 386
Morris, Ike, 316
"Mr. Vaughan," 264
Mulqueen, Tom, 331
Municipal sanitary inspector," 66
Murray, William, stockbroker, 172
My Darling Clementine (movie), 4, 293, 301, 339, 346, 347–349, 352, 363, 384, 398, 399
Myers, John
on Doc Holliday, 297–298
on Kate Elder, 298
Mythmaking, Wyatt Earp and, 396–403, 404–406

National Athletic Club, 322, 325, 326
Naughton, W. W., Sharkey-Fitzsimmons fight, 325
Neagle, Dave, 238
New York Journal, 326
New York Morning Telegraph, 340
New York Times, The
Frontier Marshal review
O.K. Corral Gunfight, 9, 16, 388
New York Tribune, The, 331
Newcomb, George "Bitter Creek," 61
Nichols, George Ward, journalist, 40
Nickel-Plated Gun Theory, The," 194, 196
Nicknames, western, 299
Nixon, Tom, buffalo hunt, 32
Niza, Fray Marcos de, 92
No Duty to Retreat - Violence and Values in American History and Society, 217–218
Nome Daily News, 332

O'Brian, Hugh, 45, 351, 354, 367, 384, 402
O'Brien, George, 345
Occidental Saloon, 166, 167
O'Connor, Richard, 267, 352
Office of Indian Affairs, 124
O.K. Corral
gunfight at, 164–176, 398–399
inquest testimony, 1–3, 50, 84, 128
reports of fight, 9, 175–176, 183–185
"Old Cack," 264
Old Kinderhook, 92
Old Mexico and Her Provinces, 151, 316
Opera House Saloon, Dodge City, 63
O'Quinn, Terry, 366
Oriental Saloon, 108, 116, 134, 147, 201, 204, 231, 367
O'Rourke, Johnnie, 130, 131, 134, 275
Otero, Miguel Antonio, on Doc Holliday, 76, 99
Outlaw, The, 343, 363
Outlaws Is Coming, The (movie), 354

Paladin, 351
Palmquist, Robert, 16, 177n.5, 228n.3–4, 229n.5–6, 328n.3, 386
Parker, Chief Quanah, 57
Parsons, George, 104–105, 126, 132–

133, 140, 143, 162, 164, 175–176,
186, 231–232, 240–241, 247, 253,
258, 269, 281, 294, 331–332, 334–
335, 337, 386
*Past Imperfect – History According to the
Movies*, 7, 387
Pat Garrett and Billy the Kid (movie),
363, 400
Paul, Bob, Pima County sheriff, 122,
129–130, 139–140, 259–260, 308–
309
Paxton, Bill, 366, 369
Payne, William, 317
Peabody, Endicott, 8
Pearce, Abel Head "Shanghai," 45–48
Peckinpah, Sam, 363, 400
Peel, Martin, 269
Pella, Iowa, Earp family, 21, 22
Pendleton, Albert S., 292, 301–302
Penn, Arthur, 363
Perine, George, Tombstone, 115
Perry, Frank, 357
Peterson, J. Y., 338
Philpot, Bud
   Benson stage coach robbery, 139,
   202–203, 204, 237
   O.K. Corral analysis, 221–222
Pickwick Papers, 293
*Picture Story of Wyatt Earp, The Most
Colorful Marshal of the Old West*, 43–
44
Pierce, Charley "Tulsa Jack," 61
Pilgrim's Progress, 293
Pinafore on Wheels, 113
"Pipe-off," 202
Pitkin, Frederick, Colorado governor,
309
*Place Where Souls Are Born, The, A
Journey into the American Southwest*,
377
Plains Indians, Earp view of, 23–24
"Point-men," 403
Police Gazette, Earp coverage, 9, 314–
315, 319–320, 388
Pollard, Michael J., 363
Posse Comitatus Act, 103, 152
Prescott Miner, Chinese laundry, 98
Price, Lyttleton, district attorney, 200
Priestly, Jason, 366
Prince of Pistoleers, The, 39, 384
Pritchard, A. J., 317
Prohibition, Earp's view of, 339

Prospecting, Earp's interest in, 317,
330, 337
Prostitution
   Dodge city, 63
   Earps and, 50–51
   Wichita, Kansas, 37
Pueblo, New Mexico, 307, 308

Quaid, Dennis, 369
Quantrill's Raider's, 36
Quinn, Anthony, 355

Rachal, Bob, cattleman, 66–67, 78, 80
Railway construction camps, boxing in,
26–27
Randall, Alder, Tombstone mayor, 123
Reagan, Ronald, as Wyatt Earp, 344,
402
"Red Light District," 88n.2
Redfield, Len, Benson stage coach
robbery, 140
Rediscovery of the Frontier, The, 403
Reilly, James, Tombstone JP, 115–116,
162, 236–237
Religion, Nicolas Earp on, 22
Republican, meaning of, 6
Republican party, Earp association
with, 6, 9, 11, 120–121, 402
"Revisionist," Earp legend, 7
Richards, Hugo, 244
Rickabaugh, Lou, gambler, 99–100,
145
Rickard, G. L. "Tex," boxing promoter,
327, 329
"Ride of Vengeance," 233
Ride the High Country (movie), 354–
355
"Ringo," 105, 279
Ringo, John Peter, cowboy, 103, 104–
106, 122, 240–242, 274–279, 292–
294
Ritter and Ream's Undertakers, 185
Roberts, Gary, 236
Robin Hood of El Dorado (movie), 346
Rocha, Guy Lewis, 15
Rogers, Roy, 351
Roosevelt, Teddy, friend of B.
Masterson, 340, 380
Rosa, Joseph G., Hickok biographer,
39, 79, 389
Rothstein, Arnold, friend of B.
Masterson, 340

Rudabaugh, Dirty Dave, 27, 72
Rule, Richard, 182, 185, 244
Russell, Kurt, 7, 364, 366, 368–369

Saga of Billy the Kid, The, 12–13, 391–392
Saint Johnson (movie), 343
Saloons
  Dodge City, 63, 313
  role of, 8–9
  Tombstone, 95, 129, 131, 166, 167, 171–173
San Bernardino, California, Earp family, 24, 25
San Carlos Apache Reservation, 108
San Diego, California, 317–318, 320
  Josephine "Sadie," Marcus in, 318–320
  Wyatt Earp in, 317–320
San Diego Daily Union, 186, 232, 318
San Francisco Call, 325, 331
San Francisco Examiner
  Earp coverage, 329, 388
  Sharkey-Fitzsimmons fight, 325, 388
  Virgil Earp interview, 112, 250
  Wyatt Earp interview, 78, 81, 311, 265, 323–324
San Francisco Exchange, 273
San Francisco
  Josephine "Sadie" Marcus in, 321
  Wyatt Earp in, 312, 321, 335
Sandy Bob stage coach robbery, 159–160
Saturday Evening Post
  Earp brothers, 382
  Frontier Marshal review, 381
  Vendetta Ride, 388
Schieffelin, Ed, Tombstone, 93–94, 108, 281–282
Schieffelin Hall, 95, 281
Schmeling, Max, referee controversies, 327
Schneider, W. P., ambush of, 130–131
Scott, Randolph, as Wyatt Earp, 343
Scribner's, Earp coverage, 9, 388
Sea Wolf, The, 329
Seattle Post-Intelligencer, 330–331
Shanssey, John, 27, 75
Sharkey, Jack, referee controversies, 327
Sharkey, Tom "Sailor," 321, 324–326, 327–328

Sharkey-Fitzsimmons fight, 324–326, 327–328
Sharp rifle, buffalo hunting, 31–32
Shaw, Bob, 72
Sherman, William Tecumseh, 56
  on Tombstone, Arizona, 95
Shestack, Melvin, 339
Shibell, Charlie, Tombstone sheriff, 97, 109, 110, 115, 121–123, 169
"Shooter rack," 77
Short, Luke, gambler, 100, 134, 146, 313–314
Shown, John, 29–30
Sierra Bonita ranch, 268–273
"Significance of the Frontier in American History, The," 403
Sills, H. F.
  Earp/Holliday trial, 208, 226
  inquest testimony, 1–3
Silver rush, Tombstone, 86, 329
Sippy, Ben
  O.K. Corral analysis, 221, 222
  Tombstone, 121, 123, 126, 131–133, 146
Sitting Bull, 54
Sizemore, Tom, as Wyatt Earp, 353
Skeleton Canyon massacre, 149, 154–156, 206
Slaughter, "Texas" John, Tombstone sheriff, 106–107, 282–283
Slotkin, Richard, 9–10
Smith, Al, 339
Smith, Bill, marshal, 49–50
"Sodom and Gomorrah of the Plains, The," 54
Solomon, S., 254–255
Sons of Katie Elder, The (movie), 299
"Southern Democratic values," 215
Southern, Terry, 6
Southwest Missourian, on Constable Earp, 29
Spangenberg's gunsmith shop, 171, 172
Spangler, Mike, Arapahoe County sheriff, 308
"Special officer," Earp as, 38
"Spectre of the Gun," Star Trek episode, 360–361, 398
Spencer, Marietta, on Morgan's death, 250–252
Spencer, Pete, 160, 205, 250–251
Spicer, Wells, judge Earp/Holliday

trial, 194, 199–200, 203, 209–214, 236–237, 281
Spoilers, The (movie), 330
"Sporting man," 321
St. Johns, Adela Rogers, 339, 340
"Stage Driver," 25
Stagecoach (movie), 279, 301, 445
Stanley, Henry M., journalist, 40
Stapp, W. W., W. Earp alias, 338
Stapp, Wyatt Berry, 21
"Steel vest," 265
Steele, Richard, referee controversies, 327
Stewart, James, as Wyatt Earp, 356
Stilwell, Frank, 159–160, 205, 252
    death of, 247–253, 258
Stilwell, William, judge, 242
Stockman, 104
Storms, Charlie, gambler, 134
"Strong Men of the West," 381
Sturges, John, 356–357
Sullivan, Barry, 400
Sunset, 70, 342, 359
Sunset Trail, The, 304
Sutherland, Keifer, 364
Sutherland, Urilla, 29
Swilling, Hank, 249, 255

Tefertiller, Casey, 15
Ten Per Cent Ring, Tombstone, 121, 237
"Texans" as cowboys, 41
"That spasm of modernism," 95
The Gunfighter (movie), 105, 279
The O.K. Corral Inquest, 15
Thomas, Augustine, 268
Thomas, Heck, 61, 399
Thomas, Susan Mckay, 292 , 301–302
Thompson, Ben, gunfighter, 38–39, 43–45
Three Guardsmen, 61
Tilghman, Bill, Dodge marshal, 13, 32, 33, 61–62, 380, 400
Tipton, Dan, 232, 253, 313
Tombstone (movie), 7, 105, 258, 298, 300–301, 303, 304, 346, 352, 364, 365–369, 397, 399
Tombstone - An Illiad of the Southwest, 12, 13, 91, 154–155, 346, 387, 390–393
Tombstone, Arizona, mining town, 86, 91–92, 93, 94–95, 108, 114, 281–283

Tombstone Citizens League, 123
Tombstone Daily Nugget, The, 110, 152, 183–185, 186, 193, 236–238, 241, 242, 244, 246, 253, 262–263, 265, 269–270, 272–273, 386–387
    on Doc Holliday, 144
Tombstone Epitaph, 7, 104, 108, 110, 150, 160, 175, 183, 236–238, 242–244, 253, 260, 262–263, 271, 272–273
    pro-Earp, 386
Tombstone, hospital, 1
Tombstone lot-jumping controversy, 118–119, 147–148
Tombstone Milling and Mining Company, 269
Tombstone Story, The, 298
Tombstone Volunteer Fire Company, 111
Tonopah, Nevada
    Josephine "Sadie," Marcus in, 333
    Wyatt Earp in, 333
Tonopah Sun, The, V. Earp, 336
Torres, Louis, Sonora, 155
Tough Nut mine, 94
Tourneur, Jacques, 349–350
Townsite Company, Tombstone, 123
Toys
    Billy the Kid related, 376
    Wyatt Earp related, 351, 375–376
Track, Ingleside, 323
Traywick, Ben, historian, 107
Trinidad, Arizona, 307, 308
Tritle, Frederick, Arizona governor, 309
Tucson Star, 306–307
    Josephine "Sadie" Marcus Earp manuscript, 386
Tucson Weekly Citizen
    cowboys, 149
    Lenoard, 142
"Turned to meet the other party," 181
Turner, Alford, 15, 192, 195–196, 289–290
Turner, Frederick Jackson, 403
Twain, Mark, on Plains Indians, 24
Tyler, Johnny, 99–100, 116
Tzu, Wang, 377

"Uncle Ned history," 53n.5, 101, 191
Undercover for Wells Fargo, 112, 275
Unruh, David, 330

Untouchables, The (movie), 6, 363–364
Uris, Leon, 252
Ute Chief, Holliday, 310

Valentine, John J., Wells Fargo
  president, 112
Van Buren, Martin, 92
Vendetta Ride (1882), 12, 233, 401–402
  newspaper coverage of, 388
Vermillion, Texas Jack, 253, 260, 261, 266, 281, 313
Vidor, King, 362
Vietnam War, influence on portray of American West, 357–359
Virginian, The, 334–335
Vogano Saloon, 131

Walcott, Jersey Joe, referee
  controversies, 326
Wallace, A.O., Tombstone judge, 169, 170
Walsh, Raoul, 341, 388
Warlock (movie), 355, 356
Waters, Frank, 5, 49, 96, 378, 402
Wayne, John, Earp legend and, 5
Webster, Ab, Dodge City mayor, 313–314
Wells Fargo
  O.K. Corral analysis, 222
  in Tombstone, 108, 111, 157, 171
  Virgil's relation with, 112
  Wyatt Earp's relationship with, 69–70, 112, 157, 241, 320
Wells Fargo agents
  Dodge, Fred, 111, 112, 140, 216, 262, 275
  Gray, Isaac, 70
  Hume, Jim, 112, 240
  Williams, Marshall, 108, 112, 143, 164, 165, 237, 245–246
West, fascination with, 403–404
Whelen, Billy, 270
White, Charlie, 98–99
White Elephant Saloon, 316
White, Fred, Tombstone city marshal, 108, 115, 117, 118
Why the West Was Wild, 50
Wichita (movie), 349, 355

Wichita Beacon, on Wyatt Earp, 48–49
Wichita, Kansas, 36–38, 45
Wichita petition, 206–207
"Wickedest Town in the West, The," 54
Wild Bill (movie), 40
Wild Bill Hickok (movie), 9, 39, 342
Wild Bill - The Man and the Myth, 389
Wild, Wooly, and Wicked, 67
Williams, Marshall, Wells Fargo agent, 108, 112, 143, 164, 165, 237, 245–246
Williams, Mike, special deputy, 40
Williams, Winfred Scott, 208–209
Wilstach, Frank, 39
Winchester '73 (movie), 32
Woods, Harry, *Daily Nugget*, 129, 269, 286
Wright, Bob, 66–68, 80
Wyatt Earp (movie), 72, 131, 298, 352, 353, 362, 369–370, 397
"Wyatt Earp attitude, a," 6
Wyatt Earp Birthplace Museum, 19, 21
Wyatt Earp Bogeyman, legend, 12, 402
Wyatt Earp Enterprises, 351
Wyatt Earp: Facts, Volume 1, 34n.2
Wyatt Earp, Frontier Marshal, 379–380
  discussion of, 5, 10–11, 13–15, 379–380, 382–384, 387
  quotations from, 25, 31, 32, 36, 42, 43, 48, 57–58, 62, 66, 232, 253
"Wyatt Earp - Justice at the O.K. Corral," 360
Wyatt Earp Superman, legend, 12
"Wyatt Earp syndrome, the," 4
Wyatt Earp - The Life Beyond the Legend, 15
"Wyatt Earp's West," CD-Rom, 4

Young Guns (movie), 72, 364
Younger, Cole, Confederate soldier, 41
Yukon, Alaska
  Josephine "Sadie," Marcus in, 329–333
  Wyatt Earp in, 329–333
Yulin, Harris, 7, 299, 358